CONTEXTS OF THE DRAMA

RICHARD GOLDSTONE
The City College
The City University of New York

McGRAW-HILL BOOK COMPANY
New York/St. Louis/San Francisco
Toronto/London/Sydney

Library of Congress Catalog Card Number 68-13092

23662

1 2 3 4 5 6 7 8 9 0 MAMM 7 5 4 3 2 1 0 6 9 8

Drawings by Rosalie Seidler.

PN
6112
.G63
1968
mar 2002
ABN 5002

ACKNOWLEDGMENTS

THE ANTIGONE OF SOPHOCLES: An English Version by Dudley Fitts and Robert Fitzgerald, copyright, 1939, by Harcourt, Brace & World, Inc., renewed, 1967, by Dudley Fitts and Robert Fitzgerald and reprinted by permission of the publishers. *Caution:* All rights, including professional, amateur, motion picture, recitation, lecturing, public reading, radio broadcasting and television are strictly reserved. Inquiries on all rights should be addressed to Harcourt, Brace & World, Inc., 757 Third Ave., New York, N.Y. 10017.
"Antigone Then and Now" by Frank Jones. *Proceedings of the IVth Congress of the International Comparative Literature Association, Fribourg, 1964,* published by Mouton & Co., The Hague, Paris, 1966.

HIPPOLYTUS by Euripides, translated by Philip Vellacott. Reprinted from *Euripides: Alcestis and Other Plays,* copyright © Philip Vellacott 1953. Published by Penguin Books Ltd., Harmondsworth, Middlesex, England.

ANTONY AND CLEOPATRA by William Shakespeare, edited by Oscar James Campbell, Alfred Rothschild, and Stuart Vaughan. Copyright © 1966 by Bantam Books, Inc. Reprinted by permission from *The Bantam Shakespeare.*
"On Anthony and Cleopatra" by Maynard Mack. Introduction to *Shakespeare: Antony and Cleopatra,* ed. Maynard Mack, Penguin, 1959. Reprinted by permission of Penguin Books Inc.

THE MISER by Molière, translated by John Wood. Reprinted from *Molière: Plays,* translated by John Wood. Published by Penguin Books Ltd., Harmondsworth, Middlesex, England.
Excerpt from "Molière." From *Sainte-Beuve: Selected Essays* translated by Francis Steegmuller and Norbert Guterman. Copyright © 1963 by Doubleday & Company, Inc. Reprinted by permission of the publishers.

PREFACE

Each of the plays that constitute this anthology are notable works, admirably representing their respective authors. Such plays are their own excuse for being; in choosing them, however, I was guided by considerations beyond their inherent excellence. Every play has proved itself in the college classroom. All twelve, moreover, form a viable teaching whole, each bearing a relationship one to the other.

Those who approach the study of literature historically, and therefore chronologically, will find that the plays in this volume fall into five periods: classical Greece is represented by two tragedies; the seventeenth century by Shakespeare and Molière; the late nineteenth and turn-of-the-century by Ibsen, Shaw, and Chekhov; the decade beginning with World War II by three American plays; and the past decade by two representations of the new drama. I regret that space limitations prevented the inclusion of other plays of other periods, most particularly, examples of Restoration and eighteenth-century English comedy.

Another approach that this selection accommodates is the generic study of drama. The major genres are included: classic and Shakespearean tragedy; classic farce; modern tragedy; realistic drama; the Shavian comedy of ideas; historical drama; theater of the absurd.

For those who prefer to focus their study of plays on major themes, each play in this text has either a thematic counterpart or antithesis in another play in this volume.

1. The conflict between personal commitment and social responsibility underlies both *Antigone* and *Becket*.

2. The power of love and the use of power are antitheses reflected in the two plays by Shakespeare and Shaw.

3. Two farces about love and money reveal the differences between the France of Louis XIV and the America of Chester A. Arthur.

4. The frustration of a woman when engaged in a mortal struggle against social custom is portrayed in both Phaedra and Hedda Gabler.

5. Romantic dreams and the nightmare of reality are the concerns of both Chekhov and Williams.

6. Two studies in loneliness and alienation are provided by O'Neill and Albee.

Other thematic relationships will undoubtedly suggest themselves.

No fewer than half the plays offered here were written by playwrights whose love of the English language is reflected in the stylistic excellence of the work which represents them. Even Eugene O'Neill, whose ear betrayed him in many of his earlier plays, became at one with the American language in his maturity. The six plays in translation are not mere renderings into English from another language. They combine fidelity to their origins with literary distinction. Because all are recent translations, the dialogue is fresh and alive without being anachronistic.

I should like to express my appreciation to Professors Beekman Cottrell, John Henry Raleigh, Philip Roddman, Sherwood Weber, and Mr. Bruce Moody for the afterwords they wrote for this volume. Also I am obligated to Messrs. Edward Albee and Thornton Wilder and to Professors Frank Jones and Maynard Mack for their permission to use articles they had prepared for other publications but which fit harmoniously into the context of this book.

I am further indebted to Professor Roddman for his reading much of the introductory material and making a number of excellent recommendations. Kenneth Fay, of Long Island University, has improved the text with his shrewd editorial suggestions. A number of my colleagues have provided me with good counsel; to each of them I offer thanks and the hope that this book fulfills their expectations. A special debt is due Rosalie Seidler, who made the drawings of the twelve playwrights in this volume.

Richard Goldstone

CONTENTS

CONTEXTS OF THE DRAMA

GENERAL INTRODUCTION

READING THE SCORE

The great, now legendary, musical conductor, Arturo Toscanini, "heard" the ideal performance of Beethoven's *Ninth Symphony* and of Verdi's *Otello* only when he studied their scores in the silent library of his home in Riverdale-on-Hudson. But even among the most ardent devotees of music, there are few who would choose a printed text in a music library over a performance in a concert hall or opera house. Most of us prefer live music; similarly, most of us prefer the staged performance of a play to a text.

Opportunities to see ideal representations of great plays are rare, alas, even for those who have access to the professional stage companies of Chicago, Los Angeles, or New York. The American theater concerns itself principally with new and ephemeral stage plays and with musical comedies. Our interest in serious drama forces us back to studying the "score."

Fortunately, unlike musicians, we need not be specialists or scholars to enjoy the reading of a play's text. To be sure, play reading makes strenuous demands upon our attention and upon our creative imaginations, and our training in the reading of fiction or poetry only partially prepares us for the demands of reading drama.

The essential difference between reading poetry or fiction, on the one hand, and drama, on the other, is that both poetry and fiction relate what the writer saw, felt, imagined—in a past time. A play is taking place as we see it; in Thornton Wilder's words, "A play visibly represents pure existing."

THE CONTEXTS OF THEATER, IDEAS, AND HISTORY

In reading a play, then, our first responsibility to the work is to visualize it in the context of theater. In our mind's eye we follow the progress of the play as it is performed in a Greek amphitheater, an Elizabethan playhouse, or on a modern proscenium stage—by actors who are not only articulating lines in varied inflections, accents, and intonations but also moving, gesticulating, physically reacting. We see costumes, settings, properties. Often there is music. Always there is an audience. A playwright composes for an audience which laughs, sighs, weeps, holds its breath, bursts into applause.

A great play, however, makes demands upon our attention that transcend mere story and spectacle. Story and spectacle, characters in conflict, are the bases of drama; but except for the simpleminded or the intellec-

1

tually undemanding, they are not enough. In addition to seeing a play in its context of theater, we view it in the context of ideas. Ultimately the moment comes when we ask ourselves: What does it all mean? Why do men do such things? Why did everything come to nothing? Who was really to blame? Could such misfortunes befall me?

No play, no work of art, of course, is lacking in some kind of thematic content. What makes a play interesting, however, is the subtlety, the complexity, the ambiguity of its ideas, preoccupations, and themes. Shakespeare's *Antony and Cleopatra* was for 200 years accounted inferior to others among the tragedies because it was supposed to have been merely a spectacular account of a man who ruined himself because of an infatuation for an unworthy woman. To reduce the work to so bald and even questionable a concept is to deny oneself the experience of a rich, noble, and surpassingly fascinating monument of art. If literature teaches us anything, it teaches us that things are not what they seem; we look behind the act for its meaning and behind the meaning for the act.

An element that makes a collection of plays such as those that are to follow interesting is the extraordinary effect that time and place have upon the textures of the different works. That is to say, we are enabled to study a play in its historical context more easily when we have several plays from different epochs to compare one with another. For example, *The Zoo Story,* by Edward Albee, turns upon an adventitious encounter in New York City's Central Park between a prosperous, conventional professional man in his forties and a slightly younger roustabout. The play, set in the present, is one that, for a number of reasons, could not have its counterpart in another century, nor even perhaps, in another country. Drama from Greece to the present has contained scenes whose impact derived from a confrontation between persons of high estate and low. Ordinarily, what we encounter are the conventional servant-master relationships (Don Juan and Sganarelle in Molière; Volpone and Mosca in Ben Jonson). When the relationship ceases to be conventional, as in Webster's *The Duchess of Malfi* (the duchess marries her steward) or in Strindberg's *Miss Julie,* tragedy is the only possible outcome.

After reading all twelve plays in this volume, one could evolve some persuasive generalizations about shifts in the concept of caste and class —and about a number of other equally important social questions that affect and are central to our aesthetic response to the drama. It is an awareness of just such questions that helps us to avoid false or irrelevant expectations of a playwright's intentions, that deepens our understanding of the dramatic experience, and that inevitably shapes our critical discussion.

THE PLAY AS LITERATURE

The limitless possibilities inherent in viewing a play in its historical context, of seeing the social-political-economic implications buried in its text, present their own peculiar dangers; for improperly used, such contexts may cause us to lose sight of the play as a work of imaginative literature. Too great a preoccupation with historical context can easily blind the student to a play's aesthetic quality. For a number of years the plays of John Galsworthy, excellent social documents, were respected, analyzed, and anthologized. The plays were the work of an objective master craftsman. But they lacked artistic distinction, and they no longer hold the stage.

But what is it that gives a play artistic distinction? What enables us to recognize a play as a work of art?

The great artists—in music, in painting, in sculpture, as well as in literature—were men who first had to achieve a mastery of their craft. Shakespeare, Molière, Ibsen, for example, began as apprentices in repertory theaters; Chekhov, Shaw, Wilder, O'Neill, writers from their youth, wrote their great plays only as they moved into middle age.

We have already noted that craftsmanship and technique are no substitute for genius; but genius without craftsmanship renders effective theater impossible. Thus, if we wish to examine the play aesthetically, we want to begin with a consideration of its structural and technical components.

PLOT AND STRUCTURE

Aristotle observed that the first element of drama is plot, the imitation of a noble action in which the events are so arranged that the audience has the sense of a beginning, a development, and an end of the action. Plot may be simple, as it generally is both in Greek tragedy and in contemporary drama; or it may be complicated, as it is in Jacobean and Restoration drama. Simple plots are not inherently better than complex plots, although we are living in an age that prefers the simple over the complex. Even implausible or unlikely turns of event do not necessarily flaw the play of a master. (Could Macbeth have really encountered witches? Does *King Oedipus* rely too exclusively on a series of improbable coincidences?)

In evaluating the plot of a play, we require:
1. That the events logically proceed one from another
2. That characters act and react to events in a manner in which their natures would dispose them to act
3. That the final resolution be not only logically inevitable but consonant with the universe inhabited by the *dramatis personae*

Closely related to the plot of a play is structure—the matter of the arrangement and emphasis of the events in the play. Structure is to drama essentially what the skeleton is to the body. And just as we are only subliminally aware of the skeleton beneath the skin, in the same manner should we be aware of dramatic structure.

Textbooks on the drama have traditionally analyzed the structure of Greek tragedy, Shakespearean tragedy, Restoration comedy, the Well-made play, the modern three-act play—analyses generally accompanied by diagrams and charted schemata. Though every play lends itself to an analysis of its structure, such analyses in themselves tell us very little about the value of a work; the analyses, moreover, are misleading because the structures of a number of the Greek plays, for example, do not conform to the pattern that texts assign to classical tragedy. Every play contains its own structure, its particular skeleton.

Thus, one might point out that Shakespeare's tragedies begin with exposition, succeeded by rising action to a turning point; that there is a falling action leading to the climax and the catastrophe. The difficulty here is not only that Shakespeare varied the structure of his plays, but that the structure of the most important dramatic work of the twentieth century is unrelated to the dramatic structure of anything that came before. Pirandello, Brecht, Thornton Wilder, and Samuel Beckett all turned their backs upon the conventions governing conventional dramatic structure. The true relation of structure to our consideration of what makes a play a work of art lies in the degree to which the dramatist allows the structure to grow organically out of character and theme rather than to base itself on contrived and outwardly imposed notions about good dramatic construction.

THE LANGUAGE OF DRAMA

The dramatist confronted by the matter of diction—the words that his characters speak—finds himself on the horns of a dilemma: he wants the language of his play to be as evocative, as pithy, as memorable, as witty as he is capable of writing; but he also requires that his characters sound like the people whom they are representing. It has been said of Shakespeare that every line of dialogue "may be assigned to the proper speaker."

Though there may be some exaggeration in that claim, there is not a great deal. Unlike most of the other seventeenth-century dramatists, Shakespeare took pains to individualize the speech of all his *dramatis personae.*

Shakespeare and his contemporaries, of course, wrote romantic drama and used the appropriate language of poetry. Because Horatio, in *Hamlet,* can say:

> But look, the morn, in russet mantle clad
> Walks o'er the dew of yon high eastward hill . . .

instead of "It's getting light," the diction of Elizabethan drama became a glory in itself. Christopher Marlowe, for example, achieved distinction as a dramatist without ever having learned how to construct a play. The force and beauty of "Marlowe's mighty line" compensate for his inadequacies of craftsmanship.

In modern drama, where the language of prose has superseded the language of poetry, the playwright must ingeniously maintain a delicate balance wherein the dialogue combines literary distinction with the illusion of actual speech. Ibsen, for example, after writing what could very well have endured as his supreme masterpiece, the poetic drama *Peer Gynt,* turned to the drama of social realism; but the poet in him remained close to the surface of his creative inspiration. Thus we find in *Hedda Gabler* recurrent references to Lövborg's manuscript as "child," to Thea's hair, to General Gabler's pistols, to vine leaves in the hair of Lövborg; what emerges from this succession of recurrent images is a level of prose inordinately arresting and individual. Chekhov weaves into the strands of dialogue *cris du coeur* that transform the banal and repetitive rambling of his characters into the most expressive dialogue of the past century. When, for example, Irena says to the homely Toozenbach, her fiancé:

> *(Weeping)* I've never loved anyone in my life. Oh, I've had such dreams about being in love; I've been dreaming about it for ever so long, day and night . . . but somehow my soul seems like an expensive piano which someone has locked up and the key's got lost . . .

the audience is both devastated and transported by Chekhov's image. Among our contemporary playwrights, startling effects are achieved through naturalistic dialogue. Jerry, the hero of *The Zoo Story,* describes the contents of his small, dingy furnished room to the prosperous and conventional Peter:

> . . . I have toilet articles, a few clothes, a hot plate that I'm not supposed to have, a can opener, one that works with a key, you know; a

knife, two forks, and two spoons, one small, one large; three plates, a cup, a saucer, a drinking glass, two picture frames, both empty, eight or nine books, a pack of pornographic playing cards, regular deck, an old Western Union typewriter that prints nothing but capital letters, and a small strongbox without a lock which has in it. . . . what? Rocks! Some rocks . . . sea-rounded rocks I picked up on the beach when I was a kid. Under which . . . weighed down . . . are some letters . . . please letters . . . please why don't you do this, and please when will you do that letters. And when letters, too. When will you write? When will you come? When? These letters are from more recent years.

This extraordinary cataloging of some meager possessions becomes both heartbreaking and illuminating.

The language of all great drama, classical, romantic, or modern, whether it be cast in verse or prose, because it is evocative, allusive, and imaginal, is the language of dramatic poetry. Often, it is the inadequate quality of language, the poverty of the writer's verbal resources, that have doomed many an otherwise respectable dramatic work to oblivion or to radio and television channels.

CHARACTERIZATION IN DRAMA

The final touchstone, perhaps the most important of all, in evaluating any play as a work of art—and most certainly in evaluating today's theater—is characterization. Contemporary dramatists such as Samuel Beckett, Jean Genêt, Eugene Ionesco have all but eliminated plot and action, ignored the idea of traditional dramatic structure, employed the barest bones of rhetoric—and still produced plays of consequence. What they have worked with, principally, are ideas and characters. But just as a play will come to life with little more than a single fully realized character, a play without a single vital person is no play at all.

How, in a play, is character established? Through:

1. Dialogue spoken by the character.
2. Dialogue spoken about the character.
3. Action taken by the character.
4. The personality and interpretation of the actor playing the role. Playwrights have often composed a role with a specific actor or actress in mind.

In the present century, playwrights such as Bernard Shaw and Eugene O'Neill have in their extended stage directions appended detailed comments and analyses of the *dramatis personae*.

Paradoxically, what makes for distinguished plays is the refusal of the characters of the play to conform precisely to the playwright's conception of them. One reason the great plays retain their immediacy is that the great characters of drama—Antigone, Phaedra, Antony, Cleopatra, Harpagon, Caesar, Hedda Gabler, Mrs. Dolly Levi among them—are subject not only to the shadings of each interpreter's art, to the interpretation of each reader, each critic, each director, but also to the changes of time itself. Plays date when the characters do not change and grow with evolving contexts of history.

An example of a character defying his author is the protagonist of *The Zoo Story*. Edward Albee specified in the stage directions that Jerry is "in his late thirties [with] a once trim . . . body [that] has begun to go to . . . fat . . . no longer handsome." In the original (1960) New York production, however, the role of Jerry was taken by George Maharis, a younger, leaner man than Albee described. Now the play means one thing if the protagonist has reached the limit of his youth; it means something else if the protagonist is on the threshold of middle age.

What we find in Jerry is a character in a play already taking on a life of his own, as Hamlet has done for centuries, becoming independent of his author, becoming instead someone we recognize, someone we know or have known, or have had glimpses or intimations of, in the progress of our own lives. But this is not to say that we ask no more of a character in a play than that we merely recognize his humanity, that we acknowledge his existence; characters in a television series, after all, are designed to remind us of neighbors and relatives. Recognition is not all.

Such is the art of a great dramatist that he persuades us not only that the creatures of his imagination have an existence through the identification we ourselves subliminally establish, but that the motives, aspirations, and passions of these imaginary men and women are identical with those passions which subconsciously influence our own lives. Might not the intelligent, well-intentioned, and heartbroken parent gain insight and even solace from Sophocles' *Antigone* just as the high-minded adolescent might gain a tolerance of the weaknesses of his elders through a compassionate reading of Euripides' *Hippolytus*? The characterizations of a Sophocles, a Shakespeare, or a Chekhov not only inform us but ennoble and develop us by enriching our understanding and enlarging our compassions.

A playwright has three principal means at his disposal for presenting character:

1. In melodrama and in farce particularly he offers his audience characters who are stock types—the earnest young lover; the miserly father; the middle-aged lecher; the meddling gossip; the helpless, credulous virgin; the faithful friend-confidant; the braggart soldier; the timorous

youth (who never wins the girl). These stereotypes, though they are the staple of farce, are employed even in high tragedy and in serious drama. Juliet's Nurse is the Meddling Gossip; Shylock, the Miserly Father; Hamlet's Horatio, the Friend-Confidant. Even the subtle Iago of *Othello* traces his ancestry back to the allegorical figure of *Vice* in the medieval morality plays. Even the extraordinary Falstaff has his origins in the *miles gloriosus*, the braggart soldier, of Greek and Roman comedy.

2. A second means of presenting character is the process of exfoliation or revelation. In melodrama the process is mainly a trick, a device, wherein a seemingly good man turns out to be evil, or a sinister character turns out to be good. But in serious drama the playwright reveals facets of character until the whole man emerges. Shakespeare's Antony, Shaw's Caesar, Anouilh's Becket are examples of protagonists who are not so much developed as exposed, layer by layer, until at the end, we discover the core of their being.

3. A third method of characterization is development. Although character development is more generally associated with the novelist's art than it is with the dramatist's, a number of memorable dramatic portraits reflect the technique of development: Aeschylus' Orestes; Shakespeare's Romeo, King Richard II, Hamlet, Lear; Ibsen's Mrs. Alving; Shaw's Cleopatra; Anouilh's King Henry II. Obviously the short span of a play's duration limits the dramatist's opportunity to develop more than one or two of his *dramatis personae*. In Anouilh's *Becket* only Henry undergoes a development. It is Henry who says to his older friend and counselor early in the play:

> You think too much . . . It's because people think that there are problems.

Later in the play, the matured, self-confident Henry contemptuously says of his faithful attendant nobles:

> Ah, my four idiots! My faithful hounds! It's warm beside you, like being in a stable. Good sweat! Comfortable nothingness! (*He taps their skulls.*) Not the least little glimmer inside to spoil the fun. And to think that before he came I was like you!

Anouilh's technique is to contrast Henry, capable of change and growth, with Becket, whose overreaching aspirations and profoundly wounded pride become clearly manifest only late in the play. Anouilh, having exploited the technique of development and revelation of character in the persons of Henry and Becket, fills out the play with types: a zealous young freedom fighter, a shrewish wife, two scheming Italian prelates, a bored and worldly king of France.

Let us ask ourselves once more: What gives a play artistic distinction?

Plot? Theme? Structure? Character? Diction? What makes a woman beautiful? A good figure? Long legs? Regular features? Large eyes? A full mouth? An ample bosom? Yes. No. Perhaps. A woman may have all those attributes and fall short of beauty. A woman may have few, possibly none, of those qualities and be beautiful. So it is in dealing with a play in the context of its aesthetic qualities. We may establish standards of plot construction, character development, elegance of style, subtlety of idea—all relevant in evaluating a play as a work of art. And the yardstick won't apply. In familiarizing ourselves with the great plays of the past, we acquire taste and the capacity to both enjoy and appreciate the drama of the present and future. For the drama has been a major art form for the past 2,500 years; the drama of tomorrow will consist of new-sprung entities with their own laws. Having read the old plays in the context of the present, we are preparing ourselves to read the new in the context of the future.

NOTES ON THE GENRES
OF THE DRAMA

TRAGEDY   Tragedy, as a literary term, refers to a form of drama that presents a man of a certain nobility who is attempting to achieve his highest aspirations but who, confronted by forces stronger than his greatest capacities, fails in his struggle.

GREEK CLASSICAL TRAGEDY   The definition of Greek tragedy is drawn from the extant plays of Aeschylus, Sophocles, and Euripides. Greek tragedy reflects the belief that all men are fated to suffer; that the greatest men suffer greatly; that suffering is exacted by the gods from men whose faults, errors, or ignorance require retributive justice; and that the depiction of man's errors and the manifestation of divine justice in drama ameliorate the state of man.

ELIZABETHAN TRAGEDY   Elizabethan tragedy, the tragedies of Marlowe and Shakespeare, incorporate the principal characteristics of Greek tragedy. Nevertheless, since the plays of Marlowe and Shakespeare are the product of a vastly different culture, as well as of a different stage tradition, there are striking differences: the chorus has all but disappeared; the unities of time, place, and action are disregarded; the classical restraints requiring the off-stage enactment of violence and passion are dismissed. Most important, Elizabethan tragedy expresses the Christian idea that suffering is conducive to redemption, that out of disorder caused by the existence of some evil force, order can be restored after the protagonist has properly expiated either his own crimes or the crimes associated with his mortal state, and that the death of the protagonist brings him to a state either of grace or of damnation.[1]

MODERN TRAGEDY   The hero of modern tragedy has been diminished in stature by the fact that he no longer transgresses against divine law as in Greek tragedy, nor does he defy outrageous fortune and his corporeal enemies as in Elizabethan tragedy. Instead, the protagonist of modern tragedy, denizen of an infinite universe, achieves meaning in

[1] Another distinction between Greek tragedy and Elizabethan (or Christian) tragedy has been drawn by W. H. Auden as follows:

> . . . first, Greek tragedy is the tragedy of necessity: i.e., the feeling aroused in the spectator is "What a pity it had to be this way"; Christian tragedy is the tragedy of possibility, "What a pity it was this way when it might have been otherwise"; secondly, the hubris which is the flaw in the Greek hero's character is the illusion of a man who knows himself strong and believes that nothing can shake that strength, while the corresponding Christian sin of Pride is the illusion of a man who knows himself weak but believes he can by his own efforts transcend that weakness and become strong.

protest against his insignificance, bravely insisting that his existence has a meaning, at least for himself.

MELODRAMA   Melodrama is tragedy *manqué,* tragedy that misses. It is not, however, contemptible. Most of the plays of Eugene O'Neill (except the last group beginning with *The Iceman Cometh*) emerge as melodramas. So do most of the plays of Lillian Hellman, Clifford Odets, Maxwell Anderson, and Tennessee Williams. In melodrama, the scale of thought and feeling is in proportion to daily life, never transcending the scale of the play—and the play can therefore rarely survive the times which produced it.

REALISTIC DRAMA   (Formerly called *tragicomedy,* in recent years called *drama*—from the French term *drame.*) Realistic drama, the predominant dramatic mode of the twentieth century, began in 1850 when Turgenev completed *A Month in the Country,* influenced, presumably, by the realistic novels of Balzac and Stendhal. Dramatic realism gained impetus in the social dramas of Ibsen and of Chekhov, the most influential architects of modern theater. Realistic drama objectively reveals men and women attempting to come to terms with a relentlessly changing environment and accepting their defeats with a shrug of resignation, with tears, or with bitter laughter. The realist playwright differs from the classicist or the romantic in that he shows us neither the glories of an idealized past nor the possibilities of an idealized future; he attempts to show us the way we live now.

COMEDY   The oldest extant comedies (425–405 B.C.), Aristophanes' so-called Old Comedy, were topical, fantastic, satiric—and funny. Their appeal was as intellectual as their intention was serious. The later plays of Aristophanes, Middle Comedy, form a bridge to the New Comedy of Menander (343–292 B.C.), who is, in fact, the father of the modern comedic tradition. Menander's impact upon the Roman dramatists, Plautus and Terence, left us the legacy of farce, romantic comedy, and the comedy of manners. Comedy, in provoking laughter, reminds us of our foibles and frailties, encouraging us to maintain a sense of proportion, a sense of fairness.

THE COMEDY OF MANNERS   The comedy of manners, previously developed by Shakespeare (in scenes of *Much Ado about Nothing, Twelfth Night,* and *The Merchant of Venice*), by Molière, and by Wycherly, was brought to a state of perfection by Congreve in the last decade of the seventeenth century. Since that time a fixed tradition of the English and the French theater, the comedy of manners has attracted the talents of Sheridan, Wilde, Bernard Shaw, and Jean Anouilh, all of whom have impressed their genius upon this aristocrat of the comic modes. The comedy of manners examines the lives of the worldly upper classes with the intention of exposing the hypocrisy of those whose manners are better than their morals and whose language is more elegant than their appetites.

THE COMEDY OF IDEAS   So closely related is the comedy of ideas to the comedy of manners that sometimes the two modes are indistinguishable. But not always. The comedy of ideas is primarily associated with the plays of George Bernard Shaw. Shavian comedy is the comedy of ideas, usually welded to the comedy of manners, but sometimes to farce, to Chekhovian drama, and even to melodrama. In the comedy of ideas Shaw deals with the logic of a system in relation to human practice; and as Shaw demonstrates, life always wins over any logical system.

FARCE   The oldest form of comedy, farce—with its devices, its situations, and its stereotyped characters—has served Aristophanes, Plautus, Shakespeare, Molière, Chekhov (for his one-act plays) , and Charlie Chaplin. The ingredients of farce, in addition to the conventionalized plots and simplification of human nature to its basic traits, are word play and idiomatic language, often vulgar or bawdy; visual humor (mimicry, pratfalls, double takes) ; outrageously cruel or absurdly licentious behavior. Although farce has been often dismissed as mindless entertainment, the targets of farce stand as figures of an implicit criticism of modes of human behavior, of social institutions and taboos. Eric Bentley, the critic and translator of Brecht, has even called farce cathartic, like tragedy, enabling the audience to savor unsavory adventures "without taking the responsibility or suffering the guilt."

OTHER GENRES   There are a number of miscellaneous genres of plays which need not be analyzed here. Some of them are chronicle plays (Laurence Housman's *Victoria Regina*); the masque (Milton's *Comus*) ; romantic drama (Rostand's *Cyrano de Bergerac*) ; agitprop—the inciting, left-wing plays of the 1930s— (Odets's *Waiting for Lefty*) ; epic drama of Bertold Brecht; expressionist fantasy (Strindberg's *The Dream Play*) ; experimental drama (Pirandello, Thornton Wilder) ; poetic drama (Yeats's "Purgatory"). There is also symbolist drama, folk drama, closet drama, and fantasy. Most recently there has been a new movement in drama, marked by experimentation in both the realistic and surrealistic modes; these new experimental dramatists, Ionesco, Genêt, Sartre, Pinter, Beckett, and Edward Albee, have been labeled practitioners of a Theater of the Absurd—a term Mr. Albee discusses in the afterword to his play *The Zoo Story,* both of which appear in this text.

SOPHOCLES

SOPHOCLES (CA. 496–406 B.C.) WAS BORN IN COLONUS, NEAR ATHENS, OF A WELL-TO-DO FAMILY. HE SERVED ATHENS AS BOTH MILITARY LEADER AND PUBLIC OFFICIAL. HIS LIFEWORK, HOWEVER, WAS THAT OF PLAYWRIGHT; HE COMPETED WITH BOTH THE OLDER AESCHYLUS AND THE YOUNGER EURIPIDES FOR THE DRAMA PRIZES AWARDED AT THE FESTIVALS OF DIONYSUS AND WON FIRST PRIZE NEARLY TWENTY TIMES. AFTER HIS DEATH, SOPHOCLES WAS VENERATED BY ATHENIANS AS A HERO OF THE STATE.

If any dramatist could challenge the supremacy of Shakespeare, it would surely be Sophocles. But of the approximately one hundred and twenty-five plays attributed to Sophocles, all but seven have been lost. The extant seven include *Ajax, Antigone, Electra, The Maidens of Trachis, Oedipus at Colonus, Oedipus Rex,* and *Philoctetes.*

Of Sophocles's surviving plays, *Antigone* is most interesting to students of the drama. First produced about 442 B.C. (a few decades after the beginning of Western drama as we know it), *Antigone* so firmly established the principle of dramatic conflict as to make it an eternal monument of play construction. Unlike Sophocles's *Oedipus Rex*—that dramatic masterpiece of remorseless self-discovery—*Antigone* involves us at least as much intellectually as it involves us emotionally in the play's action.

For example, even in our first reading of the play, we cannot help seeing how Sophocles maintains a balance in the conflict between Antigone's private conscience and Creon's sense of public responsibility. Our empathic involvement with Antigone, moreover, diminishes during the progress of the play as the reasons given by her for her acts become more diffuse. And when the play ends, for whom do we most grieve? Antigone? Haemon? Creon?

The ancient Greeks believed that supernatural forces in the universe governed their lives. Their concept of the Fates, that a family could be cursed by the gods, pervades both the *Oresteia* of Aeschylus and the three plays concerning King Oedipus and his children. The vindictiveness of Zeus is stated by Antigone in the opening lines and many times repeated by her. It may be said that Creon's misfortunes are due to his refusal to accept that awesome Fate which Antigone and the chorus insistently invoke. Compare his opening lines with those of Antigone. Is it possible that he, rather than Antigone, is the tragic hero of the play?

It is interesting to observe how the function of the Chorus changes during the progress of the play. To ignore or slight the lines of the Chorus of Greek drama, particularly in *Antigone,* is to lose the greater part of the play's poetry (translation though it be) and many of the play's implications. The magnificent third chorus, "Fortunate they whose lives have no taste of pain," inspired one of the landmarks of English poetry, Matthew Arnold's "Dover Beach."

ANTIGONE

AN ENGLISH VERSION
BY DUDLEY FITTS AND ROBERT FITZGERALD

PERSONS REPRESENTED

ANTIGONE
ISMENE
EURYDICE
CREON
HAIMON
TEIRESIAS
A SENTRY
A MESSENGER
CHORUS

SCENE: *Before the palace of Creon, King of Thebes. A central double door, and two lateral doors. A platform extends the length of the façade, and from this platform three steps lead down into the "orchestra," or chorus-ground.* TIME: *dawn of the day after the repulse of the Argive army from the assault on Thebes.*

PROLOGUE

(ANTIGONE *and* ISMENE *enter from the central door of the Palace.*)
ANTIGONE
    Ismenê, dear sister,
    You would think that we had already suffered enough
    For the curse on Oedipus:
    I cannot imagine any grief
    That you and I have not gone through. And now—
    Have they told you of the new decree of our King Creon?
ISMENE
    I have heard nothing: I know
    That two sisters lost two brothers, a double death
    In a single hour; and I know that the Argive army
    Fled in the night; but beyond this, nothing.
ANTIGONE
    I thought so. And that is why I wanted you
    To come out here with me. There is something we must do.
ISMENE
    Why do you speak so strangely?

ANTIGONE

Listen, Ismenê:
Creon buried our brother Eteoclês
With military honors, gave him a soldier's funeral,
And it was right that he should; but Polyneicês,
Who fought as bravely and died as miserably,—
They say that Creon has sworn
No one shall bury him, no one mourn for him,
But his body must lie in the fields, a sweet treasure
For carrion birds to find as they search for food.
That is what they say, and our good Creon is coming here
To announce it publicly; and the penalty—
Stoning to death in the public square!

                              There it is,
And now you can prove what you are:
A true sister, or a traitor to your family.

ISMENE

Antigonê, you are mad! What could I possibly do?

ANTIGONE

You must decide whether you will help me or not.

ISMENE

I do not understand you. Help you in what?

ANTIGONE

Ismenê, I am going to bury him. Will you come?

ISMENE

Bury him! You have just said the new law forbids it.

ANTIGONE

He is my brother. And he is your brother, too.

ISMENE

But think of the danger! Think what Creon will do!

ANTIGONE

Creon is not strong enough to stand in my way.

ISMENE

Ah sister!
Oedipus died, everyone hating him
For what his own search brought to light, his eyes
Ripped out by his own hand; and Iocastê died,
His mother and wife at once: she twisted the cords
That strangled her life; and our two brothers died,
Each killed by the other's sword. And we are left:
But oh, Antigonê,
Think how much more terrible than these
Our own death would be if we should go against Creon

And do what he has forbidden! We are only women,
We cannot fight with men, Antigonê!
The law is strong, we must give in to the law
In this thing, and in worse. I beg the Dead
To forgive me, but I am helpless: I must yield
To those in authority. And I think it is dangerous business
To be always meddling.

ANTIGONE

                If that is what you think,
I should not want you, even if you asked to come.
You have made your choice, you can be what you want to be.
But I will bury him; and if I must die,
I say that this crime is holy: I shall lie down
With him in death, and I shall be as dear
To him as he to me.

                It is the dead,
Not the living, who make the longest demands:
We die for ever . . .

                You may do as you like,
Since apparently the laws of the gods mean nothing to you.

ISMENE

They mean a great deal to me; but I have no strength
To break laws that were made for the public good.

ANTIGONE

That must be your excuse, I suppose. But as for me,
I will bury the brother I love.

ISMENE

                Antigonê,
I am so afraid for you!

ANTIGONE

                You need not be:
You have yourself to consider, after all.

ISMENE

But no one must hear of this, you must tell no one!
I will keep it a secret, I promise!

ANTIGONE

                Oh tell it! Tell everyone!
Think how they'll hate you when it all comes out
If they learn that you knew about it all the time!

ISMENE

So fiery! You should be cold with fear.

ANTIGONE

Perhaps. But I am doing only what I must.

ISMENE

But can you do it? I say that you cannot.

ANTIGONE

Very well: when my strength gives out, I shall do no more.

ISMENE

Impossible things should not be tried at all.

ANTIGONE

Go away, Ismenê:

I shall be hating you soon, and the dead will too,

For your words are hateful. Leave me my foolish plan:

I am not afraid of the danger; if it means death,

It will not be the worst of deaths—death without honor.

ISMENE

Go then, if you feel that you must.

You are unwise,

But a loyal friend indeed to those who love you.

(*Exit into the Palace.* ANTIGONE *goes off, L. Enter the* CHORUS.)

PÁRODOS

CHORUS

Now the long blade of the sun, lying   (STROPHE 1)

Level east to west, touches with glory

Thebes of the Seven Gates. Open, unlidded

Eye of golden day! O marching light

Across the eddy and rush of Dircê's stream,

Striking the white shields of the enemy

Thrown headlong backward from the blaze of morning!

CHORAGOS

Polyneicês their commander

Roused them with windy phrases,

He the wild eagle screaming

Insults above our land,

His wings their shields of snow,

His crest their marshall helms.

CHORUS

Against our seven gates in a yawning ring   (ANTISTROPHE 1)

The famished spears came onward in the night;

But before his jaws were sated with our blood,

Or pinefire took the garland of our towers,

He was thrown back; and as he turned, great Thebes—

No tender victim for his noisy power—

Rose like a dragon behind him, shouting war.

CHORAGOS

> For God hates utterly
> The bray of bragging tongues;
> And when he beheld their smiling,
> Their swagger of golden helms,
> The frown of his thunder blasted
> Their first man from our walls.

CHORUS

> We heard his shout of triumph high in the air   (STROPHE 2)
> Turn to a scream; far out in a flaming arc
> He fell with his windy torch, and the earth struck him.
> And others storming in fury no less than his
> Found shock of death in the dusty joy of battle.

CHORAGOS

> Seven captains at seven gates
> Yielded their clanging arms to the god
> That bends the battle-line and breaks it.
> These two only, brothers in blood,
> Face to face in matchless rage,
> Mirroring each the other's death,
> Clashed in long combat.

CHORUS

> But now in the beautiful morning of victory   (ANTISTROPHE 2)
> Let Thebes of the many chariots sing for joy!
> With hearts for dancing we'll take leave of war:
> Our temples shall be sweet with hymns of praise,
> And the long night shall echo with our chorus.

SCENE I

CHORAGOS

> But now at last our new King is coming:
> Creon of Thebes, Menoikeus' son.
> In this auspicious dawn of his reign
> What are the new complexities
> That shifting Fate has woven for him?
> What is his counsel? Why has he summoned
> The old men to hear him?

(*Enter* CREON *from the Palace, C. He addresses the* CHORUS *from the top step.*)

CREON

> Gentlemen: I have the honor to inform you that our Ship of State, which recent storms have threatened to destroy, has come safely to

harbor at last, guided by the merciful wisdom of Heaven. I have summoned you here this morning because I know that I can depend upon you: your devotion to King Laïos was absolute; you never hesitated in your duty to our late ruler Oedipus; and when Oedipus died, your loyalty was transferred to his children. Unfortunately, as you know, his two sons, the princes Eteoclês and Polyneicês, have killed each other in battle; and I, as the next in blood, have succeeded to the full power of the throne.

I am aware, of course that no Ruler can expect complete loyalty from his subjects until he has been tested in office. Nevertheless, I say to you at the very outset that I have nothing but contempt for the kind of Governor who is afraid, for whatever reason, to follow the course that he knows is best for the State; and as for the man who sets private friendship above the public welfare,—I have no use for him, either. I call God to witness that if I saw my country headed for ruin, I should not be afraid to speak out plainly; and I need hardly remind you that I would never have any dealings with an enemy of the people. No one values friendship more highly than I; but we must remember that friends made at the risk of wrecking our Ship are not real friends at all.

These are my principles, at any rate, and that is why I have made the following decision concerning the sons of Oedipus: Eteoclês, who died as a man should die, fighting for his country, is to be buried with full military honors, with all the ceremony that is usual when the greatest heroes die; but his brother Polyneicês, who broke his exile to come back with fire and sword against his native city and the shrines of his fathers' gods, whose one idea was to spill the blood of his blood and sell his own people into slavery—Polyneicês, I say, is to have no burial: no man is to touch him or say the least prayer for him; he shall lie on the plain, unburied; and the birds and the scavenging dogs can do with him whatever they like.

This is my command, and you can see the wisdom behind it. As long as I am King, no traitor is going to be honored with the loyal man. But whoever shows by word and deed that he is on the side of the State, —he shall have my respect while he is living, and my reverence when he is dead.

CHORAGOS

If that is your will, Creon son of Menoikeus,
You have the right to enforce it: we are yours.

CREON

That is my will. Take care that you do your part.

CHORAGOS

We are old men: let the younger ones carry it out.

CREON

I do not mean that: the sentries have been appointed.

CHORAGOS

Then what is it that you would have us do?

CREON

You will give no support to whoever breaks this law.

CHORAGOS

Only a crazy man is in love with death!

CREON

And death it is; yet money talks, and the wisest
Have sometimes been known to count a few coins too many.

(*Enter* SENTRY *from L.*)

SENTRY

I'll not say that I'm out of breath from running, King, because every
time I stopped to think about what I have to tell you, I felt like going
back. And all the time a voice kept saying, "You fool, don't you know
you're walking straight into trouble?"; and then another voice: "Yes,
but if you let somebody else get the news to Creon first, it will be even
worse than that for you!" But good sense won out, at least I hope it
was good sense, and here I am with a story that makes no sense, at all;
but I'll tell it anyhow, because, as they say, what's going to happen's
going to happen, and—

CREON

Come to the point. What have you to say?

SENTRY

I did not do it. I did not see who did it. You must not punish me for
what someone else has done.

CREON

A comprehensive defense! More effective, perhaps,
If I knew its purpose. Come: what is it?

SENTRY

A dreadful thing . . . I don't know how to put it—

CREON

Out with it!

SENTRY

       Well, then;
The dead man—
       Polyneicês—
(*Pause. The* SENTRY *is overcome, fumbles for words.* CREON *waits im-
passively.*)
       out there—
          someone,—
New dust on the slimy flesh!

(*Pause. No sign from* CREON.)

Someone has given it burial that way, and

Gone . . .

(*Long pause.* CREON *finally speaks with deadly control.*)

CREON

And the man who dared do this?

SENTRY

I swear I

Do not know! You must believe me!

Listen:

The ground was dry, not a sign of digging, no,

Not a wheeltrack in the dust, no trace of anyone.

It was when they relieved us this morning: and one of them,

The corporal, pointed to it.

There it was,

The strangest—

Look:

The body, just mounded over with light dust: you see?

Not buried really, but as if they'd covered it

Just enough for the ghost's peace. And no sign

Of dogs or any wild animal that had been there.

And then what a scene there was! Every man of us

Accusing the other: we all proved the other man did it,

We all had proof that we could not have done it.

We were ready to take hot iron in our hands,

Walk through fire, swear by all the gods,

It was not I!

I do not know who it was, but it was not I!

(CREON's *rage has been mounting steadily, but the* SENTRY *is too intent
upon his story to notice it.*)

And then, when this came to nothing, someone said

A thing that silenced us and made us stare

Down at the ground: you had to be told the news,

And one of us had to do it! We threw the dice,

And the bad luck fell to me. So here I am,

No happier to be here than you are to have me:

Nobody likes the man who brings bad news.

CHORAGOS

I have been wondering, King: can it be that the gods have done this?

CREON   (*furiously*) .

Stop!

Must you doddering wrecks

Go out of your heads entirely? "The gods!"
Intolerable!
The gods favor this corpse? Why? How had he served them?
Tried to loot their temples, burn their images,
Yes, and the whole State, and its laws with it!
Is it your senile opinion that the gods love to honor bad men?
A pious thought!—
                No, from the very beginning
There have been those who have whispered together,
Stiff-necked anarchists, putting their heads together,
Scheming against me in alleys. These are the men,
And they have bribed my own guard to do this thing.
Money!   (*Sententiously*.)
There's nothing in the world so demoralizing as money.
Down go your cities,
Homes gone, men gone, honest hearts corrupted,
Crookedness of all kinds, and all for money!
(*To* SENTRY.)
                      But you—!
I swear by God and by the throne of God,
The man who has done this thing shall pay for it!
Find that man, bring him here to me, or your death
Will be the least of your problems: I'll string you up
Alive, and there will be certain ways to make you
Discover your employer before you die;
And the process may teach you a lesson you seem to have missed:
The dearest profit is sometimes all too dear:
That depends on the source. Do you understand me?
A fortune won is often misfortune.

SENTRY

King, may I speak?

CREON

                Your very voice distresses me.

SENTRY

Are you sure that it is my voice, and not your conscience?

CREON

By God, he wants to analyze me now!

SENTRY

It is not what I say, but what has been done, that hurts you.

CREON

You talk too much.

SENTRY

              Maybe; but I've done nothing.

CREON
　　Sold your soul for some silver: that's all you've done.
SENTRY
　　How dreadful it is when the right judge judges wrong!
CREON
　　Your figures of speech
　　May entertain you now; but unless you bring me the man,
　　You will get little profit from them in the end.
(*Exit* CREON *into the Palace.*)
SENTRY
　　"Bring me the man"—!
　　I'd like nothing better than bringing him the man!
　　But bring him or not, you have seen the last of me here.
　　At any rate, I am safe!
(*Exit* SENTRY.)

ODE I

CHORUS
　　Numberless are the world's wonders, but none　　　　(STROPHE 1)
　　More wonderful than man; the stormgray sea
　　Yields to his prows, the huge crests bear him high;
　　Earth, holy and inexhaustible, is graven
　　With shining furrows where his plows have gone
　　Year after year, the timeless labor of stallions.

　　The lightboned birds and beasts that cling to cover,　　(ANTISTROPHE 1)
　　The lithe fish lighting their reaches of dim water,
　　All are taken, tamed in the net of his mind;
　　The lion on the hill, the wild horse windy-maned,
　　Resign to him; and his blunt yoke has broken
　　The sultry shoulders of the mountain bull.

　　Words also, and thought as rapid as air,　　　　　（STROPHE 2)
　　He fashions to his good use; statecraft is his,
　　And his the skill that deflects the arrows of snow,
　　The spears of winter rain: from every wind
　　He has made himself secure—from all but one:
　　In the late wind of death he cannot stand.

　　O clear intelligence, force beyond all measure!　　（ANTISTROPHE 2)
　　O fate of man, working both good and evil!
　　When the laws are kept, how proudly his city stands!

When the laws are broken, what of his city then?
Never may the anárchic man find rest at my hearth,
Never be it said that my thoughts are his thoughts.

SCENE II

(*Re-enter* SENTRY *leading* ANTIGONE.)
CHORAGOS
What does this mean? Surely this captive woman
Is the Princess, Antigonê. Why should she be taken?
SENTRY
Here is the one who did it! We caught her
In the very act of burying him.—Where is Creon?
CHORAGOS
Just coming from the house.
(*Enter* CREON, *C.*)
CREON
What has happened?
Why have you come back so soon?
SENTRY   (*expansively*) .
O King,
A man should never be too sure of anything:
I would have sworn
That you'd not see me here again: your anger
Frightened me so, and the things you threatened me with;
But how could I tell then
That I'd be able to solve the case so soon?
No dice-throwing this time: I was only too glad to come!
Here is this woman. She is the guilty one:
We found her trying to bury him.
Take her, then; question her; judge her as you will.
I am through with the whole thing now, and glád óf it.
CREON
But this is Antigonê! Why have you brought her here?
SENTRY
She was burying him, I tell you!
CREON   (*severely*) .
Is this the truth?
SENTRY
I saw her with my own eyes. Can I say more?
CREON
The details: come, tell me quickly!

SENTRY
                                        It was like this:
After those terrible threats of yours, King,
We went back and brushed the dust away from the body.
The flesh was soft by now, and stinking,
So we sat on a hill to windward and kept guard.
No napping this time! We kept each other awake.
But nothing happened until the white round sun
Whirled in the center of the round sky over us:
Then, suddenly,
A storm of dust roared up from the earth, and the sky
Went out, the plain vanished with all its trees
In the stinging dark. We closed our eyes and endured it.
The whirlwind lasted a long time, but it passed;
And then we looked, and there was Antigonê!
I have seen
A mother bird come back to a stripped nest, heard
Her crying bitterly a broken note or two
For the young ones stolen. Just so, when this girl
Found the bare corpse, and all her love's work wasted,
She wept, and cried on heaven to damn the hands
That had done this thing.
                                        And then she brought more dust
And sprinkled wine three times for her brother's ghost.

We ran and took her at once. She was not afraid,
Not even when we charged her with what she had done.
She denied nothing.
                                        And this was comfort to me,
And some uneasiness: for it is a good thing
To escape from death, but it is no great pleasure
To bring death to a friend.
                                        Yet I always say
There is nothing so comfortable as your own safe skin!
CREON   *(slowly, dangerously)* .
And you, Antigonê,
You with your head hanging,—do you confess this thing?
ANTIGONE
I do. I deny nothing.
CREON   *(to* SENTRY*)* .
                                        You may go.
(Exit SENTRY.*)*

(To ANTIGONE.)
Tell me, tell me briefly:
Had you heard my proclamation touching this matter?

ANTIGONE
It was public. Could I help hearing it?

CREON
And yet you dared defy the law.

ANTIGONE
                    I dared.
It was not God's proclamation. That final Justice
That rules the world below makes no such laws.

Your edict, King, was strong,
But all your strength is weakness itself against
The immortal unrecorded laws of God.
They are not merely now: they were, and shall be,
Operative for ever, beyond man utterly.

I knew I must die, even without your decree:
I am only mortal. And if I must die
Now, before it is my time to die,
Surely this is no hardship: can anyone
Living, as I live, with evil all about me,
Think Death less than a friend? This death of mine
Is of no importance; but if I had left my brother
Lying in death unburied, I should have suffered.
Now I do not.
                    You smile at me. Ah Creon,
Think me a fool, if you like; but it may well be
That a fool convicts me of folly.

CHORAGOS
Like father, like daughter: both headstrong, deaf to reason!
She has never learned to yield.

CREON
                    She has much to learn.
The inflexible heart breaks first, the toughest iron
Cracks first, and the wildest horses bend their necks
At the pull of the smallest curb.
                    Pride? In a slave?
This girl is guilty of a double insolence,
Breaking the given laws and boasting of it.
Who is the man here,

She or I, if this crime goes unpunished?
Sister's child, or more than sister's child,
Or closer yet in blood—she and her sister
Win bitter death for this!
(*To* SERVANTS.)
                                        Go, some of you,
Arrest Ismenê. I accuse her equally.
Bring her: you will find her sniffling in the house there.

Her mind's a traitor: crimes kept in the dark
Cry for light, and the guardian brain shudders;
But how much worse than this
Is brazen boasting of barefaced anarchy!

ANTIGONE

Creon, what more do you want than my death?

CREON
                                                        Nothing.
That gives me everything.

ANTIGONE
                            Then I beg you: kill me.
This talking is a great weariness: your words
Are distasteful to me, and I am sure that mine
Seem so to you. And yet they should not seem so:
I should have praise and honor for what I have done.
All these men here would praise me
Were their lips not frozen shut with fear of you.
(*Bitterly.*)
Ah the good fortune of kings,
Licensed to say and do whatever they please!

CREON

You are alone here in that opinion.

ANTIGONE

No, they are with me. But they keep their tongues in leash.

CREON

Maybe. But you are guilty, and they are not.

ANTIGONE

There is no guilt in reverence for the dead.

CREON

But Eteoclês—was he not your brother too?

ANTIGONE

My brother too.

CREON
                And you insult his memory?

ANTIGONE   (*softly*).
The dead man would not say that I insult it.
CREON
He would: for you honor a traitor as much as him.
ANTIGONE
His own brother, traitor or not, and equal in blood.
CREON
He made war on his country. Eteoclês defended it.
ANTIGONE
Nevertheless, there are honors due all the dead.
CREON
But not the same for the wicked as for the just.
ANTIGONE
Ah Creon, Creon,
Which of us can say what the gods hold wicked?
CREON
An enemy is an enemy, even dead.
ANTIGONE
It is my nature to join in love, not hate.
CREON   (*finally losing patience*).
Go join them, then; if you must have your love,
Find it in hell!
CHORAGOS
But see, Ismenê comes:
(*Enter* ISMENE, *guarded.*)
Those tears are sisterly, the cloud
That shadows her eyes rains down gentle sorrow.
CREON
You too, Ismenê,
Snake in my ordered house, sucking my blood
Stealthily—and all the time I never knew
That these two sisters were aiming at my throne!
                                              Ismenê,
Do you confess your share in this crime, or deny it?
Answer me.
ISMENE
Yes, if she will let me say so. I am guilty.
ANTIGONE   (*coldly*).
No, Ismenê. You have no right to say so.
You would not help me, and I will not have you help me.
ISMENE
But now I know what you meant; and I am here
To join you, to take my share of punishment.

ANTIGONE

   The dead man and the gods who rule the dead

   Know whose act this was. Words are not friends.

ISMENE

   Do you refuse me, Antigonê? I want to die with you:

   I too have a duty that I must discharge to the dead.

ANTIGONE

   You shall not lessen my death by sharing it.

ISMENE

   What do I care for life when you are dead?

ANTIGONE

   Ask Creon. You're always hanging on his opinions.

ISMENE

   You are laughing at me. Why, Antigonê?

ANTIGONE

   It's a joyless laughter, Ismenê.

ISMENE

                    But can I do nothing?

ANTIGONE

   Yes. Save yourself. I shall not envy you.

   There are those who will praise you; I shall have honor, too.

ISMENE

   But we are equally guilty!

ANTIGONE

               No more, Ismenê.

   You are alive, but I belong to Death.

CREON   *(to the* CHORUS*)* .

   Gentlemen, I beg you to observe these girls:

   One has just now lost her mind; the other,

   It seems, has never had a mind at all.

ISMENE

   Grief teaches the steadiest minds to waver, King.

CREON

   Yours certainly did, when you assumed guilt with the guilty!

ISMENE

   But how could I go on living without her?

CREON

                   You are.

   She is already dead.

ISMENE

           But your own son's bride!

CREON

   There are places enough for him to push his plow.

I want no wicked women for my sons!
ISMENE
    O dearest Haimon, how your father wrongs you!
CREON
    I've had enough of your childish talk of marriage!
CHORAGOS
    Do you really intend to steal this girl from your son?
CREON
    No; Death will do that for me.
CHORAGOS
                    Then she must die?
CREON   *(ironically)* .
    You dazzle me.
         —But enough of this talk!
    (To GUARDS.*)*
    You, there, take them away and guard them well:
    For they are but women, and even brave men run
    When they see Death coming.
(Exeunt ISMENE, ANTIGONE, *and* GUARDS.*)*

ODE II

CHORUS
    Fortunate is the man who has never tasted God's vengeance!
                               (STROPHE 1)
    Where once the anger of heaven has struck, that house is shaken
    For ever: damnation rises behind each child
    Like a wave cresting out of the black northeast,
    When the long darkness under sea roars up
    And bursts drumming death upon the windwhipped sand.

    I have seen this gathering sorrow from time long past   (ANTISTROPHE 1)
    Loom upon Oedipus' children: generation from generation
    Takes the compulsive rage of the enemy god.
    So lately this last flower of Oedipus' line
    Drank the sunlight! but now a passionate word
    And a handful of dust have closed up all its beauty.

      What mortal arrogance   (STROPHE 2)
      Transcends the wrath of Zeus?
    Sleep cannot lull him, nor the effortless long months
    Of the timeless gods: but he is young for ever,

And his house is the shining day of high Olympos.
   All that is and shall be,
   And all the past, is his.
No pride on earth is free of the curse of heaven.

   The straying dreams of men   (ANTISTROPHE 2)
      May bring them ghosts of joy:
But as they drowse, the waking embers burn them;
Or they walk with fíxed éyes, as blind men walk.
But the ancient wisdom speaks for our own time:
   Fate works most for woe
   With Folly's fairest show.
Man's little pleasure is the spring of sorrow.

SCENE III

CHORAGOS
   But here is Haimon, King, the last of all your sons.
   Is it grief for Antigonê that brings him here,
   And bitterness at being robbed of his bride?
(*Enter* HAIMON.)
CREON
   We shall soon see, and no need of diviners.
                                        —Son,
   You have heard my final judgment on that girl:
   Have you come here hating me, or have you come
   With deference and with love, whatever I do?
HAIMON
   I am your son, father. You are my guide.
   You make things clear for me, and I obey you.
   No marriage means more to me than your continuing wisdom.
CREON
   Good. That is the way to behave: subordinate
   Everything else, my son, to your father's will.
   This is what a man prays for, that he may get
   Sons attentive and dutiful in his house,
   Each one hating his father's enemies,
   Honoring his father's friends. But if his sons
   Fail him, if they turn out unprofitably,
   What has he fathered but trouble for himself
   And amusement for the malicious?
                              So you are right
   Not to lose your head over this woman.

Your pleasure with her would soon grow cold, Haimon,
And then you'd have a hellcat in bed and elsewhere.
Let her find her husband in Hell!
Of all the people in this city, only she
Has had contempt for my law and broken it.

Do you want me to show myself weak before the people?
Or to break my sworn word? No, and I will not.
The woman dies.
I suppose she'll plead "family ties." Well, let her.
If I permit my own family to rebel,
How shall I earn the world's obedience?
Show me the man who keeps his house in hand,
He's fit for public authority.
                         I'll have no dealings
With law-breakers, critics of the government:
Whoever is chosen to govern should be obeyed—
Must be obeyed, in all things, great and small,
Just and unjust! O Haimon,
The man who knows how to obey, and that man only,
Knows how to give commands when the time comes.
You can depend on him, no matter how fast
The spears come: he's a good soldier, he'll stick it out.

Anarchy, anarchy! Show me a greater evil!
This is why cities tumble and the great houses rain down,
This is what scatters armies!

No, no: good lives are made so by discipline.
We keep the laws then, and the lawmakers,
And no woman shall seduce us. If we must lose,
Let's lose to a man, at least! Is a woman stronger than we?

CHORAGOS

Unless time has rusted my wits,
What you say, King, is said with point and dignity.

HAIMON   (*boyishly earnest*) .

Father:
Reason is God's crowning gift to man, and you are right
To warn me against losing mine. I cannot say—
I hope that I shall never want to say!—that you
Have reasoned badly. Yet there are other men
Who can reason, too; and their opinions might be helpful.
You are not in a position to know everything
That people say or do, or what they feel:
Your temper terrifies them—everyone

Will tell you only what you like to hear.
But I, at any rate, can listen; and I have heard them
Muttering and whispering in the dark about this girl.
They say no woman has ever, so unreasonably,
Died so shameful a death for a generous act:
"She covered her brother's body. Is this indecent?
She kept him from dogs and vultures. Is this a crime?
Death?—She should have all the honor that we can give her!"

This is the way they talk out there in the city.

You must believe me:
Nothing is closer to me than your happiness.
What could be closer? Must not any son
Value his father's fortune as his father does his?
I beg you, do not be unchangeable:
Do not believe that you alone can be right.
The man who thinks that,
The man who maintains that only he has the power
To reason correctly, the gift to speak, the soul—
A man like that, when you know him, turns out empty.

It is not reason never to yield to reason!

In flood time you can see how some trees bend,
And because they bend, even their twigs are safe,
While stubborn trees are torn up, roots and all.
And the same thing happens in sailing:
Make your sheet fast, never slacken,—and over you go,
Head over heels and under: and there's your voyage.
Forget you are angry! Let yourself be moved!
I know I am young; but please let me say this:
The ideal condition
Would be, I admit, that men should be right by instinct;
But since we are all too likely to go astray,
The reasonable thing is to learn from those who can teach.

CHORAGOS

You will do well to listen to him, King,
If what he says is sensible. And you, Haimon,
Must listen to your father.—Both speak well.

CREON

You consider it right for a man of my years and experience
To go to school to a boy?

HAIMON

                         It is not right

If I am wrong. But if I am young, and right,
What does my age matter?

CREON

You think it right to stand up for an anarchist?

HAIMON

Not at all. I pay no respect to criminals.

CREON

Then she is not a criminal?

HAIMON

The City would deny it, to a man.

CREON

And the City proposes to teach me how to rule?

HAIMON

Ah. Who is it that's talking like a boy now?

CREON

My voice is the one voice giving orders in this City!

HAIMON

It is no City if it takes orders from one voice.

CREON

The State is the King!

HAIMON

Yes, if the State is a desert.

(*Pause.*)

CREON

This boy, it seems, has sold out to a woman.

HAIMON

If you are a woman: my concern is only for you.

CREON

So? Your "concern"! In a public brawl with your father!

HAIMON

How about you, in a public brawl with justice?

CREON

With justice, when all that I do is within my rights?

HAIMON

You have no right to trample on God's right.

CREON (*completely out of control*) .

Fool, adolescent fool! Taken in by a woman!

HAIMON

You'll never see me taken in by anything vile.

CREON

Every word you say is for her!

HAIMON (*quietly, darkly*) .

And for you.
And for me. And for the gods under the earth.

CREON

You'll never marry her while she lives.

HAIMON

Then she must die.—But her death will cause another.

CREON

Another?

Have you lost your senses? Is this an open threat?

HAIMON

There is no threat in speaking to emptiness.

CREON

I swear you'll regret this superior tone of yours!

You are the empty one!

HAIMON

                      If you were not my father,

I'd say you were perverse.

CREON

You girlstruck fool, don't play at words with me!

HAIMON

I am sorry. You prefer silence.

CREON

                 Now, by God—!

I swear, by all the gods in heaven above us,

You'll watch it, I swear you shall!

(*To the* SERVANTS.)

                  Bring her out!

Bring the woman out! Let her die before his eyes!

Here, this instant, with her bridegroom beside her!

HAIMON

Not here, no; she will not die here, King.

And you will never see my face again.

Go on raving as long as you've a friend to endure you.

(*Exit* HAIMON.)

CHORAGOS

Gone, gone.

Creon, a young man in a rage is dangerous!

CREON

Let him do, or dream to do, more than a man can.

He shall not save these girls from death.

CHORAGOS

                 These girls?

You have sentenced them both?

CREON

                No, you are right.

I will not kill the one whose hands are clean.

CHORAGOS

But Antigonê?

CREON   (*somberly*).

　　　　　　　I will carry her far away
Out there in the wilderness, and lock her
Living in a vault of stone. She shall have food,
As the custom is, to absolve the State of her death.
And there let her pray to the gods of hell:
They are her only gods:
Perhaps they will show her an escape from death,
Or she may learn,
　　　　　　　though late,
That piety shown the dead is pity in vain.

(*Exit* CREON.)

ODE III

CHORUS

Love, unconquerable   (STROPHE)
Waster of rich men, keeper
Of warm lights and all-night vigil
In the soft face of a girl:
Sea-wanderer, forest-visitor!
Even the pure Immortals cannot escape you,
And mortal man, in his one day's dusk,
Trembles before your glory.

Surely you swerve upon ruin   (ANTISTROPHE)
The just man's consenting heart,
As here you have made bright anger
Strike between father and son—
And none has conquered but Love!
A girl's glánce wórking the will of heaven:
Pleasure to her alone who mocks us,
Merciless Aphroditê.

SCENE IV

CHORAGOS   (*as* ANTIGONE *enters guarded*).

But I can no longer stand in awe of this,
Nor, seeing what I see, keep back my tears.

Here is Antigonê, passing to that chamber
Where all find sleep at last.

ANTIGONE

Look upon me, friends, and pity me   (STROPHE 1)
Turning back at the night's edge to say
Good-by to the sun that shines for me no longer;
Now sleepy Death
Summons me down to Acheron, that cold shore:
There is no bridesong there, nor any music.

CHORUS

Yet not unpraised, not without a kind of honor,
You walk at last into the underworld;
Untouched by sickness, broken by no sword.
What woman has ever found your way to death?

ANTIGONE

How often I have heard the story of Niobê,   (ANTISTROPHE 1)
Tantalos' wretched daughter, how the stone
Clung fast about her, ivy-close: and they say
The rain falls endlessly
And sifting soft snow; her tears are never done.
I feel the loneliness of her death in mine.

CHORUS

But she was born of heaven, and you
Are woman, woman-born. If her death is yours,
A mortal woman's, is this not for you
Glory in our world and in the world beyond?

ANTIGONE

You laugh at me. Ah, friends, friends,   (STROPHE 2)
Can you not wait until I am dead? O Thebes,
O men many-charioted, in love with Fortune,
Dear springs of Dircê, sacred Theban grove,
Be witnesses for me, denied all pity,
Unjustly judged! and think a word of love
For her whose path turns
Under dark earth, where there are no more tears.

CHORUS

You have passed beyond human daring and come at last
Into a place of stone where Justice sits.
I cannot tell
What shape of your father's guilt appears in this.

ANTIGONE   (ANTISTROPHE 2)

You have touched it at last: that bridal bed
Unspeakable, horror of son and mother mingling:

Their crime, infection of all our family!
O Oedipus, father and brother!
Your marriage strikes from the grave to murder mine.
I have been a stranger here in my own land:
All my life
The blasphemy of my birth has followed me.

CHORUS

Reverence is a virtue, but strength
Lives in established law: that must prevail.
You have made your choice,
Your death is the doing of your conscious hand.

ANTIGONE

Then let me go, since all your words are bitter,   (EPODE)
And the very light of the sun is cold to me.
Lead me to my vigil, where I must have
Neither love nor lamentation; no song, but silence.

(CREON *interrupts impatiently.*)

CREON

If dirges and planned lamentations could put off death,
Men would be singing for ever.

(*To the* SERVANTS.)
                                                        Take her, go!
You know your orders: take her to the vault
And leave her alone there. And if she lives or dies,
That's her affair, not ours: our hands are clean.

ANTIGONE

O tomb, vaulted bride-bed in eternal rock,
Soon I shall be with my own again
Where Persephonê welcomes the thin ghosts underground:
And I shall see my father again, and you, mother,
And dearest Polyneicês—
                                        dearest indeed
To me, since it was my hand
That washed him clean and poured the ritual wine:
And my reward is death before my time!

And yet, as men's hearts know, I have done no wrong,
I have not sinned before God. Or if I have,
I shall know the truth in death. But if the guilt
Lies upon Creon who judged me, then, I pray,
May his punishment equal my own.

CHORAGOS   O passionate heart,
Unyielding, tormented still by the same winds!

CREON

Her guards shall have good cause to regret their delaying.

ANTIGONE

Ah! That voice is like the voice of death!

CREON

I can give you no reason to think you are mistaken.

ANTIGONE

Thebes, and you my fathers' gods,
And rulers of Thebes, you see me now, the last
Unhappy daughter of a line of kings,
Your kings, led away to death. You will remember
What things I suffer, and at what men's hands,
Because I would not transgress the laws of heaven.
(*To the* GUARDS, *simply*.)
Come: let us wait no longer.
(*Exit* ANTIGONE, *L.*, *guarded*.)

ODE IV

CHORUS

All Danaê's beauty was locked away	(STROPHE 1)
In a brazen cell where the sunlight could not come:	
A small room, still as any grave, enclosed her.	
Yet she was a princess too,	
And Zeus in a rain of gold poured love upon her.	
O child, child,	
No power in wealth or war	
Or tough sea-blackened ships	
Can prevail against untiring Destiny!	

And Dryas' son also, that furious king,	(ANTISTROPHE 1)
Bore the god's prisoning anger for his pride:	
Sealed up by Dionysos in deaf stone,	
His madness died among echoes.	
So at the last he learned what dreadful power	
His tongue had mocked:	
For he had profaned the revels,	
And fired the wrath of the nine	
Implacable Sisters that love the sound of the flute.	

And old men tell a half-remembered tale	(STROPHE 2)
Of horror done where a dark ledge splits the sea	
And a double surf beats on the gráy shóres:	

How a king's new woman, sick
With hatred for the queen he had imprisoned,
Ripped out his two sons' eyes with her bloody hands
While grinning Arês watched the shuttle plunge
Four times: four blind wounds crying for revenge,

Crying, tears and blood mingled.—Piteously born,　　(ANTISTROPHE 2)
Those sons whose mother was of heavenly birth!
Her father was the god of the North Wind
And she was cradled by gales,
She raced with young colts on the glittering hills
And walked untrammeled in the open light:
But in her marriage deathless Fate found means
To build a tomb like yours for all her joy.

SCENE V

(*Enter blind* TEIRESIAS, *led by a boy. The opening speeches of* TEIRESIAS
should be in singsong contrast to the realistic lines of CREON.)

TEIRESIAS

This is the way the blind man comes, Princes, Princes,
Lock-step, two heads lit by the eyes of one.

CREON

What new thing have you to tell us, old Teiresias?

TEIRESIAS

I have much to tell you: listen to the prophet, Creon.

CREON

I am not aware that I have ever failed to listen.

TEIRESIAS

Then you have done wisely, King, and ruled well.

CREON

I admit my debt to you. But what have you to say?

TEIRESIAS

This, Creon: you stand once more on the edge of fate.

CREON

What do you mean? Your words are a kind of dread.

TEIRESIAS

Listen, Creon:
I was sitting in my chair of augury, at the place
Where the birds gather about me. They were all a-chatter,
As is their habit, when suddenly I heard
A strange note in their jangling, a scream, a

Whirring fury; I knew that they were fighting,
Tearing each other, dying
In a whirlwind of wings clashing. And I was afraid.
I began the rites of burnt-offering at the altar,
But Hephaistos failed me: instead of bright flame,
There was only the sputtering slime of the fat thighflesh
Melting: the entrails dissolved in gray smoke,
The bare bone burst from the welter. And no blaze!

This was a sign from heaven. My boy described it,
Seeing for me as I see for others.

I tell you, Creon, you yourself have brought
This new calamity upon us. Our hearts and altars
Are stained with the corruption of dogs and carrion birds
That glut themselves on the corpse of Oedipus' son.
The gods are deaf when we pray to them, their fire
Recoils from our offering, their birds of omen
Have no cry of comfort, for they are gorged
With the thick blood of the dead.
                              O my son,
These are no trifles! Think: all men make mistakes,
But a good man yields when he knows his course is wrong,
And repairs the evil. The only crime is pride.

Give in to the dead man, then: do not fight with a corpse—
What glory is it to kill a man who is dead?
Think, I beg you:
It is for your own good that I speak as I do.
You should be able to yield for your own good.

CREON

It seems that prophets have made me their especial province.
All my life long
I have been a kind of butt for the dull arrows
Of doddering fortune-tellers!

                              No, Teiresias:
If your birds—if the great eagles of God himself
Should carry him stinking bit by bit to heaven,
I would not yield. I am not afraid of pollution:
No man can defile the gods.

                              Do what you will,
Go into business, make money, speculate
In India gold or that synthetic gold from Sardis,
Get rich otherwise than by my consent to bury him.

Teiresias, it is a sorry thing when a wise man
Sells his wisdom, lets out his words for hire!
TEIRESIAS
Ah, Creon! Is there no man left in the world—
CREON
To do what?—Come, let's have the aphorism!
TEIRESIAS
No man who knows that wisdom outweights any wealth?
CREON
As surely as bribes are baser than any baseness.
TEIRESIAS
You are sick, Creon! You are deathly sick!
CREON
As you say: it is not my place to challenge a prophet.
TEIRESIAS
Yet you have said my prophecy is for sale.
CREON
The generation of prophets has always loved gold.
TEIRESIAS
The generation of kings has always loved brass.
CREON
You forget yourself! You are speaking to your King.
TEIRESIAS
I know it. You are a king because of me.
CREON
You have a certain skill; but you have sold out.
TEIRESIAS
King, you will drive me to words that—
CREON

                                    Say them, say them!
Only remember: I will not pay you for them.
TEIRESIAS
No, you will find them too costly.
CREON

                              No doubt. Speak:
Whatever you say, you will not change my will.
TEIRESIAS
Then take this, and take it to heart!
The time is not far off when you shall pay back
Corpse for corpse, flesh of your own flesh.
You have thrust the child of this world into living night,
You have kept from the gods below the child that is theirs:
The one in a grave before her death, the other,

Dead, denied the grave. This is your crime:
And the Furies and the dark gods of Hell
Are swift with terrible punishment for you.

Do you want to buy me now, Creon?

                                    Not many days,
And your house will be full of men and women weeping,
And curses will be hurled at you from far
Cities grieving for sons unburied, left to rot
Before the walls of Thebes.

These are my arrows, Creon: they are all for you.

But come, child: lead me home.
(*To* BOY.)
Let him waste his fine anger upon younger men.
Maybe he will learn at last
To control a wiser tongue in a better head.
(*Exit* TEIRESIAS.)

CHORAGOS
    The old man has gone, King, but his words
    Remain to plague us. I am old, too,
    But I cannot remember that he was ever false.

CREON
    That is true. . . . It troubles me.
    Oh it is hard to give in! but it is worse
    To risk everything for stubborn pride.

CHORAGOS
    Creon: take my advice.

CREON
                                What shall I do?

CHORAGOS
    Go quickly: free Antigonê from her vault
    And build a tomb for the body of Polyneicês.

CREON
    You would have me do this?

CHORAGOS
                                Creon, yes!
    And it must be done at once: God moves
    Swiftly to cancel the folly of stubborn men.

CREON
    It is hard to deny the heart! But I
    Will do it: I will not fight with destiny.

CHORAGOS
You must go yourself, you cannot leave it to others.
CREON
I will go.
　　　　—Bring axes, servants:
Come with me to the tomb. I buried her, I
Will set her free.
　　　　　　Oh quickly!
My mind misgives—
The laws of the gods are mighty, and a man must serve them
To the last day of his life!
(*Exit* CREON.)

PÆAN

CHORAGOS
God of many names　　　　　　　　　　　　　　　　　(STROPHE 1)
CHORUS
　　　　　　　O Iacchos
　　　　　　　　　son
of Kadmeian Sémelê
　　　　　　　　O born of the Thunder!
Guardian of the West
　　　　　　　　Regent
of Eleusis' plain
　　　　　　　　O Prince of maenad Thebes
And the Dragon Field by rippling Ismenos:
CHORAGOS
God of many names　　　　　　　　　　　　　　　(ANTISTROPHE 1)
CHORUS
　　　　　　　the flame of torches
flares on our hills
　　　　　　　the nymphs of Iacchos
dance at the spring of Castalia:
from the vine-close mountain
　　　　　　　　come ah come in ivy:
Evohé evohé! sings through the streets of Thebes
CHORAGOS
God of many names　　　　　　　　　　　　　　　　(STROPHE 2)
CHORUS
　　　　　　Iacchos of Thebes
heavenly Child

         of Sémelê bride of the Thunderer!
   The shadow of plague is upon us:
                          come
  with clement feet
              oh come from Parnasos
  down the long slopes
                 across the lamenting water

CHORAGOS

  Iô Fire! Chorister of the throbbing stars!   (ANTISTROPHE 2)
  O purest among the voices of the night!
  Thou son of God, blaze for us!

CHORUS

  Come with choric rapture of circling Maenads
  Who cry *Iô Iacche!*
            God of many names!

EXODOS

(Enter MESSENGER, *L.)*

MESSENGER

  Men of the line of Kadmos, you who live
  Near Amphion's citadel:
                 I cannot say
  Of any condition of human life "This is fixed,
  This is clearly good, or bad." Fate raises up,
  And Fate casts down the happy and unhappy alike:
  No man can foretell his Fate.
                 Take the case of Creon:
  Creon was happy once, as I count happiness:
  Victorious in battle, sole governor of the land,
  Fortunate father of children nobly born.
  And now it has all gone from him! Who can say
  That a man is still alive when his life's joy fails?
  He is a walking dead man. Grant him rich,
  Let him live like a king in his great house:
  If his pleasure is gone, I would not give
  So much as the shadow of smoke for all he owns.

CHORAGOS

  Your words hint at sorrow: what is your news for us?

MESSENGER

  They are dead. The living are guilty of their death.

CHORAGOS
Who is guilty? Who is dead? Speak!
MESSENGER

Haimon.
Haimon is dead; and the hand that killed him
Is his own hand.
CHORAGOS

His father's? or his own?
MESSENGER
His own, driven mad by the murder his father had done.
CHORAGOS
Teiresias, Teiresias, how clearly you saw it all!
MESSENGER
This is my news: you must draw what conclusions you can from it.
CHORAGOS
But look: Eurydicê, our Queen:
Has she overheard us?
(*Enter* EURYDICE *from the Palace, C.*)
EURYDICE
I have heard something, friends:
As I was unlocking the gate of Pallas' shrine,
For I needed her help today, I heard a voice
Telling of some new sorrow. And I fainted
There at the temple with all my maidens about me.
But speak again: whatever it is, I can bear it:
Grief and I are no strangers.
MESSENGER

Dearest Lady,
I will tell you plainly all that I have seen.
I shall not try to comfort you: what is the use,
Since comfort could lie only in what is not true?
The truth is always best.

I went with Creon
To the outer plain where Polyneicês was lying,
No friend to pity him, his body shredded by dogs.
We made our prayers in that place to Hecatê
And Pluto, that they would be merciful. And we bathed
The corpse with holy water, and we brought
Fresh-broken branches to burn what was left of it,
And upon the urn we heaped up a towering barrow
Of the earth of his own land.

When we were done, we ran
To the vault where Antigonê lay on her couch of stone.

One of the servants had gone ahead,
And while he was yet far off he heard a voice
Grieving within the chamber, and he came back
And told Creon. And as the King went closer,
The air was full of wailing, the words lost,
And he begged us to make all haste. "Am I a prophet?"
He said, weeping, "And must I walk this road,
The saddest of all that I have gone before?
My son's voice calls me on. Oh quickly, quickly!
Look through the crevice there, and tell me
If it is Haimon, or some deception of the gods!"

We obeyed; and in the cavern's farthest corner
We saw her lying:
She had made a noose of her fine linen veil
And hanged herself. Haimon lay beside her,
His arms about her waist, lamenting her,
His love lost under ground, crying out
That his father had stolen her away from him.

When Creon saw him the tears rushed to his eyes
And he called to him: "What have you done, child? Speak to me.
What are you thinking that makes your eyes so strange?
O my son, my son, I come to you on my knees!"
But Haimon spat in his face. He said not a word,
Staring—
　　　　　　And suddenly drew his sword
And lunged. Creon shrank back, the blade missed; and the boy,
Desperate against himself, drove it half its length
Into his own side, and fell. And as he died
He gathered Antigonê close in his arms again,
Choking, his blood bright red on her white cheek.
And now he lies dead with the dead, and she is his
At last, his bride in the houses of the dead.
(*Exit* EURYDICE *into the Palace.*)
CHORAGOS
　　She has left us without a word. What can this mean?
MESSENGER
　　It troubles me, too; yet she knows what is best,
　　Her grief is too great for public lamentation,
　　And doubtless she has gone to her chamber to weep
　　For her dead son, leading her maidens in his dirge.

CHORAGOS
  It may be so: but I fear this deep silence.
(*Pause.*)
MESSENGER
  I will see what she is doing. I will go in.
(*Exit* MESSENGER *into the Palace.*)
(*Enter* CREON *with attendants, bearing* HAIMON's *body.*)
CHORAGOS
  But here is the King himself: oh look at him,
  Bearing his own damnation in his arms.
CREON
  Nothing you say can touch me any more.
  My own blind heart has brought me
  From darkness to final darkness. Here you see
  The father murdering, the murdered son—
  And all my civic wisdom!

  Haimon my son, so young, so young to die,
  I was the fool, not you; and you died for me.
CHORAGOS
  That is the truth; but you were late in learning it.
CREON
  This truth is hard to bear. Surely a god
  Has crushed me beneath the hugest weight of heaven,
  And driven me headlong a barbaric way
  To trample out the thing I held most dear.

  The pains that men will take to come to pain!
(*Enter* MESSENGER *from the Palace.*)
MESSENGER
  The burden you carry in your hands is heavy,
  But it is not all: you will find more in your house.
CREON
  What burden worse than this shall I find there?
MESSENGER
  The Queen is dead.
CREON
  O port of death, deaf world,
  Is there no pity for me? And you, Angel of evil,
  I was dead, and your words are death again.
  Is it true, boy? Can it be true?
  Is my wife dead? Has death bred death?

MESSENGER

You can see for yourself.

(*The doors are opened, and the body of* EURYDICE *is disclosed within.*)

CREON

Oh pity!

All true, all true, and more than I can bear!

O my wife, my son!

MESSENGER

She stood before the altar, and her heart

Welcomed the knife her own hand guided,

And a great cry burst from her lips for Megareus dead,

And for Haimon dead, her sons; and her last breath

Was a curse for their father, the murderer of her sons.

And she fell, and the dark flowed in through her closing eyes.

CREON

O God, I am sick with fear.

Are there no swords here? Has no one a blow for me?

MESSENGER

Her curse is upon you for the deaths of both.

CREON

It is right that it should be. I alone am guilty.

I know it, and I say it. Lead me in,

Quickly, friends.

I have neither life nor substance. Lead me in.

CHORAGOS

You are right, if there can be right in so much wrong.

The briefest way is best in a world of sorrow.

CREON

Let it come,

Let death come quickly, and be kind to me.

I would not ever see the sun again.

CHORAGOS

All that will come when it will; but we, meanwhile,

Have much to do. Leave the future to itself.

CREON

All my heart was in that prayer!

CHORAGOS

Then do not pray any more: the sky is deaf.

CREON

Lead me away. I have been rash and foolish.

I have killed my son and my wife.

I look for comfort; my comfort lies here dead.

Whatever my hands have touched has come to nothing.
Fate has brought all my pride to a thought of dust.
(*As* CREON *is being led into the house, the* CHORAGOS *advances and speaks directly to the audience.*)
CHORAGOS
There is no happiness where there is no wisdom;
No wisdom but in submission to the gods.
Big words are always punished,
And proud men in old age learn to be wise.

ANTIGONE THEN AND NOW

FRANK JONES

The hero in Sophocles says No. Oedipus denies the certainties of his future; Ajax and Electra resist humiliation; Antigone will not let Creon shame her brother's memory. Some of these protagonists are at odds with themselves; all challenge powers greater than their own, and willingly risk rejection, loneliness, death.

Antigone is a supreme embodiment of the Sophoclean conflict. Four qualities distinguish her story in Greek tragedy and after. First: she is a protestant, and wins her case. Literature offers few such examples to those who believe that force can be broken without the use of force. Second: although Antigone is in the right, her antagonist is not entirely wrong. God, speaking through Tiresias, justifies Antigone's stand; but Creon has also aimed at justice. His decree against the rebel prince is meant to show that patriotism outweighs privilege. Third: Sophocles' play is rife with inner struggles, reversals of intention, and changes of heart. Facing death, Antigone questions the rightness of her act; Creon stubbornly upholds his decision, but Tiresias shocks him out of it; tensions between duty and feeling afflict Ismene, Haimon, the elders, the watchman, and the populace. Fourth: Antigone is the only Greek tragedy of young and innocent love, the only one in which a man kills himself for a woman, like Romeo for Juliet. In brief, this is a problem play that turns not on fate or passion but on devotion and choice. Other Greek tragedies inspire pity and fear; this one arouses sympathy.

In our epoch, which abounds in protests and rebellions, competing political principles, troubled personalities and other obstacles to love,

Frank Jones, a product of the University of Wisconsin, is chairman of the Department of Comparative Literature at the University of Washington.

Antigone's case has seemed unusually pertinent. Walter Hasenclever
wrote a pacifist *Antigone* in the Germany of 1917, and in 1922 Jean
Cocteau brought to the Paris stage what he called her *cri de la révolte
et de la raison* ("outcry of revolt and reason"). During and shortly after
the Second World War the Theban princess reappeared in plays by Jean
Anouilh, José María Pemán, and Bertolt Brecht. All three are distinguished translations of ancient symbols into modern terms.

Sophocles' heroine is a martyr to sisterly duty. Everything else in her
makeup is controlled by the demands of piety. The modern playwright,
who cannot count on religious sympathies in his audience, must make
Antigone more worldly, more "like us." Accordingly, Pemán emphasizes
her pride: lineage, blood, caste are cardinal principles for his Antigone.
Brecht makes her a sister not only to a prince but to the people: against
Creon's despotic imperialism she champions democracy and peace.
Anouilh gives the girl a fondness for her brother—*le vaurien, le révolté,
le voyou* ("the good-for-nothing, the rebel, the rascal")—which springs
from her own longing for selfhood and solitude. Yet all three playwrights
find in her an emblem of integrity, purity, and zeal. In varying degrees
she remains what she was in the beginning: a citizen of a higher world
than that in which Creon feels at home.

Brecht's *Antigone,* a free treatment of Hölderlin's 1804 translation, was
first produced in Switzerland in 1948. The Marxist poet turned Sophocles'
study of human and divine will into a political parable. Before the action
of the play begins, Creon has plunged Thebes into an unprovoked war
with Argos. Antigone's brothers both fought in the attacking forces;
Polynices, who objected to the war, was killed by Creon for desertion.
The staged action follows Sophocles, except that in the end Haimon dies
in combat, not by his own hand. But the underlying idea of the original
play—that violations of divine law are quickly punished by the gods—is
restated in purely human terms. "You are blind to the divine order of the
state," says Brecht's Creon to Antigone during the trial scene. "It may be
divine," she retorts, "but I'd rather have it human." As if to confirm her
words, Creon is punished not only by the gods but by the people he has
wronged. Thebes is defeated by Argos, and it is implied that the dictator
will soon lose his power over Thebes.

This Hitler-like tyrant is crueler than his prototype, but the political
doctrine of Brecht's version is securely founded on Sophocles. It has been
held that the original *Antigone* was a warning against totalitarian ten-
dencies, a reminder to Pericles that certain spheres of life are and must be
free from government control. Whether that is true or not, the political
direction of the play itself is clear enough—Creon knows that his refusal
to bury Polynices has roused resentment among the citizens, but he can
deal with this only by threats and terror, not persuasion. Antigone main-

tains, with some justification, that the chorus of Theban elders is on her side, though afraid to say so. And the political conflict explodes in Creon's quarrel with his son, who lets fly at him a classic statement of Athenian republicanism: "A city that belongs to one man is not a city at all."

But Brecht will not let his audience believe that Antigone's victory solves the political problem. In Sophocles, Creon is still in power at the end, though morally shaken by his losses. Brecht suggests that neither Creon's rule nor Antigone's royal line can bring Thebes "a life without fear under the trees." The Sophoclean chorus closes the play with a comment on Creon: "Great words of prideful men in old age teach the chastened to be wise." But Brecht's chorus remains dissatisfied: "There is never enough time to live from day to day and grow wise with age." History is rude to tradition and resignation. An end must be a beginning.

José María Pemán's *Antígona,* which the author calls "a very free adaptation of Sophocles' tragedy," was first performed in Madrid in 1945. The Spanish monarchist makes no change in the Greek poet's fundamental thought, but accentuates the personal conflict between the tyrant and the princess. Antigone despises Creon, and her contempt is a thorn in his side. He wants Thebes to accept him wholly, as a lover expects a woman's complete surrender; and if he cannot have this he will have revenge. Before the drawn shutters of Antigone's house he gleefully anticipates the moment when Polynices' unburied corpse will start to stink, and when the town crier hesitates to proclaim the decree in the streets, Creon bellows it himself. Sophocles' tyrant hates and distrusts womankind in general, and Antigone ironically calls him "the noble Creon." Pemán enlarges this into a feud.

But—as also happens in Sophocles—the suicide of Haimon teaches Creon that he has erred. Pemán makes Creon not only forgive his son and come close to forgiving Antigone, but also accuse himself: "Disastrous, endless loneliness of the tyrant who has ignored moderation!" This is rapid proof of Antigone's dying words: "I shall live like remorse in the anguished memories of tyrants." Pemán, like Brecht, leaves the way open for improvement after Thebes, or humanity, has learned the lesson of suffering.

No such possibility appears in the *Antigone* of Jean Anouilh, who has said he has no politics. This play, first performed in Paris in 1944, has been viewed as a tribute to French resistance under the German occupation and also as a defense of collaboration with the German authorities. It is neither. Like most of Anouilh's plays, it is a cry that happiness is fleeting at best and at worst a delusion, that love and joy and freedom must fade into the gray of duty and hard work. Creon knows how to live in this world; Antigone does not. That is her tragedy, and his.

Yet Creon, not Antigone, is the hero in Anouilh. Brecht and Pemán

make him somewhat more complex and interesting than he is in Sophocles; Anouilh turns him into a great leader and a great man. Called to
save his city from the chaos brought upon it by a mad old king and a pair
of juvenile delinquents, he has cleverly let some of the credit fall on
others by making the people believe that Eteocles was the injured party
and a brave patriot. Actually he was no better than his brother, who
struck his father after a drunken party and tried to have him killed by
thugs. Creon likes and pities Antigone, offers to hush up her disobedience,
and almost succeeds in dissuading her from dying for it. But she refuses.
Disillusioned about her brother, she still cannot disappoint herself.

Anouilh reinforces the personal side of the story by lessening its ethical,
political, and religious elements. The Theban people play no part in the
action; Anouilh's chorus is an individual commentator, and we hear
nothing of popular feeling about the judgment on Antigone. Haimon's
protest against it is actuated solely by love, and Antigone's disobedience
is due to *amor fati* as much as anything else. *"A chacun son rôle"* ("Each
must play his part"), she assures her sister. *"Lui, il doit nous faire mourir,
et nous, nous devons aller enterrer notre frère. C'est comme cela que c'a
été distribué. Qu'est-ce que tu veux que nous fassions?"* ("He has to put
us to death; we have to go bury our brother. That's the way the play has
been cast. What do you expect us to do?" And in the end the chorus declares: *"Antigone est calmée maintenant, nous ne saurons jamais de
quelle fièvre"* ("Antigone is calmed now—from what fever, we shall never
know"). Everyone likes her, but no one except Creon understands her,
and even he can be wrong about her. He thinks she simply wants to die;
but, as she has told Ismene, she is in love with life. She is less martyr than
victim. Her conflict with Creon is the battle, eternally renewed and always lost, of the romantic soul against the practical man. Her death is
not her fault but the world's.

To reach a truly critical comparison of Anouilh's innovative work with
Brecht's and Pemán's more conservative efforts, a further question must
be raised. Why should a modern playwright revert to Greek themes in
the first place? What is gained by writing a new play with old names,
especially if it subverts old meanings? This trick, of which the French
are especially fond, and in which they have reached new heights in recent
years, as witness Giraudoux' *Electra* and Sartre's *The Flies,* is perhaps
little more than a subgenre, akin to parody and travesty. Anouilh's varia-
tion of the trick is to turn villains into heroes, as he does with Creon in
Antigone and with Jason in his *Médée.* Yet, in the theatre at least,
Anouilh's *Antigone* ranks as a more serious and lasting achievement than
any other contemporary sample of this minor art; and it is certainly more
vivid and effective than the direct imitations with which I have been
comparing it.

Perhaps, then, Anouilh has broken through the barrier to which comparative critics give so many names—imitation, adaptation, recreation, even transcreation—and succeeded in making something really new from something that only appears to be old. If so, there may be an element of luck in his venture. He was fortunate in choosing to add the Sophoclean heroine to his gallery of lonely young people who are up against the banality of their elders. But the main reason for the continuing success of this work is that it preserves, albeit in a self-conscious and Pirandellian style, the essential *agon* of its model: a necessarily catastrophic conflict between irreconcilable principles, both of which we can admire, and, in different states of mind, accept as guides to action. What Anouilh really imitates in Sophocles is not his matter or his manner but his knowledge— his clear vision of the abyss over which we stretch the burning rope of moral choice.

EURIPIDES

OF THE THREE GREAT GREEK TRAGIC POETS, EURIPIDES (CA. 485–406 B.C.) IS THE ONE ABOUT WHOSE LIFE WE KNOW THE LEAST. HE IS POPULARLY SUPPOSED TO HAVE COME FROM HUMBLE ORIGINS, A SUPPOSITION INCONSISTENT WITH WHAT WE KNOW GENERALLY ABOUT LIFE IN PERICLEAN ATHENS. IN HIS PLAYS, HOWEVER, HE DOES ALLOT MORE ATTENTION AND SYMPATHY TO THE SERVANTS, SOLDIERS, AND HUMBLE PEOPLE THAN EITHER SOPHOCLES OR AESCHYLUS DOES. UNLIKE HIS PREDECESSORS, HE WAS A SKEPTIC IN RELIGIOUS MATTERS AND A PROFOUND PSYCHOLOGIST. HE DID NOT REGARD THE GODS AS AWESOME, AND HE FOUND BOTH MEN AND WOMEN, IRRESPECTIVE OF RANK, FASCINATING. AMONG HIS BEST-KNOWN PLAYS ARE *ALCESTIS, ELECTRA, IPHIGENIA IN AULIS, IPHIGENIA IN TAURIS, MEDEA,* AND *THE TROJAN WOMEN.* THE *BACCHAE* IS REGARDED AS HIS MASTERPIECE. *HIPPOLYTUS,* PERHAPS HIS MOST INFLUENTIAL AND CERTAINLY HIS MOST REPRESENTATIVE TRAGEDY, WAS WRITTEN IN 432 B.C.

Hippolytus begins with a prologue spoken by Aphrodite in which she foretells the tragic outcome of the play. Can we deduce from the prologue Euripides's attitude toward the Goddess of Love? Is it respectful? Ironic? Satiric? Casual? Does Aphrodite seem to function as a goddess, or is she merely a personification of a powerful human impulse?

We find, as the play progresses, that our attitudes toward the three principals change. Our feelings about Hippolytus, Phaedra, and Theseus are "mixed." Is the ambivalence of our attitudes intended by Euripides, or is it, perhaps, due to the fact that we live in a different time with a different set of values?

Implicit throughout the play is the supreme importance of the aristocratic ideals of honor and chastity. Does the practicality of the nurse undermine the validity of these ideals, or does she serve to reinforce them?

Who, in your opinion, emerges as the most compassionate character in the play? How may the presence or absence of compassionate feeling serve as the binding force in *Hippolytus?*

The illegitimacy of Hippolytus is emphasized by Aphrodite in the opening lines of the play. To what extent do Hippolytus's actions and reactions throughout the play seem to stem from the circumstances of his birth? From his ambiguous status in his father's household?

Hippolytus, itself a reworking of an earlier play by Euripides, finds among other dramatists composing versions of the myth Seneca (*Phaedra*), Racine (*Phèdre*), Eugene O'Neill (*Desire under the Elms*), and Robinson Jeffers (*The Cretan Woman*). In the past decade a film version with a modern-day Greek setting featured Melina Mercouri, Anthony Perkins, and Raf Vallone. Each successive reworking of the story materially altered both the character and motivations of the principals. Furthermore the Greek legend has had its counterparts both in Tristan and Isolde and in the Biblical story of Joseph and Potiphar's wife. In reading the play, then, we can ponder the psychological implications which underlie this ancient, timeless, and tragic story.

HIPPOLYTUS

TRANSLATED BY PHILIP VELLACOTT

CHARACTERS

APHRODITE, *the Goddess of Sexual Love*
HIPPOLYTUS, *bastard son of Theseus*
CHORUS *of Huntsmen attending Hippolytus*
SERVANT *of Hippolytus*
CHORUS *of Women of Troezen*
NURSE *attending Phaedra*
PHAEDRA, *wife of Theseus*
THESEUS, *King of Athens and Troezen*
MESSENGER
ARTEMIS, *the huntress Goddess of Virginity*

The scene is before the royal palace at Troezen, where Theseus is spending a year of voluntary exile to atone for bloodshed. On one side of the stage is a statue of Aphrodite, on the other a statue of Artemis. In the centre is the door of the palace.

(*Enter* APHRODITE.)
APHRODITE.   Powerful among mortals, glorious among the gods,
 I am Aphrodite, named in heaven The Cyprian.
 On earth, from the Eastern shore to the outward ocean of the West,
 Over all that see the light of the sun my rule extends.
 To those who reverence my powers I show favour,
 And throw to the earth those I find arrogant and proud.
 For gods too have their pride; and it is their nature
 To enjoy receiving honour from the mortal race.
 And that my words are true I shall show this very day.
 Hippolytus, the son whom the Amazon bore to Theseus,
 Who was trained from a child by Pittheus the Severe,—
 Hippolytus, alone among the inhabitants of Troezen,
 Calls me the most pernicious of the heavenly powers;
 He abhors the bed of love; marriage he renounces;
 Honours Apollo's sister, Artemis daughter of Zeus.
 All day with her, the virgin, he ranges the green woods,
 With his swift hounds emptying the earth of beasts,
 Too fond of company too high for mortal men.
 I do not envy them their sport—I have little cause;
 But Hippolytus has insulted me and shall suffer for it
 This very day. My plans, long laid, are well begun,

59

And little work remains.
Two years ago Hippolytus
Left Pittheus' house for Athens, the city of Pandion,
To attend the holy Mysteries and complete his initiation;
And there the noble Phaedra saw him, his father's wife,—
And a terrible lust, by my contrivance, captured her heart.
The prince came home to Troezen: Phaedra was Queen of Athens.
There on the Acropolis, on the very Rock of Pallas,
She built a temple of Love looking seaward towards Troezen,
Where her heart wandered with her beloved far away;—
Still from that time this temple bears Hippolytus' name.
But Theseus, his hands stained with the blood of the Pallantides,
To purge his guilt, consented to live one year in exile,
And sailed with Phaedra his wife from Athens here to Troezen.
She now, poor wretch, groaning and maddened with the stabs of love,
Is dying, and in silence. No one in the palace knows
Her sickness. But not in secret shall her lust's full course be run.
I will reveal the truth to Theseus; all shall be shown.
This youth, who makes war with me, his own father Theseus
Shall kill with curses, by the power Poseidon King of the Sea
Gave him, that three requests of Theseus should not fail.
Phaedra shall save her honour, but must lose her life;
For I will not yield my rights through regard for her misfortunes,
But my enemies shall pay what they owe till I am satisfied.
Now I'll retire. Here comes Hippolytus, son of Theseus,
Home after his exertions in the hunting field, and with him
His whole pack of followers in full cry at his heels,
Singing hymns to Artemis! Little he knows that Death's gates
Are open now, and to-day's light is the last he shall see.
(*Exit.*)
(*Enter* HIPPOLYTUS *with* HUNTSMEN; *also an* OLD SERVANT.)
HIPPOLYTUS.   Follow, and sing!
               Follow the bright Daughter of Heaven!
               Follow our guardian Maid,
                  Artemis!
HUNTSMEN.   Child of Leto and of Zeus,
               Virgin Goddess Artemis,
               Great and holy, hear our song!
                 Greeting, joyful greeting,
                 Loveliest of maidens!
           You who haunt your kingly father's court,
         Tread at ease the broad sky's golden floor,
             Loveliest of immortal maids,
             Joyful greeting, Artemis!

HIPPOLYTUS. Goddess, for you I have twined this crown of flowers, gathered
Fresh from a virgin meadow, where no shepherd dares
To graze his flock, nor ever yet scythe swept,
But bees thread the Spring air over the maiden meadow.
There from the running stream Chastity waters the flowers;
And those whose untaught natures Holiness claims entire
May gather garlands there; and the impure may not.
Dear Mistress, take this flowery band for your bright hair,
Offered with reverent heart. I alone among mortals
Enjoy this honour; I am your companion, speak with you,
Hear your voice; only your face I do not see.
And may the end of my life's course be as the beginning!
SERVANT. My lord!—or, Prince! for only gods must be called lord,—
would you accept a word of good advice from me?
HIPPOLYTUS. Of course! I should plainly be a fool if I would not.
SERVANT. Then—you know an old law that is laid down for men—
HIPPOLYTUS. No! What do you mean? Why are you asking me this?
SERVANT. The law that says: Abhor pride and all unfriendliness.
HIPPOLYTUS. Yes; a good law: haughtiness is always a hateful thing.
SERVANT. And surely there is a charm in being open and unreserved?
HIPPOLYTUS. Great charm; great profit too, and with little trouble.
SERVANT. Do you not think this is as true for gods as for men?
HIPPOLYTUS. Why, yes; if our mortal ways are like theirs.
SERVANT. Then why have you no prayer for—a great goddess?
HIPPOLYTUS. Be careful! A word may do harm. What goddess do you mean?
SERVANT. She stands here at your own door—Aphrodite!
HIPPOLYTUS. I greet her from afar off: I am untainted.
SERVANT. Yet she is great; and her power is known and feared.
HIPPOLYTUS. I have no love for gods worshipped by night.
SERVANT. My son, we must not neglect the honor due to the gods.
HIPPOLYTUS. Gods may choose whom they will honour: so may mortals.
SERVANT. May the gods grant you wisdom, and good fortune too!
HIPPOLYTUS. Come, men, we'll go in; it is time for food. A loaded table's
a cheerful sight after hunting. Rub down the horses: when I've had
a good meal I'll take them out with the chariot and exercise them
hard.—Your Aphrodite? No! To me she is nothing at all!
(*Exit* HIPPOLYTUS *with* HUNTSMEN.)
SERVANT. The ways of young men are not for us to copy. Queen Aphrodite! with humble hearts, as befits your servants, we worship you. You
must forgive young blood, and the bold spirit that blurts foolish words
against you. Forget that you heard him speak! You are a god: and
the wisdom of gods must be wiser than men.

(Exit.)

(Enter CHORUS *of Troezenian Women.)*

CHORUS.   You have heard of the rocky fountain   (STROPHE 1)
   Where water gushes streaming from the heart of the earth,
   Where they dip pails in the pool:
   A friend of mine was there,
   Rinsing rich-coloured clothes in the rill-water
   And laying them to dry on the sun-backed rock:
   She was the first to tell me about the Queen;

   How she pines on a sick bed,   (ANTISTROPHE 1)
   Keeps always within doors,
   Clouding her golden head in the fine folds of her veil.
   This is the third day, they say,
   That her lovely lips refuse the gift of the Earth-Mother,
   The innocent body of bread.
   What storm is wrecking her life she will not tell;
   But she longs to moor in the sad harbour of death.

     Hers is no wild ecstasy   (STROPHE 2)
     Sent by Hecate or Pan,
  Mountain-frenzy, Corybantic wandering
    By Cybele's power possessed.
      Has she sinned, neglecting
      Immemorial offerings,
  Oil and honey for the Huntress Artemis?
    Wrath of gods can range and reach
      Every shore and island
      Through the salt sea's eddies.

     Or is Theseus' heart beguiled?   (ANTISTROPHE 2)
     Is your kingly husband false,
  Following pleasure in some slave-girl's secret bed?
    Has some traveller from Crete
    Sailed with news of sorrow
    To our friendly harbour?
  Are your kindred torn with trouble far away,
    That such bitter anguish
    Makes your bed your prison?

But women are always weak, and their ways are strange;   (EPODE)
Their very being is a blend of terror and helplessness
At the pains and follies their sex inherits.
I have felt this fear thrill through my own womb;

But I cried to the heavenly helper of all women,
    Artemis of the arrows;
And always—the gods be praised!—she came to my deep need.

Look! The old Nurse is coming to the door,
Bringing Queen Phaedra into the fresh air.
Her sad face is more clouded than before.
The Queen! How weak she is, how pale!
I long to know what has so wasted her.

(*Enter, from the palace,* PHAEDRA *supported by the* NURSE. ATTENDANTS *bring a couch for her.*)

NURSE.   Oh, the sickness and pain of this cruel world!
    What can I do for you? How can I tell?
    Here you are, in the light, under the clear sky;
    We have brought your bed from the palace.
    It was here that you begged and longed to come;
    Soon you will change your mind and fret for your room again.
    Each minute cheats you, nothing gives you pleasure;
    You hate what you have, and crave for what you have not.
    Better to be sick, which is a single trouble,
    Than wait on the sick, which troubles both heart and hand.
    Man's life from birth to death is sorrow and pain,
    With never pause or relief;
    And when we are dead, is there a happier world?
    Knowledge is hidden from us in clouds and darkness.
    Since we can know no other kind of life,
    Since the world of the dead is a mystery,
    It seems we must blindly love, for what it is worth,
    Our little gleam of light,
    And follow our foolish course content with tales.
PHAEDRA.   Support me, my friends, and lift my head;
    The strength of my limbs has melted away.
    Hold my white hands, my shapely arms!
    This braided veil is a weight on my head,—
    Off with it! Now let my hair fall round my shoulders.
NURSE.   Patience, my child! Lie still, you will tire yourself!
    If you are quiet and keep a brave heart
    Your illness will be easier to bear.
    We are mortal, and so must suffer.
PHAEDRA.   If I could kneel by a well-side in the fresh dew
    And drink a cupful of clear water!
    If I could lie under the poplar-trees
    And rest deep in the waving grass!
NURSE.   Speak low, child! You must not scatter your words

So loud and recklessly! There are people here!
Your speech careers wildly on wheels of madness.
PHAEDRA.   Come, take me! I am going
  Out to the hills and the woods, the pine-forests
  Where hounds pace after blood
  And press close on the spotted deer!
  O gods! were I there, shouting to the pack,
  Lifting the lance to my hair bright in the wind,
  Hurling the barbed blade!
NURSE.   What is it, child, you are fretting for?
  What are hounds and the hunt to you?
  Why so in love with water from a spring?
  If you are thirsty,
  Here by the palace-wall a stream runs down the hill!
PHAEDRA.   Lady of the Salt Mere,
  Artemis, lover of bold horsemanship!
  O for your level rides,
  And the tamed strength of a Thessaly horse under my hand!
NURSE.   What next will you say? This is madness, child!
  You were craving first
  To hunt wild beasts in a mountain glade;
  Now, for a horse on the dry sandy track.
  Here's a task for a prophet indeed, to guess
  What god drives you beside yourself
  And strikes your senses from you!
PHAEDRA.   What have I done? I have been wandering.
  My mind went from me—where? where? I was mad,
  A god touched me with madness. Oh, my grief!
  Dear Nurse, my veil again; I am ashamed
  To think what I have said. Cover my face.
  My tears fall down, and I am hot with shame.
  To come back to a right mind is agony,
  And no less agony to remain mad.
  It is best, then, to feel nothing, and so die!
NURSE   (*veiling her*).   There, child, there! How soon
  Shall my face too be veiled with death?
  I have lived long, and learnt much.
  Since we must die, it would be better,
  In making friends, never to go too far,
  Or open the depths of our heart to anyone.
  The ties of love ought to lie loosely on us,
  Easy to break or bind.
  For one heart to endure the pain of two,

As I suffer for her, is a cruel burden.
They say that steadfast devotion
Brings with it more trouble than pleasure,
And is an enemy to life and health.
So I think that in this as in other things
It is best not to go too far;
And any wise man will say the same.

CHORUS. Madam, we see the Queen's distress and are sorry for her; but what her illness is we cannot understand. We would like to ask you, her old and trusted servant: will you not tell us?

NURSE. I know nothing. I have questioned her, but she will not speak.

CHORUS. Do you not know how, or when, this trouble first began?

NURSE. The answer is still the same: to all such questions she is silent.

CHORUS. How frail and wasted she looks!

NURSE. No wonder: she has eaten nothing for three days.

CHORUS. Is she out of her mind? Or does she mean to die?

NURSE. She means to die. She is starving herself to death.

CHORUS. Strange that her husband should accept it calmly!

NURSE. She hides her illness from him, tells him she is well.

CHORUS. Does he not look at her face and see for himself?

NURSE. Just now it happens he is away from Troezen.

CHORUS. Can you not compel her to speak? Anything, to discover the cause of this sickness and these delusions!

NURSE. I have tried everything and achieved nothing; but I want to do my best, and I will not give up even now. And you, friends, are here to witness that I am one to stand by my lady in time of trouble. (*She turns to* PHAEDRA.)

Dear child, let us both forget the things we said before. Smooth away this terrible look from your brow: be my dear daughter! Don't wander any more—I was wrong to follow you, prying into your thoughts; I will be wiser. Is your sickness something you cannot speak of openly? There are women here to help with remedies. But if your troubles can be told to a man, only speak, and we will consult doctors. Well: not a word? My dear, if I have spoken foolishly, correct me; if well, say you agree. Do not sit there dumb! Speak! One word! Look at me! It is no use. (*She weeps.*) All our trouble leads to nothing, and we are as far off as ever; she would not soften before, and still refuses. Listen to me, my lady: be if you will more stubborn than the sea,—but what of your sons, if you should die? Who will take their part? They will never inherit their father's palace—no, by Hippolyta, Queen of the riding Amazons! She has a son whom your boys will serves as slaves, a bastard nursing the ambition of his royal birth, one you know well: Hippolytus!

PHAEDRA. No! No!

NURSE. Ha! Does that touch you?

PHAEDRA. You kill me! Nurse, by all the gods I implore you never again to speak of him!

NURSE. There! You are not out of your mind, far from it! And yet you still refuse both to save your own life and to help your children.

PHAEDRA. I love my children; but something else is drowning me in despair.

NURSE. My daughter,—your hands are free from blood?

PHAEDRA. My hands are pure; but my heart is defiled.

NURSE. Defiled? What? With some wrong done to you by an enemy?

PHAEDRA. No, no enemy! It is no more his will than mine that he should destroy me.

NURSE. Theseus! Has he done you some injury?

PHAEDRA. No! May I prove as guiltless towards him!

NURSE. What then is this terror that is dragging you to your grave?

PHAEDRA. Leave me to my sin. I do not sin against *you*.

NURSE. I will not leave you if I can help it. If I fail it will be your fault.

PHAEDRA. Will you try to force me? Let my hand go!

NURSE. I will not! I will cling to you until you tell me!

PHAEDRA. Poor soul! The truth would be terrible to you too.

NURSE. What could be worse to me than to see you suffer?

PHAEDRA. To tell would kill you; but what I am doing is for my honour—

NURSE. If so, to speak of it will add to your honour before the world.

PHAEDRA. —I am finding a way to bring honour out of shame.

NURSE. Then I am right in begging you to tell me—how can you hide it?

PHAEDRA. For the gods' sake leave me and let go my hand!

NURSE. Never, while you refuse what you owe to me!

PHAEDRA. It is true! I owe it. I will tell you what you ask.

NURSE. I will be quiet. Now it is for you to speak.

PHAEDRA. O my mother! What dreadful, pitiful lust raged within you!

NURSE. You mean her lust for the bull? Or what do you mean, my child?

PHAEDRA. And you too, O my sister, whom Dionysus desired—how love made you suffer!

NURSE. Why speak of them? Those tales are best forgotten.

PHAEDRA. The curse that destroyed them I now inherit.

NURSE. You frighten me! What are you going to say now?

PHAEDRA. My misery began with them. It is no new thing.

NURSE. You tell me no more of what I long to hear.

PHAEDRA. The words that you want me to say—if only you could speak them for me!

NURSE.   I am no magician to read hidden thoughts.

PHAEDRA.   When they say that one is in love, what do they mean by love?

NURSE.   Oh, my child! It is the sweetest of all things,—yet full of pain.

PHAEDRA.   It seems I have found the pain, but no sweetness.

NURSE.   What are you saying? You love a man? What man?

PHAEDRA.   Why, who should it be? It is he! The Amazon's son!

NURSE.   Hippolytus!

PHAEDRA.   You spoke his name, not I.

NURSE.   Oh, my child! What are you saying? Oh! you have broken my heart! Oh, friends, how can I bear it? How can I go on living? Oh! this hateful life, this accursed day! (*She collapses to the ground, and the* CHORUS *come to help her.*) No! Let me fall, leave me alone; I want to die and be at peace! I am dying, my life is over! . . . What does it mean? Here is a pure-hearted woman, with no desire to do wrong, yet lusting after wickedness against her will! (*Defiantly*) Aphrodite is no goddess! No! She has brought this disaster on Phaedra and on me and on the royal house,—she is something more than a goddess—something greater!

CHORUS.   Did you hear? Oh, did you hear
          The Queen's pitiful cry,
          Born of a crueller blow
          Than human heart can bear?
          Beloved Queen, let me die
          Before my heart should know
          Your heart's despair!
          Oh, Phaedra, daughter of sorrow!
          Oh, sorrow, nurse of our race!
          Deadly calamity, dragged into sudden light!
          How can you live to face,
          Hour by hour, the horror that hangs its threat
          Over your house, unknown as yet?
          The Queen of Love sent you a strange star,
          Princess of Crete!
          We see now where it will sink and set.

PHAEDRA.   Women of Troezen, who live here on the outer threshold of Peloponnese: I have at times lain long awake in the night, thinking how other lives than mine have been shattered; and I believe that such misfortune does not arise from inborn folly, since often those who suffer are wise and good. But this is how we should regard the matter: we know and see what is right, yet fail to carry it out. Some fail through sloth, others through valuing some pleasure more than goodness; and life offers us many pleasures.

   Listen: I will tell you the path my thoughts followed. When love struck me, I searched for the best way to endure the wound. My first resolve was to let slip no word, to hide what I suffered; for there is no trusting the tongue, which knows how to instruct others in wisdom, but invites disaser by its own folly. Next, I prepared to endure this madness as I ought, by overcoming it with self-control. Finally, when I still did not succeed in mastering this love, I determined that the best plan for me, beyond all contradiction, was to die. That is the decision I have taken; that is why I did not choose to thwart my own purpose with any kind of healing drug. If I do what is right, I would not wish to hide it, any more than to display my sins before witnesses. I knew that both the thing I craved, and the craving itself, was a sin. I knew also, too well, that I was a woman: a mark for the world's contempt. Whatever woman first was false to her husband with other men, misery and death destroy her! It was from noble houses that this plague first spead among women: when the great choose dishonour, the common herd will do the same. I hate women whose tongues talk of chasity, who in secret are bold in every sin! Queen Aphrodite, born from the sea's purity! how can they look into their husband's eyes, and not shudder lest sheltering darkness and guilty walls should speak? . . .

Friends, it is for this I am dying, that I may never be found guilty of disgracing my husband and my children. I want my sons to go back to the city of cities, to Athens, and hold their heads high and speak like free men there, and not blush for their mother. To live burdened with the secret of a parent's sin will enslave the boldest spirit. Only an upright heart and a clear conscience, they say, gives a man strength to wrestle with life; while those whose hearts are evil, sooner or later— as a young girl sees the truth in her glass—so they, when Time holds up his mirror, find their own sin revealed. May I never be found among them!

CHORUS.   It is true: virtue, wherever it appears, is a beautiful thing; and the fruit of virtue in this life is a good name.

NURSE.   My lady, when I heard what had happened to you, at the first shock I was terrified: now I begin to reflect how foolish I was. In human life second thoughts often prove to be wiser. What has happened to you is nothing extraordinary or hard to understand. The fever of Aphrodite has fastened on you: you are in love. What is strange in that? Why, so are countless others! And do you therefore mean to lose your life for love? Then surely there is a hard road ahead for all lovers now and to come, if their duty is to die! When Love sweeps on in the fulness of her power, there is no resisting. She steals gently on those who yield to her; but those she finds arrogant and haughty she takes and—what do you suppose?—tramples in the dust! Love rides on clouds and strides through the swollen sea. The whole world was born from Love; she sows every seed; every living creature on earth sprang from that sweet desire which is her gift to us. Those who possess pictures drawn in times past, or who spend their days pursuing the arts,—they know that Zeus once lusted for Semele, they know that once the lovely goddess of the glowing dawn stole away Cephalus and took him to live among the gods, because she loved him. Yet Cephalus and she live in the sky, and show no haste to quit the company of gods. Events have proved too strong for them; and they, believe me, are content. And you: do you refuse to submit? Your father, it seems, should have begotten you upon terms, or looked for other gods, if you're resolved to find fault with the laws of Nature. I ask you: how many good and sensible husbands see their wives unfaithful and look the other way? How many fathers help their love-sick sons to get what they want? Why, the true wisdom for mortals is to keep faults well hidden. A builder doesn't plane and polish the rafters in the roof! and it's not for us mortals to struggle after a tiresome perfection. In any case, how do you think you're going to swim clear of this flood of trouble you've met with? You are mortal, child: if the good you find in life outweighs the ill, you will be extremely fortunate. My dear daughter, soften your stubborn heart; do not blaspheme! What is it but blasphemy, to wish yourself stronger than a god? You are in love: then bear—and dare—what the god has willed. You are stricken: turn the stroke to your own good. Why, there are spells and soothing charms; we'll find a medicine for you. Trouble may wait a long time for men to mend it, if we women take no hand in the matter.

CHORUS. Her advice is more practical, Phaedra, for your present need; yet you, I feel, are right. Though it may be my approval is harder for you to accept, and more painful to hear, than her reproaches.

PHAEDRA. This is what brings ruin on fine cities and ancient houses— fair speech, too fair by far! Instead of saying what you think will please me, show me a way to save my honour.

NURSE. This is mere high-flown talk. Fine sentiments will not help you: you must have your man! He must be told in plain words what has happened, and won over without delay. If this were not a matter of life and death, if you were still a chaste-minded woman, I would never encourage you so far for your own lust and pleasure; but now we must fight for your life,—and there is nothing wrong in this.

PHAEDRA. Nothing wrong! It is horrible! Be silent, never speak such shameful words again!

NURSE. Shameful,—maybe; but more use to you than good words. Better do what I say, and live, than die for a vain boast of chasity.

PHAEDRA. No, for god's sake! What you say is plausible, but vile. Go no further! I have disciplined my heart to endure this. If you are so eloquent for evil, I shall fall now into the very pit I shrink from.

NURSE. If you feel so,—you should not have sinned at heart. Well, you did: now obey me—and be as ungrateful as you like. I have indoors a drug for the soothing of love—I have only now thought of it; it will bring you into no disgrace, no distress of mind, but it will cure you of your passion, if only you are not faint-hearted.

PHAEDRA. This drug—is it an ointment, or a draught?

NURSE. I don't know. Look for help, my girl, not explanations.

PHAEDRA. You may be too clever, and ruin me. I dread it.

NURSE. Then you would dread anything. What is it you are afraid of?

PHAEDRA. Of your saying any word about me to Hippolytus.

NURSE. Leave that to me, child. I know what to do. (*Aside*) Great Queen Aphrodite, only stand by me now, and help! For what else I have in mind, a word to our friend in the palace will be enough.

(*Exit* NURSE. PHAEDRA *remains.*)

CHORUS.

O Love, immortal Power, (STROPHE 1)
Love, dropping desire like dew on yearning eyes,
   Love, whose triumphant arms
Ravish the conquered soul with sweetest ecstasy!
   Come not in cruelty,
Never with ruthless violence invade my life!
   Fiery stroke of star or sun
Is less to fear than Aphrodite's dart
Which flies from the hand of Love, the child of Zeus,
   To madden a mortal heart.

In vain by Alpheus' banks, (ANTISTROPHE 1)
In vain at the Pythian shrine shall sacrifice multiply,
   And the blood of bulls pour forth,
Toll from the pastures of Greece to Apollo and Artemis;
   While Eros, Master of man,
   Who holds Aphrodite's key
   To her chamber of sweet delight,—
   Him in our prayers we slight:
Love, whose coming has brought, since the world began,
   Death and calamity!

Iole, Princess of Oechalia, (STROPHE 2)
Was once a free and taintless virgin,
A maiden unmatched with man;
But Aphrodite tore her from her home,
A wild nymph, helpless and frantic;
And there, amidst blood and smoke,
With dying groans for her bridal-hymn,

Gave her to the son of Alcmene
To carry weeping across the sea.

O holy wall of Thebes, (ANTISTROPHE 2)
O lips of the Dircean spring,
You with one voice could tell
How terrible is the advent of Aphrodite!
When upon Semele thunder and flame descended,
And her womb gave birth to Bacchus, the child of Zeus,
Aphrodite laid her to sleep,
A bride in the bed of Death.
For the breath of her terror is felt in every land,
And swift as a bee's flight
Is the path of her power.

PHAEDRA. Women, be quiet! . . . Oh, the last blow has fallen!

CHORUS. We will be quiet. But this sounds ominous!

PHAEDRA. Wait! I want to hear exactly what they are saying.

CHORUS. Something terrible is happening in the palace. Phaedra, what
is it?

PHAEDRA. Oh! Why must I suffer so? It is unbearable!

CHORUS. What is unbearable?
What is this anguished cry?
Tell us, what fearful word
Fell on your ears like Fate?

PHAEDRA. It is—my death! Come, stand near the door and listen.
Do you hear what an uproar is rising there?

CHORUS. You are beside the door:
For you the house utters a voice! Tell me, then,
What horror you heard,
Tell me, what has been done?

PHAEDRA. It is the son of the riding Amazon, Hippolytus, cursing and
abusing my old servant.

CHORUS. Yes, I can hear the sound,
Yet not a word is clear!
How can I tell? Oh, it was clear to you,
The cry that came from the house!

PHAEDRA. Ah, listen! Yes, too clear! He calls her "filthy bawd," damns
her for treason to her master's bed!

CHORUS.
No, no! What shall we do?
Lady, you are betrayed!
What plan can I offer?
Your secret shown to the world,
Your life and hope laid in the dust by the hand of a friend!

PHAEDRA. She has told him the fatal truth about me. She did it for love, to cure my suffering; but it was wrong!

CHORUS. What now? What way out is there? What will you do?

PHAEDRA. I do not know,—only this: that to die at once is the sole escape from this torture.

(*Enter* HIPPOLYTUS, *followed by the* NURSE.)

HIPPOLYTUS. O Mother Earth! O unfolding radiance of the sun! What things I have heard! What words unspeakable have been spoken!

NURSE. Be quiet, lad, or someone will hear this clamour!

HIPPOLYTUS. How can I be quiet after what I have listened to?

NURSE. I beg you, I kiss your hand—dear boy, be quiet!

HIPPOLYTUS. Keep your hands off my clothes! You shall not touch me.

NURSE. For the gods' sake, have pity! Don't tell what I said to you! It would kill me.

HIPPOLYTUS. Kill you? Your words were harmless, you said!

NURSE. What I said, my son, was not for everyone to hear.

HIPPOLYTUS. Honest words should not be hushed up: let everyone hear!

NURSE. My boy, do not slight the oath you swore me!

HIPPOLYTUS. My tongue swore: the oath does not bind my heart.

NURSE. What will you do, child? Destroy your friend?

HIPPOLYTUS. Friend? God forbid I should have any such friend!

NURSE. Forgive! We are human; we cannot help doing wrong.

HIPPOLYTUS. O Zeus! Why have you plagued this world with so vile and worthless a thing as woman? If it was your pleasure to plant a mortal stock, why must women be the renewers of the race? Better that men should come to your temples and put down a price, each what he could afford,—buy themselves children in embryo for gold or silver and get their money's worth; then they could live at home like free men, without women! Why, for proof that woman is an evil pest,—her father, after begetting and bringing her up, pays out a dowry to find her a home, and so gets rid of her; while whoever welcomes the viper to his bosom gleefully decks her out with gauds and gowns like a sacred statue, heaping beauty upon hatefulness, poor wretch, and squanders his inheritance. What choice has he? If he marries noble blood, he beds with his shrew and makes the best of it; or if he finds a good wife in a worthless family, with that much comfort he counters his ill-luck. For an easy life, marry a nobody, and keep her worthless and witless on a pedestal. I hate a woman who is clever—a woman who thinks more than becomes a woman; I would not have her in my house! For passion engenders wickedness the more readily in clever women; while the simple are kept from wantonness by lack of wit. A wife should have no servant ever come near her, she should live attended by dumb savage beasts, who could neither understand her nor speak to her. As it is, unchaste wives sit at home scheming lechery, while their servants traffic their schemes out to the world:—you for one, coming like a she-devil to invite me to incest with my father's wife! I'll flush your filthy words from my ears with floods of water! Do you think I could so sin, when I feel polluted merely by hearing you?

Listen: I let you trap me into swearing silence. I fear the gods, and that saves you; otherwise I would at once have told my father the whole story. Instead, I shall now leave the palace until he comes back; and I shall say nothing; but I shall come back with my father, and then I shall observe how you and your mistress meet his eye. You at least will brazen it out—I know what you're made of.—Curse the whole race of you! I can never hate you enough. Ha! They tell me I always say the same thing: well, women, it seems, always *are* the same thing. So whoever can teach women to be chaste may forbid me to tread their name in the dust!

(*Exit.*)

CHORUS. How cruel a curse it is to be born a woman!
Who would not pity us?
What shift, what turn, what plea,
After the first faltering,
Can loose us from the clamp of guilt?

PHAEDRA. I have met what I deserved.
Earth and sunlight, show me where to fly
Out of the clutch of Fate!
Where can I hide my anguish?
What god or man can give to my guilty soul
Safety or help or counsel?
I am caught in toils of torment;
There is no escape for the living:
I sink under the scourge of Chance.

CHORUS. Lady, I weep with you. The harm is done; your servant's plans have failed disastrously.

PHAEDRA (*to* NURSE). You vile, treacherous murderess, see what you have done to me! May Zeus who gave me life blast you with fire and grind you to dust! Did I not try to prevent what you were plotting? Did I not forbid you to speak a word of what now drags me in the dirt? You spoke: and your treason robs even my death of honour. Now—some new plan. Hippolytus, white-hot with rage, will carry your foul words to his father and denounce me; go complaining to old Pittheus, fill the whole land with his outrageous tale! Curse you! Curse all officious fools who thrust their wicked help on their friends to ruin them!

NURSE. My lady, I have done you wrong; you may well blame me. The wound pricks, and overcomes your judgment. Yet, if you'll listen to me, I can speak for myself. I nursed you; I am your friend; I tried to find a remedy for your trouble; and I was unlucky. With better luck, I would have been called a wise woman. After all, wisdom is only happening to guess right.

PHAEDRA. So! This is your just amends to me—to follow up your treachery with argument!

NURSE. We are wasting time in talk. I admit I was unwise; but, my daughter, there's hope, there's life, even now!

PHAEDRA. Stop! Not another word! You gave me advice before, and help too; and both were wicked. Get out of my sight! Scheme for your own affairs, and I will set mine in order!

(*Exit* NURSE.)

Noblewomen of Troezen, I ask you to do me this favour: bury deep in silence all that you have heard here today.

CHORUS. By holy Artemis, daughter of Zeus, I swear to disclose nothing of what has happened to you.

PHAEDRA. That is well. Listen, my friends—I have said this before—: I have a remedy for my present plight; one that will ensure an honourable future for my sons, and help me in face of to-day's calamity. The royal house of Crete shall forfeit no reputation through me. After this shame, to face Theseus would be too high a price for one life.

CHORUS. What are you going to do, that is so dreadful and so final?

PHAEDRA. To die. By what means, I will decide for myself.

CHORUS. In God's name, no!

PHAEDRA. You too must school me; I know my part. To-day I'll be rid of life, and give joy to my immortal murderess. Love is without mercy: I shall die defeated. Yet my death shall be a curse on another's life, and teach him not to trample on my agony. He shall have an equal share in my suffering, and learn to be gentle!

(*Exit* PHAEDRA.)

CHORUS.

O to escape and hide (STROPHE 1)
High among steep and secret rocks!
  At the touch of a god to change,
  To rise as a bird and ride
On feathered wings among soaring flocks!
  To wander far and free
Where the lost waters of Eridanus flow deep
  Down to an unknown sea;
Where for dead Phaethon the Sun's daughters weep,

Dropping piteous tears that gleam
Like amber in the purple stream!

And O for that quiet garden by the Western sea   (ANTISTROPHE 1)
    Where the daughters of Evening sing
    Under the golden apple-tree;
    Where the bold sailor wandering
    Finds the Ocean-god has barred
His Westward path over the purple waste!
    Where huge Atlas lives to guard
    The solemn frontiers of the sky;
Where in Zeus' palace fountains of ambrosial wine
    Flow by the festal couch divine,
    While holy Earth heaps high
    Her fruits of rarest taste
To bless the immortal feast with bountiful supply!

White-winged Cretan ship,   (STROPHE 2)
That brought my lady Phaedra from her wealthy home
Over the salt swell of the pounding sea,—
    White sails for the joy of a bride,
    To veil the black fate waiting!
    Heavy with omen was her course
From Crete to Athens, queen of mainland cities,
When at Peiraeus her seamen leapt ashore
And looped their plaited hawsers on the quay;
    Dark again was the hour
When from the rocky harbour of Munychion
The royal progress parted for Troezen.

Thence on Phaedra fell the fatal curse,   (ANTISTROPHE 2)
When Aphrodite with a cruel unholy lust
    Shattered her helpless heart!
    Now the storm of her distress
    Drives her, a sinking wreck,
    Alone to her marriage-chamber.
    From the high beam she will tie
    Close round her white neck the noose:
    This her one choice, to die!
Thus with reverence learnt for her immortal enemy,
And prizing a fair name above her life,
She will win release of heart from her tormenting love.
(A voice is heard shouting from the palace.)

VOICE.   Oh, help, help! Anyone who is in the house, come and help! She is hanging—the Queen, the wife of Theseus!

CHORUS.   Oh! She has kept her word! Oh, Phaedra, Phaedra! She is dead, dead! the Queen! Hung high in a strangling rope!

VOICE.   Come quickly! Bring a knife, a sword, anything to cut this cord from her neck!

CHORUS. A.   Friends, what shall we do? Ought we to go inside and untie the noose and free her?

B. Why, where are the young men who attend her? It is never safe to interefere.

VOICE.   Poor lady, she is dead! Lay her limbs out straight. Oh, what a tale to have to tell my master!

CHORUS.   Did you hear? Poor Phaedra, she is dead; they are already lay-ing out her body.

(*Enter* THESEUS, *attended by the royal guard. His head is crowned with the garland worn by those who have received a favourable answer from an oracle.*)

THESEUS.   Tell me, women,—what was that outcry in the palace? What I heard was the voices of servants weeping. (*There is silence.*) This is strange: I return home from a solemn mission of piety—and my home receives me with shut doors, not a word of welcome or greeting! . . . I hope nothing has happened to Pittheus? He is well advanced in years; yet his departure from this house would be a grief to me.

CHORUS.   What has happened, Theseus, has not touched the old. It is the young whose death will break your heart.

THESEUS.   What? Is one of my children's lives stolen from me?

CHORUS.   No, it is still more terrible: their mother is dead.

THESEUS.   What do you say? My wife dead? What happened?

CHORUS.   She made a noose with a rope and hanged herself.

THESEUS.   But why? Was it some numbing stroke of grief? What could cause so dreadful an act?

CHORUS.   That is all I know, Theseus. I have just now come to the palace to mourn for your loss.

THESEUS.   Phaedra—dead! . . . Why have I crowned my head with this garland of leaves? *Here* is my answer from the oracle!—Ho, there! Ser-vants! Unbar the doors and open! Open them wide, let me see my dead wife, whose death is death to me!

(*The doors open, showing* PHAEDRA *dead.*)

CHORUS.

Weep for the Queen, tears for her tears!
Phaedra, your agony and your act alike
Must banish peace from this house!
How could you dare a death so hideous, so unholy,

A prey to your own pitiless hand?
Poor soul, what power dims your brightness in death?
THESEUS.   O the torture of life! In this city of exile
I have seen surely the utmost of the grief appointed for me!
O Fate, like a cruel heel crushing me and my house,
A nameless foul infection from some pursuing fiend,
Corrupting, annihilating life and the love of life!
I strain despairing eyes over my sea of misery,
And my hope of safety vanishes, for the shore is out of sight
And life is a mounting wave I have not strength to surmount.
    What reason, Phaedra, what malicious chance,
    What fated cruelty can I accuse?
    As a bird from my hand you have vanished,
Swooped swift and daring into the pit of darkness
And left me tears for your death and anguish for your despair!
    Far from here this harvest grew;
    Long ago a sin was sown;
        Fruit the gods have ripened
        For my grief I gather.
CHORUS.   King, this sorrow falls not on your soul alone:
        Many share it, weeping
        A dear wife departed.
THESEUS.
    To go into the dark! Now let me die, and pass
    To the world under the earth, into the joyless dark!
    Since you, dearer than all, are at my side no longer,
    And the death you have dealt is more than the death that has swallowed
        you.
    Who will tell me the truth? Whence, my wife, could it come,—
    This chance, whose murderous blow fell on your tortured heart?
    What happened? Shall I be told? Or does my palace harbour
    A horde of lying lackeys? Phaedra! my heart is broken!
    Friends, pity me, who have lived to see such pain
    Ravage my home! No words can speak of it,
    No human heart bear it. My life is over.
        Now my house is desolate,
        And my children motherless.
        You, the dearest, best, of all
        That the dazzling sun surveys
            Or the star-eyed evening,—
            You are gone for ever!
(*As* THESEUS *has been speaking, the* CHORUS *have noticed a letter tied to*
PHAEDRA'S *wrist.*)

CHORUS. Theseus, I pity you for the storm that wrecks your home.
Yet, while I have watched your sorrow with tear-filled eyes,
Still I tremble with deeper dread for the terror to come!

THESEUS. Look! Look here! A letter fastened to her dear hand! What does this mean? Will it tell me something new? Surely, she has written her dying wishes, begging me to remember our marriage and our children. Rest easy, Phaedra! My house and bed shall never be entered by another woman! See, the impression of her golden signet brings me her greeting from the dead! Now to untwist the cord from the seal, and see what this letter has to tell me.

CHORUS. Here is a crueller pain, a deeper horror
Sent by the gods to crown the rest! If it were I,—
Knowing the truth, how could I bear my life?
The royal house heaped in ruin, never to rise!
Gods have pity! Strike not down!
Hear and help us! . . . In his eyes,
See, so grimly staring,
Portents of disaster!

THESEUS. Oh, oh! Horror upon horror, blow upon blow! Beyond endurance, beyond speech! Oh!

CHORUS. What now? If it is for us to hear, tell us!

THESEUS.
The letter! It shrieks, it howls, horrors indelible!
I am crushed; where can I escape? What I have seen has killed me.
A voice from the letter speaks, and tells—what things! what things!

CHORUS. What are you saying, Theseus? Something dreadful must follow.

THESEUS. A thing so dreadful that I scarcely can force my tongue
To utter it. Yet I will speak now. Listen, O city!
Hippolytus has braved the holy eye of Zeus and done violence to my wife's honour!
Yes, Poseidon my father, you promised me three curses: with one of them strike down my son! If they were good curses you gave me, let him not live out this day!

CHORUS. My lord, in heaven's name, take your prayer back! You are wrong—you will know it later; only trust me!

THESEUS. There is no taking back. I will not only curse but banish him from the land. If the one fails he shall feel the other. Either Poseidon will honour my curse and send his corpse below, or else as a stranger wandering the earth, an outcast from his country, he shall drain his despicable life to the dregs.

CHORUS. Why, look! Here, this very moment, comes your son himself, Hippolytus! King Theseus, calm this dangerous anger, and consider what will be best for yourself and your family.

(*Enter* HIPPOLYTUS, *with* HUNTSMEN.)

HIPPOLYTUS.   Father, I heard your outcry and came at once. What trouble has caused your distress I do not know; but I wish you would tell me. . . . Oh! What do I see? It is your wife, Father—dead! Dead? How is it possible? I had only just left her; a short time ago she was alive! What has happened to her? How did she die? . . . Father, I am asking you to tell me! Will you not speak? This is no time to be silent! I know that to insist out of season on being told everything is called idle curiosity; but I am a friend—something more than a friend. Surely, Father, you should not hide trouble from me!

THESEUS.   Oh, the futile folly of men! Why do they teach arts innumerable, contrive and search out every other thing,—when one knowledge they cannot win, one quarry they have not caught: the skill to teach wisdom to the brutish.

HIPPOLYTUS.   He would certainly be a clever instructor who could drive sense into a fool. But, Father, this is not the time for philosophical discourse. Sorrow, I fear, is making you talk wildly.

THESEUS.   Oh, there should be somewhere a touchstone of human hearts, which men could trust to tell them the truth about their friends, who is loyal and who treacherous! Every man should have two voices, the one truthful, the other—natural; so that his lying voice might be refuted by the true; and we should not be duped.

HIPPOLYTUS.   What? Has one of your friends contrived to slander me to you and make you suspect my innocence? I am bewildered, astonished! Your words are crazed, you have taken leave of your wits!

THESEUS.   The heart of man! Is there any vileness it will turn from? Will barefaced wickedness ever find its limit? If crime is to bulk bigger with each new generation, new depths of villainy be revealed age after age, the gods will need to create a second earth to house liars and lechers. Look at this man! my own son, who would pollute my marriage-bed, —and is proved guilty by the damning witness of her dead hand. Come, show your face—foul as you are, look your father in the eyes! So you— you are the man above men who keeps the company of gods! Yours is the chaste life unsmirched with evil! Who believes your bragging? Who charges gods with such ignorance and folly? Not I! So, now flaunt your purity! Play the quack with your fleshless diets! Take Orpheus for your lord and prophet and wallow in frenzied adoration of his wordy vapourings! Yes, you are exposed! Of such men let the world take warning and beware! They pursue their prey with lofty words and low cunning.— Oh, she is dead: do you think that will save you? No, vile criminal, it is the prime evidence of your guilt. What oaths or arguments could outweigh her witness and acquit you? You will say that she hated you; that there will always be war between the bastard and the true-born. Was she so poor a bargainer with her life, that she would throw away all its sweetness to spite you? Or will you tell me that young men are free from folly, women born to it? Well I know that young men are no steadier than women, when Aphrodite stirs the hot blood in them. Indeed, their sex makes them even more headstrong.

Ah! why should I fight down your defence, when her dead body blazons its evidence to my eyes? Out of this land to exile! Go, I say! Never come near the god-built walls of Athens, cross no frontier that my sword guards! I tell you, if I weaken before this outrage, the Isthmian bandit Sinis shall deny that I killed him, and call me boaster; and the sea-washed rocks where Sciron met his end shall forget the weight of my hand against evildoers!

CHORUS.   How can any mortal man be called happy? Until to-day Hippolytus, you were first in good fortune: now everything is reversed.

HIPPOLYTUS.   Father, your passionate anger is terrible; and though what you say at first appears just, you will find it does not bear closer scrutiny. Though I have no skill to address a crowd, among a few equals I can speak with more confidence. And this is natural; just as those who seem fools among wise men can be eloquent before crowds. So, now that my whole life is in danger, I must be bold and speak.

And I will begin with the first charge you leveled at me, which you thought would leave me shattered and speechless. Look at this sky, this earth: in the length and breadth of them there is no man—deny it as you will—more pure in heart than I! I have learnt, first, to reverence the gods; then, to choose friends who keep their hands innocent, whose honour forbids them either to render me or expect from me any discreditable service. I do not mock those I live among, Father; I am the same to my friends absent or present. One sin you now think me convicted of has never touched me: to this day my body is chaste; I have not known a woman. I know nothing of such matters, more than I have heard men tell, or seen in pictures; which I have little desire to look at, for my mind is virgin. Perhaps you refuse to believe that I am pure: then it is for you to show what temptation was too strong for me. Was your wife more beautiful than all other women? Or did I hope, by winning her love, to become your heir? Any such hope would have been less vain than mad! Did I covet your place as king? For a wise man a throne has no attraction; to find pleasure in power is to be corrupted by it—there are many examples. No; my ambition is a different one: let me be first in the Grecian Games, and in politics take second place, and be happy with honest friends. In this way I am able to live my own life—and to live free from danger, which is a greater blessing than a crown.

That is all I have to say, except one thing: if a witness to my innocence were here to speak, and if Phaedra were alive to listen to my defence, then the event would guide your search for the guilty. As things are, I swear to you by Zeus, Guardian of oaths, and by the Earth, that I never touched your wife, never could have wished even to think of it. I pray that I may die in nameless dishonour, cityless, homeless, exile and vagabond,—may neither sea nor land receive my dead flesh, if there is sin in me! Whether it was fear that made Phaedra take her life I do not know; further than this it is impossible for me to speak. She kept her chastity, without possessing the virtue of chastity; I possess it, and have practised it to my own ruin.

CHORUS. Surely what you have said will suffice to clear you! Your solemn oaths to the gods must be believed.

THESEUS. Is he not a spellmonger, a cheat, hoping to master my mind with his smooth temper, after putting his father to open shame?

HIPPOLYTUS. It is *your* smooth temper that I wonder at, Father. If you were my son, and I in your place, I would have killed you, not corrected you with exile, if you had dared to touch my wife.

THESEUS. Indeed! How justly! No, you shall not die like that. Many a criminal would be glad of a quick death. No: since you have passed sentence on yourself, you shall wander an outcast from your country, on alien soil you shall drain the bitter lees of life, and earn a criminal's reward.

HIPPOLYTUS. What? You will do that? You will not wait for the witness of time to condemn me, but drive me out to-day?

THESEUS. Yes! beyond the outer ocean and the ends of the earth, if I had the power, so abominable to me is the sight of you!

HIPPOLYTUS. You spurn my sworn oath, you seek no guidance of priests, but banish me unjudged?

THESEUS. Priests! with their omens from birds that fly about overhead! To me they are nothing at all! This letter here is no soothsayer's riddle, and it proves you guilty.

HIPPOLYTUS. Why do I not unlock my lips? You gods, whom my silence honours, it is you who destroy me!—No: I will not speak. Nothing I might say now could carry weight where it would help me. To tell the truth would be to break my oath and gain nothing.

THESEUS. Still your cursed piety! It chokes me! What are you waiting for? Out of my land, I say!

HIPPOLYTUS. Out of your land? Which way shall I turn? Who of my friends will receive me, exiled on such a charge?

THESEUS. Who? Any that has a warm welcome for the defiler of men's wives, the bosom-friend of all iniquity!

HIPPOLYTUS. Oh, it is time indeed for tears and a broken heart, when my father thinks and truly believes that I am guilty.

THESEUS.   The time for you to weep and be wise was the time when you cast off shame to dishonour your father's wife!

HIPPOLYTUS.   Oh, if these walls could but cry out and speak for me, and witness whether I am so vile a man!

THESEUS.   You are careful to fly for help to dumb witnesses; but the fact needs no tongue to prove you guilty.

HIPPOLYTUS.   I wish for very pity that I could stand apart and behold myself, to shed tears for my own suffering!

THESEUS.   No doubt! You are far more practised in self-worship than in self-control and honourable conduct to your father.

HIPPOLYTUS.   My unhappy mother! I was born in bitterness of sorrow. May no one that I love ever be called bastard!

THESEUS.   Guards! take him away! Do you not hear? I have already pronounced him banished.

HIPPOLYTUS.   It will be the worse for any of them that touches me. Since you're so minded, thrust me out yourself!

THESEUS.   I will do so, unless you obey me. Your exile does not touch my tears.

(*Exit* THESEUS.)

HIPPOLYTUS.   My fate, then, is fixed. It is sad and cruel, that I know the truth, yet know no way to speak it. (*He turns to the figure of* ARTEMIS.) Goddess, daughter of Leto, most dear companion, and comrade in the hunt, I shall live exiled forever from glorious Athens! Farewell, my city; farewell, land of Erechtheus; farewell, plain of Troezen, rich in the vigorous delights of youth! I take my last look now, speak my last word to you. And you too, lads that have grown up with me here,— come, say good-bye to me and see me to the border. Though even my own father denies it, you will never meet a man more honourable.

(*Exit* HIPPOLYTUS *with his men.*)

CHORUS.

When I remember that the gods take thought   (STROPHE 1)
For human life, often in hours of grief
    To me this faith has brought
    Comfort and heart's relief.

Yet, though deep in my hope perception lies
Wistful, experience grows and faith recedes:
    Men's fortunes fall and rise
    Not answering to their deeds.

Change follows change; Fate purposeless and blind
Uproots us from familiar soil:
    The longest life can find
    No rest from travel and toil.

This is my prayer: may divine providence fulfil   (ANTISTROPHE 1)
  All my heart's will,
  And bless my days with wealth, and guard
My life from pain, and keep my soul unscarred.

The dauntless stern resolve is not for me,
Nor the fair face masking the false intent;
  Rather my choice would be
To change my ways, adapt my easy creed
  To suit to-morrow's need,
And pass my quiet days in long content.

I cannot think clearly now: (STROPHE 2)
I have seen a thing that I never thought to see,—
I have seen the brightest star of the city of Athens
Driven out by his father's anger
To look for another country.
Sandy shore fringing the city-wall,
You will not see him now;
Nor you, oak-forests to the mountain-side,
Where in the train of the immortal Huntress
He followed with swift-footed hounds to make his kill!

We shall not see him now   (ANTISTROPHE 2)
Leap up behind his trained Thessalian team,
Holding the smooth track round the shore-marshes
Breathless with the tense drumming of hooves.
The music that sang unsleeping from the plucked string
Shall be dumb in his father's palace.
The garlands will wither now
That you strewed in the deep Spring grass
Where Artemis loved to rest;
And the jealous war of girls who longed for your love,
Now you are gone, sinks into hopeless peace.

To me, Hippolytus, your fate has left   (EPODE)
A life unreal, empty of all but tears.
  Dead are the dreams that lit
  Your mother's pains with joy.
Gods immortal, mortal rage reproaches you!
  How, you sister Graces,
Can you see him hounded from his father's home,
  Innocent, and outcast—
  Righteous, and uprooted?

CHORUS. Look! Someone is running this way! It is one of Hippolytus'
men! And his eyes are full of horror!

(*Enter* MESSENGER.)

MESSENGER. Women, where can I find the King? Where is Theseus? If
you know, tell me. Is he indoors?

CHORUS. Here is the King. He is coming out now.

(*Enter* THESEUS.)

MESSENGER. Theseus, I bring grave news—grave both for you and for all
your people, whether of Athens or of Troezen.

THESEUS. What is your news? Can yet another calamity have fallen upon
our two cities?

MESSENGER. Hippolytus is dead—or dying. His life hangs in the balance.

THESEUS. Who struck him? Was it the vengeance of some man whose
wife he had dishonoured as he did his father's?

MESSENGER. It was his own chariot that killed him—and the curses
which your lips called down from your father the sea-god upon your
son.

THESEUS. By the gods!—so you have proved a true father to me,
Poseidon: you heard my curse! And how did it happen? Tell me!
How did the trap of justice close on the man who shamed me?

MESSENGER. We were on the shore, near the water's edge, combing down
the horses and smoothing their manes; and we were weeping, for we
had been told that Hippolytus was no longer free to come and go in
Troezen, but was condemned by you to the miseries of exile. He came
to us there, bringing the same tale of tears; and a great troop of friends
and followers, young men like himself, came with him. After some
time he stopped weeping and said to us, "This is folly; my father must
be obeyed. Men, yoke my horses, harness them to the chariot. This is
not my country any more." Then every man of us came with a will,
and sooner than you could say it we had the team harnessed and standing ready at the prince's side. He caught up the reins from the driving-
rail, and, dressed as he was for hunting, took his stand on the chariot.
And first he held up his hands and prayed: "Zeus, may I die if I am
a guilty man! And may my father know how he has wronged me,—if
not while I live, then after I am dead!"

And now he had gripped the goad and was urging his horses; and we
servants began running beside the bridles, to escort our master along
the straight road to Argos and Epidauria. We sped on, across the
Troezenian frontier, and reached a deserted part of the coast, beyond
which, as you know, a beach runs down to the Saronic Sea. It was
there that we heard a heavy rumbling sound, like the thunder of Zeus,
but rising out of the earth, with a deep roar that was horrible to hear.
The horses pricked their ears, lifted their heads. We youths were

terrified, wondering where the sound came from. We looked out to the
breaking surf, and there we saw a wave of unearthly size, rearing to the
sky; it hid from my view not only the Scironian headland but the
Isthmus and the Rock of Asclepius. Then, swelling still huger, and
spattering foam on every side, it rushed seething and hissing to the
shore, and straight towards the chariot and the four horses. And in
the very moment of bursting and crashing, the wave threw forth a
monstrous savage bull, whose bellow filled the whole earth with an
appalling echo, while the sight of him was too tremendous for mortal
vision. The horses were seized with a frenzy of terror. Hippolytus, using
his long experience in the ways of horses, gripped the reins, twisting
them round behind his back and dragging on them as a rower tugs
on his oar. It was no use: the beasts took the wrought-iron bits between
their teeth and careered on, as though the driver's hand and the reins
and harness and the heavy chariot were nothing at all! When he struggled to steer their hurtling course up towards the soft grass, there was
the bull in front to craze them with terror and turn them back; when
they went madly tearing towards the rocks, then the bull kept close
beside them, silent, and swerving right in upon the chariot, until the
moment when he crashed the boss of the wheel against a rock and flung
the chariot tossing in the air. Then there was wild confusion—wheels,
axle, bolts, and frame leaping high. Hippolytus, tangled in the reins,
strung fast in an inextricable knot, was dragged along, his head dashed
on the rocks, his flesh torn; while in a voice terrible to hear he shouted
to his horses, "Stop! You were reared in my own stables—will you
grind me to death?" Then he cried, "Father, why did you curse me?
I am innocent! Will no one come to help me?"

Indeed, there were many of us willing enough, but run as we might
we were left behind. At last—how I do not know—he fell clear to those
fine reins that bound him. He still breathed; though there was little
life left in him. The horses had vanished away over the rocky ground,
I cannot tell where; so had the dreadful prodigy of a bull.

My lord: I am only one of your palace slaves; but I never can nor
will believe that your son was guilty of so terrible a crime—no, not
if the whole race of women hanged themselves, not if a mountain of
letters were written to accuse him: I know that Hippolytus is a good
man.

CHORUS. The wheel has turned; disaster follows disaster. Fate is inevitable; there is no escape.

THESEUS. Because I hated the man who has suffered this, I was glad
when I heard it; but remembrance of the gods awes me: Hippolytus is
my own flesh. What has happened gives me neither pleasure nor grief.

MESSENGER. What shall we do? Shall we bring him to die here? Or what

would please you? Consider: your son is struck down. Listen to my
advice and do not be harsh to him.

THESEUS.   Bring him. Let me see face to face the man who denies that
he dishonoured my bed; so that my words and the hand of heaven may
convict him.

(*Exit* MESSENGER.)

CHORUS.   Aphrodite! You lead captive
Stubborn hearts of gods and mortals!
At your side with glinting wing
Eros, round his victim swiftly circling,
Hovers over earth and the salt sea's clear song.
When on the maddened spirit
He swoops with sweet enchantment,
Whelps of the mountain know the power of his golden wing;
Fish, and the unnumbered beasts that draw
Life from the earth's breast, warmth from the sun's eye,—
Yes, and the hearts of men,
Yield to the universal spell.
Aphrodite, you alone
Reign in power and honour,
Queen of all creation!

(THESEUS *and the* CHORUS *are facing the statue of* APHRODITE; ARTEMIS *appears beside her own statue on the other side of the stage. As she speaks all turn towards her.*)

ARTEMIS.   Theseus, royal son of Aegeus! I command you,
Listen! It is Artemis, Leto's daughter, who speaks.
Why do you, wretch, rejoice at what you have heard?
You have most sinfully murdered your own son.
You believed your wife's lies without witness: now
Witness the world how you reap your own undoing!
Will you not cower shamed in the depths of hell?
Soar to the sky to escape this chain of misery?
    In the common life of good men
    There is no place for you now.

(*She moves to centre of stage.*)

I will tell you, Theseus, the true state of your unhappy life; and my
words will not smooth your path, but sharpen your pain. My purpose
in coming is to disclose, first, your son's uprightness of heart, that he
may die with a good name; then, your wife's frenzy—or, in some sense,
her nobleness. Phaedra, plagued and goaded by that goddess whom I,
and all who love virginity, most hate—Phaedra loved your son. Reason
struggled to subdue passion. She died through schemes plotted against
her will: her nurse told Hippolytus, under oath of secrecy, the Queen's

affliction. He honourably resisted her persuasions; even when you so wronged him, still for reverence of the gods he would not abjure his oath; but Phaedra, in terror lest she be exposed, wrote that lying letter and by fraud killed your son—yes, for you believed her!

THESEUS. My son, my son!

ARTEMIS. Do my words hurt, Theseus? Listen further, for you have more to suffer. You know that your father promised you the fulfilment of three curses? The first you have most wickedly misused, cursing your son when you might have cursed an enemy. Your father the sea-god gave all that he was bound to give. He had promised; and the folly was not his. Now in his eyes and in mine you are condemned. Instead of waiting for proof, or prophetic guidance, giving no room for question or the slow scrutiny of Time, with unrighteous haste you flung your curse and killed your son.

THESEUS. Goddess, let me die!

ARTEMIS. Your sin is great. Yet even you may still find pardon for what you have done. For it was Aphrodite who, to satisfy her resentment, willed that all this should happen; and there is a law among gods, that no one of us should seek to frustrate another's purpose, but let well alone. I tell you, but that I fear Zeus and his laws, I never would have submitted to such dishonour, as to stand by and see Hippolytus go to his death; for he was dearest to me of all mortals. You did not know the truth: this, first, frees your fault from the deepest guilt. Then, your wife by her death prevented any test of what she alleged, and thus made sure that you would believe her. So this flood of misfortune has burst chiefly upon you; but I too suffer. For a good man's death is no joy to the gods; but the impious man we utterly destroy, and his house and children with him.

CHORUS. Ah, look! Here comes the piteous prince,
His young flesh torn, his fair head bruised.
Ah, suffering house! The hand of heaven has struck
Twice in one day, accomplishing
The heavy doom of your appointed pain.

(*Enter* HIPPOLYTUS, *supported by huntsmen.*)

HIPPOLYTUS. Weep for me, weep for me,
Scarred, broken, trampled under foot
By man and god alike unjust,—
My father's curse, Poseidon's power;
Weep for my death!
My forehead is pierced with the fierce pain,
My brain convulsed with the pulse of anguish.
Enough now! I am fainting; let me lie.
(*They lay him down.*)

O horses my own hand fed,
Your cursed strength has crushed the breath from my body,
Torn the life from my limbs!
Men, for God's sake have careful hands
And touch me gently where the flesh is raw.
Who stands at my right side?
Lift me softly, with a steady grip.
Fallen cursed by my father's fault—
Zeus, do you see my agony?
I, that revered the gods with a holy heart,
I that was first in innocence,
Tread my way from life to the dark world,
And Death's eyes meet me as I go.

In vain I strove with patience
To love and serve my neighbour:
Now pain sets painful foot upon my body.
Let go, hold me no longer,
But let Death come to heal me;
And, if you pity me, help me to die quickly!
I am in love with the rending spear: come, cruel edge,
Shatter my heart and lull my life asleep!
Now, through my father's fatal curse,
The hellish heritage of bloodguiltiness
Won by forgotten ancestors
Descends impatient to the appointed heir—
On me it falls! Why? Why? I have done no wrong!
What shall I say? How can I ease my soul
And reach the end of anguish?
  Lay me deep for evermore,
  Death, with sore unyielding hand,
  In the land of night and sleep!

ARTEMIS.   Poor soul, galled with a bitter yoke! It was your noble heart
  that destroyed you.
HIPPOLYTUS.   Ah, breath of divine fragrance! Goddess, I hear you, and
  my torment lightens. It is truly Artemis, here in this place?
ARTEMIS.   Poor soul, it is. You have no better friend among the gods.
HIPPOLYTUS.   Lady, you see how it is with me?
ARTEMIS.   I see; but my eyes are forbidden to shed tears.
HIPPOLYTUS.   No one now to attend you in the hunt. . . .
ARTEMIS.   No: you were my dear attendant; and you are dying.
HIPPOLYTUS.   None to graze your horses, or guard your statues.
ARTEMIS.   The wicked craft of Aphrodite has done this.

HIPPOLYTUS.   Aphrodite! So, I know what god has killed me.

ARTEMIS.   She resented your neglect and hated your purity.

HIPPOLYTUS.   It is clear to me now: she has destroyed us all three.

ARTEMIS.   You, and your father, and your father's wife.

HIPPOLYTUS.   Though my father wronged me, yet I weep for him.

ARTEMIS.   He was deceived: a god had planned it so.

HIPPOLYTUS.   Father, how you have suffered to-day!

THESEUS.   My son, my heart is broken; life is loathsome to me.

HIPPOLYTUS.   Though the fault was yours, I weep for you more than for myself.

THESEUS.   Would God I might die for you, my son!

HIPPOLYTUS.   You too had little joy of your father's gifts.

THESEUS.   O that that curse had never passed my lips!

HIPPOLYTUS.   Why? You would have killed me, you were so angry then!

THESEUS.   I was cheated by the gods out of my right mind!

HIPPOLYTUS.   Oh, if only a man's curse could touch a god!

ARTEMIS.   You need not curse. Not even the black depths
Beneath the earth shall thwart the vengeance due
For this cruel wrong that Aphrodite's rage
Wreaked on your body for your pure soul's sake.
I will requite her: with this unfailing bow
My own hand shall strike down in just return
The man her heart holds dearest in the world.
    On you, poor youth, I will bestow a place
Of highest honour in the city of Troezen.
The unmarried virgins shall, before their marriage,
Cut off their hair for you; age after age
Harvest of tears and mourning shall be yours,
Music of maidens' sorrow for your death.
And Phaedra too shall give her name to memory,
And songs shall celebrate her love for you.
    Theseus, remember your own father Aegeus:
Embrace your son and clasp him to your heart.
His death was not your will: men may well sin,
When the gods so ordain.
                                        Hippolytus,
You must not hate your father; you know now
The destiny which has destroyed your life.
Farewell: I may not look upon the dead,
Nor stain my sight with death's last agony;
And now I see that you are near your end.

HIPPOLYTUS.
Farewell, immortal Virgin! Easy it is

For you to sever our long fellowship.
Since you desire it, I forgive my father,
As in days past I have obeyed your word.
Ah!
Darkness is closing now over my eyes.
Father, take hold of me; lift me upright.

THESEUS.   What is it, dear son? Will you break my heart?

HIPPOLYTUS.   I stand before Death's gates; I see them open.

THESEUS.   And will you leave me guilty and defiled?

HIPPOLYTUS.   No, no! I here absolve you of my death!

THESEUS.   What? You will free me from the stain of blood?

HIPPOLYTUS.   I swear it by the conquering bow of Artemis.

THESEUS.   Dear son, how noble a heart you show your father!

HIPPOLYTUS.   Pray that your true-born sons may be like me!

THESEUS.   O generous soul, dying in innocence!

HIPPOLYTUS.   Farewell, my father! Farewell, and farewell!

THESEUS.   Do not forsake me now! Courage, my son!

HIPPOLYTUS.

My time for courage is past. I am gone, Father.
Cover my face now quickly with my cloak.
(*He dies.*)

THESEUS.

Land of Athens, frontiers of a famous city!
    When was man more noble?
    When was loss more bitter?
Aphrodite! with what endless tears and anguish
    Shall your cruel contriving
    Haunt my heart for ever!

CHORUS.

Grief unlooked-for now fills every heart alike;
    Tears from all eyes falling
    Shall make mournful music.
He was noble: loudly then from every tongue
    Praise and lamentation
    Through the world shall echo!

NOTES

(These notes have been kept as few and as brief as possible. In general, I have not included information which can be more satisfactorily found in a small Classical Dictionary.)

p. 59 *The Cyprian:* the Greek name "Aphrodite" is native to Homeric verse and fits awkwardly into iambics; so that "Kupris," "The Cyprian," is almost everywhere used in tragedy. (This name, in fact, frequently drops its personal meaning and becomes an abstract noun for "sexual love.") In the translation I have kept "Aphrodite" throughout for the sake of clarity.

The Amazon: the Queen of the Amazons, Hippolyta, captured in war by Theseus. Shakespeare in *A Midsummer Night's Dream* makes her Theseus' honoured bride; but in the original legend she was a virgin queen subdued by force to the bed of her conqueror. Euripides plainly has this less happy situation in mind as the psychological background of the character of Hippolytus.

P. 61 *To me she is nothing at all:* the Greek phrase is an ironically polite dismissal, "Many good-byes to her!" This blasphemy is unconsciously echoed by Theseus on p. 81, in reference to divination by means of birds. As there seems to be no suitable ironic phrase in English to fit both passages, I have used a plain statement.

P. 66 *O my mother!* Phaedra was the daughter of Pasiphaë, who gave birth to the monster called the Minotaur. For this sense of hereditary guilt compare Theseus' words on p. 77, "Far from here this harvest grew", etc.

P. 67 *The Queen's pitiful cry:* this may refer to Phaedra's words, "It is he, the Amazon's son!" But presumably during the Nurse's speech Phaedra would be audibly weeping.

And life offers us many pleasures: here follow four lines which I have ventured to omit. Their meaning is as follows: ". . . many pleasures: long gossipings and idleness, a pleasant evil; and the sense of shame. Now there are two qualities called 'sense of shame'; the one is not evil [i.e., probably, conscience, which deters men from evil]; the other is a curse to families [i.e., shameful deeds]. If these two different qualities were clearly and aptly named, they would not be represented by the same letters."

There are several passages in other plays where Euripides refers to "gossip" as a thing likely to corrupt women. There are also passages where he makes a character discuss the meaning of some word. Both kinds of passage were noted as characteristic of him, and no doubt often parodied. Here, in the middle of Phaedra's agonized confession, such banal irrelevance seems to me to go beyond anything found elsewhere in Euripides, and I therefore regard these lines as possibly or probably spurious.

P. 70 *Of your saying any word about me:* the question how far Phaedra understands the Nurse, whether she tries to deceive herself or remains innocent in intention, is purposely left ambiguous by Euripides, who thus achieves an effect far more dramatic than that of a clear decision either way.

Love, the child of Zeus: Eros.

P. 71 *You are beside the door:* the door is, of course, at the back of the stage; the Chorus are in the *Orchestra,* below and in front of the stage.

P. 76 *A solemn mission of piety:* Theseus has been enquiring formally from an oracle (probably that of Delphi) whether his expiation is now complete (see p. 60, "His hands stained with blood of the Pallantides"), and has, ironically enough, returned assured of the favour of Heaven.

That is all I know, Theseus: it was a dramatic convention that the Chorus must keep secrets entrusted to them. For them to tell at this point all that they know would be to prevent the tragedy. They are provided with an excuse for their silence by Phaedra's solemn charge to them before her last exit. Their failure to save Hippolytus by telling Theseus the truth has often been quoted as an instance of Euripides' failure to reconcile his matter with his medium. But in actual production no difficulty is felt here, because it is plain to the audience that the Chorus are partly outside the action of the plot. Besides, if Hippolytus will not break his oath, why should the Troezenian women?

P. 79 *Take Orpheus for your lord and prophet:* there seems to be no evidence for any connexion between Hippolytus and Orphism; neither does Hippolytus' remark on p. 61 ("A loaded table's a cheerful sight after hunting"), nor indeed his occupation as a hunter, suggest that he was a vegetarian. Rather Euripides presents Theseus as a middle-aged man who is ready enough to regard fancy cults as responsible for lack of principle in the younger generation—by no means an out-of-date characteristic of middle-aged man.

P. 81 *To me they are nothing at all:* see p. 61, note.

P. 82 *My unhappy mother:* the fact that it is this remark which rouses Theseus to a climax of fury gives another strong hint of the tangled emotional relationship implied by Euripides as existing between Theseus and his son. Euripides is following his usual practice of making heroic characters think and feel like fifth-century Athenians. It is noticeable that Theseus realizes he has lost control, quickly recovers himself, and goes out on a rather lame threat.

P. 84 *You have proved a true father to me:* this is the second time (see p. 78) that Theseus has claimed Poseidon for his father; but Artemis twice (pp. 86 and 89) reminds him firmly that his father was the mortal Aegeus, though in her [first] speech she refers to the giver of the three curses as "your father."

P. 87 *I never would have submitted to such dishonour:* the impregnable callousness of this and other remarks of Artemis (especially, "My own hand shall strike down," etc., p. 89) convey Euripides' emphatic valuation of the comforts of religion. Man in extremity must look to himself alone.

P. 90 *When was man more noble?* It is generally supposed that these words carried a reference to Pericles, who died the year before this play was produced.

ALIENATION IN ANCIENT ATHENS

J. SHERWOOD WEBER

Arch-rebel of the fifth-century B.C. Greek literary giants, Euripides, more than any other writer of Greek or Roman antiquity, strikes the notes characteristic of the intellectual mood of our own day: dissatisfaction with both the microscopic and macroscopic state of the world, impatience and even disgust with the Establishments (political, social, and religious) that enshrine the status quo, and compassion for men, women, and children whose politico-social circumstances compel them to suffer in an inhumane world. His some ninety plays mirror his own troubled times— times which parallel ours in ways that would have reinforced Thucydides's conviction that historical situations recur—and resemble the responses of the disaffected today. Like the host of the alienated of the 1960s, Euripides was skeptical of the traditional and venerated, despaired over the general human condition, escaped from the civic involvement expected of citizens, and criticized extensively *what is* without offering any clear conception of or program for *what should be.*

It should be obvious that Euripides was never very popular in his day

Sherwood Weber, a native of Pennsylvania, completed graduate studies at the University of Wisconsin. He is the editor of *Good Reading* and chairman of the Department of English and Humanities at Pratt Institute.

with political leaders and solid citizens: his ninety-odd plays captured only five first prizes (one of which, *Bacchae,* was posthumous). Evidence indicates, however, that he pleased his audiences—particularly the young intellectuals spawned by the Sophists and the increasingly growing numbers disenchanted by escalation and failure in the Peloponnesian War; and he unquestionably became the darling of the disaffected during the fourth century and into Roman times. Probably because he was far more frequently revived than Aeschylus or Sophocles, whose conservatism fell on increasingly unbelieving ears, more of Euripides's plays survive than those of all his peers combined.

Like the alienated of our day, Euripides opposed nearly everything held sacred by the vocal. Paradoxically, however, he was extremely patriotic about Athens as an abstraction while attacking many specific Athenian practices and conditions. Every tradition inherited and hence irrationally accepted, every religious superstition, every social convention favoring the nobility or the male sex fell victim to his dramatic and lyric verse. And like many rebels today, he projected no viable substitutes for the institutions he attacked: economic exploitation of "underdeveloped" city-states and war captives (slavery), the irrationality and inhumanity of religious beliefs and practices, the shackled status of women, the practice of war as a means of achieving peace.

Unlike many of today's critics of the Establishment, Euripides was not a youth rebelling against a world he never helped make. Born about 480 B.C., he was forty-five years younger than Aeschylus (but for a short period was his contemporary in the theater) and only fifteen years Sophocles's junior. Growing up during the economically thriving, artistically creative, and generally ebullient Periclean Golden Age, he might have been expected to share the conservatism and optimism of his fellow dramatists. But somehow he was more influenced by the liberal climate of his day: by the intellectual and social radicals among the Sophists and by the rising middle class. Of retiring and questioning temperament, he did not revere the status quo because it was "in" but held that everything warranted examination on its merits and required adjustment if found unsupportable in the cold light of reason. Like Ibsen in late nineteenth-century Europe and Existentialists such as Sartre in the post-World War II West, Euripides defied convention, championed the dispossessed, subjected the unchanged and unchanging to ceaseless scrutiny. His plays thus etch their times more sharply and clearly than do those of his peers. At various times and in a variety of ways, they delineate the spirit of free inquiry fostered by Socrates, the determined skepticism of the Sophists, the collapse of the Athenian economic empire after 435, the increasing attacks from many fronts on religious superstition, criticism of the Athenian brand of democracy both from within and from without, and the sapping of money and men by the repeated reverses during the protracted Peloponnesian War (431 to 404 B.C.). His sympathy for human beings suffering in an unreasonable and unreasoning world attracted Euripides to myths that could be molded to emphasize the inhumanity of the gods (e.g., *Helen*), the malevolence or at least indifference of the universe (e.g., *Hippolytus*), the plight of women in a male-oriented society (e.g., *Medea, Alcestis, The Suppliants, The Trojan Women*), and the brutalization of all mankind through war (e.g., *The Suppliants, The Trojan Women,* and numerous other plays dealing with the Trojan War and its aftermath).

The age-old story of the young man traduced repeatedly afforded Euripides a framework for his ideas, perhaps because it can so readily be adapted to underscore the amorality of the forces shaping the human condition. The pattern of this story is simple: An admirable young man is tempted by the wife of a man to whom he owes loyalty, refuses temptation, is accused of advances by the wife, and is punished. Versions of this story, with variant outcomes (in the end the hero usually emerges triumphant), appear in *Genesis* (Joseph and Potiphar's wife), in Homer (Bellerophon and Proetus's wife), and in Hesiod and Pindar. Euripides appears to have used the plot in several of its mytho-legendary versions in at least five plays: two versions of the Phaedra-Hippolytus story, one of which is lost; and in three lost tragedies titled *Stheneboea, Peleus,* and *Tennes*. It apparently afforded Euripides an opportunity to exploit several of his favorite themes, as even a cursory glance at *Hippolytus* reveals.

One of Euripides's recurrent ideas projects the gods as selfish, inhumane, amoral, and productive of anything except law and order. As Aphrodite's opening soliloquy clearly indicates, Phaedra is to be sacrificed for Aphrodite's revenge against Hippolytus, who has spurned her profane love for the spiritual, virginal love of Artemis. Since the gods are to Euripides somehow both human *and* symbolic of superhuman forces operative in the indifferent universe, Phaedra therefore becomes a victim both of Aphrodite's vendetta and of cosmic forces beyond human coping. Though Aphrodite does not sport with human beings, she does manipulate them for personal ends.

Euripides uses this situation to show how decent but innately faulted humans suffer from forces and circumstances neither of their own making nor completely within their control. More than once a character in *Hippolytus* projects this conception of the role of man: e.g., consider the nurse:

> Man's life from birth to death is sorrow and pain
> With never pause or relief;

And when we are dead, is there a happier world?
Knowledge is hidden from us in clouds and darkness.
Since we can know no other kind of life,
Since the world of the dead is a mystery,
It seems we must blindly love, for what it is worth,
Our little gleam of light,
And follow our foolish course content with tales.

Another Euripides theme—the plight of women in a man-made world
—is reflected both in the plot and in some of the not-always-relevant
comments on antifeminism both by characters in the play and in choral
lyrics.

Still another Euripides theme—the irrationality of man and the un-
fortunate consequences thereof—emerges from the tragedy in a number
of ways: in Phaedra's inability to control her passion even though she
knows all the reasons why she should; in Hippolytus's excessive priggish-
ness, which makes compassion impossible for him until too late; in
Theseus' impulsive condemnation and curse of Hippolytus without in-
vestigating the merits of Phaedra's epistolary charge; even in the selfish
interventions of both Aphrodite and Artemis.

All these themes emerge from Euripides's broader world view deriving
from his alienation from his society and its values, from the universe
and its laws. As Richmond Lattimore concludes in a provocative analysis
of *Hippolytus* (in *Arion,* Volume I, Number 3, pages 5–18) : "The mood
of hate for the world despite or because of love for its individual people
is very strong in this play, expressed in the constant wish for impossibili-
ties, the sense of outrage, the longing for escape." Many scattered lines
from the play voice this mood; for example:

PHAEDRA.
. . . I have at times lain long awake in the night, thinking how
other lives than mine have been shattered; and I believe that such
misfortune does not arise from inborn folly, since often those who
suffer are wise and good. But this is how we should regard the
matter: we know and see what is right, yet fail to carry it out. . . .
HIPPOLYTUS.
. . . I, that revered the gods with a holy heart,
I that was first in innocence . . .
The hellish heritage of bloodguiltiness . . .
In me it falls! Why? Why? I have done no wrong! . . .
THESEUS.
As a bird from my hand you have vanished,
Swooped swift and daring into the pit of darkness
And left me tears for your death and anguish for your despair!

Unlike any other Greek we remember through his words or for his actions, Euripides in real life escaped civic responsibilities by living a withdrawn, nonpublic existence; as a result, we know little about him directly. Similarly, the characters and chorus in *Hippolytus* long to escape the horrors of civilization to the ends of the ocean, to inaccessible cliffs and sea caves, to remote forests of virgin growth and unfished streams. These yearnings for natural edens were the Euripidean equivalents of various escape routes sought by the dispossessed and disenchanted youth of today.

That the world has some right but much less right than wrong is the incessant pessimistic message in many plays by Euripides, who exposed the tarnish of his times while others memorialized the polished gold.

SHAKESPEARE

WILLIAM SHAKESPEARE IS ENGLAND'S GREATEST DRAMATIC POET AND AMONG THE THREE OR FOUR MOST ADMIRED WRITERS OF WESTERN CIVILIZATION. BORN IN STRATFORD-ON-AVON, WARWICKSHIRE, IN 1564, SHAKESPEARE WAS EDUCATED, MARRIED, AND BURIED THERE. HE WROTE HIS PLAYS FOR LONDON'S GLOBE THEATER, WHERE HE WAS BOTH AN ACTOR AND A SHAREHOLDER. BEFORE HIS RETIREMENT TO STRATFORD IN HIS MIDDLE FORTIES, SHAKE- SPEARE COMPLETED THIRTY-ODD PLAYS, VIRTUALLY ALL OF WHICH HAVE REMAINED IN THE ACTIVE THEATER REPERTORY. AFTER HIS DEATH IN 1616, TWO FRIENDS COLLECTED HIS PLAYS AND PUBLISHED THEM IN 1623.

In *Antony and Cleopatra* Shakespeare pits personifications of corruption and luxury against the symbol of incorruptibility and civic virtue. To the discomfort of many high-minded readers, corrupt Antony and luxurious Cleopatra obtain a spiritual victory over the exemplary Octavius—the future Caesar Augustus.

That "victory" presented for earlier critics one of the central difficulties of the play. As its events unfold, the unrepentant death, transfiguration, and spiritual triumph of Antony and Cleopatra seemed to them to represent Shakespeare's sacrificing a suitable moral position to that of historical or dramatic necessity. The contemporary reader, however, does not require that the playwright perform the function of a moralizer; rather we seek for accurate portrayal of the human condition. Indeed, there is perhaps no work of imaginative literature—not *Anna Karenina,* nor *The Aeneid,* nor *Tristan and Isolde*—which so boldly illuminates a grand passion or so mercilessly lays bare the souls of its principals.

Yet, as we read the play, it is clear virtually from the first lines that Shakespeare is concerned with more than anatomizing the passions of two historical personages. Rather he is attempting something no dramatist before had dared attempt: to stage the destruction of an old, effete civilization by a new, powerful one. In *Antony and Cleopatra* we are confronted by the spectacle of two worlds in collision.

But such was the nature of Shakespeare's genius that he could simultaneously suggest that as Egypt succumbed, something precious to the soul of man was being destroyed and that triumphant Rome would, like Egypt, fall in turn a victim. *Antony and Cleopatra* deals with love, and Cleopatra is its symbol; it deals with empire, and Rome is its example. Antony is the unifying element. Does his failure consist in his loving Cleopatra more than Rome or in his failure to unite the elements of East and West? How does Shakespeare achieve a fusion of the passionate world of poetry, imagination, and intuition with the temperate world of responsibility, duty, and order?

Antony and Cleopatra remain, of course, archetypes of the noble man and woman whose passion for one another impels them to shipwreck their lives. The fact that the play encompasses so grandly tragic a theme —and something a great deal more—may account for T. S. Eliot's having called *Antony and Cleopatra* Shakespeare's "most assured artistic success."

ANTONY AND CLEOPATRA

EDITED BY
OSCAR JAMES CAMPBELL,
ALFRED ROTHSCHILD, AND
STUART VAUGHAN

CHARACTERS

MARK ANTONY ⎫
OCTAVIUS CAESAR ⎱ *trium-*
M. AEMILIUS ⎰ *virs.*
 LEPIDUS ⎭
SEXTUS POMPEIUS.
DOMITIUS ⎫
 ENOBARBUS ⎮
VENTIDIUS ⎮
EROS ⎬ *friends*
SCARUS ⎮ *of*
DERCETAS ⎮ *Antony.*
DEMETRIUS ⎮
PHILO ⎭
MECAENAS ⎫
AGRIPPA ⎮
DOLABELLA ⎬ *friends*
PROCULEIUS ⎮ *of*
THYREUS ⎮ *Caesar.*
GALLUS ⎭
MENAS ⎫ *friends*
MENECRATES ⎬ *of*
VARRIUS ⎭ *Pompey.*

TAURUS, *lieutenant-general*
 to Caesar.
CANIDIUS, *lieutenant-general*
 to Antony.
SILIUS, *an officer in*
 Ventidius's army.
EUPHRONIUS, *an ambassador*
 from Antony to Caesar.
ALEXAS ⎫
MARDIAN, ⎮ *attendants*
 a Eunuch ⎬ *on*
SELEUCUS ⎮ *Cleopatra.*
DIOMEDES ⎭
A SOOTHSAYER.
A CLOWN.
CLEOPATRA, *Queen of Egypt.*
OCTAVIA, *sister of Caesar*
 and wife of Antony.
CHARMIAN ⎫ *attendants on*
IRAS ⎭ *Cleopatra.*
OFFICERS, SOLDIERS,
 MESSENGERS, *and other*
 ATTENDANTS.

SCENE: *Several parts of the Roman Empire.*

Triumvirs: The three men forming a coalition of supreme political authority. The first triumvirate was formed by Pompey, Julius Caesar, and Crassus in 60 B.C.; the second by Mark Antony, Octavius (later the Emperor Augustus), and Lepidus in 43 B.C.

ACT I

SCENE 1. Egypt. *A hall in Cleopatra's palace at Alexandria.*

(DEMETRIUS *and* PHILO *enter.*)

PHILO.

 Nay, but this dotage of our general's

 O'erflows the measure. Those his goodly eyes.

 That o'er the files and musters * of the war   troops

 Have glowed like plated * Mars, now bend, now turn,   armor-clad

 The office and devotion of their view

 Upon a tawny * front. His captain's heart,   tanned

 Which in the scuffles of great fights hath burst

 The buckles on his breast, reneges all temper,*   self-restraint

 And is become the bellows and the fan

 To cool a gypsy's * lust.[1]   Egyptian's

(*Trumpets sound.* ANTONY *and* CLEOPATRA *enter, followed by her* LADIES *and* ATTENDANTS, *and accompanied by* SERVANTS *with fans.* PHILO *draws* DEMETRIUS *aside as procession approaches.*)

         Look, where they come: 10

 Take but good note, and you shall see in him

 The triple pillar of the world transformed

 Into a strumpet's fool![2] Behold and see.

CLEOPATRA (*to* ANTONY).

 If it be love indeed, tell me how much.

ANTONY (*to* CLEOPATRA).

 There's beggary in the love that can be reckoned.

CLEOPATRA.

 I'll set a bourn * how far to be belovèd.   boundary

ANTONY.

 Then must thou needs find out new heaven, new earth.

(*An* ATTENDANT *enters.*)

ATTENDANT.

 News, my good lord, from Rome.

ANTONY.   Grates * me: the sum.[3]   grates upon

CLEOPATRA.

 Nay, hear them, Antony.

 Fulvia perchance is angry;[4] or, who knows   20

 If the scarce-bearded Caesar[5] have not sent

 His powerful mandate to you: "Do this, or this;

 Take in that kingdom, and enfranchise that;

 Perform 't, or else we damn thee."

ANTONY.   How, my love!

CLEOPATRA.

 Perchance! Nay, and most like.

 You must not stay here longer, your dismission

 Is come from Caesar; therefore hear it, Antony.

[1] See Notes, p. 213.

Where's Fulvia's process? * Caesar's I would say? Both?   summons
Call in the messengers. As I am Egypt's queen,
Thou blushest, Antony; and that blood of thine   30
Is Caesar's homager: * else so thy cheek pays shame   vassal
When shrill-tongued Fulvia scolds. The messengers!
ANTONY.
  Let Rome in Tiber melt, and the wide arch
  Of the ranged * empire fall. Here is my space.*   well-ordered/
  Kingdoms are clay: our dungy earth alike   realm
  Feeds beast as man. The nobleness of life
  Is to do thus;
  (*Embracing her.*) when such a mutual pair
  And such a twain can do 't, in which I bind,
  On pain of punishment, the world to weet *   know
  We stand up peerless.
CLEOPATRA.   Excellent falsehood!   40
  Why did he marry Fulvia, and not love her?
  I'll seem the fool I am not; Antony
  Will be himself. *   *i.e.*, a deceiver
ANTONY.   But stirred by Cleopatra.
  Now, for the love of Love and her soft hours,
  Let's not confound * the time with conference harsh.   consume
  There's not a minute of our lives should stretch
  Without some pleasure now. What sport tonight?
CLEOPATRA.
  Hear the ambassadors
ANTONY.   Fie, wrangling queen!
  Whom everything becomes, to chide, to laugh,
  To weep; whose every passion fully strives   50
  To make itself, in thee, fair and admired!
  No messenger, but thine; and all alone
  Tonight we'll wander through the streets and note
  The qualities of people. Come, my queen;
  Last night you did desire it.
  (*To the* ATTENDANT.)   Speak not to us.
(ANTONY *leads* CLEOPATRA *out, followed by* LADIES, ATTENDANTS,
and SERVANT *with fans.*)
DEMETRIUS.
  Is Caesar with Antonius prized so slight?
PHILO.
  Sir, sometimes, when he is not Antony,
  He comes too short of that great property *   quality
  Which still should go with Antony.
DEMETRIUS.   I am full sorry

That he approves * the common liar, who   60 proves correct
Thus speaks of him at Rome; but I will hope
Of better deeds tomorrow. Rest you happy!
(*They go their separate ways.*)

SCENE 2. Cleopatra's palace. *An anteroom between a hallway and a banquet room.*

(*A* SOOTHSAYER *waits.* CHARMIAN *and* IRAS *enter with* ALEXAS.)
CHARMIAN.
   Lord Alexas, sweet Alexas, most anything Alexas, almost
   most absolute * Alexas, where's the soothsayer that you   perfect
   praised so to the queen? Oh, that I knew this husband,
   which, you say, must charge * his horns with garlands! [6]   load
ALEXAS.
   Soothsayer!
SOOTHSAYER (*approaching*).
   Your will?
CHARMIAN (*to* ALEXAS).
   Is this the man?
         (*To* SOOTHSAYER.)
                   Is 't you, sir, that know things?
SOOTHSAYER.
   In nature's infinite book of secrecy
   A little I can read.
ALEXAS (*to* CHARMIAN).   Show him your hand.   10
(ENOBARBUS *enters from the banquet room.*)
ENOBARBUS.
   Bring in the banquet * quickly; wine enough   sweetmeats
   Cleopatra's health to drink.
CHARMIAN (*holding out her hand to the* SOOTHSAYER).
   Good sir, give me good fortune.
SOOTHSAYER.
   I make not, but foresee.
CHARMIAN.
   Pray, then, foresee me one.
SOOTHSAYER (*reading her palm*).
   You shall be yet far fairer than you are.
CHARMIAN.
   He means in flesh.
IRAS.
   No, you shall paint when you are old.

CHARMIAN.

　Wrinkles forbid!

ALEXAS.

　Vex not his prescience; be attentive.　　　　　　　　20

CHARMIAN.

　Hush!

SOOTHSAYER.

　You shall be more beloving than belovèd.

CHARMIAN.

　I had rather heat my liver with drinking.[7]

ALEXAS.

　Nay, hear him.

CHARMIAN.

　Good now, some excellent fortune! Let me be married to
　three kings in a forenoon, and widow them all. Let me have
　a child at fifty, to whom Herod of Jewry may do homage:[8]
　find me to marry me with Octavius Caesar, and companion
　me with my mistress.　　　　　　　　30

SOOTHSAYER.

　You shall outlive the lady whom you serve.

CHARMIAN.

　Oh excellent! I love long life better than figs.

SOOTHSAYER.

　You have seen and proved * a fairer former fortune　　　experienced
　Than that which is to approach.

CHARMIAN.

　Then belike my children shall have no names.
　Prithee, how many boys and wenches must I have?

SOOTHSAYER.

　If every of your wishes had a womb,
　And fertile every wish, a million.　　　　　　　　39

CHARMIAN.

　Out, fool! I forgive thee for * a witch.[9]　　　exonerate thee
　　　　　　　　　　　　　　　　　　　　　　　　of being

ALEXAS.

　You think none but your sheets are privy to * your wishes.　secretly know

CHARMIAN (*to* SOOTHSAYER).

　Nay, come, tell Iras hers.

ALEXAS.

　We'll know all our fortunes.

ENOBARBUS.

　Mine, and most of our fortunes, tonight, shall be—drunk to
　bed.

IRAS (*showing her hand to the* SOOTHSAYER).

There's a palm presages chastity, if nothing else.

CHARMIAN.

E'en as the o'erflowing Nilus presageth famine.   50

IRAS (*to* CHARMIAN).

Go, you wild bedfellow, you cannot soothsay.

CHARMIAN.

Nay, if an oily palm be not a fruitful prognostication, [10] I cannot scratch mine ear. (*To* SOOTHSAYER.) Prithee, tell her but a workyday * fortune.   workaday

SOOTHSAYER.

Your fortunes are alike.

IRAS.

But how, but how? Give me particulars.

SOOTHSAYER.

I have said.

IRAS.

Am I not an inch of fortune better than she?   60

CHARMIAN.

Well, if you were but an inch of fortune better than I, where would you choose it?

IRAS.

Not in my husband's nose.

CHARMIAN.

Our worser thoughts heavens mend! Alexas—come, his fortune, his fortune! Oh, let him marry a woman that cannot go,[11] sweet Isis, I beseech thee! [12] And let her die too, and give him a worse! And let worse follow worse, till the worst of all follow him laughing to his grave, fifty-fold a cuckold!   70 Good Isis, hear me this prayer, though thou deny me a matter of more weight. Good Isis, I beseech thee!

IRAS.

Amen. Dear goddess, hear that prayer of the people—for, as it is a heartbreaking to see a handsome man loose-wived, so it is a deadly sorrow to behold a foul * knave uncuckolded.   ugly Therefore, dear Isis, keep decorum, and fortune him accordingly!

CHARMIAN.

Amen.

ALEXAS (*to* ENOBARBUS).

Lo, now, if it lay in their hands to make me a cuckold, they   80 would make themselves whores, but they'd do 't!

(ALEXAS *dismisses the* SOOTHSAYER, *who goes.*)

ENOBARBUS *(looking toward the banquet room)* .
   Hush! Here comes Antony.
CHARMIAN.   Not he: the queen.
(CLEOPATRA *enters from the banquet room.*)
CLEOPATRA.
   Saw you my lord?
ENOBARBUS.   No, lady.
CLEOPATRA.   Was he not here?
CHARMIAN.
   No, madam.
CLEOPATRA.
   He was disposed to mirth; but on the sudden
   A Roman thought hath struck him. Enobarbus!
ENOBARBUS.
   Madam?
CLEOPATRA.
   Seek him, and bring him hither. Where's Alexas?
ALEXAS *(returning from the hall door, from which the* SOOTH-
   SAYER *left)* .
   Here, at your service. My lord approaches.   90
CLEOPATRA.
   We will not look upon him. Go with us.
(CLEOPATRA *goes out to the banquet room, followed by* ALEXAS,
CHARMIAN, IRAS, *and* ENOBARBUS, *as* ANTONY *enters from the
hallway with a* MESSENGER *and* ATTENDANTS.)
MESSENGER.
   Fulvia thy wife first came into the field.
ANTONY.
   Against my brother Lucius?
MESSENGER.
   Ay:
   But soon that war had end, and the time's state *   situation
   Made friends of them, jointing their force 'gainst Caesar,
   Whose better issue * in the war, from Italy,   result
   Upon the first encounter, drave them.*   drew them
ANTONY.   Well, what worst?   together
MESSENGER.
   The nature of bad news infects the teller.
ANTONY.
   When it concerns the fool or coward. On: 100
   Things that are past are done with me. 'Tis thus:
   Who tells me true, though in his tale lie death,

I hear him as * he flattered.   *as if*

MESSENGER.   Labienus [13]—

   This is stiff news—hath, with his Parthian force,

   Extended * Asia from Euphrates,   *seized*

   His conquering banner shook from Syria

   To Lydia and to Ionia;

   Whilst—

MESSENGER.

   Antony, thou wouldst say—

MESSENGER.   Oh, my lord!

ANTONY.   *bluntly/*

   Speak to me home,* mince not the general tongue: *   *opinion*

   Name Cleopatra as she is called in Rome;   110

   Rail thou in Fulvia's phrase; and taunt my faults

   With such full license as both truth and malice

   Have power to utter. Oh, then we bring forth weeds,

   When our quick * minds lie still; and our ills told us   *fertile*

   Is as our earing. * [14] Fare thee well awhile.   *ploughing*

MESSENGER.

   At your noble pleasure.

(*The* MESSENGER *goes.*)

ANTONY (*to* ATTENDANTS *at the door*) .

   From Sicyon,[15] ho, the news! Speak there!

FIRST ATTENDANT.

   The man from Sicyon—is there such an one?

SECOND ATTENDANT.

   He stays upon your will.

ANTONY.   Let him appear.

   These strong Egyptian fetters I must break,   120

   Or lose myself in dotage.

(*A second* MESSENGER *enters.*)

                     What are you?

SECOND MESSENGER.

   Fulvia thy wife is dead.

ANTONY.   Where died she?

SECOND MESSENGER.

   In Sicyon.

   Her length of sickness, with what else more serious

   Importeth * thee to know, this bears.   *concerns*

(*Gives* ANTONY *a letter.*)

ANTONY.   Forbear * me.   *leave*

(*The* SECOND MESSENGER *leaves.*)

   There's a great spirit gone! Thus did I desire it.

What our contempt doth often hurl from us,
We wish it ours again; the present pleasure,
By revolution * lowering, does become
The opposite of itself: she's good, being gone;
The hand could pluck her back that shoved her on.
I must from this enchanting queen break off:
Ten thousand harms, more than the ills I know,
My idleness doth hatch.
(Calling toward the banquet room.)

       How now! Enobarbus!

(ENOBARBUS enters.)

ENOBARBUS.

What's your pleasure, sir?

ANTONY.

I must with haste from hence.

ENOBARBUS.

Why, then, we kill all our women: we see how mortal an
unkindness is to them; if they suffer our departure, death's
the word.

ANTONY.

I must be gone.

ENOBARBUS.

Under a compelling occasion, let women die: it were pity
to cast them away for nothing; though, between them and
a great cause, they should be esteemed nothing. Cleopatra,
catching but the least noise * of this, dies instantly: I have
seen her die twenty times upon far poorer moment. I do
think there is mettle * in death, which commits some loving
act upon her, she hath such a celerity in dying.

ANTONY.

She is cunning past man's thought.

ENOBARBUS.

Alack, sir, no; her passions are made of nothing but the
finest part of pure love. We cannot call her winds and waters sighs and tears; they are greater storms and tempests
than almanacs can report. This cannot be cunning in her;
if it be, she makes a shower of rain as well as Jove.[16]

ANTONY.

Would I had never seen her!

ENOBARBUS.

Oh, sir, you had then left unseen a wonderful piece of work,
which not to have been blest withal would have discred-
ited * your travel.

i.e., of Fortune's
130 **wheel**

140

rumor

vigor

150

159
disgraced

ANTONY.

Fulvia is dead.

ENOBARBUS.

Sir?

ANTONY.

Fulvia is dead.

ENOBARBUS.

Fulvia!

ANTONY.

Dead.

ENOBARBUS.

Why, sir, give the gods a thankful sacrifice. When it pleaseth.
their deities to take the wife of a man from him, it shows to
man the tailors of the earth; comforting therein, that when   170
old robes are worn out, there are members * to make new.   people
If there were no more women but Fulvia, then had you in-
deed a cut,* and the case to be lamented. This grief is   blow
crowned with consolation: your old smock brings forth a
new petticoat: and indeed the tears live in an onion that
should water this sorrow.

ANTONY.

The business she hath broached in the state
Cannot endure my absence.

ENOBARBUS.

And the business you have broached here cannot be without   180
you; especially that of Cleopatra's, which wholly depends on
your abode.

ANTONY.

No more light answers. Let our officers
Have notice what we purpose. I shall break
The cause of our expedience * to the queen,   haste
And get her leave to part. For not alone
The death of Fulvia, with more urgent touches,*   concerns
Do strongly speak to us; but the letters too
Of many our contriving * friends in Rome   planning
Petition us at * home: Sextus Pompeius   190 urge us
Hath given the dare to Caesar,[17] and commands
The empire of the sea. Our slippery people,
Whose love is never linked to the deserver
Till his deserts are past, begin to throw
Pompey the Great and all his dignities *   honors
Upon his son, who, high in name and power,
Higher than both in blood and life, stands up

For the main * soldier, whose quality, going on,   foremost

The sides o' the world may danger.* Much is breeding,   endanger

Which, like the courser's * hair, hath yet but life,   horse's

And not a serpent's poison.[18] Say, our pleasure,   200

To such whose place is under us, requires

Our quick remove from hence.

ENOBARBUS.

    I shall do 't.

(*They go.*)

SCENE 3. *The banquet room of Cleopatra's palace.*

(CLEOPATRA *enters, followed by* CHARMIAN, IRAS, ALEXAS, *and*
ATTENDANTS.)

CLEOPATRA.

    Where is he?

CHARMIAN.   I did not see him since.

CLEOPATRA (*to* ALEXAS) .

    See where he is, who's with him, what he does.

    I did not send you. If you find him sad,

    Say I am dancing; if in mirth, report

    That I am sudden sick. Quick, and return.

(ALEXAS *goes.*)

CHARMIAN.

    Madam, methinks, if you did love him dearly,

    You do not hold the method to enforce

    The like from him.

CLEOPATRA.   What should I do, I do not?

CHARMIAN.

    In each thing give him way, cross him in nothing.

CLEOPATRA.

    Thou teachest like a fool, the way to lose him.   10

CHARMIAN.

    Tempt him not so too far; I wish, forbear:

    In time we hate that which we often fear.

    (ANTONY *enters, holding a letter.*)

    But here comes Antony.

CLEOPATRA (*aside to* CHARMIAN *as* ANTONY *approaches*) .

                I am sick and sullen.*   gloomy

ANTONY.

    I am sorry to give breathing * to my purpose—   utterance

CLEOPATRA.
    Help me away, dear Charmian; I shall fall.
    It cannot be thus long, the sides of nature *   natural strength
    Will not sustain it.
ANTONY.   Now, my dearest queen—
CLEOPATRA.
    Pray you, stand farther from me.
ANTONY.   What's the matter?
CLEOPATRA.
    I know, by that same eye, there's some good news.
    What says the married woman? You may go—   20
    Would she had never given you leave to come!
    Let her not say 'tis I that keep you here.
    I have no power upon you: hers you are.
ANTONY.
    The gods best know—
CLEOPATRA.   Oh, never was there queen
    So mightily betrayed! Yet at the first
    I saw the treasons planted.
ANTONY.   Cleopatra—
CLEOPATRA.
    Why should I think you can be mine and true,
    Though you in swearing shake the thronèd gods,
    Who have been false to Fulvia? Riotous madness,
    To be entangled with those mouth-made vows,   30
    Which break themselves in swearing!
ANTONY.   Most sweet queen—
CLEOPATRA.
    Nay, pray you, seek no color * for your going,   pretext
    But bid farewell, and go. When you sued staying,*   to stay
    Then was the time for words; no going then!
    Eternity was in our lips and eyes,
    Bliss in our brows' bent; * none our parts so poor,   arched
    But was a race * of heaven. They are so still,   taste
    Or thou, the greatest soldier of the world,
    Art turned the greatest liar.
ANTONY.   How now, lady!
CLEOPATRA.
    I would I had thy inches; thou shouldst know   40
    There were a heart in Egypt.*   *i.e.,* Egypt's queen
ANTONY.   Hear me, queen:
    The strong necessity of time commands

Our services awhile; but my full heart
Remains in use * with you. Our Italy   on deposit
Shines o'er with civil swords:. Sextus Pompeius
Makes his approaches to the port of Rome.
Equality * of two domestic powers   *i.e.,* of resources
Breed scrupulous faction: * the hated, grown to strength,   captious strife
Are newly grown to love. The condemned Pompey,
Rich in his father's honor, creeps apace   50
Into the hearts of such as have not thrived
Upon the present state,* whose numbers threaten;   administration
And quietness, grown sick of rest, would purge
By any desperate change. My more particular,*   particular reason
And that which most with you should safe * my going,   make safe
Is Fulvia's death.

CLEOPATRA.
Though age from folly could not give me freedom,
It does from childishness: can Fulvia die?

ANTONY.
She's dead, my queen.
(Offering her the letter.)
Look here, and at thy sovereign leisure read   60
The garboils * she awaked; at the last, best: [19]   disturbances
See when and where she died.

CLEOPATRA.   O most false love!
Where be the sacred vials thou shouldst fill
With sorrowful water? [20] Now I see, I see,
In Fulvia's death, how mine received shall be.

ANTONY.
Quarrel no more, but be prepared to know
The purposes I bear; which are,* or cease,   exist
As you shall give the advice. By the fire
That quickens Nilus' slime, I go from hence
Thy soldier, servant; making peace or war   70
As thou affect'st.*   desirest

CLEOPATRA.   Cut my lace; Charmian, come.
*(*CHARMIAN *moves to release her dress, but* CLEOPATRA *stops her.)*
But let it be: I am quickly ill, and well,
So Antony loves.

ANTONY.   My precious queen, forbear;
And give true evidence to his love, which * stands   who
An honorable trial.

CLEOPATRA.   So Fulvia told me.

I prithee, turn aside and weep for her;
Then bid adieu to me, and say the tears
Belong to Egypt. Good now, play one scene
Of excellent dissembling; and let it look
Like perfect honor.

ANTONY.   You'll heat my blood: no more!   80

CLEOPATRA.
You can do better yet; but this is meetly.*   well acted

ANTONY.
Now, by my sword—

CLEOPATRA.   And target.* Still he mends;   shield
But this is not the best. Look, prithee, Charmian,
How this Herculean Roman does become
The carriage * of his chafe! * 21   acting/rage

ANTONY.
I'll leave you, lady.

(*He starts to go, but her voice stops him.*)

CLEOPATRA.   Courteous lord, one word.
Sir, you and I must part, but that's not it.
Sir, you and I have loved, but there's not it;
That you know well: something it is I would—
Oh, my oblivion is a very Antony,   90
And I am all forgotten.*   have forgotten all

ANTONY.   But that your royalty
Holds idleness your subject, I should take you
For idleness * itself.   folly

CLEOPATRA.   'Tis sweating labor
To bear such idleness so near the heart
As Cleopatra this. But, sir, forgive me;
Since my becomings * kill me, when they do not   graces
Eye * well to you. Your honor calls you hence;   look
Therefore be deaf to my unpitied folly,
And all the gods go with you! Upon your sword
Sit laurel victory! 22 And smooth success   100
Be strewed before your feet!

ANTONY.   Let us go. Come,
Our separation so abides, and flies,
That thou, residing here, go'st yet with me,
And I, hence fleeting, here remain with thee.
Away!

(*They go together followed by* CHARMIAN, IRAS, *and* ATTEN-
DANTS.)

SCENE 4.   Rome. *A room in Caesar's house.*

(OCTAVIUS CAESAR *enters, reading a letter. He is accompanied by* LEPIDUS, *and attended by various* OFFICERS, SOLDIERS, *and* SERVANTS.)

CAESAR.
    You may see, Lepidus, and henceforth know,
    It is not Caesar's natural vice to hate
    Our great competitor. From Alexandria
    This is the news: he fishes, drinks, and wastes
    The lamps of night in revel; is not more manlike
    Than Cleopatra; nor the queen of Ptolemy
    More womanly than he; [23] hardly gave audience, or
    Vouchsafed to think he had partners.
    (*Handing* LEPIDUS *the letter.*)
                                    You shall find there
    A man who is the abstract * of all faults   summary
    That all men follow.
LEPIDUS.   I must not think there are   10
    Evils enow * to darken all his goodness: enough
    His faults in him seem as the spots of heaven,
    More fiery by night's blackness; hereditary,
    Rather than purchased; * what he cannot change,   acquired
    Than what he chooses.
CAESAR.
    You are too indulgent. Let us grant, it is not
    Amiss to tumble on the bed of Ptolemy; [24]
    To give a kingdom for a mirth; * to sit   jest
    And keep the turn of tippling with a slave;
    To reel the streets at noon, and stand the buffet *   exchange blows
    With knaves that smell of sweat: say this becomes him—   21
    As his composure must be rare indeed
    Whom these things cannot blemish—yet must Antony
    No way excuse his soils,* when we do bear   stains
    So great weight in his lightness.[25] If he filled
    His vacancy * with his voluptuousness,   spare time
    Full surfeits,* and the dryness of his bones,   indigestion
    Call on him for 't; * but to confound * such time,   him to account/
    That drums him from his sport, and speaks as loud   waste
    As his own state * and ours—'tis to be chid   30   status

As we rate * boys, who, being mature in knowledge,   berate

Pawn their experience to * their present pleasure,   for

And so rebel to judgment.

(*A* MESSENGER *enters.*)

LEPIDUS.   Here's more news.

MESSENGER.

Thy biddings have been done; and every hour,

Most noble Caesar, shalt thou have report

How 'tis abroad. Pompey is strong at sea;

And it appears he is belovèd of those

That only have feared Caesar.[26] To the ports

The discontents repair, and men's reports

Give him * much wronged.   make him out

CAESAR.   I should have known no less.   40

It hath been taught us from the primal * state,   primeval

That he which is was wished until he were;

And the ebbed man, ne'er loved till ne'er worth love,

Comes deared * by being lacked.[27] This common body, *   endeared / these commoners

Like to a vagabond flag upon the stream,

Goes to and back, lackeying the varying tide, [28]

To rot itself with motion.

MESSENGER.   Caesar, I bring thee word,

Menecrates and Menas, famous pirates,

Make the sea serve them, which they ear * and wound   plow

With keels of every kind. Many hot inroads   50

They make in Italy; the borders maritime

Lack blood * to think on 't, and flush * youth revolt.   *i.e.,* turn pale / lusty

No vessel can peep forth, but 'tis as soon

Taken as seen; for Pompey's name strikes more

Than could his war resisted.

CAESAR.   Antony,

Leave thy lascivious wassails.* When thou once   carousing

Wast beaten from Modena, where thou slew'st

Hirtius and Pansa, consuls, at thy heel

Did famine follow; whom thou fought'st against,   59

Though daintily brought up, with patience * more   fortitude

Than savages could suffer. Thou didst drink

The stale * of horses, and the gilded * puddle   urine / *i.e.,* scum-covered

Which beasts would cough at. Thy palate then did deign

The roughest berry on the rudest hedge;

Yea, like the stag, when snow the pasture sheets,

The barks of trees thou browsed'st; on the Alps

It is reported thou didst eat strange flesh,

Which some did die to look on. And all this—
It wounds thine honor that I speak it now—
Was borne so like a soldier that thy cheek
So much as lanked * not.

70

thinned

LEPIDUS.   'Tis pity of him.

CAESAR.
Let his shames quickly
Drive him to Rome. 'Tis time we twain
Did show ourselves i' the field; and to that end
Assemble we immediate council. Pompey
Thrives in our idleness.

LEPIDUS.   Tomorrow, Caesar,
I shall be furnished to inform you rightly
Both what by sea and land I can be able
To front * this present time.

confront at

CAESAR.   Till which encounter,
It is my business too. Farewell.

80

LEPIDUS.
Farewell, my lord. What you shall know meantime
Of stirs abroad, I shall beseech you, sir,
To let me be partaker.

CAESAR.   Doubt not, sir;
I knew it for my bond. *

duty

(*They go their separate ways attended by* OFFICERS, SOLDIERS,
and SERVANTS.)

SCENE 5.   Egypt. *Cleopatra's bedroom in the palace at Alexandria.*

(CLEOPATRA *enters, attended by* CHARMIAN, IRAS, *and* MARDIAN.)

CLEOPATRA.
Charmian!

CHARMIAN.
Madam?

CLEOPATRA.
Ha, ha!
Give me to drink mandragora.[29]

CHARMIAN.   Why madam?

CLEOPATRA.
That I might sleep out this great gap of time
My Antony is away.

CHARMIAN.   You think of him too much.

CLEOPATRA.
  Oh, 'tis treason!
CHARMIAN.   Madam, I trust, not so.
CLEOPATRA.
  Thou, eunuch Mardian!
MARDIAN (*approaching*).
                        What's your highness' pleasure?
CLEOPATRA.
  Not now to hear thee sing; I take no pleasure
  In aught an eunuch has: 'tis well for thee,   10
  That, being unseminared,* thy freer thoughts   emasculated
  May not fly forth of Egypt.* Hast thou affections? *i.e.*, to Cleopatra
MARDIAN.
  Yes, gracious madam.
CLEOPATRA.
  Indeed!
MARDIAN.
  Not in deed, madam; for I can do nothing
  But what indeed is honest to be done—
  Yet have I fierce affections, and think
  What Venus did with Mars.
CLEOPATRA.   O Charmian,
  Where think'st thou he is now? Stands he, or sits he?
  Or does he walk? Or is he on his horse?   20
  O happy horse, to bear the weight of Antony!
  Do bravely, horse! For wot'st * thou whom thou movest—   knowest
  The demi-Atlas of this earth, the arm *   armor
  And burgonet * of men.30 He's speaking now,   helmet
  Or murmuring, "Where's my serpent of old Nile?"
  For so he calls me. Now I feed myself
  With most delicious poison. Think on me,
  That am with Phoebus' amorous pinches black,
  And wrinkled deep in time.31 Broad-fronted * Caesar,   *i.e.*, bald
  When thou wast here above the ground, I was   30
  A morsel for a monarch; and great Pompey 32
  Would stand and make his eyes grow in my brow;
  There would he anchor his aspect * and die   gaze
  With looking on his life.
(ALEXAS *enters*.)
ALEXAS.   Sovereign of Egypt, hail!
CLEOPATRA.
  How much unlike art thou Mark Antony!
  Yet, coming from him, that great medicine hath

With his tinct * gilded thee.[33]its color
How goes it with my brave Mark Antony?

ALEXAS.
Last thing he did, dear queen,
He kissed—the last of many doubled kisses—40
This orient * pearl. His speech sticks in my heart.lustrous

CLEOPATRA (takes the pearl).
Mine ear must pluck it thence.

ALEXAS."Good friend," quoth he,
"Say, the firm Roman to great Egypt sends
This treasure of an oyster; at whose foot,
To mend the petty present, I will piece *add to
Her opulent throne with kingdoms; all the east,
Say thou, shall call her mistress." So he nodded,
And soberly did mount an arm-gaunt * steed,[34]battle-hardened
Who neighed so high, that what I would have spoke
Was beastly dumbed * by him.drowned out

CLEOPATRA.What, was he sad or merry?50

ALEXAS.
Like to the time o' the year between the extremes
Of hot and cold, he was nor sad nor merry.

CLEOPATRA.
Oh well-divided disposition!
(To CHARMIAN.)
Note him,
Note him, good Charmian, 'tis the man; but * note him:just
He was not sad, for he would shine on those
That make their looks by his; he was not merry,
Which seemed to tell them his remembrance lay
In Egypt with his joy; but between both:
Oh heavenly mingle! Be'st thou sad or merry,
The violence of either thee becomes,60
So does it no man else.
(To ALEXAS.)
Met'st thou my posts? *messengers

ALEXAS.
Ay, madam, twenty several messengers.
Why do you send so thick?

CLEOPATRA.Who's born that day
When I forget to send to Antony,
Shall die a beggar. Ink and paper, Charmian.
Welcome, my good Alexas. Did I, Charmian,
Ever love Caesar so?

CHARMIAN. O that brave Caesar!

CLEOPATRA.
Be choked with such another emphasis!
Say, the brave Antony.

CHARMIAN. The valiant Caesar!

CLEOPATRA.
By Isis, I will give thee bloody teeth   70
If thou with Caesar paragon * again   compare
My man of men.

CHARMIAN. By your most gracious pardon,
I sing but after you.

CLEOPATRA. My salad days,
When I was green in judgment: cold in blood,
To say as I said then!
(*Starting to go.*)
But, come, away;
Get me ink and paper.
He shall have every day a several * greeting,   separate
Or I'll unpeople Egypt.
(*She leaves, followed by* CHARMIAN, IRAS, MARDIAN, *and* ALEXAS.)

ACT II

SCENE 1. Messina. *A room in Pompey's house.*

(POMPEY *enters with the pirates* MENECRATES *and* MENAS. *All
three wear armor.*)

POMPEY.
If the great gods be just, they shall assist
The deeds of justest men.

MENECRATES. Know, worthy Pompey,
That what they do delay, they not deny.

POMPEY.
Whiles we are suitors to their throne, decays
The thing we sue for.

MENECRATES. We, ignorant of ourselves,
Beg often our own harms, which the wise powers
Deny us for our good; so find we profit
By losing of our prayers.

POMPEY. I shall do well.
The people love me, and the sea is mine;
My powers are crescent,* and my auguring * hope   waxing/
                                                  prophesying

Says it will come to the full. Mark Antony 11
In Egypt sits at dinner, and will make
No wars without doors. Caesar gets money where
He loses hearts. Lepidus flatters both,
Of both is flattered; but he neither loves,
Nor either cares for him.

MENAS.   Caesar and Lepidus
Are in the field: a mighty strength they carry.

POMPEY.
Where have you this? 'Tis false.

MENAS.   From Silvius, sir.

POMPEY.
He dreams: I know they are in Rome together,
Looking for Antony. But all the charms of love,   20
Salt * Cleopatra, soften thy wanèd lip!   wanton
Let witchcraft join with beauty, lust with both!
Tie up the libertine in a field of feasts,
Keep his brain fuming; Epicurean cooks
Sharpen with cloyless sauce his appetite,³⁵
That sleep and feeding may prorogue his honor
Even till a Lethed * dullness! ³⁶   *i.e.,* oblivious

(VARRIUS *enters.*)
                                 How now, Varrius!

VARRIUS.
This is most certain that I shall deliver: *   report
Mark Antony is every hour in Rome
Expected. Since he went from Egypt 'tis   30
A space * for further travel.   time enough

POMPEY.   I could have given less matter
A better ear. Menas, I did not think
This amorous surfeiter would have donned his helm
For such a petty war. His soldiership
Is twice the other twain; but let us rear
The higher our opinion,* that our stirring   *i.e.,* of ourselves
Can from the lap of Egypt's widow pluck
The ne'er-lust-wearied Antony.

MENAS.   I cannot hope
Caesar and Antony shall well greet together:
His wife that's dead did trespasses to Caesar; *   *i.e.,* Octavius
His brother warred upon him,³⁷ although,   Caesar
        I think,   41
Not moved by Antony.

POMPEY.   I know not, Menas,

How lesser enmities may give way to greater.
Were 't not that we stand up against them all,   probable/square
'Twere pregnant * they should square * between themselves;   off
For they have entertainèd * cause enough   accepted as
To draw their swords: but how the fear of us
May cement their divisions and bind up
The petty difference, we yet not know.
Be 't as our gods will have 't! It only stands   50
Our lives upon to use our strongest hands.[38]
Come, Menas.
(POMPEY *and* MENAS *go, followed by* MENECRATES *and* VARRIUS.)

SCENE 2. Rome. *A room in Lepidus' house, with a table and chairs.*

(LEPIDUS *and* ENOBARBUS *enter and come to the table.*)
LEPIDUS.
Good, Enobarbus, 'tis a worthy deed,
And shall become you well, to entreat your captain
To soft and gentle speech.
ENOBARBUS.   I shall entreat him
To answer like himself. If Caesar move him,
Let Antony look over Caesar's head
And speak as loud as Mars.[39] By Jupiter,
Were I the wearer of Antonius' beard,
I would not shave 't today.
LEPIDUS   'Tis not a time
For private stomaching.*   resentment
ENOBARBUS.   Every time
Serves for the matter that is then born in 't.   10
LEPIDUS.
But small to greater matters must give way.
ENOBARBUS.
Not if the small come first.
LEPIDUS.   Your speech is passion:
But, pray you, stir no embers up.
(ANTONY *and* VENTIDIUS *enter from one door;* CAESAR *and* MECAENAS *from another.*)
                         Here comes
The noble Antony.
ANTONY   (*to* VENTIDIUS, *as they approach*) .
If we compose * well here, to Parthia: agree
Hark, Ventidius.

CAESAR   (*to* MECAENAS, *as they approach*) .
                    I do not know,
    Mecaenas; ask Agrippa.
LEPIDUS   (*to* ANTONY *and* CAESAR, *as they get to the table*) .
                    Noble friends,
    That which combined us was most great, and let not
    A leaner action rend us. What's * amiss,   whatever is
    May it be gently heard: when we debate   20
    Our trivial difference loud, we do commit
    Murder in healing wounds. Then, noble partners,
    The rather, for I earnestly beseech
    Touch you the sourest points with sweetest terms,
    Nor curstness * grow to the matter.⁴⁰   ill humor
ANTONY   (*to* LEPIDUS) .   'Tis spoken well.
    Were we before our armies, and to fight,
    I should do thus.
(*Trumpets sound.*)
CAESAR   (*to* ANTONY) .
    Welcome to Rome.
ANTONY.   Thank you.
CAESAR.   Sit.
ANTONY.   Sit, sir.
CAESAR.   Nay, then.
(*They sit at the same time.*)
ANTONY.
    I learn, you take things ill which are not so,
    Or being, concern you not.
CAESAR.   I must be laughed at,   30
    If, or for nothing or a little, I
    Should say myself offended, and with you
    Chiefly i' the world; more laughed at, that I should
    Once name you derogately,* when to sound your name   derogatorily
    It not concerned me.
ANTONY.   My being in Egypt, Caesar,
    What was 't to you?
CAESAR.
    No more than my residing here at Rome
    Might be to you in Egypt; yet, if you there
    Did practice on * my state, your being in Egypt   plot against
    Might be my question.
ANTONY.   How intend you, practiced?   40
CAESAR.
    You may be pleased to catch at mine intent
    By what did here befall me. Your wife and brother

Made wars upon me; and their contestation
Was theme for you, you were the word * of war.⁴¹   watchword
ANTONY.
   You do mistake your business; my brother never
   Did urge * me in his act. I did inquire it;   name
   And have my learning * from some true reports,   information
   That drew their swords with you. Did he not rather
   Discredit my authority with yours;
   And make the wars alike against my stomach,*   50   wish
   Having * alike your cause? Of this my letters   my having
   Before did satisfy you. If you'll patch * a quarrel,   patch together
   As matter whole you have not to make it with,
   It must not be with this.
  CAESAR.   You praise yourself
   By laying defects of judgment to me; but
   You patched up your excuses.
  ANTONY.   Not so, not so;
   I know you could not lack, I am certain on 't,
   Very necessity of this thought, that I,
   Your partner in the cause 'gainst which he fought,
   Could not with graceful * eyes attend * those wars   favorable/regard
   Which fronted mine own peace. As for my wife,   61
   I would you had her spirit in such another:
   The third o' the world is yours; which with a snaffle *   bridle bit
   You may pace * easy, but not such a wife.   control
ENOBARBUS.
   Would we had all such wives, that the men might go to
   wars with the women!
ANTONY.
   So much uncurbable, her garboils,* Caesar,   brawls
   Made out of her impatience, which not wanted
   Shrewdness of policy too, I grieving grant
   Did you too much disquiet: for that you must   70
   But say, I could not help it.
  CAESAR.   I wrote to you
   When rioting * in Alexandria; you   reveling
   Did pocket up my letters, and with taunts
   Did gibe my missive * out of audience.   messenger
  ANTONY.   Sir,
   He fell upon me ere admitted; then
   Three kings I had newly feasted, and did want
   Of what I was i' the morning. But next day
   I told him of myself; which was as much

As to have asked him pardon. Let this fellow
Be nothing of our strife; if we contend,   80
Out of our question wipe him.
CAESAR.   You have broken
The article * of your oath; which you shall never   essence
Have tongue to charge me with.
LEPIDUS.   Soft,* Caesar!   careful
ANTONY.   No,
Lepidus, let him speak:
The honor is sacred which he talks on now,
Supposing that I lack it. But, on, Caesar:
The article of my oath.
CAESAR.
To lend me arms and aid when I required them;
The which you both denied.
ANTONY.   Neglected, rather;
And then when poisoned hours had bound me up   90
From mine own knowledge. As nearly as I may,
I'll play the penitent to you, but mine honesty
Shall not make poor my greatness, nor my power
Work without it. Truth is, that Fulvia,
To have me out of Egypt, made wars here;
For which myself, the ignorant motive, do
So far ask pardon as befits mine honor
To stoop in such a case.
LEPIDUS.   'Tis noble spoken.
MECAENAS.
If it might please you, to enforce no further   99
The griefs * between ye; to forget them quite   grievances
Were to remember that the present need
Speaks to atone * you.   reconcile
LEPIDUS.   Worthily spoken, Mecaenas.
ENOBARUS   (*aside to* ANTONY).
Or, if you borrow one another's love for the instant, you
may, when you hear no more words of Pompey, return it
again. You shall have time to wrangle in when you have
nothing else to do.
ANTONY   (*aside to* ENOBARBUS).
Thou art a soldier only: speak no more.
ENOBARBUS   (*aside to* ANTONY).
That truth should be silent I had almost forgot.   110
ANTONY   (*aside to* ENOBARBUS).
You wrong this presence; * therefore speak no more.   those present

ENOBARBUS   *(aside to* ANTONY*)* .
  Go to, then: your considerate stone.⁴²
CAESAR   *(aside to* LEPIDUS*)* .
  I do not much dislike the matter, but
  The manner of his speech; for 't cannot be
  We shall remain in friendship, our conditions *   disposition
  So differing in their acts. Yet, if I knew
  What hoop should hold us stanch, from edge to edge
  O' the world I would pursue it.
AGRIPPA.   Give me leave, Caesar—
CAESAR.
  Speak, Agrippa.
AGRIPPA.
  Thou hast a sister by the mother's side,   120
  Admired Octavia: great Mark Antony
  Is now a widower.
CAESAR.   Say not so, Agrippa:
  If Cleopatra heard you, your reproof
  Were well deserved of * rashness.   by
ANTONY.
  I am not married, Caesar: let me hear
  Agrippa further speak.
AGRIPPA.
  To hold you in perpetual amity,
  To make you brothers, and to knit your hearts
  With an unslipping knot, take Antony
  Octavia to his wife; whose beauty claims   130
  No worse a husband than the best of men;
  Whose virtue and whose general graces speak
  That which none else can utter. By this marriage,
  All little jealousies, which now seem great,
  And all great fears, which now import * their dangers,   impart
  Would then be nothing: truths would be tales,
  Where now half tales be truths. Her love to both
  Would, each to other and all loves to both,
  Draw after her. Pardon what I have spoke;
  For 'tis a studied,* not a present thought,   considered
  By duty ruminated.   141
ANTONY.   Will Caesar speak?
CAESAR.
  Not till he hears how Antony is touched
  With what is spoke already.
ANTONY.   What power is in Agrippa,

If I would say, "Agrippa, be it so,"
To make this good?
CAESAR.   The power of Caesar, and
His power unto Octavia.
ANTONY.   May I never
To this good pupose, that so fairly shows,
Dream of impediment! Let me have thy hand.
Further this act of grace; * and from his hour   reconciliation
The heart of brothers govern in our loves   150
And sway our great designs!
CAESAR.   There is my hand.
(*They clasp hands.*)
A sister I bequeath you, whom no brother
Did ever love so dearly: let her live
To join our kingdoms and our hearts; and never
Fly off our loves again!
LEPIDUS.   Happily, amen!
ANTONY.
I did not think to draw my sword 'gainst Pompey,
For he hath laid strange * courtesies and great   extraordinary
Of late upon me. I must thank him only,
Lest my remembrance suffer ill report;
At heel of * that, defy him.   right after
LEPIDUS.   Time calls upon 's.   160
Of us must Pompey presently * be sought;   forthwith
Or else he seeks out us.
ANTONY.   Where lies he?
CAESAR.
About the mount Misenum.⁴³
ANTONY.
What is his strength by land?
CAESAR.
Great and increasing; but by sea
He is an absolute master.
ANTONY.   So is the fame.*   report
Would we had spoke ⁴⁴ together! Haste we for it.
Yet, ere we put ourselves in arms, dispatch we
The business we have talked of.
CAESAR.   With most gladness;
And do invite you to my sister's view,   170
Whither straight I'll lead you.
ANTONY.   Let us, Lepidus,
Not lack your company.

LEPIDUS.   Noble Antony,

Not sickness should detain me.

(*Trumpets sound.* CAESAR, ANTONY, *and* LEPIDUS *leave.*)

MECAENAS   (*to* ENOBARBUS) .

Welcome from Egypt, sir.

ENOBARBUS.

Half the heart of Caesar, worthy Mecaenas!

My honorable friend, Agrippa!

AGRIPPA.

Good Enobarbus!

MECAENAS.

We have cause to be glad that matters are so well digested.

You stayed well by 't * in Egypt.   180   with your revels

ENOBARBUS.

Ay, sir; we did sleep day out of countenance, and made the
night light with drinking.

MECAENAS.

Eight wild boars roasted whole at a breakfast, and but
twelve persons there; is this true?

ENOBARBUS.

This was but as a fly by an eagle: we had much more monstrous matter of feast, which worthily deserved noting.   189

MECAENAS.

She's a most triumphant * lady, if report be square to her.   splendid

ENOBARBUS.

When she first met Mark Antony, she pursed up * his heart,   pocketed
upon the river of Cydnus.

AGRIPPA.

There she appeared indeed; or my reporter devised well for
her.

ENOBARBUS.

I will tell you.

The barge she sat in, like a burnished throne,

Burned on the water. The poop was beaten gold;

Purple the sails, and so perfumèd that

The winds were lovesick with them; the oars were silver,

Which to the tune of flutes kept stroke, and made   200

The water which they beat to follow faster,

As amorous of their strokes. For her own person,

It beggared all description: she did lie

In her pavilion—cloth-of-gold of tissue—

O'erpicturing that Venus where we see

The fancy outwork * nature.[45] On each side her   surpass

Stood pretty dimpled boys, like smiling Cupids,

With divers-colored fans, whose wind did seem
To glow * the delicate cheeks which they did cool,   make glow
And what they undid did.
AGRIPPA.   Oh, rare for Antony!   210
ENOBARBUS.
Her gentlewomen, like the Nereides,[46]
So many mermaids, tended her i' the eyes,*   every glance
And made their bends adornings.[47] At the helm
A seeming mermaid steers: the silken tackle
Swell with the touches of those flower-soft hands,
That yarely * frame * the office. From the barge   skillfully/perform
A strange invisible perfume hits the sense
Of the adjacent wharfs.
                        The city cast
Her people out upon her; and Antony,
Enthronèd i' the marketplace, did sit alone,   220
Whistling to the air; which, but for vacancy,[48]
Had gone to gaze on Cleopatra too
And made a gap in nature.
AGRIPPA.   Rare Egyptian!
ENOBARBUS.
Upon her landing, Antony sent to her,
Invited her to supper. She replied,
It should be better he became her guest;
Which she entreated. Our courteous Antony,
Whom ne'er the word of "No" woman heard speak,
Being barbered ten times o'er, goes to the feast,
And for his ordinary * pays his heart   230   meal
For what his eyes eat only.
AGRIPPA.   Royal wench!
She made great Caesar lay his sword to bed:
He plowed her, and she cropped.
ENOBARBUS.   I saw her once
Hop forty paces through the public street;
And having lost her breath, she spoke, and panted,
That she did make defect perfection,
And, breathless, power breathe forth.
MECAENAS.
Now Antony must leave her utterly.
ENOBARBUS.
Never; he will not.
Age cannot wither her, nor custom stale   240
Her infinite variety. Other women cloy
The appetites they feed; but she makes hungry

Where most she satisfies: for vilest things
Become themselves * in her; that the holy priests   *are becoming*
Bless her when she is riggish.*   *wanton*
MECAENAS.
  If beauty, wisdom, modesty, can settle
  The heart of Antony, Octavia is
  A blessed lottery * to him.   *i.e.,* prize
AGRIPPA.   Let us go.
  Good Enobarbus, make yourself my guest
  Whilst you abide here.
ENOBARBUS.
  Humbly, sir, I thank you.
(*They leave together.*)   250

SCENE 3. Rome. *A room in Caesar's house.*

(ANTONY *and* CAESAR *enter, with* OCTAVIA *walking between
them.* ATTENDANTS *light their way, and the* SOOTHSAYER *follows.*)
ANTONY.
  The world and my great office will sometimes
  Divide me from your bosom.
OCTAVIA.   All which time
  Before the gods my knee shall bow my prayers
  To them for you.
ANTONY.   Good night, sir. My Octavia,
  Read not my blemishes in * the world's report: *according to*
  I have not kept my square; [49] but that to come   *obligations*
  Shall all be done by the rule. Good night, dear lady.
  Good night, sir.
CAESAR.
  Good night.
(CAESAR *and* OCTAVIA *leave, accompanied by* ATTENDANTS. *The*
SOOTHSAYER *comes forward.*)
  Now, sirrah; you do wish yourself in Egypt?   10
SOOTHSAYER.
  Would I had never come from thence, nor you
  Thither!
ANTONY.
  If you can, your reason?
SOOTHSAYER.   I see it in
  My motion,* have it not in my tongue: but yet   *mind's eye*
  Hie you to Egypt again.

ANTONY.   Say to me,
Whose fortunes shall rise higher, Caesar's or mine?
SOOTHSAYER.
Caesar's.
Therefore, O Antony, stay not by his side:
Thy demon, that's thy spirit which keeps * thee, is   protects
Noble, courageous, high, unmatchable,   20
Where Caesar's is not; but, near him, thy angel
Becomes a fear,* as being o'erpowered: therefore   *i.e.*, thing of fear
Make space enough between you.
ANTONY.   Speak this no more.
SOOTHSAYER.
To none but thee; no more, but when to thee.
If thou dost play with him at any game,
Thou art sure to lose; and, of that natural luck,
He beats thee 'gainst the odds. Thy luster thickens,*   dims
When he shines by. I say again, thy spirit
Is all afraid to govern thee near him;
But, he away, 'tis noble.
ANTONY.   Get thee gone!   30
Say to Ventidius I would speak with him.
(*The* SOOTHSAYER *goes.*)
He shall to Parthia.
                    Be it art or hap,*   accident
He hath spoken true: the very dice obey him;
And in our sports my better cunning faints
Under his chance.* If we draw lots, he speeds; *   luck/wins
His cocks do win the battle still of mine,
When it * is all to nought; 50 and his quails ever   *i.e.*, the odds
Beat mine, inhooped, at odds.51
                    I will to Egypt:
And though I make this marriage for my peace,
I' the east my pleasure lies.
(VENTIDIUS *enters.*)
                    Oh, come Ventidius,   40
You must to Parthia: your commission's ready.
Follow me, and receive 't.
(ANTONY *goes out, followed by* VENTIDIUS.)

SCENE 4. Rome. *A street.*

(LEPIDUS *enters with* MECAENAS *and* AGRIPPA.)

LEPIDUS.

    Trouble yourselves no further. Pray you, hasten
    Your generals after.

AGRIPPA.   Sir, Mark Antony

    Will e'en but kiss Octavia, and we'll follow.

LEPIDUS.

    Till I shall see you in your soldier's dress,
    Which will become you both, farewell.

MECAENAS.   We shall,

    As I conceive the journey, be at the Mount*   *i.e.,* Mount
    Before you, Lepidus.   Misenum

LEPIDUS.   Your way is shorter:

    My purposes do draw me much about.
    You'll win two days upon me.

MECAENAS *and* AGRIPPA.   Sir, good success!

LEPIDUS.

    Farewell.   10

(They go their separate ways.)

SCENE 5. Egypt. *A room in Cleopatra's palace at Alexandria.*

*(*CLEOPATRA *enters attended by* CHARMIAN, IRAS, ALEXAS, *and other* SERVANTS.)*

CLEOPATRA.

    Give me some music; music, moody food
    Of us that trade in love.

ATTENDANT.   The music, ho!

*(*MARDIAN, *the eunuch, enters, bringing a musical instrument.)*

CLEOPATRA.

    Let it alone; let's to billiards. Come, Charmian.

CHARMIAN.

    My arm is sore; best play with Mardian.

CLEOPATRA.

    As well a woman with an eunuch played
    As with a woman.
    (To MARDIAN.)

                  Come, you'll play with me, sir?

MARDIAN.

    As well as I can, madam.

CLEOPATRA.

    And when good will is showed, though 't come too short,
    The actor may plead pardon. I'll none now.

Give me mine angle; * we'll to the river: there,   fishing rod
My music playing far off, I will betray   11
Tawny-finned fishes; my bended hook shall pierce
Their slimy jaws; and, as I draw them up,
I'll think them every one an Antony,
And say, "Ah, ha! You're caught."
CHARMIAN.   'Twas merry when
You wagered on your angling; when your diver
Did hang a salt fish on his hook, which he
With fervency drew up.
CLEOPATRA.   That time—Oh times!—
I laughed him out of patience; and that night
I laughed him into patience; and next morn,   20
Ere the ninth hour, I drunk him to his bed;
Then put my tires * and mantles on him, whilst   headdress
I wore his sword Philippan.[52]
(*A* MESSENGER *enters.*)
                Oh, from Italy!
Ram thou thy fruitful tidings in mine ears,
That long time have been barren.
MESSENGER.   Madam, madam—
CLEOPATRA.
Antonius dead!—If thou say so, villain,
Thou kill'st thy mistress: but well and free,
If thou so yield * him, there is gold, and here   report
My bluest veins to kiss; a hand that kings
Have lipped, and trembled kissing.   30
MESSENGER.
First, madam, he is well.
CLEOPATRA.   Why, there's more gold.
But, sirrah, mark, we use
To say the dead are well: bring it * to that,   if it comes
The gold I give thee will I melt and pour
Down thy ill-uttering throat.
MESSENGER.
Good madam, hear me.
CLEOPATRA.   Well, go to, I will;
But there's no goodness in thy face: if Antony
Be free and healthful—so tart a favor *   countenance
To trumpet such good tidings! If not well,
Thou shouldst come like a Fury crowned with snakes,[53]   40
Not like a formal * man.   normal
MESSENGER.   Will 't please you hear me?

CLEOPATRA.
    I have a mind to strike thee ere thou speak'st.
    Yet, if thou say Antony lives, is well,
    Or friends with Caesar, or not captive to him,
    I'll set thee in a shower of gold, and hail
    Rich pearls upon thee.
MESSENGER.   Madam, he's well.
CLEOPATRA.   Well said.
MESSENGER.
    And friends with Caesar.
CLEOPATRA.   Thou 'rt an honest man.
MESSENGER.
    Caesar and he are greater friends than ever.
CLEOPATRA.
    Make thee a fortune from me.
MESSENGER.   But yet, madam—
CLEOPATRA.
    I do not like "But yet": it does allay   50
    The good precedence; * fie upon "But yet"!   preceding it
    "But yet" is as a jailer to bring forth
    Some monstrous malefactor. Prithee, friend,
    Pour out the pack of matter to mine ear,
    The good and bad together: he's friends with Caesar;
    In state of health thou say'st; and thou say'st free.
MESSENGER.
    Free, madam? No; I made no such report:
    He's bound unto Octavia.
CLEOPATRA.   For what good turn?
MESSENGER.
    For the best turn i' the bed.
CLEOPATRA.   I am pale, Charmian.
MESSENGER.
    Madam, he's married to Octavia.   60
CLEOPATRA.
    The most infectious pestilence upon thee!
(Strikes him down.)
MESSENGER.
    Good madam, patience.
CLEOPATRA.   What say you? Hence,
    Horrible villain!
(Striking him again.)
               Or I'll spurn * thine eyes   kick
    Like balls before me.
(Grasps him by the hair and pulls him about.)

I'll unhair thy head!
Thou shalt be whipped with wire, and stewed in brine,
Smarting in lingering pickle.
MESSENGER.   Gracious, madam,
 I that do bring the news made not the match.
CLEOPATRA.
 Say 'tis not so, a province I will give thee,
 And make thy fortunes proud: the blow thou hadst
 Shall make thy peace for moving me to rage;   70
 And I will boot thee with * what gift beside   give thee
 Thy modesty ⁵⁴ can beg.   to boot
MESSENGER.   He's married, madam.
CLEOPATRA   (*drawing a knife*) .
 Rogue, thou hast lived too long.
MESSENGER.   Nay, then I'll run.
 What mean you, madam? I have made no fault.
(*He runs out.*)
CHARMIAN.
 Good madam, keep yourself within yourself:
 The man is innocent.
CLEOPATRA.
 Some innocents 'scape not the thunderbolt.
 Melt Egypt into Nile! And kindly * creatures   of our kind
 Turn all to serpents! Call the slave again:
 Though I am mad, I will not bite him: call.   80
CHARMIAN.
 He is afeard to come.
CLEOPATRA.   I will not hurt him.
 (CHARMIAN *goes out.*)
 These hands do lack nobility, that they strike
 A meaner than myself; since I myself
 Have given myself the cause.
 (CHARMIAN *returns with the* MESSENGER.)
                    Come hither, sir.
 Though it be honest, it is never good
 To bring bad news. Give to a gracious * message   pleasing
 An host of tongues; but let ill tidings tell
 Themselves when they be felt.
MESSENGER.   I have done my duty.
CLEOPATRA.
 Is he married?
 I cannot hate thee worser than I do,   90
 If thou again say, "Yes."
MESSENGER.   He's married, madam.

CLEOPATRA.
The gods confound thee! Dost thou hold there * still?   to that
MESSENGER.
Should I lie, madam?
CLEOPATRA.   Oh, I would thou didst,
So * half my Egypt were submerged and made   even if
A cistern for scaled snakes!
                         Go, get thee, hence:
Hadst thou Narcissus in thy face, to me
Thou wouldst appear most ugly.⁵⁵ He is married?
MESSENGER.
I crave your highness' pardon.
CLEOPATRA.   He is married?
MESSENGER.
Take no offense that I would not offend you.
To punish me for what you make me do   100
Seems much unequal.* He's married to Octavia.   unjust
CLEOPATRA.
Oh, that his fault should make a knave of thee,
That art not * what thou 'rt sure of! Get thee hence: not sure
The merchandise which thou hast brought from Rome
Are all to dear for me: lie they upon thy hand,
And be undone * by 'em!   ruined
(*The* MESSENGER *leaves.*)
CHARMIAN.   Good your highness, patience.
CLEOPATRA.
In praising Antony, I have dispraised Caesar.
CHARMIAN.
Many times, madam.
CLEOPATRA.   I am paid for t' now.
Lead me from hence:
I faint.
(IRAS *and* CHARMIAN *move to support her.*)
                    O Iras, Charmian! 'Tis no matter.   110
(*To* ALEXAS.)
Go to the fellow, good Alexas; bid him
Report the feature of Octavia, her years,
Her inclination,* let him not leave out   disposition
The color of her hair. Bring me word quickly.
(ALEXAS *goes.*)
Let him forever go—let him not—Charmian,
Though he be painted one way like a Gorgon,
The other way's * a Mars.⁵⁶   *i.e.,* way he's

(*To* MARDIAN.)
Bid you Alexas

Bring me word how tall she is.
(*As* CHARMIAN *starts to speak.*)
Pity me, Charmian,

But do not speak to me. Lead me to my chamber.
(CHARMIAN *and* IRAS *help her out, followed by* SERVANTS.)

SCENE 6. *In the field, near Misenum.*

(*Trumpets and drums are heard.* POMPEY *and* MENAS, *at the head of marching* TROOPS, *enter at one side.* CAESAR, ANTONY, LEPIDUS, ENOBARBUS *and* MECAENAS, *also at the head of* TROOPS, *at the other.*)

POMPEY.
Your hostages I have, so have you mine;
And we shall talk before we fight.

CAESAR.   Most meet
That first we come to words; and therefore have we
Our written purposes before us sent;
Which, if thou hast considered, let us know
If 'twill tie up thy discontented sword,
And carry back to Sicily much tall * youth   brave
That else must perish here.

POMPEY.   To you all three,
The senators alone of this great world,   9
Chief factors * for the gods, I do not know   agents
Wherefore my fathers should revengers want,
Having a son and friends; since Julius Caesar,
Who at Philippi the good Brutus ghosted, *   haunted
There saw you laboring for him. What was't
That moved pale Cassius to conspire; and what
Made the all-honored, honest * Roman, Brutus,   honorable
With the armed rest, courtiers of beauteous freedom,
To drench the Capitol, but that they would
Have one man but a man? And that is it
Hath made me rig my navy, at whose burthen   20
The angered ocean foams; with which I meant
To scourge the ingratitude that despiteful Rome
Cast on my noble father.

CAESAR.   Take your time.
Thou canst not fear * us, Pompey, with thy sails;   frighten

We'll speak with thee at sea. At land, thou know'st
How much we do o'ercount * thee.   outnumber

POMPEY.   At land, indeed,
Thou dost o'ercount * me of my father's house; [57]   overreach
But, since the cuckoo builds not for himself,
Remain in 't as thou mayst.

LEPIDUS.   Be pleased to tell us—
For this is from the present *—how you take   beside the point
The offers we have sent you.   31

CAESAR.   There's the point.

ANTONY.
Which do not be entreated to, but weigh
What it is worth embraced.*   accepted

CAESAR.   And what may follow,
To try a larger fortune.

POMPEY.   You have made me offer
Of Sicily, Sardinia: and I must
Rid all the sea of pirates; then, to send
Measures of wheat to Rome; this 'greed upon,
To part with unhacked edges,* and bear back   *i.e.,* sword edges
Our targes * undinted.   shields

CAESAR, ANTONY, *and* LEPIDUS.
               That's our offer.

POMPEY.   Know, then,   40
I came before you here a man prepared
To take this offer; but Mark Antony
Put me to some impatience. Though I lose
The praise of it by telling, you must know,
When Caesar and your brother [58] were at blows,
Your mother came to Sicily and did find
Her welcome friendly.

ANTONY.   I have heard it, Pompey;
And am well studied * for a liberal thanks   prepared
Which I do owe you.

POMPEY.   Let me have your hand.
I did not think, sir, to have met you here.   50

ANTONY.
The beds i' the east are soft. And thanks to you,
That called me timelier than my purpose hither;
For I have gained by 't.

CAESAR.   Since I saw you last,
There is a change upon you.

POMPEY.   Well, I know not
What counts * harsh fortune casts upon my face; [59]   lines

But in my bosom shall she never come,
To make my heart her vassal.
LEPIDUS.   Well met here.
POMPEY.
I hope so, Lepidus. Thus we are agreed.
I crave our composition * may be written,   compact
And sealed between us.
CAESAR.   That's the next to do.   60
POMPEY.
We'll feast each other ere we part; and let's
Draw lots who shall begin.
ANTONY.   That will I, Pompey.
POMPEY.
No, Antony, take the lot: but, first
Or last, your fine Egyptian cookery
Shall have the fame.* I have heard that Julius Caesar   its praise
Grew fat with feasting there.
ANTONY.   You have heard much.
POMPEY.
I have fair meanings, sir.
ANTONY.   And fair words to them.
POMPEY.
Then so much have I heard:
And I have heard, Apollodorus carried ⁶⁰—
ENOBARBUS.
No more of that: he did so.
POMPEY.   What, I pray you?   70
ENOBARBUS.
A certain queen to Caesar in a mattress.
POMPEY.
I know thee now. How farest thou, soldier?
ENOBARBUS.   Well;
And well am like to do; for, I perceive,
Four feasts are toward.*   in prospect
POMPEY.   Let me shake thy hand;
I never hated thee. I have seen thee fight,
When I have envied thy behavior.
ENOBARBUS.   Sir,
I never loved you much; but I ha' praised ye,
When you have well deserved ten times as much
As I have said you did.
POMPEY.   Enjoy thy plainness,*   bluntness
It nothing ill becomes thee.   81
Aboard my galley I invite you all.

Will you lead, lords?

CAESAR, ANTONY, *and* LEPIDUS.
                          Show us the way, sir.

POMPEY.   Come.

(*All leave, except* MENAS *and* ENOBARBUS.)

MENAS   (*aside*).

Thy father, Pompey, would ne'er have made this treaty.
(*To* ENOBARBUS.) You and I have known,* sir.   met

ENOBARBUS.

At sea, I think.

MENAS.

We have, sir.

ENOBARBUS.

You have done well by water.

MENAS.

And you by land.   90

ENOBARBUS.

I will praise any man that will praise me; though it cannot
be denied what I have done by land.

MENAS.

Nor what I have done by water.

ENOBARBUS.

Yes, something you can deny for your own safety. You have
been a great thief * by sea.   *i.e.,* pirate

MENAS.

And you by land.

ENOBARBUS.

There I deny my land service. But give me your hand,
Menas. If our eyes had authority, here they might take two
thieves kissing. (*They shake hands.*)   100

MENAS.

All men's face are true, whatsome'er their hands are.

ENOBARBUS.

But there is never a fair woman has a true face.

MENAS.

No slander; they steal hearts.

ENOBARBUS.

We came hither to fight with you.

MENAS.

For my part, I am sorry it is turned to a drinking. Pompey
doth this day laugh away his fortune.   110

ENOBARBUS.

If he do, sure, he cannot weep 't back again.

MENAS.

You've said, sir. We looked not for Mark Antony here. Pray
you, is he married to Cleopatra?

ENOBARBUS.

Caesar's sister is called Octavia.

MENAS.

True, sir; she was the wife of Caius Marcellus.

ENOBARBUS.

But she is now the wife of Marcus Antonius.

MENAS.

Pray ye, sir?   120

ENOBARBUS.

'Tis true.

MENAS.

Then is Caesar and he forever knit together.

ENOBARBUS.

If I were bound to divine of this unity, I would not prophesy
so.

MENAS.

I think the policy of that purpose made * more in the mar-   **lay**
riage than the love of the parties.

ENOBARBUS.

I think so too. But you shall find, the band that seems to tie
their friendship together will be the very strangler of their   130
amity: Octavia is of a holy, cold, and still conversation.*   **behavior**

MENAS.

Who would not have his wife so?

ENOBARBUS.

Not he that himself is not so; which is Mark Antony. He
will to his Egyptian dish again. Then shall the sighs of Octavia blow the fire up in Caesar; and, as I said before, that
which is the strength of their amity shall prove the immedi-
ate author of their variance. Antony will use * his affection   **continue**
where it is: he married but his occasion * here.   **necessity**

MENAS.

And thus it may be. Come, sir, will you aboard? I have a   141
health for you.

ENOBARBUS.

I shall take it, sir: we have used our throats in Egypt.

MENAS.

Come, let's away.

(*They go.*)

SCENE 7. *On board Pompey's galley, off Misenum.*

(A table is laid, and several SERVANTS *are bringing in food and drink. Music is heard.)*

FIRST SERVANT.

Here they'll be, man. Some o' their plants are ill-rooted already; the least wind i' the world will blow them down.

SECOND SERVANT.

Lepidus is high-colored.

FIRST SERVANT.

They have made him drink alms-drink.[61]

SECOND SERVANT.

As they pinch one another by the disposition,* he cries out, "No more"; reconciles them to his entreaty, and himself to the drink.

i.e., as they fall to quarrelling

FIRST SERVANT.

But it raises the greater war between him and his discretion.

10

SECOND SERVANT.

Why, this it is to have a name in great men's fellowship. I had as lief have a reed that will do me no service as a partisan * I could not heave.

spear

FIRST SERVANT.

To be called into a huge sphere, and not to be seen to move in 't, are the holes where eyes should be, which pitifully disaster * the cheeks.

bring disaster to

(A trumpet sounds. CAESAR, ANTONY, LEPIDUS, POMPEY, AGRIPPA, MECAENAS, ENOBARBUS, MENAS, *and other* CAPTAINS *enter and go to the table.)*

ANTONY   *(to* CAESAR) .

Thus do they, sir: they take the flow o' the Nile
By certain scales i' the pyramid; they know,
By the height, the lowness, or the mean, if dearth
Or foison * follow: the higher Nilus swells,
The more it promises. As it ebbs, the seedsman
Upon the slime and ooze scatters his grain,
And shortly comes to harvest.

20

plenty

LEPIDUS.

You've strange serpents there.

ANTONY.

Ay, Lepidus.

LEPIDUS.

Your serpent of Egypt is bred now of your mud by the operation of your sun. So is your crocodile.

30

ANTONY.

They are so.

POMPEY.

Sit—and some wine! (*As they all sit.*) A health to Lepidus!

LEPIDUS.

I am not so well as I should be, but I'll ne'er out.*   give up

ENOBARBUS.

Not till you have slept; I fear me you'll be in * till then.   *i.e.,* drunk

LEPIDUS.

Nay, certainly, I have heard the Ptolemies' pyramises * are   pyramids

very goodly things; without contradiction, I have heard that.   41

MENAS   (*aside to* POMPEY).

Pompey, a word.

POMPEY   (*aside to* MENAS).

                    Say in mine ear: what is 't?

MENAS   (*aside to* POMPEY).

Forsake thy seat, I do beseech thee, captain,

And hear me speak a word.

POMPEY   (*aside to* MENAS).

Forbear me * till anon. (*To all.*) This wine for Lepidus!   leave me alone

LEPIDUS.

What manner o' thing is your crocodile?

ANTONY.

It is shaped, sir, like itself; and it is as broad as it hath

breadth; it is just so high as it is, and moves with its own

organs; it lives by that which nourisheth it; and the elements   50

once out of it, it transmigrates.

LEPIDUS.

What color is it of?

ANTONY.

Of its own color too.

LEPIDUS.

'Tis a strange serpent.

ANTONY.

'Tis so. And the tears of it are wet.

CAESAR   (*to* ANTONY).

Will this description satisfy him?

ANTONY   (*to* CAESAR).

With the health that Pompey gives him, else he is a very

epicure.

POMPEY   (*aside to* MENAS).

Go hang, sir, hang! Tell me of that? Away!

Do as I bid you.

(Calling to a SERVANT.*)*
              Where's this cup I called for?   60
MENAS   *(aside to* POMPEY*)* .
   If for the sake of merit * thou wilt hear me,   my merit
   Rise from thy stool.
POMPEY   *(aside to* MENAS*)* .
   I think thou 'rt mad. The matter?
(Rises, and walks aside with MENAS.*)*
MENAS   *(aside to* POMPEY*)* .
   I have ever held my cap off to thy fortunes.
POMPEY   *(aside to* MENAS*)* .
   Thou hast served me with much faith. What's else to say?
   (To all.)
   Be jolly, lords.
ANTONY.   These quicksands, Lepidus,
   Keep off them, for you sink.
MENAS   *(aside to* POMPEY*)* .
   Wilt thou be lord of all the world?
POMPEY   *(aside to* MENAS*)* .
                  What say'st thou?
MENAS   *(aside to* POMPEY*)* .
   Wilt thou be lord of the whole world? That's twice.
POMPEY   *(aside to* MENAS*)* .
   How should that be?
MENAS   *(aside to* POMPEY*)* .
              But entertain it,
   And, though thou think me poor, I am the man
   Will give thee all the world.   70
POMPEY   *(aside to* MENAS*)* .   Hast thou drunk well?
MENAS   *(aside to* POMPEY*)* .
   No, Pompey, I have kept me from the cup.
   Thou art, if thou darest be, the earthly Jove:
   Whate'er the ocean pales,* or sky inclips.*   encloses/embraces
   Is thine, if thou wilt ha 't.
POMPEY   *(aside to* MENAS*)* .   Show me which way.
MENAS   *(aside to* POMPEY*)* .
   These three world-sharers, these competitors,
   Are in thy vessel. Let me cut the cable;
   And, when we are put off, fall to their throats:
   All there is thine.
POMPEY   *(aside to* MENAS*)* .
            Ah, this thou shouldst have done,
   And not have spoke on 't! In me 'tis villainy;   80

In thee 't had been good service. Thou must know,
'Tis not my profit that does lead mine honor;
Mine honor, it. Repent that e'er thy tongue
Hath so betrayed thine act. Being done unknown,
I should have found it afterward well done;
But must condemn it now. Desist, and drink.
(POMPEY *leaves* MENAS *and returns to the table.*)
MENAS   (*aside*).
   For this,
   I'll never follow thy palled fortunes more.
   Who seeks, and will not take when once 'tis offered,
   Shall never find it more.
POMPEY   (*to all*).   This health to Lepidus!   90
ANTONY   (*looking at* LEPIDUS, *who has passed out*).
   Bear him ashore. I'll pledge it for him, Pompey.
ENOBARBUS   (*joining* MENAS).
   Here's to thee, Menas!
MENAS.   Enobarbus, welcome!
POMPEY.
   Fill till the cup be hid.
ENOBARBUS   (*pointing to the* ATTENDANT, *who picks up* LEPIDUS
   and carries him off).
   There's a strong fellow, Menas.
MENAS.
   Why?
ENOBARBUS.
   A' bears the third part of the world, man; see'st not?
MENAS.
   The third part, then, is drunk: would it were all,
   That it might go on wheels! [62]
ENOBARBUS.
   Drink thou: increase the reels.   100
MENAS.
   Come.
(MENAS *and* ENOBARBUS *rejoin the table.*)
POMPEY.
   This is not yet an Alexandrian feast.
ANTONY.
   It ripens toward it. Strike the vessels,* ho!   tap the casks
   Here is to Caesar!
CAESAR.   I could well forbear 't.
   It's monstrous labor, when I wash my brain,
   And it grows fouler.

ANTONY.   Be a child o' the time.

CAESAR.

Possess it,* I'll make answer;   *i.e.,* drink it up

But I had rather fast from all four days

Than drink so much in one.

ENOBARBUS   (*to* ANTONY).

Ha, my brave emperor!

Shall we dance now the Egyptian bacchanals,63   110

And celebrate our drink?

POMPEY.   Let's ha 't, good soldier.

ANTONY.

Come, let's all take hands,

Till that the conquering wine hath steeped our sense

In soft and delicate Lethe.*   *i.e.,* oblivion

ENOBARBUS.   All take hands.

Make battery to our ears with the loud music:

The while I'll place you. Then the boy shall sing;

The holding * every man shall bear as loud   refrain

As his strong sides can volley.

(*Music plays.* ENOBARBUS *places the men hand in hand. A* BOY
comes forward to sing.)

                        THE SONG

            Come, thou monarch of the vine,   120

            Plumpy Bacchus with pink eyne! *   half-closed eyes

            In thy fats * our cares be drowned,   vats

            With thy grapes our hairs be crowned.

            Cup us, till the world go round,

            Cup us, till the world go round!

CAESAR.

What would you more? Pompey, good night. Good brother,

Let me request you off: our graver business

Frowns at this levity. Gentle lords, let's part;

You see we have burnt our cheeks. Strong Enobarb

Is weaker than the wine ;and mine own tongue   130

Splits what it speaks. The wild disguise hath almost

Anticked * us all. What needs more words? Good night.   made buffoons of

Good Antony, your hand.

POMPEY.   I'll try you on the shore.

ANTONY.

And shall, sir. Give's your hand.

POMPEY.   O Antony,

You have my father's house—but what? We are friends.

Come, down into the boat.

ENOBARBUS.   Take heed you fall not.
(*After drunken embraces and handclasps, all leave except*
MENAS *and* ENOBARBUS.)
Menas, I'll not on shore.
MENAS.   No, to my cabin.
These drums! These trumpets, flutes! What!
Let Neptune hear we bid a loud farewell
To these great fellows. Sound and be hanged! Sound out!   140
(*The trumpets and drums sound a loud flourish.*)
ENOBARBUS   (*throwing his cap in the air*).
Ho! says a'. There's my cap.
MENAS.
Ho! Noble captain, come.
(*They leave.*)

ACT III

SCENE 1. Syria. *A plain.*

(VENTIDIUS *enters, with* SILIUS, *at the head of Roman* TROOPS
who triumphantly bear the dead body of PACORUS *and captured
Parthian colors.*)
VENTIDIUS.
Now, darting Parthia, art thou struck; and now
Pleased fortune does of Marcus Crassus' death
Make me revenger.[64] Bear the king's son's body
Before our army. Thy Pacorus, Orodes,
Pays this for Marcus Crassus.
SILIUS.   Noble Ventidius,
Whilst yet with Parthian blood thy sword is warm,
The fugitive Parthians follow; spur through Media,
Mesopotamia, and the shelters whither
The routed fly. So thy grand captain Antony
Shall set thee on triumphant chariots and   10
Put garlands on thy head.
VENTIDIUS.   O Silius, Silius,
I have done enough; a lower place,* note well,   placed
May make * too great an act: for learn this, Silius: perform
Better to leave undone, than by our deed
Acquire too high a fame when him we serve's away.
Caesar and Antony have ever won

More in their officer than person. Sossius,
One of my place in Syria, his lieutenant,
For quick accumulation of renown,
Which he achieved by the minute, lost his favor. 20
Who does i' the wars more than his captain can
Becomes his captain's captain; and ambition,
The soldier's virtue, rather makes choice of loss,
Than gain which darkens * him.   eclipses
I could do more to do Antonius good,
But 'twould offend him; and in his offense *   *i.e.,* taking offense
Should my performance perish.
SILIUS.   Thou hast, Ventidius, that
Without the which a soldier, and his sword,
Grants scarce distinction. Thou wilt write to Antony?
VENTIDIUS.
I'll humbly signify what in his name, 30
That magical word of war, we have effected;
How, with his banners and his well-paid ranks,
The ne'er-yet-beaten horse * of Parthia   cavalry
We have jaded out o' the field.
SILIUS.   Where is he now?
VENTIDIUS.
He purposeth to Athens, whither, with what haste
The weight we must convey with 's will permit,
We shall appear before him.
(*To the* MEN *bearing the body.*)
                              On, there; pass along!
(VENTIDIUS, SILVIUS, *and the* TROOPS *march out.*)

SCENE 2. Rome. *Courtyard of Caesar's house.*

(AGRIPPA *enters from one door, meeting* ENOBARBUS, *who enters
from another.*)
AGRIPPA.
What, are the brothers parted? *   departed
ENOBARBUS.
They have dispatched * with Pompey, he is gone;   finished
The other three are sealing.* Octavia weeps   *i.e.,* agreements
To part from Rome; Caesar is sad; and Lepidus,
Since Pompey's feast, as Menas says, is troubled
With the green sickness.⁶⁵
AGRIPPA.   'Tis a noble Lepidus.

ENOBARBUS.

A very fine one: oh, how he loves Caesar!

AGRIPPA.

Nay, but how dearly he adores Mark Antony!

ENOBARBUS.

Caesar? Why, he's the Jupiter of men.

AGRIPPA.

What's Antony? The god of Jupiter.   10

ENOBARBUS.

Spake you of Caesar? How! The nonpareil! *   unequaled

AGRIPPA.

O Antony! O thou Arabian bird! 66

ENOBARBUS.

Would you praise Caesar, say "Caesar": go no further.

AGRIPPA.

Indeed, he plied them both with excellent praises.

ENOBARBUS.

But he loves Caesar best; yet he loves Antony.
Ho! Hearts, tongues, figures, scribes, bards, poets, cannot
Think, speak, cast,* write, sing, number,* ho!   compute/versify
His love to Antony. But as for Caesar,
Kneel down, kneel down, and wonder.

AGRIPPA.   Both he loves.   19

ENOBARBUS.

They are his shards,* and he their beetle.   beetle wings
(*A trumpet call sounds.*)
                         So;
This is to horse. Adieu, noble Agrippa.

AGRIPPA.

Good fortune, worthy soldier; and farewell.
(ANTONY *and* OCTAVIA *come from the house.* CAESAR *and* LEPIDUS
accompany them.)

ANTONY.

No further, sir.

CAESAR.

You take from me a great part of myself;
Use me well in 't.
              Sister, prove such a wife
As my thoughts make thee, and as my farthest band *   bond
Shall pass on thy approof.67
              Most noble Antony,
Let not the piece * of virtue, which is set   masterpiece
Betwixt us as the cement of our love,

To keep it builded, be the ram to batter   30
The fortress of it; for better might we
Have loved without this mean, if on both parts
This be not cherished.
ANTONY.   Make me not offended
In your distrust.*   *i.e.,* of me
CAESAR.   I have said.
ANTONY.   You shall not find,
Though you be therein curious,* the least cause   searching
For what you seem to fear. So, the gods keep you,
And make the hearts of Romans serve your ends!
We will here part.
CAESAR.
Farewell, my dearest sister, fare thee well:
The elements be kind to thee, and make   40
Thy spirits all of comfort! Fare thee well.
OCTAVIA   (*weeping*).
My noble brother!
ANTONY.
The April's in her eyes: it is love's spring,
And these the showers to bring it on. Be cheerful.
OCTAVIA.
Sir, look well to my husband's house; and—
CAESAR.   What,
Octavia?
OCTAVIA.
I'll tell you in your ear.
(*Whispers in* CAESAR's *ear.*)
ANTONY.
Her tongue will not obey her heart, nor can
Her heart inform her tongue—the swan's down feather,
That stands upon the swell at full of tide,
And neither way inclines.[68]   50
ENOBARBUS (*aside to* AGRIPPA).
Will Caesar weep?
AGRIPPA (*aside to* ENOBARBUS).
He has a cloud in 's face.
ENOBARBUS (*aside to* AGRIPPA).
He were the worse for that, were he a horse;
So is he, being a man.[69]
AGRIPPA (*aside to* ENOBARBUS).
Why, Enobarbus,
When Antony found Julius Caesar dead,

He cried almost to roaring; and he wept
When at Philippi he found Brutus slain.
ENOBARBUS *(aside to* AGRIPPA*)*.
    That year, indeed, he was troubled with a rheum; *   head cold
    What willingly he did confound,* he wailed,   destroy
    Believe 't, till I wept too.
CAESAR.   No, sweet Octavia,   59
    You shall hear from me still; * the time shall not   continually
    Outgo * my thinking on you.   outstrip
ANTONY *(embracing* CAESAR*)*.   Come sir, come;
    I'll wrestle with you in my strength of love.
    Look, here I have you; thus I let you go,
    And give you to the gods.
CAESAR.   Adieu; be happy!
LEPIDUS.
    Let all the number of the stars give light
    To thy fair way!
CAESAR *(kissing* OCTAVIA*)*.
    Farewell, farewell.
ANTONY.   Farewell!
(Trumpets sound. ANTONY *and* OCTAVIA *leave, followed by*
ENOBARBUS. CAESAR, LEPIDUS, *and* AGRIPPA *watch them leave,
and then go back inside.)*

SCENE 3. Egypt. *A room in Cleopatra's palace at Alexandria.*

*(*CLEOPATRA *enters, followed by* CHARMIAN, IRAS, *and* ALEXAS.*)*
CLEOPATRA.
    Where is the fellow?
ALEXAS.   Half afeard to come.
CLEOPATRA.
    Go to, go to.
    (To the MESSENGER *as he enters.)*
           Come hither, sir.
ALEXAS.   Good majesty,
    Herod of Jewry dare not look upon you
    But when you are well pleased.
CLEOPATRA.   That Herod's head
    I'll have; but how, when Antony is gone
    Through whom I might command it? Come thou near.
MESSENGER.
    Most gracious majesty—

CLEOPATRA.
Didst thou behold Octavia?
MESSENGER.
Ay, dread queen.
CLEOPATRA.
Where?   10
MESSENGER.
Madam, in Rome;
I looked her in the face, and saw her led
Between her brother and Mark Antony.
CLEOPATRA.
Is she as tall as me?
MESSENGER.   She is not, madam.
CLEOPATRA.
Didst hear her speak? Is she shrill-tongued or low?
MESSENGER.
Madam, I heard her speak; she is low-voiced.
CLEOPATRA.
That's not so good: he cannot like her long.
CHARMIAN.
Like her! O Isis! ⁷⁰ 'Tis impossible.
CLEOPATRA.
I think so, Charmian. Dull of tongue, and dwarfish!
What majesty is in her gait? Remember,   20
If e'er thou look'dst on majesty.
MESSENGER.   She creeps:
Her motion and her station * are as one;   standing still
She shows a body rather than a life,
A statue than a breather.
CLEOPATRA.   Is this certain?
MESSENGER.
Or I have no observance.
CHARMIAN.   Three in Egypt
Cannot make better note.
CLEOPATRA.   He's very knowing;
I do perceive 't. There's nothing in her yet:
The fellow has good judgment.
CHARMIAN.   Excellent.
CLEOPATRA.
Guess at her years, I prithee.
MESSENGER.   Madam,
She was a widow—
CLEOPATRA.   Widow! Charmian, hark.   30

MESSENGER.

And I do think she's thirty.

CLEOPATRA.

Bear'st thou her face in mind? Is 't long or round?

MESSENGER.

Round even to faultiness.

CLEOPATRA.

For the most part, too, they are foolish that are so.
Her hair, what color?

MESSENGER.

Brown, madam: and her forehead
As low as she would wish it.[71]

CLEOPATRA. *(giving him money)* .

There's gold for thee.
Thou must not take my former sharpness ill.
I will employ thee back again; I find thee
Most fit for business. Go make thee ready;   40
Our letters are prepared. *(The* MESSENGER *goes.)*

CHARMIAN.   A proper * man.   handsome

CLEOPATRA.

Indeed, he is so. I repent me much
That so I harried him. Why, methinks, by him,
This creature's no such thing. *   not so much

CHARMIAN.   Nothing, madam.

CLEOPATRA.

The man hath seen some majesty, and should know.

CHARMIAN.

Hath he seen majesty? Isis else defend,*   forbid
And serving you so long!

CLEOPATRA.

I have one thing more to ask him yet, good Charmian:
But 'tis no matter; thou shalt bring him to me
Where I will write. All may be well enough.   50

CHARMIAN.

I warrant you, madam.

(CLEOPATRA *leaves, followed by* ALEXAS, CHARMIAN, *and* IRAS.)

SCENE 4. Athens. *A living room in Antony's house.*

(ANTONY *and* OCTAVIA *enter.*)

ANTONY.

Nay, nay, Octavia, not only that—

That were excusable, that, and thousands more
Of semblable * import—but he hath waged   similar
New wars 'gainst Pompey; made his will, and read it
To public ear:
Spoke scantly * of me. When perforce he could not   grudgingly
But pay me terms of honor, cold and sickly
He vented * them; most narrow measure lent me: uttered
When the best hint * was given him, he not took 't,   opportunity
Or did it from his teeth.
OCTAVIA.   O my good lord,   10
Believe not all; or, if you must believe,
Stomach * not all. A more unhappy lady,   resent
If this division chance, ne'er stood between,
Praying for both parts.
The good gods will mock me presently,*   instantly
When I shall pray, "Oh, bless my lord and husband!"
Undo that prayer, by crying out as loud,
"Oh, bless my brother!" Husband win, win brother,
Prays, and destroys the prayer; no midway
'Twixt these extremes at all.
ANTONY.   Gentle Octavia,   20
Let your best love draw to that point, which seeks
Best to preserve it. If I lose honor,
I lose myself: better I were not yours
Than yours so branchless. But, as you requested,
Yourself shall go between 's. The meantime, lady,
I'll raise the preparation of a war
Shall stain * your brother. Make your soonest haste;   dim
So your desires are yours.
OCTAVIA.   Thanks to my lord.
The Jove of power make me most weak, most weak,
Your reconciler! Wars 'twixt you twain would be   30
As if the world should cleave, and that slain men
Should solder up the rift.
ANTONY.
When it appears to you where this begins,
Turn your displeasure that way; for our faults
Can never be so equal, that your love
Can equally move with them.
                            Provide your going;
Choose your own company, and command what cost
Your heart has mind to.
(*They go out by different doors.*)

SCENE 5. Athens. *An anteroom in Antony's house.*

(ENOBARBUS *enters, meeting* EROS.)

ENOBARBUS.

How now, friend Eros!

EROS.

There's strange news come, sir.

ENOBARBUS.

What, man?

EROS.

Caesar and Lepidus have made wars upon Pompey.

ENOBARBUS.

This is old. What is the success? *   outcome

EROS.

Caesar, having made use of him in the wars 'gainst Pompey,
presently denied him rivality; * would not let him partake   equality
in the glory of the action; and not resting here, accuses him   10
of letters he had formerly wrote to Pompey; upon his own
appeal, seizes him: so the poor third is up,* till death en-   locked up
large his confine.*   prison

ENOBARBUS.

Then, world, thou hast a pair of chaps,* no more;   jaws
And throw between them all the food thou hast,
They'll grind the one the other.
                              Where's Antony?

EROS.

He's walking in the garden thus—and spurns *   kicks
The rush that lies before him; cries, "Fool Lepidus!"
And threats the throat of that his officer
That murdered Pompey.

ENOBARBUS.   Our great navy's rigged.   20

EROS.

For Italy and Caesar. More, Domitius;
My lord desires you presently. My news
I might have told hereafter.

ENOBARBUS.   'Twill be naught:
But let it be. Bring me to Antony.

EROS.

Come, sir.

(*They go.*)

SCENE 6. Rome. *A chamber in Caesar's house.*

(CAESAR *enters in conference with* AGRIPPA *and* MECAENAS.)
CAESAR.

Contemning * Rome, he has done all this, and more, despising
In Alexandria. Here's the manner of 't:
I' the market-place, on a tribunal silvered,
Cleopatra and himself in chairs of gold
Were publicly enthroned. At the feet sat
Caesarion, whom they call my father's son,[72]
And all the unlawful issue that their lust
Since then hath made between them. Unto her
He gave the stablishment * of Egypt; made her inheritance
Of lower Syria, Cyprus, Lydia, 10
Absolute queen.
MECAENAS. This in the public eye?
CAESAR.

I' the common showplace, where they exercise.
His sons he there proclaimed the kings of kings:
Great Media, Parthia, and Armenia,
He gave to Alexander; to Ptolemy he assigned
Syria, Cilicia, and Phoenicia. She
In the habiliments of the goddess Isis
That day appeared; and oft before gave audience,
As 'tis reported, so.
MECAENAS. Let Rome be thus
Informed.
AGRIPPA.

Who, queasy * with his insolence nauseated
Already, will their good thoughts call from him. 21
CAESAR.

The people know it; and have now received
His accusations.
AGRIPPA. Who does he accuse?
CAESAR.

Caesar; and that, having in Sicily
Sextus Pompeius spoiled,* we had not rated * him despoiled
His part o' the isle. Then does he say, he lent me prorated
Some shipping unrestored. Lastly, he frets
That Lepidus of the triumvirate
Should be deposed; and, being,* that we detain so being
All his revenue.
AGRIPPA. Sir, this should be answered. 30

CAESAR.

'Tis done already, and the messenger gone.
I have told him, Lepidus was grown too cruel;
That he his high authority abused,
And did deserve his change. For * what I have conquered,   as for
I grant him part; but then, in his Armenia,
And other of his conquered kingdoms, I
Demand the like.

MECAENAS.   He'll never yield to that.

CAESAR.

Nor must not then be yielded to in this.

(OCTAVIA *enters, attended by* SERVANTS.)

OCTAVIA.

Hail, Caesar, and my lord! Hail, most dear Caesar!

CAESAR.

That ever I should call thee castaway!   40

OCTAVIA.

You have not called me so, nor have you cause.

CAESAR.

Why have you stolen upon us thus? You come not
Like Caesar's sister. The wife of Antony
Should have an army for an usher, and
The neighs of horse to tell of her approach
Long ere she did appear; the trees by the way
Should have borne men; and expectation fainted,
Longing for what it had not; nay, the dust
Should have ascended to the roof of heaven,
Raised by your populous * troops. But you are come   numerous
A market maid to Rome, and have prevented   51
The ostentation of our love, which, left unshown,
Is often left unloved. We should have met you
By sea and land, supplying every stage
With an augmented greeting.

OCTAVIA.   Good my lord,

To come thus was I not constrained, but did it
On my free will. My lord, Mark Antony,
Hearing that you prepared for war, acquainted
My grieved ear withal; * whereon, I begged   with that fact
His pardon * for return.   permission

CAESAR.   Which soon he granted,   60

Being an obstruct 'tween his lust and him.

OCTAVIA.

Do not say so, my lord.

CAESAR.   I have eyes upon him,
And his affairs come to me on the wind.
Where is he now?
OCTAVIA.   My lord, in Athens.
CAESAR.
No, my most wrongèd sister; Cleopatra
Hath nodded him to her. He hath give his empire
Up to a whore; who * now are levying   *i.e.,* they
The kings o' the earth for war: he hath assembled
Bocchus, the king of Libya; Archelaus,
Of Cappadocia; Philadelphos, king   70
Of Paphlagonia; the Thracian king, Adallas;
King Malchus of Arabia; King of Pont;
Herod of Jewry; Mithridates, king
Of Comagene; Polemon and Amyntas,
The kings of Mede and Lycaonia,[73]
With a more larger list of scepters.
OCTAVIA.   Ay me, most wretched,
That have my heart parted betwixt two friends
That do afflict each other!
CAESAR.   Welcome hither:
Your letters did withhold * our breaking forth;   hold back
Till we perceived, both how you were wrong led,   80
And we in negligent danger.* Cheer your heart.   danger from
                                                                   inaction
Be you not troubled with the time, which drives
O'er your content these strong necessities;
But let determined * things to destiny   predetermined
Hold unbewailed their way. Welcome to Rome;
Nothing more dear to me. You are abused
Beyond the mark * of thought; and the high gods,   bounds
To do you justice, make them ministers
Of us and those that love you. Best of comfort;
And ever welcome to us.
AGRIPPA.   Welcome, lady.   90
MECAENAS.
Welcome, dear madam.
Each heart in Rome does love and pity you.
Only the adulterous Antony, most large
In his abominations, turns you off,
And gives his potent regiment * to a trull,*   authority/whore
That noises it against us.
OCTAVIA.   Is it so, sir?
CAESAR.
Most certain. Sister, welcome: pray you,

Be ever known to patience. My dear'st sister!
(CAESAR *leads her out, followed by* AGRIPPA, MECAENAS, *and the*
SERVANTS.)

SCENE 7. Antony's camp near Actium. *Inside Antony's tent.*

(CLEOPATRA *enters with* ENOBARBUS.)
CLEOPATRA.
    I will be even with thee, doubt it not.
ENOBARBUS.
    But why, why, why?
CLEOPATRA.
    Thou hast forspoke * my being in these wars,   spoken against
    And say'st it is not fit.
ENOBARBUS.   Well, is it, is it?
CLEOPATRA.
    If not denounced against us, why should not we
    Be there in person?
ENOBARBUS (*aside*).   Well, I could reply:
    If we should serve with horse and mares together,
    The horse were merely * lost; the mares would bear   utterly
    A soldier and his horse.
CLEOPATRA.   What is 't you say?   10
ENORABUS (*to* CLEOPATRA).
    Your presence needs must puzzle * Antony;   inhibit
    Take from his heart, take from his brain, from 's time,
    What should not then be spared. He is already
    Traduced for levity; and 'tis said in Rome
    That Photinus an eunuch and your maids
    Manage this war.
CLEOPATRA.   Sink Rome, and their tongues rot
    That speak against us! A charge * we bear i' the war,   responsibility
    And, as the president of my kingdom, will
    Appear there for a man. Speak not against it;
    I will not stay behind.
ENOBARBUS.   Nay, I have done.   20
    Here comes the emperor.
(ANTONY *enters in conference with* CANIDIUS.)
ANTONY.   Is it not strange, Canidius,
    That from Tarentum and Brundusium 74
    He could so quickly cut the Ionian sea,
    And take in Toryne? 75
                    You have heard on 't, sweet?

CLEOPATRA.
  Celerity is never more admired
  Than by the negligent.
ANTONY.   A good rebuke,
  Which might have well becomed the best of men,
  To taunt at slackness. Canidius, we
  Will fight with him by sea.
CLEOPATRA.   By sea! What else?
CANIDIUS.
  Why will my lord do so?
ANTONY.   For that he dares us to 't.   30
ENOBARBUS.
  So hath my lord dared him to single fight.
CANIDIUS.
  Ay, and to wage this battle at Pharsalia,
  Where Caesar fought with Pompey. But these offers,
  Which serve not for his vantage, he shakes off;
  And so should you.
ENOBARBUS.   Your ships are not well manned;
  Your mariners are muleters, * reapers, people   mule drivers
  Ingrossed * by swift impress; * in Caesar's fleet   amassed/
  Are those that often have 'gainst Pompey fought: conscription
  Their ships are yare; * yours, heavy. No disgrace   easy to handle
  Shall fall you for refusing him at sea,   40
  Being prepared for land.
ANTONY.   By sea, by sea.
ENOBARBUS.
  Most worthy sir, you therein throw away
  The absolute * soldiership you have by land;   perfect
  Distract * your army, which doth most consist   divide
  Of war-marked footmen; leave unexecuted
  Your own renowned knowledge; quite forgo
  The way which promises assurance; and
  Give up yourself merely * to chance and hazard,   utterly
  From firm security.
ANTONY.   I'll fight at sea.
CLEOPATRA.
  I have sixty sails, Caesar none better.   50
ANTONY.
  Our overplus of shipping will we burn;
  And, with the rest full-manned, from the head * of Actium   headland
  Beat the approaching Caesar. But if we fail,
  We then can do 't at land.

(*A* MESSENGER *enters.*)
Thy business?

MESSENGER.

The news is true, my lord; he is descried;
Caesar has taken Toryne.

ANTONY.

Can he be there in person? 'Tis impossible;
Strange that his power * should be. Canidius,   *forces*
Our nineteen legions thou shalt hold by land,
And our twelve thousand horse. We'll to our ship.   60
Away, my Thetis! [76]
(*A* SOLDIER *enters.*)
How now, worthy soldier!

SOLDIER.

O noble emperor, do not fight by sea;
Trust not to rotten planks. Do you misdoubt
This sword and these my wounds? Let the Egyptians
And the Phoenicians go a-ducking: we
Have used to conquer, standing on the earth,
And fighting foot to foot.

ANTONY.   Well, well: away!
(ANTONY, CLEOPATRA, *and* ENOBARBUS *go out.*)

SOLDIER.

By Hercules, I think I am i' the right.

CANIDIUS.

Soldier, thou art: but his whole action grows
Not in the power on 't.[77] So our leader's led,   70
And we are women's men.

SOLDIER.   You keep by land
The legions and the horse whole, do you not?

CANIDIUS.

Marcus Octavius, Marcus Justeius,
Publicola, and Caelius, are for sea,
But we keep whole by land. This speed of Caesar's
Carries beyond * belief.   *passes*

SOLDIER.   While he was yet in Rome,
His power went out in such distractions as
Beguiled all spies.

CANIDIUS.   Who's his lieutenant, hear you?

SOLDIER.

They say, one Taurus.

CANIDIUS.   Well I know the man.
(*A* MESSENGER *enters.*)

MESSENGER.
The emperor calls Canidius.   80
CANIDIUS.
With news the time's with labor, and throes forth,*   gives birth
Each minute, some.
(CANIDIUS *goes, followed by the* SOLDIER *and the* MESSENGER.)

SCENE 8. A plain near Actium.

(CAESAR *enters, meeting* TAURUS, *who is at the head of marching*
TROOPS.)
CAESAR.
Taurus!
TAURUS.
My lord?
CAESAR.
Strike not by land; keep whole: provoke not battle,
Till we have done at sea. Do not exceed
The prescript * of this scroll: our fortune lies   orders
Upon this jump.*   risk
(CAESAR, TAURUS, *and the* TROOPS *march away*.)

SCENE 9. Another part of the plain.

(ANTONY *enters, followed by* ENOBARBUS.)
ANTONY.
Set we our squadrons on yond side o' the hill,
In eye of Caesar's battle; * from which place   battle array
We may the number of the ships behold,
And so proceed accordingly.
(*They go*.)

SCENE 10. Another part of the plain.

(CANIDIUS' *and* ANTONY'S *land forces pass on their way to take
up positions to watch the coming battle.* TAURUS, *with* CAESAR'S
*land forces, marches to take up his position in the other direc-
tion. Then the sound of a sea battle is heard, followed by a
nearby sounding of triumpets and beating of drums.* ENOBARBUS
enters.)

ENOBARBUS.
   Naught, naught, all naught! I can behold no longer:
   The Antoniad, the Egyptian admiral,*   flagship
   To see 't mine eyes are blasted.
   With all their sixty, fly and turn the rudder.
(SCARUS *enters.*)
SCARUS.   Gods and goddesses,
   All the whole synod of them!
ENOBARBUS.   What's thy passion?
SCARUS.
   The greater cantle * of the world is lost   segment
   With * very ignorance; we have kissed away   from
   Kingdoms and provinces.
ENOBARBUS.   How appears the fight?
SCARUS.
   On our side like the tokened pestilence,
   Where death is sure.⁷⁸ You ribaudred * nag of Egypt—   10 ribald
   Whom leprosy o'ertake!—i' the midst o' the fight,
   When vantage like a pair of twins appeared,
   Both as the same, or rather ours the elder,
   The breese * upon her, like a cow in June,   gadfly
   Hoists sails and flies.
ENOBARBUS.
   That I beheld.
   Mine eyes did sicken at the sight, and could not
   Endure a further view.
SCARUS.   She once being loofed,*   luffed
   The noble ruin of her magic, Antony,
   Claps on his sea wing, and, like a doting mallard,   20
   Leaving the fight in height, flies after her.
   I never saw an action of such shame;
   Experience, manhood, honor, ne'er before
   Did violate so itself.
ENOBARBUS.   Alack, alack!
(CANIDIUS *enters.*)
CANIDIUS.
   Our fortune on the sea is out of breath,
   And sinks most lamentably. Had our general
   Been what he knew * himself, it had gone well.   *i.e.,* true to
   Oh, he has given example for our flight,
   Most grossly, by his own!
ENOBARBUS.   Ay, are you thereabouts? *   at that point
   Why, then, good night indeed.   30

CANIDIUS.

Toward Peloponnesus are they fled.

SCARUS.

'Tis easy to 't; * and there I will attend   to reach

What further comes.

(SCARUS *goes.*)

CANIDIUS.   To Caesar will I render

My legions and my horse. Six kings already

Show me the way of yielding.

(CANIDIUS *goes off toward* CAESAR's *armies.*)

ENOBARBUS.   I'll yet follow

The wounded chance * of Antony, though my reason   fortunes

Sits in the wind against me.

(ENOBARBUS *slips away.*)

SCENE 11. Egypt. *The throne room of Cleopatra's palace at Alexandria.*

(ANTONY *enters, followed by some* OFFICERS *and* SOLDIERS.)

ANTONY.

Hark! The land bids me tread no more upon 't;

It is ashamed to bear me!

       Friends, come hither:

I am so lated * in the world, that I   belated

Have lost my way forever. I have a ship

Laden with gold. Take that, divide it. Fly,

And make your peace with Caesar.

ALL.   Fly! Not we.

ANTONY.

I have fled myself; and have instructed cowards

To run and show their shoulders. Friends, begone;

I have myself resolved upon a course

Which has no need of you; begone.   10

My treasure's in the harbor, take it. O,

I followed that * I blush to look upon.   what

My very hairs do mutiny; for the white

Reprove the brown for rashness, and they them

For fear and doting. Friends, begone; you shall

Have letters from me to some friends that will

Sweep your way for you. Pray you, look not sad,

Nor make replies of loathness: take the hint *   opportunity

Which my despair proclaims; let that be left

Which leaves itself: to the seaside straightway.   20
I will possess you of that ship and treasure.
    Leave me, I pray, a little. Pray you now.
Nay, do so; for, indeed, I have lost command,
Therefore I pray you. I'll see you by and by.
(ANTONY *sits down. His friends leave. After a moment* CLEO-
PATRA *enters, supported by* CHARMIAN *and* IRAS, *and followed
by* EROS.)

EROS.

Nay, gentle madam, to him, comfort him.

IRAS.

Do, most dear queen.

CHARMIAN.

Do! Why, what else?

CLEOPATRA.

Let me sit down.
(*She sits some distance away from* ANTONY.)
                O Juno!

ANTONY.

No, no, no, no, no.

EROS (*going to* ANTONY).

See you here, sir?   30

ANTONY.

O fie, fie, fie!

CHARMIAN.

Madam!

IRAS.

Madam, O good empress!

EROS (*to* ANTONY).

Sir, sir—

ANTONY.

Yes, my lord, yes; he at Philippi kept
His sword e'en like a dancer; while I struck
The lean and wrinkled Cassius and 'twas I
That the mad Brutus ended: [79] he alone
Dealt * on lieutenantry, and no practice had   depended
In the brave squares * of war. Yet now—no matter.   squadrons

CLEOPATRA (*to her women*).

Ah, stand by.   41

EROS.

The queen, my lord, the queen.

IRAS.

Go to him, madam, speak to him:

He is unqualitied * with very shame.   incapacitated
CLEOPATRA (*rising*).
   Well then, sustain me. Oh!
EROS (*as* CLEOPATRA *moves toward them*).
   Most noble sir, arise; the queen approaches:
   Her head's declined, and death will seize her, but *   unless
   Your comfort makes the rescue.
ANTONY.
   I have offended reputation,
   A most unnoble swerving.
EROS.   Sir, the queen.   50
ANTONY (*looks at her*).
   Oh, whither hast thou led me, Egypt? See,
   How I convey my shame out of * thine eyes   away from
   By looking back * what I have left behind   back at
   'Stroyed in dishonor.
CLEOPATRA.   O my lord, my lord,
   Forgive my fearful * sails! I little thought   frightened
   You would have followed.
ANTONY.   Egypt, thou knew'st too well
   My heart was to thy rudder tied by the strings,
   And thou shouldst tow me after: o'er my spirit
   Thy full supremacy thou knew'st, and that
   Thy beck might from the bidding of the gods
   Command me.   60
CLEOPATRA.   Oh, my pardon!
ANTONY.   Now I must
   To the young man send humble treaties, dodge
   And palter * in the shifts of lowness, who   equivocate
   With half the bulk o' the world played as I pleased,
   Making and marring fortunes. You did know
   How much you were my conqueror; and that
   My sword, made weak by my affection, would
   Obey it on all cause.
CLEOPATRA.   Pardon, pardon!
ANTONY.
   Fall not a tear, I say; one of them rates
   All that is won and lost.
   (*Embracing her.*)
               Give me a kiss;   70
   Even this repays me. We sent our schoolmaster;
   Is he come back? 80 Love, I am full of lead.
   Some wine, within there, and our viands! Fortune knows

We scorn her most when most she offers blows.
(ANTONY *leads* CLEOPATRA *out, followed by* CHARMIAN, IRAS, *and* EROS.)

SCENE 12. Egypt. *Caesar's camp. Before Caesar's tent.*

(CAESAR *enters, attended by* DOLABELLA, THYREUS, *and various*
GUARDS *and* OFFICERS.)
CAESAR.
  Let him appear that's come from Antony.
  Know you him?
DOLABELLA.   Caesar, 'tis his schoolmaster:
  An argument * that he is plucked, when hither   indication
  He sends so poor a pinion of his wing,
  Which had superfluous kings for messengers
  Not many moons gone by.
(EUPHRONIUS, *the ambassador from* ANTONY, *enters.*)
CAESAR.   Approach, and speak.
EUPHRONIUS.
  Such as I am, I come from Antony.
  I was of late as petty to his ends
  As is the morn-dew on the myrtle leaf
  To his * grand sea.   its
CAESAR.   Be 't so. Declare thine office.   10
EUPHRONIUS.
  Lord of his fortunes he salutes thee, and
  Requires * to live in Egypt; which not granted,   requests
  He lessens his requests; and to thee sues
  To let him breathe between the heavens and earth,
  A private man in Athens. This for him.
  Next, Cleopatra does confess * thy greatness;   acknowledge
  Submits her to thy might; and of thee craves
  The circle * of the Ptolemies for her heirs,   crown
  Now hazarded to thy grace.*   mercy
CAESAR.   For Antony,
  I have no ears to his request. The queen   20
  Of * audience nor desire shall fail, so * she   neither of/if
  From Egypt drive her all-disgracèd friend,
  Or take his life there. This if she perform,
  She shall not sue unheard. So to them both.
EUPHRONIUS.
  Fortune pursue thee!

CAESAR (*to soldiers*).

Bring him through the bands.

(EUPHRONIUS *goes, escorted by* GUARDS.)

(*To* THYREUS.)

To try thy eloquence, now 'tis time: dispatch;
From Antony win Cleopatra. Promise,
And in our name, what she requires; add more,
From thine invention, offers. Women are not
In their best fortunes strong; but want will perjure *   cause to perjure
The ne'er-touched vestal. Try thy cunning, Thyreus,   31
Make thine own edict for thy pains, which we
Will answer as a law.

THYREUS.   Caesar, I go.

CAESAR.

Observe how Antony becomes his flaw,[81]
And what thou think'st his very action speaks
In every power that moves.

THYREUS.   Caesar, I shall.

(THYREUS *salutes and goes.* CAESAR *leaves, followed by* DOLA-
BELLA *and the* SOLDIERS.)

SCENE 13. Egypt. *The throne room in Cleopatra's palace at
Alexandria.*

(CLEOPATRA *enters with* ENOBARBUS, CHARMIAN, *and* IRAS.)

CLEOPATRA.

What shall we do, Enobarbus?

ENOBARBUS.   Think, and die.

CLEOPATRA.

Is Antony or we in fault for this?

ENOBARBUS.

Antony only, that would make his will *   desire
Lord of his reason. What though you fled
From that great face of war, whose several ranges *   squadrons
Frighted each other? Why should he follow?
The itch of his affection should not then
Have nicked his captainship,[82] at such a point,
When half to half the world opposed, he being   9
The meered * question. 'Twas a shame no less   entire
Than was his loss, to course * your flying flags,   chase
And leave his navy gazing.

CLEOPATRA.   Prithee, peace.

(ANTONY *enters with* EUPHRONIUS, *the ambassador.*)
ANTONY.
   Is that his answer?
EUPHRONIUS.
   Ay, my lord.
ANTONY.
   The queen shall then have courtesy so she
   Will yield us up.
EUPHRONIUS.　　　He says so.
ANTONY.　　　　　　　Let her know 't.
   (*To* CLEOPATRA.)
   To the boy Caesar send this grizzled head,
   And he will fill thy wishes to the brim
   With Principalities.
CLEOPATRA.　　　　That head, my lord?
ANTONY (*to* EUPHRONIUS).
   To him again. Tell him he wears the rose　　　　　　20
   Of youth upon him; from which the world should note
   Something particular. His coin, ships, legions,
   May be a coward's, whose ministers * would prevail　　　agents
   Under the service of a child as soon
   As i' the command of Caesar. I dare him therefore
   To lay his gay comparisons * apart,　　　　　　caparisons
   And answer me declined,* sword against sword,　　*i.e.,* declined as I
   Ourselves alone. I'll write it: follow me.　　　　　am
(ANTONY *goes out, followed by* EUPHRONIUS.)
ENOBARBUS (*aside*).
   Yes, like enough, high-battled Caesar will　　　　　29
   Unstate * his happiness, and be staged to the show,　deprive himself
   Against a sworder! * 83 I see men's judgments are　　gladiator
   A parcel * of their fortunes; and things outward　　part
   Do draw the inward quality after them,
   To suffer all alike.84 That he should dream,
   Knowing all measures,* the full Caesar will　　　　fortunes
   Answer his emptiness! 85 Caesar, thou hast subdued
   His judgment too.
(*An* ATTENDANT *enters.*)
ATTENDANT.　　　　A messenger from Caesar.
CLEOPATRA.
   What, no more ceremony? See, my women!
   Against the blown * rose may they stop their nose　overblown
   That kneeled unto the buds. Admit him, sir.　　　　40
(*The* ATTENDANT *goes.*)

ENOBARBUS (*aside*).

  Mine honesty and I begin to square.*   square off
  The loyalty well held to fools does make
  Our faith mere folly: yet he that can endure
  To follow with allegiance a fall'n lord
  Does conquer him that did his master conquer,
  And earns a place i' the story.

(THYREUS *enters.*)

CLEOPATRA.   Caesar's will?

THYREUS.

  Hear it apart.

CLEOPATRA.   None but friends. Say boldly.

THYREUS.

  So, haply, are they friends to Antony.

ENOBARBUS (*to* THYREUS).

  He needs as many, sir, as Caesar has;
  Or needs not us. If Caesar please, our master   50
  Will leap to be his friend. For us, you know
  Whose he is we are, and that is, Caesar's.

THYREUS.   So.

  (*To* CLEOPATRA.)
  Thus then, thou most renowned: Caesar entreats,
  Not to consider in what case thou stand'st,
  Further than he is Caesar.

CLEOPATRA.   Go on. Right royal.

THYREUS.

  He knows that you embrace not Antony
  As you did love, but as you feared him.

CLEOPATRA.   Oh!

THYREUS.

  The scars upon your honor, therefore, he
  Does pity, as constrainèd blemishes,
  Not as deserved.

CLEOPATRA.   He is a god, and knows   60
  What is most right: mine honor was not yielded,
  But conquered merely.

ENOBARBUS (*aside*).   To be sure of that,
  I will ask Antony. Sir, sir, thou art so leaky,
  That we must leave thee to thy sinking, for
  Thy dearest quit thee.

(*He goes.*)

THYREUS.   Shall I say to Caesar
  What you require of him? For he partly begs

To be desired to give. It much would please him,
That of his fortunes you should make a staff
To lean upon; but it would warm his spirits,
To hear from me you had left Antony,   70
And put yourself under his shrowd,*   protection
The universal landlord.

CLEOPATRA.   What's your name?

THYREUS.

My name is Thyreus.

CLEOPATRA.   Most kind messenger,
Say to great Caesar this: in deputation *   by proxy
I kiss his conquering hand; tell him, I am prompt
To lay my crown at 's feet, and there to kneel;
Tell him, from his all-obeying breath I hear
The doom * of Egypt.   fate

THYREUS.   'Tis your noblest course.
Wisdom and fortune combating together,
If that the former dare but what it can,   80
No chance may shake it. Give me grace * to lay   the favor
My duty on your hand.

CLEOPATRA (as THYREUS kisses her hand).
                         Your Caesar's father oft,
When he hath mused of taking kingdoms in,
Bestowed his lips on that unworthy place,
As * it rained kisses.   as if

(ANTONY, followed by ENOBARBUS, enters in time to see the hand kissing.)

ANTONY.   Favors, by Jove that thunders!
What art thou, fellow?

THYREUS.   One that but performs
The bidding of the fullest * man, and worthiest   best-endowed
To have command obeyed.

ENOBARBUS (aside).   You will be whipped.

ANTONY (calling to GUARDS).
Approach, there! Ah, you kite! Now, gods and devils!
Authority melts from me: of late, when I cried, "Ho!"   90
Like boys unto a muss,⁸⁶ kings would start forth,
And cry, "Your will?" Have you no ears? I am
Antony yet.

(GUARDS enter.)
                    Take hence this Jack,* and whip him.   fellow

ENOBARBUS (aside).

'Tis better playing with a lion's whelp

Than with an old one dying.

ANTONY.   Moon and stars!
Whip him. Were 't twenty of the greatest tributaries
That do acknowledge Caesar, should I find them
So saucy with the hand of she here—what's her name,
Since she was Cleopatra? Whip him, fellows,   99
Till like a boy, you see him cringe * his face,   distort
And whine aloud for mercy. Take him hence.

THYREUS (*as the* GUARDS *start to take him away*) .
Mark Antony!

ANTONY.   Tug him away. Being whipped,
Bring him again. This Jack of Caesar's shall
Bear us an errand to him.

(*The* GUARDS *take* THYREUS *away.*)
(*To* CLEOPATRA.)
You were half blasted ere I knew you: ha!
Have I my pillow left unpressed in Rome,
Forborne the getting of a lawful race,
And by a gem of women, to be abused
By one that looks on feeders? *   menials

CLEOPATRA.   Good my lord—

ANTONY.
You have been a boggler * ever: *i.e.,* fickle
But when we in our viciousness grow hard—   111
Oh misery on 't!—the wise gods seel * our eyes;   sew up
In our own filth drop our clear judgments; make us
Adore our errors; laugh at 's, while we strut
To our confusion.

CLEOPATRA.   Oh, is 't come to this?

ANTONY.
I found you as a morsel cold upon
Dead Caesar's trencher; * nay, you were a fragment   platter
Of Cneius Pompey's; besides what hotter hours,
Unregistered in vulgar fame,* you have   common report
Luxuriously * picked out: for, I am sure,   licentiously
Though you can guess what temperance should be,   121
You know not what it is.

CLEOPATRA.   Wherefore is this?

ANTONY.
To let a fellow that will take rewards
And say, "God quit * you!" be familiar with   reward
My playfellow, your hand; [87] this kingly seal
And plighter of high hearts! Oh, that I were

Upon the hill of Basan, to outroar
The hornèd herd! [88] For I have savage cause;
And to proclaim it civilly,* were like   calmly
A haltered neck which does the hangman thank   130
For being yare * about him.   adroit
(*The* GUARDS *return, supporting* THYREUS *between them.*)
                                                Is he whipped?
FIRST ATTENDANT.
   Soundly, my lord.
ANTONY.   Cried he? And begged a' pardon?
FIRST ATTENDANT.
   He did ask favor.
ANTONY   (*to* THYREUS) .
   If that thy father live, let him repent
   Thou wast not made his daughter; and be thou sorry
   To follow Caesar in his triumph, since
   Thou hast been whipped for following him. Henceforth
   The white hand of a lady fever thee,
   Shake thou to look on 't. Get thee back to Caesar,
   Tell him thy entertainment.* Look, thou say   reception
   He makes me angry with him; for he seems   141
   Proud and disdainful, harping on what I am,
   Not what he knew I was. He makes me angry;
   And at this time most easy 'tis to do 't,
   When my good stars, that were my former guides,
   Have empty left their orbs,* and shot their fires   spheres
   Into the abysm of hell. If he mislike
   My speech and what is done, tell him he has
   Hipparchus, my enfranchèd bondman, whom
   He may at pleasure whip, or hang, or torture,   150
   As he shall like, to quit me. Urge it thou.
   Hence with thy stripes, begone!
(*The* GUARDS *take* THYREUS *out.*)
CLEOPATRA.
   Have you done yet?
ANTONY.   Alack, our terrene * moon   earthly
   Is now eclipsed; and it portends alone
   The fall of Antony!
CLEOPATRA.   I must stay his time.
ANTONY.
   To flatter Caesar, would you mingle eyes
   With one that ties his points? * [89]   laces
CLEOPATRA.   Not know me yet?

ANTONY.
Coldhearted toward me?

CLEOPATRA.   Ah, dear, if I be so,
From my cold heart let heaven engender hail,
And poison it in the source; and the first stone   160
Drop in my neck: as it determines,* so   ends
Dissolve my life! The next Caesarion smite
Till by degrees the memory of my womb,*   *i.e.,* my children
Together with my brave Egyptians all,
By the discandying * of this pelleted storm   dissolving
Lie graveless, till the flies and gnats of Nile
Have buried them for prey!

ANTONY.   I am satisfied.
Caesar sits down in Alexandria, where
I will oppose his fate. Our force by land
Hath nobly held; our severed navy too   170
Have knit again, and fleet,* threatening most sealike.   are afloat
Where hast thou been, my heart? Dost thou hear, lady?
If from the field I shall return once more
To kiss these lips, I will appear in blood;
I and my sword will earn our chronicle: *   chronicle of time
There's hope in 't yet.

CLEOPATRA.   That's my brave lord!

ANTONY.
I will be treble-sinewed, hearted, breathed,
And fight maliciously: for when mine hours
Were nice * and lucky, men did ransom lives   pampered
Of me for jests; but now I'll set my teeth,   181
And send to darkness all that stop me. Come,
Let's have one other gaudy night. Call to me
All my sad captains; fill our bowls once more;
Let's mock the midnight bell.

CLEOPATRA.   It is my birthday:
I had thought to have held it poor; but, since my lord
Is Antony again, I will be Cleopatra.

ANTONY.
We will yet do well.

CLEOPATRA.
Call all his noble captains to my lord.

ANTONY.
Do so, we'll speak to them; and tonight I'll force   190
The wine peep through their scars. Come on, my queen;
There's sap in 't yet. The next time I do fight,

I'll make death love me; for I will contend
Even with his pestilent * scythe.   plague-driven
(ANTONY *leads* CLEOPATRA *away, followed by* CHARMIAN, IRAS,
and all except ENOBARBUS.)

ENOBARBUS.
    Now he'll outstare the lightning. To be furious,*   frantic
    Is to be frightened out of fear; and in that mood
    The dove will peck the estridge; * and I see still,   *i.e.,* hawk
    A diminution in our captain's brain
    Restores his heart. When valor preys on reason,
    It eats the sword it fights with. I will seek   200
    Some way to leave him.
(ENOBARBUS *goes.*)

ACT IV

SCENE 1. Egypt. *Before Caesar's camp, on the outskirts of
Alexandria.*

(CAESAR's *army is drawn up, under the command of* AGRIPPA
and MECAENAS. CAESAR *enters, reading a letter.*)

CAESAR.
    He calls me boy, and chides, as * he had power   as if
    To beat me out of Egypt; my messenger
    He hath whipped with rods; dares me to personal combat,
    Caesar to Antony. Let the old ruffian know
    I have many other ways to die; meantime
    Laugh at his challenge.

MECAENAS.   Caesar must think,
    When one so great begins to rage, he's hunted
    Even to falling. Give him no breath, but now
    Make boot * of his distraction. Never anger   take advantage
    Made good guard for itself.

CAESAR.   Let our best heads   10
    Know, that tomorrow the last of many battles
    We mean to fight. Within our files * there are,   ranks
    Of those that served Mark Antony but late,
    Enough to fetch him in. See it done.
    And feast the army; we have store to do 't,
    And they have earned the waste.* Poor Antony!   *i.e.,* right to waste
(CAESAR *leaves, followed by* MECAENAS, AGRIPPA, *and the* ARMY.)

Scene 2. Egypt. *The throne room of Cleopatra's palace in Alexandria.*

(ANTONY *enters with* ENOBARBUS, *who is followed by* CLEOPATRA, CHARMIAN, IRAS, ALEXAS, *and* ATTENDANTS.)

ANTONY.

He will not fight with me, Domitius.

ENOBARBUS.   No.

ANTONY.

Why should he not?

ENOBARBUS.

He thinks, being twenty times of better fortune,
He is twenty men to one.

ANTONY.   Tomorrow, soldier,
By sea and land I'll fight. Or * I will live,   either
Or bathe my dying honor in the blood
Shall make it live again. Woo't thou fight well?

ENOBARBUS.

I'll strike, and cry, "Take all." 90

ANTONY   (*to an* ATTENDANT) .

Well said; come on.
Call forth my household servants: let's tonight
Be bounteous at our meal.

(*At the* ATTENDANT's *signal, some* SERVANTS *come in.* ANTONY *grasps each man's hand as he speaks to him.*)

Give me thy hand,   10
Thou hast been rightly honest—so hast thou—
Thou—and thou—and thou—you have served me well,
And kings have been your fellows.

CLEOPATRA   (*aside to* ENOBARBUS) .

What means this?

ENOBARBUS   (*aside to* CLEOPATRA) .

'Tis one of those odd tricks which sorrow shoots
Out of mind.

ANTONY.   And thou art honest too.
I wish I could be made * so many men,   made into
And all of you clapped * up together in   shut
Antony, that I might do you service
So good as you have done.

ALL.   The gods forbid!

ANTONY.

Well, my good fellows, wait on me tonight.   20
Scant not my cups; and make as much of me

As when mine empire was your fellow too,
And suffered my command.
CLEOPATRA   (*aside to* ENOBARBUS) .
What does he mean?
ENOBARBUS   (*aside to* CLEOPATRA) .
To make his followers weep.
ANTONY.
  Tend me tonight;
May be it is the period * of your duty.   end
Haply you shall not see me more; or if,
A mangled shadow. Perchance tomorrow
You'll serve another master. I look on you
As one that takes his leave. Mine honest friends,
I turn you not away; but, like a master   30
Married to your good service, stay till death.
Tend me tonight two hours, I ask no more,
And the gods yield * you for 't!   reward
ENOBARBUS   (*to* ANTONY) .   What mean you, sir!
To give them this discomfort? Look, they weep;
And I, an ass, am onion-eyed. For shame,
Transform us not to women.
ANTONY.   (*laughing*) .   Ho, ho, ho!
Now the witch * take me, if I meant it thus!   devil
Grace * grow where those drops fall! My hearty friends,   goodness
You take me in too dolorous a sense;
For I spake to you for your comfort; did desire you   40
To burn this night with torches. Know, my hearts,
I hope well of tomorrow; and will lead you
Where rather I'll expect victorous life
Than death and honor. Let's to supper, come,
And drown consideration.*   brooding
(*They all go.*)

SCENE 3. Egypt. *A courtyard before Cleopatra's palace in Alexandria.*

(*Two* SOLDIERS *meet to take their places on guard.*)
FIRST SOLDIER.
  Brother, good night. Tomorrow is the day.
SECOND SOLDIER.
  It will determine one way. Fare you well.
Heard you of nothing strange about the streets?

FIRST SOLDIER.
 Nothing. What news?
SECOND SOLDIER.
 Belike 'tis but a rumor. Good night to you.
FIRST SOLDIER.
 Well, sir, good night.
(*Two more* SOLDIERS *enter to take their posts.*)
SECOND SOLDIER.
 Soldiers, have careful watch.
THIRD SOLDIER.
 And you. Good night, good night.
(*The* SOLDIERS *place themselves at the four corners of the court-yard.*)
FOURTH SOLDIER.
 Here we: and if tomorrow
 Our navy thrive, I have an absolute hope   10
 Our landmen will stand up.
THIRD SOLDIER.   'Tis a brave army,
 And full of purpose.
(*The music of hautboys is heard, as if it comes from under their feet.*)
FOURTH SOLDIER.
 Peace! What noise?
FIRST SOLDIER.   List, list!
SECOND SOLDIER.
 Hark!
FIRST SOLDIER.
 Music i' the air.
THIRD SOLDIER.   Under the earth.
FOURTH SOLDIER.
 It signs * well, does it not?   augurs
THIRD SOLDIER.   No.
FIRST SOLDIER.   Peace, I say.
 What should this mean?
SECOND SOLDIER.
 'Tis the god Hercules, whom Antony loved,
 Now leaves him.
FIRST SOLDIER.
               Walk; let's see if other watchmen
 Do hear what we do.
SECOND SOLDIER.   Hear now, masters!
ALL   (*speaking together*).
                              How now!
 How now! Do you hear this?

FIRST SOLDIER. <div align="center">Ay; is 't not strange?</div> 20
THIRD SOLDIER.
  Do you hear, masters? Do you hear?
FIRST SOLDIER.
  Follow the noise so far as we have quarter; *   our post extends
  Let's see how it will give off.*   end
ALL. Content. 'Tis strange.
(*As the music continues, the* SOLDIERS *move off, listening.*[91])

SCENE. 4. Egypt. *The banquet room in Cleopatra's palace at Alexandria.*

(ANTONY, CLEOPATRA, CHARMIAN, *and* ATTENDANTS *are discovered as if at the end of a long night's festivity.*)
ANTONY.
  Eros! Mine armour, Eros!
(EROS *enters with* ANTONY's *armor.*)
CLEOPATRA. Sleep a little.
ANTONY.
  No, my chuck. Eros, come; mine armor, Eros!
  Come, good fellow, put mine iron on.
  If fortune be not ours today, it is
  Because we brave * her. Come.   defy
(*As* EROS *starts to arm* ANTONY, CLEOPATRA *joins him.*)
CLEOPATRA. Nay, I'll help too.
(*Holding up a piece of armor.*)
  What's this for?
ANTONY.   Ah, let be, let be! Thou art
  The armorer of my heart. False, false. This, this.
CLEOPATRA.
  Sooth, la, I'll help.
  (*Finding a strap.*)
       Thus it must be.
ANTONY.   Well, well;
  We shall thrive now.
  (*To* EROS.)
       Seest thou, my good fellow?
  Go put on thy defenses.
EROS.   Briefly, sir. 10
CLEOPATRA.
  Is not this buckled well?
ANTONY.   Rarely, rarely:
  He that unbuckles this, till we do please

To daff * 't for our repose, shall hear a storm.   doff
Thou fumblest, Eros; and my queen's a squire
More tight * at this than thou. Dispatch.   skillful
(*To* CLEOPATRA.)
                        O love,
That thou couldst see my wars today, and knew'st
The royal occupation! Thou shouldst see
A workman in 't.
(*As an armed* SOLDIER *enters.*)
              Good morrow to thee. Welcome.
Thou look'st like him that knows a warlike charge.
To business that we love we rise betime,   20
And go to 't with delight.
SOLDIER.   A thousand, sir,
Early though 't be, have on their riveted trim,*   armor
And at the port * expect you.   gate
(*Shouting and trumpets are heard from outside. A* CAPTAIN
and some SOLDIERS *enter.*)
CAPTAIN.
The morn is fair. Good morrow, general.
ALL.
Good morrow, general.
ANTONY.   'Tis well blown, lads.
This morning, like the spirit of a youth
That means to be of note, begins betimes.
(*To* CLEOPATRA, *taking his gauntlets as she finishes buckling
on his sword.*)
So, so. Come, give me that. This way. Well said.*   done
Fare thee well, dame, whate'er becomes of me.
(*Kisses her.*)
This is a soldier's kiss: rebukeable   30
And worthy shameful check * it were, to stand   reproof
On more mechanic compliment; * I'll leave thee   routine ceremony
Now, like a man of steel. You that will fight,
Follow me close; I'll bring you to 't. Adieu.
(ANTONY *leaves, followed by* EROS, CAPTAIN, *and* SOLDIERS.)
CHARMIAN   (*to* CLEOPATRA) .
Please you, retire to your chamber.
CLEOPATRA.   Lead me.
He goes forth gallantly. That he and Caesar might
Determine this great war in single fight!
Then, Antony—but now—well, on!
(CLEOPATRA, CHARMIAN, *and the* ATTENDANTS *go.*)

SCENE 5. Egypt. *Before Antony's camp in Alexandria.*

(*Trumpets sound.* ANTONY *and* EROS *enter, and are met by a* SOLDIER.)

SOLDIER.
The gods make this a happy day to Antony!

ANTONY.
Would thou and those thy scars had once prevailed
To make me fight at land!

SOLDIER.   Hadst thou done so,
The kings that have revolted, and the soldier
That has this morning left thee, would have still
Followed thy heels.

ANTONY.   Who's gone this morning?

SOLDIER.   Who!
One ever near thee: call for Enobarbus,
He shall not hear thee; or from Caesar's camp
Say, "I am none of thine."

ANTONY.   What say'st thou?

SOLDIER.   Sir,
He is with Caesar.

EROS.   Sir, his chests and treasure   10
He has not with him.

ANTONY.   Is he gone?

SOLDIER.   Most certain.

ANTONY.
Go, Eros, send his treasure after; do it;
Detain no jot, I charge thee. Write to him—
I will subscribe—gentle adieus and greetings;
Say that I wish he never find more cause
To change a master. Oh, my fortunes have
Corrupted honest men! Dispatch!
(EROS *and the* SOLDIERS *go.*)
                          Enobarbus!

(ANTONY *goes.*)

SCENE 6. Egypt. *Caesar's camp before Alexandria.*

(*Trumpets sound.* CAESAR *and* AGRIPPA *enter with* ENOBARBUS, *attended by* OFFICERS *and* SOLDIERS.)

CAESAR.
Go forth, Agrippa, and begin the fight.

  Our will is Antony be took alive;
  Make it so known.

AGRIPPA.
  Caesar, I shall.

(AGRIPPA *goes.*)

CAESAR.
  The time of universal peace is near.
  Prove this a prosperous day, the three-nooked * world   three-cornered
  Shall bear the olive freely.

(*A* MESSENGER *enters.*)

MESSENGER.   Antony
  Is come into the field.

CAESAR.   Go charge Agrippa
  Plant those that have revolted in the van,
  That Antony may seem to spend his fury   10
  Upon himself.

(*The* MESSENGER *leaves, followed by* CAESAR *and all the others,*
except ENOBARBUS) .

ENOBARBUS.
  Alexas did revolt; and went to Jewry on
  Affairs of Antony ;there did persuade
  Great Herod to incline himself to Caesar,
  And leave his master Antony: for this pains
  Caesar hath hanged him. Canidius and the rest
  That fell away have entertainment,* but   service
  No honorable trust. I have done ill;
  Of which I do accuse myself so sorely,
  That I will joy no more.

(*A* SOLDIER *of* CAESAR'*s army enters.*)

SOLDIER.   Enobarbus, Antony   20
  Hath after thee sent all thy treasure, with
  His bounty overplus. The messenger
  Came on my guard; and at thy tent is now
  Unloading of his mules.

ENOBARBUS.   I give it you.

SOLDIER.
  Mock not, Enobarbus.
  I tell you true: best you safed * the bringer   rendered safe
  Out of the host; I must attend mine office,
  Or would have done 't myself. Your emperor
  Continues still a Jove.

(*The* SOLDIER *goes.*)

ENOBARBUS.

    I am alone the villain of the earth,   30

    And feel I am so most. O Antony,

    Thou mine of bounty, how wouldst thou have paid

    My better service, when my turpitude

    Thou dost so crown with gold! This blows * my heart: swells

    If swift thought break it not, a swifter mean *   means

    Shall outstrike thought: but thought will do 't, I feel.

    I fight against thee! No: I will go seek

    Some ditch wherein to die; the foul'st best fits

    My latter part of life.

(ENOBARBUS *leaves.*)

SCENE 7.   Egypt. *Field of battle before Alexandria.*

(*Trumpets and drums are heard.* AGRIPPA *enters, with some of*
CAESAR'S SOLDIERS *and* OFFICERS.)

AGRIPPA.

    Retire, we have engaged ourselves too far:

    Caesar himself has work, and our oppression *   opponents

    Exceeds what we expected.

(*They go. More trumpets and drums are heard.* ANTONY *enters*
with SCARUS, *who is wounded.*)

SCARUS.

    O my brave emperor, this is fought indeed!

    Had we done so at first, we had droven them home

    With clouts * about their heads.   cloths

ANTONY.   Thou bleed'st apace.

SCARUS.

    I had a wound here that was like a T,

    But now 'tis made an H.⁹²

ANTONY.   They do retire.

SCARUS.

    We'll beat 'em into bench * holes: I have yet   privy

    Room for six scotches * more.   10 slashes

(EROS *enters.*)

EROS.

    They are beaten, sir; and our advantage serves

    For a fair victory.

SCARUS.   Let us score * their backs,   notch

    And snatch 'em up, as we take hares, behind:

    'Tis sport to maul a runner.

ANTONY.   I will reward thee
  Once for thy spritely comfort, and tenfold
  For thy good valor. Come thee on.
SCARUS.   I'll halt * after.   limp
(ANTONY *and* EROS *rush off;* SCARUS *limps after them.*)

SCENE 8. Egypt. *Under the walls of Alexandria.*

(*Trumpets and drums are heard* ANTONY *enters, followed by*
SCARUS *and marching* TROOPS.)
ANTONY.
  We have beat him to his camp.
  (*To an* OFFICER.)
                            Run one before,
  And let the queen know of our gests.* Tomorrow,   deeds
  Before the sun shall see 's, we'll spill the blood
  That has today escaped.
  (*A* MESSENGER *is dispatched.*)
                            I thank you all;
  For doughty-handed are you, and have fought
  Not as you served the cause, but as 't had been
  Each man's like mine; you have shown * all Hectors.[93]   shown yourselves
  Enter the city, clip * your wives, your friends,   embrace
  Tell them your feasts; whilst they with joyful tears
  Wash the congealment from your wounds, and kiss   10
  The honored gashes whole.
  (*To* SCARUS.)
                            Give me thy hand—
  (CLEOPATRA *enters on the walls, attended by her* WOMEN.)
  To this great fairy I'll commend thy acts,
  Make her thanks bless thee.
  (*To* CLEOPATRA.)
                            O thou day o' the world,
  Chain mine armed neck; leap thou, attire and all,
  Through proof of harness * to my heart, and there   sword-proof
                                                                        armor
  Ride on the pants * triumphing!   heartbeats
CLEOPATRA.   Lord of lords!
  O infinite virtue,* comest thou smiling from   valor
  The world's great snare uncaught?
ANTONY.   My nightingale,
  We have beat them to their beds. What, girl! though gray
  Do something mingle with our younger brown, yet ha' we   20

A brain that nourishes our nerves,* and can   sinews
Get goal for goal of youth.⁹⁴
(*Presenting* SCARUS.)
                     Behold this man;
Commend * unto his lips thy favoring hand: commit
Kiss it, my warrior. He hath fought today
As if a god, in hate of mankind, had
Destroyed in such a shape.
CLEOPATRA   (*to* SCARUS).   I'll give thee, friend,
An armor all of gold; it was a king's.
ANTONY.
He has deserved it, were it carbuncled
Like holy Phoebus' car.⁹⁵
(*To* SCARUS.)
                    Give me thy hand:
Through Alexandria make a jolly march;   30
Bear our hacked targets * like the men that owe them.   shields
Had our great palace the capacity
To camp this host, we all would sup together,
And drink carouses * to the next day's fate,   deep draughts
Which promises royal peril.
                 Trumpeters,
With brazen din blast you the city's ear;
Make mingle with our rattling tabourines; *   drums
That heaven and earth may strike their sounds together,
Applauding our approach.
(ANTONY, SCARUS, *and the* TROOPS *enter Alexandria, to the*
sound of trumpets and drums.)

SCENE 9. Egypt. *Caesar's camp outside Alexandria.*

(SENTINELS *are discovered at their posts.*)
FIRST SOLDIER.
If we be not relieved within this hour,
We must return to the court of guard.* The night   guardhouse
Is shiny; and they say we shall embattle
By the second hour i' the morn.
SECOND SOLDIER.   This last day was
A shrewd * one to 's.   grievous
(ENOBARBUS *enters.*)
ENOBARBUS   Oh, bear me witness, night—

THIRD SOLDIER   *(aside to other* SENTINELS) .
    What man is this?
SECOND SOLDIER   *(aside to other* SENTINELS) .
                        Stand close,* and list him.   concealed
ENOBARBUS.
    Be witness to me, O thou blessèd moon,
    When men revolted shall upon record
    Bear hateful memory, poor Enobarbus did
    Before thy face repent!
FIRST SOLDIER   *(aside)* . Enobarbus!
THIRD SOLDIER   *(aside)* .   Peace!   10
    Hark further.
ENOBARBUS.
    O sovereign mistress of true melancholy,
    The poisonous damp of night disponge * upon me,   squeeze out
    That life, a very rebel to my will,
    May hang no longer on me. Throw my heart
    Against the flint and hardness of my fault;
    Which, being dried with grief, will break to powder,
    And finish all foul thoughts. O Antony,
    Nobler than my revolt is infamous,   19
    Forgive me in thine own particular; *   *i.e.,* person
    But let the world rank me in register *   its records
    A master-leaver and a fugitive.
    O Antony! O Antony!
    (Sinks down.)
SECOND SOLDIER.   Let's speak
    To him.
FIRST SOLDIER.
    Let's hear him, for the things he speaks
    May concern Caesar.
THIRD SOLDIER.   Let's do so.
(As ENOBARBUS' *body settles.)*
                        But he sleeps.
FIRST SOLDIER.
    Swoons rather; for so bad a prayer as his
    Was never yet for sleep.
SECOND SOLDIER.   Go we to him.
THIRD SOLDIER   *(moving to him and shaking him)* .
    Awake, sir, awake; speak to us.
SECOND SOLDIER.   Hear you, sir?
FIRST SOLDIER.
    The hand of death hath raught * him.   reached

(*Distant drums are heard.*)

                              Hark! The drums   30
Demurely * wake the sleepers. Let us bear him   quietly
To the court of guard; he is of note. Our hour
Is fully out.
THIRD SOLDIER.
   Come on, then;
   He may recover yet.
(*The* SENTINELS *carry the body away.*)

SCENE 10. Egypt. *Between Antony's and Caesar's camps near Alexandria.*

(ANTONY *and* SCARUS *enter at the head of their* ARMY.)
ANTONY.
   Their preparation is today by sea;
   We please them not by land.
SCARUS.   For both, my lord.
ANTONY.
   I would they'd fight i' the fire or i' the air;
   We'd fight there too. But this it is: our foot
   Upon the hills adjoining to the city
   Shall stay with us. Order for sea is given.
   They have put forth the haven * . . .   harbor
   Where their appointment * we may best discover,   equipment
   And look on their endeavor.[96]
(ANTONY, SCARUS, *and their* ARMY *leave.*)

SCENE 11. Egypt. *Another part of the field between the camps near Alexandria.*

(CAESAR *enters at the head of his* ARMY.)
CAESAR.
   But being charged,* we will be still by land,   if attacked
   Which, as I take 't, we shall; for his best force
   Is forth to man his galleys. To the vales,
   And hold our best advantage.
(*They go.*)

Scene 12. Egypt. *Another part of the field.*

(ANTONY *and* SCARUS *enter.*)

ANTONY.

   Yet they are not joined. Where yond pine does stand,
   I shall discover all. I'll bring thee word
   Straight, how 'tis like to go.

(ANTONY *goes.*)

SCARUS.   Swallows have built

   In Cleopatra's sails their nests: the augurers
   Say they know not, they cannot tell; look grimly,
   And dare not speak their knowledge. Antony
   Is valiant, and dejected; and, by starts,
   His fretted * fortunes give him hope, and fear,   worn-away
   Of what he has, and has not.

(*Trumpets and drums are heard from a distance, along with
the sounds of a sea fight.* ANTONY *returns.*)

ANTONY.   All is lost;   10

   This foul Egyptian hath betrayed me:
   My fleet hath yielded to the foe; and yonder
   They cast their caps up and carouse together
   Like friends long lost. Triple-turned whore! 97 'Tis thou
   Hast sold me to this novice; and my heart
   Makes only wars on thee. Bid them all fly;
   For when I am revenged upon my charm, *   charmer
   I have done all. Bid them all fly; begone!

(SCARUS *leaves.*)

   O sun, thy uprise shall I see no more:
   Fortune and Antony part here; even here
   Do we shake hands. All come to this? The hearts   20
   That spanieled me at heels, to whom I gave
   Their wishes, do discandy,* melt their sweets   dissolve
   On blossoming Caesar; and this pine is barked,
   That overtopped them all. Betrayed I am.
   Oh this false soul of Egypt! This grave charm—
   Whose eye becked * forth my wars, and called them home;   beckoned
   Whose bosom was my crownet,* my chief end—   coronet
   Like a right gypsy, hath, at fast and loose,
   Beguilded me to the very heart of loss.
   What, Eros, Eros!

(*As he calls for* EROS, CLEOPATRA *enters.*)

                Ah, thou spell! Avaunt!   30

CLEOPATRA.

Why is my lord enraged against his love?

ANTONY.

Vanish, or I shall give thee thy deserving,
And blemish Caesar's triumph. Let him take thee,
And hoist thee up to the shouting plèbeians.
Follow his chariot, like the greatest spot *   stain
Of all thy sex; most monsterlike,* be shown   freaklike
For poor'st diminutives,* for doits; [98] and let   small change
Patient Octavia plow thy visage up
With her preparèd nails.

(CLEOPATRA *goes.*)

        'Tis well thou 'rt gone,
If it be well to live; but better 'twere   40
Thou fell'st into * my fury, for one death   before
Might have prevented many. Eros, ho!
The shirt of Nessus is upon me: teach me,
Alcides, thou mine ancestor, thy rage.
Let me lodge Lichas on the horn o' the moon; [99]
And with those hands, that grasped the heaviest club,
Subdue my worthiest self. The witch shall die:
To the young Roman boy she hath sold me, and I fall
Under this plot; she dies for 't. Eros, ho!

(*He goes.*)

SCENE 13. Egypt. *A hall in Cleopatra's palace at Alexandria.*

(CLEOPATRA *enters, meeting* CHARMIAN, IRAS, *and* MARDIAN.)

CLEOPATRA.

Help me, my women! Oh, he is more mad
Than Telamon for his shield; [100] the boar of Thessaly
Was never so embossed. * [101]   foaming with rage

CHARMIAN.   To the monument! *   tomb
There lock yourself, and send him word you are dead.
The soul and body rive not more in parting
Than greatness going off.

CLEOPATRA.   To the monument!
Mardian, go tell him I have slain myself;
Say, that the last I spoke was "Antony,"
And word it, prithee, piteously. Hence, Mardian,
And bring me how he takes my death. To the monument! 10

(MARDIAN *goes out one way, as* CLEOPATRA, CHARMIAN, *and* IRAS *go out another.*)

SCENE 14. Egypt. *A room in Cleopatra's palace at Alexandria.*

(ANTONY *and* EROS *enter.*)

ANTONY.
   Eros, thou yet behold'st me?

EROS.   Ay, noble lord.

ANTONY.
   Sometime we see a cloud that's dragonish;
   A vapor sometime like a bear or lion,
   A towered citadel, a pendent rock,
   A forkèd mountain, or blue promontory
   With trees upon 't, that nod unto the world,
   And mock our eyes with air. Thou hast seen these signs;
   They are black vesper's * pageants.   evening's

EROS.   Ay, my lord.

ANTONY.
   That which is now a horse, even with a thought
   The rack * dislimns,* and makes it indistinct,   cloud/fades
   As water is in water.   10

EROS.   It does, my lord.

ANTONY.
   My good knave Eros, now thy captain is
   Even such a body: here I am Antony;
   Yet cannot hold this visible shape, my knave.
   I made these wars for Egypt; and the queen—
   Whose heart I thought I had, for she had mine;
   Which whilst it was mine had annexed unto 't
   A million more, now lost—she, Eros, has
   Packed * cards with Caesar, and false-played my glory   stacked
   Unto an enemy's triumph.   20
   Nay, weep not, gentle Eros; there is left us
   Ourselves to end ourselves.

(MARDIAN *enters.*)

                        Oh, thy vile lady!
   She has robbed me of my sword.

MARDIAN.   No, Antony;
   My mistress loved thee, and her fortunes mingled
   With thine entirely.

ANTONY.   Hence, saucy eunuch; peace!
   She hath betrayed me and shall die the death.

MARDIAN.

Death of one person can be paid but once,
And that she has discharged: what thou wouldst do
Is done unto thy hand. The last she spake
Was "Antony! Most noble Antony!"   30
Then in the midst a tearing groan did break
The name of Antony; it was divided
Between her heart and lips: she rendered * life,   surrendered
Thy name so buried in her.

ANTONY.   Dead, then?

MARDIAN.   Dead.

ANTONY.

Unarm, Eros; the long day's task is done,
And we must sleep.
(*To* MARDIAN.)
                    That thou depart'st hence safe,
Does pay thy labor richly; go.
(MARDIAN *goes, and* EROS *begins to help remove* ANTONY's
armor.)
                    Off, pluck off.
The sevenfold shield of Ajax cannot keep
The battery * from my heart. Oh, cleave, my sides!   39 assault
Heart, once be stronger than thy continent,*   what contains you
Crack thy frail case! Apace,* Eros, apace.   hurry
No more a soldier: bruisèd pieces, go;
You have been nobly borne. From me awhile.
(EROS *goes.*)
I will o'ertake thee, Cleopatra, and
Weep for my pardon. So it must be, for now
All length * is torture. Since the torch is out,   *i.e.,* length of life
Lie down, and stray no farther. Now all labor
Mars what it does; yea, very force entangles
Itself with strength. Seal then, and all is done.
Eros!—I come, my queen—Eros!—Stay for me: 50
Where souls do couch on flowers. we'll hand in hand,
And with our sprightly port * make the ghosts gaze.   deportment
Dido and her Aeneas shall want troops,*   lack admirers
And all the haunt be ours.[102] Come, Eros, Eros!
(EROS *returns.*)

EROS.

What would my lord?

ANTONY.   Since Cleopatra died,
I have lived in such dishonor, that the gods
Detest my baseness. I, that with my sword

Quartered the world, and o'er green Neptune's back
With ships made cities, condemn myself to lack
The courage of a woman; less noble mind   60
Than she which by her death our Caesar tells,
"I am conqueror of myself." Thou art sworn, Eros,
That, when the exigent * should come, which now   exigency
Is come indeed, when I should see behind me
The inevitable prosecution * of   pursuit
Disgrace and horror, that, on my command,
Thou then wouldst kill me. Do 't. The time is come.
Thou strikes not me, 'tis Caesar thou defeat'st.
Put color in thy cheek.
EROS.   The gods withhold me!
Shall I do that which all the Parthian darts,   70
Though enemy, lost aim, and could not?
ANTONY.   Eros,
Wouldst thou be windowed in great Rome and see
Thy master thus with pleached * arms, bending down   folded
His corrigible * neck, his face subdued   submissive
To penetrative shame, whilst the wheeled seat
Of fortunate Caesar, down before him, branded
His baseness * that ensued?   abasement
EROS.   I would not see 't.
ANTONY.
Come, then; for with a wound I must be cured.
Draw that thy honest * sword, which thou hast worn   honorable
Most useful for thy country.
EROS.   Oh, sir, pardon me!   80
ANTONY.
When I did make thee free, sworest thou not then
To do this when I bade thee? Do it at once;
Or thy precedent services are all
But accidents unpurposed. Draw, and come.
EROS.
Turn from me, then, that noble countenance,
Wherein the worship of the whole world lies.
ANTONY *(turning away)*.
Lo thee!
EROS *(drawing his sword)*.
My sword is drawn.
ANTONY.   Then let it do at once
The thing why thou hast drawn it.
EROS.   My dear master.

My captain, and my emperor, let me say,   90
Before I strike this bloody stroke, farewell.
ANTONY.
  'Tis said, man; and farewell.
EROS.
  Farewell, great chief. Shall I strike now?
ANTONY.
  Now, Eros.
EROS.
  Why, there then: thus I do escape the sorrow
  Of Antony's death.
(Falls on his own sword and dies.)
ANTONY.   Thrice nobler than myself!
  Thou teachest me, O valiant Eros, what
  I should, and thou couldst not. My queen and Eros
  Have by their brave instruction got upon * me   **gained from**
  A nobleness in record. But I will be
  A bridegroom in my death, and run into 't   100
  As to a lover's bed.
  (Drawing his sword.)
            Come, then; and, Eros,
  Thy master dies thy scholar: to do thus
  I learned of thee.
  (Falling on his sword.)
          How! Not dead? Not dead?
  The guard, ho! Oh, dispatch me!
(DERCETAS *and some* GUARDS *enter.*)
FIRST GUARD.   What's the noise?
ANTONY.
  I have done my work ill, friends. Oh, make an end
  Of what I have begun.
SECOND GUARD *(discovering where* ANTONY *has fallen)*.
          The star is fallen.
FIRST GUARD.
  And time is at his period.*   **its end**
ALL.   Alas, and woe!
ANTONY.
  Let him that loves me strike me dead.
FIRST GUARD.   Not I.
SECOND GUARD.
  Nor I.
THIRD GUARD.
  Nor anyone.   110

(*The* GUARDS *leave.*)

DERCETAS.

    Thy death and fortunes bid thy followers fly.

    (*Taking* ANTONY's *sword.*)

    This sword but shown to Caesar, with this tidings,

    Shall enter me * with him.   give me a place

(DIOMEDES *enters.*)

    Where's Antony?

DERCETAS.   There, Diomed, there.

DIOMEDES.   Lives he?

    (*Calling after* DERCETAS *as he leaves.*)

    Wilt thou not answer, man?

ANTONY.

    Art thou there, Diomed? Draw thy sword, and give me

    Sufficing strokes for death.

DIOMEDES.   Most absolute lord,

    My mistress Cleopatra sent me to thee.

ANTONY.

    When did she send thee?

DIOMEDES.   Now, my lord.

ANTONY.   Where is she?

DIOMEDES.

    Locked in her monument. She had a prophesying fear   120

    Of what hath come to pass: for when she saw—

    Which never shall be found *—you did suspect   found true

    She had disposed * with Caesar, and that your rage   come to terms

    Would not be purged, she sent you word she was dead;

    But, fearing since how it might work, hath sent

    Me to proclaim the truth; and I am come,

    I dread, too late.

ANTONY.

    Too late, good Diomed: call my guard, I prithee.

DIOMEDES (*going to the door*).

    What, ho, the emperor's guard! The guard, what, ho!

    Come, your lord calls!   130

(*Some members of* ANTONY's *guard enter.*)

ANTONY.

    Bear me, good friends, where Cleopatra bides;

    'Tis the last service that I shall command you.

FIRST GUARD.

    Woe, woe are we sir, you may not live to wear

    All your true followers out.

ALL.   Most heavy day!

ANTONY.

   Nay, good my fellows, do not please sharp fate
   To grace it with your sorrows. Bid that welcome
   Which comes to punish us, and we punish it
   Seeming to bear it lightly. Take me up.
   I have led you oft: carry me now, good friends,
   And have my thanks for all.   140
(DIOMEDES *and the* GUARDS *leave, carrying* ANTONY.)

SCENE 15. Egypt. *A monument in a courtyard of Cleopatra's palace at Alexandria.*

(CLEOPATRA, CHARMIAN, *and* IRAS *enter on top of the monument, attended by some* MAIDS.)
CLEOPATRA.

   O Charmian, I will never go from hence.
CHARMIAN.

   Be comforted, dear madam.
CLEOPATRA.   No, I will not:
   All strange and terrible events are welcome,
   But comforts we despise; our size of sorrow,
   Proportioned to our cause, must be as great
   As that which makes it.
   (*To* DIOMEDES, *who enters below.*)
                  How now! Is he dead?
DIOMEDES.

   His death's upon him, but not dead.
   Look out o' the other side your monument;
   His guard have brought him thither.
(ANTONY *is borne in, on a litter, below, by the* GUARDS.)
CLEOPATRA.   O sun,
   Burn the great sphere thou movest in! [103] Darkling * stand   10   dark
   The varying shore o' the world. O Antony,
   Antony, Antony! Help, Charmian, help, Iras, help;
   Help, friends below; let's draw him hither.
ANTONY.   Peace!
   Not Caesar's valor hath o'erthrown Antony,
   But Antony's hath triumphed on itself.
CLEOPATRA.

   So it should be, that none but Antony
   Should conquer Antony; but woe 'tis so!

ANTONY.

   I am dying, Egypt, dying; only
   I here importune death awhile, until
   Of many thousand kisses the poor last   20
   I lay upon thy lips.

CLEOPATRA.   I dare not, dear—

   Dear my lord, pardon—I dare not,
   Lest I be taken. Not the imperious * show   *imperial*
   Of the full-fortuned Caesar ever shall
   Be brooched * with me. If knife, drugs, serpents, have   *ornamented*
   Edge, sting, or operation, I am safe.
   Your wife Octavia, with her modest eyes
   And still conclusion,* shall acquire no honor   *inference*
   Demuring upon me. But come, come, Antony—
   Help me, my women—we must draw thee up: 30
   Assist, good friends.

(*The* GUARDS *below lift* ANTONY's *body high enough on the litter so that the* WOMEN *can grasp it.*)

ANTONY.   Oh, quick, or I am gone.

CLEOPATRA.

   Here's sport indeed! How heavy weighs my lord!
   Our strength is all gone into heaviness,
   That makes the weight. Had I great Juno's power,
   The strong-winged Mercury should fetch thee up,
   And set thee by Jove's side.[104] Yet come a little—
   Wishers were ever fools—oh, come, come, come;

(*The* WOMEN *succeed in getting* ANTONY *into the monument, and* CLEOPATRA, *kneeling, embraces him.*)

   And welcome, welcome! Die where thou hast lived.
   Quicken * with kissing: had my lips that power,   *revive*
   Thus would I wear them out.

ALL.   A heavy sight!   40

ANTONY.

   I am dying, Egypt, dying:
   Give me some wine, and let me speak a little.

CLEOPATRA.

   No, let me speak; and let me rail so high,
   That the false housewife Fortune break her wheel,[105]
   Provoked by my offense.

ANTONY.   One word, sweet queen:
   Of Caesar seek your honor, with your safety. Oh!

CLEOPATRA.

   They do not go together.

ANTONY.   Gentle, hear me:
   None about Caesar trust but Proculeius.
CLEOPATRA.
   My resolution and my hands I'll trust;
   None about Caesar.   50
ANTONY.
   The miserable change now at my end
   Lament nor sorrow at; but please your thoughts
   In feeding them with those my former fortunes
   Wherein I lived, the greatest prince o' the world,
   The noblest; and do now not basely die,
   Not cowardly put off my helmet to
   My countryman—a Roman by a Roman
   Valiantly vanquished. Now my spirit is going;
   I can no more.
CLEOPATRA.   Noblest of men, woo't die?
   Hast thou no care of me? Shall I abide   60
   In this dull world, which in thy absence is
   No better than a sty?
(ANTONY *dies*.)
                          Oh, see, my women,
   The crown o' the earth doth melt.
   (*Embracing his body*.)
                                My lord!
   Oh, withered is the garland of the war,
   The soldier's pole * is fall'n. Young boys and girls   **standard**
   Are level now with men; the odds * is gone,   **inequality**
   And there is nothing left remarkable
   Beneath the visiting moon.
   (*She faints*.)
CHARMIAN.   Oh, quietness, lady!
IRAS.
   She is dead too, our sovereign.
CHARMIAN.   Lady!
IRAS.   Madam!
CHARMIAN.
   O madam, madam, madam!
IRAS.   Royal Egypt,   70
   Empress!
CHARMIAN (*as* CLEOPATRA *revives*) .
   Peace, peace, Iras!
CLEOPATRA.
   No more, but e'en a woman, and commanded

By such poor passion as the maid that milks
And does the meanest chares.* It were for me   chores
To throw my scepter at the injurious gods;
To tell them that this world did equal theirs
Till they had stol'n our jewel. All's but naught;
Patience is sottish,* and impatience does   stupid
Become a dog that's mad. Then is it sin   80
To rush into the secret house of death,
Ere death dare come to us? How do you, women?
What, what! Good cheer! Why, how now, Charmian!
My noble girls! Ah, women, women, look,
Our lamp is spent, it's out!
(*To* DIOMEDES *and the* GUARDS *below.*)
                              Good sirs, take heart.
We'll bury him; and then, what's brave, what's noble,
Let's do it after the high Roman fashion,
And make death proud to take us. Come, away.
This case of that hugh spirit now is cold.
Ah, women, women! Come; we have no friend   90
But resolution, and the briefest end.
(*All leave, the* WOMEN *above bearing off* ANTONY's *body.*)

ACT V

SCENE 1. Egypt. *Caesar's camp before Alexandria. Before Caesar's tent.*

(CAESAR *enters with* AGRIPPA, DOLABELLA, MECAENAS, GALLUS, PROCULEIUS, *and various* CAPTAINS *and* SOLDIERS. *They seat themselves at a council of war.*)
CAESAR.
   Go to him, Dolabella, bid him yield;
   Being so frustrate, tell him he mocks *   makes absurd
   The pauses * that he makes.   delays
DOLABELLA.   Caesar, I shall.
(DOLABELLA *goes.* DERCETAS *enters with the sword of* ANTONY.)
CAESAR.
   Wherefore is that? And what art thou that darest
   Appear thus to us?
DERCETAS.   I am called Dercetas;
   Mark Antony I served, who best was worthy
   Best to be served. Whilst he stood up and spoke,

He was my master; and I wore my life
To spend upon his haters. If thou please
To take me to thee, as I was to him   10
I'll be to Caesar; if thou pleasest not,
I yield thee up my life.

CAESAR.   What is 't thou say'st?

DERCETAS.

I say, O Caesar, Antony is dead.

CAESAR.

The breaking of so great a thing should make
A greater crack: * the round world   noise
Should have shook lions into civil streets,[106]
And citizens to their dens. The death of Antony
Is not a single doom; in the name lay
A moiety * of the world.   one half

DERCETAS.   He is dead, Caesar;
Not by a public minister of justice,   20
Nor by a hired knife; but that self hand,
Which writ his honor in the acts it did,
Hath, with the courage which the heart did lend it,
Splitted the heart. This is his sword;
I robbed his wound of it; behold it stained
With his most noble blood.

CAESAR *(to his* OFFICERS) *.* Look you sad, friends?
The gods rebuke me, but it is tidings
To wash the eyes of kings.

AGRIPPA.   And strange it is,
That nature must compel us to lament
Our most persisted deeds.

MECAENAS.   His taints and honors   30
Waged * equal with him.   contended

AGRIPPA.   A rarer spirit never
Did steer humanity; but you, gods, will give us
Some faults to make us men.
                                   Caesar is touched.

MECAENAS.

When such a spacious mirror's set before him,
He needs must see himself.

CAESAR.   O Antony!
I have followed thee to this; but we do lance
Diseases in our bodies. I must perforce
Have shown to thee such a declining day,
Or look on thine; we could not stall * together   dwell

In the whole world; but yet let me lament,   40
With tears as sovereign * as the blood of hearts,   potent
That thou, my brother, my competitor
In top * of all design,* my mate in empire,   highest/ventures
Friend and companion in the front of war,
The arm of mine own body, and the heart
Where mine his thoughts did kindle—that our stars,
Unreconciliable, should divide *   reduce
Our equalness to this. Hear me, good friends—
(*An* EGYPTIAN *enters.*)
But I will tell you at some meeter reason:
The business of this man looks out of him: 50
We'll hear him what he says. Whence are you?
EGYPTIAN (*kneeling*).
    A poor Egyptian yet. The queen my mistress,
    Confined in all she has, her monument,
    Of thy intends desires instruction,
    That she preparedly may frame * herself   adjust
    To the way she's forced to.
CAESAR.   Bid her have good heart.
    She soon shall know of us, by some of ours,
    How honorable and how kindly we
    Determine for her; for Caesar cannot live
    To be ungentle.
EGYPTIAN.
    So the gods preserve thee!   60
(*The* EGYPTIAN *goes.*)
CAESAR.
    Come hither, Proculeius. Go and say,
    We purpose her no shame. Give her what comforts
    The quality of her passion * shall require,   emotion
    Lest, in her greatness, by some mortal stroke
    She do defeat us; for her life * in Rome   living presence
    Would be eternal in our triumph.[107] Go,
    And with your speediest bring us what she says,
    And how you find of her.
PROCULEIUS.   Caesar, I shall.
(PROCULEIUS *goes.*)
CAESAR.
    Gallus, go you along.
    (*To the others, as* GALLUS *goes.*)
                          Where's Dolabella,
    To second Proculeius?

ALL *(calling)*.   Dolabella!   70
CAESAR.
    Let him alone, for I remember now
    How he's employed. He shall in time be ready.
    Go with me to my tent, where you shall see
    How hardly * I was drawn into this war;   reluctantly
    How calm and gentle I proceeded still
    In all my writings.* Go with me, and see   communications
    What I can show in this.
(CAESAR goes into his tent, and all follow.)

SCENE 2. Egypt. *The monument in Cleopatra's courtyard at Alexandria.*

(CLEOPATRA, CHARMIAN, and IRAS enter.)
CLEOPATRA.
    My desolation does begin to make
    A better life. 'Tis paltry to be Caesar;
    Not being Fortune, he's but Fortune's knave,*   servant
    A minister of her will; and it is great
    To do that thing that ends all other deeds—
    Which shackles accidents and bolts up change;
    Which sleeps, and never palates * more the dung,   tastes
    The beggar's nurse * and Caesar's.[108]   nourishment
(PROCULEIUS, GALLUS, and some of CAESAR's SOLDIERS enter the courtyard and stop at the barred gates of the monument.)
PROCULEIUS.
    Caesar sends greetings to the Queen of Egypt;
    And bids thee study on what fair demands   10
    Thou mean'st to have him grant thee.
CLEOPATRA.   What's thy name?
PROCULEIUS.
    My name is Proculeius.
CLEOPATRA.   Antony
    Did tell me of you, bade me trust you; but
    I do not greatly care to be * deceived,   *i.e.,* whether I am
    That have no use for trusting. If your master
    Would have a queen his beggar, you must tell him,
    That majesty, to keep decorum, must
    No less beg than a kingdom. If he please
    To give me conquered Egypt for my son,

He gives me so much of mine own, as I   20
Will kneel to him with thanks.
PROCULEIUS.   Be of good cheer.
You're fall'n into a princely hand, fear nothing;
Make your full reference * freely to my lord,   appeal
Who is so full of grace, that it flows over
On all that need. Let me report to him
Your sweet dependency; * and you shall find   submission
A conqueror that will pray * in aid for kindness,[109]   invoke
Where he for grace * is kneeled to.   favor
CLEOPATRA.   Pray you, tell him
I am his fortune's vassal, and I send him
The greatness he has got. I hourly learn   30
A doctrine of obedience; and would gladly
Look him i' the face.
PROCULEIUS.   This I'll report, dear lady.
Have comfort, for I know your plight is pitied
Of him that caused it.
GALLUS *(aside to* PROCULEIUS*)*.
You see how easily she may be surprised.
(While CLEOPATRA's *attention is diverted,* PROCULEIUS *and*
SOLDIERS *succeed in entering the monument and coming up
behind* CLEOPATRA *and her* ATTENDANTS. *Some* SOLDIERS *unbar
and open the gates.[110])*
                              Guard her till Caesar comes.
(He goes.)
IRAS.
Royal queen!
CHARMIAN.
O Cleopatra! Thou art taken, queen.
CLEOPATRA *(drawing a dagger)*.
Quick, quick, good hands.
PROCULEIUS *(seizing and disarming her)*.
Do not yourself such wrong, who are in this   40
Relieved, but not betrayed.
CLEOPATRA.   What, of death too,
That rids our dogs of languish? *   lingering disease
PROCULEIUS.   Cleopatra,
Do not abuse * my master's bounty by   cheat
The undoing of yourself. Let the world see
His nobleness well acted, which your death
Will never let come forth.
CLEOPATRA.   Where art thou, death?

Come hither, come! Come, come, and take a queen
Worth many babes and beggars!
PROCULEIUS.   Oh, temperance,* lady!   self-control
CLEOPATRA.
Sir, I will eat no meat, I'll not drink, sir;
If idle talk will once * be necessary,   for once
I'll not sleep neither. This mortal house I'll ruin,   51
Do Caesar what he can. Know, sir, that I
Will not wait * pinioned at your master's court;   attend
Nor once be chastised with the sober eye
Of dull Octavia. Shall they hoist me up
And show me to the shouting varletry *   rabble
Of censuring * Rome? Rather a ditch in Egypt   judging
Be gentle grave unto me! Rather on Nilus' mud
Lay me stark naked, and let the water flies   59
Blow me into abhorring! * Rather make   a thing abhorred
My country's high pyramides my gibbet,
And hang me up in chains!
PROCULEIUS.   You do extend
These thoughts of horror further than you shall
Find cause in Caesar.
(DOLABELLA *enters*.)
DOLABELLA.   Proculeius,
What thou hast done thy master Caesar knows,
And he hath sent for thee: for the queen,
I'll take her to my guard.
PROCULEIUS.   So, Dolabella,
It shall content me best: be gentle to her.
(*To* CLEOPATRA.)
To Caesar I will speak what you shall please,
If you'll employ me to him.
CLEOPATRA.   Say, I would die.   70
(PROCULEIUS *and the* GUARDS *go*.)
DOLABELLA.
Most noble empress, you have heard of me?
CLEOPATRA.
I cannot tell.
DOLABELLA.   Assuredly you know me.
CLEOPATRA.
No matter, sir, what I have heard or known.
You laugh when boys or women tell their dreams;
Is 't not your trick?
DOLABELLA.   I understand not, madam.

CLEOPATRA.
> I dreamed there was an Emperor Antony—
> Oh, such another sleep, that I might see
> But such another man!

DOLABELLA.   If it might please ye—

CLEOPATRA.
> His face was as the heavens; and therein stuck
> A sun and moon, which kept their course, and lighted   80
> The little O, the earth.

DOLABELLA.   Most sovereign creature—

CLEOPATRA.
> His legs bestrid the ocean. His reared arm
> Crested * the world; his voict was propertied *   crowned/qualitied
> As all the tunèd spheres,¹¹¹ and that to friends;
> But when he meant to quail * and shake the orb,   cause to quail
> He was as rattling thunder. For his bounty,
> There was no winter in 't; an autumn 'twas
> That grew the more by reaping; his delights
> Were dolphinlike: they showed his back above
> The elements they lived in. In his livery   90
> Walked crowns and crownets; * realms and islands were   coronets
> As plates * dropped from his pocket.   coins

DOLABELLA.   Cleopatra!

CLEOPATRA.
> Think you there was, or might be, such a man
> As this I dreamed of?

DOLABELLA.   Gentle madam, no.

CLEOPATRA.
> You lie, up to the hearing of the gods.
> But, if there be, or ever were, one such,
> It's past the size of dreaming: nature wants stuff
> To vie strange forms with fancy; yet, to imagine
> An Antony were nature's piece * 'gainst fancy,   masterpiece
> Condemning shadows quite.¹¹²

DOLABELLA.   Hear me, good madam.   100
> Your loss is as yourself, great; and you bear it
> As answering * to the weight. Would I might never   according
> O'ertake pursued success, but I do * feel,   *i.e.,* if I do not
> By the rebound of yours, a grief that smites
> My very heart at root.

CLEOPATRA.   I thank you, sir.
> Know you what Caesar means to do with me?

DOLABELLA.

I am loath to tell you what I would you knew.

CLEOPATRA.

Nay, pray you sir—

DOLABELLA.   Though he be honorable—

CLEOPATRA.

He'll lead me, then, in triumph?

DOLABELLA.

Madam, he will; I know 't.   110

(*Trumpets are heard, and a shout of* "Make way there: Caesar!" CAESAR *enters, followed by* GALLUS, PROCULEIUS, MECAENAS,
SELEUCUS, *and others of his train.*)

CAESAR.

Which is the Queen of Egypt?

DOLABELLA.

It is the emperor, madam.

(CLEOPATRA *kneels.*)

CAESAR.

Arise, you shall not kneel.

I pray you, rise, Egypt.

CLEOPATRA.   Sirs, the gods

Will have it thus; my master and my lord

I must obey.

CAESAR.   Take to you no hard thoughts:

The record of what injuries you did us,

Though written in our flesh, we shall remember

As things but done by chance.

CLEOPATRA.   Sole sir o' the world,   120

I cannot project mine own cause so well

To make it clear; but do confess I have

Been laden with like frailties which before

Have often shamed our sex.

CAESAR.   Cleopatra, know,

We will extenuate rather than enforce.

If you apply yourself to our intents,

Which towards you are most gentle, you shall find

A benefit in this change; but if you seek

To lay * on me a cruelty, by taking   force

Antony's course, you shall bereave yourself   130

Of my good purposes, and put your children

To that destruction which I'll guard them from,

If thereon you rely. I'll take my leave.

CLEOPATRA.
 And may, through all the world. 'Tis yours; and we,
 Your scutcheons * and your signs of conquest, shall   shields
 Hang in what place you please.
 (*Hands* CAESAR *a scroll.*)
         Here, my good lord.

CAESAR.
 You shall advise me in all for Cleopatra.

CLEOPATRA.
 This is the brief * of money, plate, and jewels,   list
 I am possessed of. 'Tis exactly valued;
 Not petty things admitted.* Where's Seleucus?   omitted

SELEUCUS (*coming forward*).
 Here, madam.   141

CLEOPATRA.
 This is my treasurer: let him speak, my lord,
 Upon his peril, that I have reserved
 To myself nothing.
 (*As* SELEUCUS *examines the scroll.*)
       Speak the truth, Seleucus.

SELEUCUS.
 Madam,
 I had rather seal my lips, than, to my peril,
 Speak that which is not.

CLEOPATRA.   What have I kept back?

SELEUCUS.
 Enough to purchase what you have made known.

CAESAR.
 Nay, blush not, Cleopatra; I approve
 Your wisdom in the deed.

CLEOPATRA.   See, Caesar! Oh, behold   150
 How pomp is followed! Mine * will now be yours, *i.e.,* followers
 And, should we shift estates,* yours would be mine. positions
 The ingratitude of this Seleucus does
 Even make me wild. O slave, of no more trust
 Than love that's hired! What, goest thou back? Thou shalt
 Go back, I warrant thee; but I'll catch thine eyes,
 Though they had wings. Slave, soulless villain, dog!
 Oh rarely base!

CAESAR.   Good queen, let us entreat you.

CLEOPATRA.
 O Caesar, what a wounding shame is this,

That thou, vouchsafing here to visit me,   160
Doing the honor of thy lordliness
To one so meek, that mine own servant should
Parcel * the sum of my disgraces by   specify
Addition of his envy! * Say, good Caesar,   malice
That I some lady trifle have reserved,
Immoment * toys, things of such dignity   insignificant
As we greet modern * friends withal; and say,   casual
Some nobler token I have kept apart
For Livia and Octavia, to induce   169
Their mediation—must I be unfolded *   exposed
With * one that I have bred? The gods! It smites me   by
Beneath the fall I have.
(*To* SELEUCUS.)
                              Prithee, go hence;
Or I shall show the cinders of my spirits
Through the ashes of my chance. * Wert thou a man,   fortune
Thou wouldst have mercy on me.
CAESAR.   Forbear, Seleucus.
(SELEUCUS *leaves.*)
CLEOPATRA.
Be it known, that we, the greatest, are misthought *   misjudged
For things that others do; and, when we fall,
We answer * others' merits * in our name,   answer for/deserts
Are therefore to be pitied.
CAESAR.   Cleopatra,
Not what you have reserved, nor what acknowledged,   180
Put we 'i the roll of conquest.* Still be 't yours,   list of spoils
Bestow it at your pleasure; and believe,
Caesar's no merchant, to make prize with you
Of things that merchants sold. Therefore be cheered;
Make not your thoughts your prisons.[113] No, dear queen;
For we intend so to dispose you as
Yourself shall give us counsel. Feed, and sleep.
Our care and pity is so much upon you,
That we remain your friend. And so, adieu.
CLEOPATRA
My master, and my lord!
CAESAR.   Not so. Adieu.   190
(*Trumpets sound.* CAESAR *leaves, followed by his* OFFICERS *and*
SOLDIERS.)
CLEOPATRA.
He words me, girls, he words me, that I should not

Be noble to myself. But, hark thee, Charmian.
(*Whispers to* CHARMIAN.)

IRAS.
  Finish, good lady; the bright day is done,
  And we are for the dark.

CLEOPATRA   (*to* CHARMIAN) .
                              Hie thee again.
  I have spoke already, and it is provided;
  Go put it to the haste.

CHARMIAN.   Madam, I will.
(DOLABELLA *returns.*)

DOLABELLA.
  Where is the queen?

CHARMIAN.   Behold, sir.

CLEOPATRA.   Dolabella!

DOLABELLA.
  Madam, as thereto sworn by your command,
  Which my love makes religion to obey,
  I tell you this: Caesar through Syria   200
  Intends his journey, and within three days
  You with your children will he send before.
  Make your best use of this. I have performed
  Your pleasure and my promise.

CLEOPATRA.   Dolabella,
  I shall remain your debtor.

DOLABELLA.   I your servant.
  Adieu, good queen; I must attend on Caesar.

CLEOPATRA.
  Farewell, and thanks.
  (DOLABELLA *goes.*)
                              Now, Iras, what think'st thou?
  Thou, an Egyptian puppet, shalt be shown
  In Rome, as well as I. Mechanic slaves *   *i.e.,* laborers
  With greasy aprons, rules, and hammers, shall   210
  Uplift us to the view; in their thick breaths,
  Rank of gross diet, shall we be enclouded,
  And forced to drink their vapor.

IRAS.   The gods forbid!

CLEOPATRA.
  Nay, 'tis most certain, Iras. Saucy lictors
  Will catch at us, like strumpets; and scald * rhymers   **scurvy**
  Ballad us out o' tune; the quick * comedians,   **lively**
  Extemporally will stage us, and present

Our Alexandrian revels; Antony
Shall be brought drunken forth, and I shall see
Some squeaking Cleopatra boy my greatness   220
I' the posture of a whore.[114]
IRAS.   O the good gods!
CLEOPATRA.
  Nay, that's certain.
IRAS.
  I'll never see 't; for, I am sure, my nails
  Are stronger than mine eyes.
CLEOPATRA.   Why, that's the way
  To fool their preparation, and to conquer
  Their most absurd intents.
  (CHARMIAN *returns*.)
                          Now, Charmian!
  Show me, my women, like a queen. Go fetch
  My best attires. I am again for Cydnus,
  To meet Mark Antony. Sirrah Iras, go.   229
    Now, noble Charmian, we'll dispatch * indeed;   use dispatch
  And, when thou hast done this chare,* I'll give thee leave   chore
  To play till doomsday. Bring our crown and all.
  (*As* IRAS *goes, loud voices are heard*.)
  Wherefore's this noise?
(*A* GUARDSMAN *enters*.)
GUARDSMAN.   Here is a rural fellow
  That will not be denied your highness' presence:
  He brings you figs.
CLEOPATRA.
  Let him come in. (*The* GUARDSMAN *goes*.)
                    What * poor an instrument   how
  May do a noble deed; He brings me liberty.
  My resolution's placed,* and I have nothing   fixed
  Of woman in me. Now from head to foot
  I am marble-constant; now the fleeting moon   240
  No planet is of mine.
(*The* GUARDSMAN *returns with the* CLOWN, *a countryman carry-
ing a basket*.)
GUARDSMAN.   This is the man.
CLEOPATRA   (*to the* GUARDSMAN) .
  Avoid,* and leave him.   depart
  (*To the* CLOWN *as the* GUARDSMAN *goes*.)
  Hast thou the pretty worm * of Nilus there,   snake
  That kills and pains not?

CLOWN.

Truly, I have him; but I would not be the party that should desire you to touch him, for his biting is immortal; those that do die of it do seldom or never recover.

CLEOPATRA.

Rememberest thou any that have died on 't?

CLOWN.

Very many, men and women too. I heard of one of them no longer than yesterday: a very honest woman, but something given to lie; as a woman should not do, but in the way of honesty; how she died of the biting of it, what pain she felt. Truly, she wakes a very good report o' the worm; but he that will believe all that they say, shall never be saved by half that they do; but this is most fallible, the worm's an odd worm.   250

CLEOPATRA.

Get thee hence. Farewell.   260

CLOWN.

I wish you all joy of the worm. (*Handing up his basket.*)

CLEOPATRA.

Farewell.

CLOWN.

You must think this, look you, that the worm will do his *   according to his
kind.

CLEOPATRA.

Ay, ay. Farewell.

CLOWN.

Look you, the worm is not to be trusted but in the keeping of wise people; for, indeed, there is no goodness in the worm.

CLEOPATRA.

Take thou no care. It shall be heeded.*   looked after

CLOWN.

Very good. Give it nothing, I pray you, for it is not worth the   270
feeding.

CLEOPATRA.

Will it eat me?

CLOWN.

You must not think I am so simple but I know the devil himself will not eat a woman. I know that a woman is a dish for the gods, if the devil dress her not. But, truly, these same whoreson devils do the gods great harm in their women; for in every ten that they make, the devils mar five.

CLEOPATRA.

Well, get thee gone. Farewell.   280

CLOWN.

Yes, forsooth. I wish you joy o' the worm.

(*He goes.*)

(IRAS *returns with* CLEOPATRA*'s robe and crown.*)

CLEOPATRA.

Give me my robe, put on my crown. I have
Immortal longings in me. Now no more
The juice of Egypt's grape shall moist this lip.

(*As* IRAS *robes her.*)

Yare,* yare, good Iras; quick. Methinks I hear   **hurry**
Antony call; I see him rouse himself
To praise my noble act; I hear him mock
The luck of Caesar, which the gods give men
To excuse their after wrath.

(*As* IRAS *finishes the robing.*)

                    Husband, I come!   290
Now to that name my courage prove my title!
I am fire and air; my other elements
I give to baser life.[115]

(*Kissing* CHARMIAN *and* IRAS.)

                So; have you done?
Come then, and take the last warmth of my lips.
Farewell, kind Charmian; Iras, long farewell.

(IRAS *falls and dies.*)

Have I the aspic * in my lips? Dost fall?   **asp**
If thou and nature can so gently part,
The stroke of death is as a lover's pinch,
Which hurts, and is desired. Dost thou lie still?
If thus thou vanishest, thou tell'st the world   300
It is not worth leave-taking.

CHARMIAN.

Dissolve, thick cloud, and rain; that I may say,
The gods themselves do weep!

CLEOPATRA.   This proves me base:
If she first meet the curlèd Antony,
He'll make demand of her, and spend that kiss
Which is my heaven to have.

(*To an asp, which she takes from the basket and applies to
her breast.*)

                Come, thou mortal wretch,

With thy sharp teeth this knot intrinsicate *   **intricate**
Of life at once untie. Poor venomous fool,
Be angry, and dispatch. Oh, couldst thou speak,
That I might hear thee call great Caesar ass   310
Unpolicied! *   **lacking statecraft**
CHARMIAN.   O eastern star!
CLEOPATRA.   Peace, peace!
  Dost thou not see my baby at my breast,
  That sucks the nurse asleep?
CHARMIAN   (*weeping*).   Oh, break! Oh, break!
CLEOPATRA.
  As sweet as balm, as soft as air, as gentle—
  O Antony!
  (*Applying another asp to her arm.*)
         Nay, I will take thee too:
  What * should I stay—   **why**
(*She dies.*)
CHARMIAN.
  In this vile world? So, fare thee well.
  Now boast thee, death, in thy possession lies
  A lass unparalleled.
  (*Closing* CLEOPATRA's *eyes.*)
         Downy windows, close;
  And golden Phoebus never be beheld   320
  Of eyes again so royal!
  (*Adjusting* CLEOPATRA's *crown.*)
         Your crown's awry;
  I'll mend it, and then play.
(*Some* GUARDS *rush in below.*)
FIRST GUARD.
  Where is the queen?
CHARMIAN.   Speak softly, wake her not.
FIRST GUARD.
  Caesar hath sent—
CHARMIAN.   Too slow a messenger.
  (*Applying an asp to her bosom.*)
  Oh, come apace, dispatch! I partly feel thee.
FIRST GUARD.
  Approach, ho! All's not well. Caesar's beguiled.
SECOND GUARD.
  There's Dolabella sent from Caesar; call him.
FIRST GUARD.
  What work is here! Charmian, is this well done?

CHARMIAN.
  It is well done, and fitting for a princess
  Descended of so many royal kings.   330
  Ah, soldier! (CHARMIAN *dies.*)
(DOLABELLA *enters.*)
DOLABELLA.
  How goes it here?
SECOND GUARD.   All dead.
DOLABELLA.   Caesar, thy thoughts
  Touch their effects * in this: thyself art coming   **fulfillment**
  To see performed the dreaded act which thou
  So sought'st to hinder.
(*Shouts are heard:* "A way there, a way for Caesar!" CAESAR
enters below, followed by OFFICERS *and* SOLDIERS.)
DOLABELLA.
  O sir, you are too sure an augurer;
  That * you did fear is done.   **what**
CAESAR.   Bravest at the last,
  She leveled * at our purposes, and, being royal,   **aimed**
  Took her own way.
                        The manner of their deaths   340
  I do not see them bleed.
DORABELLA.   Who was last with them?
FIRST GUARD.
  A simple countryman, that brought her figs.
  This was his basket.
CAESAR.   Poisoned, then.
FIRST GUARD.   O Caesar,
  This Charmian lived but now; she stood and spake.
  I found her trimming up * the diadem   **straightening**
  On her dead mistress: tremblingly she stood
  And on the sudden dropped.
CAESAR.   Oh, noble weakness!
  If they had swallowed poison, 'twould appear
  By external swelling. But she looks like sleep,
  As she would catch another Antony   350
  In her strong toil of grace.*   **charm**
DOLABELLA.   Here, on her breast,
  There is a vent * of blood and something blown.*   **discharge**
  The like is on her arm.   **somewhat swollen**
FIRST GUARD.
  This is an aspic's trail; and these fig leaves
  Have slime upon them, such as the aspic leaves

Upon the caves of Nile.

CAESAR.   Most probable
That so she died; for her physician tells me
She hath pursued conclusions * infinite   experiments
Of easy ways to die.
                     Take up her bed;
And bear her women from the monument.   360
She shall be buried by her Antony;
No grave upon the earth shall clip * in it   embrace
A pair so famous. High events as these
Strike those that make them; and their story is
No less in pity than his glory which
Brought them to be lamented. Our army shall
In solemn show attend this funeral;
And then to Rome. Come, Dolabella, see
High order in this great solemnity.
(*All leave.*)

NOTES

GENERAL NOTE

In *Antony and Cleopatra,* Shakespeare takes up the political situation where he left it many years before when he wrote *Julius Caesar.* Caesar has been assassinated. Antony, joining forces with Octavius Caesar against Brutus and Cassius, the leaders in the assassination plot, defeats them so overwhelmingly that they commit suicide. The vast Roman world is left divided among three men, the so-called triumvirate: Lepidus, Octavius Caesar (who, under the name of Augustus, was to become the first Emperor of Rome) , and Antony.

Lepidus proves to be a weakling, and Octavius Caesar and Antony become locked in a struggle for supremacy. Here Shakespeare takes up the story in *Antony and Cleopatra,* where Octavius Caesar's triumph over Antony is dramatized.

Historically, events did not follow upon each other as the text of the play suggests. Caesar was assassinated in 44 B.C. Brutus and Cassius were defeated in 42 B.C., and shortly after Antony first met Cleopatra. His first wife Fulvia died in 40 B.C. He married Octavia the same year. He returned to Cleopatra in 34. The battle of Actium was in 31, and the battle of Alexandria and the death of Antony and Cleopatra all occurred in 30 B.C.

TEXT: Though Edward Blount entered *Antony and Cleopatra* in the *Stationers' Register* on May 20, 1608, the play was not published until 1623, when it appeared in the First Folio. The present text, over 3,000 lines in length, probably does not represent the actual acting version of the piece. This is an indication that it was probably set up not from the company's prompt book, but either from Shakespeare's own manuscript or from some carefully prepared transcript of it, for the Folio text is an unusually good one.

DATE: The play was probably written and produced shortly before the date of its entry in the *Stationers' Register*. Stylistically it is later than *Macbeth* (1606), so that it probably first appeared on the stage during the winter season of 1607–8.

ACT I, Scene 1

1. Line 10

   To cool a gypsy's lust. The gypsies were supposed to have come from Egypt. Actually Cleopatra was of Greek descent.

2. Lines 12–3

   The triple pillar of the world transformed
   Into a strumpet's fool!
   The triple pillar was one of the triumvirs. The other two were Lepidus, and Octavius Caesar (the grandnephew and adopted son of Julius Caesar). In 29 B.C. Octavius became the first Emperor of Rome under the name Augustus.

3. Line 18

   Grates me: the sum. Antony, annoyed by the interruption, does not want to bother to listen to the messenger and asks that the message be briefly summed up for him.

4. Line 20

   Fulvia perchance is angry. Fulvia was the wife of Antony, her third husband. She was reputed to be violent and bad-tempered (see line 32, "shrill-tongued Fulvia"). She died in 40 B.C., thus enabling Antony to marry Octavia (see I, 2, 122, and II, 2, 130 ff.).

5. Line 21

   the scarce-bearded Ceasar. Octavius at this time was only twenty-three years old.

ACT I, Scene 2

6. Line 5

   must charge his horns with garlands! This is a reference to the horns a cuckold—the husband of an unfaithful wife—was supposed to grow on his head.

7. Line 23

   I had rather heat my liver with drinking. The liver was thought to be the seat of love.

8. Line 28

   Let me have a child at fifty, to whom Herod of Jewry may do homage. The allusion is to Herod, who in the mystery plays familiar to Elizabethan audiences was always presented as a fierce and blustery tyrant.

9. Line 40

   I forgive thee for a witch. I exonerate you of being a wizard because your prophecies are so trivial. "Witch" was applied to both women and men.

10. Line 53

    if an oily palm be not a fruitful prognostication. A moist palm was supposed to be sign of a passionate disposition. Fruitful prognostication—a prophecy of fruitfulness.

11. Line 66

    Oh, let him marry a woman that cannot go. Go is used in two senses—"walk" and "be sexually responsive."

12. Lines 66–7

    sweet Isis, I beseech thee! Isis was the Egyptian goddess of fertility and maternity.

13. Line 103

Labienus. Quintus Labienus was the ambassador of Brutus and Cassius to the Parthians; later, the commander-in-chief of their army.

14. Lines 113–4

> *Oh, then we bring forth weeds,*
> *When our quick minds lie still; and our ills told us*
> *Is as our earing.*

Earing is an archaic term for plowing. The meaning is that to have our faults told to us is like a plowing that frees the fields of weeds.

15. Line 117

Sicyon. A town in Greece where Antony had left his wife.

16. Line 157

she makes a shower of rain as well as Jove. In classical mythology, Jove, the king of the gods, was the giver of rain, usually referred to in this aspect as Jupiter Pluvius.

17. Lines 190–1

> *Sextus Pompeius*
> *Hath given the dare to Caesar.*

Sextus Pompeius was a son of Pompey the Great. (See Note 32.)

18. Lines 200–1

> *Which, like the courser's hair, hath yet but life,*
> *And not a serpent's poison.*

A horse's hair, when put into water, was thought to turn into a snake. "But" here is used in the sense of "only."

ACT I, Scene 3

19. Line 61

The garboils she awaked; at the last, best. The last thing she did was the best thing she did: die.

20. Lines 63–4

> *Where be the sacred vials thou shouldst fill*
> *With sorrowful water?*

These vials are the bottles of tears that the Romans put into the burial urns of their dead.

21. Lines 84–5

> *How this Herculean Roman does become*
> *The carriage of his chafe!*

How well suited to the part of this Roman who claims descent from Hercules is his acting of rage! (See Note 99.)

22. Lines 99–100

> *Upon your sword*
> *Sit laurel victory!*

The foliage of the bay-laurel was used by the ancient Greeks to crown victors in the Pythian games—athletic contests held at Delphi in honor of Apollo. Pythius was a dragon killed by Apollo.

ACT I, Scene 4

23. Lines 4–7

> *he . . . is not more manlike*
> *Than Cleopatra; or the queen of Ptolemy*
> *More womanly than he.*

Ptolemy was the name of the kings of Egypt. Cleopatra was the daughter of

Ptolemy XI. The reference is to her effeminate brother-husband Ptolemy XIII.

24. Line 17

   tumble on the bed of Ptolemy. Cleopatra's husband, whom she is suspected of having poisoned, was Ptolemy XIII, King of Egypt.

25. Lines 24–5

when we do bear

So great weight in his lightness.

When we are so deeply involved in the consequences of his frivolity or levity.

26. Lines 37–8

   And it appears he is belovèd of those
   That only have feared Caesar.

   The meaning is that those who only fear Octavius Caesar love Pompey.

27. Lines 42–4

   That he which is was wished until he were;
   And the ebbed man, ne'er loved till ne'er worth love,
   Comes deared by being lacked.

   This passage is obscure. The general sentiment seems to be that a man whose fortunes have ebbed becomes endeared to the populace because he is missed.

28. Lines 44–6

This common body,

Like to a vagabond flag upon the stream,
Goes to and back, lackeying the varying tide.

   The common body of men, like a detached leaf of the sweet flag flower on the surface of a stream, moves to and fro, following, as a lackey follows his master, the changing movements of the water.

ACT I, Scene 5

29. Line 4

   Give me to drink mandragora. Mandragora was the juice of the mandrake root, a narcotic used as a sleeping potion.

30. Lines 23–4

   The demi-Atlas of this earth, the arm
   And burgonet of men.

   In Greek myth, Atlas, as punishment for warring against Zeus, the king of the gods, was forced to bear the earth on his head and hands. Antony, so says Cleopatra, bears half of it and Octavius the other half. She ignores Lepidus.

31. Lines 27–8

   That am with Phoebus' amorous pinches black,
   And wrinkled deep in time.

   Phoebus was an epithet of Apollo, the sun-god. Cleopatra was of pure Greek stock and less than thirty years old when she first met Antony. Her exaggeration is coquetry.

32. Line 31

   great Pompey. Great Pompey, Cneius Pompeius Magnus (106–48 B.C.) , was a member of the first triumvirate with Julius Caesar and Crassus. He later became Caesar's jealous enemy. Pompey, defeated at Pharsalia (48 B.C.) , fled to Egypt, where he was assassinated.

33. Lines 36–7

that great medicine hath

With his tinct gilded thee.

   The mere fact that you come from Antony has had the effect of a great medicine and gives you a golden tint—the allusion being to the elixer of the alchemists which was supposed to turn base metal into gold.

34. Line 48

And soberly did mount an arm-gaunt steed. An arm-gaunt steed was one made lean by much war service. This is the most satisfactory of the scores of meanings suggested by the commentators.

ACT II, Scene 1

35. Lines 24–5

Epicurean cooks
Sharpen with cloyless sauce his appetite.

May cooks satisfactory to the taste of an epicure sharpen his appetite with sauces that never satiate.

36. Line 27

Even till a Lethed dullness! In classical mythology, Lethe was a river in Hades the water of which, when drunk, caused complete forgetfulness.

37. Line 41

His brother warred upon him. This brother was Lucius Antonius, who joined with Fulvia, Anthony's first wife, to make war on Octavius. (See II, 2, 43.)

38. Lines 50–1

It only stands
Our lives upon to use our strongest hands.

Our lives depends wholly upon our using our strongest forces.

ACT II, Scene 2

39. Line 6

And speak as loud as Mars. By Jupiter. Mars was the Roman god of war, Jupiter the supreme deity.

40. Line 25

Nor curstness grow to the matter. Nor let any angry speech grow into a matter of substance.

41. Lines 43–4

and their contestation
Was theme for you, you were the word of war.

Their strife became the subject that you developed until your name became the watchword of war.

42. Line 112

your considerate stone. Equivalent to "Yours prudently silent." Enobarbus means that he is willing to drop the subject without further talk.

43. Line 163

About the mount Misenum. This was a promontory in the Bay of Naples near the ancient town of Campania. It was named for Aeneas' trumpeter, Misenus, who was drowned off the cape. His death and burial Vergil describes in the *Aeneid* (VI, 232 ff.) .

44. Line 167

Would we had spoke. The preferred meaning is "Would we had finished our discussion of the matter." A possible but less probable meaning is "Would we had settled the matter by armed conflict."

45. Lines 204–6

In her pavilion—cloth-of-gold of tissue—
O'erpicturing that Venus where we see
The fancy outwork nature.

The cloth was made of interwoven threads of silk and gold. Shakespeare apparently had in mind a picture of Venus rising from the sea, painted by the Greek artist Apelles (c. 330 B.C.), as mentioned in Pliny's *Natural History*.

46. Line 211

Her gentlewomen, like the Nereides. In Greek mythology, these were sea nymphs, fifty to one hundred in number, attendant on the sea god Poseidon.

47. Line 213

And made their bends adornings. Their obeisances were so graceful that they adorned Cleopatra.

48. Line 211

but for vacancy. But for fear of forming a vacuum (which is against nature's law).

ACT II, Scene 3

49. Line 6

I have not kept my square. I have not kept my appointed place in the social structure.

50. Line 37

When it is all to nought. When the odds are all to nothing in my favor.

51. Lines 37–8

> and his quails ever
>
> *Beat mine, inhooped, at odds.*

Quailfights were well known among the ancients. Fighting cocks or quail were sometimes enclosed in a hoop to make them stay close together and so continue fighting.

ACT II, Scene 5

52. Line 23

I wore his sword Philippan. The sword was so called because of its services in the battle of Philippi, where Antony defeated Brutus and Cassius.

53. Line 40

Thou shouldst come like a Fury crowned with snakes. The Furies or Erinyes of Greek mythology were avenging spirits who brought retribution to the guilty. There were eventually three: Alecto, Megaera, and Tisiphone, and these were conceived as snaky-haired women pursuing the offender and driving him mad.

54. Line 72

Thy modesty. Anyone of your modest resources.

55. Lines 96–7

Hadst thou Narcissus in thy face, to me

Thou wouldst appear most ugly.

In Greek mythology Narcissus was a beautiful youth who spurned the nymph Echo's love for him. He was punished by being made to fall in love with his own face which he saw reflected in the water of a fountain. He pined away in desire for his image and was changed into the flower that bears his name.

56. Lines 116–7

Though he be painted one way like a Gorgon,

The other way's a Mars.

This refers to a "perspective picture," which showed different objects when looked at from different angles. A Gorgon was one of three fabled sisters with snaky hair and countenances so terrible that they turned beholders into stone. Mars was the Roman god of war.

ACT II, Scene 6

57. Line 27

Thou dost o'ercount me of my father's house. This refers to the fact that Antony had confiscated the house of the elder Pompey (see II, 7, 133–4) .

58. Line 45

your brother. The reference is to Antony's brother Lucius Antonius (see Note 37) .

59. Line 55

What counts harsh fortune casts upon my face. The figure is from casting accounts. The counts are the lines drawn in an account book.

60. Line 69

And I have heard, Apollodorus carried. Plutarch reports that after Julius Caesar had captured Alexandria, Apollodorus tied Cleopatra, then no more than a girl, in a bundle and carried her secretly to Caesar's quarters.

ACT II, Scene 7

61. Line 5

They have made him drink alms-drink. When in a drinking bout a man took the drink in place of another in order to relieve him of his obligation to drain the cup, he was said to be drinking alms-drink.

62. Line 99

That it might go on wheels! "Go on wheels" was a proverbial expression meaning "to go smoothly."

63. Line 110

Shall we dance now the Egyptian bacchanals. A bacchanal was a wild dance accompanied by equally wild singing, a form of the worship of Bacchus, the Roman god of wine.

ACT III, Scene 1

64. Lines 1–3

and now

Pleased fortune does of Marcus Crassus' death
Make me revenger.

Marcus Crassus, member of the first triumvirate with Pompey and Julius Caesar, was defeated and slain in 53 B.C. by the forces of Orodes, King of Parthia, a country to the southeast of the Caspian Sea. Despite the Romans' attacks, it remained free and independent until A.D. 226, when the Persians conquered it. The Parthians were noted for their method of fighting on horseback. After each discharge of their arrows, they turned their horses as if in flight; hence the term, a "Parthian shot."

ACT III, Scene 2

65. Lines 4–6

and Lepidus,

Since Pompey's feast, as Menas says, is troubled
With the green sickness.

Green sickness was a kind of anemia, a disorder to which young women were supposed to be especially susceptible. It produced yellow skin, weariness, nausea, and other symptoms of a hangover.

66. Line 12

O Antony! O thou Arabian bird! This refers to the phoenix, a fabulous bird, of which according to legend there was never more than one of its kind in the world at one time.

67. Lines 25-7

> *Sister, prove such a wife*
> *As my thoughts make thee, and as my farthest band*
> *Shall pass on thy approof.*

Prove yourself as worthy a wife as you are in my thoughts and as I will pledge to the utmost you will actually prove to be.

68. Lines 47-50

> *Her tongue will not obey her heart, nor can*
> *Her heart inform her tongue—the swan's down feather,*
> *That stands upon the swell at full of tide,*
> *And neither way inclines.*

Octavia's grief at leaving her brother and her joy at following her husband are as evenly balanced as a swan's feather on the water at the turn of the tide.

69. Lines 51-3

> AGRIPPA. *He has a cloud in 's face.*
> ENOBARBUS. *He were the worse for that, were he a horse;*
> *So is he, being a man.*

A dark spot in the forehead of a horse, called a cloud in his face, was regarded as a sign of ill temper.

ACT III, Scene 3

70. Line 18

> *O Isis!* Isis was an Egyptian goddess, originally of the sky. Gradually the functions of all the goddesses were attributed to her. In the mythology of Egypt, she was the sister and wife of Osiris, who represented the sun.

71. Lines 36-7

> *and her forehead*
> *As low as she would wish it.*

This is a cant phrase meaning "lower than she would wish it." In Elizabethan times a high forehead was regarded as beautiful.

ACT III, Scene 6

72. Line 6

> *Caesarion, whom they call my father's son.* Caesarion was the son of Cleopatra and Julius Caesar; the latter adopted Octavius.

73. Lines 69-75

> *Bocchus, the king of Libya; Archelaus,*
> *Of Cappadocia; Philadelphos, king*
> *Of Paphlagonia; the Thracian king, Adallas;*
> *King Malchus of Arabia; King of Pont;*
> *Herod of Jewry; Mithridates, king*
> *Of Comagene; Polemon and Amyntas,*
> *The kings of Mede and Lycaonia.*

In this list of rules, Shakespeare did not seek geographical accuracy, but impressive-sounding names. Pont stands for Pontius; Comagene, ancient Syria; Mede, Media; and Lycaondia, country in Asia Minor.

ACT III, Scene 7

74. Line 22

> *Tarentum and Brundusium.* Ancient names for Taranto and Brindisi, towns in southern Italy.

75. Line 24.

Toryne. A town on the coast of Epirus.

76. Line 61

Away, my Thetis! In classical mythology, Thetis was a sea goddess.

77. Lines 69–70

> *but his whole action grows*
> *Not in the power on 't.*

Antony's action is not developing in a way to realize our potential power.

ACT III, Scene 10

78. Lines 9–10

> *On our side like the tokened pestilence,*
> *Where death is sure.*

Spots on a person sick of the plague were thought to be sent by a god as signs (tokens) of approaching death.

ACT III, Scene 11

79. Lines 36–8

> *while I struck*
> *The lean and wrinkled Cassius; and 'twas I*
> *That the mad Brutus ended.*

These lines refer to the deaths of Cassius and Brutus as set forth in the last act of *Julius Caesar.*

80. Lines 71–2

> *We sent our schoolmaster;*
> *Is he come back?*

Euphronius, the ambassador to whom Antony refers (see II, 12, 6) , was the tutor of Antony and Cleopatra's children.

ACT III, Scene 12

81. Line 34

Observe how Antony becomes his flaw. Observe how Antony is affected by his disaster.

ACT III, Scene 13

82. Line 8

Have nicked his captainship. It was customary to cut the hair of jesters in nicks or notches, so the phrase here means that Antony's generalship has been made to look foolish.

83. Lines 29–31

> *Yes, like enough, high-battled Caesar will*
> *Unstate his happiness, and be staged to the show,*
> *Against a sworder!*

In this speech Enobarbus says ironically that it is indeed likely Caesar will surrender the advantage of his favorable position and make a public spectacle of himself as in a duel with a gladiator.

84. Lines 32–4

> *and things outward*
> *Do draw the inward quality after them,*
> *To suffer all alike.*

The outward circumstances influence the inner self so that they both suffer alike.

85. Lines 34–6

> *That he should dream,*
> *Knowing all measures, the full Caesar will*
> *Answer his emptiness!*

Enobarbus wonders how Antony, who has experienced all the ups and downs of fortune and thus knows how they affect men's responses, can even dream that a Caesar full of power will consent to deal on even terms with Antony—who has nothing to offer but emptiness.

86. Line 91

Like boys unto a muss. A muss was a scramble for nuts or for any small objects thrown upon the ground.

87. Lines 123–5

> *To let a fellow that will take rewards*
> *And say, "God quit you!" be familiar with*
> *My playfellow, your hand.*

"God quit you" was the conventional phrase in which a beggar expressed his thanks for a gift of money.

88. Lines 126–8

> *Oh, that I were*
> *Upon the hill of Basan, to outroar*
> *The hornèd herd!*

Compare Psalms 22:12–13: "Many bulls have compassed me, strong bulls of Bashan have beset me round. They gaped upon me with their mouths, as a ravening and a roaring lion."

89. Lines 156–7

> *would you mingle eyes*
> *With one that ties his points?*

The points were the laces that attached the doublet to the breeches.

ACT IV, Scene 2

90. Line 8

I'll strike, and cry, "Take all." "Take all" was a gambler's cry, meaning "All or nothing." To take all in battle was to show no mercy.

ACT IV, Scene 3

91. Closing Stage Direction

On Shakespeare's stage this music was probably meant to continue as a bridge into the next scene, which would have shown Antony and Cleopatra "discovered," either on the upper stage or within the inner below. The music probably concluded with the fanfare at the Captain's entrance to rouse Antony (IV, 4, 23).

ACT IV, Scene 7

92. Lines 7–8

> *I had a wound here that was like a T,*
> *But now 'tis made an H.*

Scarus is punning on the word "ache," which in Elizabethan times was pronounced "aitch."

ACT IV, Scene 8

93. Line 7

you have shown all Hectors. Hector, the leader of the Trojans in the Trojan War, was famous for his power and courage in battle.

94. Lines 21–2

A brain that nourishes our nerves, and can
Get goal for goal of youth.
Make as many goals as youth in the sport of barriers, in which the contestants
fought on foot, separated by a railing.
95. Lines 28–9

were it carbuncled
Like holy Phoebus' car.
Were it set with gems like the chariot of Phoebus, the sun-god.

ACT IV, Scene 10
96. Lines 7–9
They have put forth the haven . . .
Where their appointment we may best discover,
And look on their endeavor.
Line 7 is incomplete. R. G. White has suggested "Go we up" as the completion
of it, so that the meaning of the passage would be: "They have put forth from
the harbor. Go we up where we may best observe them."

ACT IV, Scene 12
97. Line 13
Triple-turned whore! Antony accused Cleopatra of having been faithless to three
men: Pompey, Julius Caesar, and now Antony.
98. Line 37
For poor'st diminutives, for doits. A doit was a Dutch coin of very small value.
99. Lines 43–5
The shirt of Nessus is upon me: teach me,
Alcides, thou mine ancestor, thy rage.
Let me lodge Lichas on the horns o' the moon.
Alcides is another name for Hercules, from whom Antony claimed to be descended
(see Note 21). The shirt of Nessus was a shirt soaked in the poisoned blood of
the Centaur Nessus. Believing it to be a love charm, Hercules' wife Deianira sent
it to her husband by Lichas, one of his companions. When Hercules donned it,
the agony caused by the effect of the poison on his skin drove him to frenzy. He
hurled Lichas into the sea and then killed himself.

ACT IV, Scene 13
100. Lines 1–2
Oh, he is more mad
Than Telamon for his shield.
Telamon is here confounded with his son Ajax, a Greek warrior in the Trojan
War who was overcome by mad fury when the shield of Achilles was awarded to
his rival Odysseus.
101. Lines 2–3
the boar of Thessaly
Was never so embossed.
The boar sent by Diana to ravage Caledon, which Meleager slew, was never so
foam-flecked with rage as Antony.

ACT IV, Scene 14
102. Lines 53–4
Dido and her Aeneas shall want troops,
And all the haunt be ours.

In the *Aeneid,* Dido was the queen of Carthage who killed herself for grief when her lover Aeneas left her to resume his journey to Italy. Antony imagines that, when he and Cleopatra enter the world of the dead, the crowd of admiring ghosts who usually surround the up-to-then most-famous lovers, Dido and Aeneas, will leave them to crowd around Cleopatra and him.

ACT IV, Scene 15
103. Lines 9–10

O sun,
Burn the great sphere thou movest in!
According to Ptolemaic astronomy the sun was fixed in a hollow sphere that re-volved about the earth.
104. Lines 35–6

The strong-winged Mercury should fetch thee up,
And set thee by Jove's side.
In Roman mythology Mercury, whose cult was derived from that of the Greek Hermes, was the herald and messenger of the gods. He was also the god of inven-tion and trickery.
105. Line 44

That the false housewife Fortune break her wheel. Fortuna, in Roman myth, was the goddess of chance. She is a hussy ("housewife") because she never remains true to any man. She was often portrayed as riding a wheel that in its revolution brought the high low, and the low high.

ACT V, Scene 1
106. Lines 15–6

the round world
Should have shook lions into civil streets.
The earth should have been shaken severely enough to liberate lions to roam the city streets.
107. Lines 65–6

for her life in Rome
Would be eternal in our triumph.
Her presence in my triumphal procession in Rome would make it eternally glo-rious (see IV, 15, 23) .

ACT V, Scene 2
108. Lines 5–8

that thing . . .
Which sleeps, and never palates more the dung,
The beggar's nurse and Caesar's.
That thing (death) which sleeps and never again makes palatable the foul food that nourishes both beggar and Caesar. In printing the Folio reading "dung," we have deviated from the Globe text's "dug."
109. Line 27

A conqueror that will pray in aid for kindness. "Pray in aid" is a legal term mean-ing to call in a person not a party to a lawsuit. The passage means a conqueror who will call in a disinterested person to help him in thinking up acts of kind-ness in your behalf.
110. Line 35 (Stage Direction)

The Globe stage directions at this point, like those in most other editions, are confusing, involving problems of upper and lower stage levels. We have made some clarifying changes. The important thing for the reader to understand is that after the gates to the monument have been opened there is no longer any obstacle to free access to those in the monument.

111. Lines 83–4

> *his voice was propertied*
> *As all the tunèd spheres.*

His voice had the quality of the music of the spheres, for each sphere as it turned was supposed to give forth a ravishingly beautiful sound.

112. Lines 98–100

> *yet, to imagine*
> *An Antony were nature's piece 'gainst fancy,*
> *Condemning shadows quite.*

To imagine an Antony would be as if nature's masterpiece were to compete with creatures of the imagination, with nature outclassing the shadowy figures of imagination.

113. Line 185

Make not your thoughts your prisons. Do not imagine yourself a prisoner.

114. Lines 219–21

> *and I shall see*
> *Some squeaking Cleopatra boy my greatness*
> *I' the posture of a whore.*

The shrill-voiced boy actor who will take the part of Cleopatra will represent my regal dignity by imitating the conduct of a whore.

115. Lines 292–3

> *I am fire and air; my other elements*
> *I give to baser life.*

A human being was supposed to be composed of four elements: fire, air, earth, and water. The last two were the "baser elements."

A Note on Shakespeare's Grammar: In Shakespeare's day the syntax and other aspects of English grammar and vocabulary were in a state of transition from an earlier, highly inflected language. The loss of endings obscured the distinguishing marks of various parts of speech, and the result was not so much confusion as freedom. (A full exposition of the peculiarities of Elizabethan language may be found in Abbott's *A Shakespearian Grammar*, 3d ed., 1871.)

This note will reassure the reader that constructions which seem ungrammatical were justified according to the accepted canons of Elizabethan usage.

ON ANTONY AND CLEOPATRA

MAYNARD MACK

Critics have been known to speak of *Macbeth, King Lear,* and *Antony and Cleopatra* as Shakespeare's *Inferno, Purgatorio,* and *Paradiso.* The comparison is misleading if taken as a guide to Shakespeare's states of

Maynard Mack, a native of Michigan, was educated at Yale where he is now chairman and Sterling Professor of English. His books include *Tragic Themes in Western Literature* and *King Lear in Our Time.*

mind, of which we know nothing, or even as a guide to the order of the three plays, the consensus of modern opinion being that *Macbeth* (ca. 1606) falls between *King Lear* (ca. 1605) and *Antony and Cleopatra* (ca. 1607). But the notion has a certain merit if taken solely as a guide to tone.

Macbeth and *King Lear,* like *Othello* earlier, are dark plays, filled with actions taking place in what can only be called "dramatic" as well as literal night, a dark night of the soul engulfed by evil. *Antony and Cleopatra,* on the other hand, is a bright play. *Macbeth* and *King Lear,* too, are savage—if one fully responds to them, terrifying. There is no savagery in *Antony and Cleopatra;* it is moving, exhilarating, even exalting, but contains nothing that should tear an audience to tatters. The humor of *Macbeth* and *King Lear* is either grim or pitiful: a drunken porter at the gate of hell, a court jester shivering on a stormy heath. The humor of *Antony and Cleopatra* is neither grim nor pitiful, although sometimes acrid enough. Cleopatra is given qualities that make her a very unqueenly queen: she lies, wheedles, sulks, screams, and makes love, all with equal abandon. Antony is given qualities that make him in some senses more like an elderly playboy than a tragic hero. We are encouraged by Shakespeare in this play to disengage ourselves from the protagonists, to feel superior to them, even to laugh at them, as we rarely are with his earlier tragic persons.

Against laughter, however, the playwright poises sympathy and even admiration. Tawdry though he has made these seasoned old campaigners in love and war, he has also magnified and idealized them, to the point at which their mutual passion becomes glorious as well as cheap. Antony, the play tells us, has "infinite virtue," Cleopatra "infinite variety." He is the "triple pillar of the world," she is the "day o' th' world." He seems a "plated Mars," she more beautiful than Venus. His guardian spirit is called "unmatchable," she is called a "lass unparalleled." He descends from the god Hercules, she from the moon-goddess Isis. She sees him as the sun and moon, lighting this "little O, th' earth"; Charmian sees her as the "Eastern star." When Antony cries Ho! "Like boys unto a muss, kings would start forth"; Cleopatra has a hand that "kings Have lipped, and trembled kissing." When Antony will swear an oath, he cries, "Let Rome in Tiber melt and the wide arch Of the ranged empire fall!" When Cleopatra will swear, she cries, "Melt Egypt into Nile! and kindly creatures Turn all to serpents." Antony, about to die, thinks of death as a continuing amour with Cleopatra: "Where souls do couch on flowers, we'll hand in hand, And with our sprightly port make the ghosts gaze." When Cleopatra is about to die, she sees death in the same transcendent terms: "Go, fetch My best attires. I am again for Cydnus, To meet Mark Antony."

Traces of Shakespeare's duality of attitude toward his lovers may be found in Plutarch, whose *Lives of the Noble Grecians and Romans Compared Together* he had read in Thomas North's magnificent English rendering (1579) of Jacques Amyot's translation of the original into French (1559). So eloquent was North's prose that in certain instances it could be assumed into blank verse with a minimum of change, as in the following well-known description of Cleopatra going to meet Antony in her barge, which should be compared with the lines of Enobarbus (Act II, scene 2, lines 191–239) in Shakespeare's play.

> . . . She went to Antonius at the age when a woman's beauty is at the prime, and she also of best judgment. . . . She disdained to set forward otherwise but to take her barge in the river of Cydnus, the poop whereof was of gold, the sails of purple, and the oars of silver, which kept stroke in rowing after the sound of the music of flutes, hautboys, cithers, viols, and such other instruments as they played upon in the barge. And now for the person of herself: She was laid under a pavilion of cloth-of-gold of tissue, apparelled and attired like the goddess Venus commonly drawn in picture; and hard by her, on either hand of her, pretty fair boys, apparelled as painters do set forth god Cupid, with little fans in their hands, with the which they fanned wind upon her. Her ladies and gentlewomen also, the fairest of them, were apparelled like the nymphs Nereides (which are the mermaids of the waters) and like the Graces, some steering the helm, others tending the tackle and ropes of the barge, out of the which there came a wonderful passing sweet savor of perfumes that perfumed the wharf's side, pestered with innumerable multitudes of people. Some of them followed the barge all alongest the river's side, others also ran out of the city to see her coming in, so that in the end there ran such multitudes of people one after another to see her that Antonius was left post-alone in the market place in his imperial seat to give audience. And there went a rumor in the people's mouths that the goddess Venus was come to play with the god Bacchus for the general good of all Asia.

Shakespeare's play owes to Plutarch's life of Antony many of its incidents, and to North's prose the wording of occasional passages like the lines of Enobarbus referred to above. It precipitates, however, an interpretation of these materials that is spectacularly Shakespeare's own. Plutarch's narrative, for all its stress on the baffling blends of vice and virtue in great minds, is at bottom the relatively familiar story of the Great Man and the Temptress. His Antony loses the world for love, not wisely but too well, and his Cleopatra, though possibly she rises to genuine love before the end (Plutarch leaves this point undecided), is rather the instrument of a great man's downfall than a tragic figure in herself. To understand the distinctiveness of Shakespeare's treatment of her, we have only to return to the passage in Plutarch and the lines of Enobarbus already cited. Plutarch's Cleopatra is all siren, every effect calculated to ensnare the senses of the conquering Roman. Shakespeare's Cleopatra is all siren too, but she is more. The repeated paradoxes in Enobarbus's language serve notice on us that everything about her is impossible, mysteriously contradictory. Her page-boys cool her cheeks only to make them burn, "and what they undid did." Her gentlewomen are seeming mermaids, half human, half sea-creature. The silken tackle swells with a life of its own at "the touches of those flower-soft hands." The wharves come alive and have "sense," quickened by her "strange invisible perfume." The city comes alive, to "cast" its people out upon her. Antony is left sitting in the marketplace, whistling to the air, and the air itself, except that nature abhors a vacuum, would have "gone to gaze on Cleopatra too" and left a gap behind. She is a creature, says Enobarbus in conclusion, who makes defect perfection, and, when breathless, power breathes forth. Other women cloy the appetites they feed, "but she makes hungry Where most she satisfies." Even the vilest things are so becoming when she does them that "the holy priests Bless her when she is riggish."

This is clearly not a portrait of a mere intriguing woman, but a kind of absolute oxymoron: Cleopatra is glimpsed here as a force like the Lucretian Venus, whose vitality resists both definition and regulation. Yet enveloped as she is by Enobarbus's mocking tones, wise and faintly world-weary, calculating amusedly the effects of his words on these un-initiated Romans, she remains the more a trollop for that. His reliable anti-romanticism undercuts the picture he draws of her, and at the same time confirms it, because it comes from him.

The ambiguity of these lines extends to almost everything in the play. In the world the dramatist has given his lovers, nothing is stable, fixed, or sure, not even ultimate values; all is in motion. Seen from one point of view, the motion may be discerned as process, the inexorable march of causes and effects, exemplified in Antony's fall and epitomized by Caesar in commenting to Octavia on the futility of her efforts to preserve the peace: "But let determined things to destiny Hold unbewailed their way." Seen from another angle, the motion reveals itself as flux, the rest-less waxing and waning of tides, of moons, of human feeling. Especially of human feeling. Antony pursued Brutus to his death, we are re-minded by Enobarbus, yet wept when he found him slain. So within the play itself Caesar weeps, having pursued Antony to his death; and Antony, desiring that Fulvia die, finds her "good, being gone"; and Enobarbus, seeking some way to leave his master, is heart-struck when he succeeds; and the Roman populace, always fickle, "Like to a vagabond flag upon the stream, Goes to and back, lackeying the varying tide, To rot itself with motion."

In such a context, it is not surprising that the lovers' passion is subject to vicissitudes, going to and back in ever more violent oscillations of. attraction and recoil. Shakespeare nowhere disguises the unstable and ultimately destructive character of their relationship, and those who, like Shaw, have belabored him for not giving sexual infatuation the satiric treatment it deserves have read too carelessly. It is likewise not surprising that the play's structure should reflect, in its abrupt and numerous shifts of scene, so marked a quality of its leading characters—their emotional and psychological vacillation. Though these shifts have also met with criticism, some finding in them a serious threat to unity, they are easily seen in the theatre to be among the dramatist's means of conveying to us an awareness of the competing values by which the lovers, and particularly Antony, are torn. "Kingdoms are clay," he declares in Egypt; "The nobleness of life Is to do thus," and embraces Cleopatra. A few hours later, however, he says with equal earnestness, "These strong Egyptian fetters I must break Or lose myself in dotage," and he departs for Rome. Again, he declares to Octavia in Rome, hereafter everything shall "be done by th' rule," yet scarcely thirty lines later, after his interview with the soothsayer, he has added, "I will to Egypt." From this point on follows a succession of fluctuations in both war and love. In war, confidence of victory shifting to despair at loss, then to new confidence, then to new despair. In love, adorings of Cleopatra changing to recriminations, then to renewed adorings, then to fresh disgust. This aspect of the play's rhythm is vividly summed up in two speeches in the third act (Act III, scene 11). "I have offended reputation," Antony says after the first sea defeat, "A most unnoble swerving": there is the voice of Rome and the soldier. A few seconds after, he says to Cleopatra, "Fall not a tear, I say: one of them rates All that is won and lost": this is the voice of Egypt and the lover.

"All that is won *and* lost" is of course the crucial ambiguity of this tragedy. Perhaps it is one about which no two readers are likely finally to agree. Much is obviously lost by the lovers in the course of the play, and Shakespeare underscores this fact, as Plutarch had done, by placing their deaths in Cleopatra's monument—that is to say, a tomb. All those imperial ambitions that once mustered "the kings o' th' earth for war" have shrunk now to this narrow stronghold, which is also a waiting grave. Antony had said as he put his arms about Cleopatra in the opening scene, "Here is my space." Now that challenge has been taken up. This is his space indeed.

But what then, if anything, has been won? The answer to this question depends as much on what one brings to *Antony and Cleopatra* as on what one finds there, for the evidence is mixed. Antony does give his life for his love before the play ends, and we observe that there are no recriminations at his final meeting with Cleopatra; only his quiet hope that she will remember him for what was noblest in him, and her acknowledgment that he was, and is, her man of men. But then, too, his death has been precipitated by her duplicity in the false report of hers; it has among its motives a self-interested desire to evade Caesar's triumph; and the suicide is even bungled in the doing: if this is a hero's death, it is a humiliating one. Likewise, Cleopatra seems to give her life for love. As Antony will be a bridegroom in his death, "and run into't As to a lover's bed," so Cleopatra will be a bride in hers, calling, "Husband, I come," receiving darkness as if it were "a lover's pinch, Which hurts, and is desired," and breathing out, in words that could equally be describing the union of life with death or the union of lover with lover, "As sweet as balm, as soft as air, as gentle—O Antony!" This, however, is the same woman who has long studied "easy ways to die," who ends her life only after becoming convinced that Caesar means to lead her in triumph, and who has cached away with her treasurer Seleucus more than half her valuables in case of need. True, the scene with Seleucus can be so played as to indicate that she is using his confession to dupe Caesar about her intention to die. But that is precisely the point. What the actor or reader makes of her conduct here will be conditioned by what he has made of her elsewhere, by what he makes of the play as a whole, and even, perhaps, by his beliefs about human nature and the depiction of human nature in art.

Are we to take the high-sounding phrases which introduce us to this remarkable love affair in the play's first scene as amorous rant?

CLEOPATRA.   If it be love indeed, tell me how much.
ANTONY.   There's beggary in the love that can be reckoned.
CLEOPATRA.   I'll set a bourn how far to be beloved.
ANTONY.   Then must thou needs find out new heaven, new earth.

Or is there a prophetic resonance in that reference to "new heaven, new earth," which we are meant to remember when Cleopatra, dreaming of a transcendent Antony—

His face was as the heav'ns, and therein stuck
A sun and moon, which kept their course and lighted
The little O, th' earth. . . .
His legs bestrid the ocean: his reared arm
Crested the world: his voice was propertied
As all the tunèd spheres—

consigns her baser elements to "baser life"? Does the passion of these two remain a destructive element to the bitter end, doomed like all the feeling in the play "to rot itself with motion"? Or, as the world slips from them, have they a glimmering of something they could not have earlier understood, of another power besides death "Which shackles accidents and bolts up change"? Is it "paltry to be Caesar," as Cleopatra claims, since "Not being Fortune, he's but Fortune's knave"? Or is it more paltry to be Antony, and, as Caesar sees it, "give a kingdom for a mirth," as well as, eventually, the world?

To such questions, *Antony and Cleopatra,* like life itself, gives no clear-cut answers. Shakespeare holds the balance even, and does not decide for us who finally is the strumpet of the play, Antony's Cleopatra, or Caesar's Fortune, and who, therefore, is the "strumpet's fool." Those who would have it otherwise, who are "hot for certainties in this our life," as Meredith phrased it, should turn to other authors than Shakespeare, and should have been born into some other world than this.

MOLIÈRE

JEAN-BAPTISTE POQUELIN (1622–1673) WAS BORN IN PARIS, THE SON OF A WELL-TO-DO UPHOLSTERER. ALTHOUGH JEAN-BAPTISTE STUDIED LAW AND WAS ADMITTED TO THE BAR, HIS LOVE OF THE THEATER COMPELLED HIM TO BREAK AWAY FROM HIS FAMILY AND MIDDLE-CLASS ASSOCIATIONS; HE JOINED A TRAVELING COMPANY OF ACTORS AND CHANGED HIS NAME TO MOLIÈRE. AT THIRTY-THREE HE STAGED HIS FIRST MATURE PLAY, *L'ETOURDI* (*"THE BLUNDERER"*). THREE YEARS LATER, IN 1658, MOLIÈRE AND HIS COMPANY PERFORMED BEFORE LOUIS XIV; THE SUN KING'S FAVOR RESULTED IN MOLIÈRE'S COMPANY BECOMING ESTABLISHED IN THE PALAIS-ROYAL. AS THE COMÉDIE FRANÇAISE, IT IS THE OLDEST REPERTORY THEATER IN THE WORLD. MOLIÈRE'S MAJOR PLAYS INCLUDE *LES PRECIEUSES RIDICULES* (1659); *L'ECOLE DES MARIS* (1661); *L'ECOLE DES FEMMES* (1662); *DOM JUAN* (1665); *LE MISANTHROPE* (1666); *L'AVARE* (1668); *TARTUFFE* (1669); *LE BOURGEOIS GENTILHOMME* (1670); *LES FOURBERIES DE SCAPIN* (1671); *LES FEMMES SAVANTES* (1672); AND *LE MALADE IMAGINAIRE* (1673).

Between the original version as Plautus's *Aulularia* and its current incarnation as *Hello Dolly! The Miser* has enjoyed an uninterrupted three-hundred-year run in the repertory of the Comédie Française. We might speculate on the enduring appeal of *The Miser*. As farce, it belongs to the most accessible but, at the same time, the most perishable of the dramatic genres. Nowadays farce, at least in England and America, is out of favor.

Harpagon, who tyrannizes over his children, bullies his servants, bargains for a young bride, and obsessively protects his gold—this not very attractive man—enjoys as secure a position in the dramatic tradition as majestic Lear or noble Antony.

Harpagon, who dominates the play—note how his presence is felt even when he is not on stage—in actual life would be insufferable. Why, then, does he fascinate us on the stage? Is it that his avarice and self-absorption suggest an undiminished vitality which reinforces our own sense of life? Men of Harpagon's years normally communicate their awareness of their mortality. Harpagon somehow suggests that he will live forever.

In *The Miser,* Molière makes comic that aspect of life that is infrequently amusing: the eternal struggle between the generations, between the old and young, between the original have's and have-not's —fathers and sons. What does, for example, Harpagon's horde of gold represent to him? What does it represent to his children? How are we to interpret the sexual rivalry between Harpagon and Cleante? What social strategems are illustrated by Valère's tactics in dealing with Harpagon?

In essence, then, we might characterize the pull of Molière's play on generations of playgoers as deriving from the tragicomic tension between the single-mindedness of the old and the conquering assurance of the young, a conflict which Molière portrays without lamentation or tears.

THE MISER

TRANSLATION BY JOHN WOOD

PERSONS OF THE PLAY

HARPAGON, *father of Cléante and Élise, suitor for the hand of Marianne*

CLÉANTE, *his son, in love with Marianne*

ÉLISE, *his daughter, in love with Valère*

VALÈRE, *son of Anselme and in love with Élise*

MARIANNE, *in love with Cléante and courted by Harpagon*

ANSELME, *father of Valère and Marianne*

FROSINE, *an adventuress*

MASTER SIMON, *an intermediary*

MASTER JACQUES, *cook and coachman to Harpagon*

BRINDAVOINE ⎫
LA MERLUCHE ⎬ *servants to Harpagon*
DAME CLAUDE ⎭

LA FLÈCHE, *valet to Cléante*

OFFICER

OFFICER'S CLERK

The scene is in Paris.

ACT ONE

(VALÈRE, ÉLISE.)

VALÈRE.   Come, my dear Élise, surely you are not feeling sad, after giving me such generous assurance of your love? Here am I, the happiest of men, and I find you sighing! Is it because you regret having made me happy? Do you repent the promise which my ardour has won from you?

ÉLISE.   No, Valère. I could never regret anything I did for you. I cannot even bring myself to wish things were other than as they are, though I must confess I am concerned about the outcome and more than a little afraid that I may love you more dearly than I ought.

VALÈRE.   But what can you possibly have to fear from loving me, Élise?

ÉLISE.   Alas! A hundred and one things: my father's anger, the reproaches of my family, what people may say about me, but most of all, Valère, a change in your affection for me. I dread the cruel indifference with

233

which men so often requite an innocent love too ardently offered them.

VALÈRE.   Ah! Do not be so unjust as to judge me by other men. Believe me capable of anything, Élise, rather than of failure in my duty to you. I love you too dearly, and mine is a love which will last as long as life itself.

ÉLISE.   Ah, Valère, you all talk like that. Men are all alike in their promises. It is only in their deeds that they differ.

VALÈRE.   If deeds alone show what we are, then at least wait and judge my love by mine. Do not look for faults which only exist in your own fond forebodings. I implore you not to let such wounding and unjust suspicions destroy my happiness! Give me time to convince you and you shall have a thousand proofs of the sincerity of my love.

ÉLISE.   Ah! How easy it is to let ourselves be persuaded by those we love! I am convinced that you would never deceive me, Valère. I do believe you love me truly and faithfully. I have not the least wish to doubt you, and my only concern is that other people may find cause to blame me.

VALÈRE.   And why should that trouble you?

ÉLISE.   Ah, if only everyone could see you as I do, I should have nothing to fear. The qualities I see in you justify everything I do for you. My love is founded on knowledge of your virtues and sustained by my gratitude, a gratitude which Heaven itself enjoins. How can I ever forget the dreadful danger which first brought us together, your noble courage in risking your life to snatch me from the fury of the waves, your tender solicitude when you had brought me to the shore and the unremitting ardour of your love which neither time nor adversity has diminished, a love for which you neglect your parents and your country, conceal your true rank and stoop to service in my father's household merely for the sake of being near me! These are the things which weigh with me, Valère, and justify, for me, my promises to you, but the justification may not seem sufficient to others—and I cannot be certain that they will share my feelings.

VALÈRE.   Of all these things you have mentioned, only one gives me any claim on you, Élise, and that is my love. As for your scruples, surely your father has done everything he could to justify you in the eyes of the world! Surely his avarice and the miserable existence he makes his children lead, would justify still stranger things! Forgive me, my dear, for speaking of him in this way, but you know that on this issue there is nothing good one can say of him. However, if only I can find my parents again, as I hope I may, we shall have little difficulty in gaining his consent. I grow impatient for news of them, and if I do not hear soon I shall set out in search of them myself.

ÉLISE.   Oh no, Valère. Do not go away, I beseech you! Stay and give your whole attention to gaining my father's confidence.

VALÈRE. Cannot you see how I am endeavouring to do so? You know what adroitness and subservience I had to show to get into his service, what a mask of sympathy and conformity with his feelings I assumed in order to ingratiate myself with him, how in his presence I am for ever playing a part with a view to gaining his favour. And am I not, indeed, making remarkable progress? I find that the best way to win people's favour is to pretend to agree with them, to fall in with their precepts, encourage their foibles and applaud whatever they do. One need have no fear of overdoing the subservience. One can play up to them quite openly, for, when it comes to flattery, the most cunning of men are the most easily deceived, and people can be induced to swallow anything, however absurd or ridiculous, provided it is sufficiently seasoned with praise. Such methods may impair one's integrity, but if one has need of people one must accommodate oneself to them, and if there is no other way of gaining their support, well then, the blame lies less with the flatterers than with those who want to be flattered.

ÉLISE. Why don't you try to win my brother's support in case the maidservant should take it into her head to betray us?

VALÈRE. No, I couldn't handle father and son at the same time. They are so utterly different that one could not be in the confidence of both simultaneously. Do what you can with your brother and make use of your mutual affection to win him to our side. He is coming in now. I will withdraw. Take this opportunity of speaking to him, but tell him only so much of our affairs as you think fit.

ÉLISE. I don't know whether I can bring myself to take him into my confidence.

(*Enter* CLÉANTE.)

CLÉANTE. I am delighted to find you alone, sister. I have been longing for a talk with you. I want to tell you a secret.

ÉLISE. Well, here I am, ready to listen, Cléante. What have you to tell me?

CLÉANTE. Lots of things, my dear, but—to sum it up in one word—I'm in love.

ÉLISE. *You* are in love?

CLÉANTE. Yes. I'm in love, and let me say before we go any further that I am fully aware that I am dependent on my father, that as a son I must submit to his wishes, that we should never give a promise of marriage without the consent of those who brought us into the world, that Heaven made them the arbiters of our choice, that it is our duty never to bestow our affections except as they may decide, that, not being blinded by passion, they are less likely to be deceived and better able to see what is good for us than we are ourselves, that it behoves us to trust to the light of their prudence rather than to our own blind desires, and that youthful impetuosity leads, as often as not, to disaster!

I mention all this, my dear sister, to save you the trouble of saying it. The fact is that I am too much in love to listen to anything you have to say and I, therefore, ask you to spare your remonstrances.

ÉLISE. And have you actually given her your promise?

CLÉANTE. No, but I am determined to do so, and I ask you, once again, not to try to dissuade me.

ÉLISE. Am I such a strange person as that, Cléante?

CLÉANTE. No, Élise, but you aren't in love. You know nothing of the power of the tender passion over the hearts of us lovers. I am afraid you may take too prudent a view.

ÉLISE. Oh, don't talk of my prudence! There is no one who is not imprudent at some time or other, and if I were to reveal all that is in my own heart you might find I was even less prudent than you are.

CLÉANTE. Ah, if only you were like me—if only you loved—

ÉLISE. Let us deal with your troubles first. Tell me who she is.

CLÉANTE. A new-comer to our neighbourhood—the most charming person in the world. I was completely carried away from the first moment I saw her. Her name is Marianne and she lives with her invalid mother, to whom she is wonderfully devoted. She cares for and consoles her in her sufferings with the most touching devotion. She lends a charm to everything she touches and a grace to everything she does. She is so gentle, so kind, so modest—so adorable. Oh, Élise, I only wish you had seen her!

ÉLISE. Oh, I can see her very well from your description, and the fact that you love her tells me sufficiently what sort of person she is.

CLÉANTE. I have discovered, indirectly, that they are not very well off, and that, even living modestly, as they do, they are hard put to make ends meet. Just think, my dear, what a pleasure it would be if I could restore her fortunes or even discreetly supplement the modest needs of a virtuous family. Imagine, on the other hand, my despair at my inability to enjoy such a pleasure, thanks to my father's avarice, or even to offer a single token of my love.

ÉLISE. Yes, I can see how galling it must be for you.

CLÉANTE. Ah, my dear, it's worse than you could ever imagine. Could anything be more cruel than this rigorous economy he inflicts on us, this unnatural parsimony under which we perforce languish? What use will money be to us if it only comes when we are too old to enjoy it; if, to manage at all in the meantime, I have to run into debt on all sides, and, like you, am constantly reduced to going to tradesmen for help in order to clothe myself decently? I wanted to talk to you and ask you to help me to sound father about what I have in mind. If I find he is opposed to it, I'm determined to run away with my beloved and take whatever fortune Heaven may vouchsafe us. With this end in view I am trying to raise money everywhere. If you are in the same position as I am, my dear sister, and father opposes your wishes too, let us both leave him and free ourselves from the tyranny his intolerable avarice has so long imposed on us.

ÉLISE.   He certainly gives us more and more cause every day to regret our dear mother's death.

CLÉANTE.   I hear his voice. Let us go and discuss our plans somewhere else and later we can join forces in an attack on his obduracy.

(*They go out. Enter* HARPAGON *and* LA FLÈCHE.)

HARPAGON.   Get out at once! I'll have no back answers! Go on! Clear out of my house, sworn thief and gallows-bird that you are!

LA FLÈCHE   (*aside*). I never came across such a confounded old scoundrel. I reckon he is possessed of a devil, if you ask me!

HARPAGON.   What are you muttering about?

LA FLÈCHE.   What are you turning me out for?

HARPAGON.   What right have you to ask me my reasons? Get out before I throw you out.

LA FLÈCHE.   What have I done to you?

HARPAGON.   Enough for me to want to be rid of you.

LA FLÈCHE.   Your son—my master—told me to wait for him!

HARPAGON.   Go wait in the street, then! Don't let me see you in the house any more, standing there keeping a watch on everything that goes on, and an eye for anything you can pick up. I want no spy for ever watching my affairs, a sneaking dog with his confounded eyes on everything I do, devouring everything I possess and rummaging everywhere to see if there's anything he can steal.

LA FLÈCHE.   And how the deuce do you think anyone is going to steal from you? Is it likely anyone is going to steal from you when you keep everything under lock and key and stand guard day and night?

HARPAGON.   I'll lock up what I want and stand guard when I please. I never saw such a pack of prying scoundrels! They've an eye on everything one does! (*Aside*) I'm only afraid he's got wind of my money. (*To* LA FLÈCHE) You are just the man to go spreading it round that I have got money hidden, aren't you?

LA FLÈCHE.   You have money hidden?

HARPAGON.   No, you rogue—I never said so! (*Aside*) Oh, it infuriates me! (*To* LA FLÈCHE) All I'm asking is that you shan't go spreading malicious rumours that I have!

LA FLÈCHE.   What does it matter to us whether you have or you haven't? It's all the same either way.

HARPAGON.   So you'll argue, will you! (*Raising his fist*) I'll teach you to argue! Once again, get out of here!

LA FLÈCHE.   All right! I'm going.

HARPAGON.   Wait! You are not taking anything with you?

LA FLÈCHE.   What could I be taking?

HARPAGON.   Come here! Let me see! Show me your hands.

LA FLÈCHE.   There!

HARPAGON.   Now the others.

LA FLÈCHE.   The others?

HARPAGON.   Yes, the others.

LA FLÈCHE.   There you are!

HARPAGON   *(pointing to his breeches)*. Have you nothing in there?

LA FLÈCHE.   See for yourself!

HARPAGON   *(feeling at the bottom of his breeches)* . These wide breeches are the very things for hiding stolen property. They deserve hanging— whoever makes such things.

LA FLÈCHE   *(aside)* . A fellow like this deserves to get what he expects. I only wish I could have the pleasure of robbing him.

HARPAGON.   Eh?

LA FLÈCHE.   What's that?

HARPAGON.   What did you say about robbing?

LA FLÈCHE.   I said, "Have a good look and make sure I am not robbing you."

HARPAGON.   That's what I intend to do. (HARPAGON *feels in* LA FLÈCHE'S *pockets.)*

LA FLÈCHE   *(aside.)* A plague on all misers and their miserly ways.

HARPAGON.   What's that? What d'ye say?

LA FLÈCHE.   What did I say?

HARPAGON.   Yes, what did you say about misers and miserly ways?

LA FLÈCHE.   I said a plague on all misers and their miserly ways!

HARPAGON.   And who are you referring to?

LA FLÈCHE.   Misers, of course.

HARPAGON.   And who are they?

LA FLÈCHE.   Who are they? Stingy old scoundrels.

HARPAGON.   But who d'ye mean by that?

LA FLÈCHE.   What are *you* worrying about?

HARPAGON.   I am worrying about what I've a right to worry about.

LA FLÈCHE.   Did you think I meant you?

HARPAGON.   I think what I choose, but I want to know who you were talking to.

LA FLÈCHE.   To—to my hat.

HARPAGON.   Yes, and I'll talk to your thick skull.

LA FLÈCHE.   Can't I say what I like about misers?

HARPAGON.   Yes, you can if you like, but I can put a stop to your impudent nonsense! Hold your tongue.

LA FLÈCHE.   I mentioned no names.

HARPAGON. If you say a word more, I'll leather you.

LA FLÈCHE. If the cap fits—I say—

HARPAGON. Will you be quiet?

LA FLÈCHE. Yes, if I must!

HARPAGON. Ah! You—

LA FLÈCHE. (*shows a pocket in his jerkin*) . Steady on! Here's another pocket! Will that satisfy you?

HARPAGON. Come on! Hand it over without my having to search you!

LA FLÈCHE. Hand over what?

HARPAGON. Whatever it is you've taken from me!

LA FLÈCHE. I've taken nothing from you.

HARPAGON. Sure?

LA FLÈCHE. Certain!

HARPAGON. Be off, then, and go to the devil!

LA FLÈCHE. That's a nice sort of leave taking.

HARPAGON. I leave you to your conscience. (*Alone*) He's a confounded nuisance, this scoundrelly valet. I hate the sight of the limping cur! It is a terrible worry having a large sum of money in the house. Much better have one's money well invested and keep no more than is needed for current expenses. It's difficult to find a safe hiding-place in the house. I've no confidence in strong boxes. I don't trust 'em. They are just an invitation to thieves, I always think—the first things they go for. All the same I'm not sure I was wise to bury in the garden the ten thousand crowns I was paid yesterday. Ten thousand crowns in gold is a sum which . . . (*Enter* ÉLISE *and* CLÉANTE *talking together in low voices.*) Oh Heavens! Have I given myself away? I let myself be carried away by my temper—I do believe I was talking aloud. (*To* CLÉANTE) What is it?

CLÉANTE. Nothing father.

HARPAGON. Have you been here long?

ÉLISE. No, we have only just come.

HARPAGON. Did you hear—er—

CLÉANTE. Hear what, father?

HARPAGON. Just now—

ÉLISE. What was it?

HARPAGON. What I have just been saying.

CLÉANTE. No.

HARPAGON. Yes, you did, you did! You did!

CLÉANTE. Pardon me, we heard nothing.

HARPAGON. I can see you overheard something. The fact is I was just saying to myself how difficult it is nowadays to get hold of any money and how fortunate anybody is who has ten thousand crowns by him.

CLÉANTE. We hesitated to come near you for fear of interrupting you.

HARPAGON. I'm very glad of the chance to explain to you, in case you got the wrong impression and imagined I was saying that I had ten thousand crowns.

CLÉANTE. We don't concern ourselves with your affairs.

HARPAGON. I only wish I had ten thousand crowns.

CLÉANTE. I don't believe—

HARPAGON. It would be a good thing for me if I had.

ÉLISE. Such things—

HARPAGON. I could well do with a sum like that.

CLÉANTE. I think—

HARPAGON. It would come in very useful.

ÉLISE. You are—

HARPAGON. I should have less cause to complain of hard times than I have.

CLÉANTE. Good Heavens, father! You have no cause to complain. Everybody knows you are well enough off!

HARPAGON. Me? Well off! What a lie! Nothing could be further from the truth! It's scandalous to spread such tales!

ÉLISE. Well, don't be angry.

HARPAGON. It's a queer thing when my own children betray me and turn against me.

CLÉANTE. Is it turning against you to say that you are well off?

HARPAGON. Yes. What with your saying things like that and your extravagant ways someone will be coming and cutting my throat one of these days in the belief that I'm made of money.

CLÉANTE. What extravagant ways have I got?

HARPAGON. What, indeed! What could be more scandalous than the sumptuous apparel you flaunt round the town? Only yesterday I was complaining of your sister—but you are far worse! It's a crying scandal! What you are wearing now, taking you as you stand, would add up to a nice competency. I have told you a score of times already, my lad, I don't like your goings on at all: this aping of the nobility and going about dressed up as you are can only mean that you are robbing me somehow.

CLÉANTE. But how can I be robbing you?

HARPAGON. How should I know? Where do you get the money to live as you do?

CLÉANTE. Where do I get the money? From cards. I happen to be lucky and I put my winnings on my back.

HARPAGON. That's no way to go on! No way at all! If you are lucky at cards you should take advantage of it and put your winnings into some sound investment. Then they'll be there when you want 'em. But what I would like to know, never mind anything else, is what's the use of all these ribbons that you are decked out with from head to foot? Wouldn't half a dozen pins do to fasten up your breeches? Why need you spend money on a wig, when you can wear your own hair—which costs nothing? I'm willing to bet that your perukes and ribbons cost you twenty guineas at least, and twenty guineas invested bring in one pound thirteen shillings and elevenpence farthing a year at no more than eight per cent.

CLÉANTE. That's true enough.

HARPAGON. Well now, suppose we leave that and come to something else—Eh? (*Aside*) I believe they are making signs to each other to steal my purse. (*To* CLÉANTE) What do you mean by making signs like that?

ÉLISE. We are just arguing as to who should speak first. We both have something to tell you.

HARPAGON. Yes, and I have something to tell both of you.

CLÉANTE. We want to talk to you about marriage, father.

HARPAGON. Ay, and it's marriage I want to talk to you about.

ÈLISE. Oh, father!

HARPAGON. Why the "Oh, father"? Is it the word marriage or the idea of getting married yourself you are afraid of, my girl?

CLÉANTE. The word marriage might well alarm both of us. It depends on what you understand by it. We are afraid that what *we* want may not agree with what *you* want.

HARPAGON. Now do be patient. Don't get alarmed. I know what is good for both of you. Neither of you shall have any cause to complain of what I am going to do for you. First of all, do you know a young lady named Marianne who lives not far from here?

CLÉANTE. Yes, father, I do.

HARPAGON (*to* ÉLISE). And you?

ÉLISE. I have heard of her.

HARPAGON. Well now, my boy, what is your opinion of this young lady?

CLÉANTE. She is a most charming person.

HARPAGON. Her looks?

CLÉANTE. Modest and intelligent.

HARPAGON. Her manner?

CLÉANTE. Admirable, beyond question.

HARPAGON. You think a girl like that is worth serious consideration?

CLÉANTE. I do, father.

HARPAGON. An eligible match, in fact?

CLÉANTE. Most eligible.

HARPAGON. And she looks as if she'd make a good housewife?

CLÉANTE. Without a doubt.

HARPAGON. And whoever marries her can count himself a lucky man, eh?

CLÉANTE.   Assuredly.

HARPAGON.   There's one little difficulty. I'm afraid she may not bring as much money as one would like.

CLÉANTE.   Ah! What does money matter, father, when it is a question of marrying a good woman?

HARPAGON.   Oh no, I don't agree with you there! But there *is* this to be said, that if she hasn't as much money as one would wish there may be some other way of making up for it.

CLÉANTE.   Of course.

HARPAGON.   Well now, I'm very pleased to find you agree with me, because her modest ways and gentle disposition have quite won my heart. Provided that I find she has *some* money—I've made up my mind to marry her.

CLÉANTE.   Eh?

HARPAGON.   What do you mean by "Eh"?

CLÉANTE.   You have made up your mind to—what did you say?

HARPAGON.   Marry Marianne.

CLÉANTE.   You mean—you—you yourself?

HARPAGON.   Yes. Me! Me! Me myself. What about it?

CLÉANTE.   I feel faint. I must get out of here.

HARPAGON.   It will pass off. Go into the kitchen and have a good drink— of cold water. (*Exit* CLÉANTE.) There! You see what these effeminate young men are! They haven't the strength of a chicken! Well, there you are, my girl, that is what I've decided for myself. For your brother I have a certain widow in mind. Someone came to talk to me about her this morning. As for you, yourself, I mean to bestow you on Seigneur Anselme!

ÉLISE.   Seigneur Anselme.

HARPAGON.   Yes, he's a man of ripe experience, prudent and discreet, not more than fifty years of age and reputed to be very rich.

ÉLISE   (*curtseying*). If you please, father, I don't want to marry.

HARPAGON   (*imitating her*). If *you* please, my pet, I want you to marry.

ÉLISE.   Excuse me, father—

HARPAGON.   Excuse *me*, my dear—

ÉLISE.   I am Seigneur Anselme's very humble servant but, if you don't mind, I won't marry him.

HARPAGON.   And I am your very humble servant, my dear, but, if you don't mind, you *will* marry him, and this very evening too.

ÉLISE.   This evening!

HARPAGON.   This evening!

ÉLISE.   No, father, I won't.

HARPAGON.   Yes, daughter, you will.

ÉLISE.   No!

HARPAGON.   Yes!

ÉLISE.   I tell you I shan't!

HARPAGON.   But I say you shall!

ÉLISE.   I will never agree to it!

HARPAGON.   But I shall make you agree to it!

ÉLISE.   I'll kill myself rather than marry such a man.

HARPAGON.   You won't kill yourself and you shall marry him. The impertinence! Who ever heard of a daughter talking like this to her father!

ÉLISE.   Who ever heard of a father requiring his daughter to make such a marriage!

HARPAGON.   It is a most suitable match. I am willing to bet that everyone will approve of my choice.

ÉLISE.   And I am willing to bet that no reasonable person would do any such thing.

HARPAGON.   Here comes Valère. Will you agree to let him judge between us?

ÉLISE.   Yes, I agree.

HARPAGON.   You'll accept his decision?

ÉLISE.   Yes, I'll abide by whatever he says.

HARPAGON.   That's settled, then. Come here, Valère! We want you to decide which of us is in the right—my daughter here, or myself.

VALÈRE.   Oh, you sir, beyond question.

HARPAGON.   But you don't know what we are talking about!

VALÈRE.   No, but you *couldn't* be wrong. You are always in the right.

HARPAGON.   I intend to marry her this evening to a man who is both wealthy and wise, and the silly chit tells me to my face that she won't have him at any price. What d'ye say to that?

VALÈRE.   What do I say to that?

HARPAGON.   Yes.

VALÈRE.   Ah well—I—

HARPAGON.   Well?

VALÈRE.   What I say is that fundamentally I agree with you—for of course you just must be right, but, on the other hand, she isn't altogether in the wrong.

HARPAGON.   Why! Seigneur Anselme is an eligible match, well born, quiet, assured, prudent, and very well off and with no surviving children of his first marriage. What more could she want?

VALÈRE.   That's true—though she might perhaps contend that it is rather precipitate and that she ought at least to be allowed time to see if she can reconcile herself to . . .

HARPAGON.   No! An opportunity like this won't stand delay. What is more, there is a special, a unique advantage. He is willing to take her —without dowry!

VALÈRE. Without dowry?

HARPAGON. Yes.

VALÈRE. Oh! I say no more. There you are! One must agree—that's absolutely conclusive.

HARPAGON. It means a considerable saving for me.

VALÈRE. Of course, there's no gainsaying that. It is true that your daughter might contend that marriage is a more serious matter than people sometimes realize, that a lifetime's happiness or unhappiness may depend upon it and that one ought not to enter into a commitment for life without giving it serious consideration.

HARPAGON. But—without dowry!

VALÈRE. Yes, you are right! That's the important thing, of course—although there are people who would contend that in a case like this your daughter's own feelings should be considered, and that where there is such a great disparity of age, temperament, and opinions there is a risk that the marriage might turn out badly. . . .

HARPAGON. But—without dowry!

VALÈRE. Yes, one must admit there's no answer to that. There is no arguing against it. Not that there are not some fathers who would attach more importance to their daughter's happiness than the money they might have to part with and refuse to sacrifice it to mercenary considerations. They would rather seek to secure before everything else that union of mutual affection from which spring happiness, joy, and contentment—

HARPAGON. Without dowry!

VALÈRE. True. It is unanswerable. Without dowry! There's no countering that!

HARPAGON. (*aside—looking offstage*). Ah, I thought I heard a dog barking. Can it be someone after my money? (*To* VALÈRE) Don't go away. I'll be back directly. (*Goes out.*)

ÉLISE. Surely you don't mean what you are saying, Valère?

VALÈRE. If we are to get what we want from him we must avoid rubbing him the wrong way. It would ruin everything to oppose him directly. There are some people you can't deal with except by humouring them. Impatient of opposition, restive by nature, they never fail to shy at the truth and won't go about things in a common-sense fashion. The only way to lead them is to turn them gently in the direction you want them to go. Pretend to give your consent and you'll find it's the best way to get what you want.

ÉLISE. But this marriage, Valère?

VALÈRE. We will find some excuse for breaking it off.

ÉLISE. But how—when it is to take place this evening?

VALÈRE. You must pretend to be ill and have it postponed.

ÉLISE.   But they will discover the truth when they call in the doctor.

VALÈRE.   Not they! What do those fellows know about anything? Have whatever malady you like, they'll explain how you got it.

HARPAGON   *(returning—to himself)*. It's nothing, thank Heaven!

VALÈRE.   If the worst comes to the worst we must take refuge in flight, that is, if you love me well enough, my dear Élise, to face— *(seeing* HARPAGON*)* Yes, it's a daughter's duty to obey her father. It's not for her to worry about what her husband looks like; when it's a case of— without dowry—she must take what she's given.

HARPAGON.   Good! That's the way to talk.

VALÈRE.   Forgive me, sir, for letting my feelings run away with me and taking the liberty of talking to her in this way.

HARPAGON.   Not at all. I am delighted. I give you a free hand with her. *(To* ÉLISE*)* It's no use running away. I invest him with full parental authority over you. You must do whatever he tells you.

VALÈRE   *(to* ÉLISE*)*. Now will you resist my remonstrances!

(To HARPAGON*)* I'll follow her and continue the homily I was giving her.

HARPAGON.   Do. I shall be grateful to you.

VALÈRE.   It is well to keep her on a tight rein.

HARPAGON.   True. We must—

VALÈRE.   Don't worry. I think I can deal with her.

HARPAGON.   Do, by all means! I am just going to take a stroll in the town. I'll be back before long.

VALÈRE.   Yes. Money is the most precious thing in all the world! You ought to thank Heaven you have such a good father. He knows the value of things. When a man offers to take a girl without dowry there's no point in looking any further. That's the only thing that matters. "Without dowry"—it counts for more than good looks, youth, birth, honour, wisdom, and probity.

(They go out together.)

HARPAGON.   Good lad! Spoken like an oracle! How lucky I am to have such a man in my service.

ACT TWO

(CLÉANTE, LA FLÈCHE.)

CLÉANTE.   Now you scoundrel! Where have you been hiding yourself? Didn't I tell you to . . .

LA FLÈCHE.   Yes, sir, and I came in here with every intention of waiting for you, but your father, who's a most awkward old man to deal with, would chase me out willy-nilly. I very nearly got myself a hiding.

CLÉANTE.   How is our affair progressing? Things have become more pressing than ever, and since I last saw you I have found out that my father
is my rival in love.

LA FLÈCHE.   Your father in love?

CLÉANTE.   Yes, and I had the greatest difficulty in the world in preventing
him from seeing how upset I was by the discovery.

LA FLÈCHE.   Fancy his being in love! What the devil is he thinking about?
Is he trying to take a rise out of everybody? What use is love to a fellow
like him, anyway?

CLÉANTE.   It must be a judgement on me—his getting an idea like this
into his head!

LA FLÈCHE.   But why do you conceal your own love affair from him?

CLÉANTE.   To give him less cause for suspicion, to keep myself in a position to prevent this marriage of his if it comes to the point. What reply
did they give you?

LA FLÈCHE.   Upon my word, sir, borrowing money is a miserable business.
Anyone who has to go through the moneylender's hands, as you have,
must put up with some pretty queer things.

CLÉANTE.   So nothing will come of it?

LA FLÈCHE.   Oh no! Master Simon, the agent they put us in touch with,
is a keen business-like fellow, and he's moving Heaven and Earth for
you. He assures me he has taken quite a fancy to you.

CLÉANTE.   So I shall get the fifteen thousand I'm asking for?

LA FLÈCHE.   Yes—subject to a few trifling conditions you'll have to accept
if you want it to go through.

CLÉANTE.   Has he put you in touch with the actual lender?

LA FLÈCHE.   Now really, sir, that isn't the way these things are done! He's
even more anxious to conceal his identity than you are. There is more
involved in these jobs than you think. They won't give his name and
he is to have an opportunity of talking to you to-day at a house hired
for the purpose, so that he can learn from your own lips about your
means and your family. I have no doubt at all that the mere mention
of your father's name will make everything easy.

CLÉANTE.   Especially as my mother is dead and they can't stop me getting
her money.

LA FLÈCHE.   There are a few conditions here which he himself has dictated to our go-between. He wants you to see them before going any
further. "Provided that the lender shall be satisfied as to the securities
and that the borrower be of age and of a family with means sufficient,
substantial and secure, free and quit of all encumbrance there shall be
executed a proper and precise undertaking before a notary, of known
probity, who to this end and purpose shall be nominated by the lender
inasmuch as he is the more concerned that the instrument be executed
in due form."

CLÉANTE.   I have nothing to say against that.

LA FLÈCHE.   "The lender, that his conscience may be free from all reproach, proposes to make his money available at no more than five and a half per cent."

CLÉANTE.   Five and a half per cent! My goodness, but that's very reasonable. There's nothing to complain of there!

LA FLÈCHE.   True. "But—whereas the lender aforesaid has not the sum in question by him and in order to oblige the borrower is himself obliged to borrow elsewhere at the rate of twenty per cent, the aforesaid borrower shall agree to meet this interest without prejudice to the five and a half per cent aforementioned in consideration of the fact that it is only to oblige the aforesaid borrower that the lender aforesaid undertakes to borrow the aforesaid amount."

CLÉANTE.   What the devil! What sort of Jew or Turk have we got hold of? That's more than twenty-five per cent!

LA FLÈCHE.   True. That's what I said. You'd better think about it.

CLÉANTE.   What's the use of thinking about it. I need the money, so I shall have to agree to everything.

LA FLÈCHE.   That's what I told them.

CLÉANTE.   Is there anything else?

LA FLÈCHE.   Just one small clause. "Of the fifteen thousand francs which the borrower requires, the lender can only dispose of twelve thousand in cash, and for the other three thousand the borrower shall undertake to take over the effects, clothing, and miscellaneous objects as set out in the following inventory and priced by the aforesaid lender at the most moderate valuation possible."

CLÉANTE.   What does that mean?

LA FLÈCHE.   Listen to the inventory. "Item—one four-poster bed complete with hangings of Hungarian lace, very handsomely worked upon an olive-coloured material, together with six chairs and a counterpane to match, the whole in very good condition and lined in red and blue shot silk; item—one tester bed with hangings of good Aumale serge in old rose with silk fringes and valance."

CLÉANTE.   What does he expect me to do with that?

LA FLÈCHE.   Wait. "Item—one set of hangings in tapestry representing the lovers of Gombaut and Macaea; item—one large table in walnut with twelve pedestal or turned legs with drawn-out leaf at either end and fitted underneath with six stools."

CLÈANTE.   Confound it! What use is that to me?

LA FLÈCHE.   Patience, please. "Item—three muskets, inlaid in mother-of-pearl, with three assorted rests; item—one brick furnace with two retorts and three flasks, very useful for anyone interested in distilling; item—"

CLÈANTE.   Oh! It's infuriating—

LA FLÈCHE.   Now, now! "Item—one Bologna lute complete with strings or nearly so; item—one fox-and-goose board, one draughts-board, one game of mother goose as derived from the ancient Greeks, very useful for passing the time when one has nothing else to do; item—one crocodile skin three feet six inches in length and stuffed with hay, a very attractive curio for suspension from the ceiling—all the afore-mentioned articles valued at upwards of four thousand five hundred francs and reduced to three thousand at the discretion of the lender."

CLÉANTE.   Confound him and his discretion! The miserable rogue! Did you ever hear of such usury! Not content with charging outrageous interest, he must rook me three thousand francs for his collection of old junk. I shan't get two hundred for the lot, and yet I suppose I must just resign myself to agreeing to whatever he wants! He's in a position to make me put up with it. His dagger's at my throat, the scoundrel!

LA FLÈCHE.   It seems to me, master, if you don't mind my saying so, that you are going the same road to ruin as Panurge—drawing your money in advance, buying dear, selling cheap, and eating your corn in the blade.

CLÉANTE.   Well, what else can I do? That's what young men are driven to by the cursed niggardliness of their fathers. Can anyone wonder that their sons wish them dead!

LA FLÈCHE.   I must admit that your father's behavior would exasperate the mildest of men. I have no particular fancy for getting myself hanged, thank the Lord, and when I see some of my colleagues involving themselves in transactions of a certain sort I know when to keep out and steer clear of the little amusements which lead one too near the gallows, but I'm bound to say that I think his behaviour is a sheer invitation to robbery. I should even consider it a praiseworthy action to rob him.

CLÉANTE.   Give me the inventory a moment, I'll have another look at it.
(*Enter* MASTER SIMON *and* HARPAGON.)

MASTER SIMON.   Yes, as I was saying, sir, the young man is in need of money. His affairs are such that he needs it urgently, and he will agree to any conditions you like to make.

HARPAGON.   And you feel certain, Master Simon, that there's not the least risk? You know your client's name, means, and family?

MASTER SIMON.   No, I can't tell you exactly. It was only by chance that he was put in touch with me, but he will tell you it all himself, and his servant assures me that you'll be completely satisfied when you make his acquaintance. All I can tell you is that his family is very wealthy, his mother is dead, and that he'll guarantee, if need be, that his father will die within six months!

HARPAGON.   Well, that's something! After all, it's only charitable to assist people when we can, Master Simon.

MASTER SIMON. Of course.

LA FLÈCHE (*to* CLÉANTE *in a whisper*). What's the meaning of this—our Master Simon talking to your father?

CLÉANTE (*to* LA FLÈCHE *in a whisper*). Someone must have told him who I am. Could *you* betray me?

MASTER SIMON. You *are* in a hurry! Who told you this was the meeting-place? (*To* HARPAGON) I didn't disclose your name and address to them, sir, but I think there's no great harm done. They are people of discretion and you can discuss things between you here.

HARPAGON. What's this?

MASTER SIMON. This gentleman is the person I was speaking of, sir, who wants to borrow fifteen thousand francs.

HARPAGON. So it's you, is it, you blackguard? You descend to this sort of thing, do you?

CLÉANTE. So it's you, is it, father? You stoop to this kind of trade, do you?

(MASTER SIMON *and* LA FLÈCHE *go out.*)

HARPAGON. So you are the man who is ruining himself by such outrageous borrowing?

CLÉANTE. And you are the man who is enriching himself by such criminal usury!

HARPAGON. How can you ever dare to face me after this?

CLÉANTE. How will you ever dare to face anyone at all?

HARPAGON. Aren't you ashamed to stoop to such extravagance, to involve yourself in such frightful expense, to squander in this disgraceful fashion the fortune your parents have toiled so hard to accumulate for you?

CLÉANTE. Don't you blush to disgrace your position by transactions of this kind, to sacrifice your honour and reputation to your insatiable lust for piling coin on coin and outdoing anything the most notorious usurers ever invented in the way of scandalous interest!

HARPAGON. Get out of my sight, you scoundrel! Get out of my sight!

CLÉANTE. I ask you, who commits the greater crime, the man who borrows to meet his necessities, or the one who extorts money from people which he doesn't need?

HARPAGON. Go away, I tell you! You make my blood boil. (*Exit* CLÉANTE.) I'm not sorry this has happened! It's a warning to me to keep a closer watch on him than ever.

(*Enter* FROSINE.)

FROSINE. Sir—

HARPAGON. Just a minute. I'll come back and talk to you presently. (*Aside*) It's time I had a look at my money!

(*He goes out. Enter* LA FLÈCHE.)

LA FLÈCHE (*to himself*). It's a most peculiar business. He must have a regular furniture store somewhere. We didn't recognize any of the stuff in the inventory.

FROSINE.   Ah, it's you, my poor La Flèche. Fancy meeting you!

LA FLÈCHE.   Why, Frosine! What are you doing here?

FROSINE.   Following my usual occupation—acting as go-between, making myself useful to people and picking up what I can from such small abilities as I possess. You have to live on your wits in this world, you know, and those of us who have no other resources must rely on scheming and hard work.

LA FLÈCHE.   Have you some business with the master?

FROSTINE.   Yes, I'm handling a little transaction for him and hoping for some recompense.

LA FLÈCHE.   From him? My goodness! You'll be clever if you get anything out of him! Money is hard to come by in this house I warn you.

FROSINE.   But there *are* certain services which are wonderfully effective in opening the purse-strings.

LA FLÈCHE.   Well I won't contradict you, but you don't know our Mr Harpagon yet. He just isn't human at all, our Mr Harpagon—he hasn't one scrap of humanity in him! He has the hardest heart and the closest fist of any man living. There's no service of any kind, sort, or description would make him grateful enough to put his hand in his pocket. Praise, compliments, fine words, friendliness, yes, as much as you like, but money—nothing doing! You may win his favour, be in his good graces—but nothing ever comes of it. He has such a dislike of the word "giving" that he won't even give you "good morning."

FROSINE.   Good Heavens! As if I don't know how to get round men! Why, I know all there is to be known about stroking them the right way, arousing their sympathy, and finding their soft spots.

LA FLÈCHE.   Not the slightest use here. Where money's involved I defy you to make any impression. On that score he's adamant—absolutely past praying for. You could be at death's door but *he* wouldn't budge. He puts money before reputation, honour, or virtue, and the mere sight of anyone asking for money is enough to throw him into a fit. It's like inflicting a mortal wound on him, taking his heart's blood, tearing out his very entrails, and if—but he's coming back. I must be off. . . .

(*He goes out. Enter* HARPAGON.)

HARPAGON   (*to himself*).   Everything is all right. (*To* FROSINE)   Well now, Frosine, what is it?

FROSINE.   Goodness me, how well you are looking—the very picture of health.

HARPAGON.   Who? Me!

FROSINE.   I never saw you looking so fresh and so sprightly.

HARPAGON.   Really?

FROSINE.   Why, you've never looked so young in your life. I know fellows of twenty-five who are not half as youthful as you are.

HARPAGON.   Nevertheless, I'm well over sixty, Frosine.

FROSINE.   Well, what's sixty? What of it? It's the very flower of one's age. You are just coming to the prime of life.

HARPAGON.   True, but I reckon I should be no worse for being twenty years younger.

FROSINE.   What are you talking about! You need wish no such thing. You've the constitution to live to a hundred.

HARPAGON.   Do you think so?

FROSINE.   I'm certain. You have all the indications. Keep still a moment! Look what a sign of longevity that is—the line between the eyes!

HARPAGON.   Is that really so?

FROSINE.   Of course. Give me your hand. Heavens! What a line of life!

HARPAGON.   What d'ye mean?

FROSINE.   You see where that line goes to?

HARPAGON.   Well, what does that mean?

FROSINE.   Upon my word. Did I say a hundred? You'll live to a hundred and twenty!

HARPAGON.   No! Is it possible?

FROSINE.   I tell you they'll have to knock you on the head! You'll see your children buried, ay, and your children's children.

HARPAGON.   So much the better! And how is our little business getting on?

FROSINE.   Need you ask? Did you ever know me start a job and not finish it? I really have a wonderful talent for matchmaking. There's nobody I couldn't pair off, given a little time to arrange things. I really think, if I took it into my head, I could match the Grand Turk and the Venetian Republic! Not that there was anything very difficult about this little business of yours. I am friendly with the two ladies and have talked to them both about you and told the mother of the intentions you have formed in regard to Marianne from seeing her pass along the street and taking the air at her window.

HARPAGON.   And her reply?

FROSINE.   She was delighted by the proposal, and when I intimated that you would like her daughter to be present this evening at the signing of your own daughter's marriage contract she agreed without hesitation and put her in my charge.

HARPAGON.   You see, I am committed to giving a supper for Seigneur Anselme, Frosine, and I shall be very pleased if she will join the party too.

FROSINE.   Good. She is to visit your daughter after dinner and then go to the fair, which she wants to do, and return in time for supper.

HARPAGON.   Very well. I'll lend them my carriage and they can go down together.

FROSINE.   That's the very thing for her!

HARPAGON.   Now, have you sounded the mother as to what dowry she can give her daughter, Frosine? Have you told her she must make an effort to contribute something and put herself to some pinching and scraping on an occasion like this? After all, nobody is going to marry a girl unless she brings something with her.

FROSINE.   Why, this girl will bring you twelve thousand a year.

HARPAGON.   Twelve thousand a year!

FROSINE.   Yes. In the first place she's been brought up on a very spare diet. She is a girl who is used to living on salad and milk, apples and cheese, so she'll need no elaborate table, none of your rich broths or eternal barley concoctions, nor any of the delicacies other women would require, and that's no small consideration. It might well amount to three thousand francs a year at least. Moreover, her tastes are simple; She has not any hankering after extravagant dresses, expensive jewellery, or sumptuous furnishings which young women of her age are so fond of—and this item alone means more than four thousand a year. Then, again, she has a very strong objection to playing for money, a most unusual thing in a woman nowadays. I know one woman in our neighbourhood who has lost twenty thousand francs at cards this year. Suppose we reckon only a quarter of that—five thousand a year for cards and four thousand on clothes and jewellery, that's nine thousand, and another three thousand on food—that gives you your twelve thousand a year, doesn't it?

HARPAGON.   Yes, it's not bad, but all these calculations don't amount to anything tangible.

FROSINE.   Come, come! Do you mean to say that a modest appetite, a sober taste in dress, and a dislike of card playing don't amount to anything tangible? Why, they are a marriage portion and an inheritance rolled into one!

HARPAGON.   No. It's just nonsense to try and make a dowry out of the expenses she won't incur. I'll give no credit for anything I don't actually receive. I really must have something I can get my hands on.

FROSINE.   Heavens, man! You'll get your hands on plenty. They've mentioned that they have money abroad somewhere. That will come to you.

HARPAGON.   Well, we shall have to look into that, but there's another thing worrying me, Frosine. The girl is young, as you know, and young people generally prefer those of their own age and don't fancy other society. I am afraid she may not take to a man as old as I am, and that might lead to certain little domestic complications which wouldn't please me at all.

FROSINE. How little you know her! It's another thing I was going to mention. She can't bear young men at all and keeps all her affection for old ones.

HARPAGON. Does she really?

FROSINE. Yes! I only wish you could have heard her on the subject. She can't bear the sight of a young man. She declares that nothing gives her more pleasure than to see a fine old man with a venerable beard. The older men are the better she likes them, so don't go making yourself look younger than you are. She wants someone in the sixties at least. She was on the point of being married when she suddenly broke it off because the man let it out that he was no more than fifty-six and he didn't put spectacles on to sign the marriage contract.

HARPAGON. That was the only reason?

FROSINE. Yes, she says fifty-six isn't old enough for her, and she likes a nose that wears spectacles.

HARPAGON. Well, that's something entirely new to me!

FROSINE. You wouldn't believe the lengths she goes to. She has a few pictures and engravings in her room, and what do you think they are? Adonis, Cephales, Paris, or Apollo? Not at all! Pictures of Saturn, King Priam, the aged Nestor, and good old father Anchises borne on the shoulders of his son.

HARPAGON. Well, that *is* remarkable! I should never have thought it. I'm delighted to hear that her tastes run that way. I must say if I'd been a woman I should never have fancied young men.

FROSINE. I can well believe you. What poor stuff young men are for anyone to fall in love with—a lot of snotty-nosed infants and fresh-faced country bumpkins. To think of anyone feeling any attraction towards them!

HARPAGON. I can never understand it myself. I don't know how it is that women are so fond of them.

FROSINE. They must be completely mad to find young men attractive. It doesn't make sense! These young fops aren't men. How can anyone take to such creatures?

HARPAGON. That's what I'm always saying. What with their effeminate voices and their two or three wisps of beard turned up like cat's whiskers, their tow wigs, their flowing breeches and unbuttoned coats!

FROSINE. Ay! They make a poor show compared with a man like you. You are something like a man, something worth looking at. You have the sort of figure women fall in love with, and you dress the part too.

HARPAGON. You think I'm attractive?

FROSINE. Why, you are quite irresistible. Your face is a picture. Turn round a little, if you please. What could be more handsome? Let me see you walk. There's a fine figure of a man—as limber and graceful as one could wish to see! Not a thing ails you.

HARPAGON.   No, nothing very serious, Heaven be praised, except a bit of catarrh that catches me now and again.

FROSINE.   Oh, that's nothing. Your catarrh is not unbecoming. Your cough is quite charming.

HARPAGON.   Tell me now, has Marianne ever seen me? Has she not noticed me passing by?

FROSINE.   No, but we've talked a lot about you. I've described you to her and I've not failed to sing your praises and tell her how fortunate she would be to have such a husband.

HARPAGON.   You've done well. Thank you, Frosine.

FROSINE.   I should like to make one small request to you, sir. (HARPAGON *looks grave.*) I'm involved in a lawsuit, and on the point of losing it for lack of a little money. You could easily ensure that I win my case if you were disposed to help me. You've no idea how pleased she will be to see you. (HARPAGON *looks cheerful.*) How delighted she will be with you. How she'll adore that old-fashioned ruff of yours! She will be absolutely charmed with your way of wearing your breeches pinned to your doublet. A lover with pinned-up breeches will be something quite out of the ordinary for her.

HARPAGON.   I'm delighted to hear it.

FROSINE.   This lawsuit is really a serious matter for me, sir— (HARPAGON *looks grave again.*) If I lose it I'm ruined, but a very little help would retrieve my position. I only wish you could have seen how delighted she was to hear me talking about you. (HARPAGON *looks cheerful again.*) As I recounted our good qualities, her eyes filled with pleasure and in the end I made her quite impatient to have the marriage all settled.

HARPAGON.   You have been very kind, Frosine, and I can't say how much obliged I am to you.

FROSINE.   I beseech you, sir, grant me the small assistance I'm asking. (HARPAGON *looks grave again.*) It will put me on my feet again and I shall be eternally grateful to you.

HARPAGON.   Good-bye. I must finish my letters.

FROSINE.   I do assure you, sir, I am in the most urgent need of your help.

HARPAGON.   I'll give instructions for my carriage to be got ready to take you to the fair.

FROSINE.   I wouldn't trouble you if I weren't absolutely obliged to.

HARPAGON.   I'll see that we have supper early so that it won't upset any of you.

FROSINE.   Please don't refuse me. You couldn't imagine, sir, how pleased—

HARPAGON.   I'm off. There's somebody calling me. Until later— (*He goes.*)

FROSINE.   May you rot, you stingy old cur! The skinflint held out against all my attempts. Devil take him! But I won't give it up. I can always count on getting something handsome out of the other party, whatever happens.

ACT THREE

(HARPAGON, CLÉANTE, ÉLISE, VALÈRE, DAME CLAUDE, MASTER JACQUES, BRINDA-VOINE, LA MERLUCHE.)

HARPAGON.   Come along. Let us have you all in here. I want to give you your instructions for this evening and see that everybody has his job. Come here, Dame Claude, we'll start with you. (*She carries a broom.*) Good, I see you are ready for the fray. Your job is to clean up all round, and do be careful not to rub the furniture too hard. I'm afraid of your wearing it out. Then, I'm putting you in charge of the bottles during the supper. If there's a single one missing or if anything is broken I shall hold you responsible and take it out of your wages.

MASTER JACQUES   (*aside*). A shrewd penalty!

HARPAGON   (*to* DAME CLAUDE). Off you go! (*She goes.*) Now you, Brinda-voine, and you, La Merluche, I give you the job of rinsing the glasses and serving the wine, but mind, only when people are thirsty. Don't do, as some scoundrelly servants do, egg people on to drink, putting the idea into their heads when they would never have thought of it otherwise. Wait till they have asked several times and always remember to put plenty of water with it.

MASTER JACQUES   (*aside*). Yes, wine without water goes to the head.

LA MERLUCHE.   Be we to take off our aprons, master?

HARPAGON.   Yes, when you see the guests arriving, but take care not to spoil your clothes.

BRINDAVOINE.   You mind, master, that there be a great blotch of lamp oil on one side of my doublet.

LA MERLUCHE.   And my breeches be that torn behind, master, that, saving your presence, they'll see my . . .

HARPAGON.   That's enough. See that you keep it against the wall. Face the company all the time—and you—hold your hat in front of you like this when you are serving the guests. (*He shows* BRINDAVOINE *how to keep his hat over his doublet to hide the oil stain.*) As for you, my girl (*to* ÉLISE), you are to keep an eye on what is cleared away from the tables and see that nothing is wasted. That's the proper job for daughters to do. In the meantime get yourself ready to welcome my mistress. She is coming to call on you and take you to the fair. Do you hear what I'm telling you?

ÉLISE.   Yes, father.

HARPAGON.   And you, my effeminate fop of a son, I'm willing to forgive you for what happened just now, but don't you be giving her any of your black looks either.

CLÉANTE.   I give her black looks, father? Whatever for?

HARPAGON.   Oh Lord! We know very well how children carry on when their fathers marry again and what the usual attitude towards a stepmother is! If you want me to forget your last escapade, I'd advise you to put on a cheerful face for the young lady and make her as welcome as ever you can.

CLÉANTE.   I really can't promise to be glad that she should become my stepmother. I couldn't truthfully say that I am, but I can promise to obey you to the letter in putting on a cheerful face to receive her.

HARPAGON.   Well, mind that you do.

CLÉANTE.   You will find you have no cause to complain on that score.

HARPAGON.   Very well! (CLÉANTE *goes out.*) Valère, I want your help in this. Now then, Master Jacques, come along; I've kept you until last.

MASTER JACQUES.   Do you want to speak to your cook or your coachman, sir? I'm both the one and the other.

HARPAGON.   I want both.

MASTER JACQUES.   But which d'ye want first?

HARPAGON.   The cook.

MASTER JACQUES.   Just a minute, then, if you don't mind. (*He takes off his coachman's overcoat and appears dressed as a cook.*)

HARPAGON.   What the deuce is the meaning of this ceremony?

MASTER JACQUES.   At your service now, sir.

HARPAGON.   I am committed to giving a supper to-night, Master Jacques—

MASTER JACQUES.   Wonders never cease!

HARPAGON.   Now tell me, can you give us something good?

MASTER JACQUES.   Yes, if you give me plenty of money.

HARPAGON.   What the devil! It's always money. It seems to be all they can say. Money! Money! Money! It's the one word they know. Money! They are always talking of money. They can never do anything without money!

VALÈRE.   I never heard such a fatuous answer. As if there's anything in providing good food if you have plenty of money. It's the easiest thing in the world. Any fool can do that much. The man who is really good at his job can put on a good meal without spending money.

MASTER JACQUES.   Put on a good meal without spending money!

VALÈRE.   Yes.

MASTER JACQUES.   Upon my word, Mr Steward, I would like you to show how it's done. You had better take on my job as cook since it seems you want to be managing everything.

HARPAGON. Be quiet! Just tell us what we shall need.

MASTER JACQUES. Ask Mr Steward there. He is the man who can put on a meal without spending money.

HARPAGON. Hey! I want an answer from *you*.

MASTER JACQUES. How many will you be at table?

HARPAGON. We shall be eight or ten, but reckon on eight. Provide for eight and there's always plenty for ten.

VALÈRE. Of course.

MASTER JACQUES. Right. You need to provide four sorts of soup and five main courses—soups, entrées—

HARPAGON. The devil! You are not feeding the whole town.

MASTER JACQUES. Roasts—

HARPAGON (*putting his hand over his mouth*). You scoundrel. You'll eat me out of house and home.

MASTER JACQUES. Entremets—

HARPAGON. Still going on?

VALÈRE. Do you want them to burst themselves? Do you think the master is asking people to come and gorge themselves to death? Go study the rules of health! Ask the doctor whether there's anything does people more harm than overeating.

HARPAGON. How right he is!

VALÈRE. You need to learn, you, and folk like you, Master Jacques, that an overloaded table is a veritable death-trap. Anyone who is really concerned for the well-being of his guests should see that the meal that he offers them is distinguished by frugality. As the ancient philosopher has it, "One should eat to live and not live to eat."

HARPAGON. Ah, well said, well said! Come, let me embrace you for that. It is the finest precept I've ever heard—"One should live to eat and not eat to"—that's not it—how does it go?

VALÈRE. "One should eat to live and not live to eat."

HARPAGON. Yes. (*To* MASTER JACQUES) Do you hear that? (*To* VALÈRE) Who was the great man who said that?

VALÈRE. I don't remember his name just now.

HARPAGON. Remember to write the words down for me! I'll have them engraved in letters of gold over the chimney-piece in the dining-room.

VALÈRE. I won't fail to do so. As for the supper, just leave it to me. I will see that everything is as it should be.

HARPAGON. Yes, do.

MASTER JACQUES. So much the better. I shall have the less to worry about.

HARPAGON. We must have things people don't go in for much these days, things which soon fill them up—some good thick stew with dumplings and chestnuts. Have plenty of that.

VALÈRE. You may rely on me.

HARPAGON. And now, Master Jacques, I must have my carriage cleaned.

MASTER JACQUES. Just a minute. This is the coachman's job. (*Puts on his coat again.*) You were saying, sir?

HARPAGON. I must have my carriage cleaned and the horses made ready to go to the fair.

MASTER JACQUES. Your horses, master? Upon my word, they are in no state for work. I can't say that they are down on their litter because the poor creatures haven't a scrap, and that's the truth of it. You keep them on such short commons that they are no more than ghosts or shadows of horses.

HARPAGON. They are in a bad way, then—but they never do anything!

MASTER JACQUES. Because they never do anything are they never to eat anything? It would be far better for them to work more, poor creatures, if they could only eat in proportion. It fair breaks my heart to see them so thin—for the fact is, I'm fond of my horses and I suffer along with them. Not a day passes but I go short myself to feed them. A man must be very hard-hearted, master, not to have pity for his fellow-creatures.

HARPAGON. It's no great job to go as far as the fair.

MASTER JACQUES. No, I haven't the heart to drive them, master, and I should be ashamed to use the whip to them in the state they are in. How do you expect them to pull the coach when they can hardly drag themselves along?

VALÈRE. I will arrange for Le Picard next door to drive them, sir. We shall want his help in preparing the supper, too.

MASTER JACQUES. Right. I'd far rather they died under someone else's hand than mine.

VALÈRE. You are a great talker, Master Jacques.

MASTER JACQUES. And you are a great meddler, Master Steward!

HARPAGON. Be quiet!

MASTER JACQUES. I can't stand flatterers, master, and I can see that every-thing he does, all his everlasting prying into the bread and the wine and the wood and the salt and the candles is nothing but back-scratch-ing, all done to curry favour with you. That's bad enough, but on top of it all I have to put up with hearing what folk say about you and, after all, I have a soft spot for you, in spite of myself. Next to my horses I think more of you than anybody else.

HARPAGON. Would you mind telling me what people say about me?

MASTER JACQUES. Yes, master—if I could be sure it wouldn't annoy you.

HARPAGON. Not in the least.

MASTER JACQUES. Excuse me, but I know very well you'll be angry.

HARPAGON. On the contrary. I shall enjoy it. I like to know what people are saying about me.

MASTER JACQUES. Well, since you will have it, master, I'll tell you straight then—they make a laughing stock of you everywhere; we have scores of jokes thrown at us about you; there's nothing folk like better than running you down and making game of your stinginess. One tale is that you've had special almanacs printed with double the numbers of fast days and vigils so that you can save money by making your household keep additional fasts; another is that you are always ready to pick a quarrel with your servants when they have a present due to them or when they are leaving your service so that you don't have to give them anything; one fellow tells how you had the law on your neighbour's cat for eating the remains of a leg of mutton, another how you were caught one night stealing oats from your own horses and how your coachman, the one before me, gave you a drubbing in the dark and you never said anything about it; in fact, I'll tell you what it is, there's no going anywhere without hearing you pulled to pieces. You are a butt and a byword for everybody, and nobody ever refers to you except as a miser, a skinflint, and a niggardly old usurer.

HARPAGON   (*beating him*). And you are a silly, rascally, scoundrelly, impudent rogue!

MASTER JACQUES.   Ah, well! Didn't I guess as much? You wouldn't believe me. I said you'd be angry if I told you the truth.

HARPAGON.   I'll teach you to talk like that. (*He goes out.*)

VALÈRE.   You seem to have got a poor reward for your frankness, Master Jacques.

MASTER JACQUES.   Upon my word, Mr Upstart, you are mighty self-important, but it's no affair of yours. Keep your laughter for your own hidings when you get 'em. Don't come laughing at mine.

VALÈRE.   Ah, my dear Master Jacques, please don't be annoyed—

MASTER JACQUES.   (*aside*). He's climbing down. I'll put on a bold front and give him a beating if he's fool enough to be frightened. (*To* VALÈRE) *You* may laugh, but I'd have you know that I'm not laughing, and if you get me annoyed I'll make you laugh on the other side of your face. (*Drives him across stage, threatening him.*)

VALÈRE.   Go easy!

MASTER JACQUES.   How d'ye mean, go easy? Suppose I don't choose to go easy.

VALÈRE.   Please—

MASTER JACQUES.   You are an impudent fellow!!

VALÈRE.   My dear Master Jacques—

MASTER JACQUES.   I don't care tuppence for your dear Master Jacques. If I once take my stick to you I'll beat you black and blue.

VALÈRE.   How d'ye mean, your stick! (VALÈRE *makes him retreat in his turn.*)

MASTER JACQUES.   I didn't mean anything.

VALÈRE.   Just understand, my dear fat-head, that if anyone's going to feel the stick you are the one!

MASTER JACQUES.   I don't doubt it.

VALÈRE.   And that you are only a good-for-nothing cook when all's said and done.

MASTER JACQUES.   Yes, I know I am.

VALÈRE.   And that you don't half know me yet.

MASTER JACQUES.   Please forgive me!

VALÈRE.   Did you say that you'd beat me?

MASTER JACQUES.   It was only a joke.

VALÈRE.   Well, I don't like your jokes. (*Beating him.*) Your jokes are in very bad taste. Just understand that. (*He goes out.*)

MASTER JACQUES.   So much for sincerity! It's a poor sort of trade. From now on I've done with it. No more telling the truth. I can put up with my master. He's got some right to beat me, but as for this precious steward, I'll have my own back on him if I can.

(*Enter* MARIANNE *and* FROSINE.)

FROSINE.   Do you know if the master is in, Master Jacques?

MASTER JACQUES.   Ay, indeed he is. I know only too well.

FROSINE.   Please tell him that we are here. (*He goes out.*)

MARIANNE.   What a strange position to be in, Frosine! I must say I am dreading the meeting.

FROSINE.   Why? What is there to worry about?

MARIANNE.   Oh, dear! How can you ask! Can't you imagine what a girl feels when she is about to confront the fate that's in store for her.

FROSINE.   I agree that Harpagon isn't what you would choose if you wanted a pleasant sort of death, and I guess from your expression that your thoughts still turn to the young man you were telling me about.

MARIANNE.   Yes, I won't pretend to deny it, Frosine. The respectful manner in which he paid his visits to us made a most favourable impression upon me.

FROSINE.   But did you find out who he is?

MARIANNE.   No, I don't know in the least, but I do know that he is very attractive, and that if I had my own choice I would as soon have him as another. Indeed he makes me loathe this husband they have chosen for me all the more.

FROSINE.   Good Lord, yes! these young sparks are all attractive enough, and can tell a good tale, but most of them are as poor as church mice. You would do much better to take an old husband with plenty of money. I admit it may seem to fly in the face of nature and there may well be some distasteful things to put up with, but then it won't be for long. When he dies you may be sure he'll leave you in a position to choose one you like better, and he'll make up for everything.

MARIANNE. But it doesn't seem right, Frosine, that one should have to look forward to someone else dying before one can be happy. Moreover, death doesn't always fall in with our schemes.

FROSINE. Don't be silly. You only marry him on the strict understanding that he leaves you a widow before very long. That must be put in the contract. It would be most inconsiderate of him if he didn't die within, say, three months!—But here comes the man himself.

MARIANNE. Oh, Frosine! What a face!

HARPAGON. Don't be offended, my dear, if I come to meet you with my spectacles on. I know that your charms are striking enough, sufficiently visible; they need no glasses to discover them, but it is through glass that one observes the stars, you know, and you yourself are a star, I declare, the loveliest one in all the firmament. (*To* FROSINE) Frosine, she doesn't say a word, and from what I can see she doesn't seem at all pleased to see me.

FROSINE. She is a little overcome. Young girls are always shy of showing their feelings at first.

HARPAGON. Perhaps you are right. (*To* MARIANNE) Now my dearie, here is my daughter coming to greet you.

(*Enter* ÉLISE.)

MARIANNE. I fear I am late in paying my respects.

ÉLISE. On the contrary, I should have come to you first.

HARPAGON. You see what a big lass she is, but ill weeds do grow fast.

MARIANNE (*aside to* FROSINE). What a horrible man!

HARPAGON. What did my pretty one say?

FROSINE. She was saying how much she admires you.

HARPAGON.. That's very kind of you, my pet.

MARIANNE (*aside*). Oh, what a creature!

HARPAGON. Very gratifying sentiments indeed!

MARIANNE (*aside*). I can bear it no longer.

(*Enter* CLÉANTE.)

HARPAGON. This is my son. He has come to pay his respects too.

MARIANNE (*aside to* FROSINE). Ah, Frosine! What an encounter. This is the very young man I was telling you about.

FROSINE (*to* MARIANNE). How very remarkable!

HARPAGON. I see you are surprised to find I have a grown-up family, but I shall be rid of both of them before long.

CLÉANTE. I must say this is a most unexpected meeting. I was completely taken aback when my father told me of his intentions a little while ago.

MARIANNE. I am in the same position. The meeting is as much a surprise to me as to you. I was quite unprepared for such a coincidence.

CLÉANTE. Truly, madam, my father could have made no better choice, and it is indeed a pleasure to meet you. All the same I cannot bring myself to say that I should welcome your becoming my stepmother. I must admit that the honour is not one I appreciate. Indeed the title, if I may say so, is the last one I should wish you to assume. All this might appear rude to some people, but you, I am sure, will know in what sense to take it, understand how repugnant this marriage must be to me, and how contrary to all my intentions. In short, I am sure you will allow me to say, with my father's kind permission, that if I had my way this marriage would never take place.

HARPAGON.   That's a fine way of paying your respects. What a tale to be telling her!

MARIANNE.   My answer is that I feel as you do. If you are loath to see me as your stepmother I am no less opposed to having you as a stepson. Please do not think it is by any wish of mine that you are placed in such a dilemma. I should be grieved to cause you distress, and had I any freedom of choice I should never consent to a marriage which would cause you unhappiness.

HARPAGON.   She's quite right. Answer a fool according to his folly. I must apologize, my dear, for my son's silliness. He is young and foolish and doesn't yet understand what he is saying.

MARIANNE.   I am not the least offended, I assure you. On the contrary, it has been a pleasure to hear your son express his feelings so frankly. I value such an avowal coming from him. Had he spoken otherwise I should not esteem him so highly.

HARPAGON.   It's very good of you to overlook his faults. He will get more sense as he grows older, and you'll find that his feelings will change.

CLÉANTE.   Never, father! My feelings will not change. I ask the lady to believe that.

HARPAGON.   You see what an absurd fellow he is. He gets worse and worse.

CLÉANTE.   Would you have me be false to my love?

HARPAGON.   Still at it? Kindly try a different tune!

CLÉANTE.   Very well, then, since you wish me to speak in a different vein—permit me, madam, to put myself in my father's place and assure you that you are the most charming person I ever met, that the greatest happiness I could imagine would be to win your favour and that I would rather be your husband than the greatest king on earth. Yes, madam, to enjoy your love would be for me the height of good fortune, and that is indeed my only ambition. There is nothing that I would not do to achieve so enviable a purpose, and whatever the obstacles may be—

HARPAGON.   Steady on, lad, if you don't mind.

CLÉANTE.   I am addressing the lady on your behalf.

HARPAGON.   Good Lord! I have a tongue of my own. I don't need you as my advocate. Here, bring some chairs.

FROSINE.   No, I think it would be better if we set out for the fair at once, so as to get back earlier and have plenty of time to talk later.

HARPAGON.   Have the horses put in the carriage, then. Please forgive me, my dear, for not having thought to provide some refreshment before you go.

CLÉANTE.   I have arranged it, father. I told them to bring in a bowl of china oranges, lemons, and sweetmeats. I had them ordered on your behalf.

HARPAGON   (*in a whisper*). Valère!

VALÈRE   (*to* HARPAGON). He's out of his mind!

CLÉANTE.   Do you think there is not enough, father? The lady will perhaps excuse any deficiency.

MARIANNE.   There was no need to have troubled.

CLÉANTE.   Did you ever see a finer diamond, madam, than the one my father has on his finger.

MARIANNE.   It *is* very brilliant.

CLÉANTE   (*taking it from his father's finger and offering it to* MARIANNE). You need to look at it from close to.

MARIANNE.   It is certainly exquisite, so full of fire.

CLÉANTE   (*preventing* MARIANNE *from returning it*). No, no, madam. It is in hands which are worthy of it now. My father has made a present of it to you.

HARPAGON.   *I* have?

CLÉANTE.   You do wish the lady to keep it for your sake, don't you, father?

HARPAGON   (*aside to* CLÉANTE). What d'ye mean?

CLÉANTE   (*aside*). What a question! (*To* MARIANNE) He means that I am to make you accept it.

MARIANNE.   But I don't at all want to—

CLÉANTE.   You really can't mean that! He would never hear of taking it back.

HARPAGON   (*aside*). I can't bear it!

MARIANNE.   It would be—

CLÉANTE   (*still preventing her from returning it*). No, I assure you, he would be offended—

MARIANNE.   Please—

CLÉANTE.   Not at all!

HARPAGON   (*aside*). Confound the—

CLÉANTE.   You see how put out he is at your refusal.

HARPAGON   (*aside*). You traitor!

CLÉANTE.   You see! He's losing his patience.

HARPAGON   (*whispers to* CLÉANTE, *threatening him*). You scoundrel!

CLÉANTE.   It's not my fault, father; I'm doing the best I can to make her keep it, but she's very obstinate.

HARPAGON   (*furious, whispers to* CLÉANTE). You blackguard!

CLÉANTE.   You are making my father angry with me, madam.

HARPAGON   *(as before)*. You villain!

CLÉANTE.   You will make him ill. Madam, please do not refuse any further.

FROSINE.   Good Lord, what a fuss! Keep the ring since the gentleman wants you to.

MARIANNE.   Rather than cause further annoyance I will keep it for the time being, but I will find another occasion to return it.

(Enter BRINDAVOINE.*)*

BRINDAVOINE.   There's a man wanting to speak to you, sir.

HARPAGON.   Tell him I'm busy. Tell him to come back another time.

BRINDAVOINE.   He says he has some money for you.

HARPAGON.   Excuse me. I'll be back presently.

(Enter LA MERLUCHE, *running. He knocks* HARPAGON *over.)*

LA MERLUCHE.   Master!

HARPAGON.   Oh! He's killed me.

CLÉANTE.   What is it, father? Are you hurt?

HARPAGON.   The scoundrel must have been bribed to break my neck by people who owe me money.

VALÈRE.   It's nothing serious.

LA MERLUCHE.   Master, I beg your pardon, I thought I was doing right to hurry.

HARPAGON.   What did you come for, you scoundrel?

LA MERLUCHE.   To tell you that your horses have cast their shoes.

HARPAGON.   Have them taken to the smith at once.

CLÉANTE.   While they are being shod I will do the honours of the house for you, father, and take the lady into the garden. I will have the refreshments taken out there.

HARPAGON.   Valère, keep your eye on that stuff, and do, I implore you, save as much of it as you can so that it can go back to the shop.

VALÈRE.   Very good, sir.

HARPAGON   *(alone)*. Oh what a scoundrel of a son! He's determined to ruin me!

ACT FOUR

(CLÉANTE, MARIANNE, ÉLISE, FROSINE.)

CLÉANTE.   We'll do better to go in here. There's no one here to worry about, so we can talk openly.

ÉLISE.   My brother has told me about his love for you. I know how trying your position must be and I assure you that you have my whole sympathy.

MARIANNE.   It is a great comfort to know that one has the support of such a person as yourself, and I do hope you will always maintain the same friendliness for me. It is such a consolation in adversity.

FROSINE.   Upon my word, it is most unlucky for both of you that you didn't let me into your secrets a bit earlier. I could have saved you all this trouble. I would never have let matters go the way they have done.

CLÉANTE.   What's the use! It's my ill luck! It just had to happen this way. (*To* MARIANNE) What decisions have you come to, my dear?

MARIANNE.   Alas! How can I come to any decisions? Dependent as I am on other people, what more can I do than hope for the best?

CLÉANTE.   Is that all the help you can offer me? Just to hope for the best? No compassionate support? No helping hand? No positive token of your affection?

MARIANNE.   What can I say? Put yourself in my place and tell me what I should do! Advise me! Command me! I will put myself in your hands, and I know that you will not ask more of me than honour and propriety permit.

CLÉANTE.   But how can I do anything effective if you expect me to keep within the bounds of rigorous honour and scrupulous propriety?

MARIANNE.   But what would you have me do? Even if I could disregard the scruples of my sex I must still consider my mother. She has always shown me the most tender affection. I could never bring myself to give her cause for sorrow. You must persuade her. Use every endeavour to gain her approval. I give you leave to say and do whatever you think necessary, and if the issue should depend on my declaring my love for you I shall be willing to avow to her all that I feel.

CLÉANTE.   Frosine, dear Frosine, won't you help us out?

FROSINE.   Goodness me! Need you ask? I should like to—with all my heart. I'm really quite kind-hearted, you know! I'm not hard by nature, and when I see people really and truly in love I'm only too willing to help them. The question is, what can we do?

CLÉANTE.   Please, do think of something.

MARIANNE.   Do make some suggestions.

ÉLISE.   Find some way of undoing the mischief you've done.

FROSINE.   It isn't so easy. (*To* MARIANNE) Your mother isn't altogether unreasonable. She might be persuaded to transfer to the son what she intended to bestow on the father. (*To* CLÉANTE) The real difficulty, as I see it, is that your father's your father!

CLÉANTE.   Exactly!

FROSINE.   What I mean is that he'll have a grievance if he finds his offer refused, and be in no mood to agree to your marriage. What we really need is that the refusal shall come from him. We must try to find some means of making him take a dislike to you, Marianne.

CLÉANTE.   That's the idea.

FROSINE.   Yes, I know it's the right idea. That's what we need, but how the deuce can we manage it? Wait a minute. Suppose we could produce someone, an elderly woman, say, with a touch of my sort of talent who could carry off the part of a lady of quality with the help of a few scratch retainers and some fancy title or other—a Marchioness or Viscountess of Lower Brittany, should we say—I might contrive to make your father believe she was a wealthy woman with a hundred thousand crowns in ready money and landed property as well, and that she was head over heels in love with him—so anxious to marry him that she would be willing to hand over all her money under the terms of the marriage contract. I don't doubt he'd listen to that proposition, for though I know he loves you very much (*to* MARIANNE) he loves money better. Once he has swallowed the bait and agreed to all that you want it wouldn't matter that he found out the truth when he came to examine our Marchioness's possessions more closely!

CLÉANTE.   It sounds a most ingenious notion.

FROSINE.   Leave it to me. I've just remembered a friend of mine who is the very person we want.

CLÉANTE.   You can count on my showing my gratitude, Frosine, if you can carry it off. Meanwhile, dear Marianne, let us make a start by winning over your mother. It would be a great deal accomplished if we could only break off the marriage. I do implore you to do all you you can. Make use of her affection for you. Employ all your charm, and all the eloquence of looks and of speech that Heaven has endowed you with. Use all your gentle persuasions and tender entreaties, those endearing caresses of yours, and they will, I am sure, prove irresistible.

MARIANNE.   I will do all I can. I won't forget anything you tell me.

(*Enter* HARPAGON.)

HARPAGON   (*aside*). Ha! My son kissing the hand of his stepmother to be! And the stepmother to be doesn't seem to be offering much objection. Is there more in this than meets the eye?

ÉLISE.   Here comes father.

HARPAGON.   The carriage is ready. You can set out as soon as you like.

CLÉANTE.   I will go with them, father, as you are not going.

HARPAGON.   No, you stay here. They will get along very well by themselves, and I need you here.

(ÉLISE, MARIANNE, *and* FROSINE *go out.*)

HARPAGON.   Well now, forget she's your stepmother and let me hear what you think of her?

CLÉANTE.   What I think of her?

HARPAGON.   Yes, her looks, her manners, her figure, her intelligence?

CLÉANTE.   Oh—so so.

HARPAGON.   Is that all you can say?

CLÉANTE.   Well, frankly, she doesn't come up to what I expected. She's just a coquette—nothing more; her figure is not particularly graceful, her looks are no more than middling, and her intelligence is very ordinary. Don't think I'm trying to put you off, father. As stepmothers go I would as soon have her as anyone else.

HARPAGON.   But you were telling her just now that—

CLÉANTE.   Merely a few conventional compliments on your behalf, and purely to please you.

HARPAGON.   So you wouldn't fancy her for yourself, then?

CLÉANTE.   Me? Not in the least!

HARPAGON.   I'm sorry about that. It cuts across an idea that was passing through my mind. Looking at her just now I began thinking about my age and the way people would talk about my marrying a girl so young, and I was on the point of giving up the idea, but as I had asked for her hand and pledged my word to her I would have let you have her, had you not taken a dislike to her.

CLÉANTE.   You would have given her to me?

HARPAGON.   Yes, to you.

CLÉANTE.   In marriage?

HARPAGON.   In marriage.

CLÉANTE.   Listen. It's true that she's not exactly what I should choose, but, to please you, father, I am prepared to marry her if you want me to.

HARPAGON.   No, I'm not so unreasonable as you think. I have no wish to make you marry a girl against your will.

CLÉANTE.   No, but I'm willing to make the effort out of consideration for you.

HARPAGON.   No, no! There's no happiness in marriage without love.

CLÉANTE.   Well, perhaps that might come afterwards. They say that love often comes after marriage.

HARPAGON.   No, I'm against taking chances where the man is concerned. I don't want to run any risk of things turning out badly. If you'd felt any inclination for her, that would have been fine and I'd have arranged for you to marry her instead of me, but, as it is, I'll stick to my original plan and marry her myself.

CLÉANTE.   Very well, father, since that's how things stand I must disclose my real feelings and tell you our secret. The truth is that I have loved her since the first day I saw her. I was intending just now to ask your permission to marry her; it was only when you revealed your own feelings and for fear of displeasing you that I refrained from doing so.

HARPAGON.   Have you visited her home?

CLÉANTE.   Yes, father.

HARPAGON.   Often?

CLÉANTE.   Fairly often, considering what time there has been.

HARPAGON.   And were you well received?

CLÉANTE.   Very well, but without their knowing who I was. That was why Marianne was so surprised when she saw me just now.

HARPAGON.   Did you tell her you loved her and that you intended to marry her?

CLÉANTE.   Of course. I have even made some approach to her mother.

HARPAGON.   And she entertained your proposals on her daughter's behalf?

CLÉANTE.   Yes, she was very kind.

HARPAGON.   And the daughter returns your affections?

CLÉANTE.   If one may judge from appearances, I think she likes me a little.

HARPAGON   (aside). I'm very pleased to have found all this out. It is just what I wanted to know. (To CLÉANTE) Right, my lad, you want to know what the position is? It's this. You'll just put this fancy of yours out of your head if you don't mind; you'll stop paying attentions to the lady I am intending to marry myself, and marry the woman I've chosen for you—and at once.

CLÉANTE.   So that was your game, father! Very well! Since that's what things have come to, let me tell you this—I will never give up my love for Marianne, I will stop at nothing to prevent your having her, and even if you have the mother's consent I may find I have some resources on my side.

HARPAGON.   What, you rascal! You have the audacity to trespass on my preserves!

CLÉANTE.   It's you who are trespassing on mine. I was there first.

HARPAGON.   Am I not your father? Aren't you bound to defer to my wishes?

CLÉANTE.   This isn't a case where a son needs defer to his father. Love is no respecter of persons.

HARPAGON.   I'll make *you* respect *me*—with a stick!

CLÉANTE.   You will do no good with threats.

HARPAGON.   You shall give up Marianne.

CLÉANTE.   Never!

HARPAGON.   Bring me a stick—at once!

(*Enter* MASTER JACQUES.)

MASTER JACQUES.   Now, now now, gentlemen! What *is* all this? What are you thinking about?

CLÉANTE.   I'm beyond caring!

MASTER JACQUES.   Steady, sir! Steady on!

HARPAGON.   Talking to me like that! The impudence!

MASTER JACQUES (*to* HARPAGON). Now, master—please!

CLÉANTE. I won't budge an inch.

MASTER JACQUES (*to* CLÉANTE). What! To your father!

HARPAGON. Just let me get at him!

MASTER JACQUES. What! To your son! It would be different if you were talking to me!

HARPAGON. I'll make you the judge between us, Master Jacques, and prove that I'm right.

MASTER JACQUES. I agree. (*To* CLÉANTE) Just stand a bit farther away.

HARPAGON. I am in love with a young lady and mean to marry her, and now this scoundrel here has the impudence to fall in love with her too, and he wants to marry her, although I've told him he can't.

MASTER JACQUES. Oh! That's wrong of him.

HARPAGON. Don't you agree that it's shocking for a son to set up as his father's rival? Isn't he in duty bound, in respect for his father, to refrain from interfering with my intentions?

MASTER JACQUES. Oh yes, you are right, but let me have a word with him. Stay there! (*He goes across stage to* CLÉANTE.)

CLÉANTE. Very well. Since he has chosen you as the judge, I make no objection. It doesn't matter to me who it is, I'm quite willing to submit to your decision, Master Jacques.

MASTER JACQUES. That's very kind of you.

CLÉANTE. I'm in love with a young lady. She returns my affection and receives my offer of love sympathetically. Then my father decides to come along and upset everything by proposing to marry her himself.

MASTER JACQUES. Oh, that's very wrong of him!

CLÉANTE. Should he not be ashamed to be thinking of marriage at his age? Isn't it absurd for him to be falling in love? Wouldn't he do better to leave love-making to younger men, don't you think?

MASTER JACQUES. You are right. He can't really mean it! Just let me have a word with him. (*Goes across to* HARPAGON.) Now look, the lad isn't as bad as you make him out to be. He'll listen to reason. He says he knows the respect he owes to you—that he was carried away in the heat of the moment and that he is willing to do whatever you want, provided you show him more consideration and arrange for him to marry someone to his liking.

HARPAGON. Well then, Master Jacques, you can tell him that, on that understanding, he can count on me absolutely. I leave him free to choose any woman he likes—except Marianne.

MASTER JACQUES. Leave it to me. (*Crosses to* CLÉANTE.) Well now, your father is not so unreasonable as you make him out to be. He has given me to understand that it was your outburst of temper that annoyed him, and all he objects to is your method of going about things. He's ready to grant you anything you ask provided you do it nicely and show him the respect and obedience a son owes to his father.

CLÉANTE.   Well then, Master Jacques, you can assure him that if only he will let me have Marianne he'll find me obedience itself and I'll do whatever he wishes in future.

MASTER JACQUES   (*to* HARPAGON). It's all settled. He agrees to everything you said.

HARPAGON.   That's splendid!

MASTER JACQUES   (*to* CLÉANTE). Everything's settled. He's satisfied with your promises.

CLÉANTE.   Thank Heaven for that!

MASTER JACQUES.   Gentlemen! It only remains for you to talk it over together. You are now in complete agreement. You were going to fall out merely because you were misunderstanding each other.

CLÉANTE.   My dear Master Jacques, I shall be eternally grateful to you.

MASTER JACQUES.   Don't mention it, sir.

HARPAGON.   I'm very pleased with you indeed, Master Jacques, and you deserve some reward. (*He feels in his pocket.* MASTER JACQUES. *holds out his hand, but* HARPAGON *pulls out his handkerchief and says*) Well, be off. I shan't forget, I assure you.

MASTER JACQUES.   Thank you kindly, sir. (*He goes out.*)

CLÉANTE.   Father, I ask you to forgive me for having been so angry.

HARPAGON.   It doesn't matter.

CLÉANTE.   I am very sorry, I assure you.

HARPAGON.   And I'm extremely pleased, for my part, to find you so reasonable.

CLÉANTE.   It's very generous of you to forgive me so promptly.

HARPAGON.   A father can always forgive his children's faults once they remember the duty they owe him.

CLÉANTE.   What! Have you forgiven my outrageous behaviour?

HARPAGON.   I *must* forgive it now that you show such obedience and respect.

CLÉANTE.   I promise you, father, I shall remember your goodness to my dying day.

HARPAGON.   And for my part I promise you shall have anything you want from me.

CLÉANTE.   Why, father, what more can I ask now that you have given me Marianne?

HARPAGON.   What's that?

CLÉANTE.   I was saying how grateful I am, father, for what you have done for me. In giving me Marianne you have given me all I could wish for.

HARPAGON.   Who said anything about giving you Marianne?

CLÉANTE.   Why, you did, father!

HARPAGON.   I did?

CLÉANTE.   Of course!

HARPAGON.   But it's you who promised to give her up.

CLÉANTE.   Give her up?

HARPAGON.   Yes.

CLÉANTE.   Never!

HARPAGON.   You've not given her up?

CLÉANTE.   On the contrary, I'm more determined than ever to marry her.

HARPAGON.   What! Are you starting all over again, you scoundrel!

CLÉANTE.   Nothing shall ever make me change my mind.

HARPAGON.   I'll see about that, you villain!

CLÉANTE.   You can do what you like!

HARPAGON.   Clear out of my sight!

CLÉANTE.   With the greatest of pleasure.

HARPAGON.   I've finished with you!

CLÉANTE.   Right! Be finished, then.

HARPAGON.   I renounce you!

CLÉANTE.   Good!

HARPAGON.   I disinherit you!

CLÉANTE.   Anything you please.

HARPAGON.   And I give you my curse!

CLÉANTE.   Keep your gifts to yourself!

(*Exit* HARPAGON.)

LA FLÈCHE   (*coming from the garden with a strong box*).   Ah master, here you are, just in the nick of time. Quick! Follow me!

CLÉANTE.   What is it?

LA FLÈCHE.   Follow me, I tell you. We are in luck.

CLÉANTE.   How d'ye mean?

LA FLÈCHE.   Here's just what you are needing.

CLÉANTE.   What is it?

LA FLÈCHE.   I have had my eye on it all day.

CLÉANTE.   But what is it?

LA FLÈCHE.   Your father's treasure—I've lifted it!

CLÉANTE.   How did you manage it?

LA FLÈCHE.   I'll tell you all about it, but let us be off. I can hear him shouting.

(*They go.*)

HARPAGON   (*calling "Stop, thief!" in the garden. He enters hatless*).   Thieves! Robbers! Assassins! Murderers! Justice! Merciful Heavens! I'm done for! I'm murdered! They've cut my throat; they've taken my money! Whoever can it be? Where's he gone to? Where is he now?

Where is he hiding? How can I find him? Which way shall I go? Which way shan't I go? Is he here? Is he there? Who's that? Stop! (*Catching his own arm*) Give me my money back, you scoundrel! Ah, it's me! I'm going out of my mind! I don't know where I am or who I am or what I'm doing. Oh dear, my dear, darling money, my beloved, they've taken you away from me and now you are gone I have lost my strength, my joy and my consolation. It's all over with me. There's nothing left for me to do in the world. I can't go on living without you. It's the finish. I can't bear any more. I'm dying; I'm dead—and buried. Will nobody bring me to life again by giving me my beloved money back or telling me who has taken it? Eh? What d'ye say? There's nobody there! Whoever did it must have watched his opportunity well and chosen the very moment I was talking to my blackguard of a son. I must go. I'll demand justice. I'll have everyone in the house put to the torture, menservants, maidservants, son, daughter, everyone—myself included. What a crowd in here! I suspect the whole pack of 'em. They all look to me like the thief. Eh? What are they talking about over there? About the fellow that robbed me? What's that noise up there? Is the thief there? Please, I implore you, tell me if you know anything about him! Isn't he hiding among you? They are all looking at me. Now they are laughing. You'll see, they are all in it, beyond question, all involved in the robbery. Come on! Come quickly! Magistrates, police, provosts, judges, racks, gibbets, hangmen. I'll have everybody hanged, and, if I don't get my money back, I'll hang myself afterwards.

ACT FIVE

(HARPAGON, *an* OFFICER *and his* CLERK.)

OFFICER. You leave it to me! I know my job, thank the Lord! This isn't the first time I've had a case of theft to investigate. I only wish I'd as many bags of money as I've had people hanged.

HARPAGON. It's to the interest of every magistrate in the country to take hand in this case. If I don't get my money back I'll demand justice on justice itself.

OFFICER. We must go through the proper procedure. How much did you say there was in the box?

HARPAGON. Ten thousand crowns—in cash.

OFFICER. Ten thousand crowns!

HARPAGON. Ten thousand crowns!

OFFICER. A considerable theft.

HARPAGON. No punishment could be bad enough for a crime of this enormity. If it goes unpunished nothing, however sacred, will be safe.

OFFICER. In what denomination of coin was the money?

HARPAGON. In good *louis d'or* and *pistoles* of full weight.

OFFICER. And whom do you suspect of the theft?

HARPAGON. Everybody. Arrest the whole town and the suburbs as well.

OFFICER. If you'll take my advice, it's unwise to alarm people unduly. Let us try to go quietly and collect our evidence, and then—then we can proceed with the full rigour of the law to recover the sum you have lost.

MASTER JACQUES (*calling over his shoulder as he comes on stage*). I'll be coming back. Cut his throat at once and let them be singeing his feet for me and putting him in boiling water. Then string him up from the rafters.

HARPAGON. Who? The fellow who has stolen my money?

MASTER JACQUES. I was talking about the suckling pig your steward has just sent me. I mean to dress him for you according to my own special recipe.

HARPAGON. We aren't interested in all that. There are other things you have to talk to this gentleman about.

OFFICER. Now, don't be alarmed. I'm not the sort of fellow to get you into trouble. Everything shall be done quietly.

MASTER JACQUES. Is the gentleman one of your supper party?

OFFICER. In a case like this, friend, you must withhold nothing from your master.

MASTER JACQUES. Upon my word, sir, I'll show you all I know. I'll do the best that I can for you.

HARPAGON. We are not worrying about that!

MASTER JACQUES. If I don't give you as good a meal as I could wish, you must blame that steward of yours. He's clipped my wings with his economies.

HARPAGON. You scoundrel! It isn't supper we are concerned with. I want you to tell what you know about the money that has been stolen from me.

MASTER JACQUES. Has somebody stolen your money?

HARPAGON. Yes, you rogue, and I'll have you hanged if you don't give it back.

OFFICER. Good Lord! Don't be so hard on him. I can see by the look of him that he is an honest fellow, and he'll tell you what you want to know without need to put him in jail. Now, my lad, if you confess you'll come to no harm and you will get a suitable reward from your master. Someone has taken his money during the day and you must know something about it.

MASTER JACQUES   (*aside*). Here's the very thing for getting my own back on that steward of ours. Ever since he arrived he's been the favorite. They won't listen to anybody but him. Moreover, I haven't forgotten the beating I had a while back.

HARPAGON.   What are you muttering about now?

OFFICER.   Let him alone. He's getting ready to tell you what you are wanting to know. I wasn't mistaken when I said he was an honest fellow.

MASTER JACQUES.   If you want to know, master, I believe that precious steward of yours has done it.

HARPAGON.   Valère?

MASTER JACQUES.   Yes.

HARPAGON.   He who seemed so trustworthy?

MASTER JACQUES.   That's the man. I suspect he's the fellow who has robbed you.

HARPAGON.   On what grounds do you suspect him?

MASTER JACQUES.   On what grounds?

HARPAGON.   Yes.

MASTER JACQUES.   I suspect him on the grounds—that I suspect him.

OFFICER.   But you must indicate what evidence you have.

HARPAGON.   Did you see him hanging about the spot where I had put my money?

MASTER JACQUES.   Yes, I did that! Where was your money?

HARPAGON.   In the garden.

MASTER JACQUES.   Exactly. He was hanging about the garden when I saw him. What was your money in?

HARPAGON.   In a cash box.

MASTER JACQUES.   The very thing! He had a cash box. I saw him with it.

HARPAGON.   What sort of a cash box? I can easily tell if it was mine.

MASTER JACQUES.   What sort of cash box?

HARPAGON.   Yes, yes, yes.

MASTER JACQUES.   Well—a sort of—like a cash box.

OFFICER.   Yes, of course, but describe it a little so that we can see whether—

MASTER JACQUES.   It was a big one.

HARPAGON.   Mine was a small one.

MASTER JACQUES.   Ay, it was small if you are going by size, but I meant it was big in that it had a big lot of money in it.

OFFICER.   What colour was it?

MASTER JACQUES.   What colour?

OFFICER.   Yes.

MASTER JACQUES.   A sort of—what's the word? Can't you help me to describe it?

HARPAGON.   Eh?

MASTER JACQUES.   It wasn't red, was it?

HARPAGON.   No, grey.

MASTER JACQUES.   That's it, a greyish red. That's what I meant.

HARPAGON.   There's no doubt about it. It's certainly the same one. Write it down, sir, write down his evidence. Oh Lord! Whom can one trust after this? There's no certainty in anything any more. I shall begin to believe that I'm capable of robbing myself.

MASTER JACQUES.   Here he comes, master. Whatever you do, don't go and tell him I told you.

(*Enter* VALÈRE.)

HARPAGON.   Come here! Come and confess to the foulest, most dastardly crime that was ever committed.

VALÈRE.   What can I do for you, sir?

HARPAGON.   What, you scoundrel! Don't you blush for your crime?

VALÈRE.   What crime are you talking about?

HARPAGON.   What crime am I talking about! You infamous wretch! As if you didn't know very well what I'm talking about. It's no use your trying to hide it. The secret is out. I've just heard the whole story. To think of your taking advantage of my kindness and getting yourself into my household on purpose to betray me and play a trick like this on me.

VALÈRE.   Well, sir, since you know all about it I won't attempt to excuse or deny it.

MASTER JACQUES   (*aside*). So ho. Have I guessed better than I thought?

VALÈRE.   I have been meaning to speak to you about it. I was waiting for a favorable opportunity, but since things have turned out as they have I can only ask you not to be angry, but be good enough to hear what I have to say in justification.

HARPAGON.   And what sort of justification can you give, you scoundrelly thief?

VALÈRE.   Ah sir, I hardly deserve epithets of that kind. It is true that I have put myself in the wrong with you, but, after all, my fault is a pardonable one.

HARPAGON.   Pardonable! A stab in the back! A mortal injury!

VALÈRE.   Please don't be angry. When you have heard what I have to say, you'll see that there is less harm done than you think.

HARPAGON.   Less harm done than I think. My very heart's blood, you scoundrel!

VALÈRE.   On a question of blood, sir, you haven't done badly. My rank is such that I shall not disgrace your blood and there's nothing in all this that I can't make amends for.

HARPAGON.   And that's exactly what I intend that you shall do—you shall return what you've stolen from me.

VALÈRE.   Your honour shall be fully satisfied, sir.

HARPAGON.   There's no question of honour! Tell me, what on earth led you to do such a thing?

VALÈRE.   Do you really need to ask?

HARPAGON.   Of course I need to ask!

VALÈRE.   It was that little god who is always forgiven, whatever he makes people do. Love, I mean.

HARPAGON.   Love!

VALÈRE.   Of course.

HARPAGON.   A pretty sort of love! Upon my word! Love of my gold pieces.

VALÈRE.   No, sir, it was not your wealth that tempted me, not in the least. That's not what dazzled me! Let me assure you I have no aspirations whatever where your wealth is concerned, provided you let me keep the one treasure I already possess.

HARPAGON.   No, indeed! By all the devils in Hell! You shan't keep it. The impudence! Wanting to keep what he's stolen.

VALÈRE.   Do you really call it stealing?

HARPAGON.   Do I really call it stealing? A treasure like that!

VALÈRE.   Yes, a treasure indeed, and beyond question the most precious you have, but not lost to you in becoming mine. On my bended knees I beg you to accord me this most cherished of treasures. Surely you can't refuse your consent.

HARPAGON.   I'll do nothing of the sort. What on earth are you talking about?

VALÈRE.   We are promised to each other and sworn never to be parted.

HARPAGON.   A wonderful promise! A very remarkable compact, I must say!

VALÈRE.   Yes, we are bound to one another for ever.

HARPAGON.   I'll put a stop to that, I promise you.

VALÈRE.   Death alone shall part us.

HARPAGON.   He must have my money on the brain!

VALÈRE.   I have already told you, sir, that I was not moved to do what I have done by material considerations. My motive was not what you think, but a far nobler one.

HARPAGON.   He'll be telling me next that it's sheer Christian charity set him wanting my money. But I'll see to that, and the law shall give me satisfaction on you, you impudent scoundrel.

VALÈRE.   Do as you please. I am resigned to bear whatever violence you may resort to, but I do ask you to believe that if any fault has been committed I alone am guilty. Your daughter is in no way to blame.

HARPAGON.   I should think not, indeed! It would be a queer thing if my daughter were involved in a crime like this. But I want to be seeing you make restoration. Where's the hiding-place?

VALÈRE.   There's no question of restoration or of hiding-place since we have not left the house.

HARPAGON   *(aside)*. Oh, my treasure! *(To* VALÈRE*)* Not left the house, you say?

VALÈRE.   No sir.

HARPAGON.   Now tell me—you haven't been tampering—

VALÈRE.   Never! There you wrong both of us. My love is pure and honourable, and though I am so deeply in love—

HARPAGON   *(aside)*. Deeply in love—with my cash box?

VALÈRE.   I would die sooner than harbour a single thought unworthy of one so kind and so modest as—

HARPAGON   *(aside)*. Modest—my cash box?

VALÈRE.   I have asked nothing more than the pleasure of feasting my eyes upon her. Nothing base or unworthy has ever profaned the love which her beauty inspires in me.

HARPAGON   *(aside)*. Beauty—my cash box? You might think he was a lover talking of his mistress.

VALÈRE.   Dame Claude knows the truth of the matter, sir. She can bear witness.

HARPAGON.   Ha, so my servant is in the plot, is she?

VALÈRE.   Yes, sir, she was a witness to our vows. Once she found that my intentions were honorable, she helped me to persuade your daughter to give me her promise and accept mine in return.

HARPAGON   *(aside)*. Fear of justice must have turned his brain! *(To* VALÈRE*)* What has my daughter to do with it?

VALÈRE.   I am just saying, sir, that I had the greatest difficulty in persuading her to accept my advances.

HARPAGON.   Accept your advances? Who?

VALÈRE.   Why, your daughter, sir. It was not until yesterday that she gave me her promise to marry me.

HARPAGON.   *My* daughter has given her promise to marry *you?*

VALÈRE.   Yes, sir—as I gave her mine in return.

HARPAGON.   Heavens! Another disaster!!

MASTER JACQUES   *(to the* OFFICER*)*. Write it down, mister! Write it all down!

HARPAGON.   Trouble on trouble. Misfortune piled on misfortune. Come, sir, do your duty! Draw up the indictment and arrest him as a thief and a seducer as well.

VALÈRE.   I have done nothing to deserve such a description. When you know who I am—

(Enter ÉLISE, MARIANNE, FROSINE.*)*

HARPAGON.   Wretched girl! You are unworthy of a father like me. This

is how you follow my precepts! You go and fall in love with a scoundrelly thief and promise to marry him without my consent. But you
will both find you have made a mistake. (*To* ÉLISE) I'll keep you within
four walls in future (*to* VALÈRE) and you shall pay for your audacity
on the gallows.

VALÈRE. The question won't be decided by your getting angry. I shall
at least be heard before I'm condemned.

HARPAGON. I was wrong when I said the gallows. You shall be broken on
the wheel.

ÉLISE (*on her knees to* HARPAGON). Father, be merciful, I implore you.
Do not push your parental rights to the limit. Don't let yourself be carried away in the first flush of anger. Take time to consider what you are
doing. Take the trouble to find out a little more about the man you
are so incensed against. He is not what he seems. You will be less surprised that I have given him my promise when you learn that you owe
it to him that you haven't lost me already. Yes, it was he, father, who
saved me from drowning. It is to him you owe your daughter's life
and—

HARPAGON. All that amounts to nothing at all. I'd rather he had left you
to drown than do what he has done.

ÉLISE. Father, I implore you by your love for me as a father—

HARPAGON. I won't hear any more. Justice must take its course.

MASTER JACQUES (*aside*). Now you shall pay for that beating you gave
me.

FROSINE (*aside*). Here's a fine kettle of fish.

(*Enter* ANSELME.)

ANSELME. What is the trouble, Mr. Harpagon? You seem very much
upset.

HARPAGON. Ah, Mr. Anselme. You see in me the most unlucky of men.
All sorts of trouble and difficulty have arisen over the contract you have
come to sign. I have suffered deadly blows both to my fortune and my
reputation. This treacherous scoundrel here has wormed his way into
my household in defiance of every sacred obligation, stolen my money
and seduced my daughter.

VALÈRE. Who cares anything about your money that you keep making
such a song about?

HARPAGON. They've got themselves engaged to be married—that's an
insult to you, Mr. Anselme. You must bring an action against him, at
your own expense, and get your revenge for his insolence with all the
rigour of the law.

ANSELME. I have no intention of forcing anyone to marry me. I make no
claim to any affection which is already given elsewhere, but, in so far

as your own interests may be involved, you can count on me to support them as my own.

HARPAGON.   This gentleman here is a very honest officer who has assured me he'll not fail to do everything his duty requires. (*To the* OFFICER) Charge him with everything he can be charged with and see that you make things black against him.

VALÈRE.   I fail to see how loving your daughter can be accounted a crime! As for the punishment you think will be meted out to me for aspiring to her hand, when you know who I am—

HARPAGON.   I don't give a rap for your stories. The world is full of self-styled nobility nowadays, impostors who take advantage of their own obscurity to assume the first illustrious name that comes into their heads!

VALÈRE.   I should scorn to lay claim to anything that doesn't belong to me, let me tell you. Anyone in Naples can bear witness to my birth and family.

ANSELME.   Gently! Mind what you are saying. You're running more risk than you think. You are speaking in the presence of one who knows Naples well and will see through any tale you invent.

VALÈRE   (*proudly putting on his hat*). I have nothing to fear. If you know Naples you know who Don Thomas d' Alburci was.

ANSELME.   I knew him well! Few better!

HARPAGON.   I care nothing for Don Thomas or Don Martin either! (*He notices two candles burning, and blows one out.*)

ANSELME.   Please—let him speak. Let us hear what he has to say.

VALÈRE.   I say that he was my father.

ANSELME.   *Your* father?

VALÈRE.   Yes.

ANSELME.   Come now! You are joking. Try a fresh tale and you may do better. You will do yourself no good with this one.

VALÈRE.   Take care what you say! This is no tale. I don't make statements that I cannot easily prove.

ANSELME.   What! You dare pretend that you are Thomas d'Alburci's son?

VALÈRE.   I do, and I will maintain it against all comers.

ANSELME.   What astounding effrontery! Let me tell you that the man you refer to was lost at sea more than sixteen years ago with his wife and children while fleeing from the cruel persecutions which accompanied the disorders in Naples, when so many noble families were driven into exile.

VALÈRE.   Yes, and let me tell you that his son, a boy of seven years of age, was saved from the wreck along with one servant by a Spanish ship, and that it is that son who is now speaking to you. Let me tell you also that the ship's captain took compassion upon me, brought me up as his own son, and that I have followed a career of arms from my earliest years. It is only recently that I learned that my father did not perish as I had always believed. I set out in search of him, and, passing through this town, I met, by a happy chance, my beloved Élise and fell under the spell of her beauty. Such was the effect of my love and her father's intransigence that I decided to take service in his household and send someone else in search of my parents.

ANSELME.   But what proof can you offer beyond your own word that this is not just a story built upon some foundation of truth?

VALÈRE.   The Spanish captain, a ruby signet ring which belonged to my father, an agate bracelet my mother clasped on my own arm, and lastly, old Pedro himself, who escaped from the shipwreck along with me.

MARIANNE.   Now I myself can vouch for the truth of what you have told us. I realize now that you are my brother.

VALÈRE.   Can you be my sister?

MARIANNE.   Yes. My heart was strangely moved from the very moment you began to speak. My mother—how overjoyed she will be to see you— has recounted our family misfortunes to me a thousand times. Heaven so willed that we too survived that unhappy shipwreck, but we did so at the cost of our liberty. The men who saved my mother and myself from a fragment of wreckage were corsairs. After ten years of slavery we regained our freedom by a stroke of good fortune and returned to Naples. There we found that our possessions had been sold and that there was no news of my father. We took ship thence to Genoa where my mother went to collect the miserable remnants of a despoiled inheritance. Fleeing from the inhumanity of her family she came to these parts, where she has since languished.

ANSELME.   Oh Lord! How wonderful are the manifestations of thy power! How true it is that Heaven alone can accomplish miracles! Come to my arms, my children, and mingle your happiness with your father's.

VALÈRE.   You are our father?

MARIANNE.   It was you my mother so lamented?

ANSELME.   Yes, my daughter. Yes, my son. I am Don Thomas d'Alburci. By the mercy of Heaven I was saved from the waves with all the money I had with me. For sixteen years I have believed you all drowned. After many wanderings I was about to seek to renew the consolations of domestic felicity by marriage to a good woman. Uncertain of my safety if I returned to Naples, I renounced my country for ever and, having contrived to dispose of all I had there, I settled down in this place and sought, under the name of Anselme, to forget the misfortunes which the other name had brought upon me.

HARPAGON.   Is this your son?

ANSELME.   It is.

HARPAGON.   Then I shall hold you responsible for paying me the ten thousand crowns he has stolen from me.

ANSELME.   Stolen from you?

HARPAGON.   Yes, this same fellow.

VALÈRE.   Who told you that?

HARPAGON.   Master Jacques.

MASTER JACQUES.   Oh! You know I've never said a word!

HARPAGON.   Oh, yes you did, and the officer here wrote it all down.

VALÈRE.   Do you think me capable of such an action?

HARPAGON.   Capable or incapable, I want my money back.

(*Enter* CLÉANTE *and* LA FLÈCHE.)

CLÉANTE.   Don't worry any more, father. Don't accuse anybody. I have news of your money. I come to tell you you can have it all back, provided you let me marry Marianne.

HARPAGON.   Where is the money?

CLÉANTE.   Don't you worry. It is where I can answer for it. It rests entirely with me. Just say what you want to do. Take your choice. Either give me Marianne or give up your money.

HARPAGON.   Is it all there?

CLÉANTE.   Every bit. Decide whether you will agree to the marriage and join her mother in giving consent. She has left her daughter free to choose between us: you—or me.

MARIANNE.   You are overlooking the fact that my mother's consent is now not sufficient. Heaven has restored my brother to me and my father. You need his consent now.

ANSELME.   Heaven has not brought me back to you, dear children, to oppose your own wishes. Mr Harpagon, you must be aware that a young girl is likely to prefer a son to his father. Come then, don't force me to say what I would much rather not. Join me in giving consent to this double marriage.

HARPAGON.   I can't decide until I see my cash box again.

CLÉANTE.   You shall—safe and sound.

HARPAGON.   I have no money for marriage portions.

ANSELME.   Well, I have enough for both, so that needn't worry you.

HARPAGON.   And you'll undertake to meet the costs of both marriages?

ANSELME.   Yes, I agree. Now are you satisfied?

HARPAGON.   Provided you buy me new clothes for the wedding.

ANSELME.   Agreed. Come, let us go and enjoy the pleasures of this happy day.

OFFICER.   Heh! Gentlemen, just a minute, if you don't mind. Who is going to pay for my depositions?

HARPAGON.   We want nothing to do with your depositions.

OFFICER.   Yes. but I don't intend to work for nothing, not likely!

HARPAGON.   There's that fellow there! (*Pointing to* MASTER JACQUES.) Take him and hang him for payment.

MASTER JACQUES.   Oh dear! What's a fellow to do! First I'm beaten for telling the truth and now they are going to hang me for telling lies.

ANSELME.   Come, Mr Harpagon, we must forgive him his untruths.

HARPAGON.   Will you pay the officer, then?

ANSELME.   So be it, but let us go at once and share our joy with your mother.

HARPAGON.   And let me go and see my beloved cash box again.

MOLIÈRE: NEW TO EVERY GENERATION

CHARLES AUGUSTIN SAINTE-BEUVE (TRANSLATED BY FRANCIS STEEGMULLER AND NORBERT GUTERMAN)

There is a class of writers who stand out even among the greatest, a very small class comprising no more than five or six names in all. Their hallmark is universality, a sense of eternal human values which pervades their portrayal of an age's customs and passions. Spontaneous creators, forceful and prolific, they are characterized first of all by this mixture of fertility, firmness, and freedom; by deep knowledge and richness of resources; by true indifference to conventional genres and techniques— any framework, any point of departure serves their purpose. They produce copiously, spurred on by obstacles, and they often achieve perfection without working less rapidly, and without resorting to artifice.

After the great figure of Homer, who gloriously inaugurated this supreme class of writers in incarnating the primitive genius of the noblest portion of mankind, it is difficult to decide which other men of ancient Greece should be included. Sophocles, however productive he may seem to have been, however human he showed himself in the harmonious expression of feelings and sufferings, Sophocles remains so perfect a figure, so sacred, as it were, in form and attitude, that we can scarcely imagine him removed from his purely Greek pedestal. The works of the famous comic authors have been lost; all we have is the name of Menander, who was perhaps the most accomplished in the group of geniuses we are speaking about. Aristophanes's marvelous imagination, so Athenian and so charming, nonetheless detracts from his universality. In Rome I can see only Plautus belonging here, a writer whose merits have not yet

Charles Augustin Sainte-Beuve (1804–1869) was one of the most influential French critics of the nineteenth century. Although he remains widely read and appreciated in our day, his critical dicta have been challenged, most notably by Proust.

been fully appreciated. He was a profound and versatile portrayer of human nature, head of his own company, like Shakespeare and like Molière, at once an actor and an author. We must see him as one of Molière's most legitimate forebears. But Latin literature was too much of a Greek import, too artificial from the outset, to provide sufficient scope for many of these free creators to develop. Ovid and Cicero, the most prolific among the great writers of this literature, are also the most "literary" and at bottom the most rhetorical. However, ancient Rome must be credited with having contributed two admirable poets to the literature of imitation, learning, and taste—those polished, accomplished artists, Virgil and Horace.

We have to come down to the modern era, to the Renaissance, to find the other men we are looking for—Shakespeare, Cervantes, Rabelais, Molière—these, with two or three more uneven talents of a later date, complete the classification. They all have a great deal in common. Their lives were eventful, beset with difficulties; they suffered, struggled, and loved. As soldiers, as physicians, as actors, as prisoners, they knew the hardships of poverty, they knew passion, and they were harassed by all sorts of worries, including financial ones.

Molière belongs among these most illustrious names, although he fully encompassed only the comic aspect of mankind: our vices, weaknesses, and follies. When he touched on the pathetic side of life, he did so quickly, incidentally. And yet he is second to none among the most complete geniuses, so greatly did he excel in his domain and explore every conceivable vein from the freest fantasy to the most serious observation. He was sovereign in every corner of reality he chose to treat in his works—and if that was only half of life, it is the half we encounter most often and that society is most concerned with.

Molière is of the century in which he lived, in that he portrays certain of its failings and his characters wear its costumes. But he is even more the portrayer of human nature in every time and place. To take the measure of his genius, it suffices to notice that though it is easy to link him to his century, yet he is not entirely determined by it; he attuned himself to it, but he is no less great transplanted to other times and places.

Today, when we judge things from a distance and by their results, Molière seems far more radically aggressive with respect to the society of his time than he himself supposed he was. We must guard against such distortion of perspectives in judging him. Among the illustrious contemporaries mentioned, only one—the one whom we would be least tempted to liken to our poet—questioned the very foundations of French society in that age even more than Molière, and analyzed birth, status, and property without perconceived ideas. This bold thinker was Pascal. However, the only consequence Pascal drew from his insights—

rather, from his destructive analysis of everything around him—was to cling more desperately to the pillars of the temple, to embrace the Cross in his agony.

Pascal and Molière seem to us today the best observers of the society of their epoch. Molière ranged over an immense territory which extended as far as the wall of the Church; he and his troupe peeked and probed into every corner of the old society, and held up to ridicule indiscriminately the conceit of the nobles, the inequality of matrimonial rights, the speciousness of religious hypocrisy. At the same time—more frighteningly—they showed the effects of these abuses upon true piety and the marriage sacrament. Pascal, meanwhile, though he remained within the central orthodoxy of the age, in his own way shook the vault of the edifice with his cries and anguish, and there was something Samson-like about the way he clasped the sacred pillars. However, in my opinion Molière did not deliberately set out to overturn the existing order—any more than Pascal did. He was probably unaware of the ultimate implications of his attitude. Similarly, it is hardly likely that Plautus had some systematic idea at the back of his mind when he made jokes about usury, prostitution, and slavery—those vices and mainsprings of ancient society.

In short, like Shakespeare and Cervantes, like three or four superior geniuses who have appeared over the ages, Molière was essentially a portrayer of human nature as he found it—without concern for organized religion, fixed dogma, or philosophical interpretation. In treating the society of his time, he portrayed the life that is everywhere that of the majority, and in castigating certain ways of life, he happened to write for all mankind. . . .

Molière's genius will be forever one of the adornments, one of the very proofs of the genius of humanity. La Rochefoucauld said that absence extinguishes little passions but increases great ones, like a violent wind which blows out candles but fans fires: the passage of time similarly affects reputations, erasing the lesser and enhancing the greater. But even among the greatest men, whose fame survives, there are many who stand at a distance from us, so to speak—their names rather than their works remain in the memory of mankind. Molière belongs to the smaller number of those whose works are ever present, new to every new generation, every new stage of civilization. Famous men, geniuses, books may multiply; civilizations may transform themselves (provided they continue); but five or six great lifetime achievements are part of the inalienable treasure of human thought. Every man who learns to read makes one more reader of Molière.

IBSEN

HENRIK IBSEN (1828–1906), BORN IN NORWAY, DOMINATES THE REALISTIC TRA-
DITION IN MODERN DRAMA; HIS PEOPLE, HIS PRODUCTIVITY, HIS PRODIGIOUS
IMAGINATIVE POWERS ASSURE HIM A PLACE AMONG THE GREAT CREATIVE
MEN OF THE POST-RENAISSANCE WORLD. HE LEARNED ABOUT THEATER AS
THE YOUNG (TWENTY-THREE-YEAR-OLD) DIRECTOR AND RESIDENT PLAY-
WRIGHT OF THE BERGEN MUNICIPAL THEATER. HE WAS ALMOST FORTY
WHEN IN 1867 HE WROTE THE ROMANTIC VERSE DRAMA *PEER GYNT*, SOME-
TIMES REGARDED AS HIS MASTERPIECE. IBSEN THEN TURNED HIS PRINCIPAL
ATTENTION TO SOCIAL REALISM: *THE LEAGUE OF YOUTH* (1869); *PILLARS OF
SOCIETY* (1877); *A DOLL'S HOUSE* (1879); *GHOSTS* (1881); *AN ENEMY OF THE PEO-
PLE* (1882). HIS NEXT PLAY, *THE WILD DUCK* (1884), WAS ANOTHER TURNING
POINT FOR IBSEN AND INAUGURATED THE LAST SEVERAL PLAYS, WHERE
SYMBOLISM COMBINES WITH REALISM IN A SERIES OF PROFOUND, PSYCHOLOGI-
CAL DRAMATIC PORTRAITS: *ROSMERSHOLM* (1886); *HEDDA GABLER* (1890); *THE
MASTER BUILDER* (1892); *LITTLE EYOLF* (1894); *JOHN GABRIEL BORKMAN* (1896);
AND, FINALLY, *WHEN WE DEAD AWAKEN* (1899).

Ibsen most comprehensively and profoundly dramatized the spiritual-
psychic-social disorders of late nineteenth-century Protestant Europe
(with which the United States has had its strongest affinities). So deep
was the penetration of his vision that none of his plays is susceptible to
quick reading and easy analysis. Although *Hedda Gabler* is, in many
respects, his most accessible *stage* play, it remains one of the most difficult to interpret. For example, James Joyce refers to Hedda as a tragic
figure; E. M. Forster finds her vulgar in her restlessness; Henry James
sees in her a study of an exasperated woman.

Hedda Gabler is the supreme example of modern tragedy: Hedda, displaying the traditional tragic qualities of pride and arrogance, engineers
her own destruction. Living between two worlds, Hedda, in her fear of
convention on the one hand and with her incapacity to achieve a personal freedom on the other, effects the dramatic catastrophe.

The play, obviously, will not yield all its secrets to any one of us.
As we read, however, we should be asking ourselves certain questions:
What does Hedda want or seem to want above everything else? How do
we reconcile her innermost needs with her marriage to Tesman? Is there
an ambivalence in her attitude toward respectable and respected members
of the community? Does she appear to live according to some formulated
code and can we evolve the set of principles she has inherited from her
father, General Gabler, whose portrait looks down on all the proceedings?

What is our own response to Aunt Julia? To her abiding interest in
Hedda's "condition"? To her care for Tesman's bedroom slippers? Does
Thea enlist our sympathy, our admiration, or our indifference?

What is the essence of Hedda's conflict? Is Lövborg a threat to Hedda's
aspirations, or is he an ally? In what sense is the final catastrophe inevitable?

HEDDA GABLER

TRANSLATION BY UNA ELLIS-FERMOR

CHARACTERS

JÖRGEN TESMAN, *a scholar engaged in*
  research in the history of civilization
HEDDA TESMAN, *his wife*
JULIANE TESMAN, *his aunt*
MRS. ELVSTED
BRACK, *a puisne judge*
EJLERT LÖVBORG
BERTE, *the Tesmans' servant*

*The action takes place in the Tesmans' villa
on the west side of the town*

ACT ONE

*A large drawing-room, well furnished, in good taste, and decorated in
dark colours. In the back wall there is a wide doorway with its curtains
pulled back. This opening leads into a smaller room decorated in the
same style as the drawing-room. In the right wall of this outer room is a
folding door that leads into the hall. In the opposite wall, left, is a glass
door also with curtains pulled back. Through its panes can be seen part
of a veranda outside and autumn foliage. In the middle of the stage is
an oval table with a cloth on it and chairs round it. Downstage, against
the right wall are a large, dark porcelain stove, a high-backed arm-
chair, a padded foot-rest and two stools. Up in the right corner are a
corner sofa and a little round table. Downstage, left, a little way from
the wall, is a sofa. Above the glass door, a piano. On each side of the
doorway at the back stands a what-not with terra-cotta and majolica ornaments. Against the back wall of the inner room can be seen a sofa, a table
and a chair or two. Over this sofa hangs the portrait of a handsome, elderly man in a general's uniform. Over the table a hanging lamp with a
soft, opal glass shade. All round the drawing-room are bouquets of flowers
in vases and glasses; others are lying on the tables. The floors in both
rooms are covered with thick carpets. Morning light: the sun shines in
through the glass doors.*

*Miss Juliane Tesman, wearing her hat and carrying a parasol, comes
in from the hall followed by Berte carrying a bouquet wrapped in paper.*

Miss Tesman is a comely, sweet-tempered-looking woman of about sixty-five, well but simply dressed in grey outdoor clothes. Berte is a servant getting on in years, with a homely, rather countrified look.

MISS TESMAN   *(stops just inside the door, listens and says softly)*. Why, I don't believe they're up yet!

BERTE   *(softly, too)*. That's what I said, Miss. Think how late the boat came in last night. And on top of that, my goodness! All the things the young mistress *would* unpack before she'd settle down.

MISS TESMAN.   Well, well. Let them have their sleep out, of course. But they must have fresh morning air to breathe when they do come out. *(She goes over to the glass door and throws it wide open.)*

BERTE   *(standing by the table, not knowing what to do with the bouquet in her hand)*. Well, upon my word, there just isn't anywhere left for it. I think I'd better put it here, Miss. *(She stands it up on the piano.)*

MISS TESMAN.   Well now, Berte my dear, you've got a new mistress. Heaven knows it was dreadfully hard for me to part with you!

BERTE   *(nearly crying)*. What do you think it was for *me*, Miss? I just can't tell you. After all these many years I've been with you two ladies.

MISS TESMAN.   We must try to be contented, Berte. There's really nothing else to be done. You know, Jörgen must have you in the house with him. He simply *must*. You have been used to looking after him ever since he was a little boy.

BERTE.   Yes, Miss. But I keep thinking of her lying there at home. Poor thing! So helpless and all. And that new girl, too! *She'll* never learn to look after a sick person properly. Never!

MISS TESMAN.   Oh, I shall manage to train her. And, you know, I shall take over most of it myself. Berte dear, there's no need for you to worry so much about my poor sister.

BERTE.   Yes, but there's another thing, Miss. I'm really afraid I'll never manage to suit the young mistress.

MISS TESMAN.   Oh, come now! Just at first, perhaps, there may be one or two things . . .

BERTE.   Because, of course, she's a fine lady—and that particular!

MISS TESMAN.   You can understand that, can't you, with General Gabler's daughter? Think what she was accustomed to in the General's day. Do you remember her riding along the road with her father? In that long black habit? And feathers in her hat?

BERTE.   My, yes! I should think I do. But, upon my word, I never thought it would be a match between her and Mr. Jörgen. Not in those days.

MISS TESMAN.   Nor did I. But that reminds me, Berte, while I think of it —you mustn't call Jörgen "Mr." any more. You must say "Doctor."

BERTE.   Yes, the young mistress said something about that, too, as soon as they got in last night. Is it true, then, Miss?

MISS TESMAN.   Yes, perfectly true. Just think of it, Berte, they made him a doctor abroad! While he was away this time, you know. I didn't know a single word about it, not till he told me down at the pier.

BERTE.   Oh, of course, he can be anything—he can. Clever, like he is. But I never thought he'd take up doctoring too.

MISS TESMAN.   Oh, it's not *that* kind of doctor he is. (*With a nod full of meaning.*) Coming to that, you may soon be able to call him something else—something even grander.

BERTE.   You don't say, Miss! What would that be, Miss?

MISS TESMAN   (*smiling*). Ah! If you only knew! (*Touched.*) God bless us! If poor dear Jochum could look up from his grave and see what his little boy has grown up to be! (*Looking about her.*) Oh, but—I say, Berte! Why *have* you done that? Taken all the covers off the furniture?

BERTE.   The mistress said I was to. Says she can't do with covers on the chairs.

MISS TESMAN.   Are they going to use this room for every day, then?

BERTE.   So it seemed, from what the mistress said. The master—the Doctor—he didn't say anything.

(*Jörgen Tesman, humming to himself, comes into the inner room from the right. He is carrying an empty, unfastened suit-case. He is a youngish-looking man of thirty-three, middle-sized, stoutish, with a round, frank, happy face. His hair and beard are fair; he wears glasses. He is comfortably—almost carelessly—dressed, in an indoor suit.*)

MISS TESMAN.   Good morning, good morning, Jörgen!

TESMAN   (*in the doorway between the rooms*). Aunt Julle! My dear Aunt Julle! (*Goes up and shakes her hand affectionately.*) All the way out here so early! Eh?

MISS TESMAN.   Well, you can just imagine! I *had* to have a look at you both.

TESMAN.   Although you haven't had anything like a proper night's rest!

MISS TESMAN.   Oh, that doesn't make a bit of difference to me.

TESMAN.   But you did get home from the pier all right? Eh?

MISS TESMAN.   Oh yes, quite all right, I'm glad to say. Mr Brack was so very kind and saw me right to my door.

TESMAN.   We *were* so sorry we couldn't give you a lift. But you saw how it was yourself. Hedda had so much luggage that she had to have with her.

MISS TESMAN.   Yes, she certainly did have a tremendous lot of luggage.

BERTE   (*to* TESMAN). Shall I go in and ask the mistress if there's anything I could help her with?

TESMAN.   No, thanks, Berte, you needn't do that. If she wants you for anything, she says she'll ring.

BERTE   (*to the right*). Very well.

TESMAN.   Oh, but, here—take this suit-case, will you?

BERTE   *(taking it)*. I'll put it up in the attic. *(Goes out by the hall door.)*

TESMAN.   Just think, Aunt Julle, I had that whole suit-case crammed full, just with the stuff I'd copied. You wouldn't believe what I've managed to collect, going through the archives. Curious old things that no one really knows about.

MISS TESMAN.   Well, well Jörgen, you certainly haven't wasted you time on your honeymoon.

TESMAN.   No, I jolly well haven't! But take your hat off, Aunt Julle. Here, let me unfasten the bow. Eh?

MISS TESMAN   *(while he is doing it)*. Bless me! It's just as though you were still at home with us.

TESMAN   *(turning and twisting the hat in his hand)*. Why! What a fine, smart hat you've bought yourself!

MISS TESMAN.   I got it because of Hedda.

TESMAN.   Because of Hedda? Eh?

MISS TESMAN.   Yes. So that Hedda shan't be ashamed of me if we go out together.

TESMAN   *(patting her cheek)*. Dear Aunt Julle! You think of absolutely everything. *(Puts the hat on a chair by the table.)* Now, look here; let's sit on the sofa and have a little chat till Hedda comes.

(They sit down. She puts her parasol in the sofa-corner.)

MISS TESMAN   *(taking both his hands and looking at him)*. What a blessing it is to have you again, Jörgen, as large as life! My dear! Poor Jochum's own boy!

TESMAN.   So it is for me, Aunt Julle, to see *you* again! You who've been my father and my mother.

MISS TESMAN.   Yes, I know you'll always have a corner in your heart for your old aunts.

TESMAN.   But I suppose there's no improvement in Aunt Rina, eh?

MISS TESMAN.   Well, you know, we can't really expect any improvement in her, poor dear. She just lies there, the same as she has all these years. But I hope the good Lord will let me keep her a little longer. For I shan't know what to do with my life otherwise, Jörgen. Especially now, you know, that I haven't got you to look after any more.

TESMAN   *(patting her on the back)*. Come, come, come!

MISS TESMAN   *(with a sudden change)*. But just think, Jörgen, you're a married man! And to think it was you who carried off Hedda Gabler! The lovely Hedda Gabler! To think of it! She, who always had so *many* admirers.

TESMAN   *(humming a little, with a satisfied smile)*. Yes, I expect a certain number of my good friends are going about this town feeling pretty envious. Eh?

MISS TESMAN. And to think that you were able to have such a long honey-moon! Over five months. Nearly six.

TESMAN. Well, for me it's been a kind of research tour as well—with all those old records I had to hunt through. And then, you know, the enormous number of books I had to read.

MISS TESMAN. Yes, that's quite true. (*Dropping her voice a little and speaking confidentially.*) But look here, Jörgen, haven't you anything . . . anything, well, *special* to tell me?

TESMAN. About the trip?

MISS TESMAN. Yes.

TESMAN. No, I don't think there's anything else, except what I told you in my letters. About my taking my doctorate down there—well, I told you that yesterday.

MISS TESMAN. Oh yes, that kind of thing. Yes. But, I mean, haven't you any . . . well, any hopes . . . er . . . ?

TESMAN. Hopes?

MISS TESMAN. Oh, come, Jörgen! After all, I *am* your old aunt!

TESMAN. Well, yes, of course I have hopes . . .

MISS TESMAN. Ah!

TESMAN. . . . I've the very best hopes of getting a professorship one of these days.

MISS TESMAN. Oh yes, a professorship. Yes.

TESMAN. Or I might say, rather, there's a certainty of my getting it. But, my dear Aunt Julle, you know that yourself perfectly well!

MISS TESMAN (*with a little laugh*) . Yes, of course I do. You're quite right. (*Changing her tone.*) But we were talking about your travels. It must have cost a lot of money, Jörgen?

TESMAN. Ye-es. But, you know, that big fellowship took us a good bit of the way.

MISS TESMAN. But I don't see how you can possibly have made that do for two.

TESMAN. Well, no; one could hardly expect that. Eh?

MISS TESMAN. Especially when it's a lady one's travelling with. For that usually comes more expensive—very much more. I've heard.

TESMAN. Well, yes, of course. It does come rather more expensive. But Hedda had to have that trip. Aunt Julle. She really had to. Nothing else would have done.

MISS TESMAN. No, no. Of course it wouldn't. A honeymoon abroad seems quite a matter of course, nowadays. But tell me now. Have you had a chance yet to have a good look at the house?

TESMAN. You bet I have! I have been wandering round ever since it was light.

MISS TESMAN. And what do you think of it, on the whole?

TESMAN.   Splendid! Absolutely splendid! There's only one thing I can't see—what we're going to do with the two empty rooms there between the back sitting-room and Hedda's bedroom.

MISS TESMAN   *(with a little laugh)*. Oh, my dear Jörgen, there may be a use for them—all in good time.

TESMAN.   Yes, you're perfectly right, Aunt Julle! Because, by degrees, as I get a bigger library, well—Eh?

MISS TESMAN.   Of course, my dear boy. It was the library I was thinking of.

TESMAN.   I'm specially glad for Hedda's sake. She often said, before we were engaged, that she'd never care to live anywhere except in Mrs. Falk's house.

MISS TESMAN.   Yes, just fancy! And then its happening like that—the house being for sale! Just as you had started.

TESMAN.   Yes, Aunt Julle, the luck certainly was with us. Eh?

MISS TESMAN.   But expensive, my dear Jörgen! It will be expensive for you, all this.

TESMAN   *(looking at her, a little disheartened)*. Yes, I suppose it will, perhaps.

MISS TESMAN.   Goodness, yes!

TESMAN.   How much do you think? Roughly. Eh?

MISS TESMAN.   Oh, I can't possibly tell till all the bills come in.

TESMAN.   But fortunately Mr. Brack has arranged the easiest possible terms for me. He wrote and told Hedda so himself.

MISS TESMAN.   Well, don't you worry about it, my child. And as for the furniture and carpets, I have given security for them.

TESMAN.   Security? You? My dear Aunt Julle, what kind of security could you give?

MISS TESMAN.   I have given a mortgage on the annuity.

TESMAN   *(jumping up)*. What! On yours and Aunt Rina's annuity?

MISS TESMAN.   Yes. I didn't know what else to do, you see.

TESMAN   *(standing in front of her)*. But, Aunt Julle, have you gone crazy? The annuity! The only thing you and Aunt Rina have to live on!

MISS TESMAN.   Now now—don't get so upset about it. The whole thing is just a formality, you know. That's what Mr. Brack said, too. For it was he who so kindly arranged it for me. Just a formality, he said.

TESMAN.   Yes, that may be so. But all the same . . .

MISS TESMAN.   Because you've got your own salary to rely on now. And—goodness me!—suppose we did have to spend a little too—just at first? Why, it would only be a pleasure for us.

TESMAN.   Oh, Aunt Julle, you will never be tired of sacrificing yourself for me.

MISS TESMAN   *(getting up and laying her hands on his shoulders)*. Have

I any other joy in this world but in smoothing the way for you, my dear boy? You who've had neither father nor mother to turn to. And now we've reached our goal, my dear! Things may have looked black now and again. But, thank goodness, you're through that now. Jörgen.

TESMAN. Yes, it's wonderful, really, how everything has worked out.

MISS TESMAN. Yes, and the people who stood in your way, who would have stopped your getting on, you have them at your feet. They have gone down before you, Jörgen—most of all, the person who was most dangerous to you. And there he lies now, on the bed he made for himself, the poor misguided creature.

TESMAN. Have you heard anything of Ejlert? Since I went away, I mean?

MISS TESMAN. No, only that he's supposed to have brought out a new book.

TESMAN. *What?* Ejlert Lövborg? Just recently? Eh?

MISS TESMAN. Yes, so they say. I shouldn't think there can be much in it, would you? Now when *your* new book comes out, that will be quite another story, Jörgen. What is it going to be about?

TESMAN. It's going to be about domestic crafts in Brabant in the Middle Ages.

MISS TESMAN. Well, well! To think you can write about a thing like that!

TESMAN. As a matter of fact, the book may take some time yet. I've got to arrange those enormous collections of material first, you know.

MISS TESMAN. Ah yes. Arranging and collecting—that's what you're so good at. You're not dear Jochum's son for nothing.

TESMAN. I'm looking forward immensely to getting down to it. Especially now that I've got a charming house of my own, my own home to work in.

MISS TESMAN. And first and foremost, my dear, now that you've got the wife your heart was set on.

TESMAN *(giving her a hug)*. Why, of course, Aunt Julle! Hedda! Why, that's the loveliest thing of all! *(Looking towards the centre doorway.)* I think she's coming. Eh?

(Hedda comes in from the left, through the inner room. She is a woman of twenty-nine. Her face and figure show breeding and distinction, her complexion has an even pallor. Her eyes are steel-grey; cold, clear and calm. Her hair is a beautiful light brown, though not noticeably abundant. The loose-fitting morning costume she is wearing is in good style.)

MISS TESMAN *(going up to Hedda)*. Good morning, Hedda dear! A very good morning to you!

HEDDA *(holding out her hand)*. Good morning, my dear Miss Tesman. What an early visit! It was kind of you.

MISS TESMAN *(seeming a little taken aback)*. Well, has the bride slept well in her new home?

HEDDA. Oh yes, thank you. Tolerably.

TESMAN. Tolerably! I like that, Hedda! You were sleeping like a log when I got up.

HEDDA. Fortunately. In any case, one has to get used to anything new, Miss Tesman. By degrees. (*Looking to the left.*) Oh! The maid has gone and opened the veranda door! There's a perfect flood of sunlight coming in.

MISS TESMAN (*going towards the door*). Well, we'll shut it, then.

HEDDA. Oh no, don't do that, please. (*To Tesman.*) Just draw the blinds, my dear, will you? That gives a softer light.

TESMAN (*at the door*). Yes, yes. All right. There you are, Hedda. Now you've got shade *and* fresh air.

HEDDA. Yes, we certainly need fresh air in here. All these precious flowers! But—won't you sit down, Miss Tesman?

MISS TESMAN. No, thank you very much. Now I know everything is going on all right here—thank goodness!—I must see about getting home again. Poor dear, she finds the time very long, lying there.

TESMAN. Give her my love and my best wishes, won't you? And tell her I'll come over and see her later on today.

MISS TESMAN. Yes, yes, I certainly will. But that reminds me, Jörgen. (*Feeling in her bag.*) I nearly forgot it. I've brought something of yours.

TESMAN. What is it, Aunt Julle? Eh?

MISS TESMAN (*bringing out a flat newspaper package and handing it to him*). Look there, my dear boy.

TESMAN (*opening it*). Well, I'm blessed! You've kept them for me, Aunt Julle! That really is sweet of her, Hedda, isn't it? Eh?

HEDDA (*by the what-not on the right*). Yes, my dear. What is it?

TESMAN. My old morning shoes. My slippers—look!

HEDDA. Oh yes. I remember, you often spoke about them while we were away.

TESMAN. Yes, I missed them dreadfully. (*Going up to her.*) Now you shall see them, Hedda.

HEDDA (*going over to the stove*). No, thanks. It really doesn't interest me.

TESMAN (*following her*). Just think, Aunt Rina embroidered them for me in bed, lying ill like that. Oh, you can't imagine how many memories are worked into them!

HEDDA. Not for me, particularly.

MISS TESMAN. Hedda's right about that, Jörgen.

TESMAN. Yes, but I think, now she belongs to the family—

HEDDA (*interrupting*). My dear, we shall never be able to manage with this maid.

MISS TESMAN. Not manage with Berte?

TESMAN. What makes you say that, my dear? Eh?

HEDDA   (*pointing*) . Look there. She's left her old hat behind her on the chair.

TESMAN   (*dropping his slippers on the floor in his dismay*) . But, Hedda—

HEDDA.   Suppose anyone were to come in and see it?

TESMAN.   But—but, Hedda, that is Aunt Julle's hat!

HEDDA.   Oh! Is it?

MISS TESMAN   (*picking up the hat*) . Yes, it's certainly mine. And it isn't old, either, my dear little Hedda.

HEDDA.   I really didn't look at it closely, Miss Tesman.

MISS TESMAN   (*putting on the hat*) . As a matter of fact, it's the first time I've worn it. The very first, it is.

TESMAN.   And a beautiful hat it is, too. Really grand!

MISS TESMAN.   Oh, it's not all that, my dear Jörgen. (*Looking round her.*) Parasol? Ah, here it is (*Picking it up.*) For that's mine, too. (*Under her breath.*) Not Berte's.

TESMAN.   A new hat and a new parasol! Think of that, Hedda.

HEDDA.   Yes, it's very nice. Charming.

TESMAN.   Yes, isn't it? Eh? But, Aunt Julle, take a good look at Hedda before you go. See how nice and charming *she* is.

MISS TESMAN.   Ah, my dear, there's nothing new in *that*. Hedda has been lovely all her life. (*She nods and goes towards the right.*)

TESMAN   (*following her*) . Yes, but have you noticed how plump she's grown, and how well she is? How much she's filled out on our travels?

HEDDA   (*crossing the room*) . Oh, be quiet—!

MISS TESMAN   (*who has stopped and turned round*) . Filled out?

TESMAN.   Of course, you can't see it so well, Aunt Julle, now she has that dress on. But I, who have the opportunity of—

HEDDA   (*at the glass door, impatiently*). Oh, you haven't any opportunity!

TESMAN.   It must be the mountain air, down there in the Tyrol—

HEDDA   (*interrupting curtly*) . I am exactly the same as I was when I went away.

TESMAN.   Yes, so you keep on saying. But you certainly aren't. Don't you think so too, Aunt Julle?

MISS TESMAN   (*gazing at her with clasped hands*). Hedda is lovely—lovely—lovely! (*She goes up to Hedda, takes her head in both hands, and, bending it down, kisses her hair.*) May God bless and take care of our Hedda. For Jörgen's sake.

HEDDA   (*freeing herself gently*) . Oh—let me go.

MISS TESMAN   (*quietly, but with emotion*) . I shall come over and see you two every single day.

TESMAN.   Yes, do, *please*, Aunt Julle! Eh?

MISS TESMAN.   Good-bye. Good-bye.

(*She goes out by the hall door. Tesman goes with her, leaving the door half open. He can be heard repeating his messages to Aunt Rina and thanking her for the shoes. In the meanwhile Hedda crosses the room, raising her arms and clenching her hands, as if in fury. Then she pulls back the curtains from the glass door and stands there looking out. After a moment Tesman comes in again, shutting the door behind him.*)

TESMAN   (*picking up the slippers from the floor*). What are you looking at, Hedda?

HEDDA   (*calm and controlled again*). I'm just looking at the leaves. They're so yellow, and so withered.

TESMAN   (*wrapping up the shoes and putting them on the table*). Well, after all, we're well on in September now.

HEDDA   (*disturbed again*). Yes, just think. We're already in—in September.

TESMAN.   Don't you think Aunt Julle was rather unlike herself, my dear? A little bit—almost formal? Whatever do you think was the matter? Eh?

HEDDA.   I hardly know her, you see. Isn't she like that as a rule?

TESMAN.   No, not like she was today.

HEDDA   (*moving away from the glass door*). Do you think she was really upset about that business with the hat?

TESMAN.   Oh, not much. Perhaps a little, just at the moment.

HEDDA.   But what extraordinary manners! To throw her hat down here in the drawing-room. One doesn't do that kind of thing.

TESMAN.   Well, you can be sure Aunt Julle won't do it again.

HEDDA.   Anyway, I'll make it all right with her.

TESMAN.   That's sweet of you, Hedda dear! If you would!

HEDDA.   When you go in to see them presently, you might ask her over here for the evening.

TESMAN.   Yes, I certainly will. And there's another thing you could do that would please her enormously.

HEDDA.   Oh? What?

TESMAN.   If you could bring yourself to speak a little more affectionately to her—as if you were one of the family. For my sake, Hedda? Eh?

HEDDA.   No, no. You mustn't ask me to do that. I've told you that once already. I'll try to call her "Aunt," and that must be enough.

TESMAN.   Oh well, all right. Only it seems to me now that you belong to the family—

HEDDA.   Well, I really don't know. . . . (*She goes up towards the centre doorway.*)

TESMAN   (*after a pause*). Is there anything the matter, Hedda? Eh?

HEDDA.   I'm just looking at my old piano. It doesn't go very well with all these other things.

TESMAN.   When I get my first salary cheque, we'll see about an exchange.

HEDDA.   Oh no, not an exchange. I don't want to get rid of it. We can put it in there, in the back room. And we can have another in its place here. Some time or other, I mean.

TESMAN   (*a little subdued*). Yes. We can do that, of course.

HEDDA   (*picking up the bouquet from the piano*). These flowers weren't here when we came in last night.

TESMAN.   Aunt Julle must have brought them for you.

HEDDA   (*looking into the bouquet*). A visiting-card. (*Taking it out and reading it.*) "Will call again later on today." Can you guess who it's from?

TESMAN.   No. Who is it? Eh?

HEDDA.   It says "Mrs. Elvsted."

TESMAN.   Really? The wife of the District Magistrate. Miss Rysing that was.

HEDDA.   Yes. Exactly. That girl with the tiresome hair, that she was always showing off. An old flame of yours, I've heard.

TESMAN   (*laughing*). Oh, it didn't last long! And it was before I knew you, Hedda. But fancy her being in town.

HEDDA.   Odd, that she should call on us. I hardly know her, except that we were at school together.

TESMAN.   Yes, I haven't seen her either for—heaven knows how long. I wonder she can bear it up there, in that hole of a place. Eh?

HEDDA   (*thinks a moment and says suddenly*). Tell me, isn't it somewhere up there that he lives—er— Ejlert Lövborg?

TESMAN.   Yes it is. Up in those parts.

(*Berte comes in at the hall door.*)

BERTE.   She's here again, ma'am. The lady who came and left the flowers an hour ago. (*Pointing.*) The ones you've got in your hand, ma'am.

HEDDA.   Oh, is she? Show her in, will you?

(*Berte opens the door for Mrs. Elvsted and goes out herself. Mrs. Elvsted is a slender little thing with pretty, soft features. Her eyes are light blue, large, round and slightly prominent, with a startled, questioning expression. Her hair is remarkably fair, almost silver-gilt, and exceptionally thick and wavy. She is a couple of years younger than Hedda. She is wearing a dark calling costume, of a good style but not quite of the latest fashion.*)

HEDDA   (*going to meet her in a friendly way*). How are you, my dear Mrs. Elvsted? It's nice to see you once more.

MRS. ELVSTED   (*nervous, and trying to control herself*). Yes, it's a very long time since we met.

TESMAN   (*giving her his hand*). Or we two either. Eh?

HEDDA.   Thank you for your lovely flowers.

MRS. ELVSTED.   Oh, please! I would have come here at once, yesterday afternoon. But I heard that you were away.

TESMAN.   Have you only just come to town? Eh?

MRS. ELVSTED.   I got here about midday yesterday. I was absolutely in despair when I heard that you weren't at home.

HEDDA.   In despair? But why?

TESMAN.   But my dear, dear Mrs. Rysing—Mrs. Elvsted, I mean—

HEDDA.   There isn't anything the matter, is there?

MRS. ELVSTED.   Yes, there is. And I don't know a living soul to turn to here in town, except you.

HEDDA   (putting the bouquet down on the table). Come now, let's sit here on the sofa.

MRS. ELVSTED.   No, I feel too worried and restless to sit down.

HEDDA.   Oh no, you don't. Come along here (She pulls Mrs. Elvsted down onto the sofa and sits beside her.)

TESMAN.   Well now, what is it, Mrs. Elvsted?

HEDDA.   Has anything gone wrong up there, at home?

MRS. ELVSTED.   Well, it has and it hasn't. Oh, I do so want you not to misunderstand me.

HEDDA.   Then the best thing you can do, Mrs. Elvsted, is to tell us all about it.

TESMAN.   Because that's what you've come for, isn't it? Eh?

MRS. ELVSTED.   Yes, yes, it is, of course. Well, then, I must explain—if you don't know already—that Ejlert Lövborg is in town too.

HEDDA.   Lövborg is!

TESMAN.   Really? So Ejlert Lövborg's come back again! Fancy that, Hedda!

HEDDA.   Quite. I heard all right.

MRS. ELVSTED.   He's been here a week now, already. Think of it! A whole week in this dangerous town. And alone! And all the bad company he could get into here!

HEDDA.   But, my dear Mrs. Elvsted, why does he specially matter to you?

MRS. ELVSTED   (gives her a frightened glance and says quickly). He used to be the children's tutor.

HEDDA.   Your children's?

MRS. ELVSTED.   My husband's. I haven't got any.

HEDDA.   Your step-children's, then.

MRS. ELVSTED.   Yes.

TESMAN   (hesitantly). Was he . . . er . . . tolerably . . . then . . . I don't quite know how to put it . . . fairly steady in his habits—enough to be given that job? Eh?

MRS. ELVSTED.   For the last two years there hasn't been a word against him.

TESMAN.   Really! Think of that, Hedda!

HEDDA.   I heard.

MRS. ELVSTED. Not the least thing, I assure you. Nothing of any kind. But still now, when I know he's here—in this great city—and with plenty of money in his pockets . . . I'm desperately anxious about him now.

TESMAN. But why didn't he stay up there where he was, then? With you and your husband? Eh?

MRS. ELVSTED. Once the book was out he was too restless and excited to stay up there with us.

TESMAN. Oh yes, that reminds me. Aunt Julle said he'd brought out a new book.

MRS. ELVSTED. Yes, a big new book on the history of civilization; a sort general survey. It's been out a fortnight now. And now that it's gone so well and made such a tremendous stir—

TESMAN. It has, has it? It must be something he had by him from his better days, then.

MRS. ELVSTED. From some time ago, you mean?

TESMAN. Exactly.

MRS. ELVSTED. No, he wrote the whole thing up at our place. Just lately —within the last year.

TESMAN. That's good news, isn't it, Hedda? Just fancy!

MRS. ELVSTED. Yes, indeed. If only it would last.

HEDDA. Have you met him here in town?

MRS. ELVSTED. No, not yet. I had a lot of trouble finding his address. But I got it at last, this morning.

HEDDA *(looking searchingly at her)*. You know, it seems a little odd of your husband to . . . er . . .

MRS. ELVSTED *(starting nervously)*. Of my husband? What does?

HEDDA. To send you to town on an errand like this. Not to come in and look after his friend himself.

MRS. ELVSTED. Oh, not at all! My husband hasn't time for that. And then there—there was some shopping I had to do.

HEDDA *(with a slight smile)*. Ah well, that's a different matter.

MRS. ELVSTED *(getting up quickly, in some distress)*. So I do implore you, Mr. Tesman, be good to Ejlert Lövborg if he comes to you! And he's sure to, because you were such good friends in the old days. And besides, you're both working in the same field. On the same subjects, as far as I can make out.

TESMAN. Well anyway, we were at one time.

MRS. ELVSTED. Yes. And that's why I do beseech you—you really will keep a watchful eye on him too, won't you, Mr. Tesman? You do promise me?

TESMAN. Yes, I'll be only too glad to, Mrs. Rysing—

HEDDA. Elvsted.

TESMAN.   I really will do what I can for Ejlert. Everything I possibly can. You can be sure of that.

MRS. ELVSTED.   Oh, you *are* being kind! (*Clasping his hands.*) Thank you, again and again. (*Frightened.*) Because my husband is so attached to him.

HEDDA   (*getting up*). You ought to write to him, my dear. He may not come to see you of his own accord.

TESMAN.   Yes, Hedda, that probably would be best. Eh?

HEDDA.   And the sooner the better. Now—at once—I think.

MRS. ELVSTED   (*beseechingly*). Oh yes? If you *would!*

TESMAN.   I'll write this very minute. Have you his address, Mrs.—Elvsted?

MRS. ELVSTED   (*taking a small slip of paper out of her pocket and handing it to him*). Here it is.

TESMAN.   Good. Good. I'll go in, then. (*Looking round him.*) That reminds me—my slippers? Ah, here they are. (*Picks up the parcel and is just going.*)

HEDDA.   Now write really kindly and affectionately. And a good long letter, too.

TESMAN.   Yes, I certainly will.

MRS. ELVSTED.   But, please, don't say a word about my having asked you to!

TESMAN.   Of course not. That goes without saying. Eh? (*He goes through the inner room to the right.*)

HEDDA   (*goes up to Mrs. Elvsted and says softly*). That's right. Now we've killed two birds with one stone.

MRS. ELVSTED.   How do you mean?

HEDDA.   Didn't you realize I wanted to get rid of him?

MRS. ELVSTED.   Yes, to write his letter.

HEDDA.   And also so that I could talk to you alone.

MRS. ELVSTED   (*confused*). About this business?

HEDDA.   Exactly. About that.

MRS. ELVSTED   (*alarmed*). But there isn't anything more, Mrs. Tesman! Nothing at all!

HEDDA.   Oh yes there is, now. There's a lot more. That much I do realize. Come over here, and we'll sit and be cosy and friendly together.

(*She pushes Mrs. Elvsted into the easy-chair by the stove and sits on one of the stools herself.*)

MRS. ELVSTED   (*looking anxiously at her watch*). But my dear Mrs. Tesman, I really meant to go now.

HEDDA.   Oh, surely there's no hurry. Now then, suppose you tell me a little about what your home's like.

MRS. ELVSTED.   But that's the last thing in the world I wanted to talk about!

HEDDA. Not to me, my dear? After all, we were at school together.

MRS. ELVSTED. Yes, but you were a class above me. How dreadfully frightened of you I was in those days!

HEDDA. Were you frightened of me?

MRS. ELVSTED. Yes. Dreadfully frightened. Because when we met on the stairs you always used to pull my hair.

HEDDA. No, *did* I?

MRS. ELVSTED. Yes, and once you said you would burn it off.

HEDDA. Oh, that was only silly talk, you know.

MRS. ELVSTED. Yes, but I was so stupid in those days. And since then, anyhow, we have drifted such a long, long way part. Our circles were so entirely different.

HEDDA. Well, then, we'll see if we can come together again. Now, look here. When we were at school we used to talk like real close friends and call each other by our Christian names.

MRS. ELVSTED. Oh no, you're making quite a mistake.

HEDDA. I certainly am *not*. I remember it perfectly well. So we are going to tell each other everything, as we did in the old days. (*Moving nearer with her stool.*) There we are! (*Kissing her cheek.*) Now you're to talk to me like a real friend and call me "Hedda."

MRS. ELVSTED (*clasping and patting her hands*). All this goodness and kindness—it's not a bit what I'm used to.

HEDDA. There, there, there! And I'm going to treat *you* like a friend, as I did before, and call you my dear Thora.

MRS. ELVSTED. My name's Thea.

HEDDA. Yes, of course. Of course. I meant Thea. (*Looking sympathetically at her.*) So you're not used to much goodness or kindness, aren't you, Thea? Not in your own home?

MRS. ELVSTED. Ah, if I *had* a home! But I haven't one. Never have had. . . .

HEDDA (*looking at her a moment*). I rather thought it must be something of that sort.

MRS. ELVSTED (*gazing helplessly in front of her*). Yes. Yes. Yes.

HEDDA. I can't quite remember now, but wasn't it as housekeeper that you went up there in the beginning—to the District Magistrate's?

MRS. ELVSTED. Actually it was to have been as governess. But his wife— his late wife—was an invalid and was ill in bed most of the time. So I had to take charge of the house too.

HEDDA. But then, in the end, you became the mistress of the house.

MRS. ELVSTED (*drearily*). Yes, I did.

HEDDA. Let me see. . . . About how long ago is it now?

MRS. ELVSTED. Since I was married?

HEDDA. Yes.

MRS. ELVSTED.   It's five years ago now.

HEDDA.   Yes, of course. It must be that.

MRS. ELVSTED.   Ah! Those five years—or rather the last two or three. Oh, if you could only imagine, Mrs. Tesman—

HEDDA   (*giving her a little slap on the hand*). Mrs. Tesman! Come, Thea!

MRS. ELVSTED.   Oh yes; I will try! Yes, Hedda, if you had any idea—if you understood—

HEDDA   (*casually*). Ejlert Lövborg was up there too for three years or so, I believe?

MRS. ELVSTED   (*looking at her doubtfully*). Ejlert Lövborg? Why yes. He was.

HEDDA.   Did you know him already? From the old days in town?

MRS. ELVSTED.   Hardly at all. Well I mean—by name, of course.

HEDDA.   But when you were up there—then, he used to visit you and your husband?

MRS. ELVSTED.   Yes, he came over to us every day. You see, he was giving the children lessons. Because, in the long run, I couldn't manage it all myself.

HEDDA.   No, I should think not. And your husband? I suppose he is often away from home?

MRS. ELVSTED.   Yes. You see, Mrs.—er—you see, Hedda, being District Magistrate he's always having to go out on circuit.

HEDDA   (*leaning against the arm of the chair*). Thea, my poor little Thea. Now you're going to tell me all about it. Just how things are.

MRS. ELVSTED.   Very well. You ask me about it, then.

HEDDA.   What is your husband really like, Thea? You know what I mean —in everyday life? Is he nice to you?

MRS. ELVSTED   (*evasively*). He's quite sure himself that he does everything for the best.

HEDDA.   Only, it seems to me, he must be much too old for you. More than twenty years older, surely?

MRS. ELVSTED   (*irritably*). Yes, there's that too. What with one thing and another, I'm miserable with him. We haven't an idea in common, he and I. Not a thing in the world.

HEDDA.   But isn't he fond of you, all the same? I mean, in his own way?

MRS. ELVSTED.   Oh, I don't know *what* he feels. I think I'm just useful to him. After all, it doesn't cost much to keep me. I'm cheap.

HEDDA.   That's silly of you.

MRS. ELVSTED   (*shaking her head*). It can't be any different. Not with him. He isn't really fond of anyone but himself. And perhaps the children—a little.

HEDDA.   And of Ejlert Lövborg, Thea.

MRS. ELVSTED   (*looking at her*). Of Ejlert Lövborg? What makes you think that?

HEDDA. But, my dear—it seems to me, when he sends you all the way into town after him. . . . (*Smiling almost imperceptibly.*) And besides, you said so yourself to my husband.

MRS. ELVSTED (*with a nervous start*). What? Oh yes, so I did. (*Breaking out, but in a lowered voice.*) No. I might as well tell you now as later. It'll all come out, anyway.

HEDDA. But, my dear Thea—

MRS. ELVSTED. Well, to be quite frank, my husband had no idea I was coming.

HEDDA. *What!* Didn't your husband know about it?

MRS. ELVSTED. No, of course not. And, anyway, he wasn't at home. He was away too. Oh, I couldn't stand it any longer, Hedda! It was simply impossible. I should have been absolutely alone up there in future.

HEDDA. Well? So then?

MRS. ELVSTED. So I packed up some of my things, you see—the ones I needed most. Very quietly, of course. And so I left the place.

HEDDA. Just like that? Nothing more?

MRS. ELVSTED. No . . . And then I took the train straight in to town.

HEDDA. But, my dear, precious child! How did you dare risk it?

MRS. ELVSTED (*getting up and moving across the room*). Well, what on earth could I do?

HEDDA. But what do you think your husband will say when you go back again?

MRS. ELVSTED (*by the table, looking at her*). Back there, to him?

HEDDA. Yes, of course. What then?

MRS. ELVSTED. I'm never going back there to him.

HEDDA (*getting up and going nearer to her*). Then you've left in real earnest, for good and all?

MRS. ELVSTED. Yes. There didn't seem to be anything else for me to do.

HEDDA. And then—your doing it quite openly!

MRS. ELVSTED. Oh, you can't keep that kind of thing secret, in any case.

HEDDA. But, Thea, what do you think people will say about you?

MRS. ELVSTED. Heaven knows, they must say what they like. (*Sitting down on the sofa wearily and sadly.*) I have only done what I *had* to do.

HEDDA (*after a short silence*). What do you mean to do now? What kind of job are you going to get?

MRS. ELVSTED. I don't know yet. I only know that I must live here, where Ejlert Lövborg lives. That is, if I *must* live. . . .

HEDDA (*moves a chair from the table, sits beside her and strokes her hands*). Thea, my dear, how did it happen? This—this friendship between you and Ejlert Lövborg?

MRS. ELVSTED. Oh, it happened by degrees, somehow. I came to have some kind of power over him.

HEDDA. Indeed? And then?

MRS. ELVSTED.   He gave up his old habits. Not because I asked him to. I never dared do that. But of course he noticed I didn't like that kind of thing. And so he left off.

HEDDA   (*masking an involuntary sneer*). In fact, you've what they call "reclaimed him," you have, little Thea.

MRS. ELVSTED.   Yes. At least, he says so himself. And he, for his part, has made me into a real human being! Taught me to think . . . and to understand . . . one thing after another.

HEDDA.   Perhaps he gave *you* lessons, too, did he?

MRS. ELVSTED.   No, not exactly lessons. . . . But he used to talk to me about such endless numbers of things. And then came the glorious, happy moment when I began to share his work! When he let me help him.

HEDDA.   And you did, did you?

MRS. ELVSTED.   Yes. When he was writing anything, we always had to work at it together.

HEDDA.   I see. Like two good comrades.

MRS. ELVSTED   (*eagerly*). Comrades! Why, Hedda, that's just what he called it! Oh, I ought to feel so perfectly happy. But I can't, though. Because I really don't know whether it will last.

HEDDA.   Aren't you surer of him than that?

MRS. ELVSTED   (*drearily*). There's the shadow of a woman standing between Ejlert Lövborg and me.

HEDDA   (*looking intently at her*). Who can that be?

MRS. ELVSTED.   I don't know. Someone or other from—from his past. Someone he's never really forgotten.

HEDDA.   What has he said . . . about it?

MRS. ELVSTED.   He only touched on it once—and quite vaguely.

HEDDA.   Oh. And what did he say, then?

MRS. ELVSTED.   He said that when they parted she wanted to shoot him with a pistol.

HEDDA   (*cold and controlled*). How absurd! People don't do that kind of thing here.

MRS. ELVSTED.   No. And that's why I thought it must be that red-haired singer that he once—

HEDDA.   Yes, that may be.

MRS. ELVSTED.   Because I remember people used to talk about her carrying loaded firearms.

HEDDA.   Oh well, then, it's obviously she.

MRS. ELVSTED   (*wringing her hands*). Yes, but just think, Hedda, now I hear that that singer—she's in town again! Oh, I'm simply desperate!

HEDDA   (*glancing towards the inner room*). Sh! Here comes my husband.

(*Getting up and whispering.*) Thea, all this must be between our two selves.

MRS. ELVSTED (*springing up*). Why, yes! For heaven's sake! (*Jörgen Tesman, with a letter in his hand, comes in from the right through the inner room.*)

TESMAN. There we are! The letter's finished and ready.

HEDDA. That's good. But I think Mrs. Elvsted wants to go now. Wait a minute. I'm going to the garden gate with her.

TESMAN. I say, Hedda, I wonder if Berte could see to this?

HEDDA (*taking the letter*). I'll tell her to.

(*Berte comes in from the hall.*)

BERTE. Mr. Brack's here and would like to see the master and mistress, please.

HEDDA. Ask Mr. Brack if he will please come in. And—look here—put this letter in the post, will you?

BERTE (*taking the letter*). Certainly, ma'am.

(*She opens the door for* BRACK *and goes out herself. He is a man of forty-five, square but well built and light in his movements. His face is round-ish, with a fine profile. His hair, still almost black, is short and carefully waved. His eyes are lively and bright. His eyebrows are thick and so is his moustache with its clipped ends. He is dressed in a well-cut outdoor suit —a little too young for his age. He wears an eye-glass, which he now and then lets fall.*)

BRACK (*bowing, with his hat in his hand*). May one call so early at this?

HEDDA. One certainly may!

TESMAN (*clasping his hand*). You will always be welcome (*Introducing him.*) Mr. Brack, Miss Rysing.

HEDDA. Oh!

BRACK (*bowing*). A great pleasure.

HEDDA (*looking at him and laughing*). It's very nice to have a look at you by daylight, Mr. Brack.

BRACK. Any difference, do you think?

HEDDA. Yes; I think a little younger.

BRACK. Thank you—very much.

TESMAN. But what do you say to Hedda? Eh? Doesn't she look well? She's positively—

HEDDA. Oh, do leave me out of it, please. What about thanking Mr. Brack for all the trouble he has taken?

BRACK. Oh, no, no. It was only a pleasure.

HEDDA. Yes. You're a good friend. But here's Mrs. Elvsted longing to be off. Excuse me a moment; I shall be back again directly.

(*Mutual good-byes.* MRS. ELVSTED *and* HEDDA *go out by the hall door.*)

BRACK. Well now; is your wife fairly satisfied?

TESMAN.   Rather! We can't thank you enough. Of course, I gather there will have to be a little rearranging. And there's a certain amount needed still. We shall have to get a few little things.

BRACK.   Is that so? Really?

TESMAN.   But you're not to have any trouble over that. Hedda said she would see to what was needed herself. But why don't we sit down? Eh?

BRACK.   Thanks. Just for a minute. (*He sits by the table.*) There's something I rather wanted to talk to you about, Tesman.

TESMAN.   Is there? Ah, I understand! (*Sits down.*) I expect it's the serious part of the fun that's coming now. Eh?

BRACK.   Oh, there's no great hurry about the financial side. However, I could wish we'd managed things a little more economically.

TESMAN.   But that wouldn't have done at all! Think of Hedda, my dear man. You, who know her so well. I couldn't possibly ask her to live in some little suburban house.

BRACK.   No. That's just the difficulty.

TESMAN.   Besides, luckily it can't be long now before I get my appointment.

BRACK.   Well you know, a thing like that can often be a slow business.

TESMAN.   Have you heard anything further? Eh?

BRACK.   Well, nothing definite— (*Breaking off.*) But that reminds me, there's one piece of news I can tell you.

TESMAN.   Oh?

BRACK.   Your old friend, Ejlert Lövborg, has come back to town.

TESMAN.   I know that already.

BRACK.   Do you? How did you come to know?

TESMAN.   She told us. The lady who went out with Hedda.

BRACK.   Oh, I see. What was her name? I didn't quite catch it.

TESMAN.   Mrs. Elvsted.

BRACK.   Oh yes; the District Magistrate's wife. Of course, it's up there he's been living.

TESMAN.   And just think! I hear, to my great delight, that he's become perfectly steady again.

BRACK.   Yes, so I'm assured.

TESMAN.   And that he's brought out a new book. Eh?

BRACK.   Oh yes.

TESMAN.   And it's made quite an impression, too.

BRACK.   It's made quite an extraordinary impression.

TESMAN.   Well, now! Isn't that good news? He, with his remarkable gifts —I was terribly afraid he'd gone under for good.

BRACK.   Yes. That was the general opinion about him.

TESMAN.   But I can't imagine what he'll do now? What on earth can he be going to live on? Eh?

(*During the last words,* HEDDA *has come in by the hall door.*)

HEDDA (*to* BRACK, *laughing, with a touch of contempt*). My husband's always worrying about what one's going to live on.

TESMAN. Oh but, my dear, we were talking about poor Ejlert Lövborg.

HEDDA (*looking quickly at him*). Oh, were you? (*Sits in the easy-chair by the stove and asks, with a casual manner.*) What's wrong with him?

TESMAN. Well, he must have run through that money he inherited long ago. And he can't very well write a new book every year. Eh? So, you see, I really wonder what will become of him.

BRACK. Perhaps I could tell you something about that.

TESMAN. Really?

BRACK. You must remember that he has relatives with a good deal of influence.

TESMAN. Ah, but unfortunately, his relatives have completely washed their hands of him.

BRACK. Once upon a time they called him the hope of the family.

TESMAN. Once upon a time, yes! But he's wrecked all that himself.

HEDDA. Who knows? (*With a slight smile.*) After all, they've "reclaimed" him up at the Elvsteds' place.

BRACK. And then this book that's come out—

TESMAN. Ah well, let's hope to goodness they'll get something or other for him. I've just written to him. Hedda, my dear, I asked him to come out to us this evening.

BRACK. But, my dear fellow, you're coming to my bachelor party this evening. You promised last night at the pier.

HEDDA. Had you forgotten it, my dear?

TESMAN. Yes, by Jove, I had!

BRACK. In any case, you needn't worry. He isn't likely to come.

TESMAN. Why do you think he won't? Eh?

BRACK (*hesitating a little. Gets up and rests his hands on the back of the chair*). Mr. dear Tesman—and you too, Mrs. Tesman—I can't, in fairness, leave you in ignorance of something that . . . er . . . that—

TESMAN. Something that has to do with Ejlert?

BRACK. That has to do both with you and with him.

TESMAN. But, my dear Brack, tell me what it is!

BRACK. You must be prepared for your appointment not to come so quickly, perhaps, as you wish or expect it to.

TESMAN (*jumping up, uneasily*). Has anything gone wrong? Eh?

BRACK. There may be some competition—perhaps—before the post is filled.

TESMAN. Competition! Fancy that, Hedda!

HEDDA (*leaning further back in the easy-chair*). Well, well, now!

TESMAN. But with whom? Surely, never with—?

BRACK. Yes. Just so. With Ejlert Lövborg.

TESMAN *(clasping his hands)*. No, no! That's absolutely unthinkable! It's simply impossible! Eh?

BRACK. Well . . . That's what we may see, all the same.

TESMAN. But look here, Brack, it would be incredibly inconsiderate to me! *(Gesticulating with his arms.)* Because—why, just think!—I'm a married man. We married on our prospects, Hedda and I. Went and got thoroughly in debt, and borrowed money from Aunt Julle too. Why good Lord, the appointment was as good as promised to me! Eh?

BRACK. Steady, old man! No doubt you'll get the job, all right. But it will be contested first.

HEDDA *(motionless in the easy-chair)*. Think of that, my dear. It will be almost like a kind of sport.

TESMAN. But, Hedda dearest, how can you take it all so casually?

HEDDA *(as before)*. I'm not doing that at all. I'm quite excited about the result.

BRACK. At any rate, Mrs. Tesman, it's as well you should know now how things stand. I mean, before you start making those little purchases I hear you have in mind.

HEDDA. This can't make any difference.

BRACK. Oh, indeed? Then there's no more to be said. Good-bye. *(To* TESMAN.*)* When I go for my afternoon stroll, I'll come in and fetch you.

TESMAN. Oh yes. Yes. I really don't know *what* I'm going to do.

HEDDA *(lying back and reaching out her hand)*. Good-bye, Mr. Brack. And do come again.

BRACK. Many thanks! Good-bye, good-bye.

TESMAN *(going to the door with him)*. Good-bye, my dear Brack. You must excuse me. . . .

(BRACK *goes out by the hall door.*)

TESMAN *(crossing the room)*. Well, Hedda, one should never venture into the land of romance. Eh?

HEDDA *(looking at him and smiling)*. Do *you* do that?

TESMAN. Why, my dear, it can't be denied. It *was* romantic to go and get married and set up house, simply and solely on our prospects.

HEDDA. You may be right, there.

TESMAN. Well, we have our charming home, anyhow. Think, Hedda, it's the home we both used to dream of—that we fell in love with, I might almost say. Eh?

HEDDA *(getting up slowly and wearily)*. It was understood of course, that we should entertain—keep up some sort of establishment.

TESMAN. Goodness, yes! How I used to look forward to it, seeing you as hostess to a chosen circle of friends! Well, well, well. For the present we two must get along by ourselves, Hedda. Just have Aunt Julle out here every now and then. . . . Oh, my, dear, it was to have been so very, very different for you.

HEDDA.   Naturally, now I shan't get a man-servant just at first.

TESMAN.   No, I'm afraid you can't. There can be no question of keeping a man-servant, you know.

HEDDA.   And the saddle-horse that I was going to—

TESMAN   (*horrified*) . Saddle-horse!

HEDDA.   I suppose it's no use even thinking of that now.

TESMAN.   Good heavens, no! That goes without saying.

HEDDA   (*crossing the room towards the back*) . Well, anyhow, I still have one thing to kill time with.

TESMAN   (*beaming with pleasure*) . Thank heavens for that! But what is it, Hedda? Eh?

HEDDA   (*at the centre doorway, looking at him with lurking contempt*) . My pistols, Jörgen.

TESMAN   (*anxiously*) . Your pistols!

HEDDA   (*with cold eyes*) . General Gabler's pistols. (*She goes through the inner room and out to the left.*)

TESMAN   (*running to the centre doorway and calling after her*) . For goodness' sake! Hedda, darling! Don't touch those dangerous things! For my sake, Hedda! Eh?

ACT TWO

The room at the Tesmans', as in the First Act, except that the piano has been taken away and a graceful little writing-table with a book case put in its place. A smaller table has been put by the sofa on the left; most of the bouquets are gone, but Mrs. Elvsted's stands on the large table in the front of the stage. It is afternoon.

Hedda, in an afternoon dress, is alone in the room. She is standing by the open glass door, loading a pistol. The fellow to it lies in an open pistol-case on the writing-table.

HEDDA   (*looking down the garden and calling*) . How do you do again, Mr. Brack?

BRACK   (*is heard from below, at a little distance*). And you, Mrs. Tesman?

HEDDA   (*lifting the pistol and aiming*) . I'm going to shoot you, sir!

BRACK   (*calling from below*) . No, no, no! Don't stand there aiming straight at me.

HEDDA.   That comes of using the back way in. (*She shoots*) .

BRACK   (*nearer*). Are you quite crazy?

HEDDA.   Dear me! I didn't hit you, did I?

BRACK   (*still outside*). Now stop this nonsense!

HEDDA.   Well, come in then.

(BRACK, *dressed as for an informal party, comes in by the glass door. He is carrying a light overcoat on his arm.*)

BRACK.   The deuce! Do you still play that game? What are you shooting at?

HEDDA.   Oh, I just stand and shoot up into the blue.

BRACK   (*taking the pistol gently out of her hand*). If you don't mind, my dear lady. (*Looking at it.*) Ah, this one. I know it well. (*Looking round him.*) Now, where have we got the case? Ah yes, here. (*Puts the pistol away and shuts the case.*) Because we're not going to play that game any more today.

HEDDA.   Well, what in heaven's name do you expect me to do with myself?

BRACK.   Haven't you had any visitors?

HEDDA   (*shutting the glass door*). Not a soul. I suppose everybody we know is still in the country.

BRACK.   And isn't Tesman at home either?

HEDDA   (*at the writing-table, shutting up the pistol-case in the drawer*). No, the minute he had finished lunch he tore off to his aunts. He didn't expect you so soon.

BRACK.   Hm—and I didn't think of that. That was stupid of me.

HEDDA   (*turning her head and looking at him*). Why stupid?

BRACK.   Because if I had, I should have come here a little—earlier.

HEDDA   (*crossing the room*). Well, then you wouldn't have found anyone at all. I was in my room changing after lunch.

BRACK.   And there isn't so much as a tiny chink in the door that one could have communicated through?

HEDDA.   You've forgotten to arrange anything like that.

BRACK.   That was stupid of me, too.

HEDDA.   Well, we shall just have to sit down here and wait. My husband won't be home yet awhile.

BRACK.   Well, never mind. I'll be patient.

(HEDDA *sits down in the corner of the sofa.* BRACK *lays his coat over the back of the nearest chair and sits down, keeping his hat in his hand. There is a short pause. They look at each other.*)

HEDDA.   Well?

BRACK   (*in the same tone*). Well?

HEDDA.   It was I who asked first.

BRACK   (*leaning forward a little*). Come now, let's have a cosy little gossip all to ourselves—Madam Hedda.

HEDDA   (*leaning further back on the sofa*). Doesn't it feel like a whole eternity since we last talked to each other? Oh, of course, a word or two last night and this morning—but I don't count that.

BRACK. Not like this, between ourselves? Alone together, you mean?

HEDDA. Yes. More or less that.

BRACK. Here was I, every blessed day, wishing to goodness you were home again.

HEDDA. And there was I, the whole time, wishing exactly the same.

BRACK. You? Really, Madam Hedda! And I, thinking you had thoroughly enjoyed yourself on your travels!

HEDDA. You may be sure I did!

BRACK. But Tesman was always saying so in his letters.

HEDDA. Oh, *he* did all right. Rummaging in libraries is the most entrancing occupation he knows. Sitting and copying out old parchments, or whatever they are.

BRACK (*with a touch of malice*). After all, that is his vocation in life. Partly, at least.

HEDDA. Oh yes, quite; it is. And of course then one can—But as for me! No, my dear sir. I was excruciatingly bored.

BRACK. Do you really mean it? In sober earnest?

HEDDA. Well, you can just imagine it for yourself. To go a whole six months and never meet a soul even remotely connected with our circle. Not a soul to talk to about the things we're interested in.

BRACK. Well, yes. I should feel the lack of that too.

HEDDA. And then, what's the most intolerable thing of all . . .

BRACK. Well?

HEDDA. Everlastingly having to be with . . . with one and the same person. . . .

BRACK (*nodding agreement*). Early and late; I know. At every conceivable moment.

HEDDA. What I said was "everlastingly."

BRACK. Quite. But with our good friend Tesman, I should have thought one would be able . . .

HEDDA. Jörgen Tesman is—a learned man, you must remember.

BRACK. Admittedly.

HEDDA. And learned men are *not* entertaining as travelling companions. Not in the long run, anyhow.

BRACK. Not even a learned man one is in love with?

HEDDA. Oh! Don't use that sentimental word.

BRACK (*slightly taken aback*). Why, what's the matter, Madam Hedda?

HEDDA (*half laughing, half annoyed*). Well, you just try it yourself! Listening to someone talking about the history of civilization, early and late—

BRACK. —Everlastingly—

HEDDA.   Yes, exactly! And all this business about domestic crafts in the Middle Ages! That's the most awful part of all.

BRACK   (*looking searchingly at her*). But, tell me . . . I don't quite see why, in that case . . . er . . .

HEDDA.   Why Jörgen and I ever made a match of it, you mean?

BRACK.   Well, let's put it that way; yes.

HEDDA.   After all, do you think that's extraordinary?

BRACK.   Yes—and no, Madam Hedda.

HEDDA.   I had simply danced myself out, my dear sir. My time was up. (*With a little start.*) Ah, no! I'm not going to say that. Nor think it, either.

BRACK.   And by Jove, you have no reason to!

HEDDA.   Oh, reason! (*Watching him rather carefully.*) And Jörgen Tesman . . . one must admit that he's a thoroughly good creature.

BRACK.   Good and reliable. No question.

HEDDA.   And I can't see that there's anything actually ridiculous about him. Do you think there is?

BRACK.   Ridiculous? No—o. I wouldn't exactly say that.

HEDDA.   Quite so. But, anyway, he's an indefatigable researcher. And it's always possible that he may get somewhere in time, after all.

BRACK   (*looking at her a little uncertainly*). I thought you believed, like everyone else, that he was going to become a really eminent man.

HEDDA   (*with a weary expression*). Yes, so I did. And since he insisted with might and main on being allowed to support me, I don't know why I shouldn't have accepted the offer.

BRACK.   No, no. Looking at it from that point of view. . . .

HEDDA.   Anyhow, it was more than my other friends and admirers were prepared to do, my dear sir.

BRACK   (*laughing*). Well, I can't answer for all the others. But as far as I myself am concerned, you know quite well that I have always preserved a—a certain respect for the marriage-tie. In a general way; in the abstract, at least, Madam Hedda.

HEDDA   (*jesting*). Ah, but I never had any hopes with regard to you.

BRACK.   All I want is to have a pleasant, intimate circle of friends where I can be useful, in one way and another, and can come and go freely like—like a trusted friend.

HEDDA.   Of the husband, you mean?

BRACK   (*leaning forward*). To be quite frank, preferably of the wife. But of the husband, too, in the second place, of course. I assure you that sort of—shall I call it triangular relationship?—is actually a very pleasant thing for everybody concerned.

HEDDA.   Yes. Many a time I longed for a third person on that trip. Driving side by side with just one other person . . . !

BRACK.   Fortunately the wedding-journey is over now.

HEDDA   (*shaking her head*). The journey will go on for a long time yet. I have only come to a stopping-place on the way.

BRACK.   Why, then one jumps out and walks about a little, Madam Hedda.

HEDDA.   I never jump out.

BRACK.   Don't you really?

HEDDA.   No. Because there is always someone at hand who—

BRACK   (*laughing*) .—Who looks when you leap, you mean?

HEDDA.   Precisely.

BRACK.   Oh come, you know!

HEDDA   (*with a gesture of disagreement*). I don't care for that. I prefer to remain sitting where I am, alone with the other person.

BRACK.   But suppose, now, a third person were to get in and join the other two?

HEDDA.   Ah well, that's quite a different matter.

BRACK.   A trusted and sympathetic friend—

HEDDA.   —Someone who could talk entertainingly about all sorts of interesting things—

BRACK.   —And nothing learned about him!

HEDDA   (*with an audible sigh*) . Well, that certainly is a relief.

BRACK   (*hearing the hall door open and glancing towards it*) . The triangle is complete.

HEDDA   (*half aloud*) . And so the train goes on.

(JÖRGEN TESMAN, *in a grey outdoor suit and a soft felt hat, comes in from the hall. He has a number of unbound books under his arm and in his pockets.*)

TESMAN   (*going up to the table by the corner sofa*). It was pretty hot carrying that load. (*Putting the books down.*) I'm absolutely streaming, Hedda. Why, there you are, come already, Brack. Eh? Berte didn't say anything about it.

BRACK   (*getting up*) . I came up through the garden.

HEDDA.   What are those books you've brought?

TESMAN   (*standing and dipping into them*) . They are some new learned publications that I simply had to have.

HEDDA.   Learned publications?

BRACK.   Ah yes. Learned publications, Mrs. Tesman.

(BRACK *and* HEDDA *exchange an understanding smile.*)

HEDDA.   Do you need any more learned publications?

TESMAN.   Why, my dear Hedda, one can never have too many of them. One has to keep up with everything that's written and printed.

HEDDA.   Yes, of course one does.

TESMAN   (*turning over the books*) . And look here—I've got hold of

Ejlert Lövborg's new book too. (*Holding it out.*) Perhaps you'd like to have a look at it, Hedda. Eh?

HEDDA.   No, thank you very much. Or . . . well perhaps later on.

TESMAN.   I dipped into it on the way.

BRACK.   Well, what do you think of it—as a learned man?

TESMAN.   I think it's remarkable—the balance and judgement it has. He never used to write like this before. (*Gathering the books together.*) Now, I'll take all this in with me. It'll be a treat to cut the pages! And then I must tidy myself up a little, too. (*To Brack.*) I say, we don't need to start at once? Eh?

BRACK.   Goodness no! There's no hurry for some time yet.

TESMAN.   Ah well, I'll take my time, then. (*Is going out with the books, but stops in the centre doorway and turns.*) Oh, while I think of it, Hedda, Aunt Julle won't be coming out to you this evening.

HEDDA.   Won't she? Perhaps it's that business with the hat that's the trouble?

TESMAN.   Oh Lord, no! How can you think that of Aunt Julle? No, the thing is Aunt Rina's very ill.

HEDDA.   So she always is.

TESMAN.   Yes, but today she was particularly bad, poor dear.

HEDDA.   Oh, then it's only natural for the other one to stay with her. I must make the best of it.

TESMAN.   And you can't imagine, my dear, how glad Aunt Julle was, in spite of that, that you'd got so plump on your holiday.

HEDDA   (*half audibly, getting up.*) Oh! These everlasting aunts!

TESMAN.   Eh?

HEDDA   (*going to the glass door*) . Nothing.

TESMAN.   Oh, all right.

(*He goes through the inner room and out to the right.*)

BRACK.   What hat was it you were talking about?

HEDDA.   Oh, that was something that happened with Miss Tesman this morning. She had put her hat down there on the chair. (*Looking at him and smiling.*) And I pretended I thought it was the servant's.

BRACK   (*shaking his head*) . But my dear Madam Hedda, how could you do that? And to that nice old lady?

HEDDA   (*nervously, walking across the room*) . Well, you know, that kind of thing comes over me—just like that. And then I can't stop myself. (*Throwing herself down in the easy-chair by the stove.*) I don't know, myself, how to explain it.

BRACK   (*behind the easy-chair*) . You're not really happy. That's the trouble.

HEDDA   (*looking straight in front of her*) . And I don't know why I should be—happy. Perhaps you can tell me, can you?

BRACK.   Well, among other things, because you've got the very home you wished for.

HEDDA   (*looking up at him and laughing*) . Do you believe that fantasy too?

BRACK.   Isn't there something in it, though?

HEDDA.   Oh yes . . . *Some*thing.

BRACK.   Very well?

HEDDA.   There's this much in it. Last summer I used Jörgen Tesman to see me home from evening parties.

BRACK.   Unfortunately I was going quite another way.

HEDDA.   True enough. You certainly were going another way last summer.

BRACK   (*laughing*) . You ought to be ashamed of yourself, Madam Hedda! Well, but you and Tesman, then?

HEDDA.   Why, we came past here one evening. And he, poor creature, was tying himself in knots because he didn't know how to find anything to talk about. And so I felt sorry for the poor, learned man.

BRACK   (*smiling doubtfully*) . You did, did you? H'm.

HEDDA.   Yes. I really did. And so, to help him out of his misery, I just said—quite casually—that I should like to live here, in this villa.

BRACK.   No more than that?

HEDDA.   Not that evening.

BRACK.   But . . . afterwards?

HEDDA.   Yes; my thoughtlessness had its consequences, my dear sir.

BRACK.   Unfortunately, our thoughtlessness all too often has, Madam Hedda.

HEDDA.   Thank you. But, you see, it was through this passion for the villa of the late Mrs. Falk that Jörgen Tesman and I found our way to an understanding. *That* led to our engagement and marriage and wedding trip and everything. Well, well. As one makes one's bed one must lie on it, I was just going to say.

BRACK.   This is delightful! And all the time, it seems, you weren't interested in the least?

HEDDA.   No. Heaven knows, I wasn't.

BRACK.   Well, but now? Now that we have made it more or less comfortable for you?

HEDDA.   Oh! I seem to smell lavender and dried roses in all the rooms. But perhaps Aunt Julle brought the smell with her.

BRACK   (*laughing*) . No, I should think it's more likely the late Mrs. Falk bequeathed it to you!

HEDDA.   It reminds one of the departed, all right. Like one's bouquet, the day after a ball. (*Clasping her hands at the back of her neck, leaning back in her chair and looking at him.*) My friend, you can't imagine how horribly bored I'm going to be out here.

BRACK.   But won't there be some object or other in life for you to work for, like other people, Madam Hedda?

HEDDA.   An object . . . that would have something fascinating about it?

BRACK.   Preferably, of course.

HEDDA.   Lord knows what kind of an object it could be. I very often wonder— (*Breaking off.*) But that's no use either.

BRACK.   It might be. Tell me about it.

HEDDA.   Whether I could get my husband to go into politics, I was going to say.

BRACK   (*laughing*). Tesman! Oh, come now! Things like politics aren't a bit—they're not at all his line of country.

HEDDA.   No, I quite believe you. But suppose I could get him to, all the same?

BRACK.   Well, but what satisfaction would you get out of it? When he isn't made that way? Why do you want to make him do it?

HEDDA.   Because I'm bored, I tell you. (*After a pause.*) Then you think, do you, it would be absolutely impossible for him to get into the Government?

BRACK.   Well you see, my dear Madam Hedda, to do that he'd need to be a fairly rich man in the first place.

HEDDA   (*getting up impatiently*). Yes. There we have it. It's this middle-class world that I've got into. (*Crossing the stage.*) It's that that makes life so wretched! So absolutely ludicrous! Because that's what it *is*.

BRACK.   I rather fancy the trouble lies somewhere else.

HEDDA.   Where?

BRACK.   You have never gone through anything that really roused you.

HEDDA.   Nothing serious, you mean?

BRACK.   Yes, that's one way of putting it, certainly. But now perhaps that may come.

HEDDA   (*with a jerk of her head*). Oh, you're thinking of all the bother over that wretched professorship. But that's my husband's affair entirely. I'm not wasting so much as a thought on it.

BRACK.   No, no. That wasn't what I was thinking of either. But suppose now there comes what, in rather solemn language, is called a serious claim on you, one full of responsibility? (*Smiling.*) A new claim, little Madam Hedda.

HEDDA   (*angrily*). Be quiet! You'll never see anything of the kind.

BRACK   (*gently*). We'll talk about it in a year's time—at most.

HEDDA   (*shortly*). I have no gift for that kind of thing, Mr. Brack. Not for things that make claims on me!

BRACK.   Why shouldn't you have a gift, like most other women, for the calling that—?

HEDDA   (*over by the glass door*) . Oh, be quiet, I tell you! It often seems to me that I've only got a gift for one thing in the world.

BRACK   (*going nearer*) . And what is that, if I may ask?

HEDDA   (*stands looking out*) . For boring myself to death. Now you know. (*Turning and looking towards the inner room with a laugh.*) Ah, just so! Here is our professor.

BRACK   (*quietly, and with a warning*) . Now then, Madam Hedda!

(JÖRGEN TESMAN, *dressed for the party, carrying his gloves and hat, comes through the inner room from the right.*)

TESMAN.   Hedda, Ejlert Lövborg hasn't sent to say he isn't coming? Eh?

HEDDA.   No.

TESMAN.   Ah, you'll see, then. We shall have him along in a little while.

BRACK.   Do you really think he'll come?

TESMAN.   Yes, I'm almost sure he will. Because that's only a vague rumour, you know—what you told us this morning.

BRACK.   Is it?

TESMAN.   Yes. At least, Aunt Julle said she didn't for one moment believe he'd stand in my way again. Just think of it!

BRACK.   Oh well, then, everything's quite all right.

TESMAN   (*putting his hat, with his gloves in it, on a chair to the right*) . Yes, but I really must wait as long as possible for him, if you don't mind.

BRACK.   We've plenty of time for that. No one will turn up at my place before seven, or half past.

TESMAN.   Oh well, we can keep Hedda company till then. And see what happens.

HEDDA   (*putting* BRACK'S *overcoat and hat over on the corner sofa*) . And if the worst comes to the worst, Mr. Lövborg can stay here with me.

BRACK   (*trying to take his things himself*) . Please let me, Mrs. Tesman! What do you mean by "the worst"?

HEDDA.   If he won't go with you and my husband.

TESMAN   (*looking at her dubiously*) . But, Hedda dear, do you think that would quite do, for him to stay here with you? Eh? Remember, Aunt Julle can't come.

HEDDA.   No, but Mrs. Elvsted's coming. So the three of us will have tea together.

TESMAN.   Oh, that'll be all right, then.

BRACK   (*smiling*) . And perhaps that might be the wisest plan for him, too.

HEDDA.   Why?

BRACK.   Good gracious, my dear lady, you've often enough said hard things about my little bachelor parties. They weren't suitable for any but men of the strongest principles.

HEDDA.   But surely Mr. Lövborg is a man of strong enough principles now? A converted sinner—

(BERTE *appears at the hall door.*)

BERTE.   There's a gentleman, ma'am, who'd like to see you.

HEDDA.   Yes, show him in.

TESMAN   (*quietly*). I'm sure it's he. Just fancy!

(EJLERT LÖVBORG *comes in from the hall. He is slight and thin, the same age as* TESMAN *but looking older and played out. His hair and beard are dark brown, his face is long and pale but with two patches of colour on the cheek-bones. He is dressed in a well-cut black suit, quite new, and is carrying dark gloves and a top-hat. He remains standing near the door and bows abruptly. He seems a little embarrassed.*)

TESMAN   (*crossing to him and shaking his hand*). Well, my dear Ejlert, so at last we meet once more!

EJLERT LÖVBORG   (*speaking with lowered voice*). Thank you for your letter, Jörgen. (*Approaching* HEDDA.) May I shake hands with you too, Mrs. Tesman?

HEDDA   (*taking his hand*). I am glad to see you, Mr. Lövborg. (*With a gesture.*) I don't know whether you two—

LÖVBORG   (*with a slight bow*). Mr. Brack, I think.

BRACK   (*returning it*). Of course we do. Some years ago—

TESMAN   (*to* LÖVBORG, *with his hands on his shoulders*). And now you're to make yourself absolutely at home, Ejlert. Musn't he, Hedda? For you're going to settle down in town again, I hear. Eh?

LÖVBORG.   I am.

TESMAN.   Well, that's only natural. Oh, look here, I've got hold of your new book. But I really haven't had the time to read it yet.

LÖVBORG.   You may as well save yourself the trouble.

TESMAN.   Why may I?

LÖVBORG.   Because there isn't much in it.

TESMAN.   Well! Fancy your saying that!

BRACK.   But it's very highly spoken of, I hear.

LÖVBORG.   That's exactly what I wanted. So I wrote a book that every-body could agree with.

BRACK.   Very wise.

TESMAN.   Yes, but my dear Ejlert—

LÖVBORG.   Because now I'm going to try and build myself up a position again. To begin over again.

TESMAN   (*a little embarrassed*). I see; that's what it is? Eh?

LÖVBORG   (*smiling puts down his hat and takes a packet wrapped in paper out of his pocket*). But when this one comes out, Jörgen Tesman, you must read it. For this is my first real book—the first I have put my-self into.

TESMAN.   Really? And what kind of book is that?

LÖVBORG.   It's the continuation.

TESMAN.   Continuation? Of what?

LÖVBORG.   Of the book.

TESMAN.   Of the new one?

LÖVBORG.   Of course.

TESMAN.   But my dear Ejlert, that one comes down to our own times!

LÖVBORG.   It does. And this one deals with the future.

TESMAN.   With the future? But, good gracious, we don't know anything about that.

LÖVBORG.   No. But there are one or two things to be said about it, all the same. (*Opening the package.*) Here, you see—

TESMAN.   But that's not your handwriting?

LÖVBORG.   I dictated it. (*Turning over the pages.*) It's divided into two sections. The first is about the factors that will control civilization in the future. And the second part, here (*turning over the later pages*), this is about the probable direction civilization will take.

TESMAN.   Amazing! It would never occur to me to write about a thing like that.

HEDDA   (*drumming on the panes of the glass door*). Hm. No . . . it wouldn't.

LÖVBORG   (*puts the MS. into the envelope and lays the packet on the table*). I brought it with me because I thought of reading you a little of it this evening.

TESMAN.   My dear fellow, that was very good of you. But, this evening . . . ? (*He looks across at* BRACK.) I don't quite know how it's to be managed.

LÖVBORG.   Well, another time then. There's no hurry.

BRACK.   I'll explain, Mr. Lövborg. There's a little affair at my place tonight. Chiefly for Tesman, you know—

LÖVBORG   (*looking for his hat*). Ah, then I won't keep you—

BRACK.   No, look here; won't you give me the pleasure of joining us?

LÖVBORG   (*shortly and decidedly*). No, I can't do that. Thank you very much.

BRACK.   Oh, nonsense! Please do. We shall be a small, select circle. And, believe me, we shall have quite a "gay" time, as Mad—Mrs. Tesman puts it.

LÖVBORG.   I don't doubt it. But all the same—

BRACK.   So you could take your manuscript along and read it to Tesman there, at my place. I've got plenty of rooms.

TESMAN.   Yes, what about it, Ejlert? You could do that! Eh?

HEDDA   (*intervening*). But, my dear, if Mr. Lövborg really doesn't want to! I'm sure he would much rather stay here and have supper with me.

LÖVBORG   (*looking at her*) . With you, Mrs. Tesman?

HEDDA.   And with Mrs. Elvsted.

LÖVBORG.   Oh. (*Casually.*) I met her for a moment this morning.

HEDDA.   Did you? Yes, she's coming out. So it's almost imperative for you to stay, Mr. Lövborg. Otherwise she'll have no one to see her home.

LÖVBORG.   That's true. Well, thank you very much, Mrs. Tesman; then I'll stay here.

HEDDA.   I'll just have a word with the maid.

(*She goes to the hall door and rings.* BERTE *comes in.* HEDDA *talks to her in an undertone and points to the inner room.* BERTE *nods and goes out again.*)

TESMAN   (*at the same time, to* EJLERT LÖVBORG) . Look here, Ejlert, is it this new material—about the future—that you're going to lecture on?

LÖVBORG.   Yes.

TESMAN.   Because I heard at the book-shop that you are going to give a course of lectures here in the autumn.

LÖVBORG.   I am. You musn't think hardly of me for it, Tesman.

TESMAN.   Good gracious, no! But—

LÖVBORG.   I can quite understand that it must be rather annoying for you.

TESMAN   (*dispiritedly*) . Oh, I can't expect you to . . . for my sake . . .

LÖVBORG.   But I'm waiting till you've got your appointment.

TESMAN.   Waiting? Yes, but—but aren't you going to try for it, then? Eh?

LÖVBORG.   No. I only want a *succès d'estime.*

TESMAN.   But, good Lord! Aunt Julle was right after all, then! Of course that was it, I knew! Hedda! Think of it, my dear! Ejlert Lövborg isn't going to stand in our way at all!

HEDDA   (*shortly*) . Our way? Please leave me out of it.

(*She goes up towards the inner room where* BERTE *is putting a tray with decanters and glasses on the table.* HEDDA *nods approvingly and comes down again.* BERTE *goes out.*)

TESMAN   (*at the same time*) . But what about you, Judge? What do you say to this? Eh?

BRACK.   Why, I should say that honour and a *succès d'estime* . . . they can be very pleasant things—

TESMAN.   They certainly can. But all the same—

HEDDA   (*looking at* TESMAN *with a cold smile*) . You look to me as though you'd been thunderstruck.

TESMAN.   Well, something like that. . . . I almost feel . . .

BRACK.   As a matter of fact, a thunderstorm has just passed over us, Mrs. Tesman.

HEDDA   (*with a gesture towards the inner room*) . Wouldn't you men like to go in and have a glass of cold punch?

BRACK *(looking at his watch)*. By way of stirrup-cup? That wouldn't be a bad idea.

TESMAN. Good, Hedda! Excellent! I feel so light-hearted now, that—

HEDDA. Won't you too, Mr. Lövborg?

LÖVBORG *(with a gesture of refusal)*. No, thank you very much. Not for me.

BRACK. But, good Lord! Cold punch isn't poison, so far as I know.

LÖVBORG. Not for everybody, perhaps!

HEDDA. I'll entertain Mr. Lövborg in the meantime.

TESMAN. That's right, Hedda dear. You do that.

(He and BRACK *go into the inner room and sit down. During what follows they drink punch, smoke cigarettes and carry on a lively conversation.* EJLERT LÖVBORG *remains standing by the stove.* HEDDA *goes to the writing-table.)*

HEDDA *(raising her voice a little)*. I'll show you some photographs, if you like. My husband and I made a trip through the Tyrol on our way home.

(She brings an album and puts it on the table by the sofa, sitting down herself in the farthest corner. EJLERT LÖVBORG *goes nearer, stands and looks at her. Then he takes a chair and sits down on her left with his back to the inner-room.)*

HEDDA *(opening the album)*. Do you see this mountain range, Mr. Lövborg? It's the Ortler Group. My husband has written it underneath. Here it is: The Ortler Group at Meran."

LÖVBORG *(who has been looking intently at her, speaking softly and slowly)*. Hedda—Gabler.

HEDDA *(glancing quickly at him)*. Hush, now!

LÖVBORG *(repeating softly)*. Hedda Gabler.

HEDDA *(looking at the album)*. Yes, that was my name once upon a time. In the days—when we two knew one another.

LÖVBORG. And in future—for the whole of my life—then, I must break myself of the habit of saying Hedda Gabler?

HEDDA *(going on turning over the pages)*. Yes, you must. And I think you'd better practise it in good time. The sooner the better, I should say.

LÖVBORG *(with resentment in his voice)*. Hedda Gabler married? And married to—Jörgen Tesman.

HEDDA. Yes. That's what happened.

LÖVBORG. Oh, Hedda, Hedda, how could you throw yourself away like that?

HEDDA *(looking sharply at him)*. Now! None of that, please.

LÖVBORG. None of what?

*(*TESMAN *comes in and goes towards the sofa.)*

HEDDA   *(hearing him coming, and speaking indifferently)* . And this one, Mr. Lövborg, is from the Vale of Ampezzo. Just look at the mountain peaks there. *(Looking affectionately up at* TESMAN.*)* What is it these queer peaks are called, my dear?

TESMAN.   Let me see. Oh, those are the Dolomites.

HEDDA.   Oh, of course! Those are the Dolomites, Mr. Lövborg.

TESMAN.   Hedda, dear, I just wanted to ask if we shouldn't bring you a little punch? For you, at any rate. Eh?

HEDDA.   Well, yes; thank you. And a few cakes, perhaps.

TESMAN.   No cigarettes?

HEDDA.   No, thanks.

TESMAN.   Right.

(He goes into the inner room and out to the right. BRACK *stays sitting in the inner room, with an eye on* HEDDA *and* LÖVBORG *from time to time.)*

LÖVBORG   *(in a low voice, as before)* . Answer me, now, Hedda my dear. How could you go and do this?

HEDDA   *(apparently intent on the album)* . If you go on saying "dear" to me, I won't talk to you.

LÖVBORG.   Mayn't I even do it when we are alone?

HEDDA.   No. You can think it if you like. But you mustn't say it.

LÖVBORG.   Ah, I understand. It offends . . . your love for Jörgen Tesman.

HEDDA   *(glancing at him and smiling)* . Love? That's good!

LÖVBORG.   Isn't it love, then?

HEDDA.   There isn't going to be any kind of disloyalty, anyhow. I won't have that sort of thing.

LÖVBORG.   Hedda, answer me just one thing—

HEDDA.   Hush!

*(*TESMAN, *with a tray, comes from the inner room.)*

TESMAN.   Look at the good things we've got here. *(He puts the tray on the table.)*

HEDDA.   Why are you bringing it yourself?

TESMAN   *(filling the glasses)* . Why, because I think it's so jolly waiting on you, Hedda.

HEDDA.   Oh, but you've filled both glasses now. And Mr. Lövborg won't have any.

TESMAN.   No, but Mrs. Elvsted will be here soon.

HEDDA.   Oh, of course; Mrs. Elvsted—

TESMAN.   Had you forgotten her? Eh?

HEDDA.   We've got so absorbed in this. *(Showing him a picture.)* Do you remember that little village?

TESMAN.   Ah, that's the one below the Brenner Pass! It was there we stayed the night—

HEDDA. —And met all those jolly tourists.

TESMAN. That's it. It was there. Just think, if we could have had *you* with us, Ejlert! Well, well!

(*He goes in again and sits down with* BRACK.)

LÖVBORG. Answer me just this one thing, Hedda.

HEDDA. Well?

LÖVBORG. Was there no love in your feeling for me either? Not a touch—not a flicker of love in that either?

HEDDA. I wonder if there actually was? To me it seems as if we were two good comrades. Two real, close friends. (*Smiling.*) You, especially, were absolutely frank.

LÖVBORG. It was you who wanted that.

HEDDA. When I look back at it, there really was something fine, something enthralling. There was a kind of courage about it, about this hidden intimacy, this comradeship that not a living soul so much as guessed at.

LÖVBORG. Yes, there was, Hedda! Wasn't there? When I came up to see your father in the afternoons. . . . And the General used to sit right over by the window reading the papers, with his back to us . . .

HEDDA. And we used to sit on the corner sofa.

LÖVBORG. Always with the same illustrated paper in front of us.

HEDDA. Yes, for lack of an album.

LÖVBORG. Yes, Hedda; and when I used to confess to you! Told you things about myself that no one else knew in those days. Sat there and owned up to going about whole days and nights blind drunk. Days and nights on end. Oh, Hedda, what sort of power in you was it—that forced me to confess things like that?

HEDDA. Do you think it was some power in me?

LÖVBORG. Yes, how else can I account for it? And all these—these questions you used to put to me . . . indirectly.

HEDDA. And that you understood so perfectly well.

LÖVBORG. To think you could sit and ask questions like that! Quite frankly.

HEDDA. Indirectly, mind you.

LÖVBORG. Yes, but frankly, all the same. Cross-question me about . . . about all that kind of thing.

HEDDA. And to think that you could answer, Mr. Lövborg.

LÖVBORG. Yes, that's just what I can't understand, looking back. But tell me now, Hedda, wasn't it love that was at the bottom of that relationship? Wasn't it, on your side, as though you wanted to purify and absolve me, when I made you my confessor? Wasn't it that?

HEDDA. No, not quite.

LÖVBORG. What made you do it, then?

HEDDA.   Do you find it so impossible to understand, that a young girl, when there's an opportunity . . . in secret . . .

LÖVBORG.   Well?

HEDDA.   That one should want to have a glimpse of a world that . . .

LÖVBORG.   That . . . ?

HEDDA.   That one isn't allowed to know about?

LÖVBORG.   So that was it, then?

HEDDA.   That . . . that as well, I rather think.

LÖVBORG.   The bond of our common hunger for life. But why couldn't that have gone on, in any case?

HEDDA.   That was your own fault.

LÖVBORG.   It was you who broke it off.

HEDDA.   Yes, when there was imminent danger of our relationship becoming serious. You ought to be ashamed of yourself, Ejlert Lövborg. How could you take advantage of—your unsuspecting comrade!

LÖVBORG   (*clenching his hands*). Oh, why didn't you make a job of it! Why didn't you shoot me down when you threatened to!

HEDDA.   Yes . . . I'm as terrified of scandal as all that.

LÖVBORG.   Yes, Hedda; you are a coward at bottom.

HEDDA.   An awful coward. (*Changing her tone.*) But it was lucky for you. And now you have consoled yourself so delightfully up at the Elvsteds'.

LÖVBORG.   I know what Thea has told you.

HEDDA.   And you have told her something about us two?

LÖVBORG.   Not a word. She's too stupid to understand a thing like that.

HEDDA.   Stupid?

LÖVBORG.   She is stupid about that sort of thing.

HEDDA.   And I'm a coward. (*She leans nearer to him, without meeting his eyes, and says more softly*). But now *I* will confess something to *you*.

LÖVBORG   (*eagerly*). Well?

HEDDA.   That, my not daring to shoot you down—

LÖVBORG.   Yes?

HEDDA.   That wasn't my worst piece of cowardice . . . that night.

LÖVBORG   (*looks at her a moment, understands and whispers passionately*). Ah, Hedda! Hedda Gabler! Now I see a glimpse of the hidden foundation of our comradeship. You and I! Then it *was* your passion for life—

HEDDA   (*quietly, with a sharp, angry glance*). Take care! Don't assume anything like that.

(*It has begun to get dark. The hall door is opened from outside by* BERTE.)

HEDDA   (*shutting the album with a snap and calling out with a smile*). There you are at last, Thea darling! Come along in!

(MRS. ELVSTED *comes in from the hall, dressed for the evening. The door is closed behind her.*)

HEDDA *(on the sofa, stretching her arms towards her)*. My precious
Thea—you can't think how I've been longing for you to come!
(MRS. ELVSTED, *in the meanwhile, exchanges slight greetings with the men
in the inner room and then comes across to the table holding her hand
out to* HEDDA. EJLERT LÖVBORG *has got up. He and* MRS. ELVSTED *greet each
other with a silent nod.)*

MRS. ELVSTED. Oughtn't I to go in and say a word or two to your husband?

HEDDA. Not a bit of it! Let them be. They're going out directly.

MRS. ELVSTED. Are they going out?

HEDDA. Yes, they're going to make a night of it.

MRS. ELVSTED *(quickly, to* LÖVBORG*)*. You're not, are you?

LÖVBORG. No.

HEDDA. Mr. Lövborg—is staying here with us.

MRS. ELVSTED *(takes a chair and is going to sit beside him)*. Oh, it *is* nice
to be here!

HEDDA. No, no, Thea my child! Not there. You're coming over here,
right beside me. I want to be in the middle.

MRS. ELVSTED. All right; just as you like. *(She goes round the table and
sits on the sofa on* HEDDA's *right.* LÖVBORG *sits down on his chair again.)*

LÖVBORG *(to* HEDDA, *after a little pause)*. Isn't she lovely, just to look at?

HEDDA *(stroking her hair lightly)*. Only to look at?

LÖVBORG. Yes. Because *we* two—she and I—we really *are* comrades. We
trust each other absolutely. That's how it is we can sit and talk to each
other quite frankly.

HEDDA. Nothing indirect about it, Mr. Lövborg?

LÖVBORG. Oh well . . .

MRS. ELVSTED *(softly, leaning close to* HEDDA*)*. Oh, Hedda, I am so happy!
Just think, he says I have inspired him, too!

HEDDA *(looking at her with a smile)*. He says that, does he?

LÖVBORG. And then she has the courage that leads to action, Mrs. Tesman.

MRS. ELVSTED. Good gracious! *Me?* Courage?

LÖVBORG. Immense—when her comrade is concerned.

HEDDA. Ah, courage. Yes. If one only had that.

LÖVBORG. What do you mean?

HEDDA. Then perhaps one could even *live* at last. *(Changing her tone
suddenly.)* But now, Thea, my dear, you must have a nice glass of cold
punch.

MRS. ELVSTED. No, thank you. I never drink anything like that.

HEDDA. Well you, then, Mr. Lövborg.

LÖVBORG. Thank you, I don't either.

MRS. ELVSTED. No, he doesn't either.

HEDDA   (*looking at him steadily*) . But suppose I want you to?

LÖVBORG.   That wouldn't alter it.

HEDDA   (*laughing*) . So I, poor thing, have no power over you at all?

LÖVBORG.   Not where that's concerned.

HEDDA.   But, joking apart, I think you ought to, all the same. For your own sake.

MRS. ELVSTED.   Oh, but, Hedda!

LÖVBORG.   How do you mean?

HEDDA.   Or, rather, on account of other people.

LÖVBORG.   Really?

HEDDA.   Otherwise people might easily get the idea that you didn't feel absolutely secure. Not really sure of yourself.

MRS. ELVSTED   (*softly*) . Oh *no,* Hedda!

LÖVBORG.   People may think what they like, for the present.

MRS. ELVSTED   (*happily*) . Exactly!

HEDDA.   I saw it so plainly with Judge Brack just this minute.

LÖVBORG.   What did you see?

HEDDA.   That contemptuous smile of his when you were afraid to go in there with them.

LÖVBORG.   Afraid! Naturally I preferred to stay here and talk to you.

MRS. ELVSTED.   That was quite understandable, Hedda!

HEDDA.   But Judge Brack couldn't be expected to guess that. And I noticed too that he smiled and glanced at my husband when you were afraid to go to this harmless little party with them either.

LÖVBORG.   Afraid! Did you say I was afraid?

HEDDA.   I don't. But that's how Judge Brack understood it.

LÖVBORG.   Let him, then.

HEDDA.   So you're not going with them?

LÖVBORG.   I am staying here with you and Thea.

MRS. ELVSTED.   Why, yes, Hedda; of course.

HEDDA   (*smiling and nodding approvingly at* LÖVBORG) . There! Quite immovable. A man of unshaken principles, always. You know, that's what a man should be. (*Turning to* MRS. ELVSTED *and patting her.*) Now, wasn't that what I said, when you came in here this morning in such a state of distraction—

LÖVBORG   (*with surprise*) . Distraction?

MRS. ELVSTED   (*in terror*) . Hedda! Oh, Hedda!

HEDDA.   Now you see for yourself! There's not the slightest need for you to go about in this deadly anxiety— (*Breaking off.*) There! Now we can all three be cheerful.

LÖVBORG   (*who has made a startled gesture*) . What on earth is all this, Mrs. Tesman?

MRS. ELVSTED.   Oh heavens, heavens, Hedda! What are you saying? What are you doing?

HEDDA.   Keep quiet. That detestable Judge Brack has got his eye on you.

LÖVBORG.   So it was deadly anxiety . . . on my behalf.

MRS. ELVSTED   *(softly and in misery)*. Oh, Hedda! How *could* you!

LÖVBORG   *(looking intently at her for a moment, his face haggard)*. So *that* was my comrade's absolute faith in me.

MRS. ELVSTED   *(beseeching)*. Oh, my dear, my dear—you must listen to me before—

LÖVBORG   *(takes one of the filled glasses, lifts it and says softly in a strained voice)*: Your health, Thea! *(He empties his glass, puts it down and takes the other.)*

MRS ELVSTED   *(softly)*. Oh, Hedda, Hedda! Did you *want* this to happen?

HEDDA.   Want it? Are you crazy?

LÖVBORG.   And a health to you too, Mrs. Tesman. Thank you for the truth. Here's to it. *(He drains his glass and is about to fill it again.)*

HEDDA   *(pinching her arm)*. They can hear what you're saying.

MRS. ELVSTED   *(with a faint cry)*. Oh!

LÖVBORG   *(to* BRACK*)*. You were so kind as to ask me to join you.

BRACK.   Oh, are you coming, after all?

LÖVBORG.   Yes, thank you very much.

BRACK.   I'm delighted.

LÖVBORG   *(putting his parcel in his pocket and speaking to* TESMAN*)* Because I should like to show you one or two things before I hand it in.

TESMAN.   Fancy! That will be jolly. But, Hedda dear, how are you going to get Mrs. Elvsted home, eh?

HEDDA.   We'll manage that somehow.

LÖVBORG   *(looking towards the women)*. Mrs. Elvsted? I'll come back again and fetch her, of course. *(Coming nearer.)* Round about ten o'clock, Mrs. Tesman? Will that do?

HEDDA.   Certainly. That will do beautifully.

TESMAN.   Oh well, everything's all right, then. But you mustn't expect *me* as early as that, Hedda.

HEDDA.   My dear, stay—as long as ever you like.

MRS. ELVSTED   *(in suppressed anxiety)*. I shall wait here, then, Mr. Lövborg, till you come.

LÖVBORG   *(with his hat in his hand)*. All right, Mrs. Elvsted.

BRACK.   And so the procession starts, gentlemen. I hope we shall have a gay time, as a certain charming lady puts it.

HEDDA.   Ah, if only that charming lady could be there, invisible—

BRACK.   Why invisible?

HEDDA.   So as to hear a little of your gaiety—uncensored, Mr. Brack.

BRACK   (*laughing*) . I shouldn't advise the charming lady to try!

HEDDA   (*laying a hand on his arm*) . Now, then. No more for the moment. Remember you're going to a party.

MRS. ELVSTED.   No, no, no!

HEDDA.   Hush! They're looking at you.

LÖVBORG   (*putting down his glass*) . Now, Thea, my dear, tell the truth!

MRS. ELVSTED.   Yes!

LÖVBORG.   Did your husband know that you had followed me?

MRS. ELVSTED   (*wringing her hands*) . Oh, Hedda! You hear what he's asking me?

LÖVBORG.   Was it an understanding between you and him, that you should come to town and spy on me? Perhaps it was he himself who made you do it? Ah yes, no doubt he wanted me in the office again! Or did he miss me at the card-table?

MRS. ELVSTED   (*softly, with a moan*) . Oh, Ejlert, Ejlert!

LÖVBORG   (*seizing a glass and about to fill it*) . A health to the old District Magistrate, too!

HEDDA   (*checking him*) . No more now. Remember, you're going out to read your book to my husband.

LÖVBORG   (*calmly, putting down the glass*) . It was stupid of me, Thea, all this. To take it like that, I mean. And don't be angry with me; dear old friend. You shall see, you and the others, that even if I came to grief once, yet . . . Now I'm on my feet again. Thanks to your help, Thea!

MRS. ELVSTED   (*radiant with joy*) . Thank heaven!

(BRACK, *in the meantime, has looked at his watch. He and* TESMAN *get up and come into the drawing-room.*)

BRACK   (*getting his hat and overcoat*) . Well, Mrs. Tesman, our time's up now.

HEDDA.   I expect it is.

LÖVBORG   (*getting up*) . Mine too, Mr. Brack.

MRS. ELVSTED   (*softly, and imploring*) . Oh, Ejlert, don't!

TESMAN   (*laughing, too*) . Oh, Hedda, you're simply priceless! Just think!

BRACK.   Well, good-bye, good-bye, ladies.

LÖVBORG   (*taking leave with a bow*) . About ten o'clock, then.

(BRACK, LÖVBORG *and* TESMAN *go out by the hall door. At the same time* BERTE *comes in from the inner room with a lighted lamp, which she puts on the drawing-room table. She goes out again the same way.*)

MRS. ELVSTED   (*who has got up and is wandering restlessly about the room*) . Hedda, Hedda, where is all this going to end?

HEDDA.   Ten o'clock—then he will come. I can see him. With vineleaves in his hair. Flushed and confident.

MRS. ELVSTED.   Yes, if only it would be like that.

HEDDA. And then, you see, then he'll have got control of himself again. Then he will be a free man for the rest of his days.

MRS. ELVSTED. Heavens, yes. If only he would come like that. As you see him.

HEDDA. He'll come like that—"so and no otherwise." (*Getting up and going nearer.*) Go on doubting him as long as you like. I believe in him. And now we'll try . . .

MRS. ELVSTED. There's something behind all this, Hedda.

HEDDA. True; there is. I want, for once in my life, to have power over a human being's fate.

MRS. ELVSTED. But haven't you got that?

HEDDA. I have not. And never have had.

MRS. ELVSTED. Not over your husband's?

HEDDA. That *would* be worth having, wouldn't it? Ah, if you could only realize how poor I am. And here are you, offered such riches! (*Throwing her arms passionately round her.*) I think I shall burn your hair off, after all.

MRS. ELVSTED. Let go! Let go! I'm frightened of you, Hedda!

BERTE (*in the doorway between the rooms*). Tea's laid in the dining-room, ma'am.

HEDDA. Good. We're coming.

MRS. ELVSTED. No, no, no! I'd rather go home alone. At once!

HEDDA. Nonsense! You must have tea first, you little goose. And then, at ten o'clock, Ejlert Lövborg will come—with vineleaves in his hair.

(*She pulls* MRS. ELVSTED, *almost by force, toward the doorway.*)

ACT THREE

The room at the Tesmans'. The curtains across the middle door-way are closed and so are those in front of the glass door. The lamp, with its shade on, is burning, turned half-down, on the table. The door of the stove is open and there has been a fire in it, which is now nearly out.

Mrs. Elvsted, wrapped up in a large shawl with her feet on a footstool, is close to the stove, lying sunk in the easy-chair. Hedda is lying asleep on the sofa with her clothes on and a rug over her.

After a pause, Mrs. Elvsted sits up quickly in her chair and listens intently. Then she sinks back wearily again, crying softly.

MRS. ELVSTED. Not yet! Oh, heavens, heavens! Not yet! (BERTE *comes stealing in cautiously by the hall door. She has a letter in her hand.*)

MRS. ELVSTED (*turning and whispering eagerly*). Well? Has anyone come?

BERTE. Yes. A girl's just been with this letter.

MRS. ELVSTED *(quickly, holding out her hand)*. A letter! Give it to me!

BERTE. No, ma'am, it's for the Doctor.

MRS. ELVSTED. Oh.

BERTE. It was Miss Tesman's maid who came with it. I'll put it here on the table.

MRS. ELVSTED. Yes, do.

BERTE *(putting down the letter)*. I think I'd better put the lamp out. It's smoking.

MRS. ELVSTED. Yes, put it out. It'll very soon be light now.

BERTE *(putting it out)*. It's quite light, ma'am.

MRS. ELVSTED. Why, it's broad daylight! And still not back!

BERTE. Lord bless you, ma'am, I thought this was how it would be.

MRS. ELVSTED. You thought so?

BERTE. Yes. When I saw that a certain person had come back to town again, well . . . And when he went off with them . . . One's heard enough about that gentleman before today.

MRS. ELVSTED. Don't speak so loud. You'll wake Mrs. Tesman.

BERTE *(looking towards the sofa and sighing)*. Gracious, yes; let her sleep, poor thing. Shall I put a bit more on the fire?

MRS. ELVSTED. No, thank you; not for me.

BERTE. Very good. *(She goes out quietly by the hall door.)*

HEDDA *(waking as the door shuts and looking up)*. What's that?

MRS. ELVSTED. It was only the maid.

HEDDA *(looking round her)*. In here? Oh yes, I remember now. *(She sits up on the sofa, stretches and rubs her eyes.)* What's the time, Thea?

MRS. ELVSTED *(looking at her watch)*. It's past seven.

HEDDA. What time did my husband come back?

MRS. ELVSTED. He isn't back.

HEDDA. He hasn't come home yet?

MRS. ELVSTED *(getting up)*. No one's come back at all.

HEDDA. And we sat here and kept ourselves awake, waiting up for them till nearly four o'clock!

MRS. ELVSTED *(wringing her hands)*. And *how* I waited for him!

HEDDA *(yawning and speaking with her hand in front of her mouth)*. Ah, well, we might have saved ourselves that trouble.

MRS. ELVSTED. Did you get a little sleep afterwards?

HEDDA. Oh yes. I slept quite well, I think. Didn't you?

MRS. ELVSTED. Not a wink! I couldn't, Hedda! It was absolutely impossible.

HEDDA *(getting up and going across to her)*. There, there, there! There's nothing to worry about. I can see perfectly well what's happened.

MRS. ELVSTED. Why, what do you think then? Tell me! Please!

HEDDA. Well, of course they kept things up frightfully late at the Judge's.

MRS. ELVSTED.   Heavens, yes. They must have done. But, all the same—

HEDDA.   And then, you see, my husband didn't like to come home and disturb us by ringing in the middle of the night. (*Laughing.*) Perhaps he didn't much care to show himself either—not straight after making a gay night of it.

MRS. ELVSTED.   But, Hedda dear, where would he have gone?

HEDDA.   He's gone up to his aunts', of course, and slept there. They keep his old room ready.

MRS. ELVSTED.   No, he can't be with them. Because a letter came for him a little while ago from Miss Tesman. There it is.

HEDDA.   Really? (*Looking at the address.*) Yes. That's certainly from Aunt Julle; it's her handwriting. Well, then, he's stayed on at the Judge's place. And Ejlert Lövborg, he's sitting reading to him—with vineleaves in his hair.

MRS. ELVSTED.   Oh, Hedda, you're just saying things you don't believe yourself.

HEDDA.   You really are a little goose, Thea.

MRS. ELVSTED.   Well, I suppose I am—worse luck.

HEDDA.   And you look simply tired to death.

MRS. ELVSTED.   Yes, I am tired to death.

HEDDA.   Well then, you're going to do as I tell you. You're going into my room and you're going to lie down on the bed for a little while.

MRS. ELVSTED.   Oh no. I shan't sleep, anyway.

HEDDA.   Yes, you *are* to.

MRS. ELVSTED.   Yes, but surely your husband must be home soon. And then I must find out at once . . .

HEDDA.   I'll let you know all right when he comes.

MRS. ELVSTED.   Well; you promise me, Hedda?

HEDDA.   Yes, you can be sure I will. You just go in and go to sleep in the meantime.

MRS. ELVSTED.   Thank you. I'll try to, then. (*She goes out through the inner room.*)

(HEDDA *goes over to the glass door and pulls back the curtains. Broad daylight pours into the room. She takes a small hand-mirror from the writing-table, looks at herself in it and tidies her hair. Then she crosses to the hall door and presses the bell. After a moment* BERTE *comes to the door.*)

BERTE.   Is there anything you want, ma'am?

HEDDA.   Yes, will you make up the fire? I'm simply freezing here.

BERTE.   Bless us! I'll have it warm in no time.

(*She rakes the remains of the fire together and puts some wood on.*)

BERTE   (*stopping to listen*) . There was a ring at the front door, ma'am.

HEDDA.   You go and answer it, then. I'll see to the fire myself.

BERTE.   It'll soon burn up. (*She goes out by the hall door.*)

(HEDDA *kneels on the footstool and puts some more wood into the stove. After a short pause,* JÖRGEN TESMAN *comes in from the hall. He looks tired and rather grave. He steals towards the middle doorway, on tiptoe and is about to slip through the curtains.*)

HEDDA   (*at the stove, without looking up*) . Good morning.

TESMAN   (*turning*) . Hedda! (*Coming towards her.*) But what on earth! You up as early as this? Eh?

HEDDA.   Yes, I got up very early today.

TESMAN.   And I was so certain you were lying asleep still! Just fancy, Hedda!

HEDDA.   Don't speak so loudly. Mrs. Elvsted is lying down in my room.

TESMAN.   Did Mrs. Elvsted stay the night here?

HEDDA.   Of course. Nobody came to fetch her.

TESMAN.   That's true; nobody did.

HEDDA   (*shutting the door of the stove and getting up*) . Well, did you have a good time at the Judge's?

TESMAN.   Have you been worrying about me, eh?

HEDDA.   No, that would never occur to me. I was just asking whether you had a good time.

TESMAN.   Not bad. It was rather jolly for once. Mostly at the beginning, as far as I was concerned. Because then Ejlert read me some of his book. We got there more than an hour too soon. Just fancy! And Brack had so much to see to. But then Ejlert read to me.

HEDDA   (*sitting down on the right-hand side of the table*) . Well now, tell me about it.

TESMAN   (*sitting down on a footstool by the stove*) . My goodness, Hedda! You can't think what a book that's going to be! I should think it's one of the most remarkable things that's ever been written. Just think!

HEDDA.   No doubt. That doesn't interest me.

TESMAN.   I must admit one thing, Hedda. When he had read it, a perfectly detestable feeling came over me.

HEDDA.   Detestable?

TESMAN.   There I was *envying* Ejlert for having been able to write a thing like that! Just think, Hedda!

HEDDA.   Yes, yes. I am.

TESMAN.   And then to know that he, with the gifts he has . . . Yes he's quite irreclaimable. What a tragedy!

HEDDA.   You mean, I suppose, that he has more spirit than other people.

TESMAN.   Oh no. The point is —there's no moderation in him.

HEDDA.   And what happened, then, in the end?

TESMAN.   Well, I really think the best way to describe it is an orgy, Hedda.

HEDDA.   Did he have vineleaves in his hair?

TESMAN.   Vineleaves? No, I didn't notice any. But he made a long, wandering speech in honour of the woman who had inspired him in his work. Well, that was how he put it.

HEDDA.   Did he say who she was?

TESMAN.   No, he didn't do that. But I can't imagine it could be anybody but Mrs. Elvsted. You watch!

HEDDA.   Oh, well. . . . Where did you part from him, then?

TESMAN.   On the way back. We broke up—the last of us—at the same time. And Brack came along with us to get a breath of fresh air. And so, you see, we agreed to see Ejlert home. Because, to tell the truth, he'd had far more than he could carry.

HEDDA.   I can quite imagine that.

TESMAN.   But here's the extraordinary part of it, Hedda. Or rather, the sad part of it, I ought to say. I—I'm almost ashamed to tell you, for Ejlert's sake.

HEDDA.   Oh, go on! So—?

TESMAN.   Well, as we were on the way back, you see, I happened to be a little behind the others. Only for a minute or two. You see?

HEDDA.   Yes, yes. But what then?

TESMAN.   And then, as I was hurrying to catch them up, what do you think I found by the roadside. Eh?

HEDDA.   No, how could I know?

TESMAN.   Don't say anything about it to anyone, Hedda. You understand. Promise me, for Ejlert's sake. (*Taking a paper parcel out of his coat pocket.*) Just think! I found this.

HEDDA.   Isn't that the parcel he had with him yesterday?

TESMAN.   It is. It's the whole of that precious, irreplaceable manuscript of his. And that's what he'd gone and lost, without noticing it. Just think, Hedda! Such a sad—

HEDDA.   But why didn't you give the packet back to him at once, then?

TESMAN.   Well, I didn't dare to. Not in the state he was in.

HEDDA.   Didn't you tell any of the others you'd found it, either?

TESMAN.   Certainly not. I didn't want to do that for Ejlert's sake, you know.

HEDDA.   Then there's no one who knows you've got Ejlert Lövborg's manuscript?

TESMAN.   No. And no one must find out, either.

HEDDA.   What did you talk to him about afterwards, then?

TESMAN.   I didn't get a chance to talk to him again, you see. Because when we got into the streets, he and two or three others got away from us. Just think!

HEDDA.   Oh? They must have seen him home, then.

TESMAN.   Yes, it looks as if they had. And Brack went off, too.

HEDDA.   And where ever have you been since?

TESMAN.   Well, I and some of the others went on home with one of the gay lads and had morning coffee at his place. Or night coffee, it would be better to call it. Eh? But as soon as I've had a moment's rest—and when I think Ejlert's slept it off, poor fellow—I must go over to him with this.

HEDDA   (*holding out her hand for the package*). No, don't give it up! Not directly, I mean. Let me read it first.

TESMAN.   Oh, Hedda, my dear, I couldn't do that. I really couldn't.

HEDDA.   You couldn't?

TESMAN.   No. You can just imagine how frantic he will be when he wakes up and misses the manuscript. Because he's got no copy of it, you realize! He said so himself.

HEDDA   (*looking searchingly at him*). Can't a thing like that be written again, then? Re-written?

TESMAN.   No, I don't think that would ever work. It's a matter of inspiration, you know.

HEDDA.   Yes, of course. I suppose that's it. (*Casually.*) Oh, by the way, there's a letter for you here.

TESMAN.   Really?

HEDDA   (*passing it to him*). It came early this morning.

TESMAN.   Why, it's from Aunt Julle! (*He puts down the paper package on the other footstool, opens the letter, runs through it and jumps up.*) Oh, Hedda! She says poor Aunt Rina's dying.

HEDDA.   Well, that was to be expected.

TESMAN.   And that if I want to see her again I must be quick. I'll run across there at once.

HEDDA   (*checking a smile*). Run?

TESMAN.   Oh, Hedda dear, if only you could bring yourself to come along, too! Just think!

HEDDA   (*getting up and dismissing the matter wearily*). No, no. Don't ask me to do things like that. I don't want to think of illness or death. You mustn't ask me to have anything to do with ugly things.

TESMAN.   Oh well, then. (*Bustling about.*) My hat? My overcoat? Oh yes; in the hall. Oh, I do so hope I'm not going to be too late, Hedda! Eh?

(BERTE *comes to the hall door.*)

BERTE.   Judge Brack's outside, asking can he come in?

TESMAN.   At this moment! No, I really can't see him now.

HEDDA.   But I can. (*To* BERTE.) Ask the Judge to come in. (BERTE *goes out.*)

HEDDA   (*quickly, in a whisper*). The parcel! (*She snatches it from the stool.*)

TESMAN.   Yes, give it to me!

HEDDA.   No, no. I'll keep it for you till you get back.

(She crosses to the writing-table and puts it in the bookcase. TESMAN *is in such a hurry that he cannot get his gloves on.* BRACK *comes in from the hall.)*

HEDDA   *(nodding to him)* . Well, you are an early bird.

BRACK.   Yes, don't you think so? *(To* TESMAN.) Are you going out, too?

TESMAN.   Yes, I simply must go and see the Aunts. Just think, the invalid one, she's dying, poor thing.

BRACK.   Dear, dear! Is she? Then you certainly mustn't let me keep you. At such a serious moment—

TESMAN.   Yes, I really must be off. Good-bye, good-bye! *(He hurries out through the hall door.)*

HEDDA   *(coming nearer to* BRACK) . It seems to have been rather more than "gay" at your place last night, Mr. Brack.

BRACK.   So much so that I haven't had my clothes off, Madam Hedda.

HEDDA.   Not you either?

BRACK.   No, as you see. Well, what has Tesman been telling you about the night's adventures?

HEDDA.   Oh, just a dull story. That they'd gone and had coffee somewhere.

BRACK.   I know all about that coffee-party. Ejlert Lövborg wasn't with them, I think?

HEDDA.   No, they'd seen him home before that.

BRACK.   Tesman, too?

HEDDA.   No; but some of the others, he said.

BRACK   *(smiling)* . Jörgen Tesman really is a simple soul, Madam Hedda.

HEDDA.   Heaven knows he is. Is there something behind this, then?

BRACK.   Yes, It's no good denying . . .

HEDDA.   Well, then let's sit down, my friend. Then you can tell your story.

(She sits down on the left of the table, with BRACK *at the long side, near her.)*

HEDDA.   Well, now?

BRACK.   I had good reasons for keeping track of my guests last night—or rather, of some of my guests.

HEDDA.   And I suppose Ejlert Lövborg was one of them.

BRACK.   I must admit he was.

HEDDA.   Now you are making me really curious.

BRACK.   Do you know where he and a few others spent the rest of the night, Madam Hedda?

HEDDA.   If it's the sort of thing that can be told, tell me.

BRACK.   Oh yes, it can be told all right. Well, they fetched up at an extremely lively party.

HEDDA.   Of the "gay" kind?

BRACK.   Of the very gayest.

HEDDA.   Go on, please. I want to hear some more.

BRACK.   Lövborg had had an invitation beforehand as well. I knew all about that. But he'd refused to go then, because he's turned over a new leaf now—as you know.

HEDDA.   Up at the Elvsteds'. Yes. But he went, then, all the same?

BRACK.   Yes. You see, Madam Hedda, unfortunately the inspiration took him at my place last night.

HEDDA.   Yes, I gather he found inspiration there.

BRACK.   Pretty violent inspiration. Anyway, he changed his mind, I imagine. For we men are unfortunately not always so firm in our principles as we ought to be.

HEDDA.   How do you know all this?

BRACK.   From the police themselves.

HEDDA   (*gazing in front of her*). So that's how it was? Then he had no vineleaves in his hair.

BRACK.   Vineleaves, Madam Hedda?

HEDDA   (*changing her tone*). But tell me, now. What's your real reason for following up Ejlert Lövborg's movements like this?

BRACK.   Well, it obviously can't be a matter of complete indifference to me, if it comes out at the trial that he had come straight from my place.

HEDDA.   Will there be a trial too, then?

BRACK.   Of course. However, that might pass. . . . But, as a friend of the house, I felt bound to give you and Tesman a full account of his night's exploits.

HEDDA.   And why, Mr. Brack?

BRACK.   Well, because I have a shrewd misgiving that he means to use you as a kind of screen.

HEDDA.   Why, how can you imagine such a thing?

BRACK.   Good Lord, we're not blind, Madam Hedda! You watch. This Mrs. Elvsted, she won't be leaving town again in a hurry.

HEDDA.   Well, even supposing there is something between them, there must be plenty of other places where they can meet.

BRACK.   No other home. Every decent house will be closed again to Ejlert Lövborg from now onwards.

HEDDA.   And so ought mine to be, you mean?

BRACK.   Yes. I admit it would be extremely unpleasant to me if this man were on a firm footing here. If he were to force his way in, superfluous and an intruder, into—

HEDDA.   Into the triangle?

BRACK.   Precisely. It would simply amount to my finding myself without a home.

HEDDA (*looking at him with a smile*) . Ah yes. The only cock in the yard. That's your idea.

BRACK (*nodding slowly and dropping his voice*) . Yes, that is my idea. And I'll fight for that idea with all the means at my command.

HEDDA (*her smile dying away*) . You are really a dangerous person, when it comes to the point.

BRACK. Do you think so?

HEDDA. Yes, I am beginning to think so now. I'm heartily thankful you've no hold or power over me—and I hope you never will.

BRACK (*laughing equivocally*) . Well, well, Madam Hedda. You may be right there. Who knows what I mightn't prove capable of in that case?

HEDDA. Now look here, Mr. Brack. That sounds almost as though you were threatening me.

BRACK (*getting up*) . Oh, far from it! The triangle, you see, is best formed and maintained by free consent.

HEDDA. That's what I think, too.

BRACK. Yes. Well, now I've said what I wanted to and I must see about getting home again. Good-bye, Madam Hedda. (*He goes toward the glass door.*)

HEDDA (*getting up*) . Are you going through the garden?

BRACK. Yes, it's shorter for me.

HEDDA. Yes, and what's more, it's a back way.

BRACK. Quite true. I have nothing against back ways. They can be quite attractive at times.

HEDDA. When someone's practising shooting, do you mean?

BRACK (*at the door, laughing to her*) . Oh, I don't think people shoot their farmyard cocks.

HEDDA (*laughing, too*) . No, not when one has only the one.

(*They nod good-bye to each other, laughing. He goes out. She shuts the door after him.*

HEDDA *stands a moment, serious now, and looks out. Then she goes across and peeps in through the curtains over the middle doorway and then goes to the writing-table, takes the packet out of the bookcase and is just going to look through it when* BERTE'*s voice is heard, speaking loudly, in the hall.* HEDDA *turns and listens, then quickly locks the package in the drawer and puts the key on the inkstand.*

EJLERT LÖVBORG, *with his overcoat on and his hat in his hand, flings open the hall door. He looks disturbed and excited.*)

LÖVBORG (*speaking towards the hall*) . And I tell you I must go in and I will. There now!

(*He shuts the door, turns, sees* HEDDA, *controls himself at once and bows.*)

HEDDA (*at the writing-table*) . Well, Mr. Lövborg, it's rather late to come and fetch Thea.

LÖVBORG. Or rather early to come and call on you. I apologize.

HEDDA. How do you know that she is still with me?

LÖVBORG. They said at her lodgings that she had been out all night.

HEDDA (*going to the centre table*). Did you notice anything about the people, when they said that?

LÖVBORG (*looking at her inquiringly*). Notice anything about them?

HEDDA. I mean, did it look as if they were drawing their own conclusions?

LÖVBORG (*understanding suddenly*). Oh yes, of course; that's true. I am dragging her down with me. Actually, though, I didn't notice anything. Tesman isn't up yet?

HEDDA. No, I don't think so.

LÖVBORG. When did he get home?

HEDDA. Pretty late.

LÖVBORG. Did he tell you anything?

HEDDA. Yes, I gathered that things had been very merry at Judge Brack's.

LÖVBORG. Nothing more?

HEDDA. No, I don't think so. But anyhow, I was so terribly sleepy—

(MRS. ELVSTED *comes in through the curtains in the middle doorway.*)

MRS. ELVSTED (*going towards him*). Oh, Ejlert! At last!

LÖVBORG. Yes, at last. And too late.

MRS. ELVSTED (*looking anxiously at him*). What is too late?

LÖVBORG. Everything's too late now. It's all up with me.

MRS. ELVSTED. No, no! Don't say that!

LÖVSTED. You'll say so yourself when you hear.

MRS. ELVSTED. I won't hear anything.

HEDDA. Perhaps you'd rather talk to her alone? If so, I'll go.

LÖVBORG. No, you stay too, please. I beg you to.

MRS. ELVSTED. Yes, but I won't hear anything, I tell you.

LÖVBORG. It's not last night's escapades I want to talk about.

MRS. ELVSTED. What is it, then?

LÖVBORG. Just this: our ways must part now.

MRS. ELVSTED. Part?

HEDDA (*involuntarily*). I knew it!

LÖVBORG. Because I don't need you any more, Thea.

MRS. ELVSTED. And you can stand here and say that? Not need me any more! I can still help you, can't I, as I did before? Surely we are going on working together?

LÖVBORG. I don't propose to work in future.

MRS. ELVSTED (*in despair*). What shall I do with my life, then?

LÖVBORG. You must try to go on living as though you had never known me.

MRS. ELVSTED. But I *can't* do that!

LÖVBORG. Try to, Thea. You must go home again—

MRS. ELVSTED (*protesting fiercely*) . Never in this life! Where you are, there will I be too. I won't let myself be driven away like this. I will stay here and be with you when the book comes out.

HEDDA (*half audibly, in suspense*) . Ah, the book, of course!

LÖVBORG (*looking at her*) . My book and Thea's. For that is what it is.

MRS. ELVSTED. Yes, that's what I feel it is. And that's why I have the right to be with you when it comes out. I want to see respect and honour showered on you again. And the joy—I want to share the joy with you.

LÖVBORG. Thea, our book will never come out.

HEDDA. Ah!

MRS. ELVSTED. Never come out!

LÖVBORG. *Can't* ever come out.

MRS. ELVSTED (*in agonized foreboding*) . Ejlert, what have you done with the manuscript?

HEDDA (*looking intently at him*) . Yes, the manuscript?

MRS. ELVSTED. Where is it?

LÖVBORG. You'd better not ask me, Thea.

MRS. ELVSTED. But I want to know. I've a right to know, at once.

LÖVBORG. The manuscript . . . oh well, then . . . I have torn the manuscript into a thousand pieces.

MRS. ELVSTED (*shrieking*) . Oh no, no!

HEDDA (*involuntarily*) . But that's not—!

LÖVBORG (*looking at her*) . Not true, you think?

HEDDA (*controlling herself*) . I suppose it is, of course. If you say so yourself. . . . . But it sounded so fantastic.

LÖVBORG. True, all the same.

MRS. ELVSTED (*wringing her hands*) . Oh, heavens, heavens, Hedda! Torn his own work to pieces!

LÖVBORG. I have torn my own life to pieces. So I might as well tear up my life's work, too.

MRS. ELVSTED. And you did it last night, then?

LÖVBORG. Yes, I tell you. Into a thousand pieces. And scattered them out in the fjord. Far out. There at least there is clean sea water. Let them drift in it. Drift with the wind and the tides. And, after a time, they will sink. Deeper and deeper. As I shall, Thea.

MRS. ELVSTED. Do you know, Ejlert, this, what you have done to the book—all my life, it will seem to me as if you had killed a little child.

LÖVBORG. You are right. It is like murdering a child.

MRS. ELVSTED. But how could you? After all, I had a share in the child, too.

HEDDA (*scarcely audible*) . Ah, the child. . . .

MRS. ELVSTED (*with a gasp*) . It's all over, then. Well, well. I'll go now, Hedda.

HEDDA.   But you're not going to leave town?

MRS. ELVSTED.   Oh, I don't know myself what I'm going to do. Everything is dark ahead of me now.

(*She goes out by the hall door.*)

HEDDA   (*standing and waiting for a moment*) . So you are not going to see her home, Mr. Lövborg?

LÖVBORG.   I? Through the streets? Suppose people were to see her walking with me?

HEDDA.   Of course, I don't know what else happened to you last night. But is it something so absolutely irreparable?

LÖVBORG.   It won't stop at last night only. I know that well enough. But, the point is, I don't *want* to live that kind of life. I don't want to start again, any more, now. It is the courage to live, and to challenge life, that she has broken in me.

HEDDA   (*looking straight before her*) . That pretty little fool has played her part in a human being's fate. (*Looking at him.*) Still, how could you treat her so callously, all the same?

LÖVBORG.   Oh, don't say it was callous!

HEDDA.   To go and destroy what has filled her soul all this long, long time! You don't call that callous?

LÖVBORG.   I can tell you the truth, Hedda.

HEDDA.   The truth?

LÖVBORG.   Promise me first, give me your word, that Thea shall never know what I tell you.

HEDDA.   You have my word for it.

LÖVBORG.   Good. Then I will tell you that that was not the truth—the story I told you just now.

HEDDA.   About the manuscript?

LÖVBORG.   Yes. I didn't tear it to pieces. Nor throw it into the fjord, either.

HEDDA.   Well, but—where is it, then?

LÖVBORG.   I have destroyed it just the same. Utterly and completely, Hedda.

HEDDA.   I don't understand all this.

LÖVBORG.   Thea said that what I had done was as good as child-murder to her.

HEDDA.   Yes. That's what she said.

LÖVBORG.   But that—killing his child—is not the worst thing a father can do to it.

HEDDA.   *That's* not the worst?

LÖVBORG.   No. It was that worst thing that I wanted to save Thea from hearing.

HEDDA.   And what is that worst thing, then?

LÖVBORG. Suppose now, Hedda, that a man, along towards morning, say, after a wild, riotous night, came home to his child's mother and said: Look here. I have been here and there, in such-and-such places. And I took the child with me. In such-and-such places. And I lost the child. Lost it completely. The devil knows what hands it's fallen into, who's got it in his clutches.

HEDDA. Oh but, when all's said and done, this—well, this was only a book.

LÖVBORG. Thea's whole soul was in that book.

HEDDA. Yes, I understand that.

LÖVBORG. And so you understand also that there is no future before us, her and me.

HEDDA. And what are you going to do, then?

LÖVBORG. Nothing. Only make an end of the whole business. The sooner the better.

HEDDA (*a step nearer*) . Ejlert Lövborg, listen to me. Could you not see to it that—that it is done beautifully?

LÖVBORG. Beautifully? (*Smiling.*) With vineleaves in the hair, as you used to imagine once upon a time—

HEDDA. Ah, not vineleaves. I don't believe in that any more. But beautifully, nevertheless. For once. Good-bye. You must go now, and not come here again.

LÖVBORG. Good-bye, Madam. Remember me to Jörgen Tesman. (*About to go.*)

HEDDA. Wait a minute. You shall have a souvenir to take with you.
(*She goes to the writing-table and opens the drawer and the pistol-case. She comes back to* LÖVBORG *again with one of the pistols.*)

LÖVBORG (*looking at her*) . Is *that* the souvenir?

HEDDA (*nodding slowly*) . Do you recognize it? It was aimed at you once.

LÖVBORG. You should have used it then.

HEDDA. There it is. Use it yourself now.

LÖVBORG (*putting the pistol in his breast pocket*) . Thanks.

HEDDA. And beautifully, Ejlert Lövborg. Promise me that.

LÖVBORG. Good-bye, Hedda Gabler. (*He goes out by the hall door.*)
(HEDDA *listens a moment at the door. Then she goes across to the writing-table and takes out the manuscript in its package. She glances inside the wrapper, pulls some of the sheets half out and looks at them. Then she goes across and sits down in the easy-chair by the stove with the packet in her lap. After a moment, she opens the stove-door and then the packet.*)

HEDDA (*throwing some of the leaves into the fire and whispering to herself*) . Now I am burning your child, Thea. You, with your curly hair. (*Throwing a few more leaves into the stove.*) Your child and Ejlert Lövborg's. (*Throwing in the rest.*) I'm burning it—burning your child.

ACT FOUR

*The same rooms at the Tesmans' house. Evening. The drawing-room is
in darkness. The inner room is lighted by the hanging lamp over the
table. The curtains are drawn across the glass door.*

*Hedda, dressed in black, is walking to and fro in the dark room. Then
she goes into the inner room and away to the left side. A few chords on
the piano are heard. Then she comes back again and into the drawing-
room.*

*Berte comes in from the right through the inner room with a lighted
lamp, which she puts on the table in front of the corner sofa in the drawing-room. Her eyes are red with crying and she has black ribbons in her
cap. She goes quietly and discreetly out to the right. Hedda goes across to
the glass door, draws the curtain aside a little and looks out into the darkness.*

*Soon after, Miss Tesman comes in from the hall door, dressed in mourn-
ing, with a hat and veil. Hedda goes towards her and holds out her hand.*

MISS TESMAN.   Yes, Hedda, here I am dressed in mourning. Because now
my poor sister's trials are over at last.

HEDDA.   I have heard already, as you see. My husband sent a note out to
me.

MISS TESMAN.   Yes, he promised he would. But I thought all the same,
that to Hedda—here, in the house of the living—I ought myself to
bring the news of her death.

HEDDA.   It was very kind of you.

MISS TESMAN.   Ah, Rina should not have died at such a moment. Hedda's
home ought not to be sad just now.

HEDDA   (*changing the subject*). She died very peacefully, didn't she,
Miss Tesman?

MISS TESMAN.   Ah, it was such a beautiful, peaceful release! And then
she had the unspeakable happiness of seeing Jörgen once more, so that
she was really able to say good-bye to him. Perhaps he hasn't come back
yet?

HEDDA.   No. He wrote that I mustn't expect him just yet. But do sit down.

MISS TESMAN.   No, thank you, my dear, precious Hedda. I should like to,
but I have so little time. She must be prepared and made ready as well
as I can. She shall go into her grave looking beautiful.

HEDDA.   Can't I help you with anything?

MISS TESMAN.   Oh, don't think of that! Hedda Tesman mustn't do that
kind of thing. Nor dwell on the thought, either. Not at such a time.
Certainly not.

HEDDA.   Ah, thoughts . . . they are not so easily mastered.

MISS TESMAN (*going on*). Well, bless us. That's how things go in this world. At home we shall be sewing for Rina. And there will be sewing to be done here too, I think, soon. But that will be a different kind, thank God!

(JÖRGEN TESMAN *comes in by the hall door.*)

HEDDA. Ah, it's a good thing you're back at last.

TESMAN. Are you here, Aunt Julle? With Hedda? Fancy!

MISS TESMAN. I was just going again, dear boy. Well, did you see to all those things you promised to do?

TESMAN. No, I'm really afraid I've forgotten half of them, you know. I must run in and see you again tomorrow. My head is so muddled today. I can't keep my ideas together.

MISS TESMAN. But, my dear Jörgen. You mustn't take it like this.

TESMAN. No? How, then . . . do you think?

MISS TESMAN. You must be glad in your grief. Glad of what has happened. As I am.

TESMAN. Oh yes, yes. You are thinking of Aunt Rina, of course.

HEDDA. It will be lonely for you now, Miss Tesman.

MISS TESMAN. Just at first, yes. But that won't last very long, I hope. Dear Rina's little room won't stand empty, I know.

TESMAN. Really? Who do you want to take it? Eh?

MISS TESMAN. Oh, there is always some poor sick person or other who needs care and attention, unfortunately.

HEDDA. Do you really want to take a burden like that on you again?

MISS TESMAN. Burden! God forgive you, my child. It has never been a burden to me.

HEDDA. But if a strange person is going to come, why—

MISS TESMAN. Oh, one soon makes friends with sick folk. And I sadly need someone to live for—I, too. Well, thank God there may be things here, too, of one sort and another, that an old aunt can lend a hand with.

HEDDA. Oh, don't bother about things here—

TESMAN. Just think how happy we three could be together, if—

HEDDA. If—?

TESMAN (*uneasily*). Oh, nothing. It'll all come right. Let's hope so. Eh?

MISS TESMAN. Well, well. You two have plenty to talk to each other about, I expect. (*Smiling.*) And perhaps Hedda has something to tell you too, Jörgen. Good-bye. Now I must go home to Rina. (*Turning at the door.*) Dear, dear, how strange it is to think of it! Now Rina is with me and with our dear Jochum, too.

TESMAN. Yes, to think of it, Aunt Julle! Eh?

(MISS TESMAN *goes out by the hall door.*)

HEDDA (*her eyes, cold and searching, following* TESMAN). I almost think the death has affected you more than it has her.

TESMAN.   Oh, it's not only Aunt Rina's death. It's Ejlert; I'm so worried about him.

HEDDA   *(quickly)*. Has anything fresh happened to him?

TESMAN.   I meant to have run over to him this afternoon and told him that his manuscript was in safe keeping.

HEDDA.   Well, didn't you find him, then?

TESMAN.   No, he wasn't at home. But afterwards I met Mrs. Elvsted, and she told me he had been here early this morning.

HEDDA.   Yes, directly you'd gone.

TESMAN.   And he seems to have said that he had torn up the manuscript. Eh?

HEDDA.   Yes, he insisted he had.

TESMAN.   But, good heavens, he must have been absolutely off his head! And so, of course, you didn't dare give it back to him, Hedda?

HEDDA.   No, he didn't take it.

TESMAN.   But you told him, all right, that we had it?

HEDDA.   No *(Quickly.)* Did you tell Mrs. Elvsted we had?

TESMAN.   No, I didn't quite like to do that. But you ought to have told him himself. Suppose he goes off in despair and does himself some injury? Let me have the manuscript, Hedda. I will dash over to him with it at once. Where is the parcel?

HEDDA   *(cold and immovable, leaning against the easy-chair)*. I haven't got it any longer.

TESMAN.   You haven't got it. What on earth do you mean by that?

HEDDA.   I have burnt it. Every scrap of it.

TESMAN   *(with a start of terror)*. Burnt it! Burnt Ejlert Lövborg's manuscript!

HEDDA.   Don't scream like that. The maid might hear you.

TESMAN.   Burnt! But, good God! No, no, no! This is simply impossible!

HEDDA.   Well, it's true, all the same.

TESMAN.   But do you realize what you have done, Hedda? It's against the law, to treat lost property like that! Think of it! You just ask Judge Brack and he'll tell you.

HEDDA.   I shouldn't advise you to talk about it either to the Judge or to anyone else.

TESMAN.   But how could you go and do anything so unheard of? How could such an idea come into your head? How could it come over you? Tell me that. Eh?

HEDDA   *(suppressing a scarcely perceptible smile)*. I did it for your sake, Jörgen.

TESMAN.   For my sake!

HEDDA.   When you came home in the morning and told me that he'd been reading to you—

TESMAN.   Yes, yes, what about it?

HEDDA.   You admitted then that you envied him his work.

TESMAN.   Good heavens, I didn't mean it literally!

HEDDA.   All the same, I couldn't bear the thought of someone else throwing you into the shade.

TESMAN   (*in an outburst of mingled doubt and joy*). Hedda! Is it true what you're saying? Yes, but . . . but . . . I've never known you show your affection in this sort of way before.

HEDDA.   Oh well, you'd better know, then, that—just at present— (*Breaking off, violently.*) No, you can go and ask Aunt Julle. She'll tell you all about it.

TESMAN.   Ah, I rather think I understand, Hedda! (*Clasping his hands together.*) Good heavens! Good heavens! Can it be possible? Eh?

HEDDA.   Don't shout so. The maid might hear you.

TESMAN   (*laughing, beside himself with joy*). The maid! No, you really are priceless, Hedda! "The maid"! Why, it's only Berte! I'll go out and tell Berte myself.

HEDDA   (*clenching her hands in desperation*). Oh, it'll be the death of me. It'll be the death of me, all this!

TESMAN.   What will, Hedda? Eh?

HEDDA   (*cold and controlled*). All this grotesque nonsense, Jörgen.

TESMAN.   Nonsense! That I'm so delighted? But, all the same . . . perhaps I had better not say anything to Berte.

HEDDA.   Oh yes, why not that, too?

TESMAN.   No, no, not yet. But Aunt Julle must certainly know about it. And then, too, that you are beginning to call me Jörgen! Think of it! Oh, Aunt Julle *will* be so glad! So glad!

HEDDA.   When she hears that I have burnt Ejlert Lövborg's manuscript, for your sake?

TESMAN.   No, that reminds me. That business with the manuscript—no one must get to know about that, of course. But that you feel like this towards me, Hedda, Aunt Julle must certainly hear that! Still, my dear, I should like to know myself whether this kind of thing is usual with young wives. Eh?

HEDDA.   You'd better ask Aunt Julle about that, too, I think.

TESMAN.   Yes, I certainly will some time. (*Looking worried and dubious again.*) But . . . but that manuscript. Oh heavens, it's dreadful to think of poor Ejlert, all the same!

(MRS. ELVSTED, *dressed as on her first visit, with her hat and out-door clothes, comes in by the hall door.*)

MRS. ELVSTED   (*greeting them quickly and speaking in agitation*). Oh, Hedda, dear, I hope you won't mind my coming again?

HEDDA.   What's the matter, Thea?

TESMAN.   Is it something to do with Ejlert Lövborg again? Eh?

MRS. ELVSTED.   Yes, I'm terribly afraid some accident has happened to him.

HEDDA   (*seizing her by the arm*). Ah—do you think so?

TESMAN.   Bless me, whatever makes you think that, Mrs. Elvsted?

MRS. ELVSTED.   Why, because I heard them talking about him at the boarding-house, just as I came in. Oh, there are the most incredible rumours about him in town today!

TESMAN.   Yes, do you know, I heard that too. Yet I could swear that he went straight home to bed. Just fancy!

HEDDA.   Well, what did they say at the boarding-house?

MRS. ELVSTED.   I didn't gather anything definite. Either they didn't know very much or . . . They stopped talking when they saw me. And as for asking—I didn't dare do that.

TESMAN   (*walking about restlessly*). We'll hope—we'll hope you misunderstood, them, Mrs. Elvsted.

MRS. ELVSTED.   No, no, I am certain it was he they were talking about. And, as I heard it, they said something about the hospital, or—

TESMAN.   The hospital!

HEDDA.   No! That can't be true.

MRS. ELVSTED.   Oh, I was so dreadfully frightened about him. So I went to his lodgings and asked for him there.

HEDDA.   Could you bring yourself to do that, Thea?

MRS. ELVSTED.   Yes, what else was I to do? I didn't feel as if I could bear the uncertainty any longer.

TESMAN.   But you didn't find him either, did you? Eh?

MRS. ELVSTED.   No. And the people didn't know anything about him. They said he hadn't been home since yesterday afternoon.

TESMAN.   Yesterday! Fancy their saying that!

MRS. ELVSTED.   Oh, I think there's only one explanation—something dreadful must have happened to him!

TESMAN.   Hedda, my dear, suppose I were to go in and make some inquiries?

HEDDA.   No. Don't mix yourself up in this business.

(BRACK, *with his hat in his hand, comes in by the hall door, which* BERTE *opens and shuts after him. He looks grave and bows silently.*)

TESMAN.   Oh, it's you, my dear Judge? Eh?

BRACK.   Yes, it was imperative for me to see you this evening.

TESMAN.   I can see that you have had Aunt Julle's news.

BRACK.   Yes, I have heard that, too.

TESMAN.   Isn't it sad? Eh?

BRACK.   Well, my dear Tesman, it depends how you look at it.

TESMAN   (*looking doubtfully at him*). Has anything else happened?

BRACK. Yes, something else.

HEDDA (*in suspense*). Anything sad, Mr. Brack?

BRACK. That, too, depends on how you look at it, Mrs. Tesman.

MRS. ELVSTED (*breaking out, involuntarily*). Oh, it's something about Ejlert Lövborg!

BRACK (*glancing at her*). What makes you think that, Madam? Do you happen to know anything already?

MRS. ELVSTED (*confused*). No, no; not at all! But—

TESMAN. But, good heavens, man, tell us!

BRACK (*shrugging his shoulders*). Well, I'm sorry to say Ejlert Lövborg has been taken to the hospital. As a matter of fact, he's dying.

MRS. ELVSTED (*crying out*). My God! My God!

TESMAN. In hospital? And dying?

HEDDA (*involuntarily*). So quickly, then!

MRS. ELVSTED (*wailing*). And we parted in anger, Hedda!

HEDDA (*whispering*). Come now, Thea! *Thea!*

MRS. ELVSTED (*without taking any notice*). I must go to him! I must see him alive!

BRACK. It won't be any use, my dear lady. Nobody's allowed to see him.

MRS. ELVSTED. Well, at least tell me what's happened to him. What is the matter?

TESMAN. Why, surely he never did it himself! Eh?

HEDDA. I'm sure he *did*.

TESMAN. Hedda, how can you?

BRACK (*with his eyes fixed steadily on her*). Unfortunately, you have guessed quite right, Mrs. Tesman.

MRS. ELVSTED. Oh, how terrible!

TESMAN. So he did it himself! Think of it!

HEDDA. Shot himself!

BRACK. Rightly guessed again, Mrs. Tesman.

MRS. ELVSTED (*trying to control herself*). When did it happen, Mr. Brack?

BRACK. This afternoon. Between three and four.

TESMAN. But, dear, dear—where did he do it, then? Eh?

BRACK (*a little uncertainly*). Where? Why, I suppose at his lodgings.

MRS. ELVSTED. No, that can't be right. Because I was there between six and seven.

BRACK. Well, somewhere else, then. I don't exactly know; I only know that he was found. . . . He had shot himself in the chest.

MRS. ELVSTED. Oh, how dreadful to think of! That he should end like this.

HEDDA (*to* BRACK). Was it in the chest?

BRACK. Yes, as I said.

HEDDA. Not in the temple, then?

BRACK.   In the chest, Mrs. Tesman.

HEDDA.   Yes, well . . . the chest is a good place, too.

BRACK.   How do you mean, Mrs. Tesman?

HEDDA   *(evasively)* . Oh, nothing—nothing.

TESMAN.   And the wound is dangerous, you say? Eh?

BRACK.   The wound is absolutely fatal. Most likely it's all over already.

MRS. ELVSTED.   Yes, yes, I feel sure it is. It is all over! All over! Oh, Hedda!

TESMAN.   But tell me, how did you find out all this?

BRACK   *(shortly)* . From one of the police. Whom I had occasion to speak to.

HEDDA   *(in a ringing voice)* . Something done, at last!

TESMAN   *(horrified)* . Good heavens! What are you saying Hedda?

HEDDA.   That there is an element of beauty in this.

BRACK.   Hm. Mrs. Tesman—

TESMAN.   Of beauty! Fancy that!

MRS. ELVSTED.   Oh, Hedda, how can you talk of beauty in a thing like that!

HEDDA.   Ejlert Lövborg has balanced his account with himself. He has had the courage to do . . . what had to be done.

MRS. ELVSTED.   No, don't ever believe that it happened in that way. What he has done was done in a moment of madness.

TESMAN.   Done in despair.

HEDDA.   It was not. Of that I am certain.

MRS. ELVSTED.   Yes, it was. In a moment of madness. Just as when he tore up our manuscript.

BRACK   *(in surprise)* . Manuscript? The book, do you mean? Has he torn that up?

MRS. ELVSTED.   Yes, he did it last night.

TESMAN   *(whispering softly)* . Oh, Hedda, we shall never get clear of this business.

BRACK.   Hm. That was odd.

TESMAN   *(walking about the room)* . Fancy Ejlert going out of the world like that! And not even leaving behind him the book that would have made his name immortal.

MRS. ELVSTED.   Oh, if only it could be put together again!

TESMAN.   Yes, just think if it could! I don't know what I wouldn't give—

MRS. ELVSTED.   Perhaps it can, Mr. Tesman.

TESMAN.   What do you mean?

MRS. ELVSTED   *(looking in her handbag)* . Look here. I have kept the loose notes that he used for dictating from.

HEDDA   *(a step nearer)* . Ah!

TESMAN.   You've kept them, Mrs. Elvsted! Eh?

MRS. ELVSTED.   Yes, I have them here. I took them with me when I came away, and here they've been, lying in my handbag.

TESMAN. Just let me see them!

MRS. ELVSTED (*passes him a stack of small sheets*). But they're in such a muddle. All mixed up together.

TESMAN. Fancy, if we could get it straight, though! Perhaps if we help each other—

MRS. ELVSTED. Oh yes! Let's try, at any rate!

TESMAN. It *shall* be done! It *must!* I will give my life to this.

HEDDA. You, Jörgen? Your life?

TESMAN. Yes. Or, rather, all my spare time. My own stuff must wait for the present. You understand, Hedda? Eh? It's something I owe to Ejlert's memory.

HEDDA. Perhaps it is.

TESMAN. And so, my dear Mrs. Elvsted, we will pull ourselves together. Heaven knows, it's no use brooding over what's done. Eh? We must try to make our minds as calm as possible, and—

MRS. ELVSTED. Yes, yes, Mr. Tesman. I will do the best I can.

TESMAN. Well, come along. We must look over the notes at once. Where shall we sit? Here? No, in here in the back room. Excuse me, my dear Judge. Now come with me, Mrs. Elvsted.

MRS. ELVSTED. Dear God! If only it could be done!

(TESMAN *and* MRS. ELVSTED *go into the inner room. She takes off her hat and overcoat. They both sit down at the table under the hanging lamp and become absorbed in concentrated examination of the papers.* HEDDA *goes across to the stove and sits in the easy-chair. Shortly afterwards* BRACK *goes across to her.*)

HEDDA (*half-aloud*). Ah, Mr. Brack, what a feeling of release it gives one, this business with Ejlert Lövborg.

BRACK. Release, Madam Hedda? Well, it certainly is a release for him—

HEDDA. I mean for me. A feeling of release, in knowing that there really can be such a thing in the world as free and fearless action. Something irradiated with spontaneous beauty.

BRACK (*smiling*). Hm. My dear Madam Hedda—

HEDDA. Oh yes. I know what you are going to say. Because you're a professional man too, in your way, like . . . Oh well!

BRACK (*looking steadily at her*). Eljert Lövborg meant more to you than you are perhaps willing to admit to yourself. Or am I wrong there?

HEDDA. I don't answer that kind of question. I only know that Ejlert Lövborg had the courage to live life in his own way. And now—this great deed, with all its beauty? That he had the strength and will to break away from the feast of life . . . and so early.

BRACK. I am very sorry, Madam Hedda, but I must deprive you of your pretty illusion.

HEDDA. Illusion?

BRACK. Which you would have been deprived of soon, in any case.

HEDDA.   And what is it?

BRACK.   He did not shoot himself intentionally.

HEDDA.   Not intentionally?

BRACK.   No. This affair of Ejlert Lövborg did not happen quite as I described it.

HEDDA   *(in suspense)*. Have you been keeping something back? What is it?

BRACK.   For poor Mrs. Elvsted's sake I did make one or two slight modifications.

HEDDA.   What were they?

BRACK.   In the first place, he is actually dead already.

HEDDA.   In hospital?

BRACK.   Yes, and without regaining consciousness.

HEDDA.   What else did you keep back?

BRACK.   The fact that the thing didn't happen at his lodgings.

HEDDA.   Well, that doesn't really make much difference.

BRACK.   It does, rather. For I must tell you Ejlert Lövborg was found shot in—in Mademoiselle Diana's boudoir.

HEDDA   *(half gets up, but sinks back again)*. That's impossible, Mr. Brack. He can't have been *there* again today!

BRACK.   He was there this afternoon. He came to demand something that, he said, they had taken away from him. Talked wildly about a child that had been lost—

HEDDA.   Ah! So that was why . . .

BRACK.   I thought perhaps it might have been his manuscript. But I gather that he destroyed that himself. So it must have been his wallet.

HEDDA.   It must have been. And it was there, then, that he was found?

BRACK.   Yes, there. With a discharged pistol that had gone off in his breast-pocket. The shot had wounded him fatally.

HEDDA.   In the chest—yes.

BRACK.   No. It hit him in the stomach.

HEDDA   *(looking up at him with an expression of disgust)*. That too! The ridiculous and the sordid lies like a curse on everything I so much as touch.

BRACK.   There is something more, Madam Hedda. Something that can also be classed as "sordid."

HEDDA.   What is that?

BRACK.   The pistol that he had on him—

HEDDA   *(breathless)*. Well! What about it?

BRACK.   He must have stolen it.

HEDDA   *(jumping up)*. Stolen! That's not true! That he did not!

BRACK.   No other explanation is possible. He *must* have stolen it. . . . Hush!

(TESMAN *and* MRS. ELVSTED *have got up from the table in the inner room and come into the drawing-room.*)

TESMAN *(with papers in both hands)*. Look here, Hedda, it's hardly possible for me to see in there under the hanging lamp. Just think!

HEDDA. Yes. I am.

TESMAN. I wonder if you would mind our sitting at your writing-table for a little while. Eh?

HEDDA. I don't mind. *(Quickly)*. Wait a minute! Let me tidy it up first.

TESMAN. Oh, you needn't do that, Hedda. There's plenty of room.

HEDDA. No, no. Just let me tidy it, I tell you. I'll take all this in and put it on the piano for the time being. There!

(She has pulled out something covered with music paper from under the bookshelf, puts some more sheets on it and carries it all in to the left in the inner room. TESMAN *puts the loose papers on the writing-table and moves the lamp there from the corner table. He and* MRS. ELVSTED *sit down and settle to work again.* HEDDA *comes back.*)

HEDDA *(behind* MRS. ELVSTED'S *chair, ruffling her hair gently)*. Well, my precious Thea, how is Ejlert Lövborg's memorial getting on?

MRS. ELVSTED *(looking up dispiritedly)*. Oh dear! It looks as if it's going to be terribly difficult to straighten out.

TESMAN. It *must* be done. There is nothing else for it. And this—getting another man's papers in order—it's just the job for me.

*(*HEDDA *goes over to the stove and sits on one of the footstools.* BRACK *stands over her, leaning against the easy-chair.*)

HEDDA *(whispers)*. What was it you said about the pistol?

BRACK *(softly)*. That he must have stolen it.

HEDDA. Why, precisely, stolen?

BRACK. Because any other explanation ought to be impossible, Madam Hedda.

HEDDA. Really?

BRACK *(glancing at her)*. Of course, Ejlert Lövborg was here this morning. Wasn't he?

HEDDA. Yes.

BRACK. Were you alone with him?

HEDDA. Yes, for a time.

BRACK. Didn't you go out of the room while he was here?

HEDDA. No.

BRACK. Think it over. Were you never out of it for a moment?

HEDDA. Well, perhaps just for a moment—out in the hall.

BRACK. And where was your pistol-case in the meantime?

HEDDA. I kept that in . . . I had it locked in . . .

BRACK. Well, Madam Hedda?

HEDDA. The case was there on the writing-table.

BRACK. Have you looked since to see whether both pistols are there?

HEDDA. No.

BRACK. Well, there's no need. I saw the pistol Lövborg had on him. And I knew it again at once, from yesterday. And from longer ago too.

HEDDA. Have you got it?

BRACK. No, the police have it.

HEDDA. What will the police do with the pistol?

BRACK. See if they can trace the owner.

HEDDA. Do you think they can find out?

BRACK *(bending over her and whispering)*. No, Hedda Gabler. Not so long as I keep silence.

HEDDA *(looking askance at him)*. And if you do *not* keep silence—what then?

BRACK *(shrugging his shoulders)*. There is always the other way out: the pistol was stolen.

HEDDA *(firmly)*. Rather death!

BRACK *(smiling)*. That is the kind of thing one *says*. One doesn't *do* it.

HEDDA *(without answering)*. And suppose, now, the pistol isn't stolen. And the owner is discovered. Then what happens?

BRACK. Well, Hedda, what happens then is a scandal.

HEDDA. Scandal!

BRACK. Scandal. Yes! The thing you have such a deadly fear of. Of course You will have to appear in court. Both you and Mademoiselle Diana. She will have to explain how the thing happened. Whether it was accident or homicide. . . . Did he try to pull the pistol out of his pocket to threaten her? And is that how it went off? Or did she snatch the pistol out of his hand, shoot him and put it back in his pocket again? She's quite equal to that. She's a hefty young woman, that same Mademoiselle Diana.

HEDDA. But all these repulsive details don't concern me.

BRACK. No. But you will have to answer the question: Why did you give Ejlert Lövborg the pistol? And what conclusions will people draw from the fact that you did give it him?

HEDDA. *(dropping her head)*. That's true. I didn't think of that.

BRACK. Well, fortunately there is no danger, so long as I say nothing.

HEDDA *(looking up at him)*. So I am in your power, Mr. Brack. From now on, you have a hold over me.

BRACK *(whispering softly)*. My dearest Hedda, believe me I shall not abuse the position.

HEDDA. In your power, all the same. At the mercy of your will and demands. And so a slave! A slave! *(Getting up impatiently.)* No! That thought I cannot tolerate. Never!

BRACK *(looking at her half mockingly)*. And yet one usually manages to tolerate the inevitable.

HEDDA (*returning his look*). Yes, possibly. (*She goes across to the writing-table.*)

HEDDA (*suppressing an involuntary smile and imitating* TESMAN's *intonation*). Well, is it getting on all right, Jörgen? Eh?

TESMAN. The Lord only knows, my dear. In any case, there's months of work here.

HEDDA (*as before*). Well, fancy that! (*Letting her hands stray gently through* MRS. ELVSTED's *hair.*) Doesn't it feel strange to you, Thea? Here you are sitting with Jörgen Tesman just as you once sat with Ejlert Lövborg.

MRS. ELVSTED. Well, if only I could inspire your husband too—

HEDDA. Oh, that will come all right—in time.

TESMAN. Yes, do you know, Hedda, I really think I am beginning to feel something of the kind. But you go back and sit down with Judge Brack again.

HEDDA. Is there nothing here I can help you two with?

TESMAN. Not a thing in the world. (*Turning his head.*) Would you be so kind as to keep Hedda company for the time being, Judge Brack?

BRACK (*with a glance at* HEDDA). It will give me the very greatest pleasure.

HEDDA. Thanks. But I'm tired tonight. I will lie down for a little while on the sofa in there.

TESMAN. Yes do, my dear. Eh?

(HEDDA *goes into the inner room and draws the curtains after her. There is a short pause. Suddenly she is heard playing a wild dance tune on the piano.*)

MRS. ELVSTED (*jumping up from her chair*). Oh! What is that?

TESMAN (*running to the doorway*). But, Hedda, my dearest—don't play dance music this evening. Think of Aunt Rina! And of Ejlert, too!

HEDDA (*putting out her head between the hangings*). And of Aunt Julle. And of all the rest of them. I will be quiet in future. (*She pulls the curtains to again after her.*)

TESMAN (*at the writing-table*). It upsets her to see us at this sad task, of course. I tell you what, Mrs. Elvsted. You shall move into Aunt Julle's and I'll come over in the evenings. And then we can sit and work there. Eh?

MRS. ELVSTED. Yes, perhaps that would be the best plan—

HEDDA (*in the inner room*). I can hear perfectly well what you are saying. But how am I going to get through the evenings out here?

TESMAN (*turning over the papers*). Oh, I'm sure Judge Brack will be kind enough to come out and see you.

BRACK (*in the easy-chair, calling gaily*). Willingly! Every single evening, Mrs. Tesman. We shall have a very pleasant time together here, you and I.

HEDDA   *(clearly and distinctly)* . Yes, that is what you are looking forward
  to, isn't it, Mr. Brack? You, as the only cock in the yard.
(A shot is heard within. TESMAN, MRS. ELVSTED, *and* BRACK *jump up.)*
TESMAN.   Ah! Now she's playing with the pistols again.
(He pulls the curtains aside and runs in. So does MRS. ELVSTED. HEDDA *is
lying lifeless, stretched out on the sofa. Confusion and cries.* BERTE *comes
in distractedly from the right.)*
TESMAN   *(shrieking to* BRACK) . Shot herself! Shot herself in the temple!
  Think of it!
BRACK   *(half-collapsed in the easy-chair)* . But, merciful God! One doesn't
  do that kind of thing!

HEDDA GABLER: THE FAR SIDE OF TRAGEDY

PHILIP RODDMAN

I SAY, WE WILL HAVE NO MORE MARRIAGES; THOSE THAT ARE MARRIED AL-
READY, ALL BUT ONE, SHALL LIVE; THE REST WILL KEEP AS THEY ARE. *HAMLET,*
ACT III, SCENE 2.

Hamlet's anguished cry against the oldest of institutions, the family—
wrung from him not so much by Ophelia's duplicity as by his aversion
to the blood-drenched duties laid upon him as a son—reverberates savagely through the last plays of Ibsen, especially in *Ghosts, The Wild
Duck, Hedda Gabler,* and *The Master Builder.* The most challenging
theme in European literature, stated in *Hamlet* and prefigured in
Aeschylus's *Oresteia,* is the fatal clash between the tyrannical ideal of the
family and the highest ideal of civilization: self-fulfillment. To this theme
Ibsen imparts the force of physical fact and the sense of moral disaster.
His means are everyday objects placed like leitmotifs and a graphic realism that exposes incurable family diseases, horrifying conjugal relations,
fruitless sacrifices, and child murder. Ibsen, in contrast with Shakespeare's
Hamlet, condemns rather than evades the appeal of ghostly powers that
in the name of love and justice and truth batten on blood. The last plays
are the poetry of a dispossessed prince, bare, forked, true, resolved to
catch the conscience of a culture whose professed idealism disguises the
barbaric superstitions of a sacrosanct order based on race, money, and
tribal passions. Ibsen knows how false and servile idealisms and moral
philosophies can be. We now realize that the European Establishment,
convicted by Ibsen of fraud and bad faith, had been breeding the men
and forces that soon after Ibsen's death produced the slaughter of two
world wars and the inferno of the concentration camps.

Philip Roddman, a graduate of Columbia University, has written extensively on eighteenth-
and twentieth-century art. He is a professor of humanities at Pratt Institute where he teaches
the philosophical backgrounds of literature.

Ibsen is a Homeric moralist; that is, he holds that the human condition goes deeper than any ethical system. Like Homer, too, he respects any form of human life that knows itself sufficiently well to have the courage to be itself, even to choosing the kind of death it needs. It follows, therefore, that his leading characters appear in situations that are morally and physically fatal to them. Their contempt for the contagious lies of society drives them, in their self-quest, to commit mad and criminal acts that light up the far deadlier universal criminality of the powers that be. More than any other modern writer, Ibsen has liberated the age—if such disparate geniuses as Shaw, Joyce, and O'Neill may be called to witness—from the curse of power loved for its own sake, from power sentimentalized, and from the moral confusion of institutional values that are the blind side of religion. Job himself had to summon the Voice from the Whirlwind to achieve as much.

Ibsen's preoccupation, therefore, with the authentic life of the individual who is beset by the coercive powers of society—economic, legal, doctrinal, ritualistic—allies his heroes and heroines to those ambiguous criminals of Greek tragedy pursued by the buzzing Furies. Without a doubt the most impressive of the Ibsen criminals, and the most fascinating woman in the plays of the age, is Hedda Gabler, "various and sinuous and graceful . . . exasperated and infinitely perverse," in the words of Henry James. If her aristocratic appearance masks the raging sensibility of an Electra, the consuming fears of a Phaedra, and the death-dealing hand of a Medea, it somehow manages to point up—in that smug middle-class setting—her redeeming gift for examining and rejecting the lie in the heart. In the notes for the first draft of the play, Ibsen writes: "With Hedda, there is deep poetry at the bottom. But her surroundings frighten her." He adds that "the Play is about the 'insuperable,' the aspiration to and striving after something which goes against convention, against what is accepted into consciousness. . . ." And under a *Nota Bene,* followed by two exclamation points, Ibsen gives *one* of the keys to Hedda's character: "H[edda] tells that she too has always had a dread of children." Evidently Ibsen conceived Hedda from the very first in his own image, as one who condemns the institution upon which all society is based—the family. Hedda, who sees through the hypocrisy of conventions, also shares her creator's talent for recognizing the degraded symbols and mythologies with which Europe has kept its "metaphysics warm." While the hats, bedroom slippers, pistols, hair, fires, manuscripts in *Hedda Gabler*—all real things like the bodies they serve—exfoliate into multiple meanings with use, the Dionysian "vine leaves" and the athletic Dianas diminish into alcoholism and the brothel.

Hedda, Ibsen reveals, is the prisoner of a society which admires her and wishes to possess her for qualities which that same society fears and condemns. Men and women are drawn to her and feel revitalized by influences that they would never admit into their consciousness. Hedda's sex belies her nature. She has a youth's feeling for horses, pistols, wild carousals, and, especially, for the gratuitous act. Like Yeats's Irish Airman, "a lonely impulse of delight" drives her to associate herself with Eilert Lövborg's bohemianism and to aim her pistol at him when he mistakes her intentions. Hedda speaks true when she disclaims ever having desired Eilert's body. Her wish has always been for a friendship of equals, for a vital comradeship:

> HEDDA. But now I will confide something to you.
> EILERT. Well?
> HEDDA. The fact that I dared not shoot you down—
> EILERT. Yes!
> HEDDA. —that was not my most arrant cowardice—that evening.
> EILERT. Oh, Hedda! Hedda Gabler! Now I begin to see a hidden reason beneath our comradeship! You and I—! After all, it was your craving for life. . . .
> HEDDA. Take care! Believe nothing of the sort!

What Hedda certainly implies here, and what Eilert only half-understands, is that her craving for life was not a craving for sex but for a free association in the prison house of her society. The courage she lacked was the courage to point the pistol at herself upon discovering the impossibility of such an association. Judge Brack's astonished cry when she at last shoots herself—"But good God!—people don't do such things"— sums up her unique career as well as his conventional newspaper mind. She has dared to free herself, at the cost of her being, from a life that was never in her style.

As in Greek tragedy, the conflict in this play is between the natural and the free society, between Hedda Tesman and Hedda Gabler, with Hedda's dream of the free individual forever destroyed by Eilert's betrayal and defection. Aeschylus in the *Oresteia* makes the point, so well understood by Ibsen, that natural society in the guise of the family bears a heavy curse, which only reason and art can dispel. Aeschylus shows us Orestes, the slayer of his mother, saved from the Furies—who personify the irrational pull, the infectious guilt, of natural society—by the intercession of the goddess of reason, Athena, and by the lord of the muses, Apollo. Henceforth Orestes is to be his own man, the herald of a free society. Aristotle, who derives not only his aesthetic concept of the organic whole from the tragic poets but his ethical ideals as well, suggests that all men wish to live in societies where moral and spiritual affinities count for more than compulsory affections. The free man is one whose personal inclinations and choices overrule ties of blood as well as religious and racial loyalties. In short, Aristotle defines civilization as the distinction we come to make between the natural society into which each of us is born and the free society in which our spirit wishes to dwell. The goal of natural society is the caste system, known in politics as fascism and in psychology as the automatism of instinct, while the goal of free society is friendship devoid of utility, the fellowship of equals, associations for an ideal purpose—goals occasionally achieved on the college campus, on the athletic field, in intellectual unions, and on the aesthetic seacoasts of Bohemia. It may be said that all Greek tragedy, not only in *Oresteia,* is a criticism of natural society. And so, essentially, is *Hamlet,* with its company of strolling players, its band of pirates, its college chum, its young dramatist-prince—all in full flight from family ties and from the deceits of the family romance, all intent upon the repudiation of the idols of the tribe.

In *Hedda Gabler* Ibsen's gift for irony is nowhere more striking than in his decision to place a patrician woman in search of authenticity not only in the most suffocating of families, the Tesmans, but in an academic milieu as well, a milieu which by its very nature smothers the spontaneous, the irresponsible, the aesthetic, the untutored passions in what is known as official life: official duties, official interests, official knowledge, and, above all, official freedom. Hedda's despair when she catches her first glimpse of all that is in store for her is overpowering. She discovers in the short span of the play's progress that the unoriginal, well-meaning man she had married is really a climber, a bore, a sponger, who demands special privileges because of his self-imposed family obligations. Who crows like a cock when Hedda suggests that her pregnancy may have played a part in her destruction of his rival's lifework. Who invites an influential rake to cuckold him while he is advancing his career with an edition of Eilert's book, which he will certainly emasculate into an academic exercise. Her gorge rises at his every word and gesture. When Eilert Lövborg reappears, caught, as she correctly guesses, in the missionary coils of George Tesman's counterpart, the "stupid" and stubborn Thea, Hedda concentrates all her will upon releasing her sometime comrade from their common prison house, as she might release a bird from its cage. Within the day of his visit she learns that Eilert distrusts Thea, puts her off with sentimental compliments, leaves no addresses for her to follow him, and casts her aside mercilessly when he is about his own business, winning or losing. Thea's interest in Eilert expresses itself in the "I-am-my-brother's-keeper" form of possessiveness; Hedda's interest is in freeing him for whatever inspiration he is capable of. The "vine leaves" in his hair are to be his own, not hers. What she is testing is her power as a comrade, not as a *femme fatale,* not as a saintly muse, for both of which she has a Byronic contempt. Eilert's act of courage to be himself will prove to her the possibility of escape from the vulgar world that has trapped them.

When he has failed himself and she offers him the pistol, whose fellow is reserved for her, there is still, on her part, a desire to liberate him from his pathological state of self-ignorance and self-defeat. And in burning the "child" (Thea's word for the manuscript), Hedda strikes at the family romance which the plebeian Thea has imported into the transfigured world of Dionysian revelry. Hedda, a modern Medea, abhors the insolence of nature, and avenges her derogated dream by setting aflame the symbolic sprig of her mothering antagonist. After all, Eilert had been writing about the "moral doctrine of the future," when, presumably, "marriage and death and division" would no longer make barren our lives. Hedda's horror of pregnancy and childbirth is that of a woman who will not permit her body to be used as an instrument for propagation by the irrational automatism of nature; she sees herself living in a kingdom of ends. Her bitter disappointments in life have fortified her taste for sterility. Everywhere she sees the free spirit done to death by society and the wine of life alchemized into the venom of frustration. "The state is the curse of the individual. . . . Undermine the concept of the state; make voluntary participation and spiritual kinship the only essentials for a union," Ibsen wrote many years before the composition of *Hedda Gabler,* adding: "That's the beginning of a freedom worth something."

The anguish that pulses behind Hedda's outrageous acts at last detaches her from a world that is blind to what Ibsen's Maximus in *Emperor and Galilean* calls "the free necessity." To prove to us that Hedda's will to power is actually a will to freedom, Ibsen modulates the theme into a denial of the will to live, as, in her impetuous flight from a strifling environment, she is brought down by her own pistols.

Hedda Gabler is probably the subtlest of plays about a woman with a Socratic gift for self-understanding but without the means that should attend it. In her own psyche a struggle rages between the military and the explorative, between Sparta and Athens, just as in her social order there is a tug of war between barbaric custom and humane knowledge. The judgments of critics upon her criminal person have always been harsh. But a woman who so thoroughly scandalizes official morality has a great deal more to report about it than the Julias and Tesmans of this world.

Something savage, something insuperable, something inadmissible to consciousness haunts this play as it haunts, to take Ibsen at his word, his eponymous heroine. We may not accept our mysterious compact with Hedda, but we feel that it is there. Perhaps what we feel is that, like Hedda, we can neither absorb nor expend our dream energy, that we must perpetually see it dissipated by society, by life itself, perhaps by some fatal leak in the universe.

Hedda Gabler is a keystone in the arch of tragic drama. It is Shakespearean in its inspiration, Greek in its execution, and modern in its implications.

CHEKHOV

ANTON CHEKHOV (1860–1904), BORN IN THE SOUTHERN RUSSIAN CITY OF TAGANROG, SON OF AN UNSUCCESSFUL GROCER AND GRANDSON OF A SERF, PREPARED FOR HIS MEDICAL CAREER IN MOSCOW. HE BEGAN WRITING NEWSPAPER SKETCHES WHILE IN MEDICAL SCHOOL TO HELP PAY FOR HIS EDUCATION. BY THE TIME HE WAS TWENTY-SIX AND A PRACTICING PHYSICIAN, HIS SHORT STORIES HAD ALREADY WON HIM A REPUTATION. CHEKHOV'S KIND OF SHORT STORY, WHICH INFLUENCED TWO BRITISH MASTERS OF THE GENRE, KATHERINE MANSFIELD AND JAMES JOYCE, REMAINS TODAY THE CHIEF PROTOTYPE FOR SERIOUS SHORT FICTION. SIMILARLY, HIS PLAYS HAVE PROFOUNDLY AFFECTED THE ENTIRE COURSE OF TWENTIETH-CENTURY DRAMA. EVEN SHAW (IN *HEARTBREAK HOUSE*) TRIED HIS HAND AT A CHEKHOVIAN PLAY. NOT ONLY HAS HIS INFLUENCE PERVADED THE GREATER PART OF SERIOUS CONTEMPORARY THEATER, BUT HIS IMPACT IS CLEARLY SEEN IN THE "ABSURD" PLAYS OF SAMUEL BECKETT, EUGENE IONESCO, AND HAROLD PINTER. CHEKHOV'S FULL-LENGTH PLAYS INCLUDE *IVANOV* (1887); *THE SEA GULL* (1896); *UNCLE VANYA* (1899); *THE THREE SISTERS* (1901); AND *THE CHERRY ORCHARD* (1904).

Although the genius inherent in Chekov's plays has been acknowledged since their original productions in Moscow, for several decades they were supposed to lack a firm, coherent plot line. Audiences accustomed to well-made plays and to the relatively simple plots of a long-standing drama tradition had grown inattentive or perhaps even intellectually lazy. More recently we have learned to appreciate not only Chekhov's genius but his superb craftsmanship.

In reading *The Three Sisters,* we discover that what appears to be a succession of casually related incidents is, in fact, a skillfully contrived meshing of three love triangles. The resolutions of the three apparently unrelated love affairs in the play underscore the communal fate of an entire family, a communal fate which unifies everything that has gone before.

The Three Sisters has elements in common with Greek tragedy, though it is neither in mood or tone *tragic.* We see, for example, how throughout the play Olga fulfills the function of a Greek chorus. Also, the destinies of the central characters are affected by unseen but omnipresent forces: an overlord (the town mayor) ; a mentally disturbed woman; an infant.

As in so many plays, we find in *The Three Sisters* that the central conflict is between one group (the victims) and another group (the victimizers) . Can we, as we observe the struggle, identify what each of the two opposing forces represents in modern society?

Some critics consider the play to be the high-water mark of dramatic composition in our century. Although it is hazardous to place absolute valuations on works of art, could we evolve from *The Three Sisters* a set of dramatic criteria against which we can view the qualities of contemporary plays in our reading and play-going experiences?

THREE SISTERS

TRANSLATED BY ELISAVETA FEN

CHARACTERS

PROZOROV, *Andrey Serghyeevich*
NATASHA (*Natalia Ivanovna*), *his fiancée,*
  afterwards his wife
OLGA (*Olga Serghyeevna, Olia*) ⎫
MASHA (*Maria Serghyeevna*)   ⎬ *his sisters*
IRENA (*Irena Serghyeevna*)   ⎭
KOOLYGHIN, *Fiodor Ilyich, master at the*
  High School for boys, husband of Masha
VERSHININ, *Alexandr Ignatyevich, Lieuten-*
  ant-Colonel, Battery Commander
TOOZENBACH, *Nikolai Lvovich, Baron,*
  Lieutenant in the Army
SOLIONY, *Vassily Vassilich, Captain*
CHEBUTYKIN, *Ivan Romanych, Army Doctor*
FEDOTIK, *Aleksey Petrovich, Second*
  Lieutenant

RODÉ, *Vladimir Karlovich, Second Lieutenant*
FERAPONT (*Ferapont Spiridonych*), *an old*
  porter from the County Office
ANFISA, *The Prozorovs' former nurse, an*
  old woman of 80

SCENE: *The action takes place in a country town.*

ACT I

A drawing-room in the Prozorovs' house; it is separated from a large ballroom [1] *at the back by a row of columns. It is midday; there is cheerful sunshine outside. In the ballroom the table is being laid for lunch.* OLGA, *wearing the regulation dark-blue dress of a secondary school mistress, is correcting her pupils' work, standing or walking about as she does so.* MASHA, *in a black dress, is sitting reading a book, her hat on her lap.* IRENA, *in white, stands lost in thought.*

OLGA. It's exactly a year ago that Father died, isn't it? This very day, the fifth of May—your Saint's day, Irena. I remember it was very cold and it was snowing. I felt then as if I should never survive his death; and you had fainted and were lying quite still, as if you were dead.

[1] A large room, sparsely furnished, used for receptions and dances in Russian houses.

And now—a year's gone by, and we talk about it so easily. You're
wearing white, and your face is positively radiant. . . .
(*A clock strikes twelve.*)
The clock struck twelve then, too. (*A pause.*) I remember when Father
was being taken to the cemetery there was a military band, and a salute
with rifle fire. That was because he was a general, in command of a
brigade. And yet there weren't many people at the funeral. Of course,
it was raining hard, raining and snowing.

IRENA.   Need we bring up all these memories?

(BARON TOOZENBACH, CHEBUTYKIN *and* SOLIONY *appear behind the columns
by the table in the ballroom.*)

OLGA.   It's so warm to-day that we can keep the windows wide open, and
yet there aren't any leaves showing on the birch trees. Father was made
a brigadier eleven years ago, and then he left Moscow and took us with
him. I remember so well how everything in Moscow was in blossom by
now, everything was soaked in sunlight and warmth. Eleven years have
gone by, yet I remember everything about it, as if we'd only left yesterday. Oh, Heavens! When I woke up this morning and saw this flood
of sunshine, all this spring sunshine, I felt so moved and so happy! I
felt such a longing to get back home to Moscow!

CHEBUTYKIN   (*to* TOOZENBACH) . The devil you have!

TOOZENBACH.   It's nonsense, I agree.

MASHA   (*absorbed in her book, whistles a tune under her breath*) .

OLGA.   Masha, do stop whistling! How can you? (*A pause.*) I suppose I
must get this continual headache because I have to go to school every
day and go on teaching right into the evening. I seem to have the
thoughts of someone quite old. Honestly, I've been feeling as if my
strength and youth were running out of me drop by drop, day after
day. Day after day, all these four years that I've been working at the
school. . . . I just have one longing and it seems to grow stronger and
stronger. . . .

IRENA.   If only we could go back to Moscow! Sell the house, finish with
our life here, and go back to Moscow.

OLGA.   Yes, Moscow! As soon as we possibly can.

(CHEBUTYKIN *and* TOOZENBACH *laugh.*)

IRENA.   I suppose Andrey will soon get a professorship. He isn't likely to
go on living here. The only problem is our poor Masha.

OLGA.   Masha can come and stay the whole summer with us every year
in Moscow.

MASHA   (*whistles a tune under her breath*) .

IRENA.   Everything will settle itself, with God's help. (*Looks through
the window.*) What lovely weather it is to-day! Really I don't know
why there's such joy in my heart. I remembered this morning that it

was my Saint's day, and suddenly I felt so happy, and I thought of the time when we were children, and Mother was still alive. And then such wonderful thoughts came to me, such wonderful stirring thoughts!

OLGA. You're so lovely to-day, you really do look most attractive. Masha looks pretty to-day, too. Andrey could be good-looking, but he's grown so stout. It doesn't suit him. As for me, I've just aged and grown a lot thinner. I suppose it's through getting so irritated with the girls at school. But to-day I'm at home, I'm free, and my headache's gone, and I feel much younger than I did yesterday. I'm only twenty-eight, after all. . . . I suppose everything that God wills must be right and good, but I can't help thinking sometimes that if I'd got married and stayed at home, it would have been a better thing for me. (*A pause.*) I would have been very fond of my husband.

TOOZENBACH (*to* SOLIONY). Really, you talk such a lot of nonsense, I'm tired of listening to you. (*Comes into the drawing-room.*) I forgot to tell you: Vershinin, our new battery commander, is going to call on you to-day. (*Sits down by the piano.*)

OLGA. I'm very glad to hear it.

IRENA. Is he old?

TOOZENBACH. No, not particularly. Forty, forty-five at the most. (*Plays quietly.*) He seems a nice fellow. Certainly not a fool. His only weakness is that he talks too much.

IRENA. Is he interesting?

TOOZENBACH. He's all right, only he's got a wife, a mother-in-law and two little girls. What's more, she's his second wife. He calls on everybody and tells them that he's got a wife and two little girls. He'll tell you about it, too, I'm sure of that. His wife seems to be a bit soft in the head. She wears a long plait like a girl, she is always philosophizing and talking in high-flown language, and then she often tries to commit suicide, apparently just to annoy her husband. I would have run away from a wife like that years ago, but he puts up with it, and just grumbles about it.

SOLIONY (*enters the drawing-room with* CHEBUTYKIN). Now I can only lift sixty pounds with one hand, but with two I can lift two hundred pounds, or even two hundred and forty. So I conclude from that that two men are not just twice as strong as one, but three times as strong, if not more.

CHEBUTYKIN (*reads the paper as he comes in*). Here's a recipe for falling hair . . . two ounces of naphthaline, half-a-bottle of methylated spirit . . . dissolve and apply once a day. . . . (*Writes it down in a notebook.*) Must make a note of it. (*To* SOLIONY.) Well, as I was trying to explain to you, you cork the bottle and pass a glass tube through the cork. Then you take a pinch of ordinary powdered alum, and . . .

IRENA. Ivan Romanych, dear Ivan Romanych!

CHEBUTYKIN. What is it, my child, what is it?

IRENA. Tell me, why is it I'm so happy to-day? Just as if I were sailing along in a boat with big white sails, and above me the wide, blue sky, and in the sky great white birds floating around?

CHEBUTYKIN (*kisses both her hands, tenderly*) : My little white bird!

IRENA. You know, when I woke up this morning, and after I'd got up and washed, I suddenly felt as if everything in the world had become clear to me, and I knew the way I ought to live. I know it all now, my dear Ivan Romanych. Man must work by the sweat of his brow whatever his class, and that should make up the whole meaning and purpose of his life and happiness and contentment. Oh, how good it must be to be a workman, getting up with the sun and breaking stones by the roadside—or a shepherd—or a schoolmaster teaching the children—or an engine-driver on the railway. Good Heavens! it's better to be a mere ox or horse, and work, than the sort of young woman who wakes up at twelve, and drinks her coffee in bed, and then takes two hours dressing. . . . How dreadful! You know how you long for a cool drink in hot weather? Well, that's the way I long for work. And if I don't get up early from now on and really work, you can refuse to be friends with me any more, Ivan Romanych.

CHEBUTYKIN (*tenderly*) . So I will, so I will. . . .

OLGA. Father taught us to get up at seven o'clock and so Irena always wakes up at seven—but then she stays in bed till at least nine, thinking about something or other. And with such a serious expression on her face, too! (*Laughs.*)

IRENA. You think it's strange when I look serious because you always think of me as a little girl. I'm twenty, you know!

TOOZENBACH. All this longing for work. . . . Heavens! how well I can understand it! I've never done a stroke of work in my life. I was born in Petersburg, an unfriendly, idle city—born into a family where work and worries were simply unknown. I remember a valet pulling off my boots for me when I came home from the cadet school. . . . I grumbled at the way he did it, and my mother looked on in admiration. She was quite surprised when other people looked at me in any other way. I was so carefully protected from work! But I doubt whether they succeeded in protecting me for good and all—yes, I doubt it very much! The time's come: there's a terrific thunder-cloud advancing upon us, a mighty storm is coming to freshen us up! Yes, it's coming all right, it's quite near already, and it's going to blow away all this idleness and indifference, and prejudice against work, this rot of boredom that our society is suffering from. I'm going to work, and in twenty-five or thirty years' time every man and woman will be working. Every one of us!

CHEBUTYKIN. I'm not going to work.

TOOZENBACH. You don't count.

SOLIONY. In twenty-five years' time you won't be alive, thank goodness. In a couple of years you'll die from a stroke—or I'll lose my temper with you and put a bullet in your head, my good fellow. (*Takes a scent bottle from his pocket and sprinkles the scent over his chest and hands.*)

CHEBUTYKIN (*laughs*). It's quite true that I never have done any work. Not a stroke since I left the university. I haven't even read a book, only newspapers. (*Takes another newspaper out of his pocket.*) For instance, here. . . . I know from the paper that there was a person called Dobroliubov, but what he wrote about I've not the faintest idea. . . . God alone knows. . . . (*Someone knocks on the floor from downstairs.*) There! They're calling me to come down: there's someone come to see me. I'll be back in a moment. . . . (*Goes out hurriedly, stroking his beard.*)

IRENA. He's up to one of his little games.

TOOZENBACH. Yes. He looked very solemn as he left. He's obviously going to give you a present.

IRENA. I do dislike that sort of thing. . . .

OLGA. Yes, isn't it dreadful? He's always doing something silly.

MASHA. "A green oak grows by a curving shore, And round that oak hangs a golden chain" . . . (*Gets up as she sings under her breath.*)

OLGA. You're sad to-day, Masha.

MASHA (*puts on her hat, singing*).

OLGA. Where are you going?

MASHA. Home.

IRENA. What a strange thing to do.

TOOZENBACH. What! Going away from your sister's party?

MASHA. What does it matter? I'll be back this evening. Good-bye, my darling. (*Kisses* IRENA.) And once again—I wish you all the happiness in the world. In the old days when Father was alive we used to have thirty or forty officers at our parties. What gay parties we had! And to-day—what have we got to-day? A man and a half, and the place is as quiet as a tomb. I'm going home. I'm depressed to-day, I'm sad, so don't listen to me. (*Laughs through her tears.*) We'll have a talk later, but good-bye for now, my dear. I'll go somewhere or other. . . .

IRENA (*displeased*). Really, you are a . . .

OLGA (*tearfully*). I understand you, Masha.

SOLIONY. If a man starts philosophizing, you call that philosophy, or possibly just sophistry, but if a woman or a couple of women start philosophizing you call that . . . what would you call it, now? Ask me another!

MASHA.   What are you talking about? You are a disconcerting person!
SOLIONY.   Nothing.

> "He had no time to say 'Oh, oh!'
> Before that bear had struck him low" . . .

(*A pause.*)

MASHA   (*to* OLGA, *crossly*). Do stop snivelling!

(*Enter* ANFISA *and* FERAPONT, *the latter carrying a large cake.*)

ANFISA.   Come along, my dear, this way. Come in, your boots are quite
clean. (*To* IRENA.) A cake from Protopopov, at the Council Office.

IRENA.   Thank you. Tell him I'm very grateful to him. (*Takes the cake.*)

FERAPONT.   What's that?

IRENA   (*louder*). Tell him I sent my thanks.

OLGA.   Nanny, will you give him a piece of cake? Go along, Ferapont,
they'll give you some cake.

FERAPONT.   What's that?

ANFISA.   Come along with me, Ferapont Spiridonych, my dear. Come
along. (*Goes out with* FERAPONT.)

MASHA.   I don't like that Protopopov fellow. Mihail Potapych, or Ivan-
ych, or whatever it is. It's best not to invite him here.

IRENA.   I haven't invited him.

MASHA.   Thank goodness.

(*Enter* CHEBUTYKIN, *followed by a soldier carrying a silver samovar. Murmurs of astonishment and displeasure.*)

OLGA   (*covering her face with her hands*). A samovar! But this is dreadful! (*Goes through to the ballroom and stands by the table.*)

IRENA.   My dear Ivan Romanych, what are you thinking about?

TOOZENBACH   (*laughs*). Didn't I tell you?

MASHA.   Ivan Romanych, you really ought to be ashamed of yourself!

CHEBUTYKIN.   My dear, sweet girls, I've no one in the world but you.
You're dearer to me than anything in the world! I'm nearly sixty, I'm
an old man, a lonely, utterly unimportant old man. The only thing
that's worth anything in me is my love for you, and if it weren't for
you, really I would have been dead long ago. (*To* IRENA.) My dear, my
sweet little girl, haven't I known you since the very day you were born?
Didn't I carry you about in my arms? . . . didn't I love your dear
mother?

IRENA.   But why do you get such expensive presents?

CHEBUTYKIN   (*tearfully and crossly*). Expensive presents! . . . Get along
with you! (*To the* ORDERLY.) Put the samovar over there. (*Mimics*
IRENA.) Expensive presents!

(*The* ORDERLY *takes the samovar to the ballroom.*)

ANFISA   (*crosses the drawing-room*). My dears, there's a strange colonel
just arrived. He's taken off his coat and he's coming up now. Irenushka,

do be nice and polite to him, won't you? (*In the doorway.*) And it's high time we had lunch, too. . . . Oh, dear! (*Goes out.*)

TOOZENBACH. It's Vershinin, I suppose.

(*Enter* VERSHININ.)

TOOZENBACH. Lieutenant-Colonel Vershinin!

VERSHININ (*to* MASHA *and* IRENA). Allow me to introduce myself— Lieutenant-Colonel Vershinin. I'm so glad, so very glad to be here at last. How you've changed! Dear, dear, how you've changed!

IRENA. Please, do sit down. We're very pleased to see you, I'm sure.

VERSHININ (*gaily*). I'm so glad to see you, so glad! But there were three of you, weren't there?—three sisters. I remember there were three little girls. I don't remember their faces, but I knew your father, Colonel Prozorov, and I remember he had three little girls. Oh, yes, I saw them myself. I remember them quite well. How time flies! Dear, dear, how it flies!

TOOZENBACH. Alexandr Ignatyevich comes from Moscow.

IRENA. From Moscow? You come from Moscow?

VERSHININ. Yes, from Moscow. Your father was a battery commander there, and I was an officer in the same brigade. (*To* MASHA.) I seem to remember your face a little.

MASHA. I don't remember you at all.

IRENA. Olia, Olia! (*Calls toward the ballroom.*) Olia, do come!

(OLGA *enters from the ballroom.*)

IRENA. It seems that Lieutenant-Colonel Vershinin comes from Moscow.

VERSHININ. You must be Olga Serghyeevna, the eldest. And you are Maria. . . . And you are Irena, the youngest. . . .

OLGA. You come from Moscow?

VERSHININ. Yes, I studied in Moscow and entered the service there. I stayed there quite a long time, but then I was put in charge of a battery here—so I moved out here, you see. I don't really remember you, you know, I only remember that there were three sisters. I remember your father, though, I remember him very well. All I need to do is to close my eyes and I can see him standing there as if he were alive. I used to visit you in Moscow.

OLGA. I thought I remembered everybody and yet . . .

VERSHININ. My Christian names are Alexandr Ignatyevich.

IRENA. Alexandr Ignatyevich, and you come from Moscow! Well, what a surprise!

OLGA. We're going to live there, you know.

IRENA. We hope to be there by the autumn. It's our home town, we were born there. . . . In Staraya Basmannaya Street.

(*Both laugh happily.*)

MASHA. Fancy meeting a fellow townsman so unexpectedly! (*Eagerly.*)

I remember now. Do you remember, Olga, there was someone they used to call "the lovesick Major"? You were a Lieutenant then, weren't you, and you were in love with someone or other, and everyone used to tease you about it. They called you "Major" for some reason or other.

VERSHININ   (*laughs*). That's it, that's it. . . . "The lovesick Major," that's what they called me.

MASHA.   In those days you only had a moustache. . . . Oh, dear, how much older you look! (*Tearfully.*) How much older!

VERSHININ.   Yes, I was still a young man in the days when they called me "the lovesick Major." I was in love then. It's different now.

OLGA.   But you haven't got a single grey hair! You've aged, yes, but you're certainly not an old man.

VERSHININ.   Nevertheless, I'm turned forty-two. Is it long since you left Moscow?

IRENA.   Eleven years. Now what are you crying for, Masha, you funny girl? . . . (*Tearfully.*) You'll make me cry, too.

MASHA.   I'm not crying. What was the street you lived in?

VERSHININ.   In the Staraya Basmannaya.

OLGA.   We did, too.

VERSHININ.   At one time I lived in the Niemietzkaya Street. I used to walk from there to the Krasny Barracks, and I remember there was such a gloomy bridge I had to cross. I used to hear the noise of the water rushing under it. I remember how lonely and sad I felt there. (*A pause.*) But what a magnificently wide river you have here! It's a marvellous river!

OLGA.   Yes, but this is a cold place. It's cold here, and there are too many mosquitoes.

VERSHININ.   Really? I should have said you had a really good healthy climate here, a real Russian climate. Forest, river . . . birch-trees, too. The dear, unpretentious birch-trees—I love them more than any of the other trees. It's nice living here. But there's one rather strange thing, the station is fifteen miles from the town. And no one knows why.

SOLIONY.   I know why it is. (*Everyone looks at him.*) Because if the station were nearer, it wouldn't be so far away, and as it is so far away, it can't be nearer. (*An awkward silence.*)

TOOZENBACH.   You like your little joke, Vassily Vassilich.

OLGA.   I'm sure I remember you now. I know I do.

VERSHININ.   I knew your mother.

CHEBUTYKIN.   She was a good woman, God bless her memory!

IRENA.   Mamma was buried in Moscow.

OLGA.   At the convent of Novo-Dievichye.

MASHA.   You know, I'm even beginning to forget what she looked like.

I suppose people will lose all memory of us in just the same way. We'll be forgotten.

VERSHININ. Yes, we shall all be forgotten. Such is our fate, and we can't do anything about it. And all the things that seem serious, important and full of meaning to us now will be forgotten one day—or anyway they won't seem important any more. (*A pause.*) It's strange to think that we're utterly unable to tell what will be regarded as great and important in the future and what will be thought of as just paltry and ridiculous. Didn't the great discoveries of Copernicus—or of Columbus, if you like—appear useless and unimportant to begin with?—whereas some rubbish, written up by an eccentric fool, was regarded as a revelation of great truth? It may well be that in time to come the life we live to-day will seem strange and uncomfortable and stupid and not too clean, either, and perhaps even wicked. . . .

TOOZENBACH. Who can tell? It's just as possible that future generations will think that we lived our lives on a very high plane and remember us with respect. After all, we no longer have tortures and public executions and invasions, though there's still a great deal of suffering!

SOLIONY (*in a high-pitched voice as if calling to chickens*). Cluck, cluck, cluck! There's nothing our good Baron loves as much as a nice bit of philosophizing.

TOOZENBACH. Vassily Vassilich, will you kindly leave me alone? (*Moves to another chair.*) It's becoming tiresome.

SOLIONY (*as before*). Cluck, cluck, cluck! . . .

TOOZENBACH (*to* VERSHININ). The suffering that we see around us—and there's so much of it—itself proves that our society has at least achieved a level of morality which is higher. . . .

VERSHININ. Yes, yes, of course.

CHEBUTYKIN. You said just now, Baron, that our age will be called great; but people are small all the same. . . . (*Gets up.*) Look how small I am.

(*A violin is played off stage.*)

MASHA. That's Andrey playing the violin; he's our brother, you know.

IRENA. We've got quite a clever brother. . . . We're expecting him to be a professor. Papa was a military man, but Andrey chose an academic career.

OLGA. We've been teasing him to-day. We think he's in love, just a little.

IRENA. With a girl who lives down here. She'll be calling in to-day most likely.

MASHA. The way she dresses herself is awful! It's not that her clothes are just ugly and old-fashioned, they're simply pathetic. She'll put on some weird-looking, bright yellow skirt with a crude sort of fringe affair, and then a red blouse to go with it. And her cheeks look as though they've been scrubbed, they're so shiny! Andrey's not in love with her—I can't believe it; after all, he has got some taste. I think he's playing the fool, just to annoy us. I heard yesterday that she's going to get married to Protopopov, the chairman of the local council. I thought it was an excellent idea. (*Calls through the side door.*) Andrey, come here, will you? Just for a moment, dear.

(*Enter* ANDREY.)

OLGA.   This is my brother, Andrey Serghyeevich.

VERSHININ.   Vershinin.

ANDREY.   Prozorov. (*Wipes the perspiration from his face.*) I believe you've been appointed battery commander here?

OLGA.   What do you think, dear? Alexandr Ignatyevich comes from Moscow.

ANDREY.   Do you, really? Congratulations! You'll get no peace from my sisters now.

VERSHININ.   I'm afraid your sisters must be getting tired of me already.

IRENA.   Just look, Andrey gave me this little picture frame to-day. (*Shows him the frame.*) He made it himself.

VERSHININ   (*looks at the frame, not knowing what to say*) : Yes, it's . . . it's very nice indeed. . . .

IRENA.   Do you see that little frame over the piano? He made that one, too.

(ANDREY *waves his hand impatiently and walks off.*)

OLGA.   He's awfully clever, and he plays the violin, and he makes all sorts of things, too. In fact, he's very gifted all round. Andrey, please, don't go. He's got such a bad habit—always going off like this. Come here!

(MASHA *and* IRENA *take him by the arms and lead him back laughing.*)

MASHA.   Now just you come here!

ANDREY.   Do leave me alone, please do!

MASHA.   You are a silly! They used to call Alexandr Ignatyevich "the lovesick Major," and he didn't get annoyed.

VERSHININ.   Not in the least.

MASHA.   I feel like calling you a "lovesick fiddler."

IRENA.   Or a "lovesick professor."

OLGA.   He's fallen in love! Our Andriusha's in love!

IRENA   (*clapping her hands*) . Three cheers for Andriusha! Andriusha's in love!

CHEBUTYKIN   (*comes up behind* ANDREY *and puts his arms round his waist*) . "Nature created us for love alone." . . . (*Laughs loudly, still holding his paper in his hand.*)

ANDREY.   That's enough of it, that's enough. . . . (*Wipes his face.*) I couldn't get to sleep all night, and I'm not feeling too grand just now. I read till four o'clock, and then I went to bed, but nothing happened. I kept thinking about one thing and another . . . and it gets light so early; the sun just pours into my room. I'd like to translate a book from the English while I'm here during the summer.

VERSHININ.   You read English, then?

ANDREY.   Yes. My father—God bless his memory—used to simply wear us out with learning. It sounds silly, I know, but I must confess that since he died I've begun to grow stout, as if I'd been physically relieved of the strain. I've grown quite stout in a year. Yes, thanks to Father, my sisters and I know French and German and English, and Irena here knows Italian, too. But what an effort it all cost us!

MASHA.   Knowing three languages in a town like this is an unnecessary luxury. In fact, not even a luxury, but just a sort of useless encumbrance . . . it's rather like having a sixth finger on your hand. We know a lot of stuff that's just useless.

VERSHININ.   Really! (*Laughs.*) You know a lot of stuff that's useless! It seems to me that there's no place on earth, however dull and depressing it may be, where intelligence and education can be useless. Let us suppose that among the hundred thousand people in this town, all of them, no doubt, very backward and uncultured, there are just three people like yourself. Obviously, you can't hope to triumph over all the mass of ignorance around you; as your life goes by, you'll have to keep giving in little by little until you get lost in the crowd, in the hundred thousand. Life will swallow you up, but you'll not quite disappear, you'll make some impression on it. After you've gone, perhaps six more people like you will turn up, then twelve, and so on, until in the end most people will have become like you. So in two or three hundred years like on this old earth of ours will have become marvellously beautiful. Man longs for a life like that, and if it isn't here yet, he must imagine it, wait for it, dream about it, prepare for it, he must know and see more than his father and his grandfather did. (*Laughs.*) And you're complaining because you know a lot of stuff that's useless.

MASHA   (*takes off her hat*) . I'll be staying to lunch.

IRENA   (*with a sigh*) . Really, someone should have written all that down.

(ANDREY *has left the room, unnoticed.*)

TOOZENBACH.   You say that in time to come life will be marvellously beautiful. That's probably true. But in order to share in it now, at a distance so to speak, we must prepare for it and work for it.

VERSHININ   (*gets up*) . Yes. . . . What a lot of flowers you've got here! (*Looks round.*) And what a marvellous house! I do envy you! All my life I seem to have been pigging it in small flats, with two chairs and a sofa and a stove which always smokes. It's the flowers that I've missed in my life, flowers like these! . . . (*Rubs his hands.*) Oh, well, never mind!

TOOZENBACH.   Yes, we must work. I suppose you're thinking I'm a sentimental German. But I assure you I'm not—I'm Russian. I don't speak a word of German. My father was brought up in the Greek Orthodox faith. (*A pause.*)

VERSHININ   (*walks up and down the room*). You know, I often wonder what it would be like if you could start your life over again—deliberately, I mean, consciously. . . . Suppose you could put aside the life you'd lived already, as though it was just a sort of rough draft, and then start another one like a fair copy. If that happened, I think the thing you'd want most of all would be not to repeat yourself. You'd try at least to create a new environment for yourself, a flat like this one, for instance, with some flowers and plenty of light. . . . I have a wife, you know, and two little girls; and my wife's not very well, and all that. . . . Well, if I had to start my life all over again, I wouldn't marry. . . . No, no!

(*Enter* KOOLYGHIN, *in the uniform of a teacher.*)

KOOLYGHIN   (*approaches* IRENA). Congratulations, dear sister—from the bottom of my heart, congratulations on your Saint's day. I wish you good health and everything a girl of your age ought to have! And allow me to present you with this little book. . . . (*Hands her a book.*) It's the history of our school covering the whole fifty years of its existence. I wrote it myself. Quite a trifle, of course—I wrote it in my spare time when I had nothing better to do—but I hope you'll read it nevertheless. Good morning to you all! (*To* VERSHININ.) Allow me to introduce myself. Koolyghin's the name; I'm a master at the secondary school here. And a town councillor. (*To* IRENA.) You'll find a list in the book of all the pupils who have completed their studies at our school during the last fifty years. *Feci quod potui, faciant meliora potentes.* (*Kisses* MASHA.)

IRENA.   But you gave me this book last Easter!

KOOLYGHIN   (*laughs*). Did I really? In that case, give it me back—or no, better give it to the Colonel. Please do take it, Colonel. Maybe you'll read it some time when you've nothing better to do.

VERSHININ.   Thank you very much. (*Prepares to leave.*) I'm so very glad to have made your acquaintance. . . .

OLGA.   You aren't going are you? . . . Really, you mustn't.

IRENA.   But you'll stay and have lunch with us! Please do.

OLGA.   Please do.

VERSHININ   (*bows*). I see I've intruded on your Saint's day party. I didn't know. Forgive me for not offering you my congratulations.

(*Goes into the ballroom with* OLGA.)

KOOLYGHIN. To-day is Sunday, my friends, a day of rest; let us rest and enjoy it, each according to his age and position in life! We shall have to roll up the carpets and put them away till the winter. . . . We must remember to put some naphthaline on them, or Persian powder. . . . The Romans enjoyed good health because they knew how to work *and* how to rest. They had *mens sana in corpore sano.* Their life had a definite shape, a form. . . . The director of the school says that the most important thing about life is form. . . . A thing that loses its form is finished—that's just as true of our ordinary, everyday lives. (*Takes* MASHA *by the waist and laughs.*) Masha loves me. My wife loves me. Yes, and the curtains will have to be put away with the carpets, too. . . . I'm cheerful to-day, I'm in quite excellent spirits. . . . Masha, we're invited to the director's at four o'clock to-day. A country walk has been arranged for the teachers and their families.

MASHA. I'm not going.

KOOLYGHIN (*distressed*). Masha, darling, why not?

MASHA. I'll tell you later. . . . (*Crossly.*) All right, I'll come, only leave me alone now. . . . (*Walks off.*)

KOOLYGHIN. And after the walk we shall all spend the evening at the director's house. In spite of weak health, that man is certainly sparing no pains to be sociable. A first-rate, thoroughly enlightened man! A most excellent person! After the conference yesterday he said to me: I'm tired, Fiodor Ilyich. I'm tired!" (*Looks at the clock, then at his watch.*) Your clock is seven minutes fast. Yes, "I'm tired," he said.

(*The sound of the violin is heard off stage.*)

OLGA. Will you all come and sit down, please! Lunch is ready. There's a pie.

KOOLYGHIN. Ah, Olga, my dear girl! Last night I worked up to eleven o'clock, and I felt tired, but to-day I'm quite happy. (*Goes to the table in the ballroom.*) My dear Olga!

CHEBUTYKIN (*puts the newspaper in his pocket and combs his beard*). A pie? Excellent!

MASHA (*sternly to* CHEBUTYKIN). Remember, you mustn't take anything to drink to-day. Do you hear? It's bad for you.

CHEBUTYKIN. Never mind. I've got over that weakness long ago! I haven't done any heavy drinking for two years. (*Impatiently.*) Anyway, my dear, what does it matter?

MASHA. All the same, don't you dare to drink anything. Mind you don't now! (*Crossly, but taking care that her husband does not hear.*) So now I've got to spend another of those damnably boring evenings at the director's!

TOOZENBACH. I wouldn't go if I were you, and that's that.

CHEBUTYKIN. Don't you go, my dear.

MASHA. Don't go, indeed! Oh, what a damnable life! It's intolerable. . . . (*Goes into the ballroom.*)

CHEBUTYKIN (*follows her*). Well, well! . . .

SOLIONY (*as he passes* TOOZENBACH *on the way to the ballroom*). Cluck, cluck, cluck!

TOOZENBACH. Do stop it, Vassily Vassilich. I've really had enough of it. . . .

SOLIONY. Cluck, cluck, cluck! . . .

KOOLYGHIN (*gaily*). Your health, Colonel! I'm a schoolmaster . . . and I'm quite one of the family here, as it were. I'm Masha's husband. She's got a sweet nature, such a very sweet nature!

VERSHININ. I think I'll have a little of this dark vodka. (*Drinks.*) Your health! (*To* OLGA.) I do feel so happy with you people!

(*Only* IRENA *and* TOOZENBACH *remain in the drawing-room.*)

IRENA. Masha's a bit out of humour to-day. You know, she got married when she was eighteen, and then her husband seemed the cleverest man in the world to her. It's different now. He's the kindest of men, but not the cleverest.

OLGA (*impatiently*). Andrey, will you please come?

ANDREY (*off stage*). Just coming. (*Enters and goes to the table.*)

TOOZENBACH. What are you thinking about?

IRENA. Oh, nothing special. You know, I don't like this man Soliony, I'm quite afraid of him. Whenever he opens his mouth he says something silly.

TOOZENBACH. He's a strange fellow. I'm sorry for him, even though he irritates me. In fact, I feel more sorry for him than irritated. I think he's shy. When he's alone with me, he can be quite sensible and friendly, but in company he's offensive and bullying. Don't go over there just yet, let them get settled down at the table. Let me stay beside you for a bit. Tell me what you're thinking about. (*A pause.*) You're twenty . . . and I'm not thirty yet myself. What years and years we still have ahead of us, a whole long succession of years, all full of my love for you!

IRENA. Don't talk to me about love, Nikolai Lvovich.

TOOZENBACH (*not listening*). Oh, I long so passionately for life, I long to work and strive so much, and all this longing is somehow mingled with my love for you, Irena. And just because you happen to be beautiful life appears beautiful to me! What are you thinking about?

IRENA. You say that life is beautiful. Maybe it is—but what if it only seems to be beautiful? Our lives, I mean the lives of us three sisters, haven't been beautiful up to now. The truth is that life has been sti-fling us, like weeds in a garden. I'm afraid I'm crying. . . . So unnecessary. . . . (*Quickly dries her eyes and smiles.*) We must work, work! The reason we feel depressed and take such a gloomy view of life is that we've never known what it is to make a real effort. We're the children of parents who despised work. . . .

(*Enter* NATALIA IVANOVNA. *She is wearing a pink dress with a green belt.*)

NATASHA. They've gone in to lunch already. . . . I'm late. . . . (*Glances at herself in a mirror, adjusts her dress.*) My hair seems to be all right. . . . (*Catches sight of* IRENA.) My dear Irena Serghyeevna, congratulations! (*Gives her a vigorous and prolonged kiss.*) You've got such a lot of visitors. . . . I feel quite shy. . . . How do you do, Baron?

OLGA (*enters the drawing-room*). Oh, there you are, Natalia Ivanovna! How are you, my dear?

(*They kiss each other.*)

NATASHA. Congratulations! You've such a lot of people here, I feel dreadfully shy. . . .

OLGA. It's all right, they're all old friends. (*Alarmed, dropping her voice.*) You've got a green belt on! My dear, that's surely a mistake!

NATASHA. Why, is it a bad omen, or what?

OLGA. No, but it just doesn't go with your dress . . . it looks so strange. . . .

NATASHA (*tearfully*). Really? But it isn't really green, you know, it's a sort of dull colour. . . . (*Follows* OLGA *to the ballroom.*)

(*All are now seated at the table; the drawing-room is empty.*)

KOOLYGHIN. Irena, you know, I do wish you'd find yourself a good husband. In my view it's high time you got married.

CHEBUTYKIN. You ought to get yourself a nice little husband, too, Natalia Ivanovna.

KOOLYGHIN. Natalia Ivanovna already has a husband in view.

MASHA (*strikes her plate with her fork*). A glass of wine for me, please! Three cheers for our jolly old life! We keep our end up, we do!

KOOLYGHIN. Masha, you won't get more than five out of ten for good conduct!

VERSHININ. I say, this liqueur's very nice. What is it made of?

SOLIONY. Black beetles!

IRENA. Ugh! ugh! How disgusting!

OLGA. We're having roast turkey for dinner to-night, and then apple tart. Thank goodness, I'll be here all day to-day . . . this evening, too. You must all come this evening.

VERSHININ. May I come in the evening, too?

IRENA. Yes, please do.

NATASHA. They don't stand on ceremony here.

CHEBUTYKIN.   "Nature created us for love alone." . . . (*Laughs.*)

ANDREY   (*crossly*). Will you stop it, please? Aren't you tired of it yet?
(FEDOTIK *and* RODÉ *come in with a large basket of flowers.*)

FEDOTIK.   Just look here, they're having lunch already!

RODÉ   (*in a loud voice*). Having their lunch? So they are, they're having
lunch already.

FEDOTIK.   Wait half a minute. (*Takes a snapshot.*) One! Just one minute more! . . . (*Takes another snapshot.*) Two! All over now.
(*They pick up the basket and go into the ballroom where they are greeted
uproariously.*)

RODÉ   (*loudly*). Congratulations, Irena Serghyeevna! I wish you all the
best, everything you'd wish for yourself! Gorgeous weather to-day, absolutely marvellous. I've been out walking the whole morning with the
boys. You do know that I teach gym at the high school, don't you? . . .

FEDOTIK.   You may move now, Irena Serghyeevna, that is, if you want
to. (*Takes a snapshot.*) You do look attractive to-day. (*Takes a top out
of his pocket.*) By the way, look at this top. It's got a wonderful hum.

IRENA.   What a sweet little thing!

MASHA.   "A green oak grows by a curving shore, And round that oak
hangs a golden chain." . . . A green chain around that oak. . . . (*Pee-
vishly.*) Why do I keep on saying that? Those lines have been worrying
me all day long!

KOOLYGHIN.   Do you know, we're thirteen at table?

RODÉ   (*loudly*). You don't really believe in these old superstitions, do
you? (*Laughter.*)

KOOLYGHIN.   When thirteen people sit down to table, it means that some
of them are in love. Is it you, by any chance, Ivan Romanych?

CHEBUTYKIN.   Oh, I'm just an old sinner. . . . But what I can't make
out is why Natalia Ivanovna looks so embarrassed.
(*Loud laughter.* NATASHA *runs out into the drawing-room,* ANDREY *follows
her.*)

ANDREY.   Please, Natasha, don't take any notice of them! Stop . . . wait
a moment. . . . Please!

NATASHA.   I feel so ashamed. . . . I don't know what's the matter with
me, and they're all laughing at me. It's awful of me to leave the table
like that, but I couldn't help it. . . . I just couldn't. . . .
(*Covers her face with her hands.*)

ANDREY.   My dear girl, please, please don't get upset. Honestly, they
don't mean any harm, they're just teasing. My dear, sweet girl, they're
really good-natured folks, they all are, and they're fond of us both.
Come over to the window, they can't see us there. . . .
 Looks round.)

NATASHA.   You see, I'm not used to being with a lot of people.

ANDREY.   Oh, how young you are, Natasha, how wonderfully, beautifully young! My dear, sweet girl, don't get so upset! Do believe me, believe me. . . . I'm so happy, so full of love, of joy. . . . No, they can't see us here! They can't see us! How did I come to love you, when was it? . . . I don't understand anything. My precious, my sweet, my innocent girl, please—I want you to marry me! I love you, I love you as I've never loved anybody. . . . *(Kissing her.)*

(Enter two officers and seeing NATASHA *and* ANDREY *kissing, stand and stare in amazement.)*

ACT II

The scene is the same as in Act I. It is eight o'clock in the evening. The faint sound of an accordion is heard coming from the street.

The stage is unlit. Enter NATALIA IVANOVNA *in a dressing-gown, carrying a candle. She crosses the stage and stops by the door leading to* ANDREY's *room.*

NATASHA.   What are you doing, Andriusha? Reading? It's all right, I only wanted to know. . . . *(Goes to another door, opens it, looks inside and shuts it again.)* No one's left a light anywhere. . . .

ANDREY   *(enters with a book in his hand)* . What is it, Natasha?

NATASHA.   I was just going round to see if anyone had left a light anywhere. It's carnival week, and the servants are so excited about it . . . anything might happen! You've got to watch them. Last night about twelve o'clock I happened to go into the dining-room, and—would you believe it?—there was a candle alight on the table. I've not found out who lit it. *(Puts the candle down.)* What time is it?

ANDREY   *(glances at his watch)* . Quarter past eight.

NATASHA.   And Olga and Irena still out. They aren't back from work yet, poor things! Olga's still at some teachers' conference, and Irena's at the post office. *(Sighs.)* This morning I said to Irena: "Do take care of yourself, my dear." But she won't listen. Did you say it was a quarter past eight? I'm afraid Bobik is not at all well. Why does he get so cold? Yesterday he had a temperature, but today he feels quite cold when you touch him. . . . I'm so afraid!

ANDREY.   It's all right, Natasha. The boy's well enough.

NATASHA.   Still, I think he ought to have a special diet. I'm so anxious about him. By the way, they tell me that some carnival party's supposed to be coming here soon after nine. I'd rather they didn't come, Andriusha.

ANDREY.   Well, I really don't know what I can do. They've been asked to come.

NATASHA. This morning the dear little fellow woke up and looked at me, and then suddenly he smiled. He recognized me, you see. "Good morning, Bobik," I said, "good morning, darling precious!" And then he laughed. Babies understand everything, you know, they understand us perfectly well. Anyway, Andriusha, I'll tell the servants not to let that carnival party in.

ANDREY (*irresolutely*). Well . . . it's really for my sisters to decide, isn't it? It's their house, after all.

NATASHA. Yes, it's their house as well. I'll tell them, too. . . . They're so kind. . . . (*Walks off.*) I've ordered sour milk for supper. The doctors says you ought to eat nothing but sour milk, or you'll never get any thinner. (*Stops.*) Bobik feels cold. I'm afraid his room is too cold for him. He ought to move into a warmer room, at least until the warm weather comes. Irena's room, for instance—that's just a perfect room for a baby: it's dry, and it gets the sun all day long. We must tell her: perhaps she'd share Olga's room for a bit. . . . In any case, she's never at home during the day, she only sleeps there. . . . (*A pause.*) Andriusha, why don't you say anything?

ANDREY. I was just day-dreaming. . . . There's nothing to say, anyway. . . .

NATASHA. Well. . . . What was it I was going to tell you? Oh, yes! Ferapont from the Council Office wants to see you about something.

ANDREY (*yawns*). Tell him to come up.

(NATASHA *goes out.* ANDREY, *bending over the candle which she has left behind, begins to read his book. Enter* FERAPONT *in an old shabby overcoat, his collar turned up, his ears muffled in a scarf.*)

ANDREY. Hullo, old chap! What did you want to see me about?

FERAPONT. The chairman's sent you the register and a letter or something. Here they are. (*Hands him the book and the letter.*)

ANDREY. Thanks. That's all right. Incidentally, why have you come so late? It's gone eight already.

FERAPONT. What's that?

ANDREY (*raising his voice*). I said, why have you come so late? It's gone eight already.

FERAPONT. That's right. It was still daylight when I came first, but they wouldn't let me see you. The master's engaged, they said. Well, if you're engaged, you're engaged. I'm not in a hurry. (*Thinking that* ANDREY *has said something.*) What's that?

ANDREY. Nothing. (*Turns over the pages of the register.*) Tomorrow's Friday, there's no meeting, but I'll go to the office just the same . . . do some work. I'm so bored at home! . . . (*A pause.*) Yes, my dear old fellow, how things do change, what a fraud life is! So strange! To-day I picked up this book, just out of boredom, because I hadn't anything

to do. It's a copy of some lectures I attended at the University. . . .
Good Heavens! Just think—I'm secretary of the local council now, and
Protopopov's chairman, and the most I can ever hope for is to become
a member of the council myself! I—a member of the local council! I,
who dream every night that I'm a professor in Moscow University, a
famous academician, the pride of all Russia!

FERAPONT. I'm sorry, I can't tell you. I don't hear very well.

ANDREY. If you could hear properly I don't think I'd be talking to you
like this. I must talk to someone, but my wife doesn't seem to understand me, and as for my sisters . . . I'm afraid of them for some reason
or other, I'm afraid of them laughing at me and pulling my leg. . . .
I don't drink and I don't like going to pubs, but my word! how I'd
enjoy an hour or so at Tyestov's, or the Great Moscow Restaurant! Yes,
my dear fellow, I would indeed!

FERAPONT. The other day at the office a contractor was telling me about
some business men who were eating pancakes in Moscow. One of them
ate forty pancakes and died. It was either forty or fifty, I can't remember exactly.

ANDREY. You can sit in some huge restaurant in Moscow without knowing anyone, and no one knowing you; yet somehow you don't feel that
you don't belong there. . . . Whereas here you know everybody, and
everybody knows you, and yet you don't feel you belong here, you feel
you don't belong at all. . . . You're lonely and you feel a stranger.

FERAPONT. What's that? (*A pause.*) It was the same man that told me—
of course, he may have been lying—he said that there's an enormous
rope stretched right across Moscow.

ANDREY. Whatever for?

FERAPONT. I'm sorry, I can't tell you. That's what he said.

ANDREY. What nonsense! (*Reads the book.*) Have you ever been to
Moscow?

FERAPONT (*after a pause*). No. It wasn't God's wish. (*A pause.*) Shall
I go now?

ANDREY. Yes, you may go. Good-bye. (FERAPONT *goes out.*) Good-bye.
(*Reading.*) Come in the morning to take some letters. . . . You can
go now. (*A pause.*) He's gone. (*A bell rings.*) Yes, that's how it is. . . .
(*Stretches and slowly goes to his room.*)

(*Singing is heard off stage; a nurse is putting a baby to sleep. Enter* MASHA
and VERSHININ. *While they talk together, a maid lights a lamp and candles
in the ballroom.*)

MASHA. I don't know. (*A pause.*) I don't know. Habit's very important,
of course. For instance, after Father died, for a long time we couldn't
get accustomed to the idea that we hadn't any orderlies to wait on us.
But, habit apart, I think it's quite right what I was saying. Perhaps it's

different in other places, but in this town the military certainly do seem to be the nicest and most generous and best-mannered people.

VERSHININ.   I'm thirsty. I could do with a nice glass of tea.

MASHA   (*glances at her watch*). They'll bring it in presently. You see, they married me off when I was eighteen. I was afraid of my husband because he was a school-master, and I had only just left school myself. He seemed terribly learned then, very clever and important. Now it's quite different, unfortunately.

VERSHININ.   Yes. . . . I see. . . .

MASHA.   I don't say anything against my husband—I'm used to him now—but there are such a lot of vulgar and unpleasant and offensive people among the other civilians. Vulgarity upsets me, it makes me feel insulted, I actually suffer when I meet someone who lacks refinement and gentle manners, and courtesy. When I'm with the other teachers, my husband's friends, I just suffer.

VERSHININ.   Yes, of course. But I should have thought that in a town like this the civilians and the army people were equally uninteresting. There's nothing to choose between them. If you talk to any educated person here, civilian or military, he'll generally tell you that he's just worn out. It's either his wife, or his house, or his estate, or his horse, or something. . . . We Russians are capable of such elevated thoughts —then why do we have such low ideals in practical life? Why is it, why?

MASHA.   Why?

VERSHININ.   Yes, why does his wife wear him out, why do his children wear him out? And what about *him* wearing out his wife and children?

MASHA.   You're a bit low-spirited to-day, aren't you?

VERSHININ.   Perhaps. I haven't had any dinner to-day. I've had nothing to eat since morning. One of my daughters is a bit off colour, and when the children are ill, I get so worried. I feel utterly conscience-stricken at having given them a mother like theirs. Oh, if only you could have seen her this morning! What a despicable woman! We started quarrelling at seven o'clock, and at nine I just walked out and slammed the door. (*A pause.*) I never talk about these things in the ordinary way. It's a strange thing, but you're the only person I feel I dare complain to. (*Kisses her hand.*) Don't be angry with me. I've nobody, nobody but you. . . . (*A pause.*)

MASHA.   What a noise the wind's making in the stove! Just before Father died the wind howled in the chimney just like that.

VERSHININ.   Are you superstitious?

MASHA.   Yes.

VERSHININ.   How strange. (*Kisses her hand.*) You really are a wonderful creature, a marvellous creature! Wonderful, marvellous! It's quite dark here, but I can see your eyes shining.

MASHA *(Moves to another chair)*. There's more light over here.

VERSHININ. I love you, I love you, I love you. . . . I love your eyes, I love your movements. . . . I dream about them. A wonderful, marvellous being!

MASHA *(Laughing softly)*. When you talk to me like that, somehow I can't help laughing, although I'm afraid at the same time. Don't say it again, please. *(Half-audibly.)* Well, no . . . go on. I don't mind. . . . *(Covers her face with her hands.)* I don't mind. . . . Someone's coming. . . . Let's talk about something else. . . .

(Enter IRENA *and* TOOZENBACH *through the ballroom.)*

TOOZENBACH. I have a triple-barrelled name—Baron Toozenbach-Krone-Alschauer—but actually I'm a Russian. I was baptized in the Greek-Orthodox faith, just like yourself. I haven't really got any German characteristics, except maybe the obstinate patient way I keep on pestering you. Look how I bring you home every evening.

IRENA. How tired I am!

TOOZENBACH. And I'll go on fetching you from the post office and bringing you home every evening for the next twenty years—unless you send me away. . . . *(Noticing* MASHA *and* VERSHININ, *with pleasure.)* Oh, it's you! How are you?

IRENA. Well, here I am, home at last! *(To* MASHA.*)* A woman came into the post office just before I left. She wanted to send a wire to her brother in Saratov to tell him her son had just died, but she couldn't remember the address. So we had to send the wire without an address, just to Saratov. She was crying and I was rude to her, for no reason at all. "I've no time to waste," I told her. So stupid of me. We're having the carnival crowd to-day, aren't we?

MASHA. Yes.

IRENA *(sits down)*. How nice it is to rest! I am tired!

TOOZENBACH *(smiling)*. When you come back from work, you look so young, so pathetic, somehow. . . . *(A pause.)*

IRENA. I'm tired. No, I don't like working at the post office, I don't like it at all.

MASHA. You've got thinner. . . . *(Whistles.)* You look younger, too, and your face looks quite boyish.

TOOZENBACH. It's the way she does her hair.

IRENA. I must look for another job. This one doesn't suit me. It hasn't got what I always longed for and dreamed about. It's the sort of work you do without inspiration, without even thinking.

(Someone knocks at the floor from below.)

That's the Doctor knocking. (*To* TOOZENBACH.) Will you answer him, dear? . . . I can't. . . . I'm so tired.

TOOZENBACH   (*knocks on the floor.*)

IRENA.   He'll be up in a moment. We must do something about all this. Andrey and the Doctor went to the club last night and lost at cards again. They say Andrey lost two hundred roubles.

MASHA   (*with indifference*). Well, what are we to do about it?

IRENA.   He lost a fortnight ago, and he lost in December, too. I wish to goodness he'd lose everything we've got, and soon, too, and then perhaps we'd move out of this place. Good Heavens, I dream of Moscow every night. Sometimes I feel as if I were going mad. (*Laughs.*) We're going to Moscow in June. How many months are there till June? . . . February, March, April, May . . . nearly half-a-year!

MASHA.   We must take care that Natasha doesn't get to know about him losing at cards.

IRENA.   I don't think she cares.

(*Enter* CHEBUTYKIN. *He has been resting on his bed since dinner and has only just got up. He combs his beard, then sits down at the table and takes out a newspaper.*)

MASHA.   There he is. Has he paid his rent yet?

IRENA   (*laughs*). No. Not a penny for the last eight months. I suppose he's forgotten.

MASHA   (*laughs*). How solemn he looks sitting there!

(*They all laugh. A pause.*)

IRENA.   Why don't you say something, Alexandr Ignatyevich?

VERSHININ.   I don't know. I'm just longing for some tea. I'd give my life for a glass of tea! I've had nothing to eat since morning. . . .

CHEBUTYKIN.   Irena Serghyeevna!

IRENA.   What is it?

CHEBUTYKIN.   Please come here. *Venez ici!* (IRENA *goes over to him and sits down at the table.*) I can't do without you.

(IRENA *lays out the cards for a game of patience.*)

VERSHININ.   Well, if we can't have any tea, let's do a bit of philosophizing, anyway.

TOOZENBACH.   Yes, let's. What about?

VERSHININ.   What about? Well . . . let's try to imagine what life will be like after we're dead, say in two or three hundred years.

TOOZENBACH.   All right, then. . . . After we're dead, people will fly about in balloons, the cut of their coats will be different, the sixth sense will be discovered, and possibly even developed and used, for all I know. . . . But I believe, life itself will remain the same; it will still be difficult and full of mystery and full of happiness. And in a thousand years' time people will still be sighing and complaining: "How hard this business of living is!"—and yet they'll still be scared to death and un-willing to die, just as they are now.

VERSHININ *(after a moment's thought)*. Well, you know . . . how shall I put it? I think everything in the world is bound to change gradually —in fact, it's changing before our very eyes. In two or three hundred years, or maybe in a thousand years—it doesn't matter how long exactly —life will be different. It will be happy. Of course, we shan't be able to enjoy that future life, but all the same, what we're living for now is to create it, we work and . . . yes, we suffer in order to create it. That's the goal of our life, and you might say that's the only happiness we shall ever achieve.

MASHA *(laughs quietly.)*

TOOZENBACH. Why are you laughing?

MASHA. I don't know. I've been laughing all day to-day.

VERSHININ *(to TOOZENBACH)*. I went to the same cadet school as you did but I never went on to the Military Academy. I read a great deal, of course, but I never knew what books I ought to choose, and probably I read a lot of stuff that's not worth anything. But the longer I live the more I seem to long for knowledge. My hair's going grey and I'm getting on in years, and yet how little I know, how little! All the same, I think I do know one thing which is not only true but also most important. I'm sure of it. Oh, if only I could convince you that there's not going to be any happiness for our own generation, that there mustn't be and won't be. . . . We've just got to work and work. All the happiness is reserved for our descendants, our remote descendants. *(A pause.)* Anyway, if I'm not to be happy, then at least my children's children will be.

(FEDOTIK and RODÉ enter the ballroom; they sit down and sing quietly, one of them playing on a guitar.)

TOOZENBACH. So you won't even allow us to dream of happiness! But what if I *am* happy?

VERSHININ. You're not.

TOOZENBACH *(flinging up his hands and laughing)*: We don't understand one another, that's obvious. How can I convince you?

MASHA *(laughs quietly.)*

TOOZENBACH *(holds up a finger to her)*. Show a finger to her and she'll laugh! *(To VERSHININ.)* And life will be just the same as ever not merely in a couple of hundred years' time, but in a million years. Life doesn't change, it always goes on the same; it follows its own laws, which don't concern us, which we can't discover anyway. Think of the birds that migrate in the autumn, the cranes, for instance: they just fly on and on. It doesn't matter what sort of thoughts they've got in their heads, great thoughts or little thoughts, they just fly on and on, not knowing where or why. And they'll go on flying no matter how many philosophers they happen to have flying with them. Let them philosophize as much as they like, as long as they go on flying.

MASHA.   Isn't there some meaning?

TOOZENBACH.   Meaning? . . . Look out there, it's snowing. What's the meaning of that? (*A pause.*)

MASHA.   I think a human being has got to have some faith, or at least he's got to seek faith. Otherwise his life will be empty, empty. . . . How can you live and not know why the cranes fly, why children are born, why the stars shine in the sky! . . . You must either know why you live, or else . . . nothing matters . . . everything's just wild grass. . . . (*A pause.*)

VERSHININ.   All the same, I'm sorry my youth's over.

MASHA.   "It's a bore to be alive in this world, friends," that's what Gogol says.

TOOZENBACH.   And I feel like saying: it's hopeless arguing with you, friends! I give you up.

CHEBUTYKIN   (*reads out of the paper*). Balsac's marriage took place at Berdichev.[1]

IRENA   (*sings softly to herself.*)

CHEBUTYKIN.   Must write this down in my notebook. (*Writes.*) Balsac's marriage took place at Berdichev. (*Reads on.*)

IRENA   (*playing patience, pensively*). Balsac's marriage took place at Berdichev.

TOOZENBACH.   Well, I've thrown in my hand. Did you know that I'd sent in my resignation, Maria Serghyeevna?

MASHA.   Yes, I heard about it. I don't see anything good in it, either. I don't like civilians.

TOOZENBACH.   Never mind. (*Gets up.*) What sort of a soldier do I make, anyway? I'm not even good-looking. Well, what does it matter? I'll work. I'd like to do such a hard day's work that when I came home in the evening I'd fall on my bed exhausted and go to sleep at once. (*Goes to the ballroom.*) I should think working men sleep well at nights!

FEDOTIK   (*to* IRENA). I've got you some coloured crayons at Pyzhikov's, in Moscow Street. And this little penknife, too. . . .

IRENA.   You still treat me as if I were a little girl. I wish you'd remember I'm grown up now. (*Takes the crayons and the penknife, joyfully.*) They're awfully nice!

FEDOTIK.   Look, I bought a knife for myself, too. You see, it's got another blade here, and then another . . . this thing's for cleaning your ears, and these are nail-scissors, and this is for cleaning your nails. . . .

RODÉ   (*in a loud voice*). Doctor, how old are you?

[1] A town in Western Russia well known for its almost exclusively Jewish population.

CHEBUTYKIN.   I? Thirty-two.

(*Laughter.*)

FEDOTIK.   I'll show you another kind of patience. (*Sets out the cards.*)

(*The samovar is brought in, and* ANFISA *attends to it. Shortly afterwards* NATASHA *comes in and begins to fuss around the table.*)

SOLIONY   (*enters, bows to the company and sits down at the table.*)

VERSHININ.   What a wind, though!

MASHA.   Yes. I'm tired of winter! I've almost forgotten what summer is like.

IRENA   (*playing patience*). I'm going to go out. We'll get to Moscow!

FEDOTIK.   No, it's not going out. You see, the eight has to go on the two of spades. (*Laughs.*) That means you won't go to Moscow.

CHEBUTYKIN   (*reads the paper*). Tzitzikar. Smallpox is raging. . . .

ANFISA   (*goes up to* MASHA). Masha, the tea's ready, dear. (*To* VERSHININ.) Will you please come to the table, your Excellency? Forgive me, your name's slipped my memory. . . .

MASHA.   Bring it here, Nanny. I'm not coming over there.

IRENA.   Nanny!

ANFISA.   Comi-ing!

NATASHA   (*to* SOLIONY). You know, even tiny babies understand what we say perfectly well! "Good morning, Bobik," I said to him only today, "Good morning, my precious!"—and then he looked at me in such a special sort of way. You may say it's only a mother's imagination, but it isn't, I do assure you. No, no! He really is an extraordinary child!

SOLIONY.   If that child were mine, I'd cook him up in a frying pan and eat him. (*Picks up his glass, goes into the drawing-room and sits down in a corner.*)

NATASHA   (*covers her face with her hands*). What a rude, ill-mannered person!

MASHA.   People who don't even notice whether it's summer or winter are lucky! I think I'd be indifferent to the weather if I were living in Moscow.

VERSHININ.   I've just been reading the diary of some French cabinet minister—he wrote it in prison. He got sent to prison in connection with the Panama affair. He writes with such a passionate delight about the birds he can see through the prison window—the birds he never even noticed when he was a cabinet minister. Of course, now he's released he won't notice them any more. . . . And in the same way, you won't notice Moscow once you live there again. We're not happy and we can't be happy: we only want happiness.

TOOZENBACH   (*picks up a box from the table*). I say, where are all the chocolates?

IRENA.   Soliony's eaten them.

TOOZENBACH.   All of them?

ANFISA   (*serving* VERSHININ *with tea*). Here's a letter for you, Sir.

VERSHININ.   For me? (*Takes the letter.*) From my daughter. (*Reads it.*) Yes, of course. . . . Forgive me, Maria Serghyeevna, I'll just leave quietly. I won't have any tea. (*Gets up, agitated.*) Always the same thing. . . .

MASHA.   What is it? Secret?

VERSHININ   (*in a low voice*). My wife's taken poison again. I must go. I'll get away without them seeing me. All this is so dreadfully unpleasant. (*Kisses* MASHA's *hand.*) My dear, good, sweet girl. . . . I'll go out this way, quietly. . . . (*Goes out.*)

ANFISA.   Where's he off to? And I've just brought him some tea! What a queer fellow!

MASHA   (*flaring up.*) Leave me alone! Why do you keep worrying me? Why don't you leave me in peace? (*Goes to the table, cup in hand.*) I'm sick and tired of you, silly old woman!

ANFISA.   Why. . . . I didn't mean to offend you, dear.

ANDREY'S VOICE   (*off stage*). Anfisa!

ANFISA   (*mimics him*). Anfisa! Sitting there in his den! . . . (*Goes out.*)

MASHA   (*by the table in the ballroom, crossly*). Do let me sit down somewhere! (*Jumbles up the cards laid out on the table.*) You take up the whole table with your cards! Why don't you get on with your tea?

IRENA.   How bad-tempered you are, Mashka!

MASHA.   Well, if I'm bad-tempered, don't talk to me, then. Don't touch me!

CHEBUTYKIN   (*laughs*). Don't touch her! . . . Take care you don't touch her!

MASHA.   You may be sixty, but you're always gabbling some damn nonsense or other, just like a child. . . .

NATASHA   (*sighs*). My dear Masha, need you use such expressions? You know, with your good looks you'd be thought so charming, even by the best people—yes, I honestly mean it—if only you wouldn't use these expressions of yours! Je vous prie, pardonnez moi, Marie, mais vous avez des manières un peu grossières.

TOOZENBACH   (*with suppressed laughter*). Pass me . . . I say, will you please pass me. . . . Is that cognac over there, or what? . . .

NATASHA.   Il parait que mon Bobik déjà ne dort pas. . . . I think he's awake. He's not been too well to-day. I must go and see him . . . excuse me. (*Goes out.*)

IRENA.   I say, where has Alexandr Ignatyevich gone to?

MASHA.   He's gone home. His wife's done something queer again.

TOOZENBACH   (*goes over to* SOLIONY *with a decanter of cognac*). You always sit alone brooding over something or other—though what it's all about nobody knows. Well, let's make it up. Let's have cognac together. (*They drink.*) I suppose I'll have to play the piano all night to-night—a lot of rubbishy tunes, of course. . . . Never mind!

SOLIONY. Why did you say "let's make it up"? We haven't quarrelled.

TOOZENBACH. You always give me the feeling that there's something wrong between us. You're a strange character, no doubt about it.

SOLIONY (*recites*). "I am strange, but who's not so? Don't be angry, Aleko!"

TOOZENBACH. What's Aleko got to do with it? . . . (*A pause.*)

SOLIONY. When I'm alone with somebody I'm all right, I'm just like other people. But in company, I get depressed and shy, and . . . I talk all sorts of nonsense. All the same, I'm a good deal more honest and well-intentioned than plenty of others. I can prove I am.

TOOZENBACH. You often make me angry because you keep on pestering me when we're in company—but all the same, I do like you for some reason. . . . I'm going to get drunk to-night, whatever happens! Let's have another drink!

SOLIONY. Yes, let's. (*A pause.*) I've never had anything against you personally, Baron. But my temperament's rather like Lermontov's. (*In a low voice.*) I even look a little like Lermontov, I've been told. . . . (*Takes a scent bottle from his pocket and sprinkles some scent on his hands.*)

TOOZENBACH. I have sent in my resignation! Finished! I've been considering it for five years, and now I've made up my mind at last. I'm going to work.

SOLIONY (*recites*). "Don't be angry, Aleko. . . . Away, away with all your dreams!"

(*During the conversation* ANDREY *enters quietly with a book in his hand and sits down by the candle.*)

TOOZENBACH. I'm going to work!

CHEBUTYKIN (*comes into the drawing-room with* IRENA). And the food they treated me to was the genuine Caucasian stuff: onion soup, followed by chehartma—that's a meat dish, you know.

SOLIONY. Chereshma isn't meat at all; it's a plant, something like an onion.

CHEBUTYKIN. No-o, my dear friend. Chehartma isn't an onion, it's roast mutton.

CHEBUTYKIN. Well, why should I argue about it with you? You've never been to the Caucasus and you've never tasted chehartma.

SOLIONY. I haven't tasted it because I can't stand the smell of it. Chereshma stinks just like garlic.

ANDREY (*imploringly*). Do stop it, friends! Please stop it!

TOOZENBACH.   When's the carnival crowd coming along?

IRENA.   They promised to be here by nine—that means any moment now.

TOOZENBACH   (*embraces* ANDREY *and sings*). "Ah, my beautiful porch, my lovely new porch, my . . ."[2]

ANDREY   (*dances and sings*). "My new porch all made of maplewood. . . ."

CHEBUTYKIN   (*dances*). "With fancy carving over the door. . . ."

(*Laughter.*)

TOOZENBACH   (*kisses* ANDREY). Let's have a drink, the devil take it! Andriusha, let's drink to eternal friendship. I'll come with you when you go back to Moscow University.

SOLIONY.   Which university? There are two universities in Moscow.

ANDREY.   There's only one.

SOLIONY.   I tell you there are two.

ANDREY.   Never mind, make it three. The more the merrier.

SOLIONY.   There are two universities in Moscow.

(*Murmurs of protest and cries of "Hush!"*)

There are two universities in Moscow, an old one and a new one. But if you don't want to listen to what I'm saying, if my conversation irritates you, I can keep silent. In fact I can go to another room. . . . (*Goes out through one of the doors.*)

TOOZENBACH.   Bravo, bravo! (*Laughs.*) Let's get started, my friends, I'll play for you. What a funny creature that Soliony is! . . . (*Sits down at the piano and plays a waltz.*)

MASHA   (*dances alone*). The Baron is drunk, the Baron is drunk, the Baron is drunk. . . .

(*Enter* NATASHA.)

NATASHA   (*to* CHEBUTYKIN). Ivan Romanych! (*Speaks to him, then goes out quietly.* CHEBUTYKIN *touches* TOOZENBACH *on the shoulder and whispers to him.*)

IRENA.   What is it?

CHEBUTYKIN.   It's time we were going. Good-night.

IRENA.   But really. . . . What about the carnival party?

ANDREY   (*embarrassed*). The carnival party's not coming. You see, my dear, Natasha says that Bobik isn't very well, and so . . . Anyway, I don't know . . . and certainly don't care. . . .

IRENA   (*shrugs her shoulders*). Bobik's not very well! . . .

MASHA.   Never mind, we'll keep our end up! If they turn us out, out we must go! (*To* IRENA.) It isn't Bobik who's not well, it's her. . . . There! . . . (*Taps her forehead with her finger.*) Petty little bourgeois housewife!

(ANDREY *goes to his room on the right.* CHEBUTYKIN *follows him. The guests say good-bye in the ballroom.*)

[2] A traditional Russian dance-song.

FEDOTIK.   What a pity! I'd been hoping to spend the evening here, but of course, if the baby's ill. . . . I'll bring him some toys to-morrow.

RODÉ   *(in a loud voice)*. I had a good long sleep after lunch to-day on purpose, I thought I'd be dancing all night. I mean to say, it's only just nine o'clock.

MASHA.   Let's go outside and talk it over. We can decide what to do then. *(Voices are heard saying "Good-bye! God bless you!" and* TOOZENBACH *is heard laughing gaily. Everyone goes out.* ANFISA *and a maid clear the table and put out the lights. The nurse sings to the baby off stage. Enter* ANDREY, *wearing an overcoat and hat, followed by* CHEBUTYKIN. *They move quietly.)*

CHEBUTYKIN.   I've never found time to get married, somehow . . . partly because my life's just flashed past me like lightning, and partly because I was always madly in love with your mother and she was married. . . .

ANDREY.   One shouldn't marry. One shouldn't marry because it's so boring.

CHEBUTYKIN.   That may be so, but what about loneliness? You can philosophize as much as you like, dear boy, but loneliness is a dreadful thing. Although, really . . . well, it doesn't matter a damn, of course! . . .

ANDREY.   Let's get along quickly.

CHEBUTYKIN.   What's the hurry? There's plenty of time.

ANDREY.   I'm afraid my wife may try to stop me.

CHEBUTYKIN.   Ah!

ANDREY.   I won't play cards to-night, I'll just sit and watch. I'm not feeling too well. . . . What ought I to do for this breathlessness, Ivan Romanych?

CHEBUTYKIN.   Why ask me, dear boy? I can't remember—I simply don't know.

ANDREY.   Let's go through the kitchen. *(They go out. A bell rings. The ring is repeated, then voices and laughter are heard.)*

IRENA   *(coming in)*. What's that?

ANFISA   *(in a whisper)*. The carnival party. *(The bell rings again.)*

IRENA.   Tell them there's no one at home, Nanny. Apologize to them. *(* ANFISA *goes out.* IRENA *walks up and down the room, lost in thought. She seems agitated. Enter* SOLIONY.*)*

SOLIONY   *(puzzled)*. There's no one here. . . . Where is everybody?

IRENA.   They've gone home.

SOLIONY.   How strange! Then you're alone here?

IRENA.   Yes, alone. *(A pause.)* Well . . . good-night.

SOLIONY.   I know I behaved tactlessly just now, I lost control of myself. But you're different from the others, you stand out high above them—

you're pure, you can see where the truth lies. . . . You're the only person in the world who can possibly understand me. I love you. . . . I love you with a deep, infinite . . .

IRENA.   Do please go away. Good-night!

SOLIONY.   I can't live without you (*Follows her.*) Oh, it's such a delight just to look at you! (*With tears.*) Oh, my happiness! Your glorious, marvellous, entrancing eyes—eyes like no other woman's I've ever seen. . . .

IRENA.   (*coldly*) . Please stop it, Vassily Vassilich!

SOLIONY.   I've never spoken to you of my love before . . . it makes me feel as if I were living on a different planet. . . . (*Rubs his forehead.*) Never mind! I can't force you to love me, obviously. But I don't intend to have any rivals—successful rivals, I mean. . . . No, no! I swear to you by everything I hold sacred that if there's anyone else, I'll kill him. Oh, how wonderful you are!

(*Enter* NATASHA *carrying a candle.*)

NATASHA   (*pokes her head into one room, then into another, but passes the door leading to her husband's room*) . Andrey's reading in there. Better let him read. Forgive me, Vassily Vassilich, I didn't know you were here. I'm afraid I'm not properly dressed.

SOLIONY.   I don't care. Good-bye. (*Goes out.*)

NATASHA.   You must be tired, my poor dear girl. (*Kisses* IRENA) . You ought to go to bed earlier.

IRENA.   Is Bobik asleep?

NATASHA.   Yes, he's asleep. But he's not sleeping peacefully. By the way, my dear, I've been meaning to speak to you for some time but there's always been something . . . either you're not here, or I'm too busy. . . . You see, I think that Bobik's nursery is so cold and damp. . . . And your room is just ideal for a baby. Darling, do you think you could move into Olga's room?

IRENA   (*not understanding her*) . Where to?

(*The sound of bells is heard outside, as a "troika" is driven up to the house.*)

NATASHA.   You can share a room with Olia for the time being, and Bobik can have your room. He is such a darling! This morning I said to him: "Bobik, you're my very own! My very own!" And he just gazed at me with his dear little eyes. (*The door bell rings.*) That must be Olga. How late she is!

(*A maid comes up to* NATASHA *and whispers in her ear.*)

NATASHA.   Protopopov! What a funny fellow! Protopopov's come to ask me to go for a drive with him. In a troika! (*Laughs.*) Aren't these men strange creatures! . . .

(*The door bell rings again.*)

Someone's ringing. Shall I go for a short drive? Just for a quarter of an hour? (*To the maid.*) Tell him I'll be down in a minute. (*The door bell rings.*) That's the bell again. I suppose it's Olga. (*Goes out.*)

(*The maid runs out;* IRENA *sits lost in thought. Enter* KOOLYGHIN *and* OLGA, *followed by* VERSHININ.)

KOOLYGHIN. Well! What's the meaning of this? You said you were going to have a party.

VERSHININ. It's a strange thing. I left here about half an hour ago, and they were expecting a carnival party then.

IRENA. They've all gone.

KOOLYGHIN. Masha's gone, too? Where has she gone to? And why is Protopopov waiting outside in a troika? Who's he waiting for?

IRENA. Please don't ask me questions. I'm tired.

KOOLYGHIN. You . . . spoilt child!

OLGA. The conference has only just ended. I'm quite worn out. The headmistress is ill and I'm deputizing for her. My head's aching, oh, my head, my head. . . . (*Sits down.*) Andrey lost two hundred roubles at cards last night. The whole town's talking about it. . . .

KOOLYGHIN. Yes, the conference exhausted me, too. (*Sits down.*)

VERSHININ. So now my wife's taken it into her head to try to frighten me. She tried to poison herself. However, everything's all right now, so I can relax, thank goodness. . . . So we've got to go away? Well, good-night to you, all the best. Fiodor Illych, would you care to come along with me somewhere or other? I can't stay at home to-night, I really can't. . . . Do come!

KOOLYGHIN. I'm tired. I don't think I'll come. (*Gets up.*) I'm tired. Has my wife gone home?

IRENA. I think so.

KOOLYGHIN (*kisses* IRENA's *hand*). Good-night. We can rest to-morrow and the day after to-morrow, two whole days! Well, I wish you all the best. (*Going out.*) How I long for some tea! I reckoned on spending the evening in congenial company, but—*o, fallacem hominum spem!* Always use the accusative case in exclamations.

VERSHININ. Well, it looks as if I'll have to go somewhere by myself. (*Goes out with* KOOLYGHIN, *whistling.*)

OLGA. My head aches, oh, my head. . . . Andrey lost at cards . . . the whole town's talking. . . . I'll go and lie down. (*Going out.*) To-morrow I'm free, and the day after to-morrow I'm free. . . . My head's aching, oh, my poor head. . . .

IRENA (*alone*). They've all gone. No one's left.

(*Someone is playing an accordion in the street. The nurse sings in the next room.*)

NATASHA (*crosses the ballroom, wearing a fur coat and cap. She is fol-*

lowed by the maid) . I'll be back in half an hour. I'm just going for a little drive. (*Goes out.*)

IRENA   (*alone, with intense longing*) . Moscow! Moscow! Moscow!

ACT III

A bedroom now shared by OLGA *and* IRENA. *There are two beds, one on the right, the other on the left, each screened off from the center of the room. It is past two o'clock in the morning. Off stage the alarm is being sounded on account of a fire which has been raging for some time. The inmates of the house have not yet been to bed.* MASHA *is lying on a couch, dressed, as usual, in black.* OLGA *and* ANFISA *come in.*

ANFISA.   Now they're sitting down there, under the stairs. . . . I keep telling them to come upstairs, that they shouldn't sit down there, but they just cry. "We don't know where our Papa is," they say, "perhaps he's got burned in the fire." What an idea! And there are people in the yard, too . . . half dressed. . . .

OLGA   (*takes a dress out of a wardrobe*) . Take this grey frock, Nanny. . . . And this one. . . . This blouse, too. . . . And this skirt. Oh, Heavens! what is happening! Apparently the whole of the Kirsanovsky Street's been burnt down. . . . Take this . . . and this, too. . . . (*Throws the clothes into* ANFISA's *arms.*) The poor Vershinins had a fright. Their house only just escaped being burnt down. They'll have to spend the night here . . . we mustn't let them go home. Poor Fedotik's lost everything, he's got nothing left. . . .

ANFISA.   I'd better call Ferapont, Oliushka, I can't carry all this.

OLGA   (*rings*) . No one takes any notice when I ring. (*Calls through the door.*) Is anyone there? Will someone come up please!
(*A window, red with the glow of fire, can be seen through the open door. The sound of a passing fire engine is heard.*)
How dreadful it all is! And how tired of it I am! (*Enter* FERAPONT.) Take this downstairs please. . . . The Kolotilin girls are sitting under the stairs . . . give it to them. And this, too. . . .

FERAPONT.   Very good, Madam. Moscow was burned down in 1812 just the same. Mercy on us! . . . Yes, the French were surprised all right.

OLGA.   Go along now, take this down.

FERAPONT.   Very good. (*Goes out.*)

OLGA.   Give it all away, Nanny, dear. We won't keep anything, give it all away. . . . I'm so tired, I can hardly keep on my feet. We mustn't let the Vershinins go home. The little girls can sleep in the drawing-room, and Alexandr Ignatyevich can share the downstairs room with the

Baron. Fedotik can go in with the Baron, too, or maybe he'd better sleep in the ballroom. The doctor's gone and got drunk—you'd think he'd done it on purpose; he's so hopelessly drunk that we can't let anyone go into his room. Vershinin's wife will have to go into the drawing-room, too.

ANFISA (*wearily*). Don't send me away, Oliushka, darling! Don't send me away!

OLGA. What nonsense you're talking, Nanny! No one's sending you away.

ANFISA (*leans her head against* OLGA'S *breast*). My dearest girl! I do work, you know, I work as hard as I can. . . . I suppose now I'm getting weaker, I'll be told to go. But where can I go? Where? I'm eighty years old. I'm over eighty-one!

OLGA. You sit down for a while, Nanny. . . . You're tired, you poor dear. . . . (*Makes her sit down.*) Just rest a bit. You've turned quite pale.

(*Enter* NATASHA.)

NATASHA. They're saying we ought to start a subscription in aid of the victims of the fire. You know—form a society or something for the purpose. Well, why not? It's an excellent idea! In any case it's up to us to help the poor as best we can. Bobik and Sofochka are fast asleep as if nothing had happened. We've got such a crowd of people in the house; the place seems full of people whichever way you turn. There's 'flu about in the town. . . . I'm so afraid the children might catch it.

OLGA (*without listening to her*). You can't see the fire from this room; it's quiet in here.

NATASHA. Yes. . . . I suppose my hair is all over the place. (*Stands in front of the mirror.*) They say I've got stouter, but it's not true! I'm not a bit stouter. Masha's asleep . . . she's tired, poor girl. . . . (*To* ANFISA, *coldly.*) How dare you sit down in my presence? Get up! Get out of here! (ANFISA *goes out. A pause.*) I can't understand why you keep that old woman in the house.

OLGA. (*taken back*). Forgive me for saying it, but I can't understand how you . . .

NATASHA. She's quite useless here. She's just a peasant woman, her right place is in the country. You're spoiling her. I do like order in the home, I don't like having useless people about. (*Strokes* OLGA'S *cheek.*) You're tired, my poor dear! Our headmistress is tired! You know, when my Sofochka grows up and goes to school, I'll be frightened of you.

OLGA. I'm not going to be a headmistress.

NATASHA. You'll be asked to, Olechka. It's settled.

OLGA. I'll refuse. I couldn't do it. . . . I wouldn't be strong enough. (*Drinks water.*) You spoke so harshly to Nanny just now. . . . You must forgive me for saying so, but I just can't stand that sort of thing . . . it made me feel quite faint. . . .

NATASHA (*agitated*). Forgive me, Olia, forgive me. I didn't mean to upset you.

(MASHA *gets up, picks up a pillow and goes out in a huff.*)

OLGA. Please try to understand me, dear. . . . It may be that we've been brought up in a peculiar way, but anyway I just can't bear it. When people are treated like that, it gets me down, I feel quite ill. . . . I simply get unnerved. . . .

NATASHA. Forgive me, dear, forgive me! . . . (*Kisses her.*)

OLGA. Any cruel or tactless remark, even the slightest discourtesy, upsets me. . . .

NATASHA. It's quite true, I know I often say things which would be **better** left unsaid—but you must agree with me, dear, that she'd be better in the country somewhere.

OLGA. She's been with us for thirty years.

NATASHA. But she can't do any work now, can she? Either I don't understand you, or you don't want to understand me. She can't work, she just sleeps or sits about.

OLGA. Well, let her sit about.

NATASHA (*in surprise*). What do you mean, let her sit about? Surely she is a servant! (*Tearfully.*) No, I don't understand you, Olia! I have a nurse for the children and a wet nurse and we share a maid and a cook. Whatever do we want this old woman for? What for?

(*The alarm is sounded again.*)

OLGA. I've aged ten years to-night.

NATASHA. We must sort things out, Olia. You're working at your school, and I'm working at home. You're teaching and I'm running the house. And when I say anything about the servants, I know what I'm talking about. . . . That old thief, that old witch must get out of this house to-morrow! . . . (*Stamps her feet.*) How dare you vex me so? How dare you? (*Recovering her self-control.*) Really, if you don't move downstairs, we'll always be quarrellng. This is quite dreadful!

(*Enter* KOOLYGHIN.)

KOOLYGHIN. Where's Masha? It's time we went home. They say the fire's getting less fierce. (*Stretches.*) Only one block got burnt down, but to begin with it looked as if the whole town was going to be set on fire by that wind. (*Sits down.*) I'm so tired, Olechka, my dear. You know, I've often thought that if I hadn't married Masha, I'd have married you, Olechka. You're so kind. I'm worn out. (*Listens.*)

OLGA. What is it?

KOOLYGHIN. The doctor's got drunk just at if he'd done it on purpose. Hopelessly drunk. . . . As if he'd done it on purpose. (*Gets up.*) I think he's coming up here. . . . Can you hear him? Yes, he's coming up. (*Laughs.*) What a fellow, really! . . . I'm going to hide myself. (*Goes to the wardrobe and stands between it and the wall.*) What a scoundrel!

OLGA.   He's been off drinking for two years, and now suddenly he goes and gets drunk. . . . (*Walks with* NATASHA *towards the back of the room.*)

(CHEBUTYKIN *enters; walking firmly and soberly he crosses the room, stops, looks round, then goes to the wash-stand and begins to wash his hands.*)

CHEBUTYKIN   (*glumly*). The devil take them all . . . all the lot of them! They think I can treat anything just because I'm a doctor, but I know positively nothing at all. I've forgotten everything I used to know. I remember nothing, positively nothing. . . . (OLGA *and* NATASHA *leave the room without his noticing.*) The devil take them! Last Wednesday I attended a woman at Zasyp. She died, and it's all my fault that she did die. Yes. . . . I used to know a thing or two twenty-five years ago, but now I don't remember anything. Not a thing! Perhaps I'm not a man at all, but I just imagine that I've got hands and feet and a head. Perhaps I don't exist at all, and I only imagine that I'm walking about and eating and sleeping. (*Weeps.*) Oh, if only I could simply stop existing! (*Stops crying, glumly.*) God knows. . . . The other day they were talking about Shakespeare and Voltaire at the club. . . . I haven't read either, never read a single line of either, but I tried to make out by my expression that I had. The others did the same. How petty it all is! How despicable! And then suddenly I thought of the woman I killed on Wednesday. It all came back to me, and I felt such a swine, so sick of myself that I went and got drunk. . . .

(*Enter* IRENA, VERSHININ *and* TOOZENBACH. TOOZENBACH *is wearing a fashionable new civilian suit.*)

IRENA.   Let's sit down here for a while. No one will come in here.

VERSHININ.   The whole town would have been burnt down but for the soldiers. They're a fine lot of fellows! (*Rubs his hands with pleasure.*) Excellent fellows! Yes, they're a fine lot!

KOOLYGHIN   (*approaches them*). What's the time?

TOOZENBACH.   It's gone three. It's beginning to get light.

IRENA.   Everyone's sitting in the ballroom and nobody thinks of leaving. That man Soliony there, too. . . . (*To* CHEBUTYKIN.) You ought to go to bed, Doctor.

CHEBUTYKIN.   I'm all right. . . . Thanks. . . . (*Combs his beard.*)

KOOLYGHIN   (*laughs*). Half seas over, Ivan Romanych! (*Slaps him on the shoulder.*) You're a fine one! *In vino veritas,* as they used to say in Rome.

TOOZENBACH.   Everyone keeps asking me to arrange a concert in aid of the victims of the fire.

IRENA.   Well, who'd you get to perform in it?

TOOZENBACH.   It could be done if we wanted to. Maria Serghyeevna plays the piano wonderfully well, in my opinion.

KOOLYGHIN.   Yes, wonderfully well!

IRENA.   She's forgotten how to. She hasn't played for three years. . . . or maybe it's four.

TOOZENBACH.   Nobody understands music in this town, not a single person. But I do—I really do—and I assure you quite definitely that Maria Serghyeevna plays magnificently. She's almost a genius for it.

KOOLYGHIN.   You're right, Baron. I'm very fond of Masha. She's such a nice girl.

TOOZENBACH.   Fancy being able to play so exquisitely, and yet having nobody, nobody at all, to appreciate it!

KOOLYGHIN   (*sighs*).   Yes. . . . But would it be quite proper for her to play in a concert? (*A pause.*) I don't know anything about these matters, my friends. Perhaps it'll be perfectly all right. But you know, although our director is a good man, a very good man indeed, and most intelligent, I know that he does hold certain views. . . . Of course, this doesn't really concern him, but I'll have a word with him about it, all the same, if you like.

CHEBUTYKIN   (*picks up a china clock and examines it.*)

VERSHININ.   I've got my clothes in such a mess helping to put out the fire, I must look like nothing on earth. (*A pause.*) I believe they were saying yesterday that our brigade might be transferred to somewhere a long way away. Some said it was to be Poland, and some said it was Cheeta, in Siberia.

TOOZENBACH.   I heard that, too. Well, the town will seem quite deserted.

IRENA.   We'll go away, too!

CHEBUTYKIN   (*drops clock and breaks it*).   Smashed to smithereens!

(*A pause. Everyone looks upset and embarrassed.*)

KOOLYGHIN   (*picks up the pieces*).   Fancy breaking such a valuable thing! Ah, Ivan Romanych, Ivan Romanych! You'll get a bad mark for that!

IRENA.   It was my mother's clock.

CHEBUTYKIN.   Well, supposing it was. If it was your mother's, then it was your mother's. Perhaps I didn't smash it. Perhaps it only appears that I did. Perhaps it only appears to us that we exist, whereas in reality we don't exist at all. I don't know anything, no one knows anything. (*Stops at the door.*) Why are you staring at me? Natasha's having a nice little affair with Protopopov, and you don't see it. You sit here seeing nothing, and meanwhile Natasha's having a nice little affair with Protopopov. . . . (*Sings.*) Would you like a date? . . . (*Goes out.*)

VERSHININ. So. . . . (*Laughs.*) How odd it all is, really. (*A pause.*) When the fire started, I ran home as fast as I could. When I got near, I could see that our house was all right and out of danger, but the two little girls were standing there, in the doorway in their night clothes. Their mother wasn't there. People were rushing about, horses, dogs . . . and in the kiddies' faces I saw a frightened, anxious, appealing look, I don't know what! . . . My heart sank when I saw their faces. My God, I thought, what will these children have to go through in the course of their poor lives? And they may live a long time, too! I picked them up and ran back here with them, and all the time I was running, I was thinking the same thing: what will they have to go through? (*The alarm is sounded. A pause.*) When I got here, my wife was here already . . . angry, shouting!

(*Enter* MASHA *carrying a pillow; she sits down on the couch.*)

VERSHININ. And when my little girls were standing in the doorway with nothing on but their night clothes, and the street was red with the glow of the fire and full of terrifying noises, it struck me that the same sort of thing used to happen years ago, when armies used to make sudden raids on towns, and plunder them and set them on fire. . . . Anyway, is there any essential difference between things as they were and as they are now? And before very long, say, in another two or three hundred years, people may be looking at our present life just as we look at the past now, with horror and scorn. Our own times may seem uncouth to them, boring and frightfully uncomfortable and strange. . . . Oh, what a great life it'll be then, what a life! (*Laughs.*) Forgive me, I'm philosophizing my head off again . . . but may I go on, please? I'm bursting to philosophize just at the moment. I'm in the mood for it. (*A pause.*) You seem as if you've all gone to sleep. As I was saying: what a great life it will be in the future! Just try to imagine it. . . . At the present time there are only three people of your intellectual calibre in the whole of this town, but future generations will be more productive of people like you. They'll go on producing more and more of the same sort until at last the time will come when everything will be just as you'd wish it yourselves. People will live their lives in your way, and then even you may be outmoded, and a new lot will come along who will be even better than you are. . . . (*Laughs.*) I'm in quite a special mood to-day. I feel full of a tremendous urge to live. . . . (*Sings.*)

> "To Love all ages are in fee,
> The passion's good for you and me." . . . (*Laughs.*)

MASHA (*sings*). Tara-tara-tara. . . .
VERSHININ. Tum-tum. . . .
MASHA. Tara-tara . . .

VERSHININ. Tum-tum, tum-tum. . . . (*Laughs.*)

(*Enter* FEDOTIK.)

FEDOTIK (*dancing about*). Burnt, burnt! Everything I've got burnt!

(*All laugh.*)

IRENA. It's hardly a joking matter. Has everything really been burnt?

FEDOTIK (*laughs*). Everything, completely. I've got nothing left. My guitar's burnt, my photographs are burnt, all my letters are burnt. Even the little note-book I was going to give you has been burnt.

(*Enter* SOLIONY.)

IRENA. No, please go away, Vassily Vassilich. You can't come in here.

SOLIONY. Can't I? Why can the Baron come in here if I can't?

VERSHININ. We really must go, all of us. What's the fire doing?

SOLIONY. It's dying down, they say. Well, I must say it's a peculiar thing that the Baron can come in here, and I can't. (*Takes a scent bottle from his pocket and sprinkles himself with scent.*)

VERSHININ. Tara-tara.

MASHA. Tum-tum, tum-tum.

VERSHININ (*laughs, to* SOLIONY). Let's go to the ballroom.

SOLIONY. Very well, we'll make a note of this. "I hardly need to make my moral yet more clear: That might be teasing geese, I fear!"³ (*Looks at* TOOZENBACH.) Cluck, cluck, cluck! (*Goes out with* VERSHININ *and* FEDOTIK.)

IRENA. That Soliony has smoked the room out. . . . (*Puzzled.*) The Baron's asleep. Baron! Baron!

TOOZENBACH (*waking out of his doze*). I must be tired. The brick-works. . . . No, I'm not talking in my sleep. I really do intend to go to the brick-works and start working there quite soon. I've had a talk with the manager. (*To* IRENA, *tenderly.*) You are so pale, so beautiful, so fascinating. . . . Your pallor seems to light up the darkness around you, as if it were luminous, somehow. . . . You're sad, you're dissatisfied with the life you have to live. . . . Oh, come away with me, let's go away and work together!

MASHA. Nikolai Lvovich, I wish you'd go away.

TOOZENBACH (*laughs*). Oh, you're here, are you? I didn't see you. (*Kisses* IRENA's *hand.*) Good-bye, I'm going. You know as I look at you now, I keep thinking of the day—it was a long time ago, your Saint's day— when you talked to us about the joy of work. . . . You were so gay and high-spirited then. . . . And what a happy life I saw ahead of me! Where is it all now? (*Kisses her hand.*) There are tears in your eyes. You should go to bed, it's beginning to get light . . . it's almost morning. . . . Oh, if only I could give my life for you!

MASHA. Nikolai Lvovich, please go away! Really now. . . .

³ From Krylov's fable *Geese* (Translated by Bernard Pares).

TOOZENBACH.   I'm going. (*Goes out.*)

MASHA   (*lies down*). Are you asleep, Fiodor?

KOOLYGHIN.   Eh?

MASHA.   Why don't you go home?

KOOLYGHIN.   My darling Masha, my sweet, my precious Masha. . . .

IRENA.   She's tired. Let her rest a while, Fyedia.

KOOLYGHIN.   I'll go in a moment. My wife, my dear, good wife! . . . How I love you! . . . only you!

MASHA   (*crossly*). *Amo, amas, amat, amamus, amatis, amant!*

KOOLYGHIN   (*laughs*). Really, she's an amazing woman!—I've been married to you for seven years, but I feel as if we were only married yesterday. Yes, on my word of honour, I do! You really are amazing! Oh, I'm so happy, happy, happy!

MASHA.   And I'm so bored, bored, bored! (*Sits up.*) I can't get it out of my head. . . . It's simply disgusting. It's like having a nail driven into my head. No, I can't keep silent about it any more. It's about Andrey. . . . He's actually mortgaged this house to a bank, and his wife's got hold of all the money—and yet the house doesn't belong to him, it belongs to all four of us! Surely, he must realize that, if he's got any honesty.

KOOLYGHIN.   Why bring all this up, Masha? Why bother about it now? Andriusha owes money all round. . . . Leave him alone.

MASHA.   Anyway, it's disgusting. (*Lies down.*)

KOOLYGHIN.   Well, we aren't poor, Masha. I've got work, I teach at the county school, I give private lessons in my spare time. . . . I'm just a plain, honest man. . . . *Omnia mea mecum porto,* as they say.

MASHA.   I don't ask for anything, but I'm just disgusted by injustice. (*A pause.*) Why don't you go home, Fiodor?

KOOLYGHIN   (*kisses her*). You're tired. Just rest here for a while. . . . I'll go home and wait for you. . . . Go to sleep. (*Goes to the door.*) I'm happy, happy, happy! (*Goes out.*)

IRENA.   The truth is that Andrey is getting to be shallow-minded. He's aging and since he's been living with that woman he's lost all the inspiration he used to have! Not long ago he was working for a professorship, and yet yesterday he boasted of having at last been elected a member of the County Council. Fancy him a member, with Protopopov as chairman! They say the whole town's laughing at him, he's the only one who doesn't know anything or see anything. And now, you see, everyone's at the fire, while he's just sitting in his room, not taking the slightest notice of it. Just playing his violin. (*Agitated.*) Oh, how dreadful it is, how dreadful, how dreadful! I can't bear it any longer, I can't, I really can't! . . .

(*Enter* OLGA. *She starts arranging things on her bedside table.*)

IRENA (*sobs loudly*). You must turn me out of here! Turn me out; I
can't stand it any more!

OLGA (*alarmed*). What is it, darling?

IRENA (*sobbing*). Where. . . . Where has it all gone to? Where is it?
Oh, God! I've forgotten. . . . I've forgotten everything . . . there's
nothing but a muddle in my head. . . . I don't remember what the
Italian for "window" is, or for "ceiling." . . . Every day I'm forgetting
more and more, and life's slipping by, and it will never, never come
back. . . . We shall never go to Moscow. . . . I can see that we shall
never go. . . .

OLGA. Don't, my dear, don't. . . .

IRENA (*trying to control herself*). Oh, I'm so miserable! . . . I can't
work, I won't work! I've had enough of it, enough! . . . First I worked
on the telegraph, now I'm in the County Council office, and I hate
and despise everything they give me to do there. . . . I'm twenty-three
years old, I've been working all this time, and I feel as if my brain's
dried up. I know I've got thinner and uglier and older, and I find no
kind of satisfaction in anything, none at all. And the time's passing
. . . and I feel as if I'm moving away from any hope of a genuine, fine
life, I'm moving further and further away and sinking into a kind of
abyss. I feel in despair, and I don't know why I'm still alive, why I
haven't killed myself. . . .

OLGA. Don't cry, my dear child, don't cry. . . . It hurts me.

IRENA. I'm not crying any more. That's enough of it. Look, I'm not
crying now. Enough of it, enough! . . .

OLGA. Darling, let me tell you something. . . . I just want to speak as
your sister, as your friend. . . . That is, if you want my advice. . . .
Why don't you marry the Baron?

IRENA (*weeps quietly.*)

OLGA. After all, you do respect him, you think a lot of him. . . . It's
true, he's not good-looking, but he's such a decent, clean-minded sort
of man. . . . After all, one doesn't marry for love, but to fulfil a duty.
At least, I think so, and I'd marry even if I weren't in love. I'd marry
anyone that proposed to me, as long as he was a decent man. I'd even
marry an old man.

IRENA. I've been waiting all this time, imagining that we'd be moving
to Moscow, and I'd meet the man I'm meant for there. I've dreamt
about him and I've loved him in my dreams. . . . But it's all turned
out to be nonsense . . . nonsense. . . .

OLGA (*embracing her*). My darling sweetheart, I understand everything
perfectly. When the Baron resigned his commission and came to see us
in his civilian clothes, I thought he looked so plain that I actually

started to cry. . . . He asked me why I was crying. . . . How could I tell him? But, of course, if it were God's will that he should marry you, I'd feel perfectly happy about it. That's quite a different matter, quite different!

(NATASHA, *carrying a candle, comes out of the door on the right, crosses the stage and goes out through the door on the left without saying anything.*)

MASHA (*sits up*). She goes about looking as if she'd started the fire.

OLGA. You're silly, Masha. You're the stupidest person in our family. Forgive me for saying so.

(*A pause.*)

MASHA. My dear sisters, I've got something to confess to you. I must get some relief, I feel the need of it in my heart. I'll confess it to you two alone, and then never again, never to anybody! I'll tell you in a minute. (*In a low voice.*) It's a secret, but you'll have to know everything. I can't keep silent any more. (*A pause.*) I'm in love, in love. . . . I love that man. . . . You saw him here just now. . . . Well, what's the good? . . . I love Vershinin. . . .

OLGA (*goes behind her screen*). Don't say it. I don't want to hear it.

MASHA. Well, what's to be done? (*Holding her head.*) I thought he was queer at first, then I started to pity him . . . then I began to love him . . . love everything about him—his voice, his talk, his misfortunes, his two little girls. . . .

OLGA. Nevertheless, I don't want to hear it. You can say any nonsense you like, I'm not listening.

MASHA. Oh, you're stupid, Olia! If I love him, well—that's my fate! That's my destiny. . . . He loves me, too, It's all rather frightening, isn't it? Not a good thing, is it? (*Takes* IRENA *by the hand and draws her to her.*) Oh, my dear! . . . How are we going to live through the rest of our lives? What's going to become of us? When you read a novel, everything in it seems so old and obvious, but when you fall in love yourself, you suddenly discover that you don't really know anything, and you've got to make your own decisions. . . . My dear sisters, my dear sisters! . . . I've confessed it all to you, and now I'll keep quiet. . . . I'll be like that madman in the story by Gogol—silence . . . silence! . . .

(*Enter* ANDREY *followed by* FERAPONT.)

ANDREY (*crossly*). What do you want? I don't understand you.

FERAPONT (*stopping in the doorway, impatiently*). I've asked you about ten times already, Andrey Serghyeevich.

ANDREY. In the first place, you're not to call me Andrey Serghyeevich—call me "Your Honour."

FERAPONT. The firemen are asking Your Honour if they may drive through your garden to get to the river. They've been going a long way round all this time—it's a terrible business!

ANDREY. All right. Tell them it's all right. (FERAPONT *goes out.*) They keep on plaguing me. Where's Olga? (OLGA *comes from behind the screen.*) I wanted to see you. Will you give me the key to the cupboard? I've lost mine. You know the key I mean, the small one you've got. . . .

(OLGA *silently hands him the key.* IRENA *goes behind the screen on her side of the room.*)

ANDREY. What a terrific fire! It's going down though. That Ferapont annoyed me, the devil take him! Silly thing he made me say. . . . Telling him to call me "Your Honour"! . . . (*A pause.*) Why don't you say anything, Olia? (*A pause.*) It's about time you stopped this nonsense . . . sulking like this for no reason whatever. . . . You here, Masha? And Irena's here, too. That's excellent! We can talk it over then, frankly and once for all. What have you got against me? What is it?

OLGA. Drop it now, Andriusha. Let's talk it over to-morrow. (*Agitated.*) What a dreadful night!

ANDREY (*in great embarrassment*). Don't get upset. I'm asking you quite calmly, what have you got against me? Tell me frankly.

VERSHININ'S VOICE (*off stage*). Tum-tum-tum!

MASHA (*in a loud voice, getting up*). Tara-tara-tara! (*To* OLGA.) Good-bye, Olia, God bless you! (*Goes behind the screen and kisses* IRENA.) Sleep well. . . . Good-bye, Andrey. I should leave them now, they're tired . . . talk it over to-morrow. . . . (*Goes out.*)

OLGA. Really, Andriusha, let's leave it till to-morrow. . . . (*Goes behind the screen on her side of the room.*) It's time to go to bed.

ANDREY. I only want to say one thing, then I'll go. In a moment. . . . First of all, you've got something against my wife, against Natasha. I've always been conscious of it from the day we got married. Natasha is a fine woman, she's honest and straightforward and high-principled. . . . That's my opinion. I love and respect my wife. You understand that I respect her, and I expect others to respect her, too. I repeat: she's an honest, high-principled woman, and all your grievances against her —if you don't mind my saying so—are just imagination, and nothing more. . . . (*A pause.*) Secondly, you seem to be annoyed with me for not making myself a professor, and not doing any academic work. But I'm working in the Council Office, I'm a member of the County Council, and I feel my service there is just as fine and valuable as any academic work I might do. I'm a member of the County Council, and if you want to know, I'm proud of it! (*A pause.*) Thirdly . . . there's something else I must tell you. . . . I know I mortgaged the house without asking your permission. . . . That was wrong, I admit it, and I ask you to forgive me. . . . I was driven to it by my debts. . . . I'm in debt for about thirty-five thousand roubles. I don't play cards any more, I've given it up long ago. . . . The only thing I can say to justify myself is that you girls get an annuity, while I don't get anything . . . no income, I mean. . . . (*A pause.*)

KOOLYGHIN (*calling through the door*). Is Masha there? She's not there? (*Alarmed.*) Where can she be then? It's very strange. . . . (*Goes away.*)

ANDREY. So you won't listen? Natasha is a good, honest woman, I tell you. (*Walks up and down the stage, then stops.*) When I married her, I thought we were going to be happy, I thought we should all be happy. . . . But . . . oh, my God! . . . (*Weeps.*) My dear sisters, my dear, good sisters, don't believe what I've been saying, don't believe it. . . . (*Goes out.*)

KOOLYGHIN (*through the door, agitated*). Where's Masha? Isn't Masha here? Extraordinary! (*Goes away.*)

(*The alarm is heard again. The stage is empty.*)

IRENA (*speaking from behind the screen*). Olia! Who's that knocking on the floor?

OLGA. It's the doctor, Ivan Romanych. He's drunk.

IRENA. It's been one thing after another all night. (*A pause.*) Olia! (*Peeps out from behind the screen.*) Have you heard? The troops are being moved from the district . . . they're being sent somewhere a long way off.

OLGA. That's only a rumour.

IRENA. We'll be left quite alone then. . . . Olia!

OLGA. Well?

IRENA. Olia, darling, I do respect the Baron. . . . I think a lot of him, he's a very good man. . . . I'll marry him, Olia, I'll agree to marry him, if only we can go to Moscow! Let's go, please do let's go! There's nowhere in the world like Moscow. Let's go, Olia! Let's go!

ACT IV

The old garden belonging to the Prozorovs' house. A river is seen at the end of a long avenue of fir-trees, and on the far bank of the river a forest. On the right of the stage there is a verandah with a table on which champagne bottles and glasses have been left. It is midday. From time to time people from the street pass through the garden to get to the river. Five or six soldiers march through quickly.

CHEBUTYKIN, *radiating a mood of benevolence which does not leave him throughout the act, is sitting in a chair in the garden. He is wearing his army cap and is holding a walking stick, as if ready to be called away at any moment.* KOOLYGHIN, *with a decoration round his neck and with his moustache shaved off,* TOOZENBACH *and* IRENA *are standing on the verandah saying good-bye to* FEDOTIK *and* RODÉ, *who are coming down the steps. Both officers are in marching uniform.*

TOOZENBACH   (*embracing* FEDOTIK). You're a good fellow, Fedotik; we've been good friends! (*Embraces* RODÉ.) Once more, then. . . . Good-bye, my dear friends!

IRENA.   Au revoir!

FEDOTIK.   It's not "au revoir." It's good-bye. We shall never meet again!

KOOLYGHIN.   Who knows? (*Wipes his eyes, smiling.*) There! you've made me cry.

IRENA.   We'll meet some time.

FEDOTIK.   Perhaps in ten or fifteen years' time. But then we'll hardly know one another. . . . We shall just meet and say, "How are you?" coldly. . . . (*Takes a snapshot.*) Wait a moment. . . . Just one more, for the last time.

RODÉ   (*embraces* TOOZENBACH). We're not likely to meet again. . . . (*Kisses* IRENA's *hand.*) Thank you for everything . . . everything!

FEDOTIK   (*annoyed*). Do just wait a second!

TOOZENBACH.   We'll meet again if we're fated to meet. Do write to us. Be sure to write.

RODÉ   (*glancing round the garden*). Good-bye, trees! (*Shouts.*) Heigh-ho! (*A pause.*) Good-bye, echo!

KOOLYGHIN.   I wouldn't be surprised if you got married out there, in Poland. . . . You'll get a Polish wife, and she'll put her arms round you and say: Kohane! [4] (*Laughs.*)

FEDOTIK   (*glances at his watch*). There's less than an hour to go. Soliony is the only one from our battery who's going down the river on the barge. All the others are marching with the division. Three batteries are leaving to-day by road and three more to-morrow—then the town will be quite peaceful.

TOOZENBACH.   Yes, and dreadfully dull, too.

RODÉ.   By the way, where's Maria Serghyeevna?

KOOLYGHIN.   She's somewhere in the garden.

FEDOTIK.   We must say good-bye to her.

RODÉ.   Good-bye. I really must go, or I'll burst into tears. (*Quickly embraces* TOOZENBACH *and* KOOLYGHIN, *kisses* IRENA's *hand.*) Life's been very pleasant here. . . .

FEDOTIK   (*to* KOOLYGHIN). Here's something for a souvenir for you—a note-book with a pencil. . . . We'll go down to the river through here. (*They go off, glancing back.*)

[4] A Polish word meaning "beloved."

RODÉ *(shouts)*. Heigh-ho!

KOOLYGHIN *(shouts)*. Good-bye!

(At the back of the stage FEDOTIK *and* RODÉ *meet* MASHA, *and say good-bye to her; she goes off with them.)*

IRENA. They've gone. . . . *(Sits down on the bottom step of the verandah.)*

CHEBUTYKIN. They forgot to say good-bye to me.

IRENA. Well, what about you?

CHEBUTYKIN. That's true, I forgot, too. Never mind, I'll be seeing them again quite soon. I'll be leaving to-morrow. Yes . . . only one more day. And then, in a year's time I'll be retiring. I'll come back here and finish the rest of my life near you. There's just one more year to go and then I get my pension. . . . *(Puts a newspaper in his pocket and takes out another.)* I'll come back here and lead a reformed life. I'll be a nice, quiet, well-behaved little man.

IRENA. Yes, it's really time you reformed, my dear friend. You ought to live a different sort of life, somehow.

CHEBUTYKIN. Yes. . . . I think so, too. *(Sings quietly.)* Tarara-boom-di-ay. . . . I'm sitting on a tomb-di-ay. . . .

KOOLYGHIN. Ivan Romanych is incorrigible! Incorrigible!

CHEBUTYKIN. Yes, you ought to have taken me in hand. You'd have reformed me!

IRENA. Fiodor's shaved his moustache off. I can't bear to look at him.

KOOLYGHIN. Why not?

CHEBUTYKIN. If I could just tell you what your face looks like now—but I daren't.

KOOLYGHIN. Well! Such are the conventions of life! *Modus vivendi,* you know. The director shaved his moustache off, so I shaved mine off when they gave me an inspectorship. No one likes it, but personally I'm quite indifferent. I'm content. Whether I've got a moustache or not, it's all the same to me. *(Sits down.)*

ANDREY *(passes across the back of the stage pushing a pram with a child asleep in it.)*

IRENA. Ivan Romanych, my dear friend, I'm awfully worried about something. You were out in the town garden last night—tell me what happened there?

CHEBUTYKIN. What happened? Nothing. Just a trifling thing. *(Reads his paper.)* It doesn't matter anyway.

KOOLYGHIN. They say that Soliony and the Baron met in the town garden outside the theatre last night and . . .

TOOZENBACH. Don't please! What's the good? . . . *(Waves his hand at him deprecatingly and goes into the house.)*

KOOLYGHIN. It was outside the theatre. . . . Soliony started badgering the Baron, and he lost patience and said something that offended him.

CHEBUTYKIN.   I don't know anything about it. It's all nonsense.

KOOLYGHIN.   A school-master once wrote "nonsense" in Russian over a pupil's essay, and the pupil puzzled over it, thinking it was a Latin word. (*Laughs.*) Frightfully funny, you know! They say that Soliony's in love with Irena and that he got to hate the Baron more and more. . . . Well, that's understandable. Irena's a very nice girl. She's a bit like Masha, she tends to get wrapped up in her own thoughts. (*To* IRENA.) But your disposition is more easy-going than Masha's. And yet Masha has a very nice disposition, too. I love her, I love my Masha.

(*From the back of the stage comes a shout: "Heigh-ho!"*)

IRENA   (*starts*) : Anything seems to startle me to-day. (*A pause.*) I've got everything ready, too. I'm sending my luggage off after lunch. The Baron and I are going to get married to-morrow, and directly afterwards we're moving to the brick-works, and the day after to-morrow I'm starting work at the school. So our new life will begin, God willing! When I was sitting for my teacher's diploma, I suddenly started crying for sheer joy, with a sort of feeling of blessedness. . . . (*A pause*) . The carrier will be coming for my luggage in a minute. . . .

KOOLYGHIN.   That's all very well, but somehow I can't feel that it's meant to be serious. All ideas and theories, but nothing really serious. Anyway, I wish you luck from the bottom of my heart.

CHEBUTYKIN   (*moved*) . My dearest girl, my precious child! You've gone on so far ahead of me, I'll never catch you up now. I've got left behind like a bird which has grown too old and can't keep up with the rest of the flock. Fly away, my dears, fly away, and God be with you! (*A pause.*) It's a pity you've shaved your moustache off, Fiodor Illyich.

KOOLYGHIN.   Don't keep on about it, please! (*Sighs.*) Well, the soldiers will be leaving to-day, and everything will go back to what it was before. Anyway, whatever they say, Masha is a good, loyal wife. Yes, I love her dearly and I'm thankful for what God has given me. Fate treats people so differently. For instance, there's an excise clerk here called Kozyrev. He was at school with me and he was expelled in his fifth year because he just couldn't grasp the *ut consecutivum*. He's dreadfully hard up now, and in bad health, too, and whenever I meet him, I just say to him: "Hullo, *ut consecutivum!*" "Yes," he replies, "that's just the trouble—*consecutivum*" . . . and he starts coughing. Whereas I—I've been lucky all my life. I'm happy, I've actually been awarded the order of Saint Stanislav, second class—and now I'm teaching children the same old *ut consecutivum*. Of course, I'm clever, cleverer than plenty of other people, but happiness does not consist of merely being clever. . . .

(*In the house someone plays "The Maiden's Prayer."*)

IRENA. To-morrow night I shan't have to listen to "The Maiden's Prayer." I shan't have to meet Protopopov. . . . (*A pause.*) By the way, he's in the sitting-room. He's come again.

KOOLYGHIN. Hasn't our headmistress arrived yet?

IRENA. No, we've sent for her. If you only knew how difficult it is for me to live here by myself, without Olia! She lives at the school now; she's the headmistress and she's busy the whole day. And I'm here alone, bored, with nothing to do, and I hate the very room I live in. So I've just made up my mind—if I'm really not going to be able to live in Moscow, that's that. It's my fate, that's all. Nothing can be done about it. It's God's will, everything that happens, and that's the truth. Nikolai Lvovich proposed to me. . . . Well, I thought it over, and I made up my mind. He's such a nice man, it's really extraordinary how nice he is. . . . And then suddenly I felt as though my soul had grown wings, I felt more cheerful and so relieved somehow that I wanted to work again. Just to start work! . . . Only something happened yesterday, and now I feel as though something mysterious is hanging over me. . . .

CHEBUTYKIN. Nonsense!

NATASHA (*speaking through the window*). Our headmistress!

KOOLYGHIN. Our headmistress has arrived! Let's go indoors.

(*Goes indoors with* IRENA.)

CHEBUTYKIN (*reads his paper and sings quietly to himself*). Tarara-boom-di-ay. . . . I'm sitting on a tomb-di-ay. . . .

(MASHA *walks up to him;* ANDREY *passes across the back of the stage pushing the pram.*)

MASHA. You look very comfortable sitting here. . . .

CHEBUTYKIN. Well, why not? Anything happening?

MASHA (*sits down*). No nothing. (*A pause.*) Tell me something. Were you in love with my mother?

CHEBUTYKIN. Yes, very much in love.

MASHA. Did she love you?

CHEBUTYKIN (*after a pause*). I can't remember now.

MASHA. Is my man here? Our cook Marfa always used to call her policeman "my man." Is he here?

CHEBUTYKIN. Not yet.

MASHA. When you have to take your happiness in snatches, in little bits, as I do, and then lose it, as I've lost it, you gradually get hardened and bad-tempered. (*Points at her breast.*) Something's boiling over inside me, here. (*Looking at* ANDREY, *who again crosses the stage with the pram.*) There's Andrey, our dear brother. . . . All our hopes are gone. It's the same as when thousands of people haul a huge bell up into a tower. Untold labour and money is spent on it, and then suddenly it falls and gets smashed. Suddenly, without rhyme or reason. It was the same with Andrey. . . .

ANDREY. When are they going to settle down in the house? They're making such a row.

CHEBUTYKIN. They will soon. (*Looks at his watch.*) This is an old-fashioned watch: it strikes. . . . (*Winds his watch which then strikes.*) The first, second and fifth batteries will be leaving punctually at one o'clock. (*A pause.*) And I shall leave to-morrow.

ANDREY. For good?

CHEBUTYKIN. I don't know. I may return in about a year. Although, God knows . . . it's all the same. . . .

(*The sounds of a harp and a violin are heard.*)

ANDREY. The town will seem quite empty. Life will be snuffed out like a candle. (*A pause.*) Something happened yesterday outside the theatre; everybody's talking about it. I'm the only one that doesn't seem to know about it.

CHEBUTYKIN. It was nothing. A lot of nonsense. Soliony started badgering the Baron, or something. The Baron lost his temper and insulted him, and in the end Soliony had to challenge him to a duel. (*Looks at his watch.*) I think it's time to go. . . . At half-past twelve, in the forest over there, on the other side of the river. . . . Bang-bang! (*Laughs.*) Soliony imagines he's like Lermontov. He actually writes poems. But, joking apart, this is his third duel.

MASHA. Whose third duel?

CHEBUTYKIN. Soliony's.

MASHA. What about the Baron?

CHEBUTYKIN. Well, what about him? (*A pause.*)

MASHA. My thoughts are all in a muddle. . . . But what I mean to say is that they shouldn't be allowed to fight. He might wound the Baron or even kill him.

CHEBUTYKIN. The Baron's a good enough fellow, but what does it really matter if there's one Baron more or less in the world? Well, let it be! It's all the same. (*The shouts of "Ah-oo!" and "Heigh-ho!" are heard from beyond the garden.*) That's Skvortsov, the second shouting from the boat. He can wait.

ANDREY. I think it's simply immoral to fight a duel, or even to be present at one as a doctor.

CHEBUTYKIN. That's only how it seems. . . . We don't exist, nothing exists, it only seems to us that we do. . . . And what difference does it make?

MASHA. Talk, talk, nothing but talk all day long! . . . (*Starts to go.*) Having to live in this awful climate with the snow threatening to fall at any moment, and then on the top of it having to listen to all this sort of talk. . . . (*Stops.*) I won't go into the house, I can't bear going in there. . . . Will you let me know when Vershinin comes? . . . (*Walks off along the avenue.*) Look, the birds are beginning to fly away already! (*Looks up.*) Swans or geese. . . . Dear birds, happy birds. . . . (*Goes off.*)

ANDREY. Our house will seem quite deserted. The officers will go, you'll go, my sister will get married, and I'll be left alone in the house.

CHEBUTYKIN. What about your wife?

(*Enter* FERAPONT *with some papers.*)

ANDREY. My wife is my wife. She's a good, decent sort of woman . . . she's really very kind, too, but there's something about her which pulls her down to the level of an animal . . . a sort of mean, blind, thick-skinned animal—anyway, not a human being. I'm telling you this as a friend, the only person I can talk openly to. I love Natasha, it's true. But at times she appears to me so utterly vulgar, that I feel quite bewildered by it, and then I can't understand why, for what reasons I love her—or, anyway, did love her.

CHEBUTYKIN (*gets up*). Well, dear boy, I'm going away to-morrow and it may be we shall never see each other again. So I'll give you a bit of advice. Put on your hat, take a walking stick, and go away. . . . Go away, and don't ever look back. And the further you go, the better.

(SOLIONY *passes across the back of the stage accompanied by two officers. Seeing* CHEBUTYKIN, *he turns towards him, while the officers walk on.*)

SOLIONY. It's time, Doctor. Half past twelve already. (*Shakes hands with* ANDREY.)

CHEBUTYKIN. In a moment. Oh, I'm tired of you all. (*To* ANDREY.) Andriusha, if anyone asks for me, tell them I'll be back presently. (*Sighs.*) Oh-ho-ho!

SOLIONY. "He had no time to say 'Oh, oh!'
Before that bear had struck him low." . . .
(*Walks off with him.*) What are you groaning about, old man?

CHEBUTYKIN. Oh, well!

SOLIONY. How do you feel?

CHEBUTYKIN (*crossly*). Like a last year's bird's-nest.

SOLIONY. You needn't be so agitated about it, old boy. I shan't indulge in anything much, I'll just scorch his wings a little, like a woodcock's. (*Takes out a scent bottle and sprinkles scent over his hands.*) I've used up a whole bottle to-day, but my hands still smell. They smell like a corpse. (*A pause.*) Yes. . . . Do you remember that Poem of Lermontov's?

"And he, rebellious, seeks a storm,
As if in storms there were tranquillity." . . .

CHEBUTYKIN. Yes.

> "He had no time to say 'Oh, oh!'
> Before that bear had struck him low."

(*Goes out with* SOLIONY. *Shouts of "Heigh-ho!" and "Ah-oo!" are heard. Enter* ANDREY *and* FERAPONT.)

FERAPONT. Will you sign these papers, please?

ANDREY (*with irritation*). Leave me alone! Leave me alone, for Heaven's sake. (*Goes off with the pram.*)

FERAPONT. Well, what am I supposed to do with the papers then? They are meant to be signed, aren't they? (*Goes to back of stage.*)

(*Enter* IRENA *and* TOOZENBACH, *the latter wearing a straw hat.* KOOLYGHIN *crosses the stage, calling: "Ah-oo! Masha! Ah-oo!"*)

TOOZENBACH. I think he's the only person in the whole town who's glad that the army is leaving.

IRENA. That's quite understandable, really. (*A pause.*) The town will look quite empty.

TOOZENBACH. My dear, I'll be back in a moment.

IRENA. Where are you going?

TOOZENBACH. I must slip back to the town, and then . . . I want to see some of my colleagues off.

IRENA. It's not true. . . . Nikolai, why are you so absent-minded to-day? (*A pause.*) What happened outside the theatre last night?

TOOZENBACH (*with a movement of impatience*). I'll be back in an hour. . . . I'll be back with you again. (*Kisses her hands.*) My treasure! . . . (*Gazes into her eyes.*) It's five years since I first began to love you, and still I can't get used to it, and you seem more beautiful every day. What wonderful, lovely hair! What marvellous eyes! I'll take you away to-morrow. We'll work, we'll be rich, my dreams will come to life again. And you'll be happy! But—there's only one "but," only one—you don't love me!

IRENA. I can't help that! I'll be your wife, I'll be loyal and obedient to you, but I can't love you. . . . What's to be done? (*Weeps.*) I've never loved anyone in my life. Oh, I've had such dreams about being in love! I've been dreaming about it for ever so long, day and night . . . but somehow my soul seems like an expensive piano which someone has locked up and the key's got lost. (*A pause.*) Your eyes are so restless.

TOOZENBACH. I was awake all night. Not that there's anything to be afraid of in my life, nothing threatening. . . . Only the thought of that lost key torments me and keeps me awake. Say something to me. . . . (*A pause.*) Say something!

IRENA. What? What am I to say? What?

TOOZENBACH. Anything.

IRENA. Don't, my dear, don't. . . . (*A pause.*)

TOOZENBACH. Such trifles, such silly little things sometimes become so important suddenly, for no apparent reason! You laugh at them, just as you always have done, you still regard them as trifles, and yet you suddenly find they're in control, and you haven't the power to stop them. But don't let us talk about all that! Really, I feel quite elated. I feel as if I was seeing those fir-trees and maples and birches for the first time in my life. They all seem to be looking at me with a sort of inquisitive look and waiting for something. What beautiful trees— and how beautiful, when you think of it, life ought to be with trees like these! (*Shouts of "Ah-oo! Heigh-ho!" are heard.*) I must go, it's time. . . . Look at that dead tree, it's all dried-up, but it's still swaying in the wind along with the others. And in the same way, it seems to me that, if I die, I shall still have a share in life somehow or other. Good-bye, my dear. . . . (*Kisses her hands.*) Your papers, the ones you gave me, are on my desk, under the calendar.

IRENA. I'm coming with you.

TOOZENBACH (*alarmed*). No, no! (*Goes off quickly, then stops in the avenue.*) Irena!

IRENA. What?

TOOZENBACH (*not knowing what to say*). I didn't have any coffee this morning. Will you tell them to get some ready for me? (*Goes off quickly.*)

(IRENA *stands, lost in thought, then goes to the back of the stage and sits down on a swing. Enter* ANDREY *with the pram;* FERAPONT *appears.*)

FERAPONT. Andrey Serghyeech, the papers aren't mine, you know, they're the office papers. I didn't make them up.

ANDREY. Oh, where has all my past life gone to?—the time when I was young and gay and clever, when I used to have fine dreams and great thoughts, and the present and the future were bright with hope? Why do we become so dull and commonplace and uninteresting almost before we've begun to live? Why do we get lazy, indifferent, useless, unhappy? . . . This town's been in existence for two hundred years; a hundred thousand people live in it, but there's not one who's any different from all the others! There's never been a scholar or an artist or a saint in this place, never a single man sufficiently outstanding to make you feel passionately that you wanted to emulate him. People here do nothing but eat, drink and sleep. . . . Then they die and some more take their places, and they eat, drink and sleep, too,—and just to introduce a bit of variety into their lives, so as to avoid getting com-pletely stupid with boredom, they indulge in their disgusting gossip and vodka and gambling and law-suits. The wives deceive their hus-bands, and the husbands lie to their wives, and pretend they don't see anything and don't hear anything. . . . And all this overwhelming vulgarity and pettiness crushes the children and puts out any spark they might have in them, so that they, too, become miserable, half-dead creatures, just like one another and just like their parents! . . . (*To* FERAPONT, *crossly.*) What do you want?

FERAPONT.   What? Here are the papers to sign.

ANDREY.   What a nuisance you are!

FERAPONT   (*hands him the papers*). The porter at the finance department told me just now . . . he said last winter they had two hundred degrees of frost in Petersburg.

ANDREY.   I hate the life I live at present, but oh! the sense of elation when I think of the future! Then I feel so light-headed, such a sense of release! I seem to see light ahead, light and freedom. I see myself free, and my children, too,—free from idleness, free from *kvass,* free from eternal meals of goose and cabbage, free from after-dinner naps, free from all this degrading parasitism! . . .

FERAPONT.   They say two thousand people were frozen to death. They say everyone was scared stiff. It was either in Petersburg or in Moscow, I can't remember exactly.

ANDREY   (*with sudden emotion, tenderly*). My dear sisters, my dear good sisters! (*Tearfully.*) Masha, my dear sister! . . .

NATASHA   (*through the window*). Who's that talking so loudly there? Is that you, Andriusha? You'll wake Sofochka. *Il ne faut pas faire du bruit, la Sophie est dormie déjà. Vous êtes un ours.* (*Getting angry.*) If you want to talk, give the pram to someone else. Ferapont, take the pram from the master.

FERAPONT.   Yes, Madam. (*Takes the pram.*)

ANDREY   (*shamefacedly*). I was talking quietly.

NATASHA   (*in the window, caressing her small son*). Bobik! Naughty Bobik! Aren't you a naughty boy!

ANDREY   (*glancing through the papers*). All right, I'll go through them and sign them if they need it. You can take them back to the office later. (*Goes into the house, reading the papers.*)

(FERAPONT *wheels the pram into the garden.*)

NATASHA   (*in the window*). What's Mummy's name, Bobik? You darling! And who's that lady? Auntie Olia. Say: "Hullo, Auntie Olia."

(*Two street musicians, a man and a girl, enter and begin to play on a violin and a harp;* VERSHININ, OLGA *and* ANFISA *come out of the house and listen in silence for a few moments; then* IRENA *approaches them.*)

OLGA.   Our garden's like a public road; everybody goes through it. Nanny, give something to the musicians.

ANFISA   (*giving them money*). Go along now, God bless you, good people! (*The musicians bow and go away.*) Poor, homeless folk! Whoever would go dragging round the streets playing tunes if he had enough to eat? (*To* IRENA.) How are you, Irenushka? (*Kisses her.*) Ah, my child, what a life I'm having! Such comfort! In a large flat at the school with Oliushka—and no rent to pay, either! The Lord's been kind to me in my old age. I've never had such a comfortable time in my life, old sinner that I am! A big flat, and no rent to pay, and a whole room to myself, with my own bed. All free. Sometimes when I wake up in the night I begin to think, and then—Oh, Lord! Oh, Holy Mother of God!—there's no one happier in the world than me!

VERSHININ (*glances at his watch*). We shall be starting in a moment Olga Serghyeevna. It's time I went. (*A pause.*) I wish you all the happiness in the world . . . everything. . . . Where's Maria Serghyeevna?

IRENA. She's somewhere in the garden. I'll go and look for her.

VERSHININ. That's kind of you. I really must hurry.

ANFISA. I'll come and help to look for her. (*Calls out.*) Mashenka, ah-oo! (*Goes with* IRENA *towards the far end of the garden.*) Ah-oo! Ah-oo!

VERSHININ. Everything comes to an end. Well, here we are—and now it's going to be "good-bye." (*Looks at his watch.*) The city gave us a sort of farewell lunch. There was champagne, and the mayor made a speech, and I ate and listened, but in spirit I was with you here. . . . (*Glances round the garden.*) I've grown so . . . so accustomed to you.

OLGA. Shall we meet again some day, I wonder?

VERSHININ. Most likely no! (*A pause.*) My wife and the two little girls will be staying on here for a month or two. Please, if anything happens, if they need anything. . . .

OLGA. Yes, yes, of course. You needn't worry about that. (*A pause.*) To-morrow there won't be a single officer or soldier in the town. . . . All that will be just a memory, and, of course, a new life will begin for us here. . . . (*A pause.*) Nothing ever happens as we'd like it to. I didn't want to be a headmistress, and yet now I am one. It means we shan't be going to live in Moscow. . . .

VERSHININ. Well. . . . Thank you for everything. Forgive me if ever I've done anything. . . . I've talked a lot too much, far too much. . . . Forgive me for that, don't think too unkindly of me.

OLGA (*wipes her eyes*). Now . . . why is Masha so long coming?

VERSHININ. What else can I tell you now it's time to say "good-bye"? What shall I philosophize about now? . . . (*Laughs.*) Yes, life is difficult. It seems quite hopeless for a lot of us, just a kind of impasse. . . . And yet you must admit that it is gradually getting easier and brighter, and it's clear that the time isn't far off when the light will spread everywhere. (*Looks at his watch.*) Time, it's time for me to go. . . . In the old days the human race was always making war, its entire existence was taken up with campaigns, advances, retreats, victories.

. . . But now all that's out of date, and in its place there's a huge
vacuum, clamouring to be filled. Humanity is passionately seeking
something to fill it with and, of course it will find something some day.
Oh! If only it would happen soon! (*A pause.*) If only we could educate
the industrious people and make the educated people industrious. . . .
(*Looks at his watch.*) I really must go. . . .

OLGA.   Here she comes!

(*Enter* MASHA.)

VERSHININ.   I've come to say good-bye. . . .

(OLGA *walks off and stands a little to one side so as not to interfere with
their leave-taking.*)

MASHA   (*looking into his face*). Good-bye! . . . (*A long kiss.*)

OLGA.   That'll do, that'll do.

MASHA   (*sobs loudly.*)

VERSHININ.   Write to me. . . . Don't forget me! Let me go . . . it's time.
Olga Serghyeevna, please take her away . . . I must go . . . I'm late
already. . . . (*Deeply moved, kisses* OLGA'*s hands, then embraces* MASHA
once again and goes out quickly.)

OLGA.   That'll do, Masha! Don't, my dear, don't. . . .

(*Enter* KOOLYGHIN.)

KOOLYGHIN   (*embarrassed*). Never mind, let her cry, let her. . . . My
dear Masha, my dear, sweet Masha. . . . You're my wife, and I'm
happy in spite of everything. . . . I'm not complaining, I've no reproach to make—not a single one. . . . Olga here is my witness. . . .
We'll start our life over again in the same old way, and you won't hear
a word from me . . . not a hint. . . .

MASHA   (*suppressing her sobs*). "A green oak grows by a curving shore,
And round that oak hangs a golden chain." . . . "A golden chain
round that oak." . . . Oh, I'm going mad. . . . By a curving shore
. . . a green oak. . . .

OLGA.   Calm yourself, Masha, calm yourself. . . . Give her some water.

MASHA.   I'm not crying any more. . . .

KOOLYGHIN.   She's not crying any more . . . she's a good girl.

(*The hollow sound of a gun-shot is heard in the distance.*)

MASHA.   "A green oak grows by a curving shore, And round that oak
hangs a golden chain." . . . A green cat . . . a green oak . . . I've
got it all mixed up . . . (*Drinks water.*) My life's messed up. . . . I
don't want anything now. . . . I'll calm down in a moment. . . . it
doesn't matter. . . . What *is* "the curving shore"? Why does it keep
coming into my head all the time? My thoughts are all mixed up.

(*Enter* IRENA.)

OLGA.   Calm down, Masha. That's right . . . good girl! . . . Let's go
indoors.

MASHA (*irritably*) : I'm not going in there! (*Sobs, but immediately checks herself.*) I don't go into that house now, and I'm not going to. . . .

IRENA. Let's sit down together for a moment, and not talk about anything. I'm going away to-morrow, you know. . . .

(*A pause.*)

KOOLYGHIN. Yesterday I took away a false beard and a moustache from a boy in the third form. I've got them here. (*Puts them on.*) Do I look like our German teacher? . . . (*Laughs.*) I do, don't I? The boys are funny.

MASHA. It's true, you do look like that German of yours.

OLGA (*laughs*) . Yes, he does.

(MASHA *cries.*)

IRENA. That's enough, Masha!

KOOLYGHIN. Very much like him, I think!

(*Enter* NATASHA.)

NATASHA (*to the maid*) . What? Oh, yes. Mr. Protopopov is going to keep an eye on Sofochka, and Andrey Serghyeevich is going to take Bobik out in the pram. What a lot of work these children make! . . . (*To* IRENA.) Irena, you're really leaving to-morrow? What a pity! Do stay just another week, won't you? (*Catching sight of* KOOLYGHIN, *shrieks; he laughs and takes off the false beard and moustache.*) Get away with you! How you scared me! (*To* IRENA.) I've grown so accustomed to you being here. . . . You mustn't think it's going to be easy for me to be without you. I'll get Andrey and his old violin to move into your room: he can saw away at it as much as he likes there. And then we'll move Sofochka into his room. She's such a wonderful child, really! Such a lovely little girl! This morning she looked at me with such a sweet expression, and then she said: "Ma-mma!"

KOOLYGHIN. It's quite true, she is a beautiful child.

NATASHA. So to-morrow I'll be alone here. (*Sighs.*) I'll have this fir-tree avenue cut down first, then that maple tree over there. It looks so awful in the evenings. . . . (*To* IRENA.) My dear, that belt you're wearing doesn't suit you at all. Not at all in good taste. You want something brighter to go with that dress. . . . I'll tell them to put flowers all round here, lots of flowers, so that we get plenty of scent from them. . . . (*Sternly.*) Why is there a fork lying on this seat? (*Going into the house, to the maid.*) Why is that fork left on the seat there? (*Shouts.*) Don't answer me back!

KOOLYGHIN. There she goes again.

(*A band plays a military march off stage; all listen.*)

OLGA. They're going.

(*Enter* CHEBUTYKIN.)

MASHA. The soldiers are going. Well. . . . Happy journey to them! (*To her husband.*) We must go home. . . . Where's my hat and cape? . . .

KOOLYGHIN. I took them indoors. I'll bring them at once.

OLGA. Yes, we can go home now. It's time.

CHEBUTYKIN. Olga Serghyeevna!

OLGA. What is it? (*A pause.*) What?

CHEBUTYKIN. Nothing. . . . I don't know quite how to tell you. . . . (*Whispers into her ear.*)

CHEBUTYKIN. Yes . . . a bad business. . . . I'm so tired . . . quite worn out. . . . I don't want to say another word. . . . (*With annoyance.*) Anyway, nothing matters! . . .

MASHA. What's happened?

OLGA (*puts her arms round* IRENA). What a dreadful day! . . . I don't know how to tell you, dear. . . .

IRENA. What is it? Tell me quickly, what is it? For Heaven's sake! . . . (*Cries.*)

CHEBUTYKIN. The Baron's just been killed in a duel.

IRENA (*cries quietly*). I knew it, I knew it. . . .

CHEBUTYKIN (*goes to the back of the stage and sits down*). I'm tired. . . . (*Takes a newspaper out of his pocket.*) Let them cry for a bit. . . . (*Sings quietly to himself.*) Tarara-boom-di-ay, I'm sitting on a tomb-di-ay. . . . What difference does it make? . . .

(*The three sisters stand huddled together.*)

MASHA. Oh, listen to that band! They're leaving us . . . one of them's gone for good . . . for ever! We're left alone . . . to start our lives all over again. We must go on living . . . we must go on living. . . .

IRENA (*puts her head on* OLGA'S *breast*). Some day people will know why such things happen, and what the purpose of all this suffering is. . . . Then there won't be any more riddles. . . . Meanwhile we must go on living . . . and working. Yes, we must just go on working! To-morrow I'll go away alone and teach in a school somewhere; I'll give my life to people who need it. . . . It's autumn now, winter will soon be here, and the snow will cover everything . . . but I'll go on working and working! . . .

OLGA (*puts her arms round both her sisters*). How cheerfully and jauntily that band's playing—really I feel as if I wanted to live! Merciful God! The years will pass, and we shall all be gone for good and quite forgotten. . . . Our faces and our voices will be forgotten and people won't even know that there were once three of us here. . . . But our sufferings may mean happiness for the people who come after us. . . . There'll be a time when peace and happiness reign in the world, and then we shall be remembered kindly and blessed. No, my dear sisters, life isn't finished for us yet! We're going to live! The band is playing so cheerfully and joyfully—maybe, if we wait a little longer, we shall find out why we live, why we suffer. . . . Oh, if we only knew, if only we knew!

(*The music grows fainter and fainter.* KOOLYGHIN, *smiling happily, brings out the hat and the cape.* ANDREY *enters; he is pushing the pram with* BOBIK *sitting in it.*)

CHEBUTYKIN (*sings quietly to himself*). Tarara-boom-di-ay. . . . I'm sitting on a tomb-di-ay. . . . (*Reads the paper.*) What does it matter? Nothing matters!

OLGA. If only we knew, if only we knew! . . .

THE THREE SISTERS:
THE POETICS OF MODERNISM

PHILIP RODDMAN

... TO COMPLICATE THINGS IN A NEW WAY ... IS EASY, BUT TO SEE THINGS IN A NEW WAY ... IS REALLY DIFFICULT, EVERYTHING PREVENTS ONE, HABITS, SCHOOLS, DAILY LIFE, REASON, INDOLENCE, EVERYTHING PREVENTS ONE. ... THAT IS WHY GENIUSES ARE RARE. GERTRUDE STEIN, *PICASSO*.

Cultural historians tell us that the plays of Greece as well as those of the Renaissance had their source in forms of ritual. Whether natural or supernatural in import, the ritual reassured the audience of the continuity of existence: the representation of a death followed by a revival or an active life mirroring the destiny of a people. Aristotle, a century after the flowering of such tragic poets as Aeschylus, Sophocles, and Euripides, was the first to write about the genesis and the structure of drama, which he systematized into a moral conception of the universe. The materials of drama, he said, were myth, human happiness and human misery, and a recognizable pattern of heroic destiny. Myth Aristotle equated with history, happiness and misery with forms of action—that is, with public success and public failure, not as we do, with interior and secret states of being—and the pattern of destiny with a plot, the absolute logic of a situation having a beginning, a middle, and an end. The effect upon an audience of this combination of elements in tragic poetry Aristotle considered both a cathartic and an elixir: purging the audience of its fears and doubts and revitalizing it with an image of wholeness and harmony.

Until the appearance of Anton Chekhov's innovations in drama, playwrights, of both the Classic and Romantic schools, acknowledged Aristotle's *Poetics* as the primary system of art. They accepted the heroic man as the bearer of a certain kind of wisdom, a hidden knowledge of his destiny or necessary fate, which—whether interpreted in transhuman, human, or idealistic terms—implied a fixed center and a unit of history, a story that comprised a meaningful chain of events. Chekhov was the first dramatist to break with this law of art, with the concept of an inherent logic in the acts of a man or woman who is at the heart of a play. First, he considered the fixed center an illusion of perspective and the unit of history an illusion of passion and memory. Second, he dispensed with a backdrop that was a sounding board for the meaning of man's humanity; that is, he rejected the religious or philosophical bond —the ethical constant—that tied man to an immutable pattern, whose force gave to a man's acts the shape and thrust of happiness or misery. Third, he dissolved the sense of a propulsive linear time in which causes and effects signaled to one another and bore the fruit of their consummations. In other words, Chekhov turned his back on a system that balanced all accounts and that suspended the vagaries of human nature in a world of chance in order to vindicate the principle of a transfinite moral harmony.

Chekhov was the master of a new poetics because he was the master of a very old, a pre-European, vision. Perhaps Conrad's Stein in *Lord Jim* comes close to it in a famous, many-faceted sentence: "A man that is born falls into a dream like a man who falls into the sea." Chekhov brought human life into the foreground, giving it the immediacy of a dream. He made it move in a continuous present, with everything happening at once, as in a street fair. Somewhere beyond the human scene he recognized a persistence of some sort, but one totally blind to man's needs, deaf to his most glorious music and poetry, and therefore no more to be invoked than the slab of stone that seals a grave. One might call this persistence *nature*—but, of course, dissociated from the connotations added to the word by such ideals as Wordsworth's "Nature's holy plan" —and one might go on to describe it as mechanical, mindless, monotonous, forever still or forever flowing depending on one's position—like darkness, like light, like space, like gravity, detached from the humanness of human events as the waves are from the progress or destination of a sail. Against this background or upon its surface, men and women appear and disappear like bubbles of air. Out of this scientific vision Chekhov fashioned the comedy of contrasts and the tragedy of dissolutions and stitched them together in such a way as to form an art that is like a reversible fabric. In Chekhov the Socratic conviction that the genius of tragedy is the same as the genius of comedy is beautifully substantiated. On the one hand, Chekhov contrasted the warm immediacy of human presence with the substantial coldness of the vast inertia of nature. On the other hand, he made a distinction between the dream that each of his characters breathes, or the tender land for which his heart is yearning, and the concrete life of food, of sleep, of idleness, of work, of birth, of death that he actually experiences. "A man of letters," Chekhov said, "should be as objective as a chemist." As a consequence, we see in his plays the complete range of the chemistry of life's colors in the everpresent interplay between the illusions that make life bearable and the actualities that bear it up. Everything is in counterpoint between the disequilibrium of society and the equilibrium of the life cycle. The many internal and the many external worlds have no connection. When they touch, it is only to collide in frustration or in death. The house in *The Three Sisters,* for example, has an external value for Natasha and Protopopov that is antipodal to the civilization dreamed and realized inside it.

Before Chekhov's vision of life the wisdom of the schools and the art of the academies appear thin and vain. His plays read like *Ecclesiastes.* "*O fallacem hominum spem!*—accusative after an interjection," Kulygin says, after Natasha has upset everyone's plans for the evening. And indeed, for Chekhov not only are all hopes illusions—as in the Latin tag —but they are also disruptions of whatever pleasures in the midst of which there is a possibility of being pleased. Irina's hope of Moscow—the refrain of Act I, the curtain lines of Acts II and III, which bring to a focus all the passions of the play about work, about love, about the New Jerusalem that is to flower within a century or two—is the most tormenting and devouring of all the illusions. It poisons her remarkable gifts and condemns her at the end to become the feminine counterpart of the unfeeling Dr. Chebutykin. It is as a criticism of illusions, not as a criticism of life—about whose meaning or meanings Chekhov absolutely refused to speculate—that we value his art. Not only in the characters he created, but also in the old philosophies and old poetries, he wished to separate sense from nonsense. He felt that to endow life, as the old systems did, with a beauty that it did not possess and with a nobility that it did not display, was to alienate men from life as it is experienced, to make them ineffectual, violent, melancholy, or apathetic. There is something sinister, irrational, and absurd in Solyony's evoking Lermontov, in Masha's quoting Pushkin, in Vershinin's paraphrasing his harumscarum utopists. Chekhov preferred the wisdom of experience to any art or philosophy of inexperience. That is why he turned drama into life, not life into drama. His advice to young writers was that of a behaviorist in psychology. "Remember," he once said to a writer, "the subject must be new [taken from life, not from literature] and you can do without a plot."

At a time when so eminent an author as Tolstoy was sternly recalling men from the old forms of literature and art—as in *What Is Art?*—to even older forms of religion, and while another equally eminent man, George Bernard Shaw, in his esthetic socialism was extolling the old forms of literature and art as the religion of the future—witness Dubedat's dying speech in *The Doctor's Dilemma*—Chekhov, dedicated doctor that he was, calmly pursued his purpose of observing life as truly and honestly as a biologist observes a laboratory culture or as an atomic physicist studies a cloud chamber. Of his great contemporaries, it was Thomas Hardy who perhaps came closest to Chekhov's attentive interests. In a note meant only for his own eyes, Hardy wrote in his youth: "A naturalist's interest in the hatching of a queer egg or germ is the utmost introspective consideration you should allow yourself." Whatever we may think of Chekhov's positivist approach to literature, so rare in an age of symbolist mysticism on the one hand and sociological naturalism on the other, we must credit him with the courage to see things as they are—without philosophical or religious adhesions—and with an appreciation of the genuine, if very modest, possibilities of life. Instead of presenting characters whom we can emulate, instead of creating plays with which we can identify our moral and spiritual ideals, instead of documenting the inhumanity of man or the malevolence of nature, Chekhov did something much more difficult: He invented an art form that detaches us from our preconceptions about life and so extends our range of perception and sharpens the precision of our feelings. Here we have the key to the epic theater of Bertolt Brecht and to the absurdist theater of Samuel Beckett and his followers. But it is the key of the master of them all, the key of Anton Chekhov, who never luxuriates in his mind- or soul-states. If the art of the twentieth century that is subsumed under the general term of *modernism* has several fathers, surely the father of modernist dramatic literature is Anton Chekhov. It was he who first applied the leverage that replaced the old poetics of catharsis and harmony with the new poetics of detachment and precision. If the old poetics took for granted a freedom to will and to be made whole, Chekhov's poetics insisted on our freedom to think and to take the measure of our defeat. Chekhov suggested that we examine our condition before we indulge our feelings lest we convert our illusions into hallucinations. By an odd turn of history we have all become Chekhovian characters. The hostile, hopeless climate of *fin-de-siècle* Russia has persisted in one form or another until it has permeated the whole World Technopolis. Everywhere we have grown resigned to the lie on the front page, to the destruction of the canopy of trees between the ancient park and the asphalt drive, to the loss of our youth's emotional investments, to the wanderings of the dispossessed, while remaining apprehensive of the knock on the door, of the notice that we are no longer wanted, and of the inexorable marching orders. The spent Faustian dream that drifts through *The Three Sisters* has by now invaded the literary tissue of the American Dream with a frowzy *Angst*.

All the leading characters in *The Three Sisters* are the late products of a Faustian century, of Faustian habits of thought, but without the Faustian will or the Faustian faith. Although in pursuit of happiness, they no longer believe that anything they do in the present can control the future. They therefore moralize and philosophize the livelong day and far into the night in order to disinfect the air of the stale odor of futility. Of the Romantic spirit of Faustianism they have retained the feeling of contempt for the world and the capacity for being bored. But this contempt is not a mark of their superiority to an unjust world; rather, it is a screen for their confusion and ineffectuality before the facts of life mistaken for an unjust world. And their boredom is not a signal for renewed activity, as with the Romantics, but for the onset of paralysis. Gentry, demi-aristocrats, intellectuals, Chekhov's characters see themselves as the proper heirs to all civilization, refusing in their highbred egotism, much like Ezra Pound and T. S. Eliot and their epigones, to do justice to a Niagara epoch of new knowledge, new technology, new social permutations. The self-invention of the early Romantics, who cultivated the Will at the expense of the Reality Principle of science, has in Chekhov's world grown fatally confused with self-doubt; and the self-endearment of the movers and shakers of a young and blissful age has withered into self-ennui. The Faustians have suddenly become "superfluous men," and salvation by the *ewig Weibliche*—the eternal feminine—an absurdity. All these free souls in *The Three Sisters* have donned uniforms of one sort or another—enslaved to a military or pedagogical or governmental machine. And the two sisters who are not in uniform are condemned to a slavery even more fundamental: the dream of an elective sexual affinity, which may appear in an irrecoverable flash, as it does for Masha, or may elude the dreamer altogether, as it eludes Irina. The women cannot help the men because they are emotionally bankrupt, and the men cannot help the women because they are emotionally blind. Only the unselfconscious Natasha, who is set apart from the society of the play, and whose anonymous animality crushes everyone she touches, has that rough sense of thrift and ruthless insistence which, however distasteful, Chekhov finds less degrading to the human spirit than the charade of exhausted fantasies enacted among the elect. Natasha fascinates Chekhov because she is a monster, like a natural force, full of traps and ambushes; perhaps she is the true "eternal feminine." The difference between her and Irina is absolute. In the affecting scene of Act IV between Tusenbach and Irina, Tusenbach tries to draw a human cry—even if only one of despair—from the girl for whom he is about to fight a duel. But all he gets is the flattest of formulas—"the key to my heart"—transposed into a dream symbol of a costly piano. Indeed, Irina's fantasies have cost her her humanity:

> IRINA. Oh, how I dreamed of love, dreamed of it for years and years, night and day, but my heart is like a costly piano whose case is locked and the key lost.
> TUSENBACH. I didn't sleep all night. . . . Just this lost key haunts me and keeps me awake at night. Say something. (*Pause.*) Say something.
> IRINA. What shall I say? What?
> TUSENBACH. Anything.
> IRINA. No, I can't.

For once we stand outside a romantic scene—the lover going off to duel for his love—and observe its hardness, its confusion, its cruelty, its folly, and the pity of it. Chekhov, to use Blake's verse, makes "a tear . . . an intellectual thing." We feel for Tusenbach, knowing that he very likely thinks death preferable to the mixed agonies of life with Irina. At any rate, in that scene the romantic flames of love, of a very long century, expire in the smoke of a pistol shot.

The consort of voices in a Chekhov play is a web of contradictions, tautologies, irrelevances, as in life, constantly forcing us into statements of our own, into making sense of the nonsense of casual conversations. The imagery in the plays is the paraphernalia of daily living. The very familiarity of the things—cameras, keys, and fiddles, clocks, forks, and scent bottles, newspapers, belts, and old clothes, birds, trees, and flowers, sleigh bells, perambulators, and pianos, fire and snow—the very familiarity serves to bridge the pauses in the dialogue, the breaks between the short spans of attention, the intermittences of memory that the characters display. The images or objects are there to be touched, to be looked at, to be heard, to be remembered, remaining simple and indeterminate, never conspicuous, always ashimmer with air and color, like the lives that they accompany and sustain. Chekhov is an impressionist, calling upon the eye of the beholder to fuse the colors indicated by the crosslights of objects and dialogue. The human observer selects the rhythms that answer to those of his own experience. Everything is appearance, everything remains inconclusive. People go on talking, sometimes loving, forever arriving and leaving, and always dying. To Masha's question: "But, does that make sense?" Tusenbach replies: "Sense! It's snowing out there. Does that make sense?"

Chekhov is the most civilized of modern writers. He allows us to draw from his work any belief we choose. He never intimidates us with a meaning, any more than life does.

SHAW

GEORGE BERNARD SHAW (1856–1950), WHO BECAME THE BEST-KNOWN WRITER THE TWENTIETH CENTURY HAS THUS FAR PRODUCED, WAS UNPUBLISHED UNTIL HE WAS NEARLY THIRTY AND RELATIVELY UNKNOWN UNTIL HE WAS PAST FORTY. BORN IN DUBLIN OF IRISH PROTESTANT PARENTS, SHAW LEFT IRELAND FOREVER WHEN HE WAS TWENTY. THE TEN YEARS IN LONDON BEFORE SHAW ESTABLISHED HIMSELF AS A MUSIC-ART-DRAMA CRITIC WERE CRUCIAL TO HIS DEVELOPMENT. AS AN IMPOVERISHED AND UNPUBLISHED NOVELIST, SHAW DISCOVERED THE WORLD OF THE POOR AND THE DISPOSSESSED, BECOMING A LIFELONG SOCIALIST AND A FOUNDER OF THE FABIAN SOCIETY—PROGENITOR OF THE BRITISH LABOUR PARTY. HIS PLAYS ACHIEVED POPULARITY IN THE EARLY 1900S AND ENTERED THE REPERTORIES OF THEATERS THROUGHOUT THE WORLD.

Caesar and Cleopatra (1897–1898) is the first of Shaw's major plays. Although it lacks the high style of *Man and Superman,* the perfect structure of *Pygmalion,* the intellectual virtuosity of *Major Barbara,* and the near-tragic intensity of *Saint Joan, Caesar and Cleopatra* is nevertheless a formidable and absorbing play.

What fascinates us most in the work is, of course, Julius Caesar. Despite Shakespeare's denigratory portrait of him, Caesar was one of the titans of history, a genius who could command armies and successfully administer a vast empire which he himself had pieced together. The extent to which Shaw's portrait is historically accurate is beside the point: It is sufficiently accurate in broad outline, and it captures the spirit of the man. What *is* to the point is that the portrait is credible, and the credibility is the key to Shaw's achievement.

As we read the play, we observe that Shaw's portraitures of Caesar and of Cleopatra differ in technique. In Caesar, Shaw's method is exfoliation—a gradual process of revelation until at the end, we sense the hard, gemlike center of this most complex of men. Compare one's impression of Caesar in the first scene: He is like a wise and experienced high school principal taking in hand an unruly bright young pupil. But we become progressively aware of the extraordinary range and flexibility of his mind, his objectivity combined with a profound humanity.

Cleopatra's character, on the other hand, is not so much revealed as developed; the thrust of the play derives from the impulse of the mature mind to nurture the moral development of the inexperienced. The real conflict in the play arises from Cleopatra's resistance to education. A compendium of superstition, irrationality, cruelty, and fear at the outset of the play, Cleopatra—in this play the eternal adolescent, capable of learning but egocentrically selective—is no more than an expendable chesspiece for the strong men battling for the mastery of Egypt.

Is Cleopatra merely the most direct means of Caesar's achieving his ends or simply a part of the apparatus in Caesar's inspired improvisations? However we interpret Caesar's feelings toward Cleopatra, what emerges from the tension between them is the enthronement of a queen and the embarkation of a great man upon the last stage of the momentous journey toward his destiny.

CAESAR AND CLEOPATRA

ACT I

*An October night on the Syrian border of Egypt towards the end of the
XXXIII Dynasty, in the year 706 by Roman computation, afterwards
reckoned by Christian computation as 48 B.C. A great radiance of silver
fire, the dawn of a moonlit night, is rising in the east. The stars and the
cloudless sky are our own contemporaries, nineteen and a half centuries
younger than we know them; but you would not guess that from their appearance. Below them are two notable drawbacks of civilization: a palace,
and soldiers. The palace, an old, low, Syrian building of whitened mud,
is not so ugly as Buckingham Palace; and the officers in the courtyard are
more highly civilized than modern English officers: for example, they do
not dig up the corpses of their dead enemies and mutilate them, as we dug
up Cromwell and the Mahdi. They are in two groups: one intent on the
gambling of their captain Belzanor, a warrior of fifty, who, with his spear
on the ground beside his knee, is stooping to throw dice with a sly-looking
young Persian recruit; the other gathered about a guardsman who has just
finished telling a naughty story (still current in English barracks) at
which they are laughing uproariously. They are about a dozen in number, all highly aristocratic young Egyptian guardsmen, handsomely
equipped with weapons and armor, very unEnglish in point of not being
ashamed of and uncomfortable in their professional dress; on the contrary,
rather ostentatiously and arrogantly warlike, as valuing themselves on
their military caste.*

*Belzanor is a typical veteran, tough and wilful; prompt, capable and
crafty where brute force will serve; helpless and boyish when it will not:
an effective sergeant, an incompetent general, a deplorable dictator.
Would, if influentially connected, be employed in the two last capacities
by a modern European State on the strength of his success in the first. Is
rather to be pitied just now in view of the fact that Julius Caesar is invad-
ing his country. Not knowing this, is intent on his game with the Persian,
whom, as a foreigner, he considers quite capable of cheating him.*

*His subalterns are mostly handsome young fellows whose interest in the
game and the story symbolizes with tolerable completeness the main interests in life of which they are conscious. Their spears are leaning against
the walls, or lying on the ground ready to their hands. The corner of the
courtyard forms a triangle of which one side is the front of the palace,
with a doorway, the other a wall with a gateway. The storytellers are on
the palace side; the gamblers, on the gateway side. Close to the gateway,
against the wall, is a stone block high enough to enable a Nubian sentinel, standing on it, to look over the wall. The yard is lighted by a torch*

stuck in the wall. As the laughter from the group round the storyteller dies away, the kneeling Persian, winning the throw, snatches up the stake from the ground.

BELZANOR.   By Apis, Persian, thy gods are good to thee.

THE PERSIAN.   Try yet again, O captain. Double or quits!

BELZANOR.   No more. I am not in the vein.

THE SENTINEL   *(poising his javelin as he peers over the wall)*. Stand. Who goes there?

(They all start, listening. A strange voice replies from without.)

VOICE.   The bearer of evil tidings.

BELZANOR   *(calling to the sentry)*. Pass him.

THE SENTINEL   *(grounding his javelin)*. Draw near, O bearer of evil tidings.

BELZANOR   *(pocketing the dice and picking up his spear)*. Let us receive this man with honor. He bears evil tidings.

(The GUARDSMEN *seize their spears and gather about the gate, leaving a way through for the new comer.)*

PERSIAN   *(rising from his knee)*. Are evil tidings, then, so honorable?

BELZANOR.   O barbarous Persian, hear my instruction. In Egypt the bearer of good tidings is sacrificed to the gods as a thank offering; but no god will accept the blood of the messenger of evil. When we have good tidings, we are careful to send them in the mouth of the cheapest slave we can find. Evil tidings are borne by young noblemen who desire to bring themselves into notice. *(They join the rest at the gate.)*

THE SENTINEL.   Pass, O young captain; and bow the head in the House of the Queen.

VOICE.   Go anoint thy javelin with fat of swine, O Blackamoor; for before morning the Romans will make thee eat it to the very butt.

(The owner of the voice, a fairhaired dandy, dressed in a different fashion to that affected by the GUARDSMEN, *but no less extravagantly, comes through the gateway laughing. He is somewhat battlestained; and his left forearm, bandaged, comes through a torn sleeve. In his right hand he carries a Roman sword in its sheath. He swaggers down the courtyard, the* PERSIAN *on his right,* BELZANOR *on his left and the* GUARDSMEN *crowding down behind him.)*

BELZANOR.   Who art thou that laughest in the House of Cleopatra the Queen, and in the teeth of Belzanor, the captain of her guard?

THE NEW COMER.   I am Bel Affris, descended from the gods.

BELZANOR   *(ceremoniously)*. Hail, cousin!

ALL   *(except the* PERSIAN*)*. Hail, cousin!

PERSIAN.   All the Queen's guards are descended from the gods, O stranger, save myself. I am Persian, and descended from many kings.

BEL AFFRIS (*to the* GUARDSMEN). Hail, cousins! (*To the* PERSIAN, *condescendingly*) Hail, mortal!

BELZANOR. You have been in battle, Bel Affris; and you are a soldier among soldiers. You will not let the Queen's women have the first of your tidings.

BEL AFFRIS. I have no tidings, except that we shall have our throats cut presently, women, soldiers, and all.

PERSIAN (*to* BELZANOR) . I told you so.

THE SENTINEL (*who has been listening*) . Woe, alas!

BEL AFFRIS (*calling to him.*) Peace, peace, poor Ethiop: destiny is with the gods who painted thee black. (*To* BELZANOR) What has this mortal (*indicating the* PERSIAN) told you?

BELZANOR. He says that the Roman Julius Caesar, who has landed on our shores with a handful of followers, will make himself master of Egypt. He is afraid of the Roman soldiers. (*The* GUARDSMEN *laugh with boisterous scorn.*) Peasants, brought up to scare crows and follow the plough. Sons of smiths and millers and tanners! And we nobles, consecrated to arms, descended from the gods!

PERSIAN. Belzanor: the gods are not always good to their poor relations.

BELZANOR (*hotly, to the* PERSIAN). Man to man, are we worse than the slaves of Caesar?

BEL AFFRIS (*stepping between them*) . Listen, cousin. Man to man, we Egyptians are as gods above the Romans.

THE GUARDSMEN (*exultingly*) . Aha!

BEL AFFRIS. But this Caesar does not pit man against man: he throws a legion at you where you are weakest as he throws a stone from a catapult; and that legion is as a man with one head, a thousand arms, and no religion. I have fought against them; and I know.

BELZANOR (*derisively*) . Were you frightened, cousin?

(*The* GUARDSMEN *roar with laughter, their eyes sparkling at the wit of their* CAPTAIN.)

BEL AFFRIS. No, cousin; but I was beaten. They were frightened (perhaps) ; but they scattered us like chaff.

(*The* GUARDSMEN, *much damped, utter a growl of contemptuous disgust.*)

BELZANOR. Could you not die?

BEL AFFRIS. No: that was too easy to be worthy of a descendant of the gods. Besides, there was no time: all was over in a moment. The attack came just where we least expected it.

BELZANOR. That shews that the Romans are cowards.

BEL AFFRIS. They care nothing about cowardice, these Romans: they fight to win. The pride and honor of war are nothing to them.

PERSIAN. Tell us the tale of the battle. What befell?

THE GUARDSMEN   (*gathering eagerly round* BEL AFFRIS). Ay: the tale of the battle.

BEL AFFRIS.   Know then, that I am a novice in the guard of the temple of Ra in Memphis, serving neither Cleopatra nor her brother Ptolemy, but only the high gods. We went a journey to inquire of Ptolemy why he had driven Cleopatra into Syria, and how we of Egypt should deal with the Roman Pompey, newly come to our shores after his defeat by Caesar at Pharsalia. What, think ye, did we learn? Even that Caesar is coming in hot pursuit of his foe, and that Ptolemy has slain Pompey, whose severed head he holds in readiness to present to the conqueror. (*Sensation among the* GUARDSMEN.) Nay, more: we found that Caesar is already come; for we had not made half a day's journey on our way back when we came upon a city rabble flying from his legions, whose landing they had gone out to withstand.

BELZANOR.   And ye, the temple guard! did ye not withstand these legions?

BEL AFFRIS.   What man could, that we did. But there came the sound of a trumpet whose voice was as the cursing of a black mountain. Then saw we a moving wall of shields coming towards us. You know how the heart burns when you charge a fortified wall; but how if the fortified wall were to charge you?

THE PERSIAN   (*exulting in having told them so*). Did I not say it?

BEL AFFRIS.   When the wall came nigh, it changed into a line of men— common fellows enough, with helmets, leather tunics, and breastplates. Every man of them flung his javelin: the one that came my way drove through my shield as through a papyrus—lo there! (*he points to the bandage on his left arm*) and would have gone through my neck had I not stooped. They were charging at the double then, and were upon us with short swords almost as soon as their javelins. When a man is close to you with such a sword, you can do nothing with our weapons: they are all too long.

THE PERSIAN.   What did you do?

BEL AFFRIS.   Doubled my fist and smote my Roman on the sharpness of his jaw. He was but mortal after all: he lay down in a stupor; and I took his sword and laid it on. (*Drawing the sword*) Lo! a Roman sword with Roman blood on it!

THE GUARDSMEN   (*approvingly*). Good! (*They take the sword and hand it round, examining it curiously.*)

THE PERSIAN.   And your men?

BEL AFFRIS.   Fled. Scattered like sheep.

BELZANOR   (*furiously*). The cowardly slaves! Leaving the descendants of the gods to be butchered!

BEL AFFRIS   (*with acid coolness*). The descendants of the gods did not stay to be butchered, cousin. The battle was not to the strong; but the race was to the swift. The Romans, who have no chariots, sent a cloud of horsemen in pursuit, and slew multitudes. Then our high priest's captain rallied a dozen descendants of the gods and exhorted us to die fighting. I said to myself: surely it is safer to stand than to lose my breath and be stabbed in the back; so I joined our captain and stood. Then the Romans treated us with respect; for no man attacks a lion when the field is full of sheep, except for the pride and honor of war, of which these Romans know nothing. So we escaped with our lives; and I am come to warn you that you must open your gates to Caesar; for his advance guard is scarce an hour behind me; and not an Egyptian warrior is left standing between you and his legions.

THE SENTINEL. Woe, alas! (*He throws down his javelin and flies into the palace.*)

BELZANOR. Nail him to the door, quick! (*The* GUARDSMEN *rush for him with their spears; but he is too quick for them.*) Now this news will run through the palace like fire through stubble.

BEL AFFRIS. What shall we do to save the women from the Romans?

BELZANOR. Why not kill them?

PERSIAN. Because we should have to pay blood money for some of them. Better let the Romans kill them: it is cheaper.

BELZANOR (*awestruck at his brain power.*) O subtle one! O serpent!

BEL AFFRIS. But your Queen?

BELZANOR. True: we must carry off Cleopatra.

BEL AFFRIS. Will ye not await her command?

BELZANOR. Command! a girl of sixteen! Not we. At Memphis ye deem her a Queen: here we know better. I will take her on the crupper of my horse. When we soldiers have carried her out of Caesar's reach, then the priests and the nurses and the rest of them can pretend she is queen again, and put their commands into her mouth.

PERSIAN. Listen to me, Belzanor.

BELZANOR. Speak, O subtle beyond thy years.

THE PERSIAN. Cleopatra's brother Ptolemy is at war with her. Let us sell her to him.

THE GUARDSMEN. O subtle one! O serpent!

BELZANOR. We dare not. We are descended from the gods; but Cleopatra is descended from the river Nile; and the lands of our fathers will grow no grain if the Nile rises not to water them. Without our father's gifts we should live the lives of dogs.

PERSIAN. It is true: the Queen's guard cannot live on its pay. But hear me further, O ye kinsmen of Osiris.

THE GUARDSMEN. Speak, O subtle one. Hear the serpent begotten!

PERSIAN. Have I heretofore spoken truly to you of Caesar, when you thought I mocked you?

GUARDSMEN.   Truly, truly.

BELZANOR   *(reluctantly admitting it)*. So Bel Affris says.

PERSIAN.   Hear more of him, then. This Caesar is a great lover of women: he makes them his friends and counsellors.

BELZANOR.   Faugh! This rule of women will be the ruin of Egypt.

THE PERSIAN.   Let it rather be the ruin of Rome! Caesar grows old now: he is past fifty and full of labors and battles. He is too old for the young women; and the old women are too wise to worship him.

BEL AFFRIS.   Take heed, Persian. Caesar is by this time almost within earshot.

PERSIAN.   Cleopatra is not yet a woman: neither is she wise. But she already troubles men's wisdom.

BELZANOR.   Ay: that is because she is descended from the river Nile and a black kitten of the sacred White Cat. What then?

PERSIAN.   Why, sell her secretly to Ptolemy, and then offer ourselves to Caesar as volunteers to fight for the overthrow of her brother and the rescue of our Queen, the Great Grand-daughter of the Nile.

THE GUARDSMEN.   O serpent!

PERSIAN.   He will listen to us if we come with her picture in our mouths. He will conquer and kill her brother, and reign in Egypt with Cleopatra for his Queen. And we shall be her guard.

GUARDSMEN.   O subtlest of all the serpents! O admiration! O wisdom!

BEL AFFRIS.   He will also have arrived before you have done talking, O word spinner.

BELZANOR.   That is true. *(An affrighted uproar in the palace interrupts him.)* Quick: the flight has begun: guard the door. *(They rush to the door and form a cordon before it with their spears. A mob of* WOMEN-SERVANTS *and* NURSES *surges out. Those in front recoil from the spears, screaming to those behind to keep back.* BELZANOR's *voice dominates the disturbance as he shouts)* Back there. In again, unprofitable cattle.

THE GUARDSMEN.   Back, unprofitable cattle.

BELZANOR.   Send us out Ftatateeta, the Queen's chief nurse.

THE WOMAN   *(calling into the palace)*. Ftatateeta, Ftatateeta. Come, come. Speak to Belzanor.

A WOMAN.   Oh, keep back. You are thrusting me on the spearheads.

(A huge grim woman, her face covered with a network of tiny wrinkles, and her eyes old, large, and wise; sinewy handed, very tall, very strong; with the mouth of a bloodhound and the jaws of a bulldog, appears on the threshold. She is dressed like a person of consequence in the palace, and confronts the GUARDSMEN *insolently.)*

FTATATEETA.   Make way for the Queen's chief nurse.

BELZANOR   *(with solemn arrogance)*. Ftatateeta: I am Belzanor, the captain of the Queen's guard, descended from the gods.

FTATATEETA   *(retorting his arrogance with interest)*. Belzanor: I am

Ftatateeta, the Queen's chief nurse; and your divine ancestors were proud to be painted on the wall in the pyramids of the kings whom my fathers served.

(*The* WOMEN *laugh triumphantly.*)

BELZANOR (*with grim humor*). Ftatateeta: daughter of a long-tongued, swivel-eyed chameleon, the Romans are at hand. (*A cry of terror from the* WOMEN: *they would fly but for the spears.*) Not even the descendants of the gods can resist them; for they have each man seven arms, each carrying seven spears. The blood in their veins is boiling quicksilver; and their wives become mothers in three hours, and are slain and eaten the next day.

(*A shudder of horror from the* WOMEN. FTATATEETA, *despising them and scorning the soldiers, pushes her way through the crowd and confronts the spear points undismayed.*)

FTATATEETA. Then fly and save yourselves, O cowardly sons of the cheap clay gods that are sold to fish porters; and leave us to shift for ourselves.

BELZANOR. Not until you have first done our bidding, O terror of manhood. Bring out Cleopatra the Queen to us and then go whither you will.

FTATATEETA (*with a derisive laugh*). Now I know why the gods have taken her out of our hands. (*The* GUARDSMEN *start and look at one another.*) Know, thou foolish soldier, that the Queen has been missing since an hour past sun down.

BELZANOR (*furiously*). Hag: you have hidden her to sell to Caesar or her brother. (*He grasps her by the left wrist, and drags her, helped by a few of the* GUARD, *to the middle of the courtyard, where, as they fling her on her knees, he draws a murderous looking knife.*) Where is she? Where is she? or— (*He threatens to cut her throat.*)

FTATATEETA (*savagely.*) Touch me, dog; and the Nile will not rise on your fields for seven times seven years of famine.

BELZANOR (*frightened, but desperate*). I will sacrifice: I will pay. Or stay. (*To the* PERSIAN) You, O subtle one: your father's lands lie far from the Nile. Slay her.

PERSIAN (*threatening her with his knife*). Persia has but one god; yet he loves the blood of old women. Where is Cleopatra?

FTATATEETA. Persian: as Osiris lives, I do not know. I chid her for bringing evil days upon us by talking to the sacred cats of the priests, and carrying them in her arms. I told her she would be left alone here when the Romans came as a punishment for her disobedience. And now she is gone—run away—hidden. I speak the truth. I call Osiris to witness—

THE WOMEN (*protesting officiously*). She speaks the truth, Belzanor.

BELZANOR. You have frightened the child: she is hiding. Search—quick —into the palace—search every corner.

(*The* GUARDS, *led by* BELZANOR, *shoulder their way into the palace through the flying crowd of* WOMEN, *who escape through the courtyard gate.*)

FTATATEETA (*screaming*). Sacrilege! Men in the Queen's chambers! Sa— (*Her voice dies away as the* PERSIAN *puts his knife to her throat.*)

BEL AFFRIS (*laying a hand on* FTATATEETA's *left shoulder*). Forbear her yet a moment, Persian. (*To* FTATATEETA, *very significantly*) Mother: your gods are asleep or away hunting; and the sword is at your throat. Bring us to where the Queen is hid, and you shall live.

FTATATEETA (*contemptuously*). Who shall stay the sword in the hand of a fool, if the high gods put it there? Listen to me, ye young men without understanding. Cleopatra fears me; but she fears the Romans more. There is but one power greater in her eyes than the wrath of the Queen's nurse and the cruelty of Caesar; and that is the power of the Sphinx that sits in the desert watching the way to the sea. What she would have it know, she tells into the ears of the sacred cats; and on her birthday she sacrifices to it and decks it with poppies. Go ye therefore into the desert and seek Cleopatra in the shadow of the Sphinx; and on your heads see to it that no harm comes to her.

BEL AFFRIS (*to the* PERSIAN). May we believe this, O subtle one?

PERSIAN. Which way come the Romans?

BEL AFFRIS. Over the desert, from the sea, by this very Sphinx.

PERSIAN (*to* FTATATEETA). O mother of guile! O aspic's tongue! You have made up this tale so that we two may go into the desert and perish on the spears of the Romans. (*Lifting his knife*) Taste death.

FTATATEETA. Not from thee, baby. (*She snatches his ankle from under him and flies stooping along the palace wall, vanishing in the darkness within its precinct.* BEL AFFRIS *roars with laughter as the* PERSIAN *tumbles. The* GUARDSMEN *rush out of the palace with* BELZANOR *and a mob of fugitives, mostly carrying bundles.*)

PERSIAN. Have you found Cleopatra?

BELZANOR. She is gone. We have searched every corner.

THE NUBIAN SENTINEL (*appearing at the door of the palace*). Woe! Alas! Fly, fly!

BELZANOR. What is the matter now?

THE NUBIAN SENTINEL. The sacred white cat has been stolen.

ALL. Woe! Woe! (*General panic. They all fly with cries of consternation. The torch is thrown down and extinguished in the rush. Darkness. The noise of the fugitives dies away. Dead silence. Suspense. Then the blackness and stillness breaks softly into silver mist and strange airs as the windswept harp of Memnon plays at the dawning of the moon. It rises full over the desert; and a vast horizon comes into relief, broken by a huge shape which soon reveals itself in the spreading radiance as a Sphinx pedestalled on the sands. The light still clears, until the upraised eyes of the image are distinguished looking straight forward and upward in infinite fearless vigil, and a mass of color between its great paws defines itself as a heap of red poppies on which a girl lies motionless, her silken vest heaving gently and regularly with the breathing of a dreamless sleeper, and her braided hair glittering in a shaft of moonlight like a bird's wing.*

Suddenly there comes from afar a vaguely fearful sound (it might be the bellow of a Minotaur softened by great distance) and Memnon's music stops. Silence: then a few faint high-ringing trumpet notes. Then silence again. Then a man comes from the south with stealing steps, ravished by the mystery of the night, all wonder, and halts, lost in contemplation, opposite the left flank of the Sphinx, whose bosom, with its burden, is hidden from him by its massive shoulder.)

THE MAN. Hail, Sphinx: salutation from Julius Caesar! I have wandered in many lands, seeking the lost regions from which my birth into this world exiled me, and the company of creatures such as I myself. I have found flocks and pastures, men and cities, but no other Caesar, no air native to me, no man kindred to me, none who can do my day's deed, and think my night's thought. In the little world yonder, Sphinx, my place is as high as yours in this great desert; only I wander, and you sit still; I conquer, and you endure; I work and wonder, you watch and wait; I look up and am dazzled, look down and am darkened, look round and am puzzled, whilst your eyes never turn from looking out— out of the world—to the lost region—the home from which we have strayed. Sphinx, you and I, strangers to the race of men, are no strangers to one another: have I not been conscious to you and of this place since I was born? Rome is a madman's dream: this is my Reality. These starry lamps of yours I have seen from afar in Gaul, in Britain, in Spain, in Thessaly, signalling great secrets to some eternal sentinel below, whose post I never could find. And here at last is their sentinel— an image of the constant and immortal part of my life, silent, full of thoughts, alone in the silver desert. Sphinx, Sphinx: I have climbed mountains at night to hear in the distance the stealthy footfall of the winds that chase your sands in forbidden play—our invisible children, O Sphinx, laughing in whispers. My way hither was the way of destiny; for I am he of whose genius you are the symbol: part brute, part woman, and part God—nothing of man in me at all. Have I read your riddle, Sphinx?

THE GIRL *(who has wakened, and peeped cautiously from her nest to see who is speaking.)* Old gentleman.

CAESAR *(starting violently, and clutching his sword)*. Immortal gods!

THE GIRL. Old gentleman: don't run away.

CAESAR *(stupefied)*. "Old gentleman: don't run away!!!" This! to Julius Caesar!

THE GIRL *(urgently)*. Old gentleman.

CAESAR. Sphinx: you presume on your centuries. I am younger than you, though your voice is but a girl's voice as yet.

THE GIRL. Climb up here, quickly; or the Romans will come and eat you.

CAESAR (*running forward past the Sphinx's shoulder, and seeing her*). A child at its breast! a divine child!

THE GIRL. Come up quickly. You must get up at its side and creep round.

CAESAR (*amazed*). Who are you?

THE GIRL. Cleopatra, Queen of Egypt.

CAESAR. Queen of the Gypsies, you mean.

CLEOPATRA. You must not be disrespectful to me, or the Sphinx will let the Romans eat you. Come up. It is quite cosy here.

CAESAR (*to himself*). What a dream! What a magnificent dream! Only let me not wake, and I will conquer ten continents to pay for dreaming it out to the end. (*He climbs to the Sphinx's flank, and presently reappears to her on the pedestal, stepping round its right shoulder.*)

CLEOPATRA. Take care. That's right. Now sit down: you may have its other paw. (*She seats herself comfortably on its left paw.*) It is very powerful and will protect us; but (*shivering, and with plaintive loneliness*) it would not take any notice of me or keep me company. I am glad you have come: I was very lonely. Did you happen to see a white cat anywhere?

CAESAR (*sitting slowly down on the right paw in extreme wonderment*). Have you lost one?

CLEOPATRA. Yes: the sacred white cat: is it not dreadful? I brought him here to sacrifice him to the Sphinx; but when we got a little way from the city a black cat called him, and he jumped out of my arms and ran away to it. Do you think that the black cat can have been my great-great-great-grand-mother?

CAESAR (*staring at her*). Your great-great-great-grand-mother! Well, why not? Nothing would surprise me on this night of nights.

CLEOPATRA. I think it must have been. My great-grand-mother's great-grandmother was a black kitten of the sacred white cat; and the river Nile made her his seventh wife. That is why my hair is so wavy. And I always want to be let do as I like, no matter whether it is the will of the gods or not: that is because my blood is made with Nile water.

CAESAR. What are you doing here at this time of night? Do you live here?

CLEOPATRA. Of course not: I am the Queen; and I shall live in the palace at Alexandria when I have killed my brother, who drove me out of it. When I am old enough I shall do just what I like. I shall be able to poison the slaves and see them wriggle, and pretend to Ftatateeta that she is going to be put into the fiery furnace.

CAESAR.   Hm! Meanwhile why are you not at home and in bed?

CLEOPATRA.   Because the Romans are coming to eat us all. You are not at home and in bed either.

CAESAR *(with conviction)*. Yes I am. I live in a tent; and I am now in that tent, fast asleep and dreaming. Do you suppose that I believe you are real, you impossible little dream witch?

CLEOPATRA *(giggling and leaning trustfully towards him)*. You are a funny old gentleman. I like you.

CAESAR.   Ah, that spoils the dream. Why don't you dream that I am young?

CLEOPATRA.   I wish you were; only I think I should be more afraid of you. I like men, especially young men with round strong arms; but I am afraid of them. You are old and rather thin and stringy; but you have a nice voice; and I like to have somebody to talk to, though I think you are a little mad. It is the moon that makes you talk to yourself in that silly way.

CAESAR.   What! you heard that, did you? I was saying my prayers to the great Sphinx.

CLEOPATRA.   But this isn't the great Sphinx.

CAESAR *(much disappointed looking up at the statue)*. What!

CLEOPATRA.   This is only a dear little kitten of the Sphinx. Why, the great Sphinx is so big that it has a temple between its paws. This is my pet Sphinx. Tell me: do you think the Romans have any sorcerers who could take us away from the Sphinx by magic?

CAESAR.   Why? Are you afraid of the Romans?

CLEOPATRA *(very seriously)*. Oh, they would eat us if they caught us. They are barbarians. Their chief is called Julius Caesar. His father was a tiger and his mother a burning mountain; and his nose is like an elephant's trunk. (CAESAR *involuntarily rubs his nose.*) They all have long noses, and ivory tusks, and little tails, and seven arms with a hundred arrows in each; and they live on human flesh.

CAESAR.   Would you like me to show you a real Roman?

CLEOPATRA *(terrified)*. No. You are frightening me.

CAESAR.   No matter: this is only a dream——

CLEOPATRA *(excitedly)*. It is not a dream: it is not a dream. See, see. *(She plucks a pin from her hair and jabs it repeatedly into his arm.)*

CAESAR.   Ffff—Stop. *(Wrathfully)* How dare you?

CLEOPATRA *(abashed)*. You said you were dreaming. *(Whimpering)* I only wanted to shew you——

CAESAR *(gently)*. Come, come: don't cry. A queen mustn't cry. *(He rubs his arm, wondering at the reality of the smart.)* Am I awake? *(He strikes his hand against the Sphinx to test its solidity. It feels so real that he begins to be alarmed, and says perplexedly)* Yes, I— *(quite panicstricken*) no: impossible: madness, madness! (*Desperately*) Back to camp—to camp. (*He rises to spring down from the pedestal.*)

CLEOPATRA (*flinging her arms in terror round him*). No: you shan't leave me. No, no, no: don't go. I'm afraid—afraid of the Romans.

CAESAR (*as the conviction that he is really awake forces itself on him*). Cleopatra: can you see my face well?

CLEOPATRA. Yes. It is so white in the moonlight.

CAESAR. Are you sure it is the moonlight that makes me look whiter than an Egyptian? (*Grimly*) Do you notice that I have a rather long nose?

CLEOPATRA (*recoiling, paralyzed by a terrible suspicion*). Oh!

CAESAR. It is a Roman nose, Cleopatra.

CLEOPATRA. Ah! (*With a piercing scream she springs up; darts round the left shoulder of the Sphinx; scrambles down to the sand; and falls on her knees in frantic supplication, shrieking*) Bite him in two, Sphinx: bite him in two. I meant to sacrifice the white cat—I did indeed—I (CAESAR, *who has slipped down from the pedestal, touches her on the shoulder*) Ah! (*She buries her head in her arms.*)

CAESAR. Cleopatra: shall I teach you a way to prevent Caesar from eating you?

CLEOPATRA (*clinging to him piteously*). Oh do, do, do. I will steal Ftatateeta's jewels and give them to you. I will make the river Nile water your lands twice a year.

CAESAR. Peace, peace, my child. Your gods are afraid of the Romans: you see the Sphinx dare not bite me, nor prevent me carrying you off to Julius Caesar.

CLEOPATRA (*in pleading murmurings*). You won't, you won't. You said you wouldn't.

CAESAR. Caesar never eats women.

CLEOPATRA (*springing up full of hope*). What!

CAESAR (*impressively*). But he eats girls (*she relapses*) and cats. Now you are a silly little girl; and you are descended from the black kitten. You are both a girl and a cat.

CLEOPATRA (*trembling*). And will he eat me?

CAESAR. Yes; unless you make him believe that you are a woman.

CLEOPATRA. Oh, you must get a sorcerer to make a woman of me. Are you a sorcerer?

CAESAR. Perhaps. But it will take a long time; and this very night you must stand face to face with Caesar in the palace of your fathers.

CLEOPATRA. No, no. I daren't.

CAESAR. Whatever dread may be in your soul—however terrible Caesar may be to you—you must confront him as a brave woman and a great queen; and you must feel no fear. If your hand shakes: if your voice quavers; then—night and death! (*She moans.*) But if he thinks you worthy to rule, he will set you on the throne by his side and make you the real ruler of Egypt.

CLEOPATRA   (*despairingly*). No: he will find me out: he will find me out.

CAESAR   (*rather mournfully*). He is easily deceived by women. Their eyes dazzle him; and he sees them not as they are, but as he wishes them to appear to him.

CLEOPATRA   (*hopefully*). Then we will cheat him. I will put on Ftatateeta's head-dress; and he will think me quite an old woman.

CAESAR.   If you do that he will eat you at one mouthful.

CLEOPATRA.   But I will give him a cake with my magic opal and seven hairs of the white cat baked in it; and——

CAESAR   (*abruptly*). Pah! you are a little fool. He will eat your cake and you too. (*He turns contemptuously from her.*)

CLEOPATRA   (*running after him and clinging to him*). Oh, please, please! I will do whatever you tell me. I will be good! I will be your slave. (*Again the terrible bellowing note sounds across the desert, now closer at hand. It is the bucina, the Roman war trumpet.*)

CAESAR.   Hark!

CLEOPATRA   (*trembling*). What was that?

CAESAR.   Caesar's voice.

CLEOPATRA   (*pulling at his hand*). Let us run away. Come. Oh, come.

CAESAR.   You are safe with me until you stand on your throne to receive Caesar. Now lead me thither.

CLEOPATRA   (*only too glad to get away*). I will, I will. (*Again the bucina.*) Oh, come, come, come: the gods are angry. Do you feel the earth shaking?

CAESAR.   It is the tread of Caesar's legions.

CLEOPATRA   (*drawing him away*). This way, quickly. And let us look for the white cat as we go. It is he that has turned you into a Roman.

CAESAR.   Incorrigible, oh, incorrigible! Away! (*He follows her, the bucina sounding louder as they steal across the desert. The moonlight wanes: the horizon again shows black against the sky, broken only by the fantastic silhouette of the Sphinx. The sky itself vanishes in darkness, from which there is no relief until the gleam of a distant torch falls on great Egyptian pillars supporting the roof of a majestic corridor. At the further end of this corridor a Nubian* SLAVE *appears carrying the torch.* CAESAR, *still led by* CLEOPATRA, *follows him. They come down the corridor,* CAESAR *peering keenly about at the strange architecture, and at the pillar shadows between which, as the passing torch makes them hurry noiselessly backwards, figures of men with wings and hawks' heads, and vast black marble cats, seem to flit in and out of ambush. Further along, the wall turns a corner and makes a spacious transept in which* CAESAR *sees, on his right, a throne, and behind the throne a door. On each side of the throne is a slender pillar with a lamp on it.*)

CAESAR.   What place is this?

CLEOPATRA.   This is where I sit on the throne when I am allowed to wear my crown and robes. (*The* SLAVE *holds his torch to shew the throne.*)

CAESAR.   Order the slave to light the lamps.

CLEOPATRA   (*shyly*). Do you think I may?

CAESAR.   Of course. You are the Queen. (*She hesitates.*) Go on.

CLEOPATRA   (*timidly, to the* SLAVE). Light all the lamps.

FTATATEETA   (*suddenly coming from behind the throne*). Stop. (*The* SLAVE *stops. She turns sternly to* CLEOPATRA, *who quails like a naughty child.*) Who is this you have with you; and how dare you order the lamps to be lighted without my permission? (CLEOPATRA *is dumb with apprehension.*)

CAESAR.   Who is she?

CLEOPATRA.   Ftatateeta.

FTATATEETA   (*arrogantly*). Chief nurse to——

CAESAR   (*cutting her short*). I speak to the Queen. Be silent. (*To* CLEO- PATRA) Is this how your servants know their places? Send her away; and do you (*to the* SLAVE) do as the Queen has bidden. (*The* SLAVE *lights the lamps. Meanwhile* CLEOPATRA *stands hesitating, afraid of* FTATATEETA.) You are the Queen: send her away.

CLEOPATRA   (*cajoling*). Ftatateeta, dear: you must go away—just for a little.

CAESAR.   You are not commanding her to go away: you are begging her. You are no Queen. You will be eaten. Farewell. (*He turns to go.*)

CLEOPATRA   (*clutching him*). No, no, no. Don't leave me.

CAESAR.   A Roman does not stay with queens who are afraid of their slaves.

CLEOPATRA.   I am not afraid. Indeed I am not afraid.

FTATATEETA.   We shall see who is afraid here. (*Menacingly*) Cleo- patra——

CAESAR.   On your knees, woman: am I also a child that you dare trifle with me? (*He points to the floor at* CLEOPATRA's *feet.* FTATATEETA, *half cowed, half savage, hesitates.* CAESAR *calls to the* NUBIAN) Slave. (*The* NUBIAN *comes to him.*) Can you cut off a head? (*The* NUBIAN *nods and grins ecstatically, showing all his teeth.* CAESAR *takes his sword by the scabbard, ready to offer the hilt to the* NUBIAN, *and turns again to* FTATATEETA, *repeating his gesture.*) Have you remembered yourself, mistress? (FTATATEETA, *crushed, kneels before* CLEOPATRA, *who can hardly believe her eyes.*)

FTATATEETA *(hoarsely)*. O Queen, forget not thy servant in the days of thy greatness.

CLEOPATRA *(blazing with excitement)*. Go. Begone. Go away. (FTATA-TEETA *rises with stooped head, and moves backwards towards the door.* CLEOPATRA *watches her submission eagerly, almost clapping her hands, which are trembling. Suddenly she cries)* Give me something to beat her with. *(She snatches a snake-skin from the throne and dashes after* FTATATEETA, *whirling it like a scourge in the air.* CAESAR *makes a bound and manages to catch her and hold her while* FTATATEETA *escapes.)*

CAESAR. You scratch, kitten, do you?

CLEOPATRA *(breaking from him)*. I will beat somebody. I will beat him. *(She attacks the* SLAVE.*)* There, there, there! *(The* SLAVE *flies for his life up the corridor and vanishes. She throws the snake-skin away and jumps on the step of the throne with her arms waving, crying)* I am a real Queen at last—a real, real Queen! Cleopatra the Queen! (CAESAR *shakes his head dubiously, the advantage of the change seeming open to question from the point of view of the general welfare of Egypt. She turns and looks at him exultantly. Then she jumps down from the step, runs to him, and flings her arms round him rapturously, crying)* Oh, I love you for making me a Queen.

CAESAR. But queens love only kings.

CLEOPATRA. I will make all the men I love kings. I will make you a king. I will have many young kings, with round, strong arms; and when I am tired of them I will whip them to death; but you shall always be my king: my nice, kind, wise, good old king.

CAESAR. Oh, my wrinkles, my wrinkles! And my child's heart! You will be the most dangerous of all Caesar's conquests.

CLEOPATRA *(appalled)*. Caesar! I forgot Caesar. *(Anxiously)* You will tell him that I am a Queen, will you not?—a real Queen. Listen! *(stealthily coaxing him)* let us run away and hide until Caesar is gone.

CAESAR. If you fear Caesar, you are no true Queen; and though you were to hide beneath a pyramid, he would go straight to it and lift it with one hand. And then—! *(He chops his teeth together.)*

CLEOPATRA *(trembling)*. Oh!

CAESAR. Be afraid if you dare. *(The note of the bucina resounds again in the distance. She moans with fear.* CAESAR *exults in it, exclaiming)* Aha! Caesar approaches the throne of Cleopatra. Come: take your place. *(He takes her hand and leads her to the throne. She is too down-cast to speak)*. Ho, there, Teetatota. How do you call your slaves?

CLEOPATRA *(spiritlessly, as she sinks on the throne and cowers there, shaking)*. Clap your hands.

(He claps his hands. FTATATEETA *returns.)*

CAESAR.   Bring the Queen's robes, and her crown, and her women; and prepare her.

CLEOPATRA   (*eagerly—recovering herself a little*). Yes, the crown, Ftatateeta: I shall wear the crown.

FTATATEETA.   For whom must the Queen put on her state?

CAESAR.   For a citizen of Rome. A king of kings, Totateeta.

CLEOPATRA   (*stamping at her*). How dare you ask questions? Go and do as you are told. (FTATATEETA *goes out with a grim smile.* CLEOPATRA *goes on eagerly, to* CAESAR) Caesar will know that I am a Queen when he sees my crown and robes, will he not?

CAESAR.   No. How shall he know that you are not a slave dressed up in the Queen's ornaments?

CLEOPATRA.   You must tell him.

CAESAR.   He will not ask me. He will know Cleopatra by her pride, her courage, her majesty, and her beauty. (*She looks very doubtful.*) Are you trembling?

CLEOPATRA   (*shivering with dread*). No, I—I— (*in a very sickly voice*) No.

(FTATATEETA *and three* WOMEN *come in with the regalia.*)

FTATATEETA.   Of all the Queen's women, these three alone are left. The rest are fled. (*They begin to deck* CLEOPATRA, *who submits, pale and motionless.*)

CAESAR.   Good, good. Three are enough. Poor Caesar generally has to dress himself.

FTATATEETA   (*contemptuously*). The Queen of Egypt is not a Roman barbarian. (*To* CLEOPATRA) Be brave, my nursling. Hold up your head before this stranger.

CAESAR   (*admiring* CLEOPATRA, *and placing the crown on her head*). Is it sweet or bitter to be a Queen, Cleopatra?

CLEOPATRA.   Bitter.

CAESAR.   Cast out fear; and you will conquer Caesar. Tota: are the Romans at hand?

FTATATEETA.   They are at hand; and the guard has fled.

THE WOMEN   (*wailing subduedly*). Woe to us!

(*The* NUBIAN *comes running down the hall.*)

NUBIAN.   The Romans are in the courtyard. (*He bolts through the door. With a shriek, the* WOMEN *fly after him.* FTATATEETA's *jaw expresses savage resolution: she does not budge.* CLEOPATRA *can hardly restrain herself from following them.* CAESAR *grips her wrist, and looks steadfastly at her. She stands like a martyr.*)

CAESAR.   The Queen must face Caesar alone. Answer "So be it."

CLEOPATRA   (*white*). So be it.

CAESAR   (*releasing her*). Good.

(A tramp and tumult of armed men is heard. CLEOPATRA's *terror increases. The bucina sounds close at hand, followed by a formidable clangor of trumpets. This is too much for* CLEOPATRA: *she utters a cry and darts towards the door.* FTATATEETA *stops her ruthlessly.)*

FTATATEETA. You are my nursling. You have said "So be it"; and if you die for it, you must make the Queen's word good. *(She hands* CLEOPATRA *to* CAESAR, *who takes her back, almost beside herself with apprehension, to the throne.)*

CAESAR. Now, if you quail—! *(He seats himself on the throne.)*

(She stands on the step, all but unconscious, waiting for death. The ROMAN SOLDIERS *troop in tumultuously through the corridor, headed by their* ENSIGN *with his eagle, and their* BUCINATOR, *a burly fellow with his instrument coiled around his body, its brazen bell shaped like the head of a howling wolf. When they reach the transept, they stare in amazement at the throne; dress into ordered rank opposite it; draw their swords and lift them in the air with a shout of* Hail Caesar. CLEOPATRA *turns and stares wildly at* CAESAR; *grasps the situation; and, with a great sob of relief, falls into his arms.)*

ACT II

Alexandria. A hall on the first floor of the Palace, ending in a loggia approached by two steps. Through the arches of the loggia the Mediterranean can be seen, bright in the morning sun. The clean lofty walls, painted with a procession of the Egyptian theocracy, presented in profile as flat ornament, and the absence of mirrors, sham perspectives, stuffy upholstery and textiles, make the place handsome, wholesome, simple and cool, or, as a rich English manufacturer would express it, poor, bare, ridiculous and unhomely. For Tottenham Court Road civilization is to this Egyptian civilization as glass bead and tattoo civilization is to Tottenham Court Road.

The young king Ptolemy Dionysus (aged ten) is at the top of the steps, on his way in through the loggia, led by his guardian Pothinus, who has him by the hand. The court is assembled to receive him. It is made up of men and women (some of the women being officials) of various complexions and races, mostly Egyptian; some of them, comparatively fair, from lower Egypt; some, much darker, from upper Egypt; with a few Greeks and Jews. Prominent in a group on Ptolemy's right hand is Theodotus, Ptolemy's tutor. Another group, on Ptolemy's left is headed by Achillas, the general of Ptolemy's troops. Theodotus is a little old man, whose features are as cramped and wizened as his limbs, except his tall straight forehead, which occupies more space than all the rest of his face.

He maintains an air of magpie keenness and profundity, listening to what the others say with the sarcastic vigilance of a philosopher listening to the exercises of his disciples. Achillas is a tall handsome man of thirty-five, with a fine black beard curled like the coat of a poodle. Apparently not a clever man, but distinguished and dignified. Pothinus is a vigorous man of fifty, a eunuch, passionate, energetic and quick witted, but of common mind and character; impatient and unable to control his temper. He has fine tawny hair, like fur. Ptolemy, the King, looks much older than an English boy of ten; but he has the childish air, the habit of being in leading strings, the mixture of impotence and petulance, the appearance of beng excessively washed, combed and dressed by other hands, which is exhibited by court-bred princes of all ages.

All receive the King with reverences. He comes down the steps to a chair of state which stands a little to his right, the only seat in the hall. Taking his place before it, he looks nervously for instructions to Pothinus, who places himself at his left hand.

POTHINUS.   The King of Egypt has a word to speak.

THEODOTUS   *(in a squeak which he makes impressive by sheer self-opinionativeness)*. Peace for the King's word!

PTOLEMY   *(without any vocal inflexions: he is evidently repeating a lesson)*. Take notice of this all of you. I am the firstborn son of Auletes the Flute Blower who was your King. My sister Berenice drove him from his throne and reigned in his stead but—but *(he hesitates)* ——

POTHINUS   *(stealthily prompting)* —but the gods would not suffer——

PTOLEMY.   Yes—the gods would not suffer—not suffer—*(he stops; then, crestfallen)* I forgot what the gods would not suffer.

THEODOTUS.   Let Pothinus, the King's guardian, speak for the King.

POTHINUS   *(suppressing his impatience with difficulty)*. The King wished to say that the gods would not suffer the impiety of his sister to go unpunished.

PTOLEMY   *(hastily)*. Yes; I remember the rest of it. *(He resumes his monotone.)* Therefore the gods sent a stranger, one Mark Antony, a Roman captain of horsemen, across the sands of the desert and he set my father again upon the throne. And my father took Berenice my sister and struck her head off. And now that my father is dead yet another of his daughters, my sister Cleopatra, would snatch the kingdom from me and reign in my place. But the gods would not suffer (POTHINUS *coughs admonitorily)* —the gods—the gods would not suffer——

POTHINUS   *(prompting)* —will not maintain——

PTOLMEY.   Oh yes—will not maintain such iniquity, they will give her head to the axe even as her sister's. But with the help of the witch

Ftatateeta she hath cast a spell on the Roman Julius Caesar to make him uphold his false pretence to rule in Egypt. Take notice then that I will not suffer—that I will not suffer—(*pettishly, to* POTHINUS) What is it that I will not suffer?

POTHINUS   (*suddenly exploding with all the force and emphasis of political passion*). The King will not suffer a foreigner to take from him the throne of our Egypt. (*A shout of applause.*) Tell the King, Achillas, how many soldiers and horsemen follow the Roman?

THEODOTUS.   Let the King's general speak!

ACHILLAS.   But two Roman legions, O King. Three thousand soldiers and scarce a thousand horsemen.

(*The court breaks into derisive laughter; and a great chattering begins, amid which* RUFIO, *a Roman officer, appears in the loggia. He is a burly, black-bearded man of middle age, very blunt, prompt and rough, with small clear eyes, and plump nose and cheeks, which, however, like the rest, of his flesh, are in ironhard condition.*)

RUFIO   (*from the steps*). Peace, ho! (*The laughter and chatter cease abruptly.*) Caesar approaches.

THEODOTUS   (*with much presence of mind*). The King permits the Roman commander to enter!

(CAESAR, *plainly dressed, but wearing an oak wreath to conceal his baldness, enters from the loggia, attended by* BRITANNUS, *his secretary, a Briton, about forty, tall, solemn, and already slightly bald, with a heavy, drooping, hazel-colored moustache trained so as to lose its ends in a pair of trim whiskers. He is carefully dressed in blue, with portfolio, inkhorn, and reed pen at his girdle. His serious air and sense of the importance of the business in hand is in marked contrast to the kindly interest of* CAESAR, *who looks at the scene, which is new to him, with the frank curiosity of a child, and then turns to the King's chair:* BRITANNUS *and* RUFIO *posting themselves near the steps at the other side.*)

CAESAR   (*looking at* POTHINUS *and* PTOLEMY). Which is the King? the man or the boy?

POTHINUS.   I am Pothinus, the guardian of my lord the King.

CAESAR   (*patting* PTOLEMY *kindly on the shoulder*). So you are the King. Dull work at your age, eh? (*To* POTHINUS) Your servant, Pothinus. (*He turns away unconcernedly and comes slowly along the middle of the hall, looking from side to side at the courtiers until he reaches* ACHILLAS.) And this gentleman?

THEODOTUS.   Achillas, the King's general.

CAESAR   (*to* ACHILLAS, *very friendly*). A general, eh? I am a general myself. But I began too old, too old. Health and many victories, Achillas!

ACHILLAS.   As the gods will, Caesar.

CAESAR   (*turning to* THEODOTUS). And you, sir, are———?

THEODOTUS.   Theodotus, the King's tutor.

CAESAR.   You teach men how to be kings, Theodotus. That is very clever of you. (*Looking at the gods on the walls as he turns away from* THEODOTUS *and goes up again to* POTHINUS). And this place?

POTHINUS.   The council chamber of the chancellors of the King's treasury, Caesar.

CAESAR.   Ah! that reminds me. I want some money.

POTHINUS.   The King's treasury is poor, Caesar.

CAESAR.   Yes: I notice that there is but one chair in it.

RUFIO   (*shouting gruffly*). Bring a chair there, some of you, for Caesar.

PTOLEMY   (*rising shyly to offer his chair*). Caesar——

CAESAR   (*kindly*). No, no, my boy: that is your chair of state. Sit down.

(*He makes* PTOLEMY *sit down again. Meanwhile* RUFIO, *looking about him, sees in the nearest corner an image of the god Ra, represented as a seated man with the head of a hawk. Before the image is a bronze tripod, about as large as a three-legged stool, with a stick of incense burning on it.* RUFIO, *with Roman resourcefulness and indifference to foreign superstitions, promptly seizes the tripod; shakes off the incense; blows away the ash; and dumps it down behind* CAESAR, *nearly in the middle of the hall.*)

RUFIO.   Sit on that, Caesar.

(*A shiver runs through the court, followed by a hissing whisper of* Sacrilege!)

CAESAR   (*seating himself*). Now, Pothinus, to business. I am badly in want of money.

BRITANNUS   (*disapproving of these informal expressions*). My master would say that there is a lawful debt due to Rome by Egypt, contracted by the King's deceased father to the Triumvirate; and that it is Caesar's duty to his country to require immediate payment.

CAESAR   (*blandly*). Ah, I forgot. I have not made my companions known here. Pothinus: this is Britannus, my secretary. He is an islander from the western end of the world, a day's voyage from Gaul. (BRITANNUS *bows stiffly.*) This gentleman is Rufio, my comrade in arms. (RUFIO *nods.*) Pothinus: I want 1,600 talents.

(*The* COURTIERS, *appalled, murmur loudly, and* THEODOTUS *and* ACHILLAS *appeal mutely to one another against so monstrous a demand.*)

POTHINUS   (*aghast*). Forty million sesterces! Impossible. There is not so much money in the King's treasury.

CAESAR   (*encouragingly*). Only sixteen hundred talents, Pothinus. Why count it in sesterces? A sestertius is only worth a loaf of bread.

POTHINUS.   And a talent is worth a racehorse. I say it is impossible. We have been at strife here, because the King's sister Cleopatra falsely claims his throne. The King's taxes have not been collected for a whole year.

CAESAR.   Yes they have, Pothinus. My officers have been collecting them all the morning. (*Renewed whisper and sensation, not without some stifled laughter, among the courtiers.*)

RUFIO (*bluntly*). You must pay, Pothinus. Why waste words? You are getting off cheaply enough.

POTHINUS (*bitterly*). Is it possible that Caesar, the conqueror of the world, has time to occupy himself with such a trifle as our taxes?

CAESAR. My friend: taxes are the chief business of a conqueror of the world.

POTHINUS. Then take warning, Caesar. This day, the treasures of the temples and the gold of the King's treasury shall be sent to the mint to be melted down for our ransom in the sight of the people. They shall see us sitting under bare walls and drinking from wooden cups. And their wrath be on your head, Caesar, if you force us to this sacrilege!

CAESAR. Do not fear, Pothinus: the people know how well wine tastes in wooden cups. In return for your bounty, I will settle this dispute about the throne for you, if you will. What say you?

POTHINUS. If I say no, will that hinder you?

RUFIO (*defiantly*). No.

CAESAR. You say the matter has been at issue for a year, Pothinus. May I have ten minutes at it?

POTHINUS. You will do your pleasure, doubtless.

CAESAR. Good! But first, let us have Cleopatra here.

THEODOTUS. She is not in Alexandria: she is fled into Syria.

CAESAR. I think not. (*To* RUFIO) Call Totateeta.

RUFIO (*calling*). Ho there, Teetatota.

(*Ftatateeta enters the loggia, and stands arrogantly at the top of the steps.*)

FTATATEETA. Who pronounces the name of Ftatateeta, the Queen's chief nurse?

CAESAR. Nobody can pronounce it, Tota, except yourself. Where is your mistress?

(CLEOPATRA, *who is hiding behind* FTATATEETA, *peeps out at them laughing.* CAESAR *rises.*)

CAESAR. Will the Queen favor us with her presence for a moment?

CLEOPATRA (*pushing* FTATATEETA *aside and standing haughtily on the brink of the steps*). Am I to behave like a Queen?

CAESAR. Yes.

(CLEOPATRA *immediately comes down to the chair of state; seizes* PTOLEMY *and drags him out of his seat; then takes his place in the chair.* FTATATEETA *seats herself on the steps of the loggia, and sits there, watching the scene with sybilline intensity.*)

PTOLEMY (*mortified, and struggling with his tears*). Caesar: this is how she treats me always. If I am a king why is she allowed to take everything from me?

CLEOPATRA. You are not to be King, you little cry-baby. You are to be eaten by the Romans.

CAESAR (*touched by* PTOLEMY's *distress*). Come here, my boy, and stand by me.

(PTOLEMY *goes over to* CAESAR, *who, resuming his seat on the tripod, takes the boy's hand to encourage him.* CLEOPATRA, *furiously jealous, rises and glares at them.*)

CLEOPATRA (*with flaming cheeks*). Take your throne: I don't want it. (*She flings away from the chair, and approaches* PTOLEMY, *who shrinks from her.*) Go this instant and sit down in your place.

CAESAR. Go, Ptolemy. Always take a throne when it is offered to you.

RUFIO. I hope you will have the good sense to follow your own advice when we return to Rome, Caesar.

(PTOLEMY *slowly goes back to the throne, giving* CLEOPATRA *a wide berth, in evident fear of her hands. She takes his place beside* CAESAR.)

CAESAR. Pothinus——

CLEOPATRA (*interrupting him*). Are you not going to speak to me?

CAESAR. Be quiet. Open your mouth again before I give you leave; and you shall be eaten.

CLEOPATRA. I am not afraid. A queen must not be afraid. Eat my husband there, if you like: he is afraid.

CAESAR (*starting*). Your husband! What do you mean?

CLEOPATRA (*pointing to* PTOLEMY). That little thing.

(*The two* ROMANS *and the* BRITON *stare at one another in amazement.*)

THEODOTUS. Caesar: you are a stranger here, and not conversant with our laws. The kings and queens of Egypt may not marry except with their own royal blood. Ptolemy and Cleopatra are born king and consort just as they are born brother and sister.

BRITANNUS (*shocked*). Caesar: this is not proper.

THEODOTUS (*outraged*). How!

CAESAR (*recovering his self-possession*). Pardon him, Theodotus: he is a barbarian, and thinks that the customs of his tribe and island are the laws of nature.

BRITANNUS. On the contrary, it is these Egyptians who are barbarians; and you do wrong to encourage them. I say it is a scandal.

CAESAR. Scandal or not, my friend, it opens the gate of peace. (*He rises and addresses* POTHINUS *seriously*) Pothinus: hear what I propose.

RUFIO. Hear Caesar there.

CAESAR. Ptolemy and Cleopatra shall reign jointly in Egypt.

ACHILLAS. What of the King's younger brother and Cleopatra's younger sister?

RUFIO (*explaining*). There is another little Ptolemy, Caesar: so they tell me.

CAESAR. Well, the little Ptolemy can marry the other sister; and we will make them both a present of Cyprus.

POTHINUS (*impatiently*). Cyprus is of no use to anybody.

CAESAR. No matter: you shall have it for the sake of peace.

BRITANNUS (*unconsciously anticipating a later statesman*). Peace with honor, Pothinus.

POTHINUS (*mutinously*). Caesar: be honest. The money you demand is the price of our freedom. Take it; and leave us to settle our own affairs.

THE BOLDER COURTIERS (*encouraged by* POTHINUS's *tone and* CAESAR's *quietness*). Yes, yes. Egypt for the Egyptians!

(*The conference now becomes an altercation, the* EGYPTIANS *becoming more and more heated.* CAESAR *remains unruffled; but* RUFIO *grows fiercer and doggeder, and* BRITANNUS *haughtily indignant.*)

RUFIO (*contemptuously*). Egypt for the Egyptians! Do you forget that there is a Roman army of occupation here, left by Aulus Gabinius when he set up your toy king for you?

ACHILLAS (*suddenly asserting himself*). And now under my command. *I* am the Roman general here, Caesar.

CAESAR (*tickled by the humor of the situation*). And also the Egyptian general, eh?

POTHINUS (*triumphantly*). That is so, Caesar.

CAESAR (*to* ACHILLAS). So you can make war on the Egyptians in the name of Rome, and on the Romans—on me, if necessary—in the name of Egypt?

ACHILLAS. That is so, Caesar.

CAESAR. And which side are you on at present, if I may presume to ask, general?

ACHILLAS. On the side of the right and of the gods.

CAESAR. Hm! How many men have you?

ACHILLAS. That will appear when I take the field.

RUFIO (*truculently*). Are your men Romans? If not, it matters not how many there are, provided you are no stronger than 500 to ten.

POTHINUS. It is useless to try to bluff us, Rufio. Caesar has been defeated before and may be defeated again. A few weeks ago Caesar was flying for his life before Pompey: a few months hence he may be flying for his life before Cato and Juba of Numidia, the African King.

ACHILLAS (*following up* POTHINUS's *speech menacingly*). What can you do with 4,000 men?

THEODOTUS (*following up* ACHILLAS's *speech with a raucous squeak*). And without money? Away with you.

ALL THE COURTIERS (*shouting fiercely and crowding towards* CAESAR). Away with you. Egypt for the Egyptians! Begone.

(RUFIO *bites his beard, too angry to speak.* CAESAR *sits as comfortably as if he were at breakfast, and the cat were clamoring for a piece of Finnan-haddie.*)

CLEOPATRA.   Why do you let them talk to you like that, Caesar? Are you afraid?

CAESAR.   Why, my dear, what they say is quite true.

CLEOPATRA.   But if you go away, I shall not be Queen.

CAESAR.   I shall not go away until you are Queen.

POTHINUS.   Achillas: if you are not a fool, you will take that girl whilst she is under your hand.

RUFIO   (*daring them*). Why not take Caesar as well, Achillas?

POTHINUS   (*retorting the defiance with interest*). Well said, Rufio. Why not?

RUFIO.   Try, Achillas. (*Calling*) Guard there.

(*The loggia immediately fills with* CAESAR's *soldiers, who stand, sword in hand, at the top of the steps, waiting the word to charge from their centurion, who carries a cudgel. For a moment the Egyptians face them proudly: then they retire sullenly to their former places.*)

BRITANNUS.   You are Caesar's prisoners, all of you.

CAESAR   (*benevolently*). Oh no, no, no. By no means. Caesar's guests, gentlemen.

CLEOPATRA.   Won't you cut their heads off?

CAESAR.   What! Cut off your brother's head?

CLEOPATRA.   Why not? He would cut off mine, if he got the chance. Wouldn't you, Ptolemy?

PTOLEMY   (*pale and obstinate*). I would. I will, too, when I grow up.

(CLEOPATRA *is rent by a struggle between her newly-acquired dignity as a queen, and a strong impulse to put out her tongue at him. She takes no part in the scene which follows, but watches it with curiosity and wonder, fidgeting with the restlessness of a child, and sitting down on* CAESAR's *tripod when he rises.*)

POTHINUS.   Caesar: if you attempt to detain us——

RUFIO.   He will succeed, Egyptian: make up your mind to that. We hold the palace, the beach, and the eastern harbor. The road to Rome is open; and you shall travel it if Caesar chooses.

CAESAR   (*courteously*). I could do no less, Pothinus, to secure the retreat of my own soldiers. I am accountable for every life among them. But you are free to go. So are all here, and in the palace.

RUFIO   (*aghast at this clemency*). What! Renegades and all?

CAESAR   (*softening the expression*). Roman army of occupation and all, Rufio.

POTHINUS   (*desperately*). Then I make a last appeal to Caesar's justice. I shall call a witness to prove that but for us, the Roman army of occupation, led by the greatest soldier in the world, would now have Caesar at its mercy. (*Calling through the loggia*) Ho, there, Lucius Septimus (CAESAR *starts, deeply moved*): if my voice can reach you, come forth and testify before Caesar.

CAESAR (*shrinking*). No, no.

THEODOTUS. Yes, I say. Let the military tribune bear witness.

(LUCIUS SEPTIMUS, *a clean shaven, trim athlete of about* 40, *with symmetrical features, resolute mouth, and handsome, thin Roman nose, in the dress of a Roman officer, comes in through the loggia and confronts* CAESAR, *who hides his face with his robe for a moment; then, mastering himself, drops it, and confronts the tribune with dignity.*)

POTHINUS. Bear witness, Lucius Septimius. Caesar came hither in pursuit of his foe. Did we shelter his foe?

LUCIUS. As Pompey's foot touched the Egyptian shore, his head fell by the stroke of my sword.

THEODOTUS (*with viperish relish*). Under the eyes of his wife and child! Remember that, Caesar! They saw it from the ship he had just left. We have given you a full and sweet measure of vengeance.

CAESAR (*with horror*). Vengeance!

POTHINUS. Our first gift to you, as your galley came into the roadstead, was the head of your rival for the empire of the world. Bear witness, Lucius Septimius: is it not so?

LUCIUS. It is so. With this hand, that slew Pompey, I placed his head at the feet of Caesar.

CAESAR. Murderer! So would you have slain Caesar, had Pompey been victorious at Pharsalia.

LUCIUS. Woe to the vanquished, Caesar! When I served Pompey, I slew as good men as he, only because he conquered them. His turn came at last.

THEODOTUS (*flatteringly*). The deed was not yours, Caesar, but ours— nay, mine; for it was done by my counsel. Thanks to us, you keep your reputation for clemency, and have your vengeance too.

CAESAR. Vengeance! Vengeance!! Oh, if I could stoop to vengeance, what would I not exact from you as the price of this murdered man's blood. (*They shrink back, appalled and disconcerted.*) Was he not my son-in-law, my ancient friend, for 20 years the master of great Rome, for 30 years the compeller of victory? Did not I, as a Roman, share his glory? Was the Fate that forced us to fight for the mastery of the world, of our making? Am I Julius Caesar, or am I a wolf, that you fling to me the grey head of the old soldier, the laurelled conqueror, the mighty Roman, treacherously struck down by this callous ruffian, and then claim my gratitude for it! (*To* LUCIUS SEPTIMIUS) Begone: you fill me with horror.

LUCIUS (*cold and undaunted*). Pshaw! you have seen severed heads be-

fore, Caesar, and severed right hands too, I think; some thousands of
them, in Gaul, after you vanquished Vercingetorix. Did you spare him,
with all your clemency? Was that vengeance?

CAESAR. No, by the gods! would that it had been! Vengeance at least is
human. No, I say: those severed right hands, and the brave Vercingetorix basely strangled in a vault beneath the Capitol, were (*with shuddering satire*) a wise severity, a necessary protection to the common-
wealth, a duty of statemanship—follies and fictions ten times bloodier
than honest vengeance! What a fool was I then! To think that men's
lives should be at the mercy of such fools! (*Humbly*) Lucius Septimius,
pardon me: why should the slayer of Vercingetorix rebuke the slayer
of Pompey? You are free to go with the rest. Or stay if you will: I will
find a place for you in my service.

LUCIUS. The odds are against you, Caesar. I go. (*He turns to go out
through the loggia.*)

RUFIO (*full of wrath at seeing his prey escaping*). That means that he is
a Republican.

LUCIUS (*turning defiantly on the loggia steps*). And what are you?

RUFIO. A Caesarian, like all Caesar's soldiers.

CAESAR (*courteously*). Lucius: believe me, Caesar is no Caesarian. Were
Rome a true republic, then were Caesar the first of Republicans. But
you have made your choice. Farewell.

LUCIUS. Farewell. Come, Achillas, whilst there is yet time.

(CAESAR, *seeing that* RUFIO's *temper threatens to get the worse of him,
puts his hand on his shoulder and brings him down the hall out of harm's
way,* BRITANNUS *accompanying them and posting himself on* CAESAR's *right
hand. This movement brings the three in a little group to the place occupied by* ACHILLAS, *who moves haughtily away and joins* THEODOTUS *on
the other side.* LUCIUS SEPTIMIUS *goes out through the* SOLDIERS *in the
loggia.* POTHINUS, THEODOTUS *and* ACHILLAS *follow him with the* COURTIERS,
very mistrustful of the SOLDIERS, *who close up in their rear and go out
after them, keeping them moving without much ceremony. The* KING *is
left in his chair, piteous, obstinate, with twitching face and fingers. During these movements* RUFIO *maintains an energetic grumbling, as follows:—*)

RUFIO (*as* LUCIUS *departs*). Do you suppose he would let us go if he had
our heads in his hands?

CAESAR. I have no right to suppose that his ways are any baser than
mine.

RUFIO. Psha!

CAESAR. Rufio: if I take Lucius Septimius for my model, and become
exactly like him, ceasing to be Caesar, will you serve me still?

BRITANNUS. Caesar: this is not good sense. Your duty to Rome demands that her enemies should be prevented from doing further mischief. (CAESAR, *whose delight in the moral eye-to-business of his British secretary is inexhaustible, smiles indulgently.*)

RUFIO. It is no use talking to him, Britannus: you may save your breath to cool your porridge. But mark this, Caesar. Clemency is very well for you; but what is it for your soldiers, who have to fight to-morrow the men you spared yesterday? You may give what orders you please; but I tell you that your next victory will be a massacre, thanks to your clemency. *I*, for one, will take no prisoners. I will kill my enemies in the field; and then you can preach as much clemency as you please: I shall never have to fight them again. And now, with your leave, I will see these gentry off the premises. (*He turns to go.*)

CAESAR (*turning also and seeing* PTOLEMY). What! have they left the boy alone! Oh shame, shame!

RUFIO (*Taking* PTOLEMY's *hand and making him rise*). Come, your majesty!

PTOLEMY (*to* CAESAR, *drawing away his hand from* RUFIO). Is he turning me out of my palace?

RUFIO (*grimly*). You are welcome to stay if you wish.

CAESAR (*kindly*). Go, my boy. I will not harm you; but you will be safer away, among your friends. Here you are in the lion's mouth.

PTOLEMY (*turning to go*). It is not the lion I fear, but (*looking at* RUFIO) the jackal. (*He goes out through the loggia.*)

CAESAR (*laughing approvingly*). Brave boy!

CLEOPATRA (*jealous of* CAESAR's *approbation, calling after* PTOLEMY). Little silly. You think that very clever.

CAESAR. Britannus: attend the King. Give him in charge to that Pothinus fellow. (BRITANNUS *goes out after* PTOLEMY.)

RUFIO (*pointing to* CLEOPATRA). And this piece of goods? What is to be done with her? However, I suppose I may leave that to you. (*He goes out through the loggia.*)

CLEOPATRA (*flushing suddenly and turning on* CAESAR). Did you mean me go with the rest?

CAESAR (*a little preoccupied, goes with a sigh to* PTOLEMY's *chair, whilst she waits for his answer with red cheeks and clenched fists*). You are free to do just as you please, Cleopatra.

CLEOPATRA. Then you do not care whether I stay or not?

CAESAR (*smiling*). Of course I had rather you stayed.

CLEOPATRA. Much, much rather?

CAESAR (*nodding*). Much, much rather.

CLEOPATRA. Then I consent to stay, because I am asked. But I do not want to, mind.

CAESAR. That is quite understood. (*Calling*) Totateeta.

(FTATATEETA, *still seated, turns her eyes on him with a sinister expression, but does not move.*)

CLEOPATRA   (*with a splutter of laughter*). Her name is not Totateeta: it is Ftatateeta. (*Calling*) Ftatateeta. (FTATATEETA *instantly rises and comes to* CLEOPATRA.)

CAESAR   (*stumbling over the name*). Tfatafeeta will forgive the erring tongue of a Roman. Tota: the Queen will hold her state here in Alexandria. Engage women to attend upon her; and do all that is needful.

FTATATEETA.   Am I then the mistress of the Queen's household?

CLEOPATRA   (*sharply*). No: *I* am the mistress of the Queen's household. Go and do as you are told, or I will have you thrown into the Nile this very afternoon, to poison the poor crocodiles.

CAESAR   (*shocked*). Oh no, no.

CLEOPATRA.   Oh yes, yes. You are very sentimental, Caesar; but you are clever; and if you do as I tell you, you will soon learn to govern.

(CAESAR, *quite dumbfounded by this impertinence, turns in his chair and stares at her.*)

(FTATATEETA, *smiling grimly, and showing a splendid set of teeth, goes, leaving them alone together.*)

CAESAR.   Cleopatra: I really think I must eat you, after all.

CLEOPATRA   (*kneeling beside him and looking at him with eager interest, half real, half affected to shew how intelligent she is*). You must not talk to me now as if I were a child.

CAESAR.   You have been growing up since the Sphinx introduced us the other night; and you think you know more than I do already.

CLEOPATRA   (*taken down, and anxious to justify herself*). No: that would be very silly of me: of course I know that. But—(*suddenly*) are you angry with me?

CAESAR.   No.

CLEOPATRA   (*only half believing him*). Then why are you so thoughtful?

CAESAR   (*rising*). I have work to do, Cleopatra.

CLEOPATRA   (*drawing back*). Work! (*Offended*) You are tired of talking to me; and that is your excuse to get away from me.

CAESAR   (*sitting down again to appease her*). Well, well: another minute. But then—work!

CLEOPATRA.   Work! what nonsense! You must remember that you are a king now: I have made you one. Kings don't work.

CAESAR.   Oh! Who told you that, little kitten? Eh?

CLEOPATRA.   My father was King of Egypt; and he never worked. But he was a great king, and cut off my sister's head because she rebelled against him and took the throne from him.

CAESAR.   Well; and how did he get his throne back again?

CLEOPATRA   (*eagerly, her eyes lighting up*). I will tell you. A beautiful young man, with strong round arms, came over the desert with many horsemen, and slew my sister's husband and gave my father back his throne. (*Wistfully*) I was only twelve then. Oh, I wish he would come again, now that I am a queen. I would make him my husband.

CAESAR.   It might be managed, perhaps; for it was I who sent that beautiful young man to help your father.

CLEOPATRA   (*enraptured*). You know him!

CAESAR   (*nodding*). I do.

CLEOPATRA.   Has he come with you? (CAESAR *shakes his head: she is cruelly disappointed.*) Oh, I wish he had, I wish he had. If only I were a little older; so that he might not think me a mere kitten, as you do! But perhaps that is because you are old. He is many, many years younger than you, is he not?

CAESAR   (*as if swallowing a pill*). He is somewhat younger.

CLEOPATRA.   Would he be my husband, do you think, if I asked him?

CAESAR.   Very likely.

CLEOPATRA.   But I should not like to ask him. Could you not persuade him to ask me—without knowing that I wanted him to?

CAESAR   (*touched by her innocence of the beautiful young man's character*). My poor child!

CLEOPATRA.   Why do you say that as if you were sorry for me? Does he love anyone else?

CAESAR.   I am afraid so.

CLEOPATRA   (*tearfully*). Then I shall not be his first love.

CAESAR.   Not quite the first. He is greatly admired by women.

CLEOPATRA.   I wish I could be the first. But if he loves me, I will make him kill all the rest. Tell me: is he still beautiful? Do his strong round arms shine in the sun like marble?

CAESAR.   He is in excellent condition—considering how much he eats and drinks.

CLEOPATRA.   Oh, you must not say common, earthly things about him; for I love him. He is a god.

CAESAR.   He is a great captain of horsemen, and swifter of foot than any other Roman.

CLEOPATRA.   What is his real name?

CAESAR   (*puzzled*). His real name?

CLEOPATRA.   Yes. I always call him Horus, because Horus is the most beautiful of our gods. But I want to know his real name.

CAESAR.   His name is Mark Antony.

CLEOPATRA   (*musically*). Mark Antony, Mark Antony, Mark Antony! What a beautiful name! (*She throws her arms round* CAESAR's *neck.*) Oh, how I love you for sending him to help my father! Did you love my father very much?

CAESAR.   No, my child; but your father, as you say, never worked. I always work. So when he lost his crown he had to promise me 16,000 talents to get it back for him.

CLEOPATRA.   Did he ever pay you?

CAESAR.   Not in full.

CLEOPATRA.   He was quite right: it was too dear. The whole world is not worth 16,000 talents.

CAESAR.   That is perhaps true, Cleopatra. Those Egyptians who work paid as much of it as he could drag from them. The rest is still due. But as I most likely shall not get it, I must go back to my work. So you must run away for a little and send my secretary to me.

CLEOPATRA   (*coaxing*). No: I want to stay and hear you talk about Mark Antony.

CAESAR.   But if I do not get to work, Pothinus and the rest of them will cut us off from the harbor; and then the way from Rome will be blocked.

CLEOPATRA.   No matter: I don't want you to go back to Rome.

CAESAR.   But you want Mark Antony to come from it.

CLEOPATRA   (*springing up*). Oh yes, yes, yes: I forgot. Go quickly and work, Caesar; and keep the way over the sea open for my Mark Antony. (*She runs out through the loggia, kissing her hand to* MARK ANTONY *across the sea.*)

CAESAR   (*going briskly up the middle of the hall to the loggia steps*). Ho, Britannus. (*He is startled by the entry of a wounded* ROMAN SOL-DIER, *who confronts him from the upper step.*) What now?

SOLDIER   (*pointing to his bandaged head*). This, Caesar; and two of my comrades killed in the market place.

CAESAR   (*quiet, but attending*). Ay. Why?

SOLDIER.   There is an army come to Alexandria, calling itself the Roman army.

CAESAR.   The Roman army of occupation. Ay?

SOLDIER.   Commanded by one Achillas.

CAESAR.   Well?

SOLDIER.   The citizens rose against us when the army entered the gates. I was with two others in the market place when the news came. They set upon us. I cut my way out; and here I am.

CAESAR.   Good. I am glad to see you alive. (RUFIO *enters the loggia hastily, passing behind the* SOLDIER *to look out through one of the arches at the quay beneath.*) Rufio, we are besieged.

RUFIO.   What! Already?

CAESAR.   Now or to-morrow: what does it matter? We shall be besieged. (BRITANNUS *runs in.*)

BRITANNUS.   Caesar——

CAESAR   (*anticipating him*). Yes: I know. (RUFIO *and* BRITANNUS *come down the hall from the loggia at opposite sides, past* CAESAR, *who waits for a moment near the step to say to the* SOLDIER) Comrade: give the word to turn out on the beach and stand by the boats. Get your wound attended to. Go. (SOLDIER *hurries out.* CAESAR *comes down the hall between* RUFIO *and* BRITANNUS) Rufio: we have some ships in the west harbor. Burn them.

RUFIO   (*staring*) . Burn them!!

CAESAR.   Take every boat we have in the east harbor, and seize the Pharos —that island with the lighthouse. Leave half our men behind to hold the beach and the quay outside this palace: that is the way home.

RUFIO   (*disapproving strongly*) . Are we to give up the city?

CAESAR.   We have not got it, Rufio. This palace we have; and—what is that building next door?

RUFIO.   The theatre.

CAESAR.   We will have that too: it commands the strand. For the rest, Egypt for the Egyptians!

RUFIO.   Well, you know best, I suppose. Is that all?

CAESAR.   That is all. Are those ships burnt yet?

RUFIO.   Be easy: I shall waste no more time. (*He runs out.*)

BRITANNUS.   Caesar: Pothinus demands speech of you. In my opinion he needs a lesson. His manner is most insolent.

CAESAR.   Where is he?

BRITANNUS.   He waits without.

CAESAR.   Ho there! admit Pothinus.

(POTHINUS *appears in the loggia, and comes down the hall very haughtily to* CAESAR's *left hand.*)

CAESAR.   Well, Pothinus?

POTHINUS.   I have brought you our ultimatum, Caesar.

CAESAR.   Ultimatum! The door was open: you should have gone out through it before you declared war. You are my prisoner now. (*He goes to the chair and loosens his toga.*)

POTHINUS   (*scornfully.*) I your prisoner! Do you know that you are in Alexandria, and that King Ptolemy, with an army outnumbering your little troop a hundred to one, is in possession of Alexandria?

CAESAR   (*unconcernedly taking off his toga and throwing it on the chair*) . Well, my friend, get out if you can. And tell your friends not to kill any more Romans in the market place. Otherwise my soldiers, who do not share my celebrated clemency, will probably kill you. Britannus: pass the word to the guard; and fetch my armor. (BRITANNUS *runs out.* RUFIO *returns.*) Well?

RUFIO   (*pointing from the loggia to a cloud of smoke drifting over the harbor*) . See there! (POTHINUS *runs engerly up the steps to look out.*)

CAESAR.   What, ablaze already! Impossible!

RUFIO. Yes, five good ships, and a barge laden with oil grappled to each. But it is not my doing: the Egyptians have saved me the trouble. They have captured the west harbor.

CAESAR *(anxiously)*. And the east harbor? The lighthouse, Rufio?

RUFIO *(with a sudden sputter of raging ill usage, coming down to* CAESAR *and scolding him)*. Can I embark a legion in five minutes? The first cohort is already on the beach. We can do no more. If you want faster work, come and do it yourself?

CAESAR *(soothing him)*. Good, good. Patience, Rufio, patience.

RUFIO. Patience! Who is impatient here, you or I? Would I be here, if I could not oversee them from that balcony?

CAESAR. Forgive me, Rufio; and *(anxiously)* hurry them as much as——— *(He is interrupted by an outcry as of an old man in the extremity of misfortune. It draws near rapidly; and* THEODOTUS *rushes in, tearing his hair, and squeaking the most lamentable exclamations.* RUFIO *steps back to stare at him, amazed at his frantic condition.* POTHINUS *turns to listen.)*

THEODOTUS *(on the steps, with uplifted arms)*. Horror unspeakable! Woe, alas! Help!

RUFIO. What now?

CAESAR *(frowning)*. Who is slain?

THEODOTUS. Slain! Oh, worse than the death of ten thousand men! Loss irreparable to mankind!

RUFIO. What has happened, man?

THEODOTUS *(rushing down the hall between them)*. The fire has spread from your ships. The first of the seven wonders of the world perishes. The library of Alexandria is in flames.

RUFIO. Psha! *(Quite relieved, he goes up to the loggia and watches the preparations of the troops on the beach.)*

CAESAR. Is that all?

THEODOTUS *(unable to believe his senses)*. All! Caesar: will you go down to posterity as a barbarous soldier too ignorant to know the value of books?

CAESAR. Theodotus: I am an author myself; and I tell you it is better that the Egyptians should live their lives than dream them away with the help of books.

THEODOTUS *(kneeling, with genuine literary emotion: the passion of the pedant)*. Caesar: once in ten generations of men, the world gains an immortal book.

CAESAR *(inflexible)*. If it did not flatter mankind, the common executioner would burn it.

THEODOTUS. Without history, death would lay you beside your meanest soldier.

CAESAR. Death will do that in any case. I ask no better grave.

THEODOTUS.   What is burning there is the memory of mankind.

CAESAR.   A shameful memory. Let it burn.

THEODOTUS   (*wildly*) . Will you destroy the past?

CAESAR.   Ay, and build the future with its ruins. (THEODOTUS, *in despair, strikes himself on the temples with his fists.*) But harken, Theodotus, teacher of kings: you who valued Pompey's head no more than a shepherd values an onion, and who now kneel to me, with tears in your old eyes, to plead for a few sheepskins scrawled with errors. I cannot spare you a man or a bucket of water just now; but you shall pass freely out of the palace. Now, away with you to Achillas; and borrow his legions to put out the fire. (*He hurries him to the steps.*)

POTHINUS   (*significantly*) . You understand, Theodotus: I remain a prisoner.

THEODOTUS.   A prisoner!

CAESAR.   Will you stay to talk whilst the memory of mankind is burning? (*Calling through the loggia*) Ho there! Pass Theodotus out. (*To* THEODOTUS) Away with you.

THEODOTUS   (*to* POTHINUS) . I must go to save the library. (*He hurries out.*)

CAESAR.   Follow him to the gate, Pothinus. Bid him urge your people to kill no more of my soldiers, for your sake.

POTHINUS.   My life will cost you dear if you take it, Caesar. (*He goes out after* THEODOTUS.)

(RUFIO, *absorbed in watching the embarkation, does not notice the departure of the two* EGYPTIANS.)

RUFIO   (*shouting from the loggia to the beach*) . All ready, there?

A CENTURION   (*from below*) . All ready. We wait for Caesar.

CAESAR.   Tell them Caesar is coming—the rogues! (*Calling*) Britannicus. (*This magniloquent version of his secretary's name is one of* CAESAR's *jokes. In later years it would have meant, quite seriously and officially, Conqueror of Britain.*)

RUFIO   (*calling down*) . Push off, all except the longboat. Stand by it to embark, Caesar's guard there. (*He leaves the balcony and comes down into the hall.*) Where are those Egyptians? Is this more clemency? Have you let them go?

CAESAR   (*chuckling*) . I have let Theodotus go to save the library. We must respect literature, Rufio.

RUFIO   (*raging*) . Folly on folly's head! I believe if you could bring back all the dead of Spain, Gaul and Thessaly to life, you would do it that we might have the trouble of fighting them over again.

CAESAR.   Might not the gods destroy the world if their only thought were to be at peace next year? (RUFIO, *out of all patience, turns away in anger.* CAESAR *suddenly grips his sleeve, and adds slyly in his ear*) Besides, my friend: every Egyptian we imprison means imprisoning two Roman soldiers to guard him. Eh?

RUFIO. Agh? I might have known there was some fox's trick behind your fine talking. (*He gets away from* CAESAR *with an ill-humored shrug, and goes to the balcony for another look at the preparations; finally goes out.*)

CAESAR. Is Britannus asleep? I sent him for my armor an hour ago. (*Calling*) Britannicus, thou British islander. Britannicus!

(CLEOPATRA *runs in through the loggia with* CAESAR's *helmet and sword, snatched from* BRITANNUS, *who follows her with a cuirass and greaves. They come down to* CAESAR, *she to his left hand,* BRITANNUS *to his right.*)

CLEOPATRA. I am going to dress you, Caesar. Sit down. (*He obeys.*) These Roman helmets are so becoming! (*She takes off his wreath.*) Oh! (*She bursts out laughing at him.*)

CAESAR. What are you laughing at?

CLEOPATRA. You're bald (*beginning with a big B, and ending with a splutter*).

CAESAR (*almost annoyed*). Cleopatra! (*He rises, for the convenience of* BRITANNUS, *who puts the cuirass on him.*)

CLEOPATRA. So that is why you wear the wreath—to hide it.

BRITANNUS. Peace, Egyptian: they are the bays of the conqueror. (*He buckles the cuirass.*)

CLEOPATRA. Peace, thou: islander! (*To* CAESAR) You should rub your head with strong spirits of sugar, Caesar. That will make it grow.

CAESAR (*with a wry face*). Cleopatra: do you like to be reminded that you are very young?

CLEOPATRA (*pouting*). No.

CAESAR (*sitting down again, and setting out his leg for* BRITANNUS, *who kneels to put on his greaves*). Neither do I like to be reminded that I am—middle aged. Let me give you ten of my superfluous years. That will make you 26, and leave me only—no matter. Is it a bargain?

CLEOPATRA. Agreed. 26, mind. (*She puts the helmet on him.*) Oh! How nice! You look only about 50 in it!

BRITANNUS (*looking up severely at* CLEOPATRA). You must not speak in this manner to Caesar.

CLEOPATRA. Is it true that when Caesar caught you on that island you were painted all over blue?

BRITANNUS. Blue is the color worn by all Britons of good standing. In war we stain our bodies blue; so that though our enemies may strip us of our clothes and our lives, they cannot strip us of our respectability. (*He rises.*)

CLEOPATRA (*with* CAESAR's *sword*). Let me hang this on. Now you look splendid. Have they made any statues of you in Rome?

CAESAR. Yes, many statues.

CLEOPATRA. You must send for one and give it to me.

RUFIO (*coming back into the loggia, more impatient than ever*). Now Caesar: have you done talking? The moment your foot is aboard there will be no holding our men back: the boats will race one another for the lighthouse.

CAESAR (*drawing his sword and trying the edge*). Is this well set to-day, Britannicus? At Pharsalia it was as blunt as a barrel-hoop.

BRITANNUS. It will split one of the Egyptian's hairs to-day, Caesar. I have set it myself.

CLEOPATRA (*suddenly throwing her arms in terror round* CAESAR). Oh, you are not really going into battle to be killed?

CAESAR. No, Cleopatra. No man goes to battle to be killed.

CLEOPATRA. But they do get killed. My sister's husband was killed in battle. You must not go. Let him go (*pointing to* RUFIO. *They all laugh at her*). Oh please, please don't go. What will happen to me if you never come back?

CAESAR (*gravely*). Are you afraid?

CLEOPATRA (*shrinking*). No.

CAESAR (*with quiet authority*). Go to the balcony; and you shall see us take the Pharos. You must learn to look on battles. Go. (*She goes, downcast, and looks out from the balcony*) That is well. Now, Rufio. March.

CLEOPATRA (*suddenly clapping her hands*). Oh, you will not be able to go!

CAESAR. Why? What now?

CLEOPATRA. They are drying up the harbor with buckets—a multitude of soldiers—over there (*pointing out across the sea to her left*) —they are dipping up the water.

RUFIO (*hastening to look*). It is true. The Egyptian army! Crawling over the edge of the west harbor like locusts. (*With sudden anger he strides down to* CAESAR.) This is your accursed clemency, Caesar. Theodotus has brought them.

CAESAR (*delighted at his own cleverness*). I meant him to, Rufio. They have come to put out the fire. The library will keep them busy whilst we seize the lighthouse. Eh? (*He rushes out buoyantly through the loggia, followed by* BRITANNUS.)

RUFIO (*disgustedly*). More foxing! Agh! (*He rushes off. A shout from the* SOLDIERS *announces the appearance of* CAESAR *below.*)

CENTURION (*below*). All aboard. Give way there. (*Another shout.*)

CLEOPATRA (*waving her scarf through the loggia arch*). Goodbye, goodbye, dear Caesar. Come back safe. Goodbye!

ACT III

The edge of the quay in front of the palace, looking out west over the east harbor of Alexandria to Pharos island, just off the end of which, and connected with it by a narrow mole, is the famous lighthouse, a gigantic square tower of white marble diminishing in size storey by storey to the top, on which stands a cresset beacon. The island is joined to the main land by the Heptastadium, a great mole or causeway five miles long bounding the harbor on the south.

In the middle of the quay a Roman sentinel stands on guard, pilum in hand, looking out to the lighthouse with strained attention, his left hand shading his eyes. The pilum is a stout wooden shaft 4½ feet long, with an iron spit about three feet long fixed in it. The sentinel is so absorbed that he does not notice the approach from the north end of the quay of four Egyptian market porters carrying rolls of carpet, pre- ceded by Ftatateeta and Apollodorus the Sicilian. Apollodorus is a dash- ing young man of about 24, handsome and debonair, dressed with de- liberate æstheticism in the most delicate purples and dove greys, with ornaments of bronze, oxydized silver, and stones of jade and agate. His sword, designed as carefully as a medieval cross, has a blued blade show- ing through an openwork scabbard of purple leather and filagree. The porters, conducted by Ftatateeta, pass along the quay behind the sentinel to the steps of the palace, where they put down their bales and squat on the ground. Apollodorus does not pass along with them: he halts, amused by the preoccupation of the sentinel.

APOLLODORUS   *(calling to the* SENTINEL*)* . Who goes there, eh?

SENTINEL   *(starting violently and turning with his pilum at the charge, revealing himself as a small, wiry, sandy-haired, conscientious young man with an elderly face)* . What's this? Stand. Who are you?

APOLLODORUS.   I am Apollodorus the Sicilian. Why, man, what are you dreaming of? Since I came through the lines beyond the theatre there, I have brought my caravan past three sentinels, all so busy staring at the lighthouse that not one of them challenged me. Is this Roman dis- cipline?

SENTINEL.   We are not here to watch the land but the sea. Caesar has just landed on the Pharos. *(Looking at* FTATATEETA*)* What have you here? Who is this piece of Egyptian crockery?

FTATATEETA.   Apollodorus: rebuke this Roman dog; and bid him bridle his tongue in the presence of Ftatateeta, the mistress of the Queen's household.

APOLLODORUS.   My friend: this is a great lady, who stands high with **Caesar.**

SENTINEL *(not at all impressed, pointing to the carpets)*. And what is all this truck?

APOLLODORUS. Carpets for the furnishing of the Queen's apartments in the palace. I have picked them from the best carpets in the world; and the Queen shall choose the best of my choosing.

SENTINEL. So you are the carpet merchant?

APOLLODORUS *(hurt)*. My friend: I am a patrician.

SENTINEL. A patrician! A patrician keeping a shop instead of following arms!

APOLLODORUS. I do not keep a shop. Mine is a temple of the arts. I am a worshipper of beauty. My calling is to choose beautiful things for beautiful Queens. My motto is Art for Art's sake.

SENTINEL. That is not the password.

APOLLODORUS. It is a universal password.

SENTINEL. I know nothing about universal passwords. Either give me the password for the day or get back to your shop.

(FTATATEETA, roused by his hostile tone, steals towards the edge of the quay with the step of a panther, and gets behind him.)

APOLLODORUS. How if I do neither?

SENTINEL. Then I will drive this pilum through you.

APOLLODORUS. At your service, my friend. *(He draws his sword, and springs to his guard with unruffled grace.)*

FTATATEETA *(suddenly seizing the SENTINEL's arms from behind)*. Thrust your knife into the dog's throat, Apollodorus. *(The chivalrous APOLLODORUS laughingly shakes his head; breaks ground away from the SENTINEL towards the palace; and lowers his point.)*

SENTINEL *(struggling vainly)*. Curse on you! Let me go. Help ho!

FTATATEETA *(lifting him from the ground)*. Stab the little Roman reptile. Spit him on your sword.

(A couple of ROMAN SOLDIERS, with a CENTURION, come running along the edge of the quay from the north end. They rescue their comrade, and throw off FATATATEETA, who is sent reeling away on the left hand of the SENTINEL.)

CENTURION *(an unattractive man of fifty, short in his speech and manners, with a vine wood cudgel in his hand)*. How now? What is all this?

FTATATEETA *(to APOLLODORUS)*. Why did you not stab him? There was time!

APOLLODORUS. Centurion: I am here by order of the Queen to——

CENTURION *(interrupting him)*. The Queen! Yes, yes: *(to the SENTINEL)* pass him in. Pass all these bazaar people in to the Queen, with their goods. But mind you pass no one out that you have not passed in—not even the Queen herself.

SENTINEL. This old woman is dangerous: she is as strong as three men. She wanted the merchant to stab me.

APOLLODORUS.   Centurion: I am not a merchant. I am a patrician and a votary of art.

CENTURION.   Is the woman your wife?

APOLLODORUS   (*horrified*). No, no! (*Correcting himself politely*) Not that the lady is not a striking figure in her own way. But (*emphatically*) she is not my wife.

FTATATEETA   (*to the* CENTURION). Roman: I am Ftatateeta, the mistress of the Queen's household.

CENTURION.   Keep your hands off our men, mistress; or I will have you pitched into the harbor, though you were as strong as ten men. (*To his* MEN) To your posts: march! (*He returns with his* MEN *the way they came.*)

FTATATEETA   (*looking malignantly after him*). We shall see whom Isis loves best: her servant Ftatateeta or a dog of a Roman.

SENTINEL   (*to* APOLLODORUS, *with a wave of his pilum towards the pallace*). Pass in there; and keep your distance. (*Turning to* FTATATEETA) Come within a yard of me, you old crocodile; and I will give you this (*the pilum*) in your jaws.

CLEOPATRA   (*calling from the palace*). Ftatateeta, Ftatateeta.

FTATATEETA   (*looking up, scandalized*). Go from the window, go from the window. There are men here.

CLEOPATRA.   I am coming down.

FTATATEETA   (*distracted*). No, no. What are you dreaming of? O ye gods, ye gods! Apollodorus: bid your men pick up your bales; and in with me quickly.

APOLLODORUS.   Obey the mistress of the Queen's household.

FTATATEETA   (*impatiently, as the* PORTERS *stoop to lift the bales*). Quick, quick: she will be out upon us. (CLEOPATRA *comes from the palace and runs across the quay to* FTATATEETA.) Oh that ever I was born!

CLEOPATRA   (*eagerly*). Ftatateeta: I have thought of something. I want a boat—at once.

FTATATEETA.   A boat! No, no: you cannot. Apollodorus: speak to the Queen.

APOLLODORUS   (*gallantly*). Beautiful queen: I am Apollodorus the Sicilian, your servant, from the bazaar. I have brought you the three most beautiful Persian carpets in the world to choose from.

CLEOPATRA.   I have no time for carpets to-day. Get me a boat.

FTATATEETA.   What whim is this? You cannot go on the water except in the royal barge.

APOLLODORUS.   Royalty, Ftatateeta, lies not in the barge but in the Queen. (*To* CLEOPATRA) The touch of your majesty's foot on the gunwale of the meanest boat in the harbor will make it royal. (*He turns to the harbor and calls seaward*) Ho there, boatman! Pull in to the steps.

CLEOPATRA. Apollodorus: you are my perfect knight; and I will always buy my carpets through you. (APOLLODORUS *bows joyously. An oar appears above the quay; and the* BOATMAN, *a bullet-headed, vivacious, grinning fellow, burnt almost black by the sun, comes up a flight of steps from the water on the* SENTINEL'S *right, oar in hand, and waits at the top.*) Can you row, Apollodorus?

APOLLODORUS. My oars shall be your majesty's wings. Whither shall I row my Queen?

CLEOPATRA. To the lighthouse. Come. (*She makes for the steps.*)

SENTINEL (*opposing her with his pilum at the charge*) . Stand. You cannot pass.

CLEOPATRA (flushing angrily) . How dare you? Do you know that I am the Queen?

SENTINEL. I have my orders. You cannot pass.

CLEOPATRA. I will make Caesar have you killed if you do not obey me.

SENTINEL. He will do worse to me if I disobey my officer. Stand back.

CLEOPATRA. Ftatateeta: strangle him.

SENTINEL (*alarmed—looking apprehensively at* FTATATEETA, *and brandishing his pilum*) . Keep off, there.

CLEOPATRA (*running to* APOLLODORUS) . Apollodorus: make your slaves help us.

APOLLODORUS. I shall not need their help, lady. (*He draws his sword.*) Now, soldier: choose which weapon you will defend yourself with. Shall it be sword against pilum, or sword against sword?

SENTINEL. Roman against Sicilian, curse you. Take that. (*He hurls his pilum at* APOLLODORUS, *who drops expertly on one knee. The pilum passes whizzing over his head and falls harmless.* APOLLODORUS, *with a cry of triumph, springs up and attacks the* SENTINEL, *who draws his sword and defends himself, crying*) Ho there, guard. Help!

   CLEOPATRA, *half frightened, half delighted, takes refuge near the palace, where the* PORTERS *are squatting among the bales. The* BOATMAN, *alarmed, hurries down the steps out of harm's way, but stops, with his head just visible above the edge of the quay, to watch the fight. The* SENTINEL *is handicapped by his fear of an attack in the rear from* FTATATEETA. *His swordsmanship, which is of a rough and ready sort, is heavily taxed, as he has occasionally to strike at her to keep her off between a blow and a guard with* APOLLODORUS. *The* CENTURION *returns with several* SOLDIERS. APOLLODORUS *springs back towards* CLEOPATRA *as this reinforcement confronts him.*

CENTURION (*coming to the* SENTINEL'S *right hand*) . What is this? What now?

SENTINEL (*panting*) . I could do well enough by myself if it weren't for the old woman. Keep her off me: that is all the help I need,

CENTURION. Make your report, soldier. What has happened?

FTATATEETA. Centurion: he would have slain the Queen.

SENTINEL (*bluntly*). I would, sooner than let her pass. She wanted to take boat, and go—so she said—to the lighthouse. I stopped her, as I was ordered to; and she set this fellow on me. (*He goes to pick up his pilum and returns to his place with it.*)

CENTURION (*turning to* CLEOPATRA). Cleopatra: I am loth to offend you; but without Caesar's express order we dare not let you pass beyond the Roman lines.

APOLLODORUS. Well, Centurion; and has not the lighthouse been within the Roman lines since Caesar landed there?

CLEOPATRA. Yes, yes. Answer that, if you can.

CENTURION (*to* APOLLODORUS). As for you, Apollodorus, you may thank the gods that you are not nailed to the palace door with a pilum for your meddling.

APOLLODORUS (*urbanely*). My military friend, I was not born to be slain by so ugly a weapon. When I fall, it will be (*holding up his sword*) by this white queen of arms, the only weapon fit for an artist. And now that you are convinced that we do not want to go beyond the lines, let me finish killing your sentinel and depart with the Queen.

CENTURION (*as the* SENTINEL *makes an angry demonstration*). Peace there. Cleopatra. I must abide by my orders, and not by the subtleties of this Sicilian. You must withdraw into the palace and examine your carpets there.

CLEOPATRA (*pouting*). I will not: I am the Queen. Caesar does not speak to me as you do. Have Caesar's centurions changed manners with his scullions?

CENTURION (*sulkily*). I do my duty. That is enough for me.

APOLLODORUS. Majesty: when a stupid man is doing something he is ashamed of, he always declares that it is his duty.

CENTURION (*angry*). Apollodorus—

APOLLODORUS (*interrupting him with defiant elegance*). I will make amends for that insult with my sword at fitting time and place. Who says artist, says duellist. (*To* CLEOPATRA) Hear my counsel, star of the east. Until word comes to these soldiers from Caesar himself, you are a prisoner. Let me go to him with a message from you, and a present; and before the sun has stooped half way to the arms of the sea, I will bring you back Caesar's order of release.

CENTURION (*sneering at him*). And you will sell the Queen the present, no doubt.

APOLLODORUS. Centurion: the Queen shall have from me, without payment, as the unforced tribute of Sicilian taste to Egyptian beauty, the richest of these carpets for her present to Caesar.

CLEOPATRA (*exultantly, to the* CENTURION). Now you see what an ignorant common creature you are!

CENTURION (*curtly*). Well, a fool and his wares are soon parted. (*He turns to his* MEN). Two more men to this post here; and see that no one leaves the palace but this man and his merchandize. If he draws his sword again inside the lines, kill him. To your posts. March.

(*He goes out, leaving two auxiliary* SENTINELS *with the other.*)

APOLLODORUS (*with polite goodfellowship*). My friends: will you not enter the palace and bury our quarrel in a bowl of wine? (*He takes out his purse, jingling the coins in it.*) The Queen has presents for you all.

SENTINEL (*very sulky*). You heard our orders. Get about your business.

FIRST AUXILIARY. Yes: you ought to know better. Off with you.

SECOND AUXILIARY (*looking longingly at the purse—this* SENTINEL *is a hooknosed man, unlike his* COMRADE, *who is squab faced*). Do not tantalize a poor man.

APOLLODORUS (*to* CLEOPATRA). Pearl of Queens: the Centurion is at hand; and the Roman soldier is incorruptible when his officer is looking. I must carry your word to Caesar.

CLEOPATRA (*who has been meditating among the carpets*). Are these carpets very heavy?

APOLLODORUS. It matters not how heavy. There are plenty of porters.

CLEOPATRA. How do they put the carpets into boats? Do they throw them down?

APOLLODORUS. Not into small boats, majesty. It would sink them.

CLEOPATRA. Not into that man's boat, for instance? (*Pointing to the* BOATMAN.)

APOLLODORUS. No. Too small.

CLEOPATRA. But you can take a carpet to Caesar in it if I send one?

APOLLODORUS. Assuredly.

CLEOPATRA. And you will have it carried gently down the steps and take great care of it?

APOLLODORUS. Depend on me.

CLEOPATRA. Great, great care?

APOLLODORUS. More than of my own body.

CLEOPATRA. You will promise me not to let the porters drop it or throw it about?

APOLLODORUS. Place the most delicate glass goblet in the palace in the heart of the roll, Queen; and if it be broken, my head shall pay for it.

CLEOPATRA. Good. Come, Ftatateeta. (FTATATEETA *comes to her.* APOLLODORUS *offers to squire them into the palace.*) No, Apollodorus, you must not come. I will choose a carpet for myself. You must wait here. (*She runs into the palace.*)

APOLLODORUS (*to the* PORTERS). Follow this lady (*indicating* FTATA-TEETA) ; and obey her.

(*The* PORTERS *rise and take up their bales.*)

FTATATEETA (*addressing the* PORTERS *as if they were vermin*). This way. And take your shoes off before you put your feet on those stairs.

(*She goes in, followed by the* PORTERS *with the carpets. Meanwhile* APOLLO-DORUS *goes to the edge of the quay and looks out over the harbor. The* SENTINELS *keep their eyes on him malignantly.*)

APOLLODORUS (*addressing the* SENTINEL). My friend——

SENTINEL (*rudely*). Silence there.

FIRST AUXILIARY. Shut your muzzle, you.

SECOND AUXILIARY (*in a half whisper, glancing apprehensively towards the north end of the quay*). Can't you wait a bit?

APOLLODORAS. Patience, worthy three-headed donkey. (*They mutter ferociously; but he is not at all intimidated.*) Listen: were you set here to watch me, or to watch the Egyptians?

SENTINEL. We know our duty.

APOLLODORUS. Then why don't you do it? There is something going on over there. (*Pointing southwestward to the mole.*)

SENTINEL (*sulkily*). I do not need to be told what to do by the like of you.

APOLLODORUS. Blockhead. (*He begins shouting*) Ho there, Centurion. Hoiho!

SENTINEL. Curse your meddling. (*Shouting*) Hoiho! Alarm! Alarm!

FIRST AND SECOND AUXILIARIES. Alarm! alarm! Hoiho!

(*The* CENTURION *comes running in with his* GUARD.)

CENTURION. What now? Has the old woman attacked you again? (*Seeing* APOLLODORUS) Are you here still?

APOLLODORUS (*pointing as before*). See there. The Egyptians are moving. They are going to recapture the Pharos. They will attack by sea and land: by land along the great mole; by sea from the west harbor. Stir yourselves, my military friends: the hunt is up. (*A clangor of trumpets from several points along the quay.*) Aha! I told you so.

CENTURION (*quickly*). The two extra men pass the alarm to the south posts. One man keep guard here. The rest with me—quick.

(*The two auxiliary* SENTINELS *run off to the south. The* CENTURION *and his* GUARD *run off northward; and immediately afterwards the bucina sounds. The four* PORTERS *come from the palace carrying a carpet, followed by* FTATATEETA.)

SENTINEL (*handling his pilum apprehensively*). You again! *The* POR-TERS *stop.*)

FTATATEETA. Peace, Roman fellow: you are now single-handed. Apollodorus: this carpet is Cleopatra's present to Caesar. It has rolled up in it ten precious goblets of the thinnest Iberian crystal, and a hundred eggs of the sacred blue pigeon. On your honor, let not one of them be broken.

APOLLODORUS. On my head be it. (*To the* PORTERS) Into the boat with them carefully.

(*The* PORTERS *carry the carpet to the steps.*)

FIRST PORTER (*looking down at the boat*). Beware what you do, sir. Those eggs of which the lady speaks must weigh more than a pound apiece. This boat is too small for such a load.

BOATMAN (*excitedly rushing up the steps*). Oh thou injurious porter! Oh thou unnatural son of a she-camel! (*To* APOLLODORUS) My boat, sir, hath often carried five men. Shall it not carry your lordship and a bale of pigeons' eggs? (*To the* PORTER) Thou mangey dromedary, the gods shall punish thee for this envious wickedness.

FIRST PORTER (*stolidly*). I cannot quit this bale now to beat thee; but another day I will lie in wait for thee.

APOLLODORUS (*going between them*). Peace there. If the boat were but a single plank, I would get to Caesar on it.

FTATATEETA (*anxiously*). In the name of the gods, Apollodorus, run no risks with that bale.

APOLLODORUS. Fear not, thou venerable grotesque: I guess its great worth. (*To the* PORTERS) Down with it, I say; and gently; or ye shall eat nothing but stick for ten days.

(*The* BOATMAN *goes down the steps, followed by the* PORTERS *with the bale:* FTATATEETA *and* APOLLODORUS *watching from the edge.*)

APOLLODORUS. Gently, my sons, my children— (*with sudden alarm*) gently, ye dogs. Lay it level in the stern—so—'tis well.

FTATATEETA (*screaming down at one of the* PORTERS). Do not step on it, do not step on it. Oh thou brute beast!

FIRST PORTER (*ascending*). Be not excited, mistress: all is well.

FTATATEETA (*panting*). All well! Oh, thou hast given my heart a turn! (*She clutches her side, gasping.*)

(*The four* PORTERS *have now come up and are waiting at the stairhead to be paid.*)

APOLLODORUS. Here, ye hungry ones. (*He gives money to the first* PORTER, *who holds it in his hand to shew to the others. They crowd greedily to see how much it is, quite prepared, after the Eastern fashion, to protest to heaven against their* PATRON's *stinginess. But his liberality overpowers them.*)

FIRST PORTER. O bounteous prince!

SECOND PORTER. O lord of the bazaar!

THIRD PORTER. O favored of the gods!

FOURTH PORTER. O father to all the porters of the market!

SENTINEL (*enviously, threatening them fiercely with his pilum*). Hence, dogs: off. Out of this. (*They fly before him northward along the quay.*)

APOLLODORUS. Farewell, Ftatateeta. I shall be at the lighthouse before the Egyptians. (*He descends the steps.*)

FTATATEETA. The gods speed thee and protect my nursling!

(*The* SENTRY *returns from chasing the* PORTERS *and looks down at the boat, standing near the stairhead lest* FTATATEETA *should attempt to escape.*)

APOLLODORUS (*from beneath, as the boat moves off.*) Farewell valiant pilum pitcher.

SENTINEL. Farewell, shopkeeper.

APOLLODORUS. Ha, ha! Pull, thou brave boatman, pull. Soho-o-o-o-o! (*He begins to sing in barcarolle measure to the rhythm of the oars*)

> My heart, my heart, spread out thy wings:
> Shake off thy heavy load of love—

Give me the oars, O son of a snail.

SENTINEL (*threatening* FTATATEETA). Now mistress: back to your hen-house. In with you.

FTATATEETA (*falling on her knees and stretching her hands over the water*). Gods of the seas, bear her safely to the shore!

SENTINEL. Bear who safely? What do you mean?

FTATATEETA (*looking darkly at him*). Gods of Egypt and of Vengeance, let this Roman fool be beaten like a dog by his captain for suffering her to be taken over the waters.

SENTINEL. Accursed one: is she then in the boat? (*He calls over the sea*) Hoiho, there, boatman! Hoiho!

APOLLODORUS (*singing in the distance*).

> My heart, my heart, be whole and free:
> Love is thine only enemy.

(*Meanwhile* RUFIO, *the morning's fighting done, sits munching dates on a faggot of brushwood outside the door of the lighthouse, which towers gigantic 'o the clouds on his left. His helmet, full of dates, is between his knees; and a leathern bottle of wine is by his side. Behind him the great stone pedestal of the lighthouse is shut in from the open sea by a low stone parapet, with a couple of steps in the middle to the broad coping. A huge chain with a hook hangs down from the lighthouse crane above his head. Faggots like the one he sits on lie beneath it ready to be drawn up to feed the beacon.*

CAESAR is standing on the step at the parapet looking out anxiously, evidently ill at ease. BRITANNUS comes out of the lighthouse door.)

RUFIO. Well, my British islander. Have you been up to the top?

BRITANNUS. I have. I reckon it at 200 feet high.

RUFIO. Anybody up there?

BRITANNUS. One elderly Tyrian to work the crane; and his son, a well conducted youth of 14.

RUFIO (*looking at the chain*). What! An old man and a boy work that! Twenty men, you mean.

BRITANNUS. Two only, I assure you. They have counterweights, and a machine with boiling water in it which I do not understand: it is not of British design. They use it to haul up barrels of oil and faggots to burn in the brazier on the roof.

RUFIO. But——

BRITANNUS. Excuse me: I came down because there are messengers coming along the mole to us from the island. I must see what their business is. (*He hurries out past the lighthouse.*)

CAESAR (*coming away from the parapet, shivering and out of sorts*). Rufio: this has been a mad expedition. We shall be beaten. I wish I knew how our men are getting on with that barricade across the great mole.

RUFIO (*angrily*). Must I leave my food and go starving to bring you a report?

CAESAR (*soothing him nervously*). No, Rufio, no. Eat, my son, eat. (*He takes another turn.* RUFIO *chewing dates meanwhile.*) The Egyptians cannot be such fools as not to storm the barricade and swoop down on us here before it is finished. It is the first time I have ever run an avoidable risk. I should not have come to Egypt.

RUFIO. An hour ago you were all for victory.

CAESAR (*apologetically*). Yes: I was a fool—rash, Rufio—boyish.

RUFIO. Boyish! Not a bit of it. Here. (*Offering him a handful of dates.*)

CAESAR. What are these for?

RUFIO. To eat. That's what's the matter with you. When a man comes to your age, he runs down before his midday meal. Eat and drink; and then have another look at our chances.

CAESAR (*taking the dates*). My age! (*He shakes his head and bites a date.*) Yes, Rufio: I am an old man—worn out now—true, quite true. (*He gives way to melancholy contemplation, and eats another date.*) Achillas is still in his prime: Ptolemy is a boy. (*He eats another date, and plucks up a little.*) Well, every dog has his day; and I have had mine: I cannot complain. (*With sudden cheerfulness*) These dates are not bad, Rufio. (BRITANNUS *returns, greatly excited, with a leathern bag.* CAESAR *is himself again in a moment.*) What now?

BRITANNUS (*triumphantly*). Our brave Rhodian mariners have captured a treasure. There! (*He throws the bag down at* CAESAR'S *feet.*) Our enemies are delivered into our hands.

CAESAR. In that bag?

BRITANNUS. Wait till you hear, Caesar. This bag contains all the letters which have passed between Pompey's party and the army of occupation here.

CAESAR. Well?

BRITANNUS (*impatient of* CAESAR's *slowness to grasp the situation*). Well, we shall now know who your foes are. The name of every man who has plotted against you since you crossed the Rubicon may be in these papers, for all we know.

CAESAR. Put them in the fire.

BRITANNUS. Put them— (*he gasps*) !!!!

CAESAR. In the fire. Would you have me waste the next three years of my life in proscribing and condemning men who will be my friends when I have proved that my friendship is worth more than Pompey's was—than Cato's is. O incorrigible British islander: am I a bull dog, to seek quarrels merely to shew how stubborn my jaws are?

BRITANNUS. But your honor—the honor of Rome——

CAESAR. I do not make human sacrifices to my honor, as your Druids do. Since you will not burn these, at least I can drown them. (*He picks up the bag and throws it over the parapet into the sea.*)

BRITANNUS. Caesar: this is mere eccentricity. Are traitors to be allowed to go free for the sake of a paradox?

RUFIO (*rising*). Caesar: when the islander has finished preaching, call me again. I am going to have a look at the boiling water machine. (*He goes into the lighthouse.*)

BRITANNUS (*with genuine feeling*). O Caesar, my great master, if I could but persuade you to regard life seriously, as men do in my country!

CAESAR. Do they truly do so, Britannus?

BRITANNUS. Have you not been there? Have you not seen them? What Briton speaks as you do in your moments of levity? What Briton neglects to attend the services at the sacred grove? What Briton wears clothes of many colors as you do, instead of plain blue, as all solid, well esteemed men should? These are moral questions with us.

CAESAR. Well, well, my friend: some day I shall settle down and have a blue toga, perhaps. Meanwhile, I must get on as best I can in my flippant Roman way. (APOLLODORUS *comes past the lighthouse.*) What now?

BRITANNUS (*turning quickly, and challenging the* STRANGER *with official haughtiness*). What is this? Who are you? How did you come here?

APOLLODORUS. Calm yourself, my friend: I am not going to eat you. I have come by boat, from Alexandria, with precious gifts for Caesar.

CAESAR. From Alexandria!

BRITANNUS (*severely*). That is Caesar, sir.

RUFIO (*appearing at the lighthouse door*). What's the matter now?

APOLLODORUS. Hail, great Caesar! I am Apollodorus the Sicilian, an artist.

BRITANNUS. An artist! Why have they admitted this vagabond?

CAESAR. Peace, man. Apollodorus is a famous patrician amateur.

BRITANNUS (*disconcerted*). I crave the gentleman's pardon. (*To* CAESAR) I understood him to say that he was a professional. (*Somewhat out of countenance, he allows* APOLLODORUS *to approach* CAESAR, *changing places with him.* RUFIO, *after looking* APOLLODORUS *up and down with marked disparagement, goes to the other side of the platform.*)

CAESAR. You are welcome, Apollodorus. What is your business?

APOLLODORUS. First, to deliver to you a present from the Queen of Queens.

CAESAR. Who is that?

APOLLODORUS. Cleopatra of Egypt.

CAESAR (*taking him into his confidence in his most winning manner*). Apollodorus: this is no time for playing with presents. Pray you, go back to the Queen, and tell her that if all goes well I shall return to the palace this evening.

APOLLODORUS. Caesar: I cannot return. As I approached the lighthouse, some fool threw a great leathern bag into the sea. It broke the nose of my boat; and I had hardly time to get myself and my charge to the shore before the poor little cockleshell sank.

CAESAR. I am sorry, Apollodorus. The fool shall be rebuked. Well, well: what have you brought me? The Queen will be hurt if I do not look at it.

RUFIO. Have we time to waste on this trumpery? The Queen is only a child.

CAESAR. Just so: that is why we must not disappoint her. What is the present, Apollodorus?

APOLLODORUS. Caesar: it is a Persian carpet—a beauty! And in it are— so I am told—pigeons' eggs and crystal goblets and fragile precious things. I dare not for my head have it carried up that narrow ladder from the causeway.

RUFIO. Swing it up by the crane, then. We will send the eggs to the cook; drink our wine from the goblets; and the carpet will make a bed for Caesar.

APOLLODORUS. The crane! Caesar: I have sworn to tender this bale of carpet as I tender my own life.

CAESAR (*cheerfully*). Then let them swing you up at the same time; and if the chain breaks, you and the pigeons' eggs will perish together. (*He goes to the chain and looks up along it, examining it curiously.*)

APOLLODORUS (*to* BRITANNUS). Is Caesar serious?

BRITANNUS. His manner is frivolous because he is an Italian; but he means what he says.

APOLLODORUS. Serious or not, he spake well. Give me a squad of soldiers to work the crane.

BRITANNUS. Leave the crane to me. Go and await the descent of the chain.

APOLLODORUS. Good. You will presently see me there (*turning to them all and pointing with an eloquent gesture to the sky above the parapet*) rising like the sun with my treasure.

(*He goes back the way he came.* BRITANNUS *goes into the lighthouse.*)

RUFIO (*ill-humoredly*). Are you really going to wait here for this foolery, Caesar?

CAESAR (*backing away from the crane as it gives signs of working*). Why not?

RUFIO. The Egyptians will let you know why not if they have the sense to make a rush from the shore end of the mole before our barricade is finished. And there we are waiting like children to see a carpet full of pigeons' eggs.

(*The chain rattles, and is drawn up high enough to clear the parapet. It then swings round out of sight behind the lighthouse.*)

CAESAR. Fear not, my son Rufio. When the first Egyptian takes his first step along the mole, the alarm will sound; and we two will reach the barricade from our end before the Egyptians reach it from their end—we two, Rufio: I, the old man, and you, his biggest boy. And the old man will be there first. So peace; and give me some more dates.

APOLLODORUS (*from the causeway below*). Soho, haul away. So-ho-o-o-o!
(*The chain is drawn up and comes round again from behind the lighthouse.* APOLLODORUS *is swinging in the air with his bale of carpet at the end of it. He breaks into song as he soars above the parapet*)

> Aloft, aloft, behold the blue
> That never shone in woman's eyes—

Easy there: stop her. (*He ceases to rise.*) Further round! (*The chain comes forward above the platform.*)

RUFIO (*calling up*). Lower away there. (*The chain and its load begins to descend.*)

APOLLODORUS (*calling up*). Gently—slowly—mind the eggs.

RUFIO (*calling up*). Easy there—slowly—slowly.

(APOLLODORUS *and the bale are deposited safely on the flags in the middle of the platform.* RUFIO *and* CAESAR *help* APOLLODORUS *to cast off the chain from the bale.*)

RUFIO. Haul up.

(*The chain rises clear of their heads with a rattle. Britannus comes from the lighthouse and helps them to uncord the carpet.*)

APOLLODORUS (*when the cords are loose*). Stand off, my friends: let Caesar see. (*He throws the carpet open.*)

RUFIO. Nothing but a heap of shawls. Where are the pigeons' eggs?

APOLLODORUS. Approach, Caesar; and search for them among the shawls.

RUFIO (*drawing his sword*). Ha, treachery! Keep back, Caesar: I saw the shawl move: there is something alive there.

BRITANNUS (*drawing his sword*). It is a serpent.

APOLLODORUS. Dares Caesar thrust his hand into the sack where the serpent moves?

RUFIO (*turning on him*). Treacherous dog——

CAESAR. Peace. Put up your swords. Apollodorus: your serpent seems to breathe very regularly. (*He thrusts his hand under the shawls and draws out a bare arm.*) This is a pretty little snake.

RUFIO (*drawing out the other arm*). Let us have the rest of you.

(*They pull* CLEOPATRA *up by the wrists into a sitting position.* BRITANNUS, *scandalized, sheathes his sword with a drive of protest.*)

CLEOPATRA (*gasping*). Oh, I'm smothered. Oh Caesar; a man stood on me in the boat; and a great sack of something fell upon me out of the sky; and then the boat sank, and then I was swung up into the air and bumped down.

CAESAR (*petting her as she rises and takes refuge on his breast*). Well, never mind: here you are safe and sound at last.

RUFIO. Ay; and now that she is here, what are we to do with her?

BRITANNUS. She cannot stay here, Caesar, without the companionship of some matron.

CLEOPATRA (*jealously, to* CAESAR, *who is obviously perplexed*). Aren't you glad to see me?

CAESAR. Yes, yes; *I* am very glad. But Rufio is very angry; and Britannus is shocked.

CLEOPATRA (*contemptuously*). You can have their heads cut off, can you not?

CAESAR. They would not be so useful with their heads cut off as they are now, my sea bird.

RUFIO (*to* CLEOPATRA). We shall have to go away presently and cut some of your Egyptians' heads off. How will you like being left here with the chance of being captured by that little brother of yours if we are beaten?

CLEOPATRA. But you mustn't leave me alone. Caesar you will not leave me alone, will you?

RUFIO. What! not when the trumpet sounds and all our lives depend on Caesar's being at the barricade before the Egyptians reach it? Eh?

CLEOPATRA. Let them lose their lives: they are only soldiers.

CAESAR (*gravely*). Cleopatra: when that trumpet sounds, we must take every man his life in his hand, and throw it in the face of Death. And of my soldiers who have trusted me there is not one whose hand I shall not hold more sacred than your head (CLEOPATRA *is overwhelmed. Her eyes fill with tears.*) Apollodorus: you must take her back to the palace.

APOLLODORUS. Am I a dolphin, Caesar, to cross the seas with young ladies on my back? My boat is sunk: all yours are either at the barricade or have returned to the city. I will hail one if I can: that is all I can do. (*He goes back to the causeway.*)

CLEOPATRA (*struggling with her tears*). It does not matter. I will not go back. Nobody cares for me.

CAESAR. Cleopatra——

CLEOPATRA. You want me to be killed.

CAESAR (*still more gravely*). My poor child: your life matters little here to anyone but yourself. (*She gives way altogether at this, casting herself down on the faggots weeping. Suddenly a great tumult is heard in the distance, bucinas and trumpets sounding through a storm of shouting.* BRITANNUS *rushes to the parapet and looks along the mole.* CAESAR *and* RUFIO *turn to one another with quick intelligence.*)

CAESAR. Come, Rufio.

CLEOPATRA (*scrambling to her knees and clinging to him*). No, no. Do not leave me, Caesar. (*He snatches his skirt from her clutch.*) Oh!

BRITANNUS (*from the parapet*). Caesar: we are cut off. The Egyptians have landed from the west harbor between us and the barricade!!!

RUFIO (*running to see*). Curses! It is true. We are caught like rats in a trap.

CAESAR (*ruthfully*). Rufio, Rufio: my men at the barricade are between the sea party and the shore party. I have murdered them.

RUFIO (*coming back from the parapet to* CAESAR's *right hand*). Ay: that comes of fooling with this girl here.

APOLLODORUS (*coming up quickly from the causeway*). Look over the parapet, Caesar.

CAESAR. We have looked, my friend. We must defend ourselves here.

APOLLODORUS. I have thrown the ladder into the sea. They cannot get in without it.

RUFIO. Ay; and we cannot get out. Have you thought of that?

APOLLODORUS. Not get out! Why not? You have ships in the east harbor.

BRITANNUS (*hopefully, at the parapet*). The Rhodian galleys are standing in towards us already. (CAESAR *quickly joins* BRITANNUS *at the parapet.*)

RUFIO (*to* APOLLODORUS, *impatiently*). And by what road are we to walk to the galleys, pray?

APOLLODORUS. *(with gay, defiant rhetoric)*. By the road that leads every-where—the diamond path of the sun and moon. Have you never seen the child's shadow play of The Broken Bridge? "Ducks and geese with ease get over"—eh? *(He throws away his cloak and cap, and binds his sword on his back.)*

RUFIO. What are you talking about?

APOLLODORUS. I will shew you. *(Calling to* BRITANNUS*)* how far off is the nearest galley?

BRITANNUS. Fifty fathom.

CAESAR. No, no: they are further off than they seem in this clear air to your British eyes. Nearly quarter of a mile, Apollodorus.

APOLLODORUS. Good. Defend yourselves here until I send you a boat from that galley.

RUFIO. Have you wings, perhaps?

APOLLODORUS. Water wings, soldier. Behold!

(He runs up the steps between CAESAR *and* BRITANNUS *to the coping of the parapet; springs into the air; and plunges head foremost into the sea.)*

CAESAR *(like a schoolboy—wildly excited)*. Bravo, bravo! *(Throwing off his cloak)* By Jupiter, I will do that too.

RUFIO *(seizing him)*. You are mad. You shall not.

CAESAR. Why not? Can I not swim as well as he?

RUFIO *(frantic)*. Can an old fool drive and swim like a young one? He is twenty-five and you are fifty.

CAESAR *(breaking loose from* RUFIO*)*. Old!!!

BRITANNUS *(shocked)*. Rufio: you forget yourself.

CAESAR. I will race you to the galley for a week's pay, father Rufio.

CLEOPATRA. But me! me!! me!!! what is to become of me?

CAESAR. I will carry you on my back to the galley like a dolphin. Rufio: when you see me rise to the surface, throw her in: I will answer for her. And then in with you after her, both of you.

CLEOPATRA. No, no, NO. I shall be drowned.

BRITANNUS. Caesar: I am a man and a Briton, not a fish. I must have a boat. I cannot swim.

CLEOPATRA. Neither can I.

CAESAR *(to* BRITANNUS*)*. Stay here, then, alone, until I recapture the lighthouse: I will not forget you. Now, Rufio.

RUFIO. You have made up your mind to this folly?

CAESAR. The Egyptians have made it up for me. What else is there to do? And mind where you jump: I do not want to get your fourteen stone in the small of my back as I come up. *(He runs up the steps and stands on the coping.)*

BRITANNUS *(anxiously)*. One last word, Caesar. Do not let yourself be seen in the fashionable part of Alexandria until you have changed your clothes.

CAESAR (*calling over the sea*). Ho, Apollodorus: (*he points skyward and quotes the barcarolle*)

> The white upon the blue above—

APOLLODORUS (*swimming in the distance*)

> Is purple on the green below—

CAESAR (*exultantly*). Aha! (*He plunges into the sea.*)

CLEOPATRA (*running excitedly to the steps*). Oh, let me see. He will be drowned. (RUFIO *seizes her.*) Ah—ah—ah—ah! (*He pitches her screaming into the sea.* RUFIO *and* BRITANNUS *roar with laughter.*)

RUFIO (*looking down after her*). He has got her. (*To* BRITANNUS) Hold the fort, Briton. Caesar will not forget you. (*He springs off.*)

BRITANNUS (*running to the steps to watch them as they swim*). All safe, Rufio?

RUFIO (*swimming*). All safe.

CAESAR (*swimming further off*). Take refuge up there by the beacon; and pile the fuel on the trap door, Britannus.

BRITANNUS (*calling in reply*). I will first so do, and then commend myself to my country's gods. (*A sound of cheering from the sea.* BRITANNUS *gives full vent to his excitement*) The boat has reached him: Hip, hip, hip, hurrah!

ACT IV

Cleopatra's sousing in the east harbor of Alexandria was in October 48 B.C. *In March* 47 *she is passing the afternoon in her boudoir in the palace, among a bevy of her ladies, listening to a slave girl who is playing the harp in the middle of the room. The harpist's master, an old musician, with a lined face, prominent brows, white beard, moustache and eyebrows twisted and horned at the ends, and a consciously keen and pretentious expression, is squatting on the floor close to her on her right, watching her performance. Ftatateeta is in attendance near the door, in front of a group of female slaves. Except the harp player all are seated: Cleopatra in a chair opposite the door on the other side of the room; the rest on the ground. Cleopatra's ladies are all young, the most conspicuous being Charmian and Iras, her favorites. Charmian is a hatchet faced, terra cotta colored little goblin, swift in her movements, and neatly finished at the hands and feet. Iras is a plump, goodnatured creature, rather fatuous, with a profusion of red hair, and a tendency to giggle on the slightest provocation.*

CLEOPATRA. Can I——

FTATATEETA (*insolently, to the* PLAYER). Peace, thou! The Queen speaks. (*The* PLAYER *stops.*)

CLEOPATRA (*to the old* MUSICIAN). I want to learn to play the harp with my own hands. Caesar loves music. Can you teach me?

MUSICIAN. Assuredly I and no one else can teach the Queen. Have I not discovered the lost method of the ancient Egyptians, who could make a pyramid tremble by touching a bass string? All the other teachers are quacks: I have exposed them repeatedly.

CLEOPATRA. Good: you shall teach me. How long will it take?

MUSICIAN. Not very long: only four years. Your Majesty must first become proficient in the philosophy of Pythagoras.

CLEOPATRA. Has she (*indicating the* SLAVE) become proficient in the philosophy of Pythagoras?

MUSICIAN. Oh, she is but a slave. She learns as a dog learns.

CLEOPATRA. Well, then, I will learn as a dog learns; for she plays better than you. You shall give me a lesson every day for a fortnight. (*The* MUSICIAN *hastily scrambles to his feet and bows profoundly.*) After that, whenever I strike a false note you shall be flogged; and if I strike so many that there is not time to flog you, you shall be thrown into the Nile to feed the crocodiles. Give the girl a piece of gold; and send them away.

MUSICIAN (*much taken aback*). But true art will not be thus forced.

FTATATEETA (*pushing him out*). What is this? Answering the Queen, forsooth. Out with you.

(*He is pushed out by* FTATATEETA, *the* GIRL *following with her harp, amid the laughter of the* LADIES *and* SLAVES.)

CLEOPATRA. Now, can any of you amuse me? Have you any stories or any news?

IRAS. Ftatateeta——

CLEOPATRA. Oh, Ftatateeta, Ftatateeta, always Ftatateeta. Some new tale to set me against her.

IRAS. No: this time Ftatateeta has been virtuous. (*All the* LADIES *laugh —not the* SLAVES.) Pothinus has been trying to bribe her to let him speak with you.

CLEOPATRA (*wrathfully*). Ha! you all sell audiences with me, as if I saw whom you please, and not whom I please. I should like to know how much of her gold piece that harp girl will have to give up before she leaves the palace.

IRAS. We can easily find out that for you.

(*The* LADIES *laugh.*)

CLEOPATRA (*frowning*). You laugh; but take care, take care. I will find out some day how to make myself served as Caesar is served.

CHARMIAN.   Old hooknose! (*They laugh again.*)

CLEOPATRA   (*revolted*). Silence. Charmian: do not you be a silly little
Egyptian fool. Do you know why I allow you all to chatter imperti-
nently just as you please, instead of treating you as Ftatateeta would
treat you if she were Queen?

CHARMIAN.   Because you try to imitate Caesar in everything; and he lets
everybody say what they please to him.

CLEOPATRA.   No; but because I asked him one day why he did so; and
he said "Let your women talk; and you will learn something from
them." What have I to learn from them? I said. "What they are,"
said he; and oh! you should have seen his eye as he said it. You would
have curled up, you shallow things. (*They laugh. She turns fiercely on*
IRAS) At whom are you laughing—at me or at Caesar?

IRAS.   At Caesar.

CLEOPATRA.   If you were not a fool, you would laugh at me; and if you
were not a coward you would not be afraid to tell me so. (FTATATEETA
returns.) Ftatateeta: they tell me that Pothinus has offered you a bribe
to admit him to my presence.

FTATATEETA   (*protesting*). Now by my father's gods——

CLEOPATRA   (*cutting her short despotically*). Have I not told you not
to deny things? You would spend the day calling your father's gods to
witness to your virtues if I let you. Go take the bribe; and bring in
Pothinus. (FTATATEETA *is about to reply.*) Don't answer me. Go.

FTATATEETA *goes out; and* CLEOPATRA *rises and begins to prowl to and
fro between her chair and the door, meditating. All rise and stand.*

IRAS   (*as she reluctantly rises*). Heigho! I wish Caesar were back in
Rome.

CLEOPATRA   (*threateningly*). It will be a bad day for you all when he
goes. Oh, if I were not ashamed to let him see that I am as cruel at
heart as my father, I would make you repent that speech! Why do
you wish him away?

CHARMIAN.   He makes you so terribly prosy and serious and learned
and philosophical. It is worse than being religious, at our ages. (*The*
LADIES *laugh.*)

CLEOPATRA.   Cease that endless cackling, will you. Hold your tongues.

CHARMIAN   (*with mock resignation*). Well, well: we must try to live
up to Caesar.

They laugh again. CLEOPATRA *rages silently as she continues to prowl
to and fro.* FTATATEETA *comes back with* POTHINUS, *who halts on the
threshold.*)

FTATATEETA   (*at the door*). Pothinus craves the ear of the——

CLEOPATRA.   There, there: that will do: let him come in. (*She resumes her seat. All sit down except* POTHINUS, *who advances to the*

middle of the room. FTATATEETA *takes her former place.*) Well, Pothinus: what is the latest news from your rebel friends?

POTHINUS (*haughtily*). I am no friend of rebellion. And a prisoner does not receive news.

CLEOPATRA. You are no more a prisoner than I am—than Caesar is. These six months we have been besieged in this palace by my subjects. You are allowed to walk on the beach among the soldiers. Can I go further myself, or can Caesar?

POTHINUS. You are but a child, Cleopatra, and do not understand these matters.

(*The* LADIES *laugh.* CLEOPATRA *looks inscrutably at him.*)

CHARMIAN. I see you do not know the latest news, Pothinus.

POTHINUS. What is that?

CHARMIAN. That Cleopatra is no longer a child. Shall I tell you how to grow much older, and much, much wiser in one day?

POTHINUS. I should prefer to grow wiser without growing older.

CHARMIAN. Well, go up to the top of the lighthouse; and get somebody to take you by the hair and throw you into the sea. (*The* LADIES *laugh.*)

CLEOPATRA. She is right, Pothinus: you will come to the shore with much conceit washed out of you. (*The* LADIES *laugh.* CLEOPATRA *rises impatiently.*) Begone, all of you. I will speak with Pothinus alone. Drive them out, Ftatateeta. (*They run out laughing.* FTATATEETA *shuts the door on them.*) What are you waiting for?

FTATATEETA. It is not meet that the Queen remain alone with——

CLEOPATRA (*interrupting her*). Ftatateeta: must I sacrifice you to your father's gods to teach you that *I* am Queen of Egypt, and not you?

FTATATEETA (*indignantly*). You are like the rest of them. You want to be what these Romans call a New Woman. (*She goes out, banging the door.*)

CLEOPATRA (*sitting down again*). Now, Pothinus: why did you bribe Ftatateeta to bring you hither?

POTHINUS (*studying her gravely*). Cleopatra: what they tell me is true. You are changed.

CLEOPATRA. Do you speak with Caesar every day for six months: and you will be changed.

POTHINUS. It is the common talk that you are infatuated with this old man.

CLEOPATRA. Infatuated? What does that mean? Made foolish, is it not? Oh no: I wish I were.

POTHINUS. You wish you were made foolish! How so?

CLEOPATRA. When I was foolish, I did what I liked, except when Ftatateeta beat me; and even then I cheated her and did it by stealth.

Now that Caesar has made me wise, it is no use my liking or disliking;
I do what must be done, and have no time to attend to myself. That is
not happiness; but it is greatness. If Caesar were gone, I think I could
govern the Egyptians; for what Caesar is to me, I am to the fools
around me.

POTHINUS   (*looking hard at her*). Cleopatra: this may be the vanity of
youth.

CLEOPATRA.   No, no: it is not that I am so clever, but that the others are
so stupid.

POTHINUS   (*musingly*). Truly, that is the great secret.

CLEOPATRA.   Well, now tell me what you came to say?

POTHINUS   (*embarrassed*). I! Nothing.

CLEOPATRA.   Nothing!

POTHINUS.   At least—to beg for my liberty: that is all.

CLEOPATRA.   For that you would have knelt to Caesar. No, Pothinus: you
came with some plan that depended on Cleopatra being a little nursery
kitten. Now that Cleopatra is a Queen, the plan is upset.

POTHINUS   (*bowing his head submissively*). It is so.

CLEOPATRA   (*exultant*). Aha!

POTHINUS   (*raising his eyes keenly to hers*). Is Cleopatra then indeed a
Queen, and no longer Caesar's prisoner and slave?

CLEOPATRA.   Pothinus: we are all Caesar's slaves—all we in this land of
Egypt—whether we will or no. And she who is wise enough to know
this will reign when Caesar departs.

POTHINUS.   You harp on Caesar's departure.

CLEOPATRA.   What if I do?

POTHINUS.   Does he not love you?

CLEOPATRA.   Love me! Pothinus: Caesar loves no one. Who are those
we love? Only those whom we do not hate: all people are strangers and
enemies to us except those we love. But it is not so with Caesar. He
has no hatred in him: he makes friends with everyone as he does with
dogs and children. His kindness to me is a wonder: neither mother,
father, nor nurse have ever taken so much care for me, or thrown open
their thoughts to me so freely.

POTHINUS.   Well: is not this love?

CLEOPATRA.   What! When he will do as much for the first girl he meets
on his way back to Rome? Ask his slave, Britannus: he has been just
as good to him. Nay, ask his very horse! His kindness is not for anything in me: it is in his own nature.

POTHINUS.   But how can you be sure that he does not love you as men
love women?

CLEOPATRA.   Because I cannot make him jealous. I have tried.

POTHINUS.   Hm! Perhaps I should have asked, then, do you love him?

CLEOPATRA. Can one love a god? Besides, I love another Roman: one whom I saw long before Caesar—no god, but a man—one who can love and hate—one whom I can hurt and who would hurt me.

POTHINUS. Does Caesar know this?

CLEOPATRA. Yes.

POTHINUS. And he is not angry.

CLEOPATRA. He promises to send him to Egypt to please me!

POTHINUS. I do not understand this man.

CLEOPATRA *(with superb contempt)*. You understand Caesar! How could you? *(Proudly)* I do—by instinct.

POTHINUS *(deferentially, after a moment's thought)*. Your Majesty caused me to be admitted to-day. What message has the Queen for me?

CLEOPATRA. This. You think that by making my brother king, you will rule in Egypt, because you are his guardian and he is a little silly.

POTHINUS. The Queen is pleased to say so.

CLEOPATRA. The Queen is pleased to say this also. That Caesar will eat up you, and Achillas, and my brother, as a cat eats up mice; and that he will put on this land of Egypt as a shepherd puts on his garment. And when he has done that, he will return to Rome, and leave Cleopatra here as his viceroy.

POTHINUS *(breaking out wrathfully)*. That he will never do. We have a thousand men to his ten; and we will drive him and his beggarly legions into the sea.

CLEOPATRA *(with scorn, getting up to go)*. You rant like any common fellow. Go, then, and marshal your thousands; and make haste; for Mithridates of Pergamos is at hand with reinforcements for Caesar. Caesar has held you at bay with two legions: we shall see what he will do with twenty.

POTHINUS. Cleopatra——

CLEOPATRA. Enough, enough: Caesar has spoiled me for talking to weak things like you. *(She goes out. POTHINUS, with a gesture of rage, is following, when FTATATEETA enters and stops him.)*

POTHINUS. Let me go forth from this hateful place.

FTATATEETA. What angers you?

POTHINUS. The curse of all the gods of Egypt be upon her! She has sold her country to the Roman, that she may buy it back from him with her kisses.

FTATATEETA. Fool: did she not tell you that she would have Caesar gone?

POTHINUS. You listened?

FTATATEETA. I took care that some honest woman should be at hand whilst you were with her.

POTHINUS. Now by the gods——

FTATATEETA. Enough of your gods! Caesar's gods are all powerful here,

It is no use you coming to Cleopatra: you are only an Egyptian. She will not listen to any of her own race: she treats us all as children.

POTHINUS. May she perish for it!

FTATATEETA (*balefully*). May your tongue wither for that wish! Go! send for Lucius Septimius, the slayer of Pompey. He is a Roman: may be she will listen to him. Begone!

POTHINUS (*darkly*). I know to whom I must go now.

FTATATEETA (*suspiciously*). To whom, then?

POTHINUS. To a greater Roman than Lucius. And mark this mistress. You thought, before Caesar came, that Egypt should presently be ruled by you and your crew in the name of Cleopatra. I set myself against it——

FTATATEETA (*interrupting him—wrangling*). Ay; that it might be ruled by you and your crew in the name of Ptolemy.

POTHINUS. Better me, or even you, than a woman with a Roman heart; and that is what Cleoparta is now become. Whilst I live, she shall never rule. So guide yourself accordingly. (*He goes out.*)

(*It is by this time drawing on to dinner time. The table is laid on the roof of the palace; and thither* RUFIO *is now climbing, ushered by a majestic* PALACE OFFICIAL, *wand of office in hand, and followed by a* SLAVE *carrying an inlaid stool. After many stairs they emerge at last into a massive colonnade on the roof. Light curtains are drawn between the columns on the north and east to soften the westering sun. The* OFFICIAL *leads* RUFIO *to one of these shaded sections. A cord for pulling the curtains apart hangs down between the pillars.*)

THE OFFICIAL (*bowing*). The Roman commander will await Caesar here.

(*The* SLAVE *sets down the stool near the southernmost column, and slips out through the curtains.*)

RUFIO (*sitting down, a little blown*). Pouf! That was a climb. How high have we come?

THE OFFICIAL. We are on the palace roof, O Beloved of Victory!

RUFIO. Good! the Beloved of Victory has no more stairs to get up.

(*A second* OFFICIAL *enters from the opposite end, walking backwards.*)

THE SECOND OFFICIAL. Caesar approaches.

(CAESAR, *fresh from the bath, clad in a new tunic of purple silk, comes in, beaming and festive, followed by two* SLAVES *carrying a light couch, which is hardly more than an elaborately designed bench. They place it near the northmost of the two curtained columns. When this is done they slip out through the curtains; and the two* OFFICIALS, *formally bowing, follow them.* RUFIO *rises to receive* CAESAR.)

CAESAR (*coming over to him*). Why, Rufio! (*Surveying his dress with an air of admiring astonishment*) A new baldrick! A new golden pommel to your sword! And you have had your hair cut! But not your beard—? impossible! (*He sniffs at* RUFIO's *beard.*) Yes, perfumed, by Jupiter Olympus!

RUFIO   (*growling*). Well: is it to please myself?

CAESAR   (*affectionately*). No, my son Rufio, but to please me—to celebrate my birthday.

RUFIO   (*contemptuously*). Your birthday! You always have a birthday when there is a pretty girl to be flattered or an ambassador to be conciliated. We had seven of them in ten months last year.

CAESAR   (*contritely*). It is true, Rufio! I shall never break myself of these petty deceits.

RUFIO.   Who is to dine with us—besides Cleopatra?

CAESAR.   Apollodorus the Sicilian.

RUFIO.   That popinjay!

CAESAR.   Come! the popinjay is an amusing dog—tells a story; sings a song; and saves us the trouble of flattering the Queen. What does she care for old politicians and camp-fed bears like us? No: Apollodorus is good company, Rufio, good company.

RUFIO.   Well, he can swim a bit and fence a bit: he might be worse, if he only knew how to hold his tongue.

CAESAR.   The gods forbid he should ever learn! Oh, this military life! this tedious, brutal life of action! That is the worst of us Romans: we are mere doers and drudgers: a swarm of bees turned into men. Give me a good talker—one with wit and imagination enough to live without continually doing something!

RUFIO.   Ay! a nice time he would have of it with you when dinner was over! Have you noticed that I am before my time?

CAESAR.   Aha! I thought that meant something. What it is?

RUFIO.   Can we be overheard here?

CAESAR.   Our privacy invites eavesdropping. I can remedy that. (*He claps his hands twice. The curtains are drawn, revealing the roof garden with a banqueting table set across in the middle for four persons, one at each end, and two side by side. The side next* CAESAR *and* RUFIO *is blocked with golden wine vessels and basins. A gorgeous* MAJOR-DOMO *is superintending the laying of the table by a staff of* SLAVES. *The colonnade goes round the garden at both sides to the further end, where a gap in it, like a great gateway, leaves the view open to the sky beyond the western edge of the roof, except in the middle, where a life size image of Ra, seated on a huge plinth, towers up, with hawk head and crown of asp and disk. His altar, which stands at his feet, is a simple white stone.*) Now everybody can see us, nobody will think of listening to us. (*He sits down on the bench left by the two* SLAVES.)

RUFIO   (*sitting down on his stool*). Pothinus wants to speak to you. I advise you to see him: there is some plotting going on here among the women.

CAESAR. Who is Pothinus?

RUFIO. The fellow with hair like squirrel's fur—the little King's bear leader, whom you kept prisoner.

CAESAR *(annoyed)*. And has he not escaped?

RUFIO. No.

CAESAR *(rising imperiously)*. Why not? You have been guarding this man instead of watching the enemy. Have I not told you always to let prisoners escape unless there are special orders to the contrary? Are there not enough mouths to be fed without him?

RUFIO. Yes; and if you would have a little sense and let me cut his throat, you would save his rations. Anyhow, he won't escape. Three sentries have told him they would put a pilum through him if they saw him again. What more can they do? He prefers to stay and spy on us. So would I if I had to do with generals subject to fits of clemency.

CAESAR *(resuming his seat, argued down)*. Hm! And so he wants to see me.

RUFIO. Ay. I have brought him with me. He is waiting there *(jerking his thumb over his shoulder)* under guard.

CAESAR. And you want me to see him?

RUFIO *(obstinately)*. I don't want anything. I daresay you will do what you like. Don't put it on to me.

CAESAR *(with an air of doing it expressly to indulge* RUFIO*)*. Well, well: let us have him.

RUFIO *(calling)*. Ho there, guard! Release your man and send him up. *(Beckoning)* Come along!

(POTHINUS *enters and stops mistrustfully between the two, looking from one to the other.*)

CAESAR *(graciously)*. Ah, Pothinus! You are welcome. And what is the news this afternoon?

POTHINUS. Caesar: I come to warn you of a danger, and to make you an offer.

CAESAR. Never mind the danger. Make the offer.

RUFIO. Never mind the offer. What's the danger?

POTHINUS. Caesar: you think that Cleopatra is devoted to you.

CAESAR *(gravely)*. My friend: I already know what I think. Come to your offer.

POTHINUS. I will deal plainly. I know not by what strange gods you have been enabled to defend a palace and a few yards of beach against a city and an army. Since we cut you off from Lake Mareotis, and you dug wells in the salt sea sand and brought up buckets of fresh water from them, we have known that your gods are irresistible, and that you are a worker of miracles. I no longer threaten you——

RUFIO *(sarcastically)*. Very handsome of you, indeed.

POTHINUS. So be it: you are the master. Our gods sent the north west winds to keep you in our hands; but you have been too strong for them.

CAESAR (*gently urging him to come to the point*). Yes, yes, my friend. But what then?

RUFIO. Spit it out man. What have you to say?

POTHINUS. I have to say that you have a traitress in your camp. Cleopatra——

THE MAJOR-DOMO (*at the table, announcing*). The Queen!

(CAESAR *and* RUFIO *rise.*)

RUFIO (*aside to* POTHINUS). You should have spat it out sooner, you fool. Now it is too late.

(CLEOPATRA, *in gorgeous raiment, enters in state through the gap in the colonnade, and comes down past the image of Ra and past the table to* CAESAR. *Her retinue, headed by* FTATATEETA, *joins the staff at the table.* CAESAR *gives* CLEOPATRA *his seat, which she takes.*)

CLEOPATRA (*quickly, seeing* POTHINUS). What is he doing here?

CAESAR (*seating himself beside her, in the most amiable of tempers*). Just going to tell me something about you. You shall hear it. Proceed, Pothinus.

POTHINUS (*disconcerted*). Caesar— (*He stammers.*)

CAESAR. Well, out with it.

POTHINUS. What I have to say is for your ear, not for the Queen's.

CLEOPATRA (*with subdued ferocity*). There are means of making you speak. Take care.

POTHINUS (*defiantly*). Caesar does not employ those means.

CAESAR. My friend: when a man has anything to tell in this world, the difficulty is not to make him tell it, but to prevent him from telling it too often. Let me celebrate my birthday by setting you free. Farewell: we shall not meet again.

CLEOPATRA (*angrily*). Caesar: this mercy is foolish.

POTHINUS (*to* CAESAR). Will you not give me a private audience? Your life may depend on it. (CAESAR *rises loftily.*)

RUFIO (*aside to* POTHINUS). Ass! Now we shall have some heroics.

CAESAR (*oratorically*). Pothinus——

RUFIO (*interrupting him*). Caesar: the dinner will spoil if you begin preaching your favourite sermon about life and death.

CLEOPATRA (*priggishly*). Peace, Rufio. I desire to hear Caesar.

RUFIO (*bluntly*). Your Majesty has heard it before. You repeated it to Apollodorus last week; and he thought it was all your own. (CAESAR's *dignity collapses. Much tickled, he sits down again and looks roguishly at* CLEOPATRA, *who is furious.* RUFIO *calls as before*) Ho there, guard! Pass the prisoner out. He is released. (*To* POTHINUS) Now off with you. You have lost your chance.

POTHINUS (*his temper overcoming his prudence*). I will speak.

CAESAR   (*to* CLEOPATRA). You see. Torture would not have wrung a word from him.

POTHINUS.   Caesar: you have taught Cleopatra the arts by which the Romans govern the world.

CAESAR.   Alas! they cannot even govern themselves. What then?

POTHINUS.   What then? Are you so besotted with her beauty that you do not see that she is impatient to reign in Egypt alone, and that her heart is set on your departure?

CLEOPATRA   (*rising*). Liar!

CAESAR   (*shocked*). What! Protestations! Contradictions!

CLEOPATRA   (*ashamed, but trembling with suppressed rage*). No. I do not deign to contradict. Let him talk. (*She sits down again.*)

POTHINUS.   From her own lips I have heard it. You are to be her catspaw: you are to tear the crown from her brother's head and set it on her own, delivering us all into her hand—delivering yourself also. And then Caesar can return to Rome, or depart through the gate of death, which is nearer and surer.

CAESAR   (*calmly*). Well, my friend; and is not this very natural?

POTHINUS   (*astonished*). Natural! Then you do not resent treachery?

CAESAR.   Resent! O thou foolish Egyptian, what have I to do with resentment? Do I resent the wind when it chills me, or the night when it makes me stumble in the darkness? Shall I resent youth when it turns from age, and ambition when it turns from servitude? To tell me such a story as this is but to tell me that the sun will rise tomorrow.

CLEOPATRA   (*unable to contain herself*). But it is false—false. I swear it.

CAESAR.   It is true, though you swore it a thousand times, and believed all you swore. (*She is convulsed with emotion. To screen her, he rises and takes* POTHINUS *to* RUFIO, *saying*) Come, Rufio: let us see Pothinus past the guard. I have a word to say to him. (*Aside to them*) We must give the Queen a moment to recover herself. (*Aloud*) Come. (*He takes* POTHINUS *and* RUFIO *out with him, conversing with them meanwhile.*) Tell your friends, Pothinus, that they must not think I am opposed to a reasonable settlement of the country's affairs— (*They pass out of hearing.*)

CLEOPATRA   (*in a stifled whisper*). Ftatateeta, Ftatateeta.

FTATATEETA   (*hurrying to her from the table and petting her*). Peace, child: be comforted——

CLEOPATRA   (*interrupting her*). Can they hear us?

FTATATEETA.   No, dear heart, no.

CLEOPATRA.   Listen to me. If he leaves the Palace alive, never see my face again.

FTATATEETA.   He? Poth——

CLEOPATRA   (*striking her on the mouth*). Strike his life out as I strike his name from your lips. Dash him down from the wall. Break him on the stones. Kill, kill, kill him.

FTATATEETA   (*shewing all her teeth*). The dog shall perish.

CLEOPATRA.   Fail in this, and you go out from before me for ever.

FTATATEETA   (*resolutely*). So be it. You shall not see my face until his eyes are darkened.

(CAESAR *comes back, with* APOLLODORUS, *exquisitely dressed, and* RUFIO.)

CLEOPATRA   (*to* FTATATEETA). Come soon—soon. (FTATATEETA *turns her meaning eyes for a moment on her mistress; then goes grimly away past Ra and out.* CLEOPATRA *runs like a gazelle to* CAESAR) So you have come back to me, Caesar. (*Caressingly*) I thought you were angry. Welcome, Apollodorus. (*She gives him her hand to kiss, with her other arm about* CAESAR.)

APOLLODORUS.   Cleopatra grows more womanly beautiful from week to week.

CLEOPATRA.   Truth, Apollodorus?

APOLLODORUS.   Far, far short of the truth! Friend Rufio threw a pearl into the sea: Caesar fished up a diamond.

CAESAR.   Caesar fished up a touch of rheumatism, my friend. Come: to dinner! (*They move towards the table.*)

CLEOPATRA   (*skipping like a young fawn*). Yes, to dinner. I have ordered such a dinner for you, Caesar!

CAESAR.   Ay? What are we to have?

CLEOPATRA.   Peacocks' brains.

CAESAR   (*as if his mouth watered*). Peacocks' brains, Apollodorus!

APOLLODORUS.   Not for me. I prefer nightingales' tongues.

(*He goes to one of the two covers set side by side.*)

CLEOPATRA.   Roast boar, Rufio!

RUFIO   (*gluttonously*). Good! (*He goes to the seat next* APOLLODORUS, *on his left.*)

CAESAR   (*looking at his seat, which is at the end of the table, to Ra's left hand*). What has become of my leathern cushion?

CLEOPATRA   (*at the opposite end*). I have got new ones for you.

THE MAJOR-DOMO.   These cushions, Caesar, are of Maltese gauze, stuffed with rose leaves.

CAESAR.   Rose leaves! Am I a caterpillar? (*He throws the cushions away and seats himself on the leather mattress underneath.*)

CLEOPATRA.   What a shame! My new cushions!

THE MAJOR-DOMO   (*at* CAESAR'*s elbow*). What shall we serve to whet Caesar's appetite?

CAESAR.   What have you got?

THE MAJOR-DOMO.   Sea hedgehogs, black and white sea acorns, sea nettles, beccaficoes, purple shellfish——

CAESAR.   Any oysters?

THE MAJOR-DOMO.   Assuredly.

CAESAR.   British oysters?

THE MAJOR-DOMO   *(assenting)*. British oysters, Caesar.

CAESAR.   Oysters, then. *(The* MAJOR-DOMO *signs to a* SLAVE *at each order; and the* SLAVE *goes out to execute it.)* I have been in Britain—that western land of romance—the last piece of earth on the edge of the ocean that surrounds the world. I went there in search of its famous pearls. The British pearl was a fable; but in searching for it I found the British oyster.

APOLLODORUS.   All posterity will bless you for it. *(To the* MAJOR-DOMO) Sea hedgehogs for me.

RUFIO.   Is there nothing solid to begin with?

THE MAJOR-DOMO.   Fieldfares with asparagus——

CLEOPATRA   *(interrupting)*. Fattened fowls! have some fattened fowls, Rufio.

RUFIO.   Ay, that will do.

CLEOPATRA   *(greedily)*. Fieldfares for me.

THE MAJOR-DOMO.   Caesar will deign to choose his wine? Sicilian, Lesbian, Chian——

RUFIO   *(contemptuously)*. All Greek.

APOLLODORUS.   Who would drink Roman wine when he could get Greek? Try the Lesbian, Caesar.

CAESAR.   Bring me my barley water.

RUFIO   *(with intense disgust)*. Ugh! Bring me my Falernian. *(The Falernian is presently brought to him.)*

CLEOPATRA   *(pouting)*. It is waste of time giving you dinners, Caesar. My scullions would not condescend to your diet.

CAESAR   *(relenting)*. Well, well: let us try the Lesbian. *(The* MAJOR-DOMO *fills* CAESAR's *goblet; then* CLEOPATRA's *and* APOLLODORUS's*)*. But when I return to Rome, I will make laws against these extravagances. I will even get the laws carried out.

CLEOPATRA   *(coaxingly)*. Never mind. To-day you are to be like other people: idle, luxurious, and kind. *(She stretches her hand to him along the table.)*

CAESAR.   Well, for once I will sacrifice my comfort— *(kissing her hand)* there! *(He takes a draught of wine.)* Now are you satisfied?

CLEOPATRA.   And you no longer believe that I long for your departure for Rome?

CAESAR.   I no longer believe anything. My brains are asleep. Besides, who knows whether I shall return to Rome?

RUFIO *(alarmed)*. How? Eh? What?

CAESAR. What has Rome to shew me that I have not seen already? One year of Rome is like another, except that I grow older, whilst the crowd in the Appian Way is always the same age.

APOLLODORUS. It is no better here in Egypt. The old men, when they are tired of life, say "We have seen everything except the source of the Nile."

CAESAR *(his imagination catching fire)*. And why not see that? Cleopatra: will you come with me and track the flood to its cradle in the heart of the regions of mystery? Shall we leave Rome behind us— Rome, that has achieved greatness only to learn how greatness destroys nations of men who are not great! Shall I make you a new kingdom, and build you a holy city there in the great unknown?

CLEOPATRA *(rapturously)*. Yes, yes. You shall.

RUFIO. Ay: now he will conquer Africa with two legions before we come to the roast boar.

APOLLODORUS. Come: no scoffing. This is a noble scheme: in it Caesar is no longer merely the conquering soldier, but the creative poet-artist. Let us name the holy city, and consecrate it with Lesbian wine.

CAESAR. Cleopatra shall name it herself.

CLEOPATRA. It shall be called Caesar's Gift to his Beloved.

APOLLODORUS. No, no. Something vaster than that—something universal, like the starry firmament.

CAESAR *(prosaically)*. Why not simply The Cradle of the Nile?

CLEOPATRA. No: the Nile is my ancestor; and he is a god. Oh! I have thought of something. The Nile shall name it himself. Let us call upon him. *(To the* MAJOR-DOMO*)* Send for him. *(The three* MEN *stare at one another; but the* MAJOR-DOMO *goes out as if he had received the most matter-of-fact order.)* And *(to the* RETINUE*)* away with you all. *(The* RETINUE *withdraws, making obeisance.)*

(A PRIEST *enters, carrying a miniature sphinx with a tiny tripod before it. A morsel of incense is smoking in the tripod. The* PRIEST *comes to the table and places the image in the middle of it. The light begins to change to the magenta purple of the Egyptian sunset, as if the god had brought a strange colored shadow with him. The three* MEN *are determined not to be impressed; but they feel curious in spite of themselves.)*

CAESAR. What hocus-pocus is this?

CLEOPATRA. You shall see. And it is not hocus-pocus. To do it properly, we should kill something to please him; but perhaps he will answer Caesar without that if we spill some wine to him.

APOLLODORUS *(turning his head to look up over his shoulder at Ra)*. Why not appeal to our hawkheaded friend here?

CLEOPATRA *(nervously)*. Sh! He will hear you and be angry.

RUFIO (*phlegmatically*). The source of the Nile is out of his district, I expect.

CLEOPATRA. No: I will have my city named by nobody but my dear little sphinx, because it was in its arms that Caesar found me asleep. (*She languishes at* CAESAR; *then turns curtly to the* PRIEST) Go. I am a priestess, and have power to take your charge from you. (*The* PRIEST *makes a reverence and goes out.*) Now let us call on the Nile all together. Perhaps he will rap on the table.

CAESAR. What! table rapping! Are such superstitions still believed in this year 707 of the Republic?

CLEOPATRA. It is no superstition: our priests learn lots of things from the tables. Is it not so, Apollodorus?

APOLLODORUS. Yes: I profess myself a converted man. When Cleopatra is priestess, Apollodorus is devotee. Propose the conjuration.

CLEOPATRA. You must say with me "Send us thy voice, Father Nile."

ALL FOUR (*holding their glasses together before the idol*). Send us thy voice, Father Nile.

(*The death cry of a man in mortal terror and agony answers them. Appalled, the* MEN *set down their glasses, and listen. Silence. The purple deepens in the sky.* CAESAR, *glancing at* CLEOPATRA, *catches her pouring out her wine before the god, with gleaming eyes, and mute assurances of gratitude and worship.* APOLLODORUS *springs up and runs to the edge of the roof to peer down and listen.*)

CAESAR (*looking piercingly at* CLEOPATRA). What was that?

CLEOPATRA (*petulantly*). Nothing. They are beating some slave.

CAESAR. Nothing?

RUFIO. A man with a knife in him, I'll swear.

CAESAR (*rising*). A murder!

APOLLODORUS (*at the back, waving his hand for silence*). S-sh! Silence. Did you hear that?

CAESAR. Another cry?

APOLLODORUS (*returning to the table*). No, a thud. Something fell on the beach, I think.

RUFIO (*grimly, as he rises*). Something with bones in it, eh?

CAESAR (*shuddering*). Hush, hush, Rufio. (*He leaves the table and returns to the colonnade:* RUFIO *following at his left elbow, and* APOLLODORUS *at the other side.*)

CLEOPATRA (*still in her place at the table*). Will you leave me, Caesar? Apollodorus: are you going?

APOLLODORUS. Faith, dearest Queen, my appetite is gone.

CAESAR. Go down to the courtyard, Apollodorus; and find out what has happened.

(APOLLODORUS *nods and goes out, making for the staircase by which* RUFIO *ascended.*)

CLEOPATRA. Your soldiers have killed somebody, perhaps. What does it matter?

The murmur of a crowd rises from the beach below. CAESAR *and* RUFIO *look at one another.*

CAESAR. This must be seen to. (*He is about to follow* APOLLODORUS *when* RUFIO *stops him with a hand on his arm as* FTATATEETA *comes back by the far end of the roof, with dragging steps, a drowsy satiety in her eyes and in the corners of the bloodhound lips. For a moment* CAESAR *suspects that she is drunk with wine. Not so* RUFIO: *he knows well the red vintage that has inebriated her.*)

RUFIO (*in a low tone*). There is some mischief between those two.

FTATATEETA. The Queen looks again on the face of her servant.

(CLEOPATRA *looks at her for a moment with an exultant reflection of her murderous expression. Then she flings her arm round her; kisses her repeatedly and savagely; and tears off her jewels and heaps them on her. The two* MEN *turn from the spectacle to look at one another.* FTATATEETA *drags herself sleepily to the altar; kneels before Ra; and remains there in prayer.* CAESAR *goes to* CLEOPATRA, *leaving* RUFIO *in the colonnade.*)

CAESAR (*with searching earnestness*). Cleopatra: what has happened?

CLEOPATRA (*in mortal dread of him, but with her utmost cajolery*). Nothing, dearest Caesar. (*With sickly sweetness, her voice almost failing*) Nothing. I am innocent. (*She approaches him affectionately.*) Dear Caesar: are you angry with me? Why do you look at me so? I have been here with you all the time. How can I know what has happened?

CAESAR (*reflectively*). That is true.

CLEOPATRA (*greatly relieved, trying to caress him*). Of course it is true. (*He does not respond to the caress.*) You know it is true, Rufio.

(*The murmur without suddenly swells to a roar and subsides.*)

RUFIO. I shall know presently.' (*He makes for the altar in the burly trot that serves him for a stride, and touches* FTATATEETA *on the shoulder.*) Now, mistress: I shall want you. (*He orders her, with a gesture, to go before him.*)

FTATATEETA (*rising and glowering at him*). My place is with the Queen.

CLEOPATRA. She has done no harm, Rufio.

CAESAR (*to* RUFIO). Let her stay.

RUFIO (*sitting down on the altar*). Very well. Then my place is here too; and you can see what is the matter for yourself. The city is in a pretty uproar, it seems.

CAESAR (*with grave displeasure*). Rufio: there is a time for obedience.

RUFIO. And there is a time for obstinacy. (*He folds his arms doggedly.*)

CAESAR   (*to* CLEOPATRA) . Send her away.

CLEOPATRA   (*whining in her eagerness to propitiate him*) . Yes, I will. I will do whatever you ask me, Caesar, always, because I love you. Ftatateeta: go away.

FTATATEETA.   The Queen's word is my will. I shall be at hand for the Queen's call. (*She goes out past Ra, as she came.*)

RUFIO   (*following her*) . Remember, Caesar, your bodyguard also is within call. (*He follows her out.*)

(CLEOPATRA, *presuming upon* CAESAR's *submission to* RUFIO, *leaves the table and sits down on the bench in the colonnade.*)

CLEOPATRA.   Why do you allow Rufio to treat you so? You should teach him his place.

CAESAR.   Teach him to be my enemy, and to hide his thoughts from me as you are now hiding yours.

CLEOPATRA   (*her fears returning*) . Why do you say that, Caesar? Indeed, indeed, I am not hiding anything. You are wrong to treat me like this. (*She stifles a sob.*) I am only a child; and you turn into stone because you think some one has been killed. I cannot bear it. (*She purposely breaks down and weeps. He looks at her with profound sadness and complete coldness. She looks up to see what effect she is producing. Seeing that he is unmoved, she sits up, pretending to struggle with her emotion and to put it bravely away.*) But there: I know you hate tears: you shall not be troubled with them. I know you are not angry, but only sad; only I am so silly, I cannot help being hurt when you speak coldly. Of course you are quite right: it is dreadful to think of anyone being killed or even hurt; and I hope nothing really serious has— (*Her voice dies away under his contemptuous penetration.*)

CAESAR.   What has frightened you into this? What have you done? (*A trumpet sounds on the beach below.*) Aha! that sounds like the answer.

CLEOPATRA   (*sinking back trembling on the bench and covering her face with her hands*) . I have not betrayed you, Caesar: I swear it.

CAESAR.   I know that. I have not trusted you. (*He turns from her, and is about to go out when* APOLLODORUS *and* BRITANNUS *drag in* LUCIUS SEPTIMIUS *to him.* RUFIO *follows.* CAESAR *shudders.*) Again, Pompey's murderer!

RUFIO.   The town has gone mad, I think. They are for tearing the palace down and driving us into the sea straight away. We laid hold of this renegade in clearing them out of the courtyard.

CAESAR.   Release him. (*They let go his arms.*) What has offended the citizens, Lucius Septimius?

LUCIUS.   What did you expect, Caesar? Pothinus was a favorite of theirs.

CAESAR.   What has happened to Pothinus? I set him free, here, not half an hour ago. Did they not pass him out?

LUCIUS. Ay, through the gallery arch sixty feet above ground, with three inches of steel in his ribs. He is as dead as Pompey. We are quits now, as to killing—you and I.

CAESAR (*shocked*). Assassinated!—our prisoner, our guest! (*He turns reproachfully on* RUFIO) Rufio——

RUFIO (*emphatically—anticipating the question*). Whoever did it was a wise man and a friend of yours (CLEOPATRA *is greatly emboldened*); but none of us had a hand in it. So it is no use to frown at me. (CAESAR *turns and looks at* CLEOPATRA.)

CLEOPATRA (*violently—rising*). He was slain by order of the Queen of Egypt. I am not Julius Caesar the dreamer, who allows every slave to insult him. Rufio has said I did well: now the others shall judge me too. (*She turns to the others*) This Pothinus sought to make me conspire with him to betray Caesar to Achillas and Ptolemy. I refused; and he cursed me and came privily to Caesar to accuse me of his own treachery. I caught him in the act; and he insulted me—me, the Queen! to my face. Caesar would not avenge me: he spoke him fair and set him free. Was I right to avenge myself? Speak, Lucius.

LUCIUS. I do not gainsay it. But you will get little thanks from Caesar for it.

CLEOPATRA. Speak, Apollodorus. Was I wrong?

APOLLODORUS. I have only one word of blame, most beautiful. You should have called upon me, your knight; and in fair duel I should have slain the slanderer.

CLEOPATRA (*passionately*). I will be judged by your very slave, Caesar. Britannus: speak. Was I wrong?

BRITANNUS. Were treachery, falsehood, and disloyalty left unpunished, society must become like an arena full of wild beasts, tearing one another to pieces. Caesar is in the wrong.

CAESAR (*with quiet bitterness*). And so the verdict is against me, it seems.

CLEOPATRA (*vehemently*). Listen to me, Caesar. If one man in all Alexandria can be found to say that I did wrong, I swear to have myself crucified on the door of the palace by my own slaves.

CAESAR. If one man in all the world can be found, now or forever, to know that you did wrong, that man will have either to conquer the world as I have, or be crucified by it. (*The uproar in the streets again reaches them.*) Do you hear? These knockers at your gate are also believers in vengeance and in stabbing. You have slain their leader: it is right that they shall slay you. If you doubt it, ask your four counsellors here. And then in the name of that right (*he emphasizes the word with great scorn*) shall I not slay them for murdering their Queen, and be slain in my turn by their countrymen as the invader of their fatherland? Can Rome do less then than slay these slayers too, to shew the world how Rome avenges her sons and her honor? And so, to the end of history, murder shall breed murder, always in the name of right and honor and peace, until the gods are tired of blood and create a race that can understand. (*Fierce uproar.* CLEOPATRA *becomes white with terror.*) Hearken, you who must not be insulted. Go near enough to catch their words: you will find them bitterer than the tongue of Pothinus. (*Loftily wrapping himself up in an impenetrable dignity.*) Let the Queen of Egypt now give her orders for vengeance, and take her measures for defence; for she has renounced Caesar. (*He turns to go.*)

CLEOPATRA (*terrified, running to him and falling on her knees*). You will not desert me, Caesar. You will defend the palace.

CAESAR. You have taken the powers of life and death upon you. I am only a dreamer.

CLEOPATRA. But they will kill me.

CAESAR. And why not?

CLEOPATRA. In pity——

CAESAR. Pity! What! has it come to this so suddenly, that nothing can save you now but pity? Did it save Pothinus?

(*She rises, wringing her hands, and goes back to the bench in despair.* APOLLODORUS *shews his sympathy with her by quietly posting himself behind the bench. The sky has by this time become the most vivid purple, and soon begins to change to a glowing pale orange, against which the colonnade and the great image show darklier and darklier.*)

RUFIO. Caesar: enough of preaching. The enemy is at the gate.

CAESAR (*turning on him and giving way to his wrath*). Ay; and what has held him baffled at the gate all these months? Was it my folly, as you deem it, or your wisdom? In this Egyptian Red Sea of blood, whose hand has held all your heads above the waves? (*Turning on* CLEOPATRA) And yet, when Caesar says to such an one, "Friend, go free," you, clinging for your little life to my sword, dare to steal out and stab him in the back? And you, soldiers and gentlemen, and honest servants as you forget that you are, applaud this assassination, and say "Caesar is in the wrong." By the gods, I am tempted to open my hand and let you all sink into the flood.

CLEOPATRA (*with a ray of cunning hope*). But, Caesar, if you do, you will perish yourself.

(CAESAR's *eyes blaze.*)

RUFIO (*greatly alarmed*). Now, by great Jove, you filthy little Egyptian rat, that is the very word to make him walk out alone into the city and leave us here to be cut to pieces. (*Desperately, to* CAESAR) Will you desert us because we are a parcel of fools? I mean no harm by killing: I do it as a dog kills a cat, by instinct. We are all dogs at your heels; but we have served you faithfully.

CAESAR   (relenting). Alas, Rufio, my son, my son: as dogs we are like to perish now in the streets.

APOLLODORUS   (at his post behind CLEOPATRA's seat). Caesar, what you say has an Olympian ring in it: it must be right; for it is fine art. But I am still on the side of Cleopatra. If we must die, she shall not want the devotion of a man's heart nor the strength of a man's arm.

CLEOPATRA   (sobbing). But I don't want to die.

CAESAR   (sadly). Oh, ignoble, ignoble!

LUCIUS   (coming forward between CAESAR and CLEOPATRA). Harken to me, Caesar. It may be ignoble; but I also mean to live as long as I can.

CAESAR.   Well, my friend, you are likely to outlive Caesar. Is it any magic of mine, think you, that has kept your army and this whole city at bay for so long? Yesterday, what quarrel had they with me that they should risk their lives against me? But to-day we have flung them down their hero, murdered; and now every man of them is set upon clearing out this nest of assassins—for such we are and no more. Take courage then; and sharpen your sword. Pompey's head has fallen; and Caesar's head is ripe.

APOLLODORUS.   Does Caesar despair?

CAESAR   (with infinite pride). He who has never hoped can never despair. Caesar, in good or bad fortune, looks his fate in the face.

LUCIUS.   Look it in the face, then; and it will smile as it always has on Caesar.

CAESAR   (with involuntary haughtiness). Do you presume to encourage me?

LUCIUS.   I offer you my services. I will change sides if you will have me.

CAESAR   (suddenly coming down to earth again, and looking sharply at him, divining that there is something behind the offer). What! At this point?

LUCIUS   (firmly). At this point.

RUFIO.   Do you suppose Caesar is mad, to trust you?

LUCIUS.   I do not ask him to trust me until he is victorious. I ask for my life, and for a command in Caesar's army. And since Caesar is a fair dealer, I will pay in advance.

CAESAR.   Pay! How?

LUCIUS.   With a piece of good news for you.

(CAESAR divines the news in a flash.)

RUFIO.   What news?

CAESAR   (with an elate and buoyant energy which makes CLEOPATRA sit *up and stare)* . What news! What news, did you say, my son Rufio? The relief has arrived: what other news remains for us? Is it not so, Lucius Septimius? Mithridates of Pergamos is on the march.

LUCIUS.   He has taken Pelusium.

CAESAR   *(delighted)* . Lucius Septimius: you are henceforth my officer. Rufio: the Egyptians must have sent every soldier from the city to prevent Mithridates crossing the Nile. There is nothing in the streets now but mob—mob!

LUCIUS.   It is so. Mithridates is marching by the great road to Memphis to cross above the Delta. Achillas will fight him there.

CAESAR   *(all audacity)* . Achillas shall fight Caesar there. See, Rufio. *(He runs to the table; snatches a napkin; and draws a plan on it with his finger dipped in wine, whilst* RUFIO *and* LUCIUS SEPTIMIUS *crowd about him to watch, all looking closely, for the light is now almost gone.)* Here is the palace *(pointing to his plan)* : here is the theatre. You *(to* RUFIO) take twenty men and pretend to go by that street *(pointing it out)* ; and whilst they are stoning you, out go the cohorts by this and this. My streets are right, are they, Lucius?

LUCIUS.   Ay, that is the fig market——

CAESAR   *(too much excited to listen to him)* . I saw them the day we arrived. Good! *(He throws the napkin on the table and comes down again into the colonnade.)* Away, Britannus: tell Petronius that within an hour half our forces must take ship for the western lake. See to my horse and armor. *(*BRITANNUS *runs out.)* With the rest, *I* shall march round the lake and up the Nile to meet Mithridates. Away, Lucius; and give the word.

*(*LUCIUS *hurries out after* BRITANNUS.)*

RUFIO.   Come: this is something like business.

CAESAR   *(buoyantly)* . Is it not, my only son? *(He claps his hands. The* SLAVES *hurry in to the table.)* No more of this mawkish revelling: away with all this stuff: shut it out of my sight and be off with you. *(The* SLAVES *begin to remove the table; and the curtains are drawn, shutting in the colonnade.)* You understand about the streets, Rufio?

RUFIO.   Ay, I think I do. I will get through them, at all events.

(The bucina sounds busily in the courtyard beneath.)

CAESAR.   Come, then: we must talk to the troops and hearten them. You down to the beach: I to the courtyard. *(He makes for the staircase.)*

CLEOPATRA   *(rising from her seat, where she has been quite neglected all this time, and stretching out her hands timidly to him)* . Caesar.

CAESAR   *(turning)* . Eh?

CLEOPATRA.   Have you forgotten me?

CAESAR   *(indulgently)* . I am busy now, my child, busy. When I return your affairs shall be settled. Farewell; and be good and patient. (*He goes, preoccupied and quite indifferent. She stands with clenched fists, in speechless rage and humiliation.*)

RUFIO. That game is played and lost, Cleopatra. The woman always gets the worst of it.

CLEOPATRA   (*haughtily*). Go. Follow your master.

RUFIO   (*in her ear, with rough familiarity*). A word first. Tell your executioner that if Pothinus had been properly killed—in the throat—he would not have called out. Your man bungled his work.

CLEOPATRA   (*enigmatically*). How do you know it was a man?

RUFIO   (*startled, and puzzled*). It was not you: you were with us when it happened. (*She turns her back scornfully on him. He shakes his head, and draws the curtains to go out. It is now a magnificent moonlit night. The table has been removed.* FTATATEETA *is seen in the light of the moon and stars, again in prayer before the white altar-stone of Ra.* RUFIO *starts; closes the curtains again softly; and says in a low voice to* CLEOPATRA) Was it she? with her own hand?

CLEOPATRA   (*threateningly*). Whoever it was, let my enemies beware of her. Look to it, Rufio, you who dare make the Queen of Egypt a fool before Caesar.

RUFIO   (*looking grimly at her*). I will look to it, Cleopatra. (*He nods in confirmation of the promise, and slips out through the curtains, loosening his sword in its sheath as he goes.*)

ROMAN SOLDIERS   (*in the courtyard below*). Hail, Caesar! Hail, hail!

(CLEOPATRA *listens. The bucina sounds again, followed by several trumpets.*)

CLEOPATRA   (*wringing her hands and calling*). Ftatateeta. Ftatateeta. It is dark; and I am alone. Come to me. (*Silence.*) Ftatateeta. (*Louder.*) Ftatateeta. (*Silence. In a panic she snatches the cord and pulls the curtains apart.*)

(FTATATEETA *is lying dead on the altar of Ra, with her throat cut. Her blood deluges the white stone.*)

ACT V

High noon. Festival and military pageant on the esplanade before the palace. In the east harbor Caesar's galley, so gorgeously decorated that it seems to be rigged with flowers, is alongside the quay, close to the steps Apollodorus descended when he embarked with the carpet. A Roman guard is posted there in charge of a gangway, whence a red floorcloth is laid down the middle of the esplanade, turning off to the north opposite the central gate in the palace front, which shuts in the esplanade on the south side. *The broad steps of the gate, crowded with Cleopatra's ladies, all in their gayest attire, are like a flower garden. The façade is lined by her guard, officered by the same gallants to whom Bel Affris announced the coming of Caesar six months before in the old palace on the Syrian border. The north side is lined by Roman soldiers, with the townsfolk on tiptoe behind them, peering over their heads at the cleared esplanade, in which the officers stroll about, chatting. Among these are Belzanor and the Persian; also the Centurion, vinewood cudgel in hand, battle worn, thick-booted, and much outshone, both socially and decoratively, by the Egyptian officers.*

Apollodorus makes his way through the townsfolk and calls to the officers from behind the Roman line.

APOLLODORUS. Hullo! May I pass?

CENTURION. Pass Apollodorus the Sicilian there! (*The* SOLDIERS *let him through.*)

BELZANOR. Is Caesar at hand?

APOLLODORUS. Not yet. He is still in the market place. I could not stand any more of the roaring of the soldiers! After half an hour of the enthusiasm of an army, one feels the need of a little sea air.

PERSIAN. Tell us the news. Hath he slain the priests?

APOLLODORUS. Not he. They met him in the market place with ashes on their heads and their gods in their hands. They placed the gods at his feet. The only one that was worth looking at was Apis: a miracle of gold and ivory work. By my advice he offered the chief priest two talents for it.

BELZANOR (*appalled*) . Apis the all-knowing for two talents! What said the chief priest?

APOLLODORUS. He invoked the mercy of Apis, and asked for five.

BELZANOR. There will be famine and tempest in the land for this.

PERSIAN. Pooh! Why did not Apis cause Caesar to be vanquished by Achillas? Any fresh news from the war, Apollodorus?

APOLLODORUS. The little King Ptolemy was drowned.

BELZANOR. Drowned! How?

APOLLODORUS. With the rest of them. Caesar attacked them from three sides at once and swept them into the Nile. Ptolemy's barge sank.

BELZANOR. A marvelous man, this Caesar! Will he come soon, think you?

APOLLODORUS. He was settling the Jewish question when I left.

(*A flourish of trumpets from the north, and commotion among the townsfolk, announces the approach of* CAESAR.)

PERSIAN. He has made short work of them. Here he comes. (*He hurries to his post in front of the Egyptian lines.*)

BELZANOR (*following him*) . Ho there! Caesar comes.

(*The* SOLDIERS *stand at attention, and dress their lines.* APOLLODORUS *goes to the Egyptian line.*)

CENTURION (*hurrying to the* GANGWAY GUARD). Attention there! Caesar comes.

(CAESAR *arrives in state with* RUFIO: BRITANNUS *following. The* SOLDIERS *receive him with enthusiastic shouting.*)

CAESAR. I see my ship awaits me. The hour of Caesar's farewell to Egypt has arrived. And now, Rufio, what remains to be done before I go?

RUFIO (*at his left hand*). You have not yet appointed a Roman governor for this province.

CAESAR (*looking whimsically at him, but speaking with perfect gravity*). What say you to Mithridates of Pergamos, my reliever and rescuer, the great son of Eupator?

RUFIO. Why, that you will want him elsewhere. Do you forget that you have some three or four armies to conquer on your way home?

CAESAR. Indeed! Well, what say you to yourself?

RUFIO (*incredulously*). I! I a governor! What are you dreaming of? Do you not know that I am only the son of a freedman?

CAESAR (*affectionately*). Has not Caesar called you his son? (*Calling to the whole assembly*) Peace awhile there; and hear me.

THE ROMAN SOLDIERS. Hear Caesar.

CAESAR. Hear the service, quality, rank and name of the Roman governor. By service, Caesar's shield; by quality, Caesar's friend; by rank, a Roman soldier. (*The* ROMAN SOLDIERS *give a triumphant shout.*) By name, Rufio. (*They shout again.*)

RUFIO (*kissing* CAESAR's *hand*). Ay: I am Caesar's shield; but of what use shall I be when I am no longer on Caesar's arm? Well, no matter— (*He becomes husky, and turns away to recover himself.*)

CAESAR. Where is that British Islander of mine?

BRITANNUS (*coming forward on* CAESAR's *right hand*). Here, Caesar.

CAESAR. Who bade you, pray, thrust yourself into the battle of the Delta, uttering the barbarous cries of your native land, and affirming yourself a match for any four of the Egyptians, to whom you applied unseemly epithets?

BRITANNUS. Caesar: I ask you to excuse the language that escaped me in the heat of the moment.

CAESAR. And how did you, who cannot swim, cross the canal with us when we stormed the camp?

BRITANNUS. Caesar: I clung to the tail of your horse.

CAESAR. These are not the deeds of a slave, Britannicus, but of a free man.

BRITANNUS. Caesar: I was born free.

CAESAR. But they call you Caesar's slave.

BRITANNUS. Only as Caesar's slave have I found real freedom.

CAESAR (*moved*). Well said. Ungrateful that I am, I was about to set you free; but now I will not part from you for a million talents. (*He claps him friendly on the shoulder.* BRITANNUS, *gratified, but a trifle shamefaced, takes his hand and kisses it sheepishly.*)

BELZANOR (*to the* PERSIAN). This Roman knows how to make men serve him.

PERSIAN. Ay: men too humble to become dangerous rivals to him.

BELZANOR. O subtle one! O cynic!

CAESAR (*seeing* APOLLODORUS *in the Egyptian corner and calling to him*). Apollodorus: I leave the art of Egypt in your charge. Remember: Rome loves art and will encourage it ungrudgingly.

APOLLODORUS. I understand, Caesar. Rome will produce no art itself; but it will buy up and take away whatever the other nations produce.

CAESAR. What! Rome produce no art! Is peace not an art? is war not an art? is government not an art? is civilization not an art? All these we give you in exchange for a few ornaments. You will have the best of the bargain. (*Turning to* RUFIO) And now, what else have I to do before I embark? (*Trying to recollect*) There is something I cannot remember: what can it be? Well, well: it must remain undone: we must not waste this favorable wind. Farewell, Rufio.

RUFIO. Caesar: I am loth to let you go to Rome without your shield. There are too many daggers there.

CAESAR. It matters not: I shall finish my life's work on my way back; and then I shall have lived long enough. Besides: I have always disliked the idea of dying: I had rather be killed. Farewell.

RUFIO (*with a sigh, raising his hands and giving* CAESAR *up as incorrigible*). Farewell. (*They shake hands.*)

CAESAR (*waving his hand to* APOLLODORUS). Farewell, Apollodorus, and my friends, all of you. Aboard!

(*The gangway is run out from the quay to the ship. As* CAESAR *moves towards it,* CLEOPATRA, *cold and tragic, cunningly dressed in black, without ornaments or decoration of any kind, and thus making a striking figure among the brilliantly dressed bevy of ladies as she passes through it, comes from the palace and stands on the steps.* CAESAR *does not see her until she speaks.*)

CLEOPATRA. Has Cleopatra no part in this leave taking?

CAESAR (*enlightened*). Ah, I knew there was something. (*To* RUFIO) How could you let me forget her, Rufio? (*Hastening to her*) Had I gone without seeing you, I should never have forgiven myself. (*He takes her hands, and brings her into the middle of the esplanade. She submits stonily.*) Is this mourning for me?

CLEOPATRA. No.

CAESAR (*remorsefully*). Ah, that was thoughtless of me! It is for your brother.

CLEOPATRA. No.

CAESAR. For whom, then?

CLEOPATRA. Ask the Roman governor whom you have left us.

CAESAR. Rufio?

CLEOPATRA. Yes: Rufio. (*She points at him with deadly scorn.*) He who is to rule here in Caesar's name, in Caesar's way, according to Caesar's boasted laws of life.

CAESAR (*dubiously*). He is to rule as he can, Cleopatra. He has taken the work upon him, and will do it in his own way.

CLEOPATRA. Not in your way, then?

CAESAR (*puzzled*). What do you mean by my way?

CLEOPATRA. Without punishment. Without revenge. Without judgment.

CAESAR (*approvingly*). Ay: that is the right way, the great way, the only possible way in the end. (*To* RUFIO) Believe it, Rufio, if you can.

RUFIO. Why, I believe it, Caesar. You have convinced me of it long ago. But look you. You are sailing for Numidia to-day. Now tell me: if you meet a hungry lion there, you will not punish it for wanting to eat you?

CAESAR (*wondering what he is driving at*). No.

RUFIO. Nor revenge upon it the blood of those it has already eaten.

CAESAR. No.

RUFIO. Nor judge it for its guiltiness.

CAESAR. No.

RUFIO. What, then, will you do to save your life from it?

CAESAR (*promptly*). Kill it, man, without malice, just as it would kill me. What does this parable of the lion mean?

RUFIO. Why, Cleopatra had a tigress that killed men at her bidding. I thought she might bid it kill you some day. Well, had I not been Caesar's pupil, what pious things might I not have done to that tigress? I might have punished it. I might have revenged Pothinus on it.

CAESAR (*interjects*). Pothinus!

RUFIO (*continuing*). I might have judged it. But I put all these follies behind me; and, without malice, only cut its throat. And that is why Cleopatra comes to you in mourning.

CLEOPATRA (*vehemently*). He has shed the blood of my servant Ftatateeta. On your head be it as upon his, Caesar, if you hold him free of it.

CAESAR (*energetically*). On my head be it, then; for it was well done. Rufio: had you set yourself in the seat of the judge, and with hateful ceremonies and appeals to the gods handed that woman over to some hired executioner to be slain before the people in the name of justice, never again would I have touched your hand without a shudder. But this was natural slaying: I feel no horror at it.

(RUFIO, *satisfied, nods at* CLEOPATRA, *mutely inviting her to mark that.*)

CLEOPATRA   *(pettish and childish in her impotence)*. No: not when a Roman slays an Egyptian. All the world will now see how unjust and corrupt Caesar is.

CAESAR   *(taking her hands coaxingly)*. Come: do not be angry with me. I am sorry for that poor Totateeta. *(She laughs in spite of herself.)* Aha! you are laughing. Does that mean reconciliation?

CLEOPATRA   *(angry with herself for laughing)*. No, no, NO!! But it is so ridiculous to hear you call her Totateeta.

CAESAR.   What! As much a child as ever, Cleopatra! Have I not made a woman of you after all?

CLEOPATRA.   Oh, it is you who are a great baby: you make me seem silly because you will not behave seriously. But you have treated me badly; and I do not forgive you.

CAESAR.   Bid me farewell.

CLEOPATRA.   I will not.

CAESAR   *(coaxing)*. I will send you a beautiful present from Rome.

CLEOPATRA   *(proudly)*. Beauty from Rome to Egypt indeed! What can Rome give me that Egypt cannot give me?

APOLLODORUS.   That is true, Caesar. If the present is to be really beautiful, I shall have to buy it for you in Alexandria.

CAESAR.   You are forgetting the treasures for which Rome is most famous, my friend. You cannot buy them in Alexandria.

APOLLODORUS.   What are they, Caesar?

CAESAR.   Her sons. Come, Cleopatra: forgive me and bid me farewell; and I will send you a man, Roman from head to heel and Roman of the noblest; not old and ripe for the knife; not lean in the arms and cold in the heart; not hiding a bald head under his conqueror's laurels; not stooped with the weight of the world on his shoulders; but brisk and fresh, strong and young, hoping in the morning, fighting in the day, and revelling in the evening. Will you take such an one in exchange for Caesar?

CLEOPATRA   *(palpitating)*. His name, his name?

CAESAR.   Shall it be Mark Antony? *(She throws herself into his arms.)*

RUFIO.   You are a bad hand at a bargain, mistress, if you will swap Caesar for Antony.

CAESAR.   So now you are satisfied.

CLEOPATRA.   You will not forget.

CAESAR. I will not forget. Farewell: I do not think we shall meet again. Farewell. *(He kisses her on the forehead. She is much affected and begins to sniff. He embarks.)*

THE ROMAN SOLDIERS   (*as he sets his foot on the gangway*) . Hail, Caesar;
and farewell!
(*He reaches the ship and returns* RUFIO's *wave of the hand.*)
APOLLODORUS   (*to* CLEOPATRA) . No tears, dearest Queen: they stab your
servant to the heart. He will return some day.
CLEOPATRA.   I hope not. But I can't help crying, all the same. (*She waves
her handkerchief to* CAESAR; *and the ship begins to move.*)
THE ROMAN SOLDIERS   (*drawing their swords and raising them in the
air*) . Hail, Caesar!

BETTER THAN SHAKESPEAR

BERNARD SHAW

. . . The very name of Cleopatra suggests at once a tragedy of Circe,
with the horrible difference that whereas the ancient myth rightly represents Circe as turning heroes into hogs, the modern romantic convention
would represent her as turning hogs into heroes. Shakespear's Antony
and Cleopatra . . . is vaguely distressing to the ordinary healthy citizen, because, after giving a faithful picture of the soldier broken down
by debauchery, and the typical wanton in whose arms such men perish,
Shakespear finally strains all his huge command of rhetoric and stage
pathos to give a theatrical sublimity to the wretched end of the business,
and to persuade foolish spectators that the world was well lost by the
twain. Such falsehood is not to be borne except by the real Cleopatras
and Antonys (they are to be found in every public house *) who would
no doubt be glad enough to be transfigured by some poet as immortal
lovers. Woe to the poet who stoops to such folly! The lot of the man
who sees life truly and thinks about it romantically is Despair. How well
we know the cries of that despair! Vanity of vanities, all is vanity!
moans the Preacher, when life has at last taught him that Nature will
not dance to his moralist-made tunes. Thackeray, scores of centuries
later, is still baying the moon in the same terms. Out, out, brief candle!
cries Shakespear, in his tragedy of modern literary man as murderer
and witch consulter. Surely the time is past for patience with writers
who, having to choose between giving up life in despair and discarding
the trumpery moral kitchen scales in which they try to weigh the universe, superstitiously stick to the scales, and spend the rest of the lives
they pretend to despise in breaking men's spirits. But even in pessimism
there is a choice between intellectual honesty and dishonesty. Hogarth

* neighborhood bar

drew the rake and the harlot without glorifying their end. Swift, accepting our system of morals and religion, delivering the inevitable verdict of that system on us through the mouth of the king of Brobdingnag, and described man as the Yahoo, shocking his superior the horse by his every action. Strindberg, the only living genuine Shakespearean dramatist, shows that the female Yahoo, measured by romantic standards, is viler than her male dupe and slave. I respect these resolute tragi-comedians: they are logical and faithful: they force you to face the fact that you must either accept their conclusions as valid (in which case it is cowardly to continue living) or admit that your way of judging conduct is absurd. But when your Shakespears and Thackerays huddle up the matter at the end by killing somebody and covering your eyes with the undertaker's handkerchief, duly onioned with some pathetic phrase, as The flight of angels sing thee to thy rest, or Adsum, or the like, I have no respect for them at all: such maudlin tricks may impose on tea-drunkards, not on me.

Besides, I have a technical objection to making sexual infatuation a tragic theme. Experience proves that it is only effective in the comic spirit. We can bear to see Mrs. Quickly pawing her plate for love of Falstaff, but not Antony running away from the battle of Actium for love of Cleopatra. Let realism have its demonstration, comedy its criticism, or even bawdry its horselaugh at the expense of sexual infatuation, if it must; but to ask us to subject our souls to its ruinous glamor, to worship it, deify it, and imply that it alone makes our life worth living, is nothing but folly gone mad erotically—a thing compared to which Falstaff's unbeglamored drinking and drabbing is respectable and right-minded. Whoever, then, expects to find Cleopatra a Circe and Cæsar a hog in these pages, had better lay down my book and be spared a disappointment.

In Cæsar, I have used another character with which Shakespear has been beforehand. But Shakespear, who knew human weakness so well, never knew human strength of the Cæsarian type. His Cæsar is an admitted failure; his Lear is a masterpiece. The tragedy of disillusion and doubt, of the agonized stuggle for a foothold on the quicksand made by an acute observation striving to verify its vain attribution of morality and respectability to Nature, of the faithless will and the keen eyes that the faithless will is too weak to blind; all this will give you a Hamlet or a Macbeth, and win you great applause from literary gentlemen; but it will not give you a Julius Cæsar. Cæsar was not in Shakespear, nor in the epoch, now fast waning, which he inaugurated. It cost Shakespear no pang to write Cæsar down for the merely technical purpose of writing Brutus up. And what a Brutus! A great Girondin, mirrored in Shakespear's art two hundred years before the real thing came to maturity and talked and stalked and had its head duly cut off by the coarser Antonys and Octaviuses of its time, who at least knew the difference between life and rhetoric.

It will be said that these remarks can bear no other construction than an offer of my Cæsar to the public as an improvement on Shakespear's. And in fact, that is their precise purport. But here let me give a friendly warning to those scribes who have so often exclaimed against my criticisms of Shakespear as blasphemies against a hitherto unquestioned Perfection and Infallibility. Such criticisms are no more new than the creed of my Diabolonian Puritan or my revival of the humors of Cool as a Cucumber. Too much surprise at them betrays an acquaintance with Shakespear criticism so limited as not to include even the prefaces of Dr. Johnson and the utterances of Napoleon. I have merely repeated in the dialect of my own time and in the light of its philosophy what they said in the dialect and light of theirs. Do not be misled by the Shakespear fanciers who, ever since his own time, have delighted in his plays just as they might have delighted in a particular breed of pigeons if they had never learnt to read. His genuine critics, from Ben Jonson to Mr. Frank Harris, have always kept as far on this side idolatry as I. . . .

It does not follow, however, that the right to criticize Shakespear involves the power of writing better plays. And in fact—do not be surprised at my modesty—I do not profess to write better plays. The writing of practicable stage plays does not present an infinite scope to human talent; and the dramatists who magnify its difficulties are humbugs. The summit of their art has been attained again and again. No man will ever write a better tragedy than Lear, a better comedy than Le Festin de Pierre or Peer Gynt, a better opera than Don Giovanni, a better music drama than The Nibelung's Ring, or, for the matter of that, better fashionable plays and melodramas than are now being turned out by writers whom nobody dreams of mocking with the word immortal. It is the philosophy, the outlook on life, that changes, not the craft of the playwright. . . . What is the use of writing plays or painting frescoes if you have nothing more to say or shew than was said and shewn by Shakespear, Michael Angelo, and Raphael? If these had not seen things differently, for better or worse, from the dramatic poets of the Townley mysteries, or from Giotto, they could not have produced their works: no, not though their skill of pen and hand had been double what it was. After them there was no need (and *need* alone nerves men to face the persecution in the teeth of which new art is brought to birth) to redo the already done, until in due time, when their philosophy wore itself out, a new race of nineteenth century poets and critics, from Byron to William Morris, began, first to speak coldly of Shakespear and Raphael, and then to rediscover, in the medieval art which these Renascence mas-

ters had superseded, certain forgotten elements which were germinating
again for the new harvest. What is more, they began to discover that the
technical skill of the masters was by no means superlative. Indeed, I
defy anyone to prove that the great epoch makers in fine art have
owed their position to their technical skill. It is true that when we
search for examples of a prodigious command of language and of
graphic line, we can think of nobody better than Shakespear and Michael Angelo. But both of them laid their arts waste for centuries by
leading later artists to seek greatness in copying their technique. The
technique was acquired, refined on, and surpassed over and over again;
but the supremacy of the two great exemplars remained undisputed. As
a matter of easily observable fact, every generation produces men of extraordinary special faculty, artistic, mathematical, and linguistic, who
for lack of new ideas, or indeed of any ideas worth mentioning, achieve
no distinction outside music halls and class rooms, although they can do
things easily that the great epoch makers did clumsily or not at all. The
contempt of the academic pedant for the original artist is often founded
on a genuine superiority of technical knowledge and aptitude; he is
sometimes a better anatomical draughtsman than Raphael, a better
hand at triple counterpoint than Beethoven, a better versifier than
Byron. Nay, this is true not merely of pedants, but of men who have
produced works of art of some note. If technical facility were the secret
of greatness in art, Mr. Swinburne would be greater than Browning and
Byron rolled into one, Stevenson greater than Scott or Dickens, Men-
delssohn than Wagner, Maclise than Madox Brown. Besides, new ideas
make their technique as water makes its channel; and the technician
without ideas is as useless as the canal constructor without water, though
he may do very skilfully what the Mississippi does very rudely. To clinch
the argument, you have only to observe that the epoch maker himself
has generally begun working professionally before his new ideas have
mastered him sufficiently to insist on constant expression by his art. In
such cases you are compelled to admit that if he had by chance died
earlier, his greatness would have remained unachieved, although his
technical qualifications would have been well enough established. The
early imitative works of great men are usually conspicuously inferior to
the best works of their forerunners. Imagine Wagner dying after composing Rienzi, or Shelley after Zastrozzi! Would any competent critic
then have rated Wagner's technical aptitude as high as Rossini's, Spon-
tini's, or Meyerbeer's; or Shelley's as high as Moore's? Turn the problem
another way: does anyone suppose that if Shakespear had conceived
Goethe's or Ibsen's ideas, he would have expressed them any worse than
Goethe or Ibsen? Human faculty being what it is, is it likely that in our
time any advance, except in external conditions, will take place in the

arts of expression sufficient to enable an author, without making himself ridiculous, to undertake to say what he has to say better than Homer or Shakespear? But the humblest author, and much more a rather arrogant one like myself, may profess to have something to say by this time that neither Homer nor Shakespear said. And the playgoer may reasonably ask to have historical events and persons presented to him in the light of his own time, even though Homer and Shakespear have already shewn them in the light of their time. For example, Homer presented Achilles and Ajax as heroes to the world in the Iliad. In due time came Shakespear, who said, virtually: I really cannot accept this selfish hound and this brawny brute as great men merely because Homer flattered them in playing to the Greek gallery. Consequently we have, in Troilus and Cressida, the verdict of Shakespear's epoch (our own) on the pair. This did not in the least involve any pretence on Shakespear's part to be a greater poet than Homer.

When Shakespear in turn came to deal with Henry V and Julius Cæsar, he did so according to his own essentially knightly conception of a great statesman-commander. But in the XIX century comes the German historian Mommsen, who also takes Cæsar for his hero, and explains the immense difference in scope between the perfect knight Vercingetorix and his great conqueror Julius Cæsar. In this country, Carlyle, with his vein of peasant inspiration, apprehended the sort of greatness that places the true hero of history so far beyond the mere *preux chevalier,* whose fanatical personal honor, gallantry and self-sacrifice, are founded on a passion for death born of inability to bear the weight of a life that will not grant ideal conditions to the liver. This one ray of perception became Carlyle's whole stock-in-trade; and it sufficed to make a literary master of him. In due time, when Mommsen is an old man, and Carlyle dead, come I, and dramatize the by-this-time familiar distinction in Arms and the Man, with its comedic conflict be-between the knightly Bulgarian and the Mommsenite Swiss captain. Whereupon a great many playgoers who have not yet read Shakespear, much less Mommsen and Carlyle, raise a shriek of concern for their knightly ideal as if nobody had ever questioned its sufficiency since the middle ages. Let them thank me for educating them so far. And let them allow me to set forth Cæsar in the same modern light, taking the same liberty with Shakespear as he with Homer, and with no thought of pretending to express the Mommsenite view of Cæsar any better than Shakespear expressed a view which was not even Plutarchian, and must, I fear, be referred to the tradition in stage conquerors established by Marlowe's Tamerlane as much as to even the chivalrous conception of heroism dramatized in Henry V.

For my own part, I can avouch that such powers of invention, humor

and stage ingenuity as I have been able to exercise in Plays, Pleasant
and Unpleasant, and in these Three Plays for Puritans, availed me not
at all until I saw the old facts in a new light. Technically, I do not find
myself able to proceed otherwise than as former playwrights have done.
True, my plays have the latest mechanical improvements: the action is
not carried on by impossible soliloquys and asides; and my people get
on and off the stage without requiring four doors to a room which in
real life would have only one. But my stories are the old stories; my
characters are the familiar harlequin and columbine, clown and panta-
loon (note the harlequin's leap in the third act of Cæsar and Cleopatra);
my stage tricks and suspenses and thrills and jests are the ones in vogue
when I was a boy, by which time my grandfather was tired of them. To
the young people who make their acquaintance for the first time in my
plays, they may be as novel as Cyrano's nose to those who have never
seen Punch; whilst to older playgoers the unexpectedness of my attempt
to substitute natural history for conventional ethics and romantic logic
may so transfigure the eternal stage puppets and their inevitable dilem-
mas as to make their identification impossible for the moment. If so, so
much the better for me: I shall perhaps enjoy a few years of immortal-
ity. But the whirligig of time will soon bring my audiences to my own
point of view; and then the next Shakespear that comes along will turn
these petty tentatives of mine into masterpieces final for their epoch. By
that time my twentieth century characteristics will pass unnoticed as a
matter of course, whilst the eighteenth century artificiality that marks
the work of every literary Irishman of my generation will seem anti-
quated and silly. It is a dangerous thing to be hailed at once, as a few
rash admirers have hailed me, as above all things original: what the
world calls originality is only an unaccustomed method of tickling it.
Meyerbeer seemed prodigiously original to the Parisians when he first
burst on them. To-day, he is only the crow who followed Beethoven's
plough. I am a crow who have followed many ploughs. No doubt I seem
prodigiously clever to those who have never hopped, hungry and curious, across the fields of philosophy, politics and art. Karl Marx said of
Stuart Mill that his eminence was due to the flatness of the surrounding
country. In these days of Board Schools, universal reading, cheap newspapers, and the inevitable ensuing demand for notabilities of all sorts,
literary, military, political and fashionable, to write paragraphs about,
that sort of eminence is within the reach of very moderate ability. Reputations are cheap nowadays. Even were they dear, it would still be impossible for any public-spirited citizen of the world to hope that his
reputation might endure; for this would be to hope that the flood of
general enlightenment may never rise above his miserable high-water
mark. I hate to think that Shakespear has lasted 300 years, though he

got no further than Koheleth the Preacher, who died many centuries before him; or that Plato, more than 2,000 years old, is still ahead of our voters. We must hurry on: we must get rid of reputations: they are weeds in the soil of ignorance. Cultivate that soil, and they will flower more beautifully, but only as annuals. If this preface will at all help to get rid of mine, the writing of it will have been well worth the pains.

O'NEILL

IN THE REALM OF DRAMATIC ART, THE UNITED STATES REMAINED AN ENGLISH AND EUROPEAN COLONY UNTIL 1916 WHEN THE PROVINCETOWN (MASSACHU-SETTS) WHARF THEATER STAGED A ONE-ACT PLAY BY A TWENTY-EIGHT-YEAR-OLD ALCOHOLIC DRIFTER, A GREENWICH VILLAGE WRITER-TURNED-DERELICT, EUGENE O'NEILL (1888–1953). O'NEILL'S SHORT PLAY, *BOUND EAST FOR CARDIFF*, NOT ONLY REVOLUTIONIZED AMERICAN THEATER BUT SALVAGED A GREAT MAN. IT IS A MEASURE OF O'NEILL'S ARTISTIC TRIUMPH THAT HE WAS ABLE TO EXPLOIT HIS PERSONAL HISTORY AND TRANSFORM IT INTO THE MATERIAL OF HIS ART. HIS ALIENATION FROM HIS FAMILY, FROM MIDDLE-CLASS LIFE AND VALUES, AND HIS IDENTIFICATION WITH THE MISFITS, THE HOMELESS, THE UNCOMPROMISING ARTIST-BOHEMIAN, CONSTITUTE THE SUBJECT OF MOST OF HIS FORTY-ODD PLAYS.

O'Neill's present reputation, however, rests principally on the seven plays written in his maturity between 1929 and 1943 (when illness ended his life as a writer). The plays of O'Neill which show most likelihood of survival—in addition to the one-act plays of the sea—are *Mourning Becomes Electra* (1929–1931); *Ah, Wilderness!* (1932); *The Iceman Cometh* (1939); *A Moon for the Misbegotten* (1940); *Long Day's Journey into Night* (1941); *A Touch of the Poet* (1942); and *Hughie* (1942).

Hughie differs from the remainder of O'Neill's late work in its brevity but not in its thematic concerns. Erie Smith and Charlie Hughes are men who have chosen roads that have led them in opposite directions. We know little about Charlie, but we know a great deal about his predecessor, Hughie. Are all three men basically content with the life they lead, or is there a yearning for "the road not taken"? Was there a conscious choice? That is, was Erie truly victimized by the girl who "nearly had [him] hooked for the shotgun ceremony"? Or were his aimless, unrooted wanderings inherent in his nature?

Another theme in *Hughie* concerns the self-deceptions which men practice upon themselves. Not everything that Erie says is true; we are —and sometimes so is he—aware of inconsistencies and exaggerations. How important are these lies, evasions, and distortions? What impact would a real self-awareness have upon him? Does Erie illustrate the gallantry of the human spirit, man's capacity to defy those elements which would drag him down? Or rather, does he personify the cheap, parasitic hangers-on who constitute an affront to the hard-working, responsible, and decent members of the community? Or is he merely pathetic, the portrait of a man who has failed to make a life for himself?

HUGHIE

CHARACTERS

"ERIE" SMITH, *a teller of tales*
A NIGHT CLERK

SCENE: *The desk and a section of lobby of a small hotel on a West Side street in midtown New York. It is between 3 and 4 A.M. of a day in the summer of 1928.*

It is one of those hotels, built in the decade 1900–10 on the side streets of the Great White Way sector, which began as respectable second class but soon were forced to deteriorate in order to survive. Following the First World War and Prohibition, it had given up all pretense of respectability, and now is anything a paying guest wants it to be, a third class dump, catering to the catch-as-catch-can trade. But still it does not prosper. It has not shared in the Great Hollow Boom of the twenties. The Everlasting Opulence of the New Economic Law has over-looked it. It manages to keep running by cutting the overhead for service, repairs, and cleanliness to a minimum.

The desk faces left along a section of seedy lobby with shabby chairs. The street entrance is off-stage, left. Behind the desk are a telephone switchboard and the operator's stool. At right, the usual numbered tiers of mailboxes, and above them a clock.

The Night Clerk sits on the stool, facing front, his back to the switch-board. There is nothing to do. He is not thinking. He is not sleepy. He simply droops and stares acquiescently at nothing. It would be dis-couraging to glance at the clock. He knows there are several hours to go before his shift is over. Anyway, he does not need to look at clocks. He has been a night clerk in New York hotels so long he can tell time by sounds in the street.

He is in his early forties. Tall, thin, with a scrawny neck and jutting Adam's apple. His face is long and narrow, greasy with perspiration, sallow, studded with pimples from ingrowing hairs. His nose is large and without character. So is his mouth. So are his ears. So is his thinning brown hair, powdered with dandruff. Behind horn-rimmed spectacles, his blank brown eyes contain no discernible expression. One would say they had even forgotten how it feels to be bored. He wears an ill-fitting blue serge suit, white shirt and collar, a blue tie. The suit is old and shines at the elbows as if it had been waxed and polished.

Footsteps echo in the deserted lobby as someone comes in from the street. The Night Clerk rises wearily. His eyes remain empty but his

513

gummy lips part automatically in a welcoming The-Patron-Is-Always-
Right grimace, intended as a smile. His big uneven teeth are in bad con-
dition.

Erie Smith enters and approaches the desk. He is about the same age
as the Clerk and has the same pasty, perspiry, night-life complexion.
There the resemblance ends. Erie is around medium height but appears
shorter because he is stout and his fat legs are too short for his body. So
are his fat arms. His big head squats on a neck which seems part of his
beefy shoulders. His face is round, his snub nose flattened at the tip. His
blue eyes have drooping lids and puffy pouches under them. His sandy
hair is falling out and the top of his head is bald. He walks to the desk
with a breezy, familiar air, his gait a bit waddling because of his short
legs. He carries a Panama hat and mops his face with a red and blue silk
handkerchief. He wears a light grey suit cut in the extreme, tight-
waisted, Broadway mode, the coat open to reveal an old and faded but
expensive silk shirt in a shade of blue that sets teeth on edge, and a
gay red and blue foulard tie, its knot stained by perspiration. His
trousers are held up by a braided brown leather belt with a brass buckle.
His shoes are tan and white, his socks white silk.

In manner, he is consciously a Broadway sport and a Wise Guy—the
type of small fry gambler and horse player, living hand to mouth on the
fringe of the rackets. Infesting corners, doorways, cheap restaurants, the
bars of minor speakeasies, he and his kind imagine they are in the Real
Know, cynical oracles of the One True Grapevine.

Erie usually speaks in a low, guarded tone, his droop-lidded eyes suspi-
ciously wary of nonexistent eavesdroppers. His face is set in the prescribed
pattern of gambler's dead pan. His small, pursy mouth is always crooked
in the cynical leer of one who possesses superior, inside information, and
his shifty once-over glances never miss the price tags he detects on every-
thing and everybody. Yet there is something phoney about his characteri-
zation of himself, some sentimental softness behind it which doesn't be-
long in the hard-boiled picture.

Erie avoids looking at the Night Clerk, as if he resented him.

ERIE (*peremptorily*). Key (*Then as the* NIGHT CLERK *gropes with his
    memory—grudgingly.*) Forgot you ain't seen me before. Erie Smith's
    the name. I'm an old timer in this fleabag. 492.
NIGHT CLERK   (*in a tone of one who is wearily relieved when he does not
    have to remember anything—he plucks out the key*). 492. Yes, sir.
ERIE   (*taking the key, gives the* CLERK *the once-over. He appears not un-
    favorably impressed but his tone still holds resentment*). How long
    you been on the job? Four, five days, huh? I been off on a drunk. Come
    to now, though. Tapering off. Well, I'm glad they fired that young

squirt they took on when Hughie got sick. One of them fresh wise punks. Couldn't tell him nothing. Pleased to meet you, Pal. Hope you stick around.

(*He shoves out his hand. The* NIGHT CLERK *takes it obediently.*)

NIGHT CLERK   (*with a compliant, uninterested smile*). Glad to know you, Mr. Smith.

ERIE   What's your name?

NIGHT CLERK   (*as if he had forgotten because what did it matter, anyway?*) Hughes. Charlie Hughes.

ERIE   (*starts*). Huh? Hughes? Say, is that on the level?

NIGHT CLERK   Charlie Hughes.

ERIE   Well, I be damned! What the hell d'you know about that! (*Warming toward the* CLERK.) Say, now I notice, you don't look like Hughie, but you remind me of him somehow. You ain't by any chance related?

NIGHT CLERK   You mean to the Hughes who had this job so long and died recently? No, sir. No relation.

ERIE   (*gloomily*). No, that's right. Hughie told me he didn't have no relations left—except his wife and kids, of course. (*He pauses—more gloomily.*) Yeah. The poor guy croaked last week. His funeral was what started me off on a bat. (*Then boastfully, as if defending himself against gloom.*) Some drunk! I don't go on one often. It's bum dope in my book. A guy gets careless and gabs about things he knows and when he comes to he's liable to find there's guys who'd feel easier if he wasn't around no more. That's the trouble with knowing things. Take my tip, Pal. Don't never know nothin'. Be a sap and stay healthy.

(*His manner has become secretive, with sinister undertones. But the* NIGHT CLERK *doesn't notice this. Long experience with guests who stop at his desk in the small hours to talk about themselves has given him a foolproof technique of self-defense. He appears to listen with agreeable submissiveness and be impressed, but his mind is blank and he doesn't hear unless a direct question is put to him, and sometimes not even then.* ERIE *thinks he is impressed.*)

But hell, I always keep my noggin working, booze or no booze. I'm no sucker. What was I sayin'? Oh, some drunk. I sure hit the high spots. You shoulda seen the doll I made night before last. And did she take me to the cleaners! I'm a sucker for blondes.

(*He pauses—giving the* NIGHT CLERK *a cynical, contemptuous glance.*)

You're married, ain't you?

NIGHT CLERK   (*Long ago he gave up caring whether questions were personal or not.*) Yes, sir.

ERIE   Yeah, I'd'a laid ten to one on it. You got that old look. Like Hughie had. Maybe that's the resemblance. (*He chuckles contemptuously.*) Kids, too, I bet?

NIGHT CLERK Yes, sir. Three.

ERIE You're worse off than Hughie was. He only had two. Three, huh?
Well, that's what comes of being careless!

(*He laughs. The* NIGHT CLERK *smiles at a* GUEST. *He had been a little offended when a guest first made that crack—must have been ten years
ago—yes, Eddie, the oldest, is eleven now—or is it twelve?* ERIE *goes on
with good-natured tolerance.*)

Well, I suppose marriage ain't such a bum racket, if you're made for
it. Hughie didn't seem to mind it much, although if you want my
low-down, his wife is a bum—in spades! Oh, I don't mean cheatin'.
With her puss and figure, she'd never make no one except she raided
a blind asylum.

(*The* NIGHT CLERK *feels that he has been standing a long time and his
feet are beginning to ache and he wishes 492 would stop talking and go
to bed so he can sit down again and listen to the noises in the street and
think about nothing.* ERIE *gives him an amused, condescending glance.*)

How old are you? Wait! Let me guess. You look fifty or over but I'll
lay ten to one you're forty-three or maybe forty-four.

NIGHT CLERK I'm forty-three. (*He adds vaguely.*) Or maybe it is forty-
four.

ERIE (*elated*). I win, huh? I sure can call the turn on ages, Buddy. You
ought to see the dolls get sored up when I work it on them! You're
like Hughie. He looked like he'd never see fifty again and he was only
forty-three. Me, I'm forty-five. Never think it, would you? Most of the
dames don't think I've hit forty yet.

(*The* NIGHT CLERK *shifts his position so he can lean more on the desk.
Maybe those shoes he sees advertised for fallen arches— But they cost
eight dollars, so that's out— Get a pair when he goes to heaven.* ERIE *is
sizing him up with another cynical, friendly glance.*)

I make another bet about you. Born and raised in the sticks, wasn't
you?

NIGHT CLERK (*faintly aroused and defensive*). I come originally from
Saginaw, Michigan, but I've lived here in the Big Town so long I consider myself a New Yorker now.

(*This is a long speech for him and he wonders sadly why he took the
trouble to make it.*)

ERIE I don't deserve no medal for picking that one. Nearly every guy
I know on the Big Stem—and I know most of 'em—hails from the
sticks. Take me. You'd never guess it but I was dragged up in Erie,
P-a. Ain't that a knockout! Erie, P-a! That's how I got my moniker.
No one calls me nothing but Erie. You better call me Erie, too, Pal,
or I won't know when you're talkin' to me.

NIGHT CLERK All right, Erie.

ERIE   Atta Boy. (*He chuckles.*) Here's another knockout. Smith is my
real name. A Broadway guy like me named Smith and it's my real
name! Ain't that a knockout! (*He explains carefully so there will be
no misunderstanding.*) I don't remember nothing much about Erie,
P-a, you understand—or want to. Some punk burg! After grammar
school, my Old Man put me to work in his store, dealing out groceries.
Some punk job! I stuck it till I was eighteen before I took a run-out
powder.

(*The* NIGHT CLERK *seems turned into a drooping waxwork, draped along
the desk. This is what he used to dread before he perfected his technique
of not listening: The Guest's Story of His Life. He fixes his mind on his
aching feet.* ERIE *chuckles.*)

Speaking of marriage, that was the big reason I ducked. A doll nearly
had me hooked for the old shotgun ceremony. Closest I ever come to
being played for a sucker. This doll in Erie—Daisy's her name—was
one of them dumb wide-open dolls. All the guys give her a play. Then
one day she wakes up and finds she's going to have a kid. I never
figured she meant to frame me in particular. Way I always figured, she
didn't have no idea who, so she holds a lottery all by herself. Put about
a thousand guys' names in a hat—all she could remember—and drew
one out and I was it. Then she told her Ma, and her Ma told her Pa, and
her Pa come round looking for me. But I was no fall guy even in them
days. I took it on the lam. For Saratoga, to look the bangtails over.
I'd started to be a horse player in Erie, though I'd never seen a track.
I been one ever since. (*With a touch of bravado.*) And I ain't done
so bad, Pal. I've made some killings in my time the gang still gab about.
I've been in the big bucks. More'n once, and I will be again. I've had
tough breaks too, but what the hell, I always get by. When the horses
won't run for me, there's draw or stud. When they're bad, there's a
crap game. And when they're all bad, there's always bucks to pick up
for little errands I ain't talkin' about, which they give a guy who can
keep his clam shut. Oh, I get along, Buddy. I get along fine.

(*He waits for approving assent from the* NIGHT CLERK, *but the latter is
not hearing so intently he misses his cue until the expectant silence
crashes his ears.*)

NIGHT CLERK   (*hastily, gambling on "yes"*). Yes, Sir.

ERIE   (*bitingly*). Sorry if I'm keeping you up, Sport. (*With an aggrieved
air.*) Hughie was a wide-awake guy. He was always waiting for me to
roll in. He'd say, "Hello, Erie, how'd the bangtails treat you?" Or,
"How's luck?" Or, "Did you make the old bones behave?" Then I'd
tell him how I'd done. He'd ask, "What's new along the Big Stem?"
and I'd tell him the latest off the grapevine. (*He grins with affectionate
condescension.*) It used to hand me a laugh to hear old Hughie

crackin' like a sport. In all the years I knew him, he never bet a buck on nothin'. (*Excusingly.*) But it ain't his fault. He'd have took a chance, but how could he with his wife keepin' cases on every nickel of his salary? I showed him lots of ways he could cross her up, but he was too scared. (*He chuckles.*) The biggest knockout was when he'd kid me about dames. He'd crack, "What? No blonde to-night, Erie? You must be slippin'." Jeez, you never see a guy more bashful with a doll around than Hughie was. I used to introduce him to the tramps I'd drag home with me. I'd wise them up to kid him along and pretend they'd fell for him. In two minutes, they'd have him hanging on the ropes. His face'd be red and he'd look like he wanted to crawl under the desk and hide. Some of them dolls was raw babies. They'd make him pretty raw propositions. He'd stutter like he was paralyzed. But he ate it up, just the same. He was tickled pink. I used to hope maybe I could nerve him up to do a little cheatin'. I'd offer to fix it for him with one of my dolls. Hell, I got plenty, I wouldn't have minded. I'd tell him, "Just let that wife of yours know you're cheatin', and she'll have some respect for you." But he was too scared. (*He pauses—boastfully.*) Some queens I've brought here in my time, Brother—frails from the Follies, or the Scandals, or the Frolics, that'd knock your eye out! And I still can make 'em. You watch. I ain't slippin'.

(*He looks at the* NIGHT CLERK *expecting reassurance, but the* CLERK's *mind has slipped away to the changing bounce of garbage cans in the outer night. He is thinking: "A job I'd like. I'd bang those cans louder than they do! I'd wake up the whole damned city!"* ERIE *mutters disgustedly to himself.*)

Jesus, what a dummy! (*He makes a move in the direction of the elevator, off right front—gloomily.*) Might as well hit the hay, I guess.

NIGHT CLERK (*comes to—with the nearest approach to feeling he has shown in many a long night—approvingly*). Good night, Mr. Smith. I hope you have a good rest.

(*But* ERIE *stops, glancing around the deserted lobby with forlorn distaste, jiggling the room key in his hand.*)

ERIE What a crummy dump! What did I come back for? I shoulda stayed on a drunk. You'd never guess it, Buddy, but when I first come here this was a classy hotel—and clean, can you believe it? (*He scowls.*) I've been campin' here, off and on, fifteen years, but I've got a good notion to move out. It ain't the same place since Hughie was took to the hospital. (*Gloomily.*) Hell with going to bed! I'll just lie there worrying—

(*He turns back to the desk. The* CLERK's *face would express despair, but the last time he was able to feel despair was back around World War days when the cost of living got so high and he was out of a job for three months.* ERIE *leans on the desk—in a dejected, confidential tone.*)

Believe me, Brother, I never been a guy to worry, but this time I'm on a spot where I got to, if I ain't a sap.

NIGHT CLERK *(in the vague tone of a corpse which admits it once overheard a favorable rumor about life).* That's too bad, Mr. Smith. But they say most of the things we worry about never happen. *(His mind escapes to the street again to play bouncing cans with the garbage men.)*

ERIE *(grimly).* This thing happens, Pal. I ain't won a bet at nothin' since Hughie was took to the hospital. I'm jinxed. And that ain't all— But to hell with it! You're right, at that. Something always turns up for me. I was born lucky. I ain't worried. Just moaning low. Hell, who don't when they're getting over a drunk? You know how it is. The Brooklyn Boys march over the bridge with bloodhounds to hunt you down. And I'm still carrying the torch for Hughie. His checking out was a real K.O. for me. Damn if I know why. Lots of guys I've been pals with, in a way, croaked from booze or something, or got rubbed out, but I always took it as part of the game. Hell, we all gotta croak. Here today, gone tomorrow, so what's the good of beefin'? When a guy's dead, he's dead. He don't give a damn, so why should anybody else? *(But this fatalistic philosophy is no comfort and* ERIE *sighs.)* I miss Hughie, I guess. I guess I'd got to like him a lot. *(Again he explains carefully so there will be no misunderstanding.)* Not that I was ever real pals with him, you understand. He didn't run in my class. He didn't know none of the answers. He was just a sucker. *(He sighs again.)* But I sure am sorry he's gone. You missed a lot not knowing Hughie, Pal. He sure was one grand little guy.

(He stares at the lobby floor. The NIGHT CLERK *regards him with vacant, bulging eyes full of vague envy for the blind. The garbage men have gone their predestined way. Time is that much older. The* CLERK's *mind remains in the street to greet the noise of a far-off El train. Its approach is pleasantly like a memory of hope; then it roars and rocks and rattles past the nearby corner, and the noise pleasantly deafens memory; then it recedes and dies, and there is something melancholy about that. But there is hope. Only so many El trains pass in one night, and each one passing leaves one less to pass, so the night recedes, too, until at last it must die and join all the other long nights in Nirvana, the Big Night of Nights. And that's life. "What I always tell Jess when she nags me to worry about something: 'That's life, isn't it? What can you do about it?' "* ERIE *sighs again—then turns to the* CLERK, *his foolishly wary, wise-guy eyes defenseless, his poker face as self-betraying as a hurt dog's— appealingly.)*

Say, you do remind me of Hughie somehow, Pal. You got the same look on your map. *(But the* CLERK's *mind is far away attending the obsequies of night, and it takes it some time to get back.* ERIE *is hurt*

—*contemptuously.*) But I guess it's only that old night clerk look! There's one of 'em born every minute!

NIGHT CLERK   (*His mind arrives just in time to catch this last—with a bright grimace.*) Yes, Mr. Smith. That's what Barnum said, and it's certainly true, isn't it?

ERIE   (*grateful even for this sign of companionship, growls*). Nix on the Mr. Smith stuff, Charlie. There's ten of *them* born every minute. Call me Erie, like I told you.

NIGHT CLERK   (*automatically, as his mind tiptoes into the night again*). All right, Erie.

ERIE   (*encouraged, leans on the desk, clacking his room key like a castanet*). Yeah. Hughie was one grand little guy. All the same, like I said, he wasn't the kind of guy you'd ever figger a guy like me would take to. Because he was a sucker, see—the kind of sap you'd take to the cleaners a million times and he'd never wise up he was took. Why, night after night, just for a gag, I'd get him to shoot crap with me here on the desk. With *my* dice. And he'd never ask to give 'em the once-over. Can you beat that! (*He chuckles—then earnestly.*) Not that I'd ever ring in no phoneys on a pal. I'm no heel. (*He chuckles again.*) And anyway, I didn't need none to take Hughie because he never even made me knock 'em against nothing. Just a roll on the desk here. Boy, if they'd ever let me throw 'em that way in a real game, I'd be worth ten million dollars. (*He laughs.*) You'da thought Hughie woulda got wise something was out of order when, no matter how much he'd win on a run of luck like suckers have sometimes, I'd always take him to the cleaners in the end. But he never suspicioned nothing. All he'd say was "Gosh, Erie, no wonder you took up gambling. You sure were born lucky." (*He chuckles.*) Can you beat that? (*He hastens to explain earnestly.*) Of course, like I said, it was only a gag. We'd play with real jack, just to make it look real, but it was all my jack. He never had no jack. His wife dealt him four bits a day for spending money. So I'd stake him at the start to half of what I got—in chicken feed, I mean. We'd pretend a cent was a buck, and a nickel was a fin and so on. Some big game! He got a big kick out of it. He'd get all het up. It give me a kick, too—especially when he'd say, "Gosh, Erie, I don't wonder you never worry about money, with your luck." (*He laughs.*) That guy would believe anything! Of course, I'd stall him off when he'd want to shoot nights when I didn't have a goddamned nickel. (*He chuckles.*) What laughs he used to hand me! He'd always call horses "the bangtails," like he'd known 'em all his life—and he'd never seen a race horse, not till I kidnaped him one day and took him down to Belmont. What a kick he got out of that! I got scared he'd pass out with excitement. And he wasn't doing no betting either. All

he had was four bits. It was just the track, and the crowd, and the
horses got him. Mostly the horses. (*With a surprised, reflective air.*)
Y'know, it's funny how a dumb, simple guy like Hughie will all of
a sudden get something right. He says, "They're the most beautiful
things in the world, I think." And he wins! I tell you, Pal, I'd rather
sleep in the same stall with old Man o' War than make the whole damn
Follies. What do you think?

NIGHT CLERK   (*His mind darts back from a cruising taxi and blinks bewilderedly in the light: "Say yes."*) Yes, I agree with you, Mr.—I mean,
Erie.

ERIE   (*with good-natured contempt*). Yeah? I bet you never seen one,
except back at the old Fair Grounds in the sticks. I don't mean them
kind of turtles. I mean a real horse.

(*The* CLERK *wonders what horses have to do with anything—or for that
matter, what anything has to do with anything—then gives it up.* ERIE
takes up his tale.)

And what d'you think happened the next night? Damned if Hughie
didn't dig two bucks out of his pants and try to slip 'em to me. "Let
this ride on the nose of whatever horse you're betting on tomorrow,"
he told me. I got sore. "Nix," I told him, "if you're going to start
playin' sucker and bettin' on horse races, you don't get no assist from
me." (*He grins wryly.*) Was that a laugh! Me advising a sucker not to
bet when I've spent a lot of my life tellin' saps a story to make 'em
bet! I said, "Where'd you grab this dough? Outa the Little Woman's
purse, huh? What tale you going to give her when you lose it? She'll
start breaking up the furniture with you!" "No," he says, "she'll just
cry." "That's worse," I said, "no guy can beat that racket. I had a doll
cry on me once in a restaurant full of people till I had to promise her
a diamond engagement ring to sober her up." Well, anyway, Hughie
sneaked the two bucks back in the Little Woman's purse when he went
home that morning, and that was the end of that. (*Cynically.*) Boy
Scouts got nothin' on me, Pal, when it comes to good deeds. That was
one I done. It's too bad I can't remember no others.

(*He is well wound up now and goes on without noticing that the* NIGHT
CLERK's *mind has left the premises in his sole custody.*)

Y'know I had Hughie sized up for a sap the first time I see him. I'd
just rolled in from Tia Juana. I'd make a big killing down there and
I was lousy with jack. Came all the way in a drawing room, and I
wasn't lonely in it neither. There was a blonde movie doll on the
train—and I was lucky in them days. Used to follow the horses South
every winter. I don't no more. Sick of traveling. And I ain't as lucky
as I was— (*Hastily.*) Anyway, this time I'm talkin' about, soon as I hit
this lobby I see there's new night clerk, and while I'm signing up for

the bridal suite I make a bet with myself he's never been nothin' but a night clerk. And I win. At first, he wouldn't open up. Not that he was cagey about gabbin' too much. But like he couldn't think of nothin' about himself worth saying. But after he'd seen me roll in here the last one every night, and I'd stop to kid him along and tell him the tale of what I'd win that day, he got friendly and talked. He'd come from a hick burg upstate. Graduated from high school, and had a shot at different jobs in the old home town but couldn't make the grade until he was took on as night clerk in the hotel there. Then he made good. But he wasn't satisfied. Didn't like being only a night clerk where everybody knew him. He'd read somewhere—in the Sucker's Almanac, I guess—that all a guy had to do was come to the Big Town and Old Man Success would be waitin' at the Grand Central to give him the key to the city. What a gag that is! Even I believed that once, and no one could ever call me a sap. Well, anyway, he made the break and come here and the only job he could get was night clerk. Then he fell in love—or kidded himself he was—and got married. Met her on a subway train. It stopped sudden and she was jerked into him, and he put his arms around her, and they started talking, and the poor boob never stood a chance. She was a sales girl in some punk department store, and she was sick of standing on her dogs all day, and all the way home to Brooklyn, too. So, the way I figger it, knowing Hughie and dames, she proposed and said "yes" for him, and married him, and after that, of course, he never dared stop being a night clerk, even if he could. (*He paused.*) Maybe you think I ain't giving her a square shake. Well, maybe I ain't. She never give me one. She put me down as a bad influence, and let her chips ride. And maybe Hughie couldn't have done no better. Dolls didn't call him no riot. Hughie and her seemed happy enough the time he had me out to dinner in their flat. Well, not happy. Maybe contented. No, that's boosting it, too. Resigned comes nearer, as if each was givin' the other a break by thinking, "Well, what more could I expect?"

(*Abruptly he addresses the* NIGHT CLERK *with contemptuous good nature.*) How d'you and your Little Woman hit it off, Brother?

NIGHT CLERK   (*his mind has been counting the footfalls of the cop on the beat as they recede, sauntering longingly toward the dawn's release. "If he'd only shoot it out with a gunman some night! Nothing exciting has happened in any night I've ever lived through!" He stammers gropingly among the echoes of* ERIE'S *last words.*) Oh—you mean *my* wife? Why, we get along all right, I guess.

ERIE   (*disgustedly*). Better lay off them headache pills, Pal. First thing you know, some guy is going to call you a dope.

(*But the* NIGHT CLERK *cannot take this seriously. It is years since he cared what anyone called him. So many guests have called him so many things. The Little Woman has, too. And, of course, he has, himself. But that's all past. Is daybreak coming now? No, too early yet. He can tell by the sound of that surface car. It is still lost in the night. Flat wheeled and tired. Distant the carbarn, and far away the sleep.* ERIE, *having soothed resentment with his wisecrack, goes on with a friendly grin.*)

Well, keep hoping, Pal. Hughie was as big a dope as you until I give him some interest in life. (*Slipping back into narrative.*) That time he took me home to dinner. Was that a knockout! It took him a hell of a while to get up nerve to ask me. "Sure, Hughie," I told him, "I'll be tickled to death." I was thinking, I'd rather be shot. For one thing, he lived in Brooklyn, and I'd sooner take a trip to China. Another thing, I'm a guy that likes to eat what I order and not what somebody deals me. And he had kids and a wife, and the family racket is out of my line. But Hughie looked so tickled I couldn't welsh on him. And it didn't work out so bad. Of course, what he called home was only a dump of a cheap flat. Still, it wasn't so bad for a change. His wife had done a lot of stuff to doll it up. Nothin' with no class, you understand. Just cheap stuff to make it comfortable. And his kids wasn't the gorillas I'd expected, neither. No throwin' spitballs in my soup or them kind of gags. They was quiet like Hughie. I kinda liked 'em. After dinner I started tellin' 'em a story about a race horse a guy I know owned once. I thought it was up to me to put out something, and kids like animal stories, and this one was true, at that. This old turtle never wins a race, but he was as foxy as ten guys, a natural born crook, the goddamnedest thief, he'd steal anything in reach that wasn't nailed down— Well, I didn't get far. Hughie's wife butt in and stopped me cold. Told the kids it was bedtime and hustled 'em off like I was giving 'em measles. It got my goat, kinda. I coulda liked her—a little— if she'd give me a chance. Not that she was nothin' Ziegfeld would want to glorify. When you call her plain, you give her all the breaks. (*Resentfully.*) Well, to hell with it. She had me tagged for a bum, and seein' me made her sure she was right. You can bet she told Hughie never invite me again, and he never did. He tried to apologize, but I shut him up quick. He says, "Irma was brought up strict. She can't help being narrow-minded about gamblers." I said, "What's it to me? I don't want to hear your dame troubles. I got plenty of my own. Remember that doll I brung home night before last? She gives me an argument I promised her ten bucks. I told her, 'Listen, Baby, I got an impediment in my speech. Maybe it sounded like ten, but it was two, and that's all you get. Hell, I don't want to buy your soul! What would I do with it?' Now she's peddling the news along Broadway I'm a rat and a chiseler, and of course the all rats and chiselers believe her.

Before she's through, I won't have a friend left." (*He pauses—confidentially.*) I switched the subject on Hughie, see, on purpose. He never did beef to me about his wife again. (*He gives a forced chuckle.*) Believe me, Pal, I can stop guys that start telling me their family troubles!

NIGHT CLERK   (*His mina has hopped an ambulance clanging down Sixth, and is asking without curiosity: "Will he die, Doctor, or isn't he lucky?" "I'm afraid not, but he'll have to be absolutely quiet for months and months." "With a pretty nurse taking care of him?" "Probably not pretty." "Well, anyway, I claim he's lucky. And now I must get back to the hotel. 492 won't go to bed and insists on telling me jokes. It must have been a joke because he's chuckling." He laughs with a heartiness which has forgotten that heart is more than a word used in "Have a heart," an old slang expression.*) Ha— Ha! That's a good one, Erie. That's the best I've heard in a long time!

ERIE   (*for a moment is so hurt and depressed he hasn't the spirit to make a sarcastic crack. He stares at the floor, twirling his room key—to himself.*) Jesus, this sure is a dead dump. About as homey as the Morgue. (*He glances up at the clock.*) Gettin' late. Better beat it up to my cell and grab some shut eye.

(*He makes a move to detach himself from the desk but fails and remains wearily glued to it. His eyes prowl the lobby and finally come to rest on the* CLERK's *glistening, sallow face. He summons up strength for a withering crack.*)

Why didn't you tell me you was deaf, Buddy? I know guys is sensitive about them little afflictions, but I'll keep it confidential.

(*But the* CLERK's *mind has rushed out to follow the siren wail of a fire engine. "A fireman's life must be exciting." His mind rides the engine, and asks a fireman with disinterested eagerness: "Where's the fire? Is it a real good one this time? Has it a good start? Will it be big enough, do you think?"* ERIE *examines his face—bitingly.*)

Take my tip, Pal, and don't never try to buy from a dope peddler. He'll tell you you had enough already.

(*The* CLERK's *mind continues its dialogue with the fireman: "I mean, big enough to burn down the whole damn city?" "Sorry, Brother, but there's no chance. There's too much stone and steel. There'd always be something left." "Yes, I guess you're right. There's too much stone and steel. I wasn't really hoping, anyway. It really doesn't matter to me."* ERIE *gives him up and again attempts to pry himself from the desk, twirling his key frantically as if it were a fetish which set him free.*)

Well, me for the hay. (*But he can't dislodge himself—dully.*) Christ, it's lonely. I wish Hughie was here. By God, if he was, I'd tell him a tale that'd make his eyes pop! The bigger the story the harder he'd fall.

He was that kind of sap. He thought gambling was romantic. I guess he saw me like a sort of dream guy, the sort of guy he'd like to be if he could take a chance. I guess he lived a sort of double life listening to me gabbin' about hittin' the high spots. Come to figger it, I'll bet he even cheated on his wife that way, using me and my dolls. (*He chuckles.*) No wonder he liked me, huh? And the bigger I made myself the more he lapped it up. I went easy on him at first. I didn't lie—not any more'n a guy naturally does when he gabs about the bets he wins and the dolls he's made. But I soon see he was cryin' for more, and when a sucker cries for more, you're a dope if you don't let him have it. Every tramp I made got to be a Follies' doll. Hughie liked 'em to be Follies' dolls. Or in the Scandals or Frolics. He wanted me to be the Sheik of Araby, or something that any blonde 'd go round-heeled about. Well, I give him plenty of that. And I give him plenty of gambling tales. I explained my campin' in this dump was because I don't want to waste jack on nothin' but gambling. It was like dope to me, I told him. I couldn't quit. He lapped that up. He liked to kid himself I'm mixed up in the racket. He thought gangsters was romantic. So I fed him some baloney about highjacking I'd done once. I told him I knew all the Big Shots. Well, so I do, most of 'em, to say hello, and sometimes they hello back. Who wouldn't know 'em that hangs round Broadway and the joints? I run errands for 'em sometimes, because there's dough in it, but I'm cagey about gettin' in where it ain't healthy. Hughie wanted to think me and Legs Diamond was old pals. So I give him that too. I give him anything he cried for. (*Earnestly.*) Don't get the wrong idea, Pal. What I fed Hughie wasn't all lies. The tales about gambling wasn't. They was stories of big games and killings that really happened since I've been hangin' round. Only I wasn't in on 'em like I made out—except one or two from way back when I had a run of big luck and was in the bucks for a while until I was took to the cleaners. (*He stops to pay tribute of a sigh to the memory of brave days that were and that never were—then meditatively.*) Yeah, Hughie lapped up my stories like they was duck soup, or a beakful of heroin. I sure took him around with me in tales and showed him one hell of a time. (*He chuckles—then seriously.*) And, d'you know, it done me good, too, in a way. Sure. I'd get to seein' myself like he seen me. Some nights I'd come back here without a buck, feeling lower than a snake's belly, and first thing you know I'd be lousy with jack, bettin' a grand a race. Oh, I was wise I was kiddin' myself. I ain't a sap. But what the hell, Hughie loved it, and it didn't cost nobody nothin', and if every guy along Broadway who kids himself was to drop dead there wouldn't be nobody left. Ain't it the truth, Charlie?

(*He again stares at the* NIGHT CLERK *appealingly, forgetting past rebuffs. The* CLERK's *face is taut with vacancy. His mind has been trying to fasten itself to some noise in the night, but a rare and threatening pause of silence has fallen on the city, and here he is, chained behind a hotel desk forever, awake when everyone else in the world is asleep, except Room 492, and he won't go to bed, he's still talking, and there is no escape.*)

NIGHT CLERK   (*His glassy eyes stare through* ERIE's *face. He stammers deferentially.*) Truth? I'm afraid I didn't get—What's the truth?

ERIE   (*hopelessly*) . Nothing, Pal. Not a thing.

(*His eyes fall to the floor. For a while he is too defeated even to twirl his room key. The* CLERK's *mind still cannot make a getaway because the city remains silent, and the night vaguely reminds him of death, and he is vaguely frightened, and now that he remembers, his feet are giving him hell, but that's no excuse not to act as if the* GUEST *is always right:* "I should have paid 492 more attention. After all, he is company. He is awake and alive. I should use him to help me live through the night. What's he been talking about? I must have caught some of it without meaning to." *The* NIGHT CLERK's *forehead puckers perspiringly as he tries to remember. Erie begins talking again but this time it is obviously aloud to himself, without hope of a listener.*)

I could tell by Hughie's face before he went to the hospital, he was through. I've seen the same look on guys' faces when they knew they was on the spot, just before guys caught up with them. I went to see him twice in the hospital. The first time, his wife was there and give me a dirty look, but he cooked up a smile and said, "Hello, Erie, how're the bangtails treating you?" I see he wants a big story to cheer him, but his wife butts in and says he's weak and he mustn't get excited. I felt like crackin', "Well, the Docs in this dump got the right dope. Just leave you with him and he'll never get excited." The second time I went, they wouldn't let me see him. That was near the end. I went to his funeral, too. There wasn't nobody but a coupla his wife's relations. I had to feel sorry for her. She looked like she ought to be parked in a coffin, too. The kids was bawlin'. There wasn't no flowers but a coupla lousy wreaths. It woulda been a punk showing for poor old Hughie, if it hadn't been for my flower piece. (*He swells with pride.*) That was some display, Pal. It'd knock your eye out! Set me back a hundred bucks, and no kiddin'! A big horseshoe of red roses! I knew Hughie'd want a horseshoe because that made it look like he'd been a horse player. And around the top printed in forget-me-nots was "Good-by, Old Pal." Hughie liked to kid himself he was my pal. (*He adds sadly.*) And so he was, at that—even if he was a sucker.

(*He pauses, his false poker face as nakedly forlorn as an organ grinder's monkey's. Outside, the spell of abnormal quiet presses suffocatingly upon the street, enters the deserted, dirty lobby. The* NIGHT CLERK's *mind cowers away from it. He cringes behind the desk, his feet aching like hell. There is only one possible escape. If his mind could only fasten onto something 492 has said. "What's he been talking about? A clerk should always be attentive. You even are duty bound to laugh at a guest's smutty jokes, no matter how often you've heard them. That's the policy of the hotel. 492 has been gassing for hours. What's he been telling me? I must be slipping. Always before this I've been able to hear without bothering to listen, but now when I need company— Ah! I've got it! Gambling! He said a lot about gambling. That's something I've always wanted to know more about, too. Maybe he's a professional gambler. Like Arnold Rothstein."*)

NIGHT CLERK   (*Blurts out with an uncanny, almost lifelike eagerness.*) I beg your pardon, Mr.—Erie—but did I understand you to say you are a gambler by profession? Do you, by any chance, know the Big Shot, Arnold Rothstein?

(*But this time it is* ERIE *who doesn't hear him. And the* CLERK's *mind is now suddenly impervious to the threat of Night and Silence as it pursues an ideal of fame and glory within itself called Arnold Rothstein.*)

ERIE   (*with mournful longing*). Christ, I wish Hughie was alive and kickin'. I'd tell him I win ten grand from the bookies, and ten grand at stud, and ten grand in a crap game! I'd tell him I bought one of those Mercedes sport roadsters with nickel pipes sticking out of the hood! I'd tell him I lay three babes from the Follies—two blondes and one brunette!

(*The* NIGHT CLERK *dreams, a rapt hero worship transfiguring his pimply face: "Arnold Rothstein! He must be some guy! I read a story about him. He'll gamble for any limit on anything, and always wins. The story said he wouldn't bother playing in a poker game unless the smallest bet you could make—one white chip!—was a hundred dollars. Christ, that's going some! I'd like to have the dough to get in a game with him once! The last pot everyone would drop out but him and me. I'd say, 'Okay, Arnold, the sky's the limit,' and I'd raise him five grand, and he'd call, and I'd have a royal flush to his four aces. Then I'd say, 'Okay, Arnold, I'm a good sport, I'll give you a break. I'll cut you double or nothing. Just one cut. I want quick action for my dough.' And I'd cut the ace of spades and win again." Beatific vision swoons on the empty pools of the* NIGHT CLERKS'S *eyes. He resembles a holy saint, recently elected to Paradise.* ERIE *breaks the silence—bitterly resigned.*)

But Hughie's better off, at that, being dead. He's got all the luck. He needn't do no worryin' now. He's out of the racket. I mean, the whole goddamned racket. I mean life.

NIGHT CLERK   (*kicked out of his dream—with detached, pleasant acqui-*

escence) . Yes, it is a goddamned racket when you stop to think, isn't it, 492? But we might as well make the best of it, because— Well, you can't burn it all down, can you? There's too much steel and stone. There'd always be something left to start it going again.

ERIE   (*scowls bewilderedly*) . Say, what is this? What the hell you talkin' about?

NIGHT CLERK   (*at a loss—in much confusion*) . Why, to be frank, I really don't—Just something that came into my head.

ERIE   (*bitingly, but showing he is comforted at having made some sort of contact*) . Get it out of your head quick, Charlie, or some guys in uniform will walk in here with a butterfly net and catch you. (*He changes the subject—earnestly.*) Listen, Pal, maybe you guess I was kiddin' about that flower piece for Hughie costing a hundred bucks? Well, I ain't! I didn't give a damn what it cost. It was up to me to give Hughie a big-time send-off, because I knew nobody else would.

NIGHT CLERK   Oh, I'm not doubting your word, Erie. You won the money gambling, I suppose— I mean, I beg your pardon if I'm mistaken, but you are a gambler, aren't you?

ERIE   (*preoccupied*) . Yeah, sure, when I got scratch to put up. What of it? But I don't win that hundred bucks. I don't win a bet since Hughie was took to the hospital. I had to get down on my knees and beg every guy I know for a sawbuck here and a sawbuck there until I raised it.

NIGHT CLERK   (*his mind concentrated on the Big Ideal—insistently*) . Do you by any chance know—Arnold Rothstein?

ERIE   (*his train of thought interrupted—irritably*) . Arnold? What's he got to do with it? He wouldn't loan a guy like me a nickel to save my grandmother from streetwalking.

NIGHT CLERK   (*with humble awe*) . Then you do know him!

ERIE   Sure I know the bastard. Who don't on Broadway? And he knows me—when he wants to. He uses me to run errands when there ain't no one else handy. But he ain't my trouble, Pal. My trouble is, some of these guys I put the bite on is dead wrong G's, and they expect to be paid back next Tuesday, or else I'm outa luck and have to take it on the lam, or I'll get beat up and maybe sent to a hospital. (*He suddenly rouses himself and there is something pathetically but genuinely gallant about him.*) But what the hell. I was wise I was takin' a chance. I've always took a chance, and if I lose I pay, and no welshing! It sure was worth it to give Hughie the big send-off.

(*He pauses. The* NIGHT CLERK *hasn't paid any attention except to his own dream. A question is trembling on his parted lips, but before he can get it out* ERIE *goes on gloomily*) .

But even that ain't my big worry, Charlie. My big worry is the run of bad luck I've had since Hughie got took to the hospital. Not a win.

That ain't natural. I've always been a lucky guy—lucky enough to get by and pay up, I mean. I wouldn't never worry about owing guys, like I owe them guys. I'd always know I'd make a win that'd fix it. But now I got a lousy hunch when I lost Hughie I lost my luck—I mean, I've lost the old confidence. He used to give me confidence. (*He turns away from the desk.*) No use gabbin' here all night. You can't do me no good.

(*He starts toward the elevator.*)

NIGHT CLERK (*pleadingly*). Just a minute, Erie, if you don't mind. (*With awe.*) So you're an old friend of Arnold Rothstein! Would you mind telling me if it's really true when Arnold Rothstein plays poker, one white chip is—a hundred dollars?

ERIE (*dully exasperated*). Say, for Christ's sake, what's it to you—?

(*He stops abruptly, staring probingly at the* CLERK. *There is a pause. Suddenly his face lights up with a saving revelation. He grins warmly and saunters confidently back to the desk.*)

Say, Charlie, why didn't you put me wise before, you was interested in gambling? Hell, I got you all wrong, Pal. I been tellin' myself, this guy ain't like old Hughie. He ain't got no sportin' blood. He's just a dope. (*Generously.*) Now I see you're a right guy. Shake.

(*He shoves out his hand which the* CLERK *clasps with a limp pleasure.* ERIE *goes on with gathering warmth and self-assurance.*)

That's the stuff. You and me'll get along. I'll give you all the breaks, like, I give Hughie.

NIGHT CLERK (*gracefully*). Thank you, Erie. (*Then insistently.*) Is it true when Arnold Rothstein plays poker, one white chip—

ERIE (*with magnificent carelessness*). Sets you back a hundred bucks? Sure. Why not? Arnold's in the bucks, ain't he? And when you're in the bucks, a C note is chicken feed. I ought to know, Pal. I was in the bucks when Arnold was a piker. Why, one time down in New Orleans I lit a cigar with a C note, just for a gag, y'understand. I was with a bunch of high class dolls and I wanted to see their eyes pop out—and believe me, they sure popped! After that, I coulda made 'em one at a time or all together! Hell, I once win twenty grand on a single race. That's action! A good crap game is action, too. Hell, I've been in games where there was a hundred grand in real folding money lying around the floor. That's travelin'!

(*He darts a quick glance at the* CLERK'*s face and begins to hedge warily. But he needn't. The* CLERK *sees him now as the Gambler in 492, the Friend of Arnold Rothstein—and nothing is incredible.* ERIE *goes on.*)

Of course, I wouldn't kid you. I'm not in the bucks now—not right this moment. You know how it is, Charlie. Down today and up tomorrow. I got some dough ridin' on the nose of a turtle in the 4th at Saratoga. I hear a story he'll be so full of hop, if the joc can keep him from jumpin' over the grandstand, he'll win by a mile. So if I roll in here with a blonde that'll knock your eyes out, don't be surprised. (*He winks and chuckles.*)

NIGHT CLERK (*ingratiatingly pally, smiling*). Oh, you can't surprise me that way. I've been a night clerk in New York all my life, almost. (*He tries out a wink himself.*) I'll forget the house rules, Erie.

ERIE (*dryly*). Yeah. The manager wouldn't like you to remember something he ain't heard of yet. (*Then slyly feeling his way.*) How about shootin' a little crap, Charlie? I mean just in fun, like I used to with Hughie. I know you can't afford takin' no chances. I'll stake you, see? I got a coupla bucks. We gotta use real jack or it don't look real. It's all my jack, get it? You can't lose. I just want to show you how I'll take you to the cleaners. It'll give me confidence. (*He has taken two one-dollar bills and some change from his pocket. He pushes most of it across to the* CLERK.) Here y'are. (*He produces a pair of dice—carelessly.*) Want to give these dice the once-over before we start?

NIGHT CLERK (*earnestly*). What do you think I am? I know I can trust you.

ERIE (*smiles*). You remind me a lot of Hughie, Pal. He always trusted me. Well, don't blame me if I'm lucky. (*He clicks the dice in his hand —thoughtfully.*) Y'know, it's time I quit carryin' the torch for Hughie. Hell, what's the use? It don't do him no good. He's gone. Like we all gotta go. Him yesterday, me or you tomorrow, and who cares, and what's the difference? It's all in the racket, huh? (*His soul is purged of grief, his confidence restored.*) I shoot two bits.

NIGHT CLERK (*manfully, with an excited dead-pan expression he hopes resembles Arnold Rothstein's*). I fade you.

ERIE (*throws the dice*). Four's my point. (*Gathers them up swiftly and throws them again.*) Four it is. (*He takes the money.*) Easy when you got my luck—and know how. Huh, Charlie?

(*He chuckles, giving the* NIGHT CLERK *the slyly amused, contemptuous, affectionate wink with which a Wise Guy regales a Sucker.*)

HUGHIE: A DRAUGHT OF THE FINEST VINTAGE

JOHN HENRY RALEIGH

Hughie was written in 1942 and was one of O'Neill's last creative efforts. Although he was to live until 1953, O'Neill suffered during his last years

John Henry Raleigh, a professor of English at the University of California, Berkeley, is the author of a full-length study of Eugene O'Neill.

from a mysterious nervous ailment which progressively robbed him of motor control. The first symptom was a trembling of the hands, which for a writer who could compose only in a longhand (he attempted dictation but could not function that way) was peculiarly tragic. His dramatic ambitions had been immense, including a vast cycle of from nine to eleven plays covering American history from 1789 to the 1930s and detailing the lives of the successive generations of an Irish-American family. But he only succeeded in finishing *A Touch of the Poet*. When it became apparent that he would be physically unable to complete the rest of the plays, many of which existed in fairly advanced and detailed form, he destroyed the manuscripts. (*More Stately Mansions,* unfinished, alone survived, by accident and was produced in New York in 1967.) He had also planned, in a more minor key, a series of from six to eight one-act plays to be called *By Way of Orbit*. Of these only *Hughie* was finished and thus survived. What the others would have been we can only guess, but the presumption is that they would have been similar to *Hughie.* As O'Neill put it, in rather general terms in a letter to the dramatic critic George Jean Nathan, who had read and approved the manuscript of *Hughie:* "It [*Hughie*] has its own quality, I think which makes it a bit different from anything else of that kind—at least, as far as my knowledge goes. And it gives you an idea of how the others in the series will be done."

Hughie is simultaneously a compendium of familiar O'Neill themes and devices and a new departure into new realms. As for the familiar, first, O'Neill had gained his initial fame during the years of World War I with a series of one-act plays about the sea and sailors. In these plays the characters were "bottom dogs"; the mood was often elegiac or sad although punctuated by humor; and the dialogue, American slang or racial dialects, was the opposite of standard English. *Hughie* then is, in some senses, a return to the mode and the mood that began his career. Further, O'Neill had in his early days written one one-act play, *Before Breakfast,* that had only two characters in it and whose action consisted of a monologue by one of them.

Moreover, in his career as a whole, O'Neill was consistently occupied with the themes and concerns that are embodied in *Hughie.* If all these concerns could be subsumed under one heading or generalization, it would be simply that life is a tragic affair. A friend of O'Neill once remarked that the playwright had ". . . six senses. Sight, smell, taste, touch, hearing, and tragedy. The last is by far the most highly developed." This tragic sense was not so much a matter of one single factor, as, for example, in the novels of Thomas Hardy a blind Fate or Necessity arbitrarily rules over the destinies of individuals, as it is a concatenation of inescapable circumstances that comprise the human condition. No one circumstance has priority, but an abstract enumeration of them all would go something like this: Individual men and women are born and remain incurably lonely. They crave social converse and real communion with others, but they have almost insuperable difficulties in communicating with one another or in reaching one another in any way except in a superficial or conventional fashion. The fact of death, one's own and that of others, is *the* ubiquitous fact of human life and constitutes the only certainty for all human beings; from nothing, through nothing, to nothing is the paradigm of life. Society is heartless, indifferent, and ruthless: Early it separates those who are not strong enough or tough enough for the merciless scramble for worldly success and drives them to the wall. Especially is this true of the modern city where "the bottom dog" is reduced to the very fringes of material and emotional existence and must live a life of intolerable boredom (the Night Clerk) or of extraordinarily hand-to-mouth precariousness (Erie). In the face of all this, the only defense the individual has is the cultivation of illusions, the palliation of reality by an act of the imagination, the harmless, primordial, all-too-human indulgence of the daydream. And the dreams themselves can be both negative and positive: Thus the Night Clerk imagines how much pleasure it would give him if all of New York burned down, while Erie dreams of the imagined felicities of a royal flush with a big pot on the gambling table.

But, obviously, this brief abstraction of the nature of the human tragedy in O'Neill's world does not fully explain or encompass the meaning of *Hughie,* which, in its totality, is one of the few essentially optimistic or "happy" plays that O'Neill ever wrote.

Thus as *Hughie* is familiar O'Neill in some ways, it is a new departure in others, both in the content and in the form. As for the content, first, most of O'Neill's tragedies come to rest on the fact that, in Sartre's phrase, there is "no way out." Although the tragedy is inescapable, illusions are only illusions and as defenses against the monstrous onslaughts of reality, they are not only useless but pernicious since they lead away from the truth. This is one of the themes of *Beyond the Horizon* (1920), O'Neill's first full-length tragedy. O'Neill was a young man when he wrote this play, but when he wrote *Hughie* he was in his fifties, was suffering from a progressive and inexorable disease, was just about at the end of his writing career, and had learned something about the role and function of illusions in human life and about the relationship between them and reality that was simultaneously wiser, more pathetic, and, strangely enough, happier than his previous assumptions. For one thing, he learned that there was no such thing as a permanent and unequivocal commitment to either illusion or reality, or, to put it another way, that a bearable life was some kind of constantly shifting compromise between the claims of the real and those of the illusory. As his contemporary Theodore Dreiser expressed it, paradoxically: "Woe to him who places his faith in illusion—the only reality—and woe to him who does not." Further he had learned that there can be a kind of communism of illusions, a joint-stock relationship whereby two human beings can share in the illusion capital of one, as the deceased Hughie and the living Charlie Hughes vicariously participate in the imaginary glamour of Erie's really pathetic existence. Finally, O'Neill had learned that the ultimate horror of human existence was loneliness and that the means by which two human beings came together and formed a relationship did not matter. All that mattered was the relationship itself. Thus the turning point of *Hughie* comes when a strange and terrible silence falls upon the night, and with Erie finally silent and dejected, the Night Clerk suddenly realizes that another human being has been trying to step into his consciousness: "I should have paid 492 more attention. After all, he is company. He is awake and alive. I should use him to help me live through the night." Thus Erie is enabled finally to turn from death, his obsequies for Hughie, to life; and a new, unique, and momentarily joyful human relationship, founded and nourished on fantasy, is formed between two human beings. As Henry Hewes said in his review of the Stockholm production of *Hughie,* "The interdependence of human beings, even when it is selfishly motivated, contains a divine element of love."

The form of *Hughie* also represents a new departure in that a good part of it, the inner consciousness of the Night Clerk, is unspoken. O'Neill himself was aware of this problem for the production of the play and suggested that perhaps in addition to the spoken monologue of Erie there would have to be as well a sound track or a filmed background to convey the thoughts of the Clerk. "It would require tremendous imagination," he said. "Let whoever does it figure it out. I won't be around to see it." *Hughie* has now been produced twice, once in Sweden and once in the United States, with Jason Robards as Erie. The American production was magnificent, simultaneously very funny and very sad, and those who saw it realized that O'Neill's last work was a great play, ranking with the one-act plays of Chekhov or Strindberg, even though, with a mostly silent Night Clerk, a very important part of the play was missing. It is still then, in the full sense of the word, "unproduced," awaiting that "tremendous imagination" to put it fully on the stage.

WILDER

THORNTON WILDER (1897–   ) WAS BORN IN MADISON, WISCONSIN. HIS DRA-
MATIC WRITINGS CONSIST OF ONLY FIVE PRODUCED AND PUBLISHED FULL-
LENGTH PLAYS, ABOUT A DOZEN ONE-ACT PLAYS, AND A FEW TRANSLATIONS
AND ADAPTATIONS.* DESPITE SO MODEST A CORPUS OF STAGE WORKS, WILDER
ENJOYS ONE OF THE MOST DURABLE REPUTATIONS WHICH, LIKE O'NEILL'S, IS
TRULY INTERNATIONAL. A TEACHER OF FRENCH WHEN THE SUCCESS OF *THE
BRIDGE OF SAN LUIS REY*, IN 1927, MADE HIM FAMOUS AT THIRTY, HE PUBLISHED
HIS MOST RECENT NOVEL, *THE EIGHTH DAY*, IN 1967. IN THE FORTY YEARS
BETWEEN, HE WROTE HIS PLAYS: *THE LONG CHRISTMAS DINNER AND OTHER
ONE-ACT PLAYS* (1931); *OUR TOWN* (1938); *THE SKIN OF OUR TEETH* (1942);
THE MATCHMAKER (1954); *A LIFE IN THE SUN* (*THE ALCESTIAD*) (1955); AND
PLAYS FOR BLEECKER STREET (1962). WILDER HAS TAUGHT AT BOTH THE
UNIVERSITY OF CHICAGO AND HARVARD AND SERVED IN BOTH WORLD WARS.

In contrast with Eugene O'Neill, whose plays are closely interwoven with
the fabric of his personal life, Wilder is an objectivist, dramatizing life
that is characteristically American but in no sense autobiographical. He
combines the impressions of a keen observer with the recollections of an
appreciative reader and, through the filter of his highly inventive imagination, fashions plays which are uniquely his own.

The Matchmaker, for example, has an ancestry so complicated that
only a scholar grounded in Greek, Roman, French, English, and Austrian drama could recognize all its sources. Although Wilder based his
play on Nestroy's *Einen Jux Will Es Sich Machen,* he was conscious
enough of Molière's *The Miser* to incorporate from it a scene between
Frosine and Harpagon. Frosine is clearly a prototype of Dolly Levi, just
as Harpagon is of Vandergelder. But Dolly is ultimately Wilder's creation, as memorable and original as one of Dickens' great comic characters.

In restructuring his play from his sources so that the focus shifts from
the merchant to the matchmaker, Wilder has materially altered the entire tone of his farce. The cutting edge of Molière's rational comedy-
satire is transformed into a gentler, more affirmative observation about
the conflict between the generations.

It can be said that Wilder transforms essentially European farce materials into authentic Americana. Do the comic effects of *The Matchmaker* stem from the universality of the characters and situations, or do
we recognize in them a commentary on some of the absurd but somehow
endearing aspects of our national attitudes and behavior? What are
those aspects?

Wilder, we observed, takes an affirmative view of life. Affirmation is
often associated with sentimentality and evasions of reality. How does
Wilder avoid—if you believe he does—false sentiment and false optimism?

* One of the five, *The Trumpet Shall Sound,* is a youthful work written when Wilder was an
undergraduate. The *Alcestiad* has not been produced nor published in the United States.

THE MATCHMAKER

CHARACTERS

HORACE VANDERGELDER,   *a merchant*
  of Yonkers, New York
CORNELIUS HACKL ⎤
BARNABY TUCKER ⎬ *clerks in his store*
MALACHI STACK   ⎦
AMBROSE KEMPER, *an artist*
JOE SCANLON, *a barber*
RUDOLPH ⎤
AUGUST ⎬ *waiters*
A CABMAN ⎦

MRS. DOLLY LEVI   ⎤ *friends of*
                           ⎬ *Vandergelder's*
MISS FLORA VAN HUYSEN ⎦ *late wife*
MRS. IRENE MOLLOY, *a milliner*
MINNIE FAY, *her assistant*
ERMENGARDE, *Vandergelder's niece*
GERTRUDE, *Vandergelder's housekeeper*
MISS VAN HUYSEN'S COOK

TIME: *The early 80's.*

ACT I

*Living room of Mr. Vandergelder's house, over his hay, feed and provision
store in Yonkers, fifteen miles north of New York City. Articles from the
store have overflowed into this room; it has not been cleaned for a long
time and is in some disorder, but it is not sordid or gloomy.*

*There are three entrances. One at the center back leads into the princi-
pal rooms of the house. One on the back right (all the directions are
from the point of view of the actors) opens on steps which descend to
the street door. One on the left leads to Ermengarde's room.*

*In the center of the room is a trap door; below it is a ladder descend-
ing to the store below.*

*Behind the trap door and to the left of it is a tall accountant's desk; to
the left of it is an old-fashioned stove with a stovepipe going up into the
ceiling. Before the desk is a tall stool. On the right of the stage is a table
with some chairs about it.*

*Mr. Vandergelder's Gladstone bag, packed for a journey, is beside the
desk.*

It is early morning.

(VANDERGELDER, *sixty, choleric, vain and sly, wears a soiled dressing gown. He is seated with a towel about his neck, in a chair beside the desk, being shaved by* JOE SCANLON. VANDERGELDER *is smoking a cigar and holding a hand mirror.* AMBROSE KEMPER *is angrily striding about the room.*)

VANDERGELDER   (*loudly*). I tell you for the hundreth time you will never marry my niece.

AMBROSE   (*thirty; dressed as an "artist"*). And I tell you for the thousandth time that I will marry your niece; and right soon, too.

VANDERGELDER.   Never!

AMBROSE.   Your niece is of age, Mr. Vandergelder. Your niece has consented to marry me. This is a free country, Mr. Vandergelder—not a private kingdom of your own.

VANDERGELDER.   There are no free countries for fools, Mr. Kemper. Thank you for the honor of your visit—good morning.

JOE   (*fifty; lanky, mass of gray hair falling into his eyes*). Mr. Vandergelder, will you please sit still one minute? If I cut your throat it'll be practically unintentional.

VANDERGELDER.   Ermengarde is not for you, nor for anybody else who can't support her.

AMBROSE.   I tell you I can support her. I make a very good living.

VANDERGELDER.   No, sir! a living is made, Mr. Kemper, by selling something that everybody needs at least once a year. Yes, sir! And a million is made by producing something that everybody needs every day. You artists produce something that nobody needs at any time. You may sell a picture once in a while, but you'll make no living. Joe, go over there and stamp three times. I want to talk to Cornelius. (JOE *crosses to trap door and stamps three times.*)

AMBROSE.   Not only can I support her now, but I have considerable expectations.

VANDERGELDER.   *Expectations!* We merchants don't do business with them. I don't keep accounts with people who promise somehow to pay something someday, and I don't allow my niece to marry such people.

AMBROSE.   Very well, from now on you might as well know that I regard any way we can find to get married is right and fair. Ermengarde is of age, and there's no law . . . (VANDERGELDER *rises and crosses toward* AMBROSE. JOE SCANLON *follows him complainingly and tries to find a chance to cut his hair even while he is standing.*)

VANDERGELDER.   Law? Let me tell you something, Mr. Kemper: most of the people in the world are fools. The law is there to prevent crime; we men of sense are there to prevent foolishness. It's I, and not the law, that will prevent Ermengarde from marrying you, and I've taken some steps already. I've sent her away to get this nonsense out of her head.

AMBROSE. Ermengarde's . . . not here?

VANDERGELDER. She's gone—east, west, north, south. I thank you for the honor of your visit. (*Enter* GERTRUDE—*eighty; deaf; half blind; and very pleased with herself.*)

GERTRUDE. Everything's ready, Mr. Vandergelder. Ermengarde and I have just finished packing the trunk.

VANDERGELDER. Hold your tongue! (JOE *is shaving* VANDERGELDER'*s throat, so he can only wave his hands vainly.*)

GERTRUDE. Yes, Mr. Vandergelder, Ermengarde's ready to leave. Her trunk's all marked. Care Miss Van Huysen, 8 Jackson Street, New York.

VANDERGELDER (*breaking away from Joe*). Hell and damnation! Didn't I tell you it was a secret?

AMBROSE (*picks up hat and coat—kisses* GERTRUDE). Care Miss Van Huysen, 8 Jackson Street, New York. Thank you very much. Good morning, Mr. Vandergelder. (*Exit* AMBROSE, *to the street.*)

VANDERGELDER. It won't help you, Mr. Kemper— (*To* GERTRUDE.) Deaf! And blind! At least you can do me the favor of being dumb!

GERTRUDE. Chk—chk! Such a temper! Lord save us! (CORNELIUS *puts his head up through the trap door. He is thirty-three; mock-deferential— he wears a green apron and is in his shirt-sleeves.*)

CORNELIUS. Yes, Mr. Vandergelder?

VANDERGELDER. Go in and get my niece's trunk and carry it over to the station. Wait! Gertrude, has Mrs. Levi arrived yet? (CORNELIUS *comes up the trap door, and steps into the room and closes the trap door behind him.*)

GERTRUDE. Don't shout. I can hear perfectly well. Everything's clearly marked. (*Exit left.*)

VANDERGELDER. Have the buggy brought round to the front of the store in half an hour.

CORNELIUS. Yes, Mr. Vandergelder.

VANDERGELDER. . . This morning I'm joining my lodge parade and this afternoon I'm going to New York. Before I go, I have something important to say to you and Barnaby. Good news. Fact is—I'm going to promote you. How old are you?

CORNELIUS. Thirty-three, Mr. Vandergelder.

VANDERGEDLER. What?

CORNELIUS. Thirty-three.

VANDERGELDER. That all? That's a foolish age to be at. I thought you were forty.

CORNELIUS. Thirty-three.

VANDERGELDER. A man's not worth a cent until he's forty. We just pay 'em wages to make mistakes—don't we, Joe?

JOE. You almost lost an ear on it, Mr. Vandergelder.

VANDERGELDER. I was thinking of promoting you to chief clerk.

CORNELIUS. What am I now, Mr. Vandergelder?

VANDERGELDER. You're an impertinent fool, that's what you are. Now, if you behave yourself, I'll promote you from impertinent fool to chief clerk, with a raise in your wages. And Barnaby may be promoted from idiot apprentice to incompetent clerk.

CORNELIUS. Thank you, Mr. Vandergelder.

VANDERGELDER. However, I want to see you again before I go. Go in and get my niece's trunk.

CORNELIUS. Yes, Mr. Vandergelder, (*Exit* CORNELIUS, *left.*)

VANDERGELDER. Joe—the world's getting crazier every minute. Like my father used to say: the horses'll be taking over the world soon.

JOE (*presenting mirror*). I did what I could, Mr. Vandergelder, what with you flying in and out of the chair. (*He wipes the last of the soap from* VANDERGELDER's *face.*)

VANDERGELDER. Fine, fine, Joe, you do a fine job, the same fine job you've done me for twenty years. Joe . . . I've got special reasons for looking my best today . . . isn't there something a little extry you could do, something a little special? I'll pay you right up to fifty cents —see what I mean? Do some of those things you do to the young fellas. Touch me up; smarten me up a bit.

JOE. All I know is fifteen cents' worth, like usual, Mr. Vandergelder; and that includes everything that's decent to do to a man.

VANDERGELDER. Now hold your horses, Joe—all I meant was . . .

JOE. I've shaved you for twenty years and you never asked me no such question before.

VANDERGELDER. Hold your horses, I say, Joe! I'm going to tell you a secret. But I don't want you telling it to that riffraff down to the barbershop what I'm going to tell you now. All I ask of you is a little extry because I'm thinking of getting married again; and this very afternoon I'm going to New York to call on my intended, a very refined lady.

JOE. Your gettin' married is none of my business, Mr. Vandergelder. I done everything to you I know, and the charge is fifteen cents like it always was, and . . . (CORNELIUS *crosses, left to right, and exit, carrying a trunk on his shoulder.* ERMENGARDE *and* GERTRUDE *enter from left*). I don't dye no hair, not even for fifty cents I don't!

VANDERGELDER. Joe Scanlon, get out!

JOE. And lastly, it looks to me like you're pretty rash to judge which is fools and which isn't fools, Mr. Vandergelder. People that's et onions is bad judges of who's et onions and who ain't. Good morning, ladies; good morning, Mr. Vandergelder. (*Exit* JOE.)

VANDERGELDER. Well, what do you want?

ERMENGARDE (*twenty-four; pretty, sentimental*). Uncle! You said you wanted to talk to us.

VANDERGELDER. Oh yes. Gertrude, go and get my parade regalia—the uniform for my lodge parade.

GERTRUDE. What? Oh yes. Lord have mercy! (*Exit* GERTRUDE, *back center.*)

VANDERGELDER. I had a talk with that artist of yours. He's a fool. (ERMENGARDE *starts to cry.*) Weeping! Weeping! You can go down and weep for a while in New York where it won't be noticed. (*He sits on desk chair, puts tie round neck and calls her over to tie it for him.*) Ermengarde! I told him that when you were old enough to marry you'd marry someone who could support you. I've done you a good turn. You'll come and thank me when you're fifty.

ERMENGARDE. But Uncle, I love him!

VANDERGELDER. I tell you you don't.

ERMENGARDE. But I *do!*

VANDERGELDER. And I tell you you don't. Leave those things to me.

ERMENGARDE. If I don't marry Ambrose I know I'll die.

VANDERGELDER. What of?

ERMENGARDE. A broken heart.

VANDERGELDER. Never heard of it. Mrs. Levi is coming in a moment to take you to New York. You are going to stay two or three weeks with Miss Van Huysen, an old friend of your mother's. (GERTRUDE *re-enters with coat, sash and sword. Enter from the street, right,* MALACHI STACK.) You're not to receive any letters except from me. I'm coming to New York myself today and I'll call on you tomorrow. (*To* MALACHI.) Who are you?

MALACHI (*fifty. Sardonic. Apparently innocent smile; pretense of humility*). Malachi Stack, your honor. I heard you wanted an apprentice in the hay, feed, provision and hardware business.

VANDERGELDER. An apprentice at your age?

MALACHI. Yes, your honor; I bring a lot of experience to it.

VANDERGELDER. Have you any letters of recommendation?

MALACHI (*extending a sheaf of soiled papers*). Yes, indeed, your honor! First-class recommendation.

VANDERGELDER. Ermengarde! Are you ready to start?

ERMENGARDE. Yes.

VANDERGELDER. Well, go and get ready some more. Ermengarde! Let me know the minute Mrs. Levi gets here.

ERMENGARDE. Yes, Uncle Horace. (ERMENGARDE *and* GERTRUDE *exit.* VANDERGELDER *examines the letters, putting them down one by one.*)

VANDERGELDER. I don't want an able seaman. Nor a typesetter. And I don't want a hospital cook.

MALACHI. No, your honor, but it's all experience. Excuse me! (*Selects a letter.*) This one is from your former partner, Joshua Van Tuyl, in Albany. (*He puts letters from table back into pocket.*)

VANDERGELDER. ". . . for the most part honest and reliable . . . occasionally willing and diligent." There seems to be a certain amount of hesitation about these recommendations.

MALACHI. Businessmen aren't writers, your honor. There's only one businessman in a thousand that can write a good letter of recommendation, your honor. Mr. Van Tuyl sends his best wishes and wants to know if you can use me in the provision and hardware business.

VANDERGELDER. Not so fast, not so fast! What's this "your honor" you use so much?

MALACHI. Mr. Van Tuyl says you're President of the Hudson River Provision Dealers' Recreational, Musical and Burial Society.

VANDERGELDER. I am; but there's no "your honor" that goes with it. Why did you come to Yonkers?

MALACHI. I heard that you'd had an apprentice that was a good-for-nothing, and that you were at your wit's end for another.

VANDERGELDER. Wit's end, wit's end! There's no dearth of good-for-nothing apprentices.

MALACHI. That's right, Mr. Vandergelder. It's employers there's a dearth of. Seems like you hear of a new one dying every day.

VANDERGELDER. What's that? Hold your tongue. I see you've been a barber, and a valet too. Why have you changed your place so often?

MALACHI. Changed my place, Mr. Vandergelder? When a man's interested in experience . . .

VANDERGELDER. Do you drink?

MALACHI. No, thanks. I've just had breakfast.

VANDERGELDER. I didn't ask you whether—Idiot! I asked you if you were a drunkard.

MALACHI. No, sir! No! Why, looking at it from all sides I don't even like liquor.

VANDERGELDER. Well, if you keep on looking at it from all sides, out you go. Remember that. Here. (*Gives him remaining letters.*) With all your faults, I'm going to give you a try.

MALACHI. You'll never regret it, Mr. Vandergelder. You'll never regret it.

VANDERGELDER. Now today I want to use you in New York. I judge you know your way around New York.

MALACHI. Do I know New York? Mr. Vandergelder, I know every hole and corner in New York.

VANDERGELDER. Here's a dollar. A train leaves in a minute. Take that bag to the Central Hotel on Water Street, have them save me a room. Wait for me. I'll be there about four o'clock.

MALACHI. Yes, Mr. Vandergelder. (*Picks up the bag, starts out, then comes back.*) Oh, but first, I'd like to meet the other clerks I'm to work with.

VANDERGELDER. You haven't time. Hurry now. The station's across the street.

MALACHI. Yes, sir. Away—then back once more. You'll see, sir, you'll never regret it. . . .

VANDERGELDER. I regret it already. Go on. Off with you. (*Exit* MALACHI, *right. The following speech is addressed to the audience. During it* MR. VANDERGELDER *takes off his dressing gown, puts on his scarlet sash, his sword and his bright-colored coat. He is already wearing light blue trousers with a red stripe down the sides.*)

VANDERGELDER. Ninety-nine per cent of the people in the world are fools and the rest of us are in great danger of contagion. But I wasn't always free of foolishness as I am now. I was once young, which was foolish; I fell in love, which was foolish; and I got married, which was foolish; and for a while I was poor, which was more foolish than all the other things put together. Then my wife died, which was foolish of her; I grew older, which was sensible of me; then I became a rich man, which is as sensible as it is rare. Since you see I'm a man of sense, I guess you were surprised to hear that I'm planning to get married again. Well, I've two reasons for it. In the first place, I like my house run with order, comfort and economy. That's a woman's work; but even a woman can't do it well if she's merely being paid for it. In order to run a house well, a woman must have the feeling that she owns it. Marriage is a bribe to make a housekeeper think she's a householder. Did you ever watch an ant carry a burden twice its size? What excitement! What patience! What will! Well, that's what I think of when I see a woman running a house. What giant passions in those little bodies— what quarrels with the butcher for the best cut—what fury at discovering a moth in a cupboard! Believe me!—if women could harness their natures to something bigger than a house and a baby carriage— tck! tck!—they'd change the world. And the second reason, ladies and gentlemen? Well, I see by your faces you've guessed it already. There's nothing like mixing with women to bring out all the foolishness in a man of sense. And that's a risk I'm willing to take. I've just turned sixty, and I've just laid side by side the last dollar of my first half million. So if I should lose my head a little, I still have enough money to buy it back. After many years' caution and hard work, I have earned a right to a little risk and adventure, and I'm thinking of getting married. Yes, like all you other fools, I'm willing to risk a little security for a certain amount of adventure. Think it over. (*Exit back center.* AMBROSE *enters from the street, crosses left, and whistles softly.* ERMENGARDE *enters from left.*)

ERMENGARDE. Ambrose! If my uncle saw you!

AMBROSE. Sh! Get your hat.

ERMENGARDE. My hat!

AMBROSE. Quick! Your trunk's at the station. Now quick! We're running away.

ERMENGARDE. Running away!

AMBROSE. Sh.

ERMENGARDE. Where?

AMBROSE. To New York. To get married.

ERMENGARDE. Oh, Ambrose, I can't do that. Ambrose dear—it wouldn't be proper!

AMBROSE. Listen. I'm taking you to my friend's house. His wife will take care of you.

ERMENGARDE. But, Ambrose, a girl can't go on a train with a man. I can see you don't know anything about girls.

AMBROSE. But I'm telling you we're going to get married!

ERMENGARDE. Married! But what would *Uncle* say?

AMBROSE. We don't care what Uncle'd say—we're eloping.

ERMENGARDE. Ambrose Kemper! How can you use such an awful word!

AMBROSE. Ermengarde, you have the soul of a field mouse.

ERMENGARDE. Ambrose, why do you say such cruel things to me? (*Enter* MRS. LEVI, *from the street, right. She stands listening.*)

AMBROSE. For the last time I beg you—get your hat and coat. The train leaves in a few minutes. Ermengarde, we'll get married tomorrow. . . .

ERMENGARDE. Oh, Ambrose! I see you don't understand anything about weddings. Ambrose, don't you *respect* me? . . .

MRS. LEVI (*uncertain age; mass of sandy hair; impoverished elegance; large, shrewd but generous nature, an assumption of worldly cynicism conceals a tireless amused enjoyment of life. She carries a handbag and a small brown paper bag*) . Good morning, darling girl—how are you? (*They kiss.*)

ERMENGARDE. Oh, good morning, Mrs. Levi.

MRS. LEVI. And who is this gentleman who is so devoted to you?

ERMENGARDE. This is Mr. Kemper, Mrs. Levi. Ambrose, this is . . . Mrs. Levi . . . she's an old friend. . . .

MRS. LEVI. Mrs. Levi, born Gallagher. Very happy to meet you, Mr. Kemper.

AMBROSE. Good morning, Mrs. Levi.

MRS. LEVI. Mr. Kemper, *the artist!* Delighted! Mr. Kemper, may I say something very frankly?

AMBROSE. Yes, Mrs. Levi.

MRS. LEVI. This thing you were planning to do is a very great mistake.

ERMENGARDE. Oh, Mrs. Levi, please explain to Ambrose—of *course!* I want to marry him, but to *elope!* . . . How . . .

MRS. LEVI. Now, my dear girl, you go in and keep one eye on your uncle.

I wish to talk to Mr. Kemper for a moment. You give us a warning when you hear your Uncle Horace coming. . . .

ERMENGARDE. Ye-es, Mrs. Levi. (*Exit* ERMENGARDE, *back center.*)

MRS. LEVI. Mr. Kemper, I was this dear girl's mother's oldest friend. Believe me, I am on your side. I hope you two will be married very soon, and I think I can be of real service to you. Mr. Kemper, I always go right to the point.

AMBROSE. What is the point, Mrs. Levi?

MRS. LEVI. Mr. Vandergelder is a very rich man, Mr. Kemper, and Ermengarde is his only relative.

AMBROSE. But I am not interested in Mr. Vandergelder's money. I have enough to support a wife and family.

MRS. LEVI. Enough? How much is enough when one is thinking about children and the future? The future is the most expensive luxury in the world, Mr. Kemper.

AMBROSE. Mrs. Levi, what is the point.

MRS. LEVI. Believe me, Mr. Vandergelder wishes to get rid of Ermengarde, and if you will follow my suggestions he will even permit her to marry you. You see, Mr. Vandergelder is planning to get married himself.

AMBROSE. What? That monster!

MRS. LEVI. Mr. Kemper!

AMBROSE. Married! To you, Mrs. Levi?

MRS. LEVI (*taken aback*). Oh, no, no . . . NO! I am merely arranging it. I am helping him find a suitable bride.

AMBROSE. For Mr. Vandergelder there are no suitable brides.

MRS. LEVI. I think we can safely say that Mr. Vandergelder will be married to someone by the end of next week.

AMBROSE. What are you suggesting, Mrs. Levi?

MRS. LEVI. I am taking Ermengarde to New York on the next train. I shall not take her to Miss Van Huysen's, as is planned; I shall take her to my house. I wish you to call for her at my house at five thirty. Here is my card.

AMBROSE. "Mrs. Dolly Gallagher Levi. Varicose veins reduced."

MRS. LEVI (*trying to take back card*). I beg your pardon . . .

AMBROSE (*holding card*). I beg *your* pardon. "Consultations free."

MRS. LEVI. I meant to give you my other card. Here.

AMBROSE. "Mrs. Dolly Gallagher Levi. Aurora Hosiery. Instruction in the guitar and mandolin." You do all these things, Mrs. Levi?

MRS. LEVI. Two and two make four, Mr. Kemper—always did. So you will come to my house at five thirty. At about six I shall take you both with me to the Harmonia Gardens Restaurant on the Battery; Mr. Vandergelder will be there and everything will be arranged.

AMBROSE. How?

MRS. LEVI. Oh, I don't know. One thing will lead to another.

AMBROSE. How do I know that I can trust you, Mrs. Levi? You could easily make our situation worse.

MRS. LEVI. Mr. Kemper, your situation could not possibly be worse.

AMBROSE. I wish I knew what you get out of this, Mrs. Levi.

MRS. LEVI. That is a very proper question. I get two things: profit and pleasure.

AMBROSE. How?

MRS. LEVI. Mr. Kemper, I am a woman who arranges things. At present I am arranging Mr. Vandergelder's domestic affairs. Out of it I get— shall we call it: little pickings? I need little pickings, Mr. Kemper, and especially just now, when I haven't got my train fare back to New York. You see: I am frank with you.

AMBROSE. That's your profit, Mrs. Levi; but where do you get your pleasure?

MRS. LEVI. My pleasure? Mr. Kemper, when you artists paint a hillside or a river you change everything a little, you make thousands of little changes, don't you? Nature is never completely satisfactory and must be corrected. Well, I'm like you artists. Life as it is is never quite interesting enough for me—I'm bored, Mr. Kemper, with life as it is— and so I do things. I put my hand in here, and I put my hand in there, and I watch and listen—and often I'm very much amused.

AMBROSE *(rises)*. Not in my affairs, Mrs. Levi.

MRS. LEVI. Wait, I haven't finished. There's another thing. I'm very interested in this household here—in Mr. Vandergelder and all that idle, frozen money of his. I don't like the thought of it lying in great piles, useless, motionless, in the bank, Mr. Kemper. Money should circulate like rain water. It should be flowing down among the people, through dressmakers and restaurants and cabmen, setting up a little business here, and furnishing a good time there. Do you see what I mean?

AMBROSE. Yes, I do.

MRS. LEVI. New York should be a very happy city, Mr. Kemper, but it isn't. My late husband came from Vienna; now there's a city that understands this. I want New York to be more like Vienna and less like a collection of nervous and tired ants. And if you and Ermengarde get a good deal of Mr. Vandergelder's money, I want you to see that it starts flowing in and around a lot of people's lives. And for that reason I want you to come with me to the Harmonia Gardens Restaurant tonight. *(Enter* ERMENGARDE.*)*

ERMENGARDE. Mrs. Levi, Uncle Horace is coming.

MRS. LEVI. Mr. Kemper, I think you'd better be going. . . . (AMBROSE *crosses to trap door and disappears down the ladder, closing trap as he goes.*) Darling girl, Mr. Kemper and I have had a very good talk. You'll see: Mr. Vandergelder and I will be dancing at your wedding very soon —(*Enter* VANDERGELDER *at back. He has now added a splendid plumed hat to his costume and is carrying a standard or small flag bearing the initials of his lodge.*) Oh, Mr. Vandergelder, how handsome you look! You take my breath away. Yes, my dear girl, I'll see you soon. (*Exit* ERMENGARDE *back center.*) Oh, Mr. Vandergelder, I wish Irene Molloy could see you now. But then! I don't know what's come over you lately. You seem to be growing younger every day.

VANDERGELDER. Allowing for exaggeration, Mrs. Levi. If a man eats careful there's no reason why he should look old.

MRS. LEVI. You never said a truer word.

VANDERGELDER. I'll never see fifty-five again.

MRS. LEVI. Fifty-five! Why, I can see at a glance that you're the sort that will be stamping about at a hundred—and eating five meals a day, like my Uncle Harry. At fifty-five my Uncle Harry was a mere boy. I'm a judge of hands, Mr. Vandergelder—show me your hand. (*Looks at it.*) Lord in heaven! What a life line!

VANDERGELDER. Where?

MRS. LEVI. From *here* to *here*. It runs right off your hand. I don't know where it goes. They'll have to hit you on the head with a mallet. They'll have to stifle you with a sofa pillow. You'll bury us all! However, to return to our business—Mr. Vandergelder, I suppose you've changed your mind again. I suppose you've given up all idea of getting married.

VANDERGELDER (*complacently*). Not at all, Mrs. Levi. I have news for you.

MRS. LEVI. News?

VANDERGELDER. Mrs. Levi, I've practically decided to ask Mrs. Molloy to be my wife.

MRS. LEVI (*taken aback*). You have?

VANDERGELDER. Yes, I have.

MRS. LEVI. Oh, you have! Well, I guess that's just about the best news I ever heard. So there's nothing more for me to do but wish you every happiness under the sun and say good-by. (*Crosses as if to leave.*)

VANDERGELDER (*stopping her*). Well—Mrs. Levi—Surely I thought—

MRS. LEVI. Well, I did have a little suggestion to make—but I won't. You're going to marry Irene Molloy, and that closes the matter.

VANDERGELDER. What suggestion was that, Mrs. Levi?

MRS. LEVI. Well—I *had* found *another* girl for you.

VANDERGELDER. Another?

MRS. LEVI. The most wonderful girl, the ideal wife.

VANDERGELDER. Another, eh? What's her name?

MRS. LEVI. Her name?

VANDERGELDER. Yes!

MRS. LEVI *(groping for it)*. Err . . . er . . . her *name?*—Ernestina—
Simple. *Miss* Ernestina Simple. But now of course all that's too late.
After all, you're engaged—you're practically engaged to marry Irene
Molloy.

VANDERGELDER. Oh, I ain't engaged to Mrs. Molloy!

MRS. LEVI. Nonsense! You can't break poor Irene's heart now and change
to another girl. . . . When a man at your time of life calls four times
on an attractive widow like that—and sends her a pot of geraniums—
that's practically an engagement!

VANDERGELDER. That ain't an engagement!

MRS. LEVI. And yet—! If only you were free! I've found this treasure of
a girl. Every moment I felt like a traitor to Irene Molloy—but let me
tell you: I couldn't help it. I told this girl all about you, just as though
you were a free man. Isn't that dreadful? The fact is: she has fallen in
love with you already.

VANDERGELDER. Ernestina?

MRS. LEVI. Ernestina Simple.

VANDERGELDER. Ernestina Simple.

MRS. LEVI. Of course she's a very different idea from Mrs. Molloy, Ernestina is. Like her name—simple, domestic, practical.

VANDERGELDER. Can she cook?

MRS. LEVI. Cook, Mr. Vandergelder? I've had two meals from her hands,
and—as I live—I don't know what I've done that God should reward
me with such meals.

MRS. LEVI *(continues)*. Her duck! Her steak!

VANDERGELDER. Eh! Eh! In this house we don't eat duck and steak every
day, Mrs. Levi.

MRS. LEVI. But didn't I tell you?—that's the wonderful part about it.
Her duck—what was it? Pigeon! I'm alive to tell you. I don't know
how she does it. It's a secret that's come down in her family. The great-
est chefs would give their right hands to know it. And the steaks?
Shoulder of beef—four cents a pound. Dogs wouldn't eat. But when
Ernestina passes her hands over it—! !

VANDERGELDER. Allowing for exaggeration, Mrs. Levi.

MRS. LEVI. No exaggeration. I'm the best cook in the world myself, and
know what's good.

VANDERGELDER. Hm. How old is she, Mrs. Levi?

MRS. LEVI. Nineteen, well—say twenty.

VANDERGELDER. Twenty, Mrs. Levi? Girls of twenty are apt to favor
young fellows of their own age.

MRS. LEVI. But you don't listen to me. And you don't know the girl. Mr.

Vandergelder, she has a positive horror of flighty, brainless young men. A fine head of gray hair, she says, is worth twenty shined up with goose grease. No, sir. "I like a man that's *settled*"—in so many words she said it.

VANDERGELDER. That's . . . that's not usual, Mrs. Levi.

MRS. LEVI. Usual? I'm not wearing myself to the bone hunting up *usual* girls to interest you, Mr. Vandergelder. Usual, indeed. Listen to me. Do you know the sort of pictures she has on her wall? Is it any of these young Romeos and Lochinvars? No!—it's Moses on the Mountain— that's what she's got. If you want to make her happy, you give her a picture of Methuselah surrounded by his grandchildren. That's my advice to you.

VANDERGELDER. I hope . . . hm . . . that she has some means, Mrs. Levi. I have a large household to run.

MRS. LEVI. Ernestina? She'll bring you five thousand dollars a year.

VANDERGELDER. Eh! Eh!

MRS. LEVI. Listen to me, Mr. Vandergelder. You're a man of sense, I hope. A man that can reckon. In the first place, she's an orphan. She's been brought up with a great saving of food. What does she eat herself? Apples and lettuce. It's what she's been used to eat and what she likes best. She saves you two thousand a year right there. Secondly, she makes her own clothes—out of old tablecloths and window curtains. And she's tne best-dressed woman in Brooklyn this minute. She saves you a thousand dollars right there. Thirdly, her health is of iron—

VANDERGELDER. But, Mrs. Levi, that's not money in the pocket.

MRS. LEVI. We're talking about marriage, aren't we, Mr. Vandergelder? The money she saves while she's in Brooklyn is none of your affair— but if she were your wife that would be *money*. Yes, sir, that's money.

VANDERGELDER. What's her family?

MRS. LEVI. Her father?—God be good to him! He was the best—what am I trying to say?—the best undertaker in Brooklyn, respected, esteemed. He knew all the best people—knew them well, even before they died. So—well, that's the way it is. (*Lowering her voice, intimately.*) Now let me tell you a little more of her appearance. Can you hear me: as I say, a beautiful girl, beautiful, I've seen her go down the street—you know what I mean?—the young men get dizzy. They have to lean against lampposts. And she? Modest, eyes on the ground—I'm not going to tell you any more. . . . Couldn't you come to New York today?

VANDERGELDER. I was thinking of coming to New York this afternoon. . . .

MRS. LEVY. You were? Well, now, I wonder if something could be arranged—oh, she's so eager to see you! Let me see . . .

VANDERGELDER. Could I . . . Mrs. Levi, could I give you a little dinner, maybe?

MRS. LEVI.   Really, come to think of it, I don't see where I could get the time. I'm so busy over that wretched lawsuit of mine. Yes. If I win it, I don't mind telling you, I'll be what's called a very rich woman. I'll own half of Long Island, that's a fact. But just now I'm at my wit's end for a little help, just enough money to finish it off. My wit's end. (*She looks in her handbag. In order not to hear this,* VANDERGELDER *has a series of coughs, sneezes and minor convulsions.*) But perhaps I could arrange a little dinner; I'll see. Yes, for that lawsuit all I need is fifty dollars, and Staten Island's as good as mine. I've been trotting all over New York for you, trying to find you a suitable wife.

VANDERGELDER.   Fifty dollars! !

MRS. LEVI.   Two whole months I've been . . .

VANDERGELDER.   Fifty dollars, Mrs. Levi . . . is no joke. (*Producing purse*). I don't know where money's gone to these days. It's in hiding. . . . There's twenty . . . well, there's twenty-five. I can't spare no more, not now I can't.

MRS. LEVI.   Well, this will help—will help somewhat. Now let me tell you what we'll do. I'll bring Ernestina to that restaurant on the Battery. You know it: the Harmonia Gardens. It's good, but it's not flashy. Now, Mr. Vandergelder, I think it'd be nice if just this once you'd order a real nice dinner. I guess you can afford it.

VANDERGELDER.   Well, just this once.

MRS. LEVI.   A chicken wouldn't hurt.

VANDERGELDER.   Chicken! !—Well, just this once.

MRS. LEVI.   And a little wine.

VANDERGELDER.   Wine? Well, just this once.

MRS. LEVI.   Now about Mrs. Molloy—what do you think? Shall we call that subject closed?

VANDERGELDER.   No, not at all, Mrs. Levi, I want to have dinner with Miss . . . with Miss . . .

MRS. LEVI.   Simple.

VANDERGELDER.   With Miss Simple; but first I want to make another call on Mrs. Molloy.

MRS. LEVY.   Dear, dear, dear! And Miss Simple? What races you make me run! Very well; I'll meet you on one of those benches in front of Mrs. Molloy's hat store at four thirty, as usual. (*Trap door rises, and* COR-NELIUS' *head appears.*)

CORNELIUS.   The buggy's here, ready for the parade, Mr. Vandergelder.

VANDERGELDER.   Call Barnaby. I want to talk to both of you.

CORNELIUS.   Yes, Mr. Vandergelder. (*Exit* CORNELIUS *down trap door. Leaves trap door open.*)

MRS. LEVI.   Now do put your thoughts in order, Mr. Vandergelder. I can't keep upsetting and disturbing the finest women in New York City unless you mean business.

VANDERGELDER.   Oh, I mean business all right!

MRS. LEVI.   I hope so. Because, you know, you're playing a very dangerous game.

VANDERGELDER.   Dangerous?—Dangerous, Mrs. Levi?

MRS. LEVI.   Of course, it's dangerous—and there's a name for it! You're
tampering with these women's affections, aren't you? And the only
way you can save yourself now is to be married to *someone* by the end
of next week. So think that over! (*Exit center back. Enter* CORNELIUS
and BARNABY, *by the trap door.*)

VANDERGELDER.   This morning I'm joining my lodge parade, and this
afternoon I'm going to New York. When I come back, there are going
to be some changes in the house here. I'll tell you what the change is,
but I don't want you discussing it amongst yourselves: you're going to
have a mistress.

BARNABY   (*seventeen; round-faced, wide-eyed innocence; wearing a green
apron*) . I'm too young, Mr. Vandergelder! !

VANDERGELDER.   Not yours! Death and damnation! Not yours, idiot—
mine! (*Then, realizing*) Hey! Hold your tongue until you're spoken
to! I'm thinking of getting married.

CORNELIUS   (*crosses, hand outstretched*) . Many congratulations, Mr.
Vandergelder, and my compliments to the lady.

VANDERGELDER.   That's none of your business. Now go back to the store.
(*The* BOYS *start down the ladder,* BARNABY *first.*) Have you got any
questions you want to ask before I go?

CORNELIUS.   Mr. Vandergelder—er—Mr. Vandergelder, does the chief
clerk get one evening off every week?

VANDERGELDER.   So that's the way you begin being chief clerk, is it?
When I was your age I got up at five; I didn't close the shop until ten
at night, and then I put in a good hour at the account books. The
world's going to pieces. You elegant ladies lie in bed until six and at
nine o'clock at night you rush to close the door so fast the line of customers bark their noses. No, sir—you'll attend to the store as usual,
and on Friday and Saturday nights you'll remain open until ten—now
hear what I say! This is the first time I've been away from the store
overnight. When I come back I want to hear that you've run the place
perfectly in my absence. If I hear of any foolishness, I'll discharge you.
An evening free! Do you suppose that *I* had evenings free? (*At the
top of his complacency.*) If I'd had evenings free I wouldn't be what I
am now! (*He marches out, right.*)

BARNABY   (*watching him go*) . The horses nearly ran away when they
saw him. What's the matter, Cornelius?

CORNELIUS   (*sits in dejected thought*) . Chief clerk! Promoted from chief
clerk to chief clerk.

BARNABY.   Don't you like it?

CORNELIUS.   Chief clerk!—and if I'm good, in ten years I'll be promoted to chief clerk again. Thirty-three years old and I still don't get an evening free? When am I going to begin to live?

BARNABY.   Well—ah . . . you can begin to live on Sundays, Cornelius.

CORNELIUS.   That's not living. Twice to church, and old Wolf-trap's eyes on the back of my head the whole time. And as for holidays! What did we do last Christmas? All those canned tomatoes went bad and exploded. We had to clean up the mess all afternoon. Was that living?

BARNABY   (holding his nose at the memory of the bad smell). No! !

CORNELIUS   (rising with sudden resolution). Barnaby, how much money have you got—where you can get at it?

BARNABY.   Oh—three dollars. Why, Cornelius?

CORNELIUS.   You and I are going to New York.

BARNABY.   Cornelius! ! ! We can't! Close the store?

CORNELIUS.   Some more rotten-tomato cans are going to explode.

BARNABY.   Holy cabooses! How do you know?

CORNELIUS.   I know they're rotten. All you have to do is to light a match under them. They'll make such a smell that customers can't come into the place for twenty-four hours. That'll get us an evening free. We're going to New York too, Barnaby, we're going to live! I'm going to have enough adventures to last me until I'm *partner*. So go and get your Sunday clothes on.

BARNABY.   Wha-a-a-t?

CORNELIUS.   Yes, I mean it. We're going to have a good meal; and we're going to be in danger; and we're going to get almost arrested; and we're going to spend all our money.

BARNABY.   Holy cabooses! !

CORNELIUS.   And one more thing: we're not coming back to Yonkers until we've kissed a girl.

BARNABY.   Kissed a girl! Cornelius, you can't do that. You don't know any girls.

CORNELIUS.   I'm thirty-three. I've got to begin sometime.

BARNABY.   I'm only seventeen, Cornelius. It isn't so urgent for me.

CORNELIUS.   Don't start backing down now—if the worst comes to the worst and we get discharged from here we can always join the Army.

BARNABY.   Uh—did I hear you say that you'd be old Wolftrap's partner?

CORNELIUS.   How can I help it? He's growing old. If you go to bed at nine and open the store at six, you get promoted upward whether you like it or not.

BARNABY.   My! Partner.

CORNELIUS.   Oh, there's no way of getting away from it. You and I will be Vandergelders.

BARNABY.   I? Oh, no—I may rise a little, but I'll never be a Vandergelder.

CORNELIUS. Listen—everybody thinks when he gets rich he'll be a different kind of rich person from the rich people he sees around him, later on he finds out there's only one kind of rich person, and he's it.

BARNABY. Oh, but I'll—

CORNELIUS. No. The best of all would be a person who has all the good things a poor person has, and all the good meals a rich person has, but that's never been known. No, you and I are going to be Vandergelders; all the more reason, then, for us to try and get some living and some adventure into us now—will you come, Barnaby?

BARNABY (*in a struggle with his fears, a whirlwind of words*). But Wolf-trap—KRR-pt, Gertrude-KRR-pt— (*With a sudden cry of agreement.*) Yes, Cornelius! (*Enter* MRS. LEVI, ERMENGARDE *and* GERTRUDE *from back center. The* BOYS *start down the ladder,* CORNELIUS *last.*)

MRS. LEVI. Mr. Hackl, is the trunk waiting at the station?

CORNELIUS. Yes, Mrs. Levi. (*Closes the trap door.*)

MRS. LEVI. Take a last look, Ermengarde.

ERMENGARDE. What?

MRS. LEVI. Take a last look at your girlhood home, dear. I remember when I left my home. I gave a whinny like a young colt, and off I went (ERMENGARDE *and* GERTRUDE *exit.*)

ERMENGARDE (*as they go*). Oh, Gertrude, do you think I ought to get married this way? A young girl has to be so careful! (MRS. LEVI *is alone. She addresses the audience.*)

MRS. LEVI. You know, I think I'm going to have this room with *blue* wallpaper,—yes, in blue! (*Hurries out after the others.* BARNABY *comes up trap door, looks off right, then lies on floor, gazing down through the trap door.*)

BARNABY. All clear up here, Cornelius! Cornelius—hold the candle steady a minute—the bottom row's all right—but try the top now . . . they're swelled up like they are ready to bust! *BANG.* Holy CABOOSES! *BANG, BANG.* Cornelius! I can smell it up here! (*Rises and dances about, holding his nose.*)

CORNELIUS (*rushing up the trap door*). Get into your Sunday clothes, Barnaby. We're going to New York! (*As they run out . . . there is a big explosion. A shower of tomato cans comes up from below, as— the curtain falls.*)

ACT II

Mrs. Molloy's hat shop, New York City.

There are two entrances. One door at the extreme right of the back wall, to Mrs. Molloy's workroom; one at the back left corner, to the street. The whole left wall is taken up with the show windows, filled with hats. It is separated from the shop by a low brass rail, hung with net; during the act both Mrs. Molloy and Barnaby stoop under the rail and go into the shop window. By the street door stands a large cheval glass. In the middle of the back wall is a large wardrobe or clothes cupboard, filled with ladies' coats, large enough for Cornelius to hide in. At the left, beginning at the back wall, between the wardrobe and the workroom door, a long counter extends toward the audience, almost to the footlights. In the center of the room is a large round table with a lowhanging red cloth. There are a small gilt chair by the wardrobe and two chairs in front of the counter. Over the street door and the workroom door are bells which ring when the doors are opened.

As the curtain rises, Mrs. Molloy is in the window, standing on a box, reaching up to put hats on the stand. Minnie Fay is sewing by the counter. Mrs. Molloy has a pair of felt overshoes, to be removed later.

MRS. MOLLOY. Minnie, you're a fool. Of course I shall marry Horace Vandergelder.

MINNIE. Oh, Mrs. Molloy! I didn't ask you. I wouldn't dream of asking you such a personal question.

MRS. MOLLOY. Well, it's what you meant, isn't it? And there's your answer. I shall certainly marry Horace Vandergelder if he asks me. (*Crawls under window rail, into the room, singing loudly.*)

MINNIE. I know it's none of my business . . .

MRS. MOLLOY. Speak up, Minnie, can't hear you.

MINNIE. . . . but do you . . . do you . . . ?

MRS. MOLLOY (*having crossed the room, is busy at the counter*) . Minnie, you're a fool. Say it: Do I love him? Of course, I don't love him. But I have two good reasons for marrying him just the same. Minnie, put something on that hat. It's not ugly enough. (*Throws hat over counter.*)

MINNIE (*catching and taking hat to table*) . Not ugly enough!

MRS. MOLLOY. I couldn't sell it. Put a . . . put a sponge on it.

MINNIE. Why, Mrs. Molloy, you're in such a *mood* today.

MRS. MOLLOY. In the first place I shall marry Mr. Vandergelder to get away from the millinery business. I've hated it from the first day I had anything to do with it. Minnie, I hate hats. (*Sings loudly again.*)

MINNIE. Why, what's the matter with the millinery business?

MRS. MOLLOY (*crossing to window with two hats*) . I can no longer stand being suspected of being a wicked woman, while I have nothing to show for it. I can't stand it. (*She crawls under rail into window.*)

MINNIE. Why, no one would dream of suspecting you—

MRS. MOLLOY (*on her knees, she looks over the rail*) . Minnie, you're a

fool. All millineresses are suspected of being wicked women. Why, half
the time all those women come into the shop merely to look at me.

MINNIE. Oh!

MRS. MOLLOY. They enjoy the suspicion. But they aren't certain. If they
were *certain* I was a wicked woman, they wouldn't put foot in this
place again. Do I go to restaurants? No, it would be bad for business.
Do I go to balls, or theatres, or operas? No, it would be bad for business. The only men I ever meet are feather merchants. (*Crawls out of
window, but gazes intently into the street.*) What are those two young
men doing out there on that park bench? Take my word for it, Minnie,
either I marry Horace Vandergelder, or I break out of this place like
a fire engine. I'll go to every theatre and ball and opera in New York
City. (*Returns to counter, singing again.*)

MINNIE. But Mr. Vandergelder's not . . .

MRS. MOLLOY. Speak up, Minnie, I can't hear you.

MINNIE. . . . I don't think he's attractive.

MRS. MOLLOY. But what I think he is—and it's very important—I think
he'd make a good fighter.

MINNIE. Mrs. Molloy!

MRS. MOLLOY. Take my word for it, Minnie: the best part of married
life is the fights. The rest is merely so-so.

MINNIE (*fingers in ears*). I won't listen.

MRS. MOLLOY. Peter Molloy—God rest him!—was a fine arguing man.
I pity the woman whose husband slams the door and walks out of the
house at the beginning of an argument. Peter Molloy would stand up
and fight for hours on end. He'd even throw things, Minnie, and
there's no pleasure to equal that. When I felt tired I'd start a good
bloodwarming fight and it'd take ten years off my age; now Horace
Vandergelder would put up a good fight; I know it. I've a mind to
marry him.

MINNIE. I think they're just awful, the things you're saying today.

MRS. MOLLOY. Well, I'm enjoying them myself, too.

MINNIE (*at the window*). Mrs. Molloy, those two men out in the street—

MRS. MOLLOY. What?

MINNIE. Those men. It looks as if they meant to come in here.

MRS. MOLLOY. Well now, it's time some men came into this place. I give
you the younger one, Minnie.

MINNIE. Aren't you terrible! (MRS. MOLLY *sits on center table, while*
MINNIE *takes off her felt overshoes.*)

MRS. MOLLOY. Wait till I get my hands on that older one! Mark my
words, Minnie, we'll get an adventure out of this yet. Adventure, adventure! Why does everybody have adventures except me, Minnie? Because

I have no spirit, I have no gumption. Minnie, they're coming in here. Let's go into the workroom and make them wait for us for a minute.

MINNIE. Oh, but Mrs. Molloy . . . my work! . . .

MRS. MOLLOY (*running to workroom*). Hurry up, be quick now, Minnie! (*They go out to workroom.* BARNABY *and* CORNELIUS *run in from street, leaving front door open. They are dressed in the stiff discomfort of their Sunday clothes.* CORNELIUS *wears a bowler hat,* BARNABY *a straw hat too large for him.*)

BARNABY. No one's here.

CORNELIUS Some women were here a minute ago. I saw them. (*They jump back to the street door and peer down the street.*) That's Wolf-trap all right! (*Coming back.*) Well, we've got to hide here until he passes by.

BARNABY. He's sitting down on that bench. It may be quite a while.

CORNELIUS. When these women come in, we'll have to make conversation until he's gone away. We'll pretend we're buying a hat. How much money have you got now?

BARNABY (*counting his money*). Forty cents for the train— seventy cents for dinner—twenty cents to see the whale—and a dollar I lost—I have seventy cents.

CORNELIUS. And I have a dollar seventy-five. I wish I knew how much hats cost!

BARNABY. Is this an adventure, Cornelius?

CORNELIUS. No, but it may be.

BARNABY. I think it is. There we wander around New York all day and nothing happens; and then we come to the quietest street in the whole city and suddenly Mr. Vandergelder turns the corner. (*Going to door.*) I think that's an adventure. I think . . . Cornelius! That Mrs. Levi is there now. She's sitting down on the bench with him.

CORNELIUS. What do you know about that! We know only one person in all New York City, and there she is!

BARNABY. Even if our adventure came along now I'd be too tired to enjoy it. Cornelius, why isn't this an adventure?

CORNELIUS. Don't be asking that. When you're in an adventure, you'll know it all right.

BARNABY. Maybe I wouldn't. Cornelius, let's arrange a signal for you to give me when an adventure's really going on. For instance, Cornelius, you say . . . uh . . . uh . . . *pudding;* you say *pudding* to me as if it's an adventure we're in.

CORNELIUS. I wonder where the lady who runs this store is? What's her name again?

BARNABY. Mrs. Molloy, hats for ladies.

CORNELIUS. Oh yes. I must think over what I'm going to say when she comes in. (*To counter.*) "Good afternoon, Mrs. Molloy, wonderful weather we're having. We've been looking everywhere for some beautiful hats."

BARNABY. That's fine, Cornelius!

CORNELIUS. "Good afternoon, Mrs. Molloy; wonderful weather . . ." We'll make her think we're very rich. (*One hand in trouser pocket, the other on back of chair.*) "Good afternoon, Mrs. Molloy . . ." You keep one eye on the door the whole time. "We've been looking everywhere for . . ." (*Enter* MRS. MOLLOY *from the workroom.*)

MRS. MOLLOY (*behind the counter*). Oh, I'm sorry. Have I kept you waiting? Good afternoon, gentlemen.

CORNELIUS (*hat off*). Here, Cornelius Hackl.

BARNABY (*hat off*). Here, Barnaby Tucker.

MRS. MOLLOY. I'm very happy to meet you. Perhaps I can help you. Won't you sit down?

CORNELIUS. Thank you, we will. (*The* BOYS *place their hats on the table, then sit down at the counter facing* MRS. MOLLOY.) You see. Mrs. Molloy, we're looking for hats. We've looked everywhere. Do you know what we heard? Go to Mrs. Molloy's, they said. So we came here. Only place we *could* go . . .

MRS. MOLLOY. Well, now, that's *very* complimentary.

CORNELIUS. . . . and we were right. Everybody was right.

MRS. MOLLOY. You wish to choose some hats for a friend?

CORNELIUS. Yes, exactly. (*Kicks* BARNABY.)

BARNABY. Yes, exactly.

CORNELIUS. We were thinking of five or six, weren't we, Barnaby?

BARNABY. Er—five.

CORNELIUS. You see, Mrs. Molloy, money's no object with us. None at all.

MRS. MOLLOY. Why, Mr. Hackl . . .

CORNELIUS (*rises and goes toward street door*). . . . I beg your pardon, what an interesting street! Something happening every minute. Passersby, and . . . (BARNABY *runs to join him.*)

MRS. MOLLOY. You're from out of town, Mr. Hackl?

CORNELIUS (*coming back*). Yes, ma'am—Barnaby, just keep your eye on the street, will you? You won't see that in Yonkers every day. (BARNABY *remains kneeling at street door.*)

BARNABY. Oh yes, I will.

CORNELIUS. Not all of it.

MRS. MOLLOY. Now this friend of yours—couldn't she come in with you someday and choose her hats herself?

CORNELIUS (*sits at counter*). No. Oh, no. It's a surprise for her.

MRS. MOLLOY. Indeed? That may be a little difficult, Mr. Hackl. It's not entirely customary—Your friend's very interested in the street, Mr. Hackl.

CORNELIUS. Oh yes. Yes. He has reason to be.

MRS. MOLLOY. You said you were from out of town?

CORNELIUS. Yes, we're from Yonkers.

MRS. MOLLOY. Yonkers?

CORNELIUS. Yonkers . . . yes, Yonkers. (*He gazes rapt into her eyes.*) You should know Yonkers, Mrs. Molloy. Hudson River; Palisades; drives; some say it's the most beautiful town in the world; that's what they say.

MRS. MOLLOY. Is that so!

CORNELIUS (*rises*). Mrs. Molloy, if you ever had a Sunday free, I'd . . . we'd like to show you Yonkers. Y'know, it's very historic, too.

MRS. MOLLOY. That's very kind of you. Well, perhaps . . . now about those hats. (*Takes two hats from under counter, and crosses to back center of the room.*)

CORNELIUS (*follows*). Is there . . . Have you a . . . Maybe Mr. Molloy would like to see Yonkers too?

MRS. MOLLOY. Oh, I'm a widow, Mr. Hackl.

CORNELIUS (*joyfully*). You are! (*With sudden gravity.*) Oh, that's too bad. Mr. Molloy would have enjoyed Yonkers.

MRS. MOLLOY. Very likely. Now about these hats. Is your friend dark or light?

CORNELIUS. Don't think about that for a minute. Any hat you'd like would be perfectly all right with her.

MRS. MOLLOY. Really! (*She puts one on.*) Do you like this one?

CORNELIUS (*in awe-stuck admiration*). Barnaby! (*In sudden anger.*) Barnaby! Look! (BARNABY *turns; unimpressed, he laughs vaguely, and turns to door again.*) Mrs. Molloy, that's the most beautiful hat I ever saw. (BARNABY *now crawls under the rail into the window.*)

MRS. MOLLOY. Your friend is acting very strangely, Mr. Hackl.

CORNELIUS. Barnaby, stop acting strangely. When the street's quiet and empty, come back and talk to us. What was I saying? Oh yes: Mrs. Molloy, you should know Yonkers.

MRS. MOLLOY (*hat off*). The fact is, I have a friend in Yonkers. Perhaps you know him. It's always so foolish to ask in cases like that, isn't it? (*They both laugh over this with increasing congeniality.* MRS. MOLLOY *goes to counter with hats from table.* CORNELIUS *follows.*) It's a Mr. Vandergelder.

CORNELIUS (*stops abruptly*). What was that you said?

MRS. MOLLOY. Then you do know him?

CORNELIUS. Horace Vandergelder?

MRS. MOLLOY. Yes, that's right.

CORNELIUS. Know him! (*Look to* BARNABY.) Why, no. No!

BARNABY. No! No!

CORNELIUS (*starting to glide about the room, in search of a hiding place*). I beg your pardon, Mrs. Molloy—what an attractive shop you have! (*Smiling fixedly at her he moves to the workshop door.*) And where does this door lead to? (*Opens it, and is alarmed by the bell which rings above it.*)

MRS. MOLLOY. Why, Mr. Hackl, that's my workroom.

CORNELIUS. Everything here is so interesting. (*Looks under counter.*) Every corner. Every door, Mrs. Molloy. Barnaby, notice the interesting doors and cupboards. (*He opens the cupboard door.*) Deeply interesting. Coats for ladies. (*Laughs.*) Barnaby, make a note of the table. Precious piece of furniture, with a low-hanging cloth, I see. (*Stretches his leg under table.*)

MRS. MOLLOY (*taking a hat from box left of wardrobe*). Perhaps your friend might like some of this new Italian straw. Mr. Vandergelder's a substantial man and very well liked, they tell me.

CORNELIUS. A lovely man, Mrs. Molloy.

MRS. MOLLOY. Oh yes—charming, charming!

CORNELIUS (*smiling sweetly*). Has only one fault, as far as I know; he's hard as nails; but apart from that, as you say, a charming nature, ma'am.

MRS. MOLLOY. And a large circle of friends—?

CORNELIUS. Yes, indeed, yes indeed—five or six.

BARNABY. Five!

CORNELIUS. He comes and calls on you here from time to time, I suppose.

MRS. MOLLOY (*turns from mirror where she has been putting a hat on*). This summer we'll be wearing ribbons down our back. Yes, as a matter of fact I am expecting a call from him this afternoon. (*Hat off.*)

BARNABY. I think . . . Cornelius! I think . . . !!

MRS. MOLLOY. Now to show you some more hats—

BARNABY. Look out! (*He takes a flying leap over the rail and flings himself under the table.*)

CORNELIUS. Begging your pardon, Mrs. Molloy. (*He jumps into the cupboard.*)

MRS. MOLLOY. Gentlemen! Mr. Hackl! Come right out of there this minute!

CORNELIUS (*sticking his head out of the wardrobe door*). Help us just this once, Mrs. Molloy! We'll explain later!

MRS. MOLLOY. Mr. Hackl!

BARNABY. We're as innocent as can be, Molloy.

MRS. MOLLOY.   But really! Gentlemen! I can't have this! *What are you doing?*

BARNABY.   Cornelius! Cornelius! Pudding?

CORNELIUS   *(a shout)*. Pudding! *(They disappear. Enter from the street* MRS. LEVI, *followed by* MR. VANDERGELDER. VANDERGELDER *is dressed in a too-bright checked suit, and wears a green derby—or bowler—hat. He is carrying a large ornate box of chocolates in one hand, and a cane in the other.)*

MRS. LEVI.   Irene, my darling child, how *are* you? Heaven be good to us, how well you look! *(They kiss.)*

MRS. MOLLOY.   But what a surprise! And Mr. Vandergelder in New York —what a pleasure!

VANDERGELDER   *(swaying back and forth on his heels complacently)*. Good afternoon, Mrs. Molloy. *(They shake hands.* MRS. MOLLOY *brings chair from counter for him. He sits at left of table.)*

MRS. LEVI.   Yes, Mr. Vandergelder's in New York. Yonkers lies up there —*decimated* today. Irene, we thought we'd pay you a very short call. Now you'll tell us if it's inconvenient, won't you?

MRS MOLLOY   *(placing a chair for* MRS. LEVI *at right of table)*. Inconvenient, Dolly! The idea! Why, it's sweet of you to come. *(She notices the boys' hats on the table—sticks a spray of flowers into crown of* CORNELIUS' *bowler and winds a piece of chiffon round* BARNABY's *panama.)*

VANDERGELDER.   We waited outside a moment.

MRS. LEVI.   Mr. Vandergelder thought he saw two customers coming in —two men.

MRS. MOLLOY.   Men! Men, Mr. Vandergelder? Why, what will you be saying next?

MRS. LEVI.   Then we'll sit down for a minute or two. . . .

MRS. MOLLOY   *(wishing to get them out of the shop into the workroom)*. Before you sit down— *(She pushes them both.)* Before you sit down, there's something I want to show you. I want to show Mr. Vandergelder my workroom, too.

MRS. LEVI.   I've seen the workroom a hundred times. I'll stay right here and try on some of these hats.

MRS. MOLLOY.   No, Dolly, you come too. I have something for you. Come along, everybody. *(Exit* MRS. LEVI *to workroom.)* Mr. Vandergelder, I want your advice. You don't know how helpless a woman in business is. Oh, I feel I need advice every minute from a fine business head like yours. *(Exit* VANDERGELDER *to workroom.* MRS. MOLLOY *shouts this line and then slams the workroom door.)* Now I shut the door!! *(Exit* MRS. MOLLOY. CORNELIUS *puts his head out of the wardrobe door and gradually comes out into the room, leaving door open.)*

CORNELIUS. Hsst!

BARNABY *(pokes his head out under the table)*. Maybe she wants us to go, Cornelius?

CORNELIUS. Certainly I won't go. Mrs. Molloy would think we were just thoughtless fellows. No, all I want is to stretch a minute.

BARNABY. What are you going to do when he's gone, Cornelius? Are we just going to run away?

CORNELIUS. Well . . . I don't know yet. I like Mrs. Molloy a lot. I wouldn't like her to think badly of me. I think I'll buy a hat. We can walk home to Yonkers, even if it takes us all night. I wonder how much hats cost. Barnaby, give me all the money you've got. *(As he leans over to take the money, he sneezes. Both return to their hiding places in alarm; then emerge again.)* My, all those perfumes in that cupboard tickle my nose! But I like it in there . . . it's a woman's world, and very different.

BARNABY. I like it where I am, too; only I'd like it better if I had a pillow.

CORNELIUS *(taking coat from wardrobe)*. Here, take one of these coats. I'll roll it up for you so it won't get mussed. Ladies don't like to have their coats mussed.

BARNABY. That's fine. Now I can just lie here and hear Mr. Vandergelder talk. *(CORNELIUS goes slowly above table towards cheval mirror, repeating MRS. MOLLOY's line dreamily.)*

CORNELIUS. This summer we'll be wearing ribbons down our back. . . .

BARNABY. Can I take off my shoes, Cornelius? *(CORNELIUS does not reply. He comes to the footlights and addresses the audience, in completely simple naïve sincerity)*.

CORNELIUS. Isn't the world full of wonderful things. There we sit cooped up in Yonkers for years and years and all the time wonderful people like Mrs. Molloy are walking around in New York and we don't know them at all. I don't know whether—from where you're sitting—you can see—well, for instance, the way *(He points to the edge of his right eye.)* her eye and forehead and cheek come together, up here. Can you? And the kind of fireworks that shoot out of her eyes all the time. I tell you right now: a fine woman is the greatest work of God. You can talk all you like about Niagara Falls and the Pyramids; they aren't in it at all. Of course, up there at Yonkers they came into the store all the time, and bought this and that, and I said, "Yes, ma'am," and "That'll be seventy-five cents, ma'am"; and I *watched* them. But today I've talked to one, equal to equal, equal to equal, and to the finest one that ever existed, in my opinion. They're so different from men! Everything that they say and do is so different that you feel like laughing all the time. *(He laughs.)* Golly, they're different from men. And they're awfully mysterious, too. You never can be really sure what's going on in their heads. They have a kind of wall around them all the time—of pride and a sort of play-acting: I bet you could know a woman a hundred years without ever being really sure whether she liked you or not. This minute I'm in danger. I'm in danger of losing my job and my future and everything that people think is important; but I don't care. Even if I have to dig ditches for the rest of my life, I'll be a ditch digger who once had a wonderful day.

Barnaby!

BARNABY.   Oh, you woke me up!

CORNELIUS   (*kneels*). Barnaby, we can't go back to Yonkers yet and you know why.

BARNABY.   Why not?

CORNELIUS.   We've had a good meal. We've had an adventure. We've been in danger of getting arrested. There's only one more thing we've got to do before we go back to be successes in Yonkers.

BARNABY.   Cornelius! You're never going to kiss Mrs. Molloy!

CORNELIUS.   Maybe.

BARNABY.   But she'll scream.

CORNELIUS.   Barnaby, you don't know anything at all. You might as well know right now that everybody except us goes through life kissing right and left all the time.

BARNABY   (*pauses for reflection*). *humbly*: Well, thanks for telling me, Cornelius. I often wondered. (*Enter* MRS. LEVI *from workroom*.)

MRS. LEVI.   Just a minute, Irene. I must find my handkerchief. (CORNELIUS, *caught by the arrival of* MRS. LEVI, *drops to his hands and knees, and starts very slowly to crawl back to the wardrobe, as though the slowness rendered him invisible.* MRS. LEVI, *leaning over the counter, watches him. From the cupboard he puts his head out of it and looks pleadingly at her.*) Why, Mr. Hackl, I thought you were up in Yonkers.

CORNELIUS.   I almost always am, Mrs. Levi. Oh, Mrs. Levi, don't tell Mr. Vandergelder! I'll explain everything later.

BARNABY   (*puts head out*). We're terribly innocent, Mrs. Levi.

MRS. LEVI.   Why, who's that?

BARNABY.   Barnaby Tucker—just paying a call.

MRS. LEVI   (*looking under counter and even shaking out her skirts*). Well, who else is here?

CORNELIUS.   Just the two of us, Mrs. Levi, that's all.

MRS. LEVI.   Old friends of Mrs. Molloy's, is that it?

CORNELIUS.   We never knew her before a few minutes ago, but we like her a lot—don't we, Barnaby? In fact, I think she's . . . I think she's the finest person in the world. I'm ready to tell that to anybody.

MRS. LEVI.   And does she think *you're* the finest person in the world?

CORNELIUS. Oh, no. I don't suppose she even notices that I'm alive.

MRS. LEVI. Well, I think she must notice that you're alive in that cupboard, Mr. Hackl. Well, if I were you, I'd get back into it right away. Somebody could be coming in any minute. (CORNELIUS *disappears. She sits unconcernedly in chair right. Enter* MRS. MOLLOY.)

MRS. MOLLOY (*leaving door open and looking about in concealed alarm*). Can I help you, Dolly?

MRS. LEVI. No, no, no. I was just blowing my nose. (*Enter* VANDERGELDER *from workroom.*)

VANDERGELDER. Mrs. Molloy, I've got some advice to give you about your business. (MRS. MOLLOY *comes to the center of the room and puts* BARNABY'S *hat on floor in window, then* CORNELIUS' *hat on the counter.*)

MRS. LEVI. Oh, advice from Mr. Vandergelder! The whole city should hear this.

VANDERGELDER (*standing in the workroom door pompously*). In the first place, the aim of business is to make profit.

MRS. MOLLOY. Is that so?

MRS. LEVI. I never heard it put so clearly before. Did you hear it?

VANDERGELDER (*crossing the room to the left*). You pay those girls of yours too much. You pay them as much as men. Girls like that enjoy their work. Wages, Mrs. Molloy, are paid to make people do work they don't want to do.

MRS. LEVI. Mr. Vandergelder thinks so ably. And that's exactly the way his business is run up in Yonkers.

VANDERGELDER (*patting her hand*). Mrs. Molloy, I'd like for you to come up to Yonkers.

MRS. MOLLOY. That would be very nice. (*He hands her the box of chocolates.*) Oh, thank you. As a matter of fact, I know someone from Yonkers, someone else.

VANDERGELDER (*hangs hat on the cheval mirror*). Oh? Who's that? (MRS. MOLLOY *puts chocolates on table and brings gilt chair forward and sits center at table facing the audience.*)

MRS. MOLLOY. Someone quite well-to-do, I believe, though a little free and easy in his behavior. Mr. Vandergelder, do you know Mr. Cornelius Hackl in Yonkers?

VANDERGELDER. I know him like I know my own boot. He's my head clerk.

MRS. MOLLOY. Is that so?

VANDERGELDER. He's been in my store for ten years.

MRS. MOLLOY. Well, I never!

VANDERGELDER. Where would you have known him? (MRS. MOLLOY *is in silent confusion. She looks for help to* MRS. LEVI, *seated at right end of table.*)

MRS. LEVI   (*groping for means to help* MRS. MOLLOY). Err . . . blah . . . err . . . bl . . . er . . . Oh, just one of those chance meetings, I suppose.

MRS. MOLLOY.   Yes, oh yes! One of those chance meetings.

VANDERGELDER.   What? Chance meetings? Cornelius Hackl has no right to chance meetings. Where was it?

MRS. MOLLOY.   Really, Mr. Vandergelder, it's very unlike you to question me in such a way. I think Mr. Hackl is better known than you think he is.

VANDERGELDER.   Nonsense.

MRS. MOLLOY.   He's in New York often, and he's very well liked.

MRS. LEVI   (*having found her idea, with decision*). Well, the truth might as well come out now as later. Mr. Vandergelder, Irene is quite right. Your head clerk is often in New York. Goes everywhere; has an army of friends. Everybody knows Cornelius Hackl.

VANDERGELDER   (*laughs blandly and sits in chair at left of table*). He never comes to New York. He works all day in my store and at nine o'clock at night he goes to sleep in the bran room.

MRS. LEVI.   So you think. But it's not true.

VANDERGELDER.   Dolly Gallagher, you're crazy.

MRS. LEVI.   Listen to me. You keep your nose so deep in your account books you don't know what goes on. Yes, by day, Cornelius Hackl is your faithful trusted clerk—that's true; but by night! Well, he leads a double life, that's all! He's here at the opera; at the great restaurants; in all the fashionable homes . . . why, he's at the Harmonia Gardens Restaurant three nights a week. The fact is, he's the wittiest, gayest, naughtiest, most delightful man in New York. Well, he's just *the* famous Cornelius Hackl!

VANDERGELDER   (*sure of himself*). It ain't the same man. If I ever thought Cornelius Hackl came to New York, I'd discharge him.

MRS. LEVI.   Who took the horses out of Jenny Lind's carriage and pulled her through the streets?

MRS. MOLLOY.   Who?

MRS. LEVI.   Cornelius Hackl! Who dressed up as a waiter at the Fifth Avenue Hotel the other night and took an oyster and dropped it right down Mrs. . . . (*Rises.*) No, it's too wicked to tell you!

MRS. MOLLOY.   Oh yes, Dolly, tell it! Go on!

MRS. LEVI.   No. But it *was* Cornelius Hackl.

VANDERGELDER   (*loud*). It ain't the same man. Where'd he get the money?

MRS. LEVI.   But he's very rich.

VANDERGELDER   (*rises*). Rich! I keep his money in my own safe. He has a hundred and forty-six dollars and thirty-five cents.

MRS. LEVI.   Oh, Mr. Vandergelder, you're killing me! Do come to your senses. He's one of *the* Hackls. (MRS. MOLLOY *sits at chair right of table where* MRS. LEVI *has been sitting.*)

VANDERGELDER.   *The* Hackls?

MRS. LEVI.   They built the Raritan Canal.

VANDERGELDER.   Then why should he work in my store?

MRS. LEVI.   Well, I'll tell you. (*Sits at the center of the table, facing the audience.*)

VANDERGELDER (*striding about*). I don't want to hear! I've got a headache! I'm going home. *It ain't the same man!!* He sleeps in my bran room. You can't get away from facts. I just made him my chief clerk.

MRS. LEVI.   If you had any sense you'd make him partner. (*Rises, crosses to* MRS. MOLLOY.) Now Irene, I can see you were as taken with him as everybody else is.

MRS. MOLLOY.   Why, I only met him once, very hastily.

MRS. LEVI.   Yes, but I can see that you were taken with him. Now don't you be thinking of marrying him!

MRS. MOLLOY (*her hands on her cheeks*). Dolly! What are you saying! Oh!

MRS. LEVI.   Maybe it'd be fine. But think it over carefully. He breaks hearts like hickory nuts.

VANDERGELDER.   Who?

MRS. LEVI.   Cornelius Hackl!

VANDERGELDER.   Mrs. Molloy, how often has he called on you?

MRS. MOLLOY.   Oh, I'm telling the truth. I've only seen him once in my life. Dolly Levi's been exaggerating so. I don't know where to look! (*Enter* MINNIE *from workroom and crosses to window.*)

MINNIE.   Excuse me, Mrs. Molloy. I must get together that order for Mrs. Parkinson.

MRS. MOLLOY.   Yes, we must get that off before closing.

MINNIE.   I want to send it off by the errand girl. (*Having taken a hat from the window.*) Oh, I almost forgot the coat. (*She starts for the wardrobe.*)

MRS. MOLLOY (*running to the wardrobe to prevent her*). Oh, oh! I'll do that, Minnie! (*But she is too late.* MINNIE *opens the right-hand cupboard door and falls back in terror, and screams.*)

MINNIE.   Oh, Mrs. Molloy! Help! There's a man! (MRS. MOLLOY *with the following speech pushes her back to the workroom door.* MINNIE *walks with one arm pointing at the cupboard. At the end of each of* MRS. MOLLOY'*s sentences she repeats—at the same pitch and degree—the words: There's a man!*)

MRS. MOLLOY (*slamming cupboard door*). Minnie, you imagined it. You go back in the workroom and lie down. Minnie, you're a fool; hold your tongue!

MINNIE.   There's a man! (*Exit* MINNIE *to workroom.* MRS. MOLLOY *returns to the front of the stage.* VANDERGELDER *raises his stick threateningly.*)

VANDERGELDER. If there's a man there, we'll get him out. Whoever you
are, come out of there! (*Strikes table with his stick.*)

MRS. LEVI (*goes masterfully to the cupboard—sweeps her umbrella
around among the coats and closes each door as she does so*). Nonsense!
There's no man there. See! Miss Fay's nerves have been playing tricks
on her. Come now, let's sit down again. What were you saying, Mr.
Vandergelder? (*They sit,* MRS. MOLLOY *right,* MRS. LEVI *center,* VAN-
DERGELDER *left. A sneeze is heard from the cupboard. They all rise, look
towards cupboard, then sit again.*) Well now . . . (*Another tremendous sneeze.*) *With a gesture that says, "I can do no more":* God bless
you! (*They all rise.* MRS. MOLLOY *stands with her back to the cupboard.*)

MRS. MOLLOY (*to* VANDERGELDER). Yes, there is a man in there. I'll explain it all to you another time. Thank you very much for coming to
see me. Good afternoon. Dolly. Good afternoon, Mr. Vandergelder.

VANDERGELDER. You're protecting a man in there!

MRS. MOLLOY (*with back to cupboard*). There's a very simple explanation, but for the present, good afternoon. (BARNABY *now sneezes twice,
lifting the table each time.* VANDERGELDER, *right of table, jerks off the
tablecloth.* BARNABY *pulls cloth under table and rolls himself up in it.*
MRS. MOLLOY *picks up the box of chocolates, which has rolled on to the
floor.*)

MRS. LEVI. Lord, the whole room's *crawling* with men! I'll never get
over it.

VANDERGELDER. The world is going to pieces! I can't believe my own
eyes!

MRS. LEVI. Come, Mr. Vandergelder. Ernestina Simple is waiting for us.

VANDERGELDER (*finds his hat and puts it on*). Mrs. Molloy, I shan't
trouble you again, and *vice versa.* (MRS. MOLLOY *is standing transfixed
in front of cupboard, clasping the box of chocolates.* VANDERGELDER
snatches the box from her and goes out.)

MRS. LEVI (*crosses to her*). Irene, when I think of all the interesting
things you have in this room! (*Kisses her.*) Make the most of it, dear.
(*Raps cupboard.*) Good-by! (*Raps on table with umbrella.*) Good-by!
(*Exit* MRS. LEVI. MRS. MOLLOY *opens door of cupboard.* CORNELIUS *steps
out.*)

MRS. MOLLOY. So that was one of your practical jokes, Mr. Hackl?

CORNELIUS. No, no, Mrs. Molloy!

MRS. MOLLOY. Come out from under that, Barnaby Tucker, you troublemaker! (*She snatches the cloth and spreads it back on table.* MINNIE
enters.) There's nothing to be afraid of, Minnie, I know all about these
gentlemen.

CORNELIUS.   Mrs. Molloy, we realize that what happened here—

MRS. MOLLOY.   You think because you're rich you can make up for all the harm you do, is that it?

CORNELIUS.   No, no!

BARNABY *(on the floor putting shoes on)*. No, no!

MRS. MOLLOY.   Minnie, this is the famous Cornelius Hackl who goes round New York tying people into knots; and that's Barnaby Tucker, another troublemaker.

BARNABY.   How d'you do?

MRS. MOLLOY.   Minnie, choose yourself any hat and coat in the store. We're going out to dinner. If this Mr. Hackl is so rich and gay and charming, he's going to be rich and gay and charming to us. He dines three nights a week at the Harmonia Gardens Restaurant, does he? Well, he's taking us there now.

MINNIE.   Mrs. Molloy, are you sure it's safe?

MRS. MOLLOY.   Minnie, hold your tongue. We're in a position to put these men into jail if they so much as squeak.

CORNELIUS.   Jail, Mrs. Molloy?

MRS. MOLLOY.   Jail, Mr. Hackl. Officer Cogarty does everything I tell him to do. Minnie, you and I have been respectable for years; now we're in disgrace, we might as well make the most of it. Come into the workroom with me; I know some ways we can perk up our appearances. Gentlemen, we'll be back in a minute.

CORNELIUS.   Uh—Mrs. Molloy, I hear there's an awfully good restaurant at the railway station.

MRS. MOLLOY *(high indignation)*. Railway station? Railway station? Certainly not! No, sir! You're going to give us a good dinner in the heart of the fashionable world. Go on in, Minnie! Don't you boys forget that you've made us lose our reputations, and now the fashionable world's the only place we can eat. (MRS. MOLLOY *exits to workroom.*)

BARNABY.   She's angry at us, Cornelius. Maybe we'd better run away now.

CORNELIUS.   No, I'm going to go through with this if it kills me. Barnaby, for a woman like that a man could consent to go back to Yonkers and be a success.

BARNABY.   All I know is no woman's going to make a success out of me.

CORNELIUS.   Jail or no jail, we're going to take those ladies out to dinner. So grit your teeth. (*Enter* MRS. MOLLOY *and* MINNIE *from workroom dressed for the street.*)

MRS. MOLLOY.   Gentlemen, the cabs are at the corner, so forward march! (*She takes a hat—which will be* BARNABY's *at the end of Act III—and gives it to* MINNIE.)

CORNELIUS.   Yes, ma'am. (BARNABY *stands shaking his empty pockets warningly.*) Oh, Mrs. Molloy . . . is it far to the restaurant? Couldn't we walk?

MRS. MOLLOY (*pauses a moment, then*). Minnie, take off your things. We're not going.

OTHERS. Mrs. Molloy!

MRS. MOLLOY. Mr. Hackl, I don't go anywhere I'm not wanted. Good night. I'm not very happy to have met you. (*She crosses the stage as though going to the workroom door.*)

OTHERS. Mrs. Molloy!

MRS. MOLLOY. I suppose you think we're not fashionable enough for you? Well, I won't be a burden to you. Good night, Mr. Tucker. (*The others follow her behind counter:* CORNELIUS, BARNABY, *then* MINNIE.)

CORNELIUS. We want you to come with us more than anything in the world, Mrs. Molloy. (MRS. MOLLOY *turns and pushes the three back. They are now near the center of the stage, to the right of the table,* MRS. MOLLOY *facing the audience.*)

MRS. MOLLOY. No, you don't! Look at you! Look at the pair of them, Minnie! Scowling, both of them!

CORNELIUS. Please, Mrs. Molloy!

MRS. MOLLOY. Then smile. (*To* BARNABY.) Go on, smile! No, that's not enough. Minnie, you come with me and we'll get our own supper.

CORNELIUS. Smile, Barnaby, you lout!

BARNABY. My face can't smile any stronger than that.

MRS. MOLLOY. Then do something! Show some interest. Do something lively: sing!

CORNELIUS. I can't sing, really I can't.

MRS. MOLLOY. We're wasting our time, Minnie. They don't want us.

CORNELIUS. Barnaby, what can you sing? Mrs. Molloy, all we know are sad songs.

MRS. MOLLOY. That doesn't matter. If you want us to go out with you; you've got to sing something. (*All this has been very rapid; the boys turn up to counter, put their heads together, confer and abruptly turn, stand stiffly and sing "Tenting tonight; tenting tonight; tenting on the old camp ground." The four of them now repeat the refrain, softly harmonizing. At the end of the song, after a pause,* MRS. MOLLOY, *moved, says:*)

MRS. MOLLOY. We'll come! (*The boys shout joyfully.*) You boys go ahead. (CORNELIUS *gets his hat from counter; as he puts it on he discovers the flowers on it.* BARNABY *gets his hat from window. They go out whistling.* MINNIE *turns and puts her hat on at the mirror.*) Minnie, get the front door key—I'll lock the workroom. (MRS. MOLLOY *goes to workroom.* MINNIE *takes key from hook left of wardrobe and goes to* MRS. MOLLOY, *at the workroom door. She turns her around.*)

MINNIE.   Why, Mrs. Molloy, you're crying! (MRS. MOLLOY *flings her arms round Minnie.*)

MRS. MOLLOY.   Oh, Minnie, the world is full of wonderful things. Watch me, dear, and tell me if my petticoat's showing. (*She crosses to door, followed by* MINNIE, *as—*)

the curtain falls.

ACT III

Veranda at the Harmonia Gardens Restaurant on the Battery, New York. This room is informal and rustic. The main restaurant is indicated to be off stage back right.

There are three entrances: swinging double doors at the center of the back wall leading to the kitchen; one on the right wall (perhaps up a few steps and flanked by potted palms) to the street; one on the left wall to the staircase leading to the rooms above.

On the stage are two tables, left and right, each with four chairs. It is now afternoon and they are not yet set for dinner. Against the back wall is a large folding screen. Also against the back wall are hat and coat racks.

As the curtain rises, Vandergelder is standing, giving orders to Rudolph, a waiter. Malachi Stack sits at table left.

VANDERGELDER.   Now, hear what I say. I don't want you to make any mistakes. I want a table for three.

RUDOLPH (*tall "snob" waiter, alternating between cold superiority and rage. German accent.*)   For three.

VANDERGELDER.   There'll be two ladies and myself.

MALACHI.   It's a bad combination, Mr. Vandergelder. You'll regret it.

VANDERGELDER.   And I want a chicken.

MALACHI.   A chicken. You'll regret it.

VANDERGELDER.   Hold your tongue. Write it down: chicken.

RUDOLPH.   Yes, sir. Chicken Esterhazy? Chicken cacciatore? Chicken à la crème?

VANDERGELDER (*exploding*).   A chicken! A chicken like everybody else has. And with the chicken I want a bottle of wine.

RUDOLPH.   Moselle? Chablis? Vouvray?

MALACHI.   He doesn't understand you, Mr. Vandergelder. You'd better speak louder.

VANDERGELDER (*spelling*).   W-I-N-E.

RUDOLPH.   Wine.

VANDERGELDER.   Wine! And I want this table removed. We'll eat at that table alone. (*Exit* RUDOLPH *through service door at back.*)

MALACHI. There are some people coming in here now, Mr. Vandergelder. (VANDERGELDER *goes to back right to look at the newcomers.*)

VANDERGELDER. What! Thunder and damnation! It's my niece Ermengarde! What's she doing here?!—Wait till I get my hands on her.

MALACHI (*running up to him*). Mr. Vandergelder! You must keep your temper!

VANDERGELDER. And there's that rascal artist with her. Why it's a plot. I'll throw them in jail.

MALACHI. Mr. Vandergelder! They're old enough to come to New York. You can't throw people into jail for coming to New York.

VANDERGELDER. And there's Mrs. Levi! What's she doing with them? It's a plot. It's a conspiracy! What's she saying to the cabman? Go up and hear what she's saying.

MALACHI (*listening at entrance, right*). She's telling the cabman to wait, Mr. Vandergelder. She's telling the young people to come in and have a good dinner, Mr. Vandergelder.

VANDERGELDER. I'll put an end to this.

MALACHI. Now, Mr. Vandergelder, if you lose your temper, you'll make matters worse. Mr. Vandergelder, come here and take my advice.

VANDERGELDER. Stop pulling on my coat. What's your advice?

MALACHI. Hide, Mr. Vandergelder. Hide behind this screen, and listen to what they're saying.

VANDERGELDER (*being pulled behind the screen*). Stop pulling at me. (*They hide behind the screen as* MRS. LEVI, ERMENGARDE *and* AMBROSE *enter from the right.* AMBROSE *is carrying* ERMENGARDE'*s luggage.*)

ERMENGARDE. But I don't want to eat in a restaurant. It's not proper.

MRS. LEVI. Now, Ermengarde, dear, there's nothing wicked about eating in a restaurant. There's nothing wicked, even, about being in New York. Clergymen just make those things up to fill out their sermons.

ERMENGARDE. Oh, I wish I were in Yonkers, where *nothing* ever happens!

MRS. LEVI. Ermengarde, you're hungry. That's what's troubling you.

ERMENGARDE. Anyway, after dinner you must promise to take me to Aunt Flora's. She's been waiting for me all day and she must be half dead of fright.

MRS. LEVI. All right but of course, you know at Miss Van Huysen's you'll be back in your uncle's hands.

AMBROSE (*hands raised to heaven*). I can't stand it.

MRS. LEVI (*to* AMBROSE). Just keep telling yourself how pretty she is. Pretty girls have very little opportunity to improve their other advantages.

AMBROSE. Listen, Ermengarde! You don't want to go back to your uncle. Stop and think! That old man with one foot in the grave!

MRS. LEVI. And the other three in the cashbox.

AMBROSE. Smelling of oats—

MRS. LEVI. And axle grease.

MALACHI. That's not true. It's only partly true.

VANDERGELDER *(loudly)*. Hold your tongue! I'm going to teach them a lesson.

MALACHI *(whisper)*. Keep your temper, Mr. Vandergelder. Listen to what they say.

MRS. LEVI *(hears this; throws a quick glance toward the screen; her whole manner changes)*. Oh dear, what was I saying? The Lord be praised, how glad I am that I found you two dreadful children just as you were about to break poor dear Mr. Vandergelder's heart.

AMBROSE. He's got no heart to break!

MRS. LEVI *(vainly signaling)*. Mr. Vandergelder's a much kinder man than you think.

AMBROSE. Kinder? He's a wolf.

MRS. LEVI. Remember that he leads a very lonely life. Now you're going to have dinner upstairs. There are some private rooms up there,—just meant for shy timid girls like Ermengarde. Come with me. *(She pushes the young people out left,* AMBROSE *carrying the luggage.)*

VANDERGELDER *(coming forward)*. I'll show them! *(He sits at table right.)*

MALACHI. Everybody should eavesdrop once in a while, I always say. There's nothing like eavesdropping to show you that the world outside your head is different from the world inside your head.

VANDERGELDER *(producing a pencil and paper)*. I want to write a note. Go and call that cabman in here. I want to talk to him.

MALACHI. No one asks advice of a cabman, Mr. Vandergelder. They see so much of life that they have no ideas left.

VANDERGELDER. Do as I tell you.

MALACHI. Yes, sir. Advice of a cabman! *(Exit right.* VANDERGELDER *writes his letter.)*

VANDERGELDER. "My dear Miss Van Huysen" *(To audience.)* Everybody's dear in a letter. It's enough to make you give up writing 'em. "My dear Miss Van Huysen. This is Ermengarde and that rascal Ambrose Kemper. They are trying to run away. Keep them in your house until I come." *(MALACHI returns with an enormous* CABMAN *in a high hat and a long coat. He carries a whip.)*

CABMAN *(entering)*. What's he want?

VANDERGELDER. I want to talk to you.

CABMAN. I'm engaged. I'm waiting for my parties.

VANDERGELDER *(folding letter and writing address)*. I know you are. Do you want to earn five dollars?

CABMAN. Eh?

VANDERGELDER.   I asked you, do you want to earn five dollars?

CABMAN.   I don't know. I never tried.

VANDERGELDER.   When those parties of yours come downstairs, I want you to drive them to this address. Never mind what they say, drive them to this address. Ring the bell: give this letter to the lady of the house: see that they get in the door and keep them there.

CABMAN.   I can't make people go into a house if they don't want to.

VANDERGELDER   (*producing purse*). Can you for ten dollars?

CABMAN.   Even for ten dollars, I can't do it alone.

VANDERGELDER.   This fellow here will help you.

MALACHI   (*sitting at table left*). Now I'm pushing people into houses.

VANDERGELDER.   There's the address: Miss Flora Van Huysen, 8 Jackson Street.

CABMAN.   Even if I get them in the door I can't be sure they'll stay there.

VANDERGELDER.   For fifteen dollars you can.

MALACHI.   Murder begins at twenty-five.

VANDERGELDER.   Hold your tongue! (*To* CABMAN.) The lady of the house will help you. All you have to do is to sit in the front hall and see that the man doesn't run off with the girl. I'll be at Miss Van Huysen's in an hour or two and I'll pay you then.

CABMAN.   If they call the police, I can't do anything.

VANDERGELDER.   It's perfectly honest business. Perfectly honest.

MALACHI.   Every man's the best judge of his own honesty.

VANDERGELDER.   The young lady is my niece. (*The* CABMAN *laughs, skeptically*.) The young lady is my niece!! (*The* CABMAN *looks at* MALACHI *and shrugs*.) She's trying to run away with a good-for-nothing and we're preventing it.

CABMAN.   Oh, I know them, sir. They'll win in the end. Rivers don't run uphill.

MALACHI.   What did I tell you, Mr. Vandergelder? Advice of a cabman.

VANDERGELDER   (*hits table with his stick*). Stack! I'll be back in half an hour. See that the table's set for three. See that nobody else eats here. Then go and join the cabman on the box.

MALACHI.   Yes, sir. (*Exit* VANDERGELDER *right*.)

CABMAN.   Who's your friend?

MALACHI.   Friend!! That's not a friend; that's an employer I'm trying out for a few days.

CABMAN.   You won't like him.

MALACHI.   I can see you're in business for yourself because you talk about liking employers. No one's ever liked an employer since business began.

CABMAN.   AW—!

MALACHI.   No, sir. I suppose you think *your horse* likes you?

CABMAN.   My old Clementine? She'd give her right feet for me.

MALACHI.   That's what all employers think. You imagine it. The streets of New York are full of cab horses winking at one another. Let's go in the kitchen and get some whiskey. I can't push people into houses when I'm sober. No, I've had about fifty employers in my life, but this is the most employer of them all. He talks to everybody as though he were paying them.

CABMAN.   I had an employer once. He watched me from eight in the morning until six at night—just sat there and watched me. Oh, dear! Even my mother didn't think I was as interesting as that. (CABMAN *exits through service door.*)

MALACHI   (*following him off*). Yes, being employed is like being loved: you know that somebody's thinking about you the whole time. (*Exits. Enter right,* MRS. MOLLOY, MINNIE, BARNABY *and* CORNELIUS.)

MRS. MOLLOY.   See! Here's the place I meant! Isn't it fine? Minnie, take off your things; we'll be here for hours.

CORNELIUS   (*stopping at door*). Mrs. Molloy, are you sure you'll like it here? I think I feel a draught.

MRS. MOLLOY.   Indeed, I do like it. We're going to have a fine dinner right in this room; it's private, and it's elegant. Now we're all going to forget our troubles and call each other by our first names. Cornelius! Call the waiter.

CORNELIUS.   Wait—wait—I can't make a sound. I must have caught a cold on that ride. Wai—No! It won't come.

MRS. MOLLOY.   I don't believe you. Barnaby, you call him.

BARNABY   (*boldly*). Waiter! Waiter! (CORNELIUS *threatens him.* BARNABY *runs left.*)

MINNIE.   I never thought I'd be in such a place in my whole life. Mrs. Molloy, is this what they call a "café"?

MRS. MOLLOY   (*sits at table left, facing audience*). Yes, this is a café. Sit down, Minnie. Cornelius, Mrs. Levi gave us to understand that every waiter in New York knew you.

CORNELIUS.   They will. (BARNABY *sits at chair left;* MINNIE *in chair back to audience. Enter* RUDOLPH *from service door.*)

RUDOLPH.   Good evening, ladies and gentlemen.

CORNELIUS   (*shaking his hand*). How are you, Fritz? How are you, my friend?

RUDOLPH.   I am Rudolph.

CORNELIUS.   Of course. Rudolph, of course. Well, Rudolph, these ladies want a little something to eat—you know what I mean? Just if you can find the time—we know how busy you are.

MRS. MOLLOY.   Cornelius, there's no need to be so familiar with the waiter. (*Takes menu from* RUDOLPH.)

CORNELIUS. Oh, yes, there is.

MRS. MOLLOY *(passing menu across)*. Minnie, what do you want to eat?

MINNIE. Just anything, Irene.

MRS. MOLLOY. No, speak up, Minnie. What do you want?

MINNIE. No, really, I have no appetite at all. *(Swings round in her chair and studies the menu, horrified at the prices.)* Oh . . . Oh . . . I'd like some sardines on toast and a glass of milk.

CORNELIUS *(takes menu from her)*. Great grindstones! What a sensible girl. Barnaby, shake Minnie's hand. She's the most sensible girl in the world. Rudolph, bring us gentlemen two glasses of beer, a loaf of bread and some cheese.

MRS. MOLLOY *(takes menu)*. I never heard such nonsense. Cornelius, we've come here for a good dinner and a good time. Minnie, have you ever eaten pheasant?

MINNIE. Pheasant? N-o-o-o!

MRS. MOLLOY. Rudolph, have you any pheasant?

RUDOLPH. Yes, ma'am. Just in from New Jersey today.

MRS. MOLLOY. Even the pheasants are leaving New Jersey. *(She laughs loudly, pushing* CORNELIUS, *then* RUDOLPH; *not from menu.)* Now Rudolph, write this down: mock turtle soup; pheasant; mashed chestnuts; green salad; and some nice red wine. (RUDOLPH *repeats each item after her.)*

CORNELIUS *(losing all his fears, boldly)*. All right, Barnaby, you watch me. *(He reads from the bill of fare.)* Rudolph, write this down: Neapolitan ice cream; hothouse peaches; champagne . . .

ALL. Champagne! (BARNABY *spins round in his chair.)*

CORNELIUS *(holds up a finger)* . . . and a German band. Have you got a German band?

MRS. MOLLOY. No, Cornelius, I won't let you be extravagant. Champagne, but no band. Now, Rudolph, be quick about this. We're hungry. *(Exit* RUDOLPH *to kitchen.* MRS. MOLLOY *crosses to right.)* Minnie, come upstairs. I have an idea about your hair. I think it'd be nice in two wee horns—

MINNIE *(hurrying after her, turns and looks at the boys)*. Oh! Horns! *(They go out right. There is a long pause.* CORNELIUS *sits staring after them.)*

BARNABY. Cornelius, in the Army, you have to peel potatoes all the time.

CORNELIUS *(not turning)*. Oh, that doesn't matter. By the time we get out of jail we can move right over to the Old Men's Home. *(Another waiter,* AUGUST, *enters from service door bearing a bottle of champagne in cooler, and five glasses.* MRS. MOLLOY *re-enters right, followed by* MINNIE, *and stops* AUGUST.)

MRS. MOLLOY.   Waiter! What's that? What's that you have?

AUGUST   (*young waiter; baby face; is continually bursting into tears*). It's some champagne, ma'am.

MRS. MOLLOY.   Cornelius, it's our champagne. (ALL *gather round* AUGUST.)

AUGUST.   No, no. It's for His Honor the Mayor of New York and he's very impatient.

MRS. MOLLOY.   Shame on him! The Mayor of New York has more important things to be impatient about. Cornelius, open it. (CORNELIUS *takes the bottle, opens it and fills the glasses*).

AUGUST.   Ma'am, he'll kill me.

MRS. MOLLOY.   Well, have a glass first and die happy.

AUGUST   (*sits at table right, weeping*). He'll kill me. (RUDOLPH *lays the cloth on the table, left.*)

MRS. MOLLOY.   I go to a public restaurant for the first time in ten years and all the waiters burst into tears. There, take that and stop crying, love. (*She takes a glass to* AUGUST *and pats his head, then comes back.*) Barnaby, make a toast!

BARNABY   (*center of the group, with naïve sincerity*). I? . . . uh . . To all the ladies in the world . . . may I get to know more of them . . . and . . . may I get to know them better. (*There is a hushed pause.*)

CORNELIUS   (*softly*). To the ladies!

MRS. MOLLOY.   That's *very* sweet and *very* refined. Minnie, for that I'm going to give Barnaby a kiss.

MINNIE.   Oh!

MRS. MOLLOY.   Hold your tongue, Minnie. I'm old enough to be his mother, and—(*Indicating a height three feet from the floor*) a dear wee mother I would have been too. Barnaby, this is for you from all the ladies in the world. (*She kisses him.* BARNABY *is at first silent and dazed, then:*)

BARNABY.   Now I can go back to Yonkers, Cornelius. Pudding. Pudding. Pudding! (*He spins round and falls on his knees.*)

MRS. MOLLOY.   Look at Barnaby. He's not strong enough for a kiss. His head can't stand it. (*Exit* AUGUST, *right service door, with tray and cooler. The sound of "Les Patineurs" waltz comes from off left.* CORNELIUS *sits in chair facing audience, top of table.* MINNIE *at left.* BARNABY *at right and* MRS. MOLLOY *back to audience.*) Minnie, I'm enjoying myself. To think that this goes on in hundreds of places every night, while I sit at home darning my stockings. (MRS. MOLLOY *rises and dances, alone, slowly about the stage.*) Cornelius, dance with me.

CORNELIUS   (*rises*). Irene, the Hackls don't dance. We're Presbyterian.

MRS. MOLLOY.   Minnie, you dance with me. (MINNIE *joins her.* CORNELIUS *sits again.*)

MINNIE.   Lovely music.

MRS. MOLLOY.   Why, Minnie, you dance beautifully.

MINNIE.   We girls dance in the workroom when you're not looking, Irene.

MRS. MOLLOY.   You thought I'd be angry! Oh dear, no one in the world understands anyone else in the world. (*The girls separate.* MINNIE *dances off to her place at the table.* MRS. MOLLOY *sits thoughtfully at table right. The music fades away.*) Cornelius! Jenny Lind and all those other ladies—do you see them all the time?

CORNELIUS   (*rises and joins her at table right*).   Irene, I've put them right out of my head. I'm interested in . . . (RUDOLPH *has entered by the service door. He now flings a tablecloth between them on table.*)

MRS. MOLLOY.   Rudolph, what are you doing?

RUDOLPH.   A table's been reserved here. Special orders.

MRS. MOLLOY.   Stop right where you are. That party can eat inside. This veranda's ours.

RUDOLPH.   I'm very sorry. This veranda is open to anybody who wants it. Ah, there comes the man who brought the order. (*Enter* MALACHI *from the kitchen, drunk.*)

MRS. MOLLOY   (*to* MALACHI).   Take your table away from here. We got here first, Cornelius, throw him out.

MALACHI.   Ma'am, my employer reserved this room at four o'clock this afternoon. You can go and eat in the restaurant. My employer said it was very important that he have a table alone.

MRS. MOLLOY.   No, sir. We got here first and we're going to stay here— alone, too. (MINNIE *and* BARNABY *come forward.*)

RUDOLPH.   Ladies and gentlemen!

MRS. MOLLOY.   Shut up, you! (*To* MALACHI.) You're an impertinent, idi- otic kill-joy.

MALACHI   (*very pleased*).   That's an insult!

MRS. MOLLOY.   All the facts about you are insults. (*To* CORNELIUS.) Cor- nelius, do something. Knock it over! The table.

CORNELIUS.   Knock it over. (*After a shocked struggle with himself* COR- NELIUS *calmly overturns the table.* AUGUST *rights the table and picks up cutlery, weeping copiously.*)

RUDOLPH   (*in cold fury*).   I'm sorry, but this room can't be reserved for anyone. If you want to eat alone, you must go upstairs. I'm sorry, but that's the rule.

MRS. MOLLOY.   We're having a nice dinner alone and we're going to stay here. Cornelius, knock it over. (CORNELIUS *overturns the table again. The* GIRLS *squeal with pleasure. The waiter* AUGUST *again scrambles for the silver.*)

MALACHI. Wait till you see my employer!

RUDOLPH *(bringing screen down)*. Ladies and gentlemen! I'll tell you what we'll do. There's a big screen here. We'll put the screen up between the tables. August, come and help me.

MRS. MOLLOY. I won't eat behind a screen. I won't. Minnie, make a noise. We're not animals in a menagerie. Cornelius, no screen. Minnie, there's a fight. I feel ten years younger. No screen! No screen! *(During the struggle with the screen all talk at once.)*

MALACHI *(loud and clear and pointing to entrance at right)*. Now you'll learn something. There comes my employer now, getting out of that cab.

CORNELIUS *(coming to him, taking off his coat)*. Where? I'll knock him down too. (BARNABY *has gone up to right entrance. He turns and shouts clearly:*)

BARNABY. Cornelius, it's Wolf-trap. Yes, it is!

CORNELIUS. Wolf-trap! Listen, everybody. I think the screen's a good idea. Have you got any more screens, Rudolph? We could use three or four. *(He pulls the screen forward again.)*

MRS. MOLLOY. Quiet down, Cornelius, and stop changing your mind. Hurry up, Rudolph, we're ready for the soup. *(During the following scene* RUDOLPH *serves the meal at the table left, as unobtrusively as possible. The stage is now divided in half. The quartet's table is at the left. Enter* VANDERGELDER *from the right. Now wears overcoat and carries the box of chocolates.)*

VANDERGELDER. Stack! What's the meaning of this? I told you I wanted a table alone. What's that? (VANDERGELDER *hits the screen twice with his stick.* MRS. MOLLOY *hits back twice with a spoon. The four young people sit:* BARNABY *facing audience;* MRS. MOLLOY *right,* MINNIE *left, and* CORNELIUS *back to audience.)*

MALACHI. Mr. Vandergelder, I did what I could. Mr. Vandergelder, you wouldn't believe what wild savages the people of New York are. There's a woman over there, Mr. Vandergelder—civilization hasn't touched her.

VANDERGELDER. Everything's wrong. You can't even manage a thing like that. Help me off with my coat. Don't kill me. Don't kill me. *(During the struggle with the overcoat* MR. VANDERGELDER's *purse flies out of his pocket and falls by the screen.* VANDERGELDER *goes to the coat tree and hangs his coat up.)*

MRS. MOLLOY. Speak up! I can't hear you.

CORNELIUS. My voice again. Barnaby, how's your throat? Can you speak?

BARNABY. Can't make a sound.

MRS. MOLLOY. Oh, all right. Bring your heads together, and we'll whisper.

VANDERGELDER. Who are those people over there?

MALACHI.   Some city sparks and their girls, Mr. Vandergelder. What goes
on in big cities, Mr. Vandergelder—best not think of it.

VANDERGELDER.   Has that couple come down from upstairs yet? I hope
they haven't gone off without your seeing them.

MALACHI.   No, sir. Myself and the cabman have kept our eyes on everything.

VANDERGELDER *(sits at right of table, profile to the audience)*. I'll sit
here and wait for my guests. You go out to the cab.

MALACHI.   Yes, sir. (VANDERGELDER *unfurls newspaper and starts to read.*
MALACHI *sees the purse on the floor and picks it up.*) Eh? What's that?
A purse. Did you drop something, Mr. Vandergelder?

VANDERGELDER.   No. Don't bother me any more. Do as I tell you.

MALACHI *(stooping over. Coming center)*. A purse. That fellow over
there must have let it fall during the misunderstanding about the
screen. No, I won't look inside. Twenty-dollar bills, dozens of them. I'll
go over and give it to him. (*Starts toward* CORNELIUS, *then turns and
says to audience:*) You're surprised? You're surprised to see me getting
rid of this money so quickly, eh? I'll explain it to you. There was a
time in my life when my chief interest was picking up money that
didn't belong to me. The law is there to protect property, but—sure,
the law doesn't care whether a property owner deserves his property or
not, and the law has to be corrected. There are several thousands of
people in this country engaged in correcting the law. For a while, I
too was engaged in the redistribution of superfluities. A man works all
his life and leaves a million to his widow. She sits in hotels and eats
great meals and plays cards all afternoon and evening, with ten dia-
monds on her fingers. Call in the robbers! Call in the robbers! Or a
man leaves it to his son who stands leaning against bars all night boring a bartender. Call in the robbers! Stealing's a weakness. There are
some people who say you shouldn't have any weaknesses at all—no
vices. But if a man has no vices, he's in great danger of making vices
out of his virtues, and there's a spectacle. We've all seen them: men
who were monsters of philanthropy and women who were dragons of
purity. We've seen people who told the truth, though the Heavens
fall,—and the Heavens fell. No, no—nurse one vice in your bosom.
Give it the attention it deserves and let your virtues spring up modestly
around it. Then you'll have the miser who's no liar; and the drunkard
who's the benefactor of a whole city. Well, after I'd had that weakness
of stealing for a while, I found another: I took to whisky—whisky took
to me. And then I discovered an important rule that I'm going to pass
on to you: Never support two weaknesses at the same time. It's your
combination sinners—your lecherous liars and your miserly drunkards
—who dishonor the vices and bring them into bad repute. So now you

see why I want to get rid of this money: I want to keep my mind free
to do the credit to whisky that it deserves. And my last word to you,
ladies and gentlemen, is this: one vice at a time. (*Goes over to* COR-
NELIUS.) Can I speak to you for a minute?

CORNELIUS (*rises*). You certainly can. We all want to apologize to you
about that screen—that little misunderstanding. (*They all rise, with
exclamations of apology.*) What's your name, sir?

MALACHI. Stack, sir. Malachi Stack. If the ladies will excuse you, I'd like
to speak to you for a minute. (*Draws* CORNELIUS *down to front of
stage.*) Listen, boy, have you lost . . . ? Come here . . . (*Leads him
further down, out of* VANDERGELDER's *hearing.*) Have you lost something?

CORNELIUS. Mr. Stack, in this one day I've lost everything I own.

MALACHI. There it is. (*Gives him purse.*) Don't mention it.

CORNELIUS. Why, Mr. Stack . . . you know what it is? It's a miracle.
(*Looks toward the ceiling.*)

MALACHI. Don't mention it.

CORNELIUS. Barnaby, come here a minute. I want you to shake hands
with Mr. Stack. (BARNABY, *napkin tucked into his collar, joins them.*)
Mr. Stack's just found the purse I lost, Barnaby. You know—the purse
full of money.

BARNABY (*shaking his hand vigorously*). You're a wonderful man, Mr.
Stack.

MALACHI. Oh, it's nothing—nothing.

CORNELIUS. I'm certainly glad I went to church all these years. You're
a good person to know, Mr. Stack. In a way. Mr. Stack, where do you
work?

MALACHI. Well, I've just begun. I work for a Mr. Vandergelder in
Yonkers. (CORNELIUS *is thunderstruck. He glances at* BARNABY *and
turns to* MALACHI *with awe. All three are swaying slightly, back and
forth.*)

CORNELIUS. You do? It's a miracle. (*He points to the ceiling.*) Mr. Stack,
I know you don't need it—but can I give you something for . . . for
the good work?

MALACHI (*putting out his hand*). Don't mention it. It's nothing. (*Starts
to go left.*)

CORNELIUS. Take that. (*Hands him a note.*)

MALACHI (*taking note*). Don't mention it.

CORNELIUS. And that. (*Another note.*)

MALACHI (*takes it and moves away*). I'd better be going.

CORNELIUS. Oh, here. And that.

MALACHI (*hands third note back*). No . . . I might get to like them.
(*Exit left.* CORNELIUS *bounds exultantly back to table.*)

CORNELIUS   Irene, I feel a lot better about everything. Irene, I feel so
well that I'm going to tell the truth.

MRS. MOLLOY.   I'd forgotten that, Minnie. Men get drunk so differently
from women. All right, what is the truth?

CORNELIUS.   If I tell the truth, will you let me . . . will you let me put
my arm around your waist? (MINNIE *screams and flings her napkin
over her face.*)

MRS. MOLLOY.   Hold your tongue, Minnie. All right, you can put your
arm around my waist just to show it can be done in a gentlemanly way;
but I might as well warn you: a corset is a corset.

CORNELIUS   (*his arm around her; softly*). You're a wonderful person,
Mrs. Molloy.

MRS. MOLLOY.   Thank you. (*She removes his hand from around her
waist.*) All right, now that's enough. What is the truth?

CORNELIUS.   Irene, I'm not as rich as Mrs. Levi said I was.

MRS. MOLLOY.   Not rich!

CORNELIUS.   I almost never came to New York. And I'm not like she said
I was,—bad. And I think you ought to know that at this very minute
Mr. Vandergelder's sitting on the other side of that screen.

MRS. MOLLOY.   What! Well, he's not going to spoil any party of mine. So
that's why we have been whispering? Let's forget all about Mr. Vandergelder and have some more wine. (*They start to sing softly: "The
Sidewalks of New York." Enter* MRS. LEVI, *from the street, in an elaborate dress.* VANDERGELDER *rises.*)

MRS. LEVI.   Good evening, Mr. Vandergelder.

VANDERGELDER.   Where's—where's Miss Simple?

MRS. LEVI.   Mr. Vandergelder, I'll never trust a woman again as long as I
live.

VANDERGELDER.   Well? What is it?

MRS. LEVI.   She ran away this afternoon and got married!

VANDERGELDER.   She did?

MRS. LEVI.   Married, Mr. Vandergelder, to a young boy of fifty.

VANDERGELDER.   She did?

MRS. LEVI.   Oh, I'm as disappointed as you are. I-can't-eat-a-thing-what-
have-you-ordered?

VANDERGELDER.   I ordered what you told me to, a chicken. (*Enter* AU-
GUST. *He goes to* VANDERGELDER's *table.*)

MRS. LEVI.   I don't think I could face a chicken. Oh, waiter. How do you
do? What's your name?

AUGUST.   August, ma'am.

MRS. LEVI.   August, this is Mr. Vandergelder of Yonkers—Yonkers' most
influential citizen, in fact. I want you to see that he's served with the

best you have and served promptly. And there'll only be the two of us. (MRS. LEVI *gives one set of cutlery to* AUGUST. VANDERGELDER *puts chocolate box under table.*) Mr. Vandergelder's been through some trying experiences today—what with men hidden all over Mrs. Molloy's store—like Indians in ambush.

VANDERGELDER (*between his teeth*). Mrs. Levi, you don't have to tell him everything about me. (*The* QUARTET *commences singing again very softly.*)

MRS. LEVI. Mr. Vandergelder, if you're thinking about getting married, you might as well learn right now you have to let women be women. Now, August, we want excellent service.

AUGUST. Yes, ma'am. (*Exits to kitchen.*)

VANDERGELDER. You've managed things very badly. When I plan a thing it takes place. (MRS. LEVI *rises.*) Where are you going?

MRS. LEVI. Oh, I'd just like to see who's on the other side of that screen. (MRS. LEVI *crosses to the other side of the stage and sees the* QUARTET. *They are frightened and fall silent.*)

CORNELIUS (*rising*). Good evening, Mrs. Levi. (MRS. LEVI *takes no notice, but, taking up the refrain where they left off, returns to her place at the table right.*)

VANDERGELDER. Well, who was it?

MRS. LEVI. Oh, just some city sparks entertaining their girls, I guess.

VANDERGELDER. Always wanting to know everything; always curious about everything; always putting your nose into other people's affairs. Anybody who lived with you would get as nervous as a cat.

MRS. LEVI. What? What's that you're saying?

VANDERGELDER. I said anybody who lived with you would—

MRS. LEVI. Horace Vandergelder, get that idea right out of your head this minute. I'm surprised that you even mentioned such a thing. Understand once and for all that I have no intention of marrying you.

VANDERGELDER. I didn't mean that.

MRS. LEVI. You've been hinting around at such a thing for some time, but from now on put such ideas right out of your head.

VANDERGELDER. Stop talking that way. That's not what I meant at all.

MRS. LEVI. I hope not. I should hope not. Horace Vandergelder, you go your way (*Points a finger.*) and I'll go mine. (*Points in same direction.*) I'm not some Irene Molloy, whose head can be turned by a pot of geraniums. Why, the idea of you even suggesting such a thing.

VANDERGELDER. Mrs. Levi, you misunderstood me.

MRS. LEVI. I certainly hope I did. If I had any intention of marrying again it would be to a far more pleasure-loving man than you. Why I'd marry Cornelius Hackl before I'd marry you. (CORNELIUS *raises his head in alarm. The others stop eating and listen.*) However, we won't discuss it any more. (*Enter* AUGUST *with a tray.*) Here's August with our food. I'll serve it, August.

AUGUST. Yes, ma'am. (*Exit* AUGUST.)

MRS. LEVI. Here's some white meat for you, and some giblets, very tender and very good for you. No, as I said before, you go your way and I'll go mine.—Start right in on the wine. I think you'll feel better at once. However, since you brought the matter up, there's one more thing I think I ought to say.

VANDERGELDER (*rising in rage*). I didn't bring the matter up at all.

MRS. LEVI. We'll have forgotten all about it in a moment, but—sit down, sit down, we'll close the matter forever in just a moment, but there's one more thing I ought to say. (VANDERGELDER *sits down.*) It's true, I'm a woman who likes to know everything that's going on; who likes to manage things, you're perfectly right about that. But I wouldn't like to manage anything as disorderly as your household, as out of control, as untidy. You'll have to do that yourself, God helping you.

VANDERGELDER. It's not out of control.

MRS. LEVI. Very well, let's not say another word about it. Take some more of that squash, it's good. No, Horace, a complaining, quarrelsome, friendless soul like you is no sort of companion for me. You go your way (*Peppers her own plate.*) and I'll go mine. (*Peppers his plate.*)

VANDERGELDER. Stop saying that.

MRS. LEVI. I won't say another word.

VANDERGELDER. Besides . . . I'm not those things you said I am.

MRS. LEVI. What?—Well, I guess you're friendless, aren't you? Ermengarde told me this morning you'd even quarreled with your barber— a man who's held a razor to your throat for twenty years! Seems to me that that's sinking pretty low.

VANDERGELDER. Well, . . . but . . . my clerks, they . . .

MRS. LEVI. They like you? Cornelius Hackl and that Barnaby? Behind your back they call you Wolf-trap. (*Quietly the* QUARTET *at the other table have moved up to the screens—bringing chairs for* MRS. MOLLOY *and* MINNIE. *Wine glasses in hand, they overhear this conversation.*)

VANDERGELDER (*blanching*). They don't.

MRS. LEVI. No, Horace. It looks to me as though I were the last person in the world that liked you, and even I'm just so-so. No, for the rest of my life I intend to have a good time. You'll be able to find some housekeeper who can prepare you three meals for a dollar a day—it can be done, you know, if you like cold baked beans. You'll spend your last days listening at keyholes, for fear someone's cheating you. Take some more of that.

VANDERGELDER. Dolly, you're a damned exasperating woman.

MRS. LEVI. There! You see? That's the difference between us. I'd be nagging you all day to get some spirit into you. You could be a perfectly charming, witty, amiable man, if you wanted to.

VANDERGELDER *(rising, bellowing)*. I don't want to be charming.

MRS. LEVI. But you are. Look at you now. You can't hide it.

VANDERGELDER *(sits)*. Listen at keyholes! Dolly, you have no right to say such things to me.

MRS. LEVI. At your age you ought to enjoy hearing the honest truth.

VANDERGELDER. My age! My age! You're always talking about my age.

MRS. LEVI. I don't know what your age is, but I do know that up at Yonkers with bad food and bad temper you'll double it in six months. Let's talk of something else; but before we leave the subject there's one more thing I *am* going to say.

VANDERGELDER. Don't!

MRS. LEVI. Sometimes, just sometimes, I think I'd be tempted to marry you out of sheer pity; and if the confusion in your house gets any worse I may *have* to.

VANDERGELDER. I haven't asked you to marry me.

MRS. LEVI. Well, *please don't.*

VANDERGELDER. And my house is not in confusion.

MRS. LEVI. What? With your niece upstairs in the restaurant right now?

VANDERGELDER. I've fixed that better than you know.

MRS. LEVI. And your clerks skipping around New York behind your back?

VANDERGELDER. They're in Yonkers where they always are.

MRS. LEVI. Nonsense!

VANDERGELDER. What do you mean, nonsense?

MRS. LEVI. Cornelius Hackl's the other side of that screen this very minute.

VANDERGELDER. It ain't the same man!

MRS. LEVI. All right. Go on. Push it, knock it down. Go and see.

VANDERGELDER *(goes to screen, pauses in doubt, then returns to his chair again)*. I don't believe it.

MRS. LEVI. All right. All right. Eat your chicken. Of course, Horace, if your affairs went from bad to worse and you became actually miserable, I might feel that it was my duty to come up to Yonkers and be of some assistance to you. After all, I was your wife's oldest friend.

VANDERGELDER. I don't know how you ever got any such notion. Now understand, once and for all, I have *no intention of marrying anybody.* Now, I'm tired and I don't want to talk. (CORNELIUS *crosses to extreme left,* MRS. MOLLOY *following him.*)

MRS. LEVI. I won't say another word, either.

CORNELIUS. Irene, I think we'd better go. You take this money and pay the bill. Oh, don't worry, it's not mine.

MRS. MOLLOY. No, no, I'll tell you what we'll do. You boys put on our coats and veils, and if he comes stamping over here, he'll think you're girls.

CORNELIUS. What! Those things!

MRS. MOLLOY. Yes. Come on. (*She and* MINNIE *take the clothes from the stand.*)

VANDERGELDER (*rises*). I've got a headache. I've had a bad day. I'm going to Flora Van Huysen's, and then I'm going back to my hotel. (*Reaches for his purse.*) So, here's the money to pay for the dinner. (*Searching another pocket.*) Here's the money to pay for the . . . (*Going through all his pockets.*) Here's the money . . . I've lost my purse!!

MRS. LEVI. Impossible! I can't imagine you without your purse.

VANDERGELDER. It's been stolen. (*Searching overcoat.*) Or I left it in the cab. What am I going to do? I'm new at the hotel; they don't know me. I've never been here before . . . Stop eating the chicken, I can't pay for it!

MRS. LEVI (*laughing gaily*). Horace, I'll be able to find some money. Sit down and calm yourself.

VANDERGELDER. Dolly Gallagher, I gave you twenty-five dollars this morning.

MRS. LEVI. I haven't a cent. I gave it to my lawyer. We can borrow it from Ambrose Kemper, upstairs.

VANDERGELDER. I wouldn't take it.

MRS. LEVI. Cornelius Hackl will lend it to us.

VANDERGELDER. He's in Yonkers.—Waiter! (CORNELIUS *comes forward dressed in* MRS. MOLLOY'*s coat, thrown over his shoulder like a cape.* MRS. LEVI *is enjoying herself immensely.* VANDERGELDER *again goes to back wall to examine the pockets of his overcoat.*)

MRS. MOLLOY. Cornelius, is that Mr. Vandergelder's purse?

CORNELIUS. I didn't know it myself. I thought it was money just wandering around loose that didn't belong to anybody.

MRS. MOLLOY. Goodness! That's what politicians think!

VANDERGELDER. Waiter! (*A band off left starts playing a polka.* BARNABY *comes forward dressed in* MINNIE'*s hat, coat and veil.*)

MINNIE. Irene, doesn't Barnaby make a lovely girl? He just ought to stay that way. (MRS. LEVI *and* VANDERGELDER *move their table upstage while searching for the purse.*)

MRS. MOLLOY. Why should we have our evening spoiled? Cornelius, I can teach you to dance in a few minutes. Oh, he won't recognize you.

MINNIE. Barnaby, it's the easiest thing in the world. (*They move their table up against the back wall.*)

MRS. LEVI.   Horace, you danced with me at your wedding and you danced with me at mine. Do you remember?

VANDERGELDER.   No. Yes.

MRS. LEVI.   Horace, you were a good dancer then. Don't confess to me that you're too old to dance.

VANDERGELDER.   I'm not too old. I just don't want to dance.

MRS. LEVI.   Listen to that music. Horace, do you remember the dances in the firehouse at Yonkers on Saturday night? You gave me a fan. Come, come on! (VANDERGELDER *and* MRS. LEVI *start to dance.* CORNELIUS, *dancing with* MRS. MOLLOY, *bumps into* VANDERGELDER, *back to back.* VANDERGELDER, *turning, fails at first to recognize him, then does and roars:*)

VANDERGELDER.   You're discharged! Not a word! You're fired! Where's that idiot, Barnaby Tucker? He's fired, too. (*The four young people, laughing, start rushing out the door to the street.* VANDERGELDER, *pointing at* MRS. MOLLOY, *shouts:*) You're discharged!

MRS. MOLLOY   (*pointing at him*). You're discharged! (*Exit.*)

VANDERGELDER.   You're discharged! (*Enter from left,* AMBROSE *and* ERMENGARDE. *To* ERMENGARDE:) I'll lock you up for the rest of your life, young lady.

ERMENGARDE.   Uncle! (*She faints in* AMBROSE'S *arms.*)

VANDERGELDER   (*to* AMBROSE). I'll have you arrested. Get out of my sight. I never want to see you again.

AMBROSE   (*carrying* ERMENGARDE *across to exit right*). You can't do anything to me, Mr. Vandergelder. (*Exit* AMBROSE *and* ERMENGARDE.)

MRS. LEVI   (*who has been laughing heartily, follows the distraught* VANDERGELDER *about the stage as he continues to hunt for his purse*). Well, there's your life, Mr. Vandergelder! Without niece—without clerks— without bride—and without your purse. *Will you marry me now?*

VANDERGELDER.   No! (*To get away from her, he dashes into the kitchen.* MRS. LEVI, *still laughing, exclaims to the audience:*)

MRS. LEVI.   Damn!! (*And rushes off right.*)

The curtain falls.

ACT IV

Miss Flora Van Huysen's house.

   This is a prosperous spinster's living room and is filled with knick-knacks, all in bright colors, and hung with family portraits, bird cages, shawls, etc.

   There is only one entrance—a large double door in the center of the back wall. Beyond it one sees the hall which leads left to the street door and right to the kitchen and the rest of the house. On the left are big

windows hung with lace curtains on heavy draperies. Front left is Miss
Van Huysen's sofa, covered with bright-colored cushions, and behind it
a table. On the right is another smaller sofa. Miss Van Huysen is lying
on the sofa. The cook is at the window, left. Miss Van Huysen, fifty,
florid, stout and sentimental, is sniffing at smelling salts. Cook (enor-
mous) holds a china mixing bowl.

COOK.　No, ma'am. I could swear I heard a cab drawing up to the door.

MISS VAN H.　You imagined it. Imagination. Everything in life . . . like
　　that . . . disappointment . . . illusion. Our plans . . . our hopes
　　. . . what becomes of them? Nothing. The story of my life. (*She sings*
　　for a moment.)

COOK.　Pray God nothing's happened to the dear girl. Is it a long jour-
　　ney from Yonkers?

MISS VAN H.　No; but long enough for a thousand things to happen.

COOK.　Well, we've been waiting all day. Don't you think we ought to
　　call the police about it?

MISS VAN H.　The police! If it's God's will, the police can't prevent it. Oh,
　　in three days, in a week, in a year, we'll know what's happened. . . .
　　And if anything *has* happened to Ermengarde, it'll be a lesson to *him*
　　—that's what it'll be.

COOK.　To who?

MISS VAN H.　To that cruel uncle of hers, of course,—to Horace Vander-
　　gelder, and to everyone else who tries to separate young lovers. Young
　　lovers have enough to contend with as it is. Who should know that bet-
　　ter than I? No one. The story of my life. (*Sings for a moment, then:*)
　　There! Now I hear a cab. Quick!

COOK.　No. No, ma'am. I don't see anything.

MISS VAN H.　There! What did I tell you? Everything's imagination—illu-
　　sion.

COOK.　But surely, if they'd changed their plans Mr. Vandergelder would
　　have sent you a message.

MISS VAN H.　Oh, I know what's the matter. That poor child probably
　　thought she was coming to another prison—to another tyrant. If she'd
　　known that I was her friend, and a friend of all young lovers, she'd be
　　here by now. Oh, yes, she would. Her life shall not be crossed with
　　obstacles and disappointments as . . . Cook, a minute ago my smelling
　　salts were on this table. Now they've completely disappeared.

COOK.　Why, there they are, ma'am, right there in your hand.

MISS VAN H.　Goodness! How did they get there? I won't inquire. Stranger
　　things have happened!

COOK. I suppose Mr. Vandergelder was sending her down with someone?

MISS VAN H. Two can go astray as easily as . . . (*She sneezes.*)

COOK. God bless you! (*Runs to window.*) Now, here's a carriage stopping. (*The doorbell rings.*)

MISS VAN H. Well, open the door, Cook. (COOK *exits.*) It's probably some mistake. (*Sneezes again.*) God bless you! (*Sounds of altercation off in hall.*) It almost sounds as though I heard voices.

CORNELIUS (*off*). I don't want to come in. This is a free country, I tell you.

CABMAN (*off*). Forward march!

MALACHI (*off*). In you go. We have orders.

CORNELIUS (*off*). You can't make a person go where he doesn't want to go. (*Enter* MALACHI, *followed by* COOK. *The* CABMAN *bundles* BARNABY *and* CORNELIUS *into the room, but they fight their way back into the hall.* CORNELIUS *has lost* MRS. MOLLOY's *coat, but* BARNABY *is wearing* MINNIE's *clothes.*)

MALACHI. Begging your pardon, ma'am, are you Miss Van Huysen?

MISS VAN H. Yes, I am, unfortunately. What's all this noise about?

MALACHI. There are two people here that Mr. Vandergelder said must be brought to this house and kept here until he comes. And here's his letter to you.

MISS VAN H. No one has any right to tell me whom I'm to keep in my house if they don't want to stay.

MALACHI. You're right, ma'am. Everybody's always talking about people breaking into houses, ma'am; but there are more people in the world who want to break out of houses, that's what I always say.—Bring them in, Joe. (*Enter* CORNELIUS *and* BARNABY *being pushed by the* CABMAN.)

CORNELIUS. This young lady and I have no business here. We jumped into a cab and asked to be driven to the station and these men brought us to the house and forced us to come inside. There's been a mistake.

CABMAN. Is your name Miss Van Huysen?

MISS VAN H. Everybody's asking me if my name's Miss Van Huysen. I think that's a matter I can decide for myself. Now will you all be quiet while I read this letter? . . . "This is Ermengarde and that rascal Ambrose Kemper . . ." Now I know who you two are, anyway. "They are trying to run away . . ." Story of my life. "Keep them in your house until I come." Mr. Kemper, you have nothing to fear. (*To* CABMAN.) Who are you?

CABMAN. I'm Joe. I stay here until the old man comes. He owes me fifteen dollars.

MALACHI. That's right, Miss Van Huysen, we must stay here to see they don't escape.

MISS VAN H (*to* BARNABY). My dear child, take off your things. We'll all have some coffee. (*To* MALACHI *and* CABMAN.) You two go out and wait in the hall. I'll send coffee out to you. Cook, take them. (COOK *pushes* MALACHI *and* CABMAN *into the hall.*)

CORNELIUS. Ma'am, we're not the people you're expecting, and there's no reason . . .

MISS VAN H. Mr. Kemper, I'm not the tyrant you think I am. . . . You don't have to be afraid of me. . . . I know you're trying to run away with this innocent girl. . . . All my life I have suffered from the interference of others. You shall not suffer as I did. So put yourself entirely in my hands. (*She lifts* BARNABY's *veil.*) Ermengarde! (*Kisses him on both cheeks.*) Where's your luggage?

BARNABY. It's—uh—uh—it's . . .

CORNELIUS. Oh, I'll find it in the morning. It's been mislaid.

MISS VAN H. Mislaid! How like life! Well, Ermengarde; you shall put on some of my clothes.

BARNABY. Oh, I know I wouldn't be happy, really.

MISS VAN H. She's a shy little thing, isn't she? Timid little darling! . . . Cook! Put some gingerbread in the oven and get the coffee ready . . .

COOK. Yes, ma'am. (*Exits to kitchen.*)

MISS VAN H. . . . while I go and draw a good hot bath for Ermengarde.

CORNELIUS. Oh, oh—Miss Van Huysen . . .

MISS VAN H. Believe me, Ermengarde, your troubles are at an end. You two will be married tomorrow. (*To* BARNABY.) My dear, you look just like I did at your age, and your sufferings have been as mine. While you're bathing, I'll come and tell you the story of my life.

BARNABY. Oh, I don't want to take a bath. I always catch cold.

MISS VAN H. No, dear, you won't catch cold. I'll slap you all over. I'll be back in a minute. (*Exit.*)

CORNELIUS (*looking out of window*). Barnaby, do you think we could jump down from this window?

BARNABY. Yes—we'd kill ourselves.

CORNELIUS. We'll just have to stay here and watch for something to happen. Barnaby, the situation's desperate.

BARNABY. It began getting desperate about half-past four and it's been getting worse ever since. Now I have to take a bath and get slapped all over. (*Enter* MISS VAN HUYSEN *from kitchen.*)

MISS VAN H. Ermengarde, you've still got those wet things on. Your bath's nearly ready. Mr. Kemper, you come into the kitchen and put your feet in the oven. (*The doorbell rings. Enter* COOK.) What's that? It's the doorbell. I expect it's your uncle.

COOK. There's the doorbell. (*At window.*) It's *another* man and a girl in a cab!

MISS VAN H. Well, go and let them in, Cook. Now, come with me, you two. Come, Ermengarde. (*Exit* COOK. MISS VAN HUYSEN *drags* CORNELIUS *and the protesting* BARNABY *off into the kitchen.*)

COOK (*off*). No, that's impossible. Come in, anyway. (*Enter* ERMENGARDE, *followed by* AMBROSE, *carrying the two pieces of luggage.*) There's some mistake. I'll tell Miss Van Huysen, but there's some mistake.

ERMENGARDE. But, I tell you, I *am* Mr. Vandergelder's niece; I'm Ermengarde.

COOK. Beg your pardon, Miss, but you *can't* be Miss Ermengarde.

ERMENGARDE. But—but—here I *am*. And that's my baggage.

COOK. Well, I'll tell Miss Van Huysen who you *think* you are, but she won't like it. (*Exits.*)

AMBROSE. You'll be all right now, Ermengarde. I'd better go before she sees me.

ERMENGARDE. Oh, no. You must stay. I feel so strange here.

AMBROSE. I know, but Mr. Vandergelder will be here in a minute. . . .

ERMENGARDE. Ambrose, you can't go. You can't leave me in this crazy house with those drunken men in the hall. Ambrose . . . Ambrose, let's say you're someone else that my uncle sent down to take care of me. Let's say you're—you're Cornelius Hackl!

AMBROSE. Who's Cornelius Hackl?

ERMENGARDE. You know. He's chief clerk in Uncle's store.

AMBROSE. I don't want to be Cornelius Hackl. No, no, Ermengarde, come away with me now. I'll take you to my friend's house. Or I'll take you to Mrs. Levi's house.

ERMENGARDE. Why, it was Mrs. Levi who threw us right at Uncle Horace's face. Oh, I wish I were back in Yonkers where nothing ever happens. (*Enter* MISS VAN HUYSEN.)

MISS VAN H. What's all this I hear? Who do you say you are?

ERMENGARDE. Aunt Flora . . . don't you remember me? I'm Ermengarde.

MISS VAN H. And you're Mr. Vandergelder's niece?

ERMENGARDE. Yes, I am.

MISS VAN H. Well, that's very strange indeed, because he has just sent me another niece named Ermengarde. She came with a letter from him, explaining everything. Have you got a letter from him?

ERMENGARDE. No . . .

MISS VAN H. Really!—And who is this?

ERMENGARDE. This is Cornelius Hackl, Aunt Flora.

MISS VAN H. Never heard of him.

ERMENGARDE. He's chief clerk in Uncle's store.

MISS VAN H.   Never heard of him. The other Ermengarde came with the
man she's in love with, and that *proves* it. She came with Mr. Ambrose
Kemper.

AMBROSE   (*shouts*). Ambrose Kemper!

MISS VAN H.   Yes, Mr. Hackl, and Mr. Ambrose Kemper is in the kitchen
there now *with his feet in the oven.* (ERMENGARDE *starts to cry.* MISS
VAN HUYSEN *takes her to the sofa. They both sit.*) Dear child, what is
your trouble?

ERMENGARDE.   Oh, dear. I don't know what to do.

MISS VAN H.   (*in a low voice*). Are you in love with this man?

ERMENGARDE.   Yes, I am.

MISS VAN H.   I could see it—and are people trying to separate you?

ERMENGARDE.   Yes, they are.

MISS VAN H.   I could see it—who? Horace Vandergelder?

ERMENGARDE.   Yes.

MISS VAN H.   That's enough for me. I'll put a stop to Horace Vandergelder's goings on. (MISS VAN HUYSEN *draws* AMBROSE *down to sit on her
other side.*) Mr. Hackl, think of me as your friend. Come in the
kitchen and get warm. . . . (*She rises and starts to go out.*) We can
decide later who everybody is. My dear, would you like a good hot
bath?

ERMENGARDE.   Yes, I would.

MISS VAN H.   Well, when Ermengarde comes out you can go in. (*Enter*
CORNELIUS *from the kitchen.*)

CORNELIUS.   Oh, Miss Van Huysen . . .

ERMENGARDE.   Why, Mr. Hack—!!

CORNELIUS   (*sliding up to her, urgently*). Not yet! I'll explain. I'll explain everything.

MISS VAN H.   Mr. Kemper!—Mr. Kemper! This is Mr. Cornelius Hackl.
(*To* AMBROSE.) Mr. Hackl, this is Mr. Ambrose Kemper. (*Pause, while
the men glare at one another.*) Perhaps you two know one another?

AMBROSE.   No!

CORNELIUS.   No, we don't.

AMBROSE   (*hotly*). Miss Van Huysen, I know that man is not Ambrose
Kemper.

CORNELIUS   (*ditto*). And he's not Cornelius Hackl.

MISS VAN H.   My dear young men, what does it matter what your names
are? The important thing is that you are you. (*To* AMBROSE.) You are
alive and breathing, aren't you, Mr. Hackl? (*Pinches* AMBROSE's *left
arm.*)

AMBROSE.   Ouch, Miss Van Huysen.

MISS VAN H.   This dear child imagines she is Horace Vandergelder's niece
Ermengarde.

ERMENGARDE. But I am.

MISS VAN H. The important thing is that you're all in love. Everything else is illusion. (*She pinches* CORNELIUS' *arm.*)

CORNELIUS. Ouch! Miss Van Huysen!

MISS VAN H. (*comes down and addresses the audience*). Everybody keeps asking me if I'm Miss Van Huys . . . (*She seems suddenly to be stricken with doubt as to who she is; her face shows bewildered alarm. She pinches herself on the upper arm and is abruptly and happily relieved.*) Now, you two gentlemen sit down and have a nice chat while this dear child has a good hot bath. (*The doorbell rings.* ERMENGARDE *exits,* MISS VAN HUYSEN *about to follow her, but stops. Enter* COOK.)

COOK. There's the doorbell again.

MISS VAN H. Well, answer it. (*She and* ERMENGARDE *exit to kitchen.*)

COOK (*at window, very happy about all these guests*). It's a cab and three ladies. I never saw such a night. (*Exit to front door.*)

MISS VAN H. Gentlemen, you can rest easy. I'll see that Mr. Vandergelder lets his nieces marry you both. (*Enter* MRS. LEVI.)

MRS. LEVI. Flora, how are you?

MISS VAN H. Dolly Gallagher! What brings you here?

MRS. LEVI. Great Heavens, Flora, what are those two drunken men doing in your hall?

MRS. VAN H. I don't know. Horace Vandergelder sent them to me.

MRS. LEVI. Well, I've brought you two girls in much the same condition. Otherwise they're the finest girls in the world. (*She goes up to the door and leads in* MRS. MOLLOY. MINNIE *follows.*) I want you to meet Irene Molloy and Minnie Fay.

MISS VAN H. Delighted to know you.

MRS. LEVI. Oh, I see you two gentlemen are here, too. Mr. Hackl, I was about to look for you (*Pointing about the room.*) somewhere here.

CORNELIUS. No, Mrs. Levi. I'm ready to face anything now.

MRS. LEVI. Mr. Vandergelder will be here in a minute. He's downstairs trying to pay for a cab without any money.

MRS. MOLLOY (*holding* VANDERGELDER'S *purse*). Oh, I'll help him.

MRS. LEVI. Yes, will you, dear? You had to pay the restaurant bills. You must have hundreds of dollars there it seems.

MRS. MOLLOY. This is his own purse he lost. I can't give it back to him without seeming . . .

MRS. LEVI. I'll give it back to him.—There, you help him with this now. (*She gives* MRS. MOLLOY *a bill and puts the purse airily under her arm.*)

VANDERGELDER (*off*). Will somebody please pay for this cab? (MRS. MOLLOY *exits to front door.*)

MRS. MOLLOY (*off stage*). I'll take care of that, Mr. Vandergelder. (*As*

MR. VANDERGELDER *enters,* MALACHI *and the* CABMAN *follow him in.* VAN-
DERGELDER *carries overcoat, stick and box of chocolates.*)

CABMAN.   Fifteen dollars, Mr. Vandergelder.

MALACHI.   Hello, Mr. Vandergelder.

VANDERGELDER   (*to* MALACHI). You're discharged! (*To* CABMAN.) You
too! (MALACHI *and* CABMAN *go out and wait in the hall.*) So I've caught
up with you at last! (*To* AMBROSE.) I never want to see you again! (*To*
CORNELIUS.) You're discharged! Get out of the house, both of you. (*He
strikes sofa with his stick; a second after,* MISS VAN HUYSEN *strikes him
on the shoulder with a folded newspaper or magazine.*)

MISS VAN H.   (*forcefully*). Now then you. Stop ordering people out of
my house. You can shout and carry on in Yonkers, but when you're
in my house you'll behave yourself.

VANDERGELDER.   They're both dishonest scoundrels.

MISS VAN H.   Take your hat off. Gentlemen, you stay right where you
are.

CORNELIUS.   Mr. Vandergelder, I can explain—

MISS VAN H.   There aren't going to be any explanations. Horace, stop
scowling at Mr. Kemper and forgive him.

VANDERGELDER.   That's not Kemper, that's a dishonest rogue named
Cornelius Hackl.

MISS VAN H.   You're crazy. (*Points to* AMBROSE.) That's Cornelius Hackl.

VANDERGELDER.   I guess I know my own chief clerk.

MISS VAN H.   I don't care what their names are. You shake hands with
them both, or out you go.

VANDERGELDER.   Shake hands with those dogs and scoundrels!

MRS. LEVI.   Mr. Vandergelder, you've had a hard day. You don't want to
go out in the rain now. Just for form's sake, you shake hands with
them. You can start quarreling with them tomorrow.

VANDERGELDER   (*gives* CORNELIUS *one finger to shake*). There! Don't regard that as a handshake. (*He turns to* AMBROSE, *who mockingly offers
him one finger.*) Hey! I never want to see you again. (MRS. MOLLOY
enters from front door.)

MRS. MOLLOY.   Miss Van Huysen.

MISS VAN H.   Yes, dear?

MRS. MOLLOY.   Do I smell coffee?

MISS VAN H.   Yes, dear.

MRS. MOLLOY.   Can I have some, good and black?

MISS VAN H.   Come along, everybody. We'll all go into the kitchen and
have some coffee. (*As they all go:*) Horace, you'll be interested to know
there are two Ermengardes in there. . . .

VANDERGELDER.   Two!! (*Last to go is* MINNIE, *who revolves about the
room dreamily waltzing, a finger on her forehead.* MRS. LEVI *has been*

standing at one side. She now comes forward, in thoughtful mood. MINNIE *continues her waltz round the left sofa and out to the kitchen.* MRS. LEVI, *left alone, comes to the front, addressing an imaginary Ephraim.*)

MRS. LEVI.   Ephraim Levi, I'm going to get married again. Ephraim, I'm marrying Horace Vandergelder for his money. I'm going to send his money out doing all the things you taught me. Oh, it won't be a marriage in the sense that we had one—but I shall certainly make him happy, and Ephraim—I'm tired. I'm tired of living from hand to mouth, and I'm asking your permission, Ephraim—will you give me away? (*Now addressing the audience, she holds up the purse.*) Money! Money!—it's like the sun we walk under; it can kill or cure.—Mr. Vandergelder's money! Vandergelder's never tired of saying most of the people in the world are fools, and in a way he's right, isn't he? Himself, Irene, Cornelius, myself! But there comes a moment in everybody's life when he must decide whether he'll live among human beings or not—a fool among fools or a fool alone.

As for me, I've decided to live among them.

I wasn't always so. After my husband's death I retired into myself. Yes, in the evenings, I'd put out the cat, and I'd lock the door, and I'd make myself a little rum toddy; and before I went to bed I'd say a little prayer, thanking God that I was independent—that no one else's life was mixed up with mine. And when ten o'clock sounded from Trinity Church tower, I fell off to sleep and I was a perfectly contented woman. And one night, after two years of this, an oak leaf fell out of my Bible. I had placed it there on the day my husband asked me to marry him; a perfectly good oak leaf—but without color and without life. And suddenly I realized that for a long time I had not shed one tear; nor had I been filled with the wonderful hope that something or other would turn out well. I saw that I was like that oak leaf, and on that night I decided to rejoin the human race.

Yes, we're all fools and we're all in danger of destroying the world with our folly. But the surest way to keep us out of harm is to give us the four or five human pleasures that are our right in the world,—and that takes a little *money!*

The difference between a little money and no money at all is enormous—and can shatter the world. And the difference between a little money and an enormous amount of money is very slight—and that, also, can shatter the world.

Money, I've always felt, money—pardon my expression—is like manure; it's not worth a thing unless it's spread about encouraging young things to grow.

Anyway,—that's the opinion of the second Mrs. Vandergelder. (VAN-

DERGELDER *enters with two cups of coffee. With his back, he closes both doors.*)

VANDERGELDER.   Miss Van Huysen asked me to bring you this.

MRS. LEVI.   Thank you both. Sit down and rest yourself. What's been going on in the kitchen?

VANDERGELDER.   A lot of foolishness. Everybody falling in love with everybody. I forgave 'em; Ermengarde and that artist.

MRS. LEVI.   I knew you would.

VANDERGELDER.   I made Cornelius Hackl my partner.

MRS. LEVI.   You won't regret it.

VANDERGELDER.   Dolly, you said some mighty unpleasant things to me in the restaurant tonight . . . all that about my house . . . and everything.

MRS. LEVI.   Let's not say another word about it.

VANDERGELDER.   Dolly, you have a lot of faults—

MRS. LEVI.   Oh, I know what you mean.

VANDERGELDER.   You're bossy, scheming, inquisitive . . .

MRS. LEVI.   Go on.

VANDERGELDER.   But you're a wonderful woman. Dolly, marry me.

MRS. LEVI.   Horace! (*Rises.*) Stop right there.

VANDERGELDER.   I know I've been a fool about Mrs. Molloy, and that other woman. But, Dolly, forgive me and marry me. (*He goes on his knees.*)

MRS. LEVI.   Horace, I don't dare. No. I don't dare.

VANDERGELDER.   What do you mean?

MRS. LEVI.   You know as well as I do that you're the first citizen of Yonkers. Naturally, you'd expect your wife to keep open house, to have scores of friends in and out all the time. Any wife of yours should be used to that kind of thing.

VANDERGELDER (*after a brief struggle with himself*). Dolly, you can live any way you like.

MRS. LEVI.   Horace, you can't deny it, your wife would have to be a *somebody.* Answer me: am I a somebody?

VANDERGELDER.   You are . . . you are. Wonderful woman.

MRS. LEVI.   Oh, you're partial. (*She crosses, giving a big wink at the audience, and sits on sofa right.* VANDERGELDER *follows her on his knees.*) Horace, it won't be enough for you to load your wife with money and jewels; to insist that she be a benefactress to half the town. (*He rises and, still struggling with himself, coughs so as not to hear this.*) No, she must be a somebody. Do you really think I have it in me to be a credit to you?

VANDERGELDER.   Dolly, everybody knows that you could do anything you wanted to do.

MRS. LEVI. I'll try. With your help, I'll try—and by the way, I found your purse. (*Holds it up.*)

VANDERGELDER. Where did you—! Wonderful woman!

MRS. LEVI. It just walked into my hand. I don't know how I do it. Sometimes I frighten myself. Horace, take it. Money walks out of my hands, too.

VANDERGELDER. Keep it. Keep it.

MRS. LEVI. Horace! (*Half laughing, half weeping, and with an air of real affection for him.*) I never thought . . . I'd ever . . . hear you say a thing like that! (BARNABY *dashes in from the kitchen in great excitement. He has discarded* MINNIE'S *clothes.*)

BARNABY. Oh! Excuse me. I didn't know anybody was here.

VANDERGELDER (*bellowing*). Didn't know anybody was here. Idiot!

MR. LEVI (*putting her hand on* VANDERGELDER'S *arm; amiably*). Come in, Barnaby. Come in. (VANDERGELDER *looks at her a minute; then says, imitating her tone:*)

VANDERGELDER. Come in, Barnaby. Come in.

BARNABY. Cornelius is going to marry Mrs. Molloy!!

MRS. LEVI. Isn't that fine! Horace! . . . (MRS. LEVI *rises, and indicates that he has an announcement to make.*)

VANDERGELDER. Barnaby, go in and tell the rest of them that Mrs. Levi has consented—

MRS. LEVI. *Finally* consented!

VANDERGELDER. Finally consented to become my wife.

BARNABY. Holy cabooses. (*Dashes back to the doorway.*) Hey! Listen, everybody! Wolf-trap—I mean—Mr. Vandergelder is going to marry Mrs. Levi. (MISS VAN HUYSEN *enters followed by all the people in this act. She is now carrying the box of chocolates.*)

MISS VAN H. Dolly, that's the best news I ever heard. (*She addresses the audience.*) There isn't any more coffee; there isn't any more gingerbread; but there are three couples in my house and they're all going to get married. And do you know, one of those Ermengardes wasn't a dear little girl at all—she was a boy! Well, that's what life is: disappointment, illusion.

MRS. LEVI (*to audience*). There isn't any more coffee; there isn't any more gingerbread, and there isn't any more play—but there is one more thing we have to do. . . . Barnaby, come here. (*She whispers to him, pointing to the audience. Then she says to the audience:*) I think the youngest person here ought to tell us what the moral of the play is. (BARNABY *is reluctantly pushed forward to the footlights.*)

BARNABY. Oh, I think it's about . . . I think it's about adventure. The test of an adventure is that when you're in the middle of it, you say to yourself, "Oh, now I've got myself into an awful mess; I wish I were sitting quietly at home." And the sign that something's wrong with you is when you sit quietly at home wishing you were out having lots of adventure. What we would like for you is that you have just the right amount of sitting quietly at home and just the right amount of—adventure! So that now we all want to thank you for coming tonight, and we all hope that in your lives you have just the right amount of—adventure!

The curtain falls.

ABOUT MY PLAYS

THORNTON WILDER

Toward the end of the twenties I began to lose pleasure in going to the theatre. I ceased to believe in the stories I saw presented there. When I did go it was to admire some secondary aspect of the play, the work of a great actor or director or designer. Yet at the same time the conviction was growing in me that the theatre was the greatest of all the arts. I felt that something had gone wrong with it in my time and that it was fulfilling only a small part of its potentialities. I was filled with admiration for presentations of classical works by Max Reinhardt and Louis Jouvet and the Old Vic, as I was by the best plays of my own time, like *Desire Under the Elms* and *The Front Page;* but at heart I didn't believe a word of them. I was like a schoolmaster grading a paper; to each of these offerings I gave an A+, but the condition of mind of one grading a paper is not that of one being overwhelmed by an artistic creation. The response we make when we "believe" a work of the imagination is that of saying: "This is the way things are. I have always known it without being fully aware that I knew it. Now in the presence of this play or novel or poem (or picture or piece of music) I know that I know it." It is this form of knowledge which Plato called "recollection." We have all murdered, in thought; and been murdered. We have all seen the ridiculous in estimable persons and in ourselves. We have all known terror as well as enchantment. Imaginative literature has nothing to say to those who do not recognize—who cannot be *reminded*—of such conditions. Of all the arts the theatre is best endowed to awaken this recollection within us—to believe is to say "yes"; but in the theatres of my time I did not feel myself prompted to any such grateful and self-forgetting acquiescence.

This dissatisfaction worried me. I was not ready to condemn myself as blasé and overfastidious, for I knew that I was still capable of belief. I believed every word of *Ulysses* and of Proust and of *The Magic Mountain,* as I did of hundreds of plays when I read them. It was on the stage that imaginative narration became false. Finally, my dissatisfaction passed into resentment. I began to feel that the theatre was not only inadequate, it was evasive; it did not wish to draw upon its deeper potentialities. I found the word for it: it aimed to be *soothing.* The tragic had no heat; the comic had no bite; the social criticism failed to indict us with responsibility. I began to search for the point where the theatre had run off the track, where it had chosen—and been permitted—to become a minor art and an inconsequential diversion.

The trouble began in the nineteenth century and was connected with the rise of the middle classes—they wanted their theatre soothing. There's nothing wrong with the middle classes in themselves. We know that now. The United States and Scandinavia and Germany are middle-class countries, so completely so that they have lost the very memory of their once despised and ludicrous inferiority (they had been inferior not only to the aristocracy but, in human dignity, to the peasantry). When a middle class is new, however, there is much that is wrong with it. When it is emerging from under the shadow of an aristocracy, from the myth and prestige of those well-born Higher-ups, it is alternately insecure and aggressively complacent. It must find its justification and reassurance in making money and displaying it. To this day, members of the middle classes in England, France and Italy feel themselves to be a little ridiculous and humiliated. The prestige of aristocracies is based upon a dreary untruth that moral superiority and the qualifications for leadership are transmittable through the chromosomes, and the secondary lie, that the environment afforded by privilege and leisure tends to nurture the flowers of the spirit. An aristocracy, defending and fostering its lie, extracts from the arts only such elements as can further its interests, the aroma and not the sap, the grace and not the trenchancy. Equally harmful to culture is the newly arrived middle class. In the English-speaking world the middle classes came into power early in the nineteenth century and gained control over the theatre. They were pious, law-abiding, and industrious. They were assured of eternal life in the next world and, in this, they were squarely seated on Property and the privileges that accompany it. They were attended by devoted servants who knew their place. They were benevolent within certain limits, but chose to ignore wide tracts of injustice and stupidity in the world about them; and they shrank from contemplating those elements within themselves that were ridiculous, shallow, and harmful. They distrusted the passions and tried to deny them. Their questions about the nature of life seemed to be sufficiently answered by the demonstration of financial status and by conformity to some clearly established rules of decorum. These were precarious positions; abysses yawned on either side. The air was loud with questions that must not be asked. These audiences fashioned a theatre which could not disturb them. They thronged to melodrama (which deals with tragic possibilities in such a way that you know from the beginning that all will end happily) and to sentimental drama (which accords a total license to the supposition that the wish is father to the thought) and to comedies in which the characters were so represented that they always resembled someone else and not oneself. Between the plays that Sheridan wrote in his twenties and the first works of Wilde and Shaw there was no play of even moderate interest written in the English language. (Unless you happen to admire and except Shelley's *The Cenci*.) These audiences, however, also thronged to Shakespeare. How did they shield themselves against his probing? How did they smother the theatre—and with such effect that it smothers us still? The box set was already there, the curtain, the proscenium, but not taken "seriously"—it was a convenience in view of the weather in northern countries. They took it seriously and emphasized and enhanced everything that thus removed, cut off, and boxed the action; they increasingly shut the play up into a museum showcase.

Let us examine why the box-set stage stifles the life in drama and why and how it militates against belief.

Every action which has ever taken place—every thought, every emotion—has taken place only once, at one moment in time and place. "I love you," "I rejoice," "I suffer," have been said and felt many billions of times, and never twice the same. Every person who has ever lived has lived an unbroken succession of unique occasions. Yet the more one is aware of this individuality in experience (innumerable! innumerable!) the more one becomes attentive to what these disparate moments have in common, to repetitive patterns. As an artist (or listener or beholder) which "truth" do you prefer—that of the isolated occasion, or that which includes and resumes the innumerable? Which truth is more worth telling? Every age differs in this. Is the Venus de Milo "one woman"? Is the play *Macbeth* the story of "one destiny"? The theatre is admirably fitted to tell both truths. It has one foot planted firmly in the particular, since each actor before us (even when he wears a mask!) is indubitably a living, breathing "one"; yet it tends and strains to exhibit a general truth since its relation to a specific "realistic" truth is confused and undermined by the fact that it is an accumulation of untruths, pretenses and fiction. The novel is pre-eminently the vehicle of the unique occasion, the theatre of the generalized one. It is through the theatre's power to raise the exhibited individual action into the realm of idea and type and universal that it is able to evoke our belief. But power is precisely what those nineteenth-century audiences did not—dared not—confront. They tamed it and drew its teeth; squeezed it into that removed showcase. They loaded the stage with specific objects, because every concrete object on the stage fixes and narrows the action to one moment in time and place. (Have you ever noticed that in the plays of Shakespeare no one—except occasionally a ruler—ever sits down? There were not even chairs on the English or Spanish stages in the time of Elizabeth I.) So it was by a jugglery with time that the middle classes devitalized the theatre. When you emphasize *place* in the theatre, you drag down and limit and harness time to it. You thrust the action back into past time, whereas it is precisely the glory of the stage that it is always "now" there. Under such production methods the characters are all dead before the action starts. You don't have to pay deeply from your heart's participation. No great age in the theatre ever attempted to capture the audiences' belief through this kind of specification and localization. I became dissatisfied with the theatre because I was unable to lend credence to such childish attempts to be "real."

I began writing one-act plays that tried to capture not verisimilitude but reality. In *The Happy Journey to Trenton and Camden* four kitchen chairs represent an automobile and a family travels seventy miles in twenty minutes. Ninety years go by in *The Long Christmas Dinner*. In *Pullman Car Hiawatha* some more plain chairs serve as berths and we hear the very vital statistics of the towns and fields that passengers are traversing; we hear their thoughts; we even hear the planets over their heads. In Chinese drama a character, by straddling a stick, conveys to us that he is on horseback. In almost every No play of the Japanese an actor makes a tour of the stage and we know that he is making a long journey. Think of the ubiquity that Shakespeare's stage afforded for the battle scenes at the close of *Julius Caesar* and *Antony and Cleopatra*. As we see them today what a cutting and hacking of the text takes place—what condescension, what contempt for his dramaturgy.

Our Town is not offered as a picture of life in a New Hampshire village; or as a speculation about the conditions of life after death (that element I merely took from Dante's *Purgatory*). It is an attempt to find a value above all price for the smallest events in our daily life. I have made the claim as preposterous as possible, for I have set the village against the largest dimensions of time and place. The recurrent words in this play (few have noticed it) are "hundreds," "thousands," and "millions." Emily's joys and griefs, her algebra lessons and her birthday presents—what are they when we consider all the billions of girls who have lived, who are living, and who will live? Each individual's assertion to an absolute reality can only be inner, very inner. And here the method of staging finds its justification—in the first two acts there are at least a few chairs and tables; but when she revisits the earth and the kitchen to which she descended on her twelfth birthday, the very chairs and table are gone. Our claim, our hope, our despair are in the mind —not in things, not in "scenery." Molière said that for the theatre all he needed was a platform and a passion or two. The climax of this play needs only five square feet of boarding and the passion to know what life means to us.

The Matchmaker is an only slightly modified version of *The Merchant of Yonkers,* which I wrote in the year after I had written *Our Town.* One way to shake off the nonsense of the nineteenth-century staging is to make fun of it. This play parodies the stock-company plays that I used to see at Ye Liberty Theatre, Oakland, California, when I was a boy. I have already read small theses in German comparing it with the great Austrian original on which it is based. The scholars are very bewildered. There is most of the plot (except that our friend Dolly Levi is not in Nestroy's play); there are some of the tags; but it's all "about" quite different matters. My play is about the aspirations of the young (and not only of the young) for a fuller, freer participation in life. Imagine an Austrian pharmacist going to the shelf to draw from a bottle which he knows to contain a stinging corrosive liquid, guaranteed to remove warts and wens; and imagine his surprise when he discovers that it has been filled overnight with very American birch-bark beer.

The Skin of Our Teeth begins, also, by making fun of old-fashioned playwriting; but the audience soon perceives that he is seeing "two times at once." The Antrobus family is living both in prehistoric times and in a New Jersey commuters' suburb today. Again, the events of our homely daily life—this time the family life—are depicted against the vast dimensions of time and place. It was written on the eve of our entrance into the war and under strong emotion and I think it mostly comes alive under conditions of crisis. It has been often charged with being a bookish fantasia about history, full of rather bloodless schoolmasterish jokes. But to have seen it in Germany soon after the war, in the shattered churches and beerhalls that were serving as theatres, with audiences whose price of admission meant the loss of a meal and for whom it was of absorbing interest that there was a "recipe for grass soup that did not cause the diarrhea," was an experience that was not so cool. I am very proud that this year it has received a first and overwhelming reception in Warsaw. The play is deeply indebted to James Joyce's *Finnegans Wake.* I should be very happy if, in the future, some author should feel similarly indebted to any work of mine. Literature has always more resembled a torch race than a furious dispute among heirs.

The theatre has lagged behind the other arts in finding the "new ways" to express how men and women think and feel in our time. I am not one of the new dramatists we are looking for. I wish I were. I hope I have played a part in preparing the way for them. I am not an innovator but a rediscoverer of forgotten goods and I hope a remover of obtrusive bric-a-brac. And as I view the work of my contemporaries I seem to feel that I am exceptional in one thing—I give (don't I?) the impression of having enormously enjoyed it.

WILLIAMS

TENNESSEE (BORN THOMAS LANIER) WILLIAMS (1914–   ), A NATIVE OF MISSIS-
SIPPI, WHOSE ADOLESCENCE WAS SPENT IN ST. LOUIS AND AT THE UNIVERSITY
OF MISSOURI, EMERGED AFTER A DECADE OF WANDERING AT THE END OF
WORLD WAR II AS THE FIRST OF A NEW GENERATION OF AMERICAN PLAY-
WRIGHTS. HE WAS SOON TO BE JOINED BY ARTHUR MILLER, ARTHUR LAU-
RENTS, WILLIAM INGE, AND EVENTUALLY EDWARD ALBEE. AMERICAN THEATER
UP TO 1945 HAD BEEN PRINCIPALLY COMMITTED TO THE REALISTIC-NATURAL-
ISTIC MODE OF CLIFFORD ODETS–ELMER RICE–LILLIAN HELLMAN AND TO THE
WELL-MADE COMEDY OF MANNERS. WILLIAMS BROUGHT TO AMERICAN DRAMA A
SYMBOLISM UNOBTRUSIVELY WORKED INTO THE TEXTURE OF LANGUAGE AND
GESTURE. HE EVOKES A NOSTALGIA FOR THE GENTLE AND THE BEAUTIFUL
WITHOUT AVOIDING A DIRECT GLANCE AT THE HARSH, OFTEN SINISTER AS-
PECTS OF AMERICAN LIFE. WILLIAMS'S SUBJECT AND THEMATIC MATERIALS ARE
RELATED TO THOSE OF A GROUP OF SOUTHERN NOVELISTS: WILLIAM FAULK-
NER, ERSKINE CALDWELL, LILLIAN SMITH, CARSON MCCULLERS, AND THOMAS
WOLFE. WILLIAMS'S PLAYS INCLUDE *THE GLASS MENAGERIE* (1945); *A STREET-
CAR NAMED DESIRE* (1947); *THE ROSE TATTOO* (1950); *CAMINO REAL* (1953);
CAT ON A HOT TIN ROOF (1955); *ORPHEUS DESCENDING* (1957); *SWEET BIRD OF
YOUTH* (1959); *PERIOD OF ADJUSTMENT* (1960).

Summer and Smoke deals with two pilgrimages: one being's quest for
spiritual and intellectual fulfillment; another's for sensual gratification.
There are no reversals, no exchanges in aspiration. The spiritual quest,
from the very first line, is that of John Buchanan—the eternal male. The
desire to achieve sensual gratification is that of Alma—the eternal
woman.

The prologue establishes the relationship between the two principals;
a bright, motherless boy seeks out the preacher's daughter. Note his puzzled awareness of her abiding interest in him. Despite her retreat behind
evasions and tactless references to his disorderliness, he persists in thinking that she can pluck the heart out of mysteries. Finally, disappointed
by her incapacity to minister to his hungry soul, he runs off.

Note that the concluding scene of the first act (Scene 6) corresponds
to the conclusion of the prologue. How does the parallel relate to the
basic theme of the play? At what moment do we understand that John's
is a spiritual quest while Alma's need is to satisfy an emotional-sexual
hunger? Why does John come to the group meeting in the Rectory, and
why does he leave?

Rosa, understanding John better than Alma, mutilates him when they
make love "because I know I can't hold you." John's sexuality is an op-
pressive burden to him. Why does he reveal that fact about himself to
Rosa but conceal it from Alma—who imagines him to be a profligate
libertine?

Is John's ultimate choice of a wife psychologically credible, consistent
with everything that has gone before? Are we to assume that Alma's life
is destroyed by her parents, the community, and her own inability to respond to the great need in John? Or is the final scene more hopeful than
pathetic?

SUMMER AND SMOKE

PART ONE—A SUMMER

PART TWO—A WINTER

The entire action of the play takes place in Glorious Hill, Mississippi. The time is the turn of the century through 1916.

PART ONE—A SUMMER

PROLOGUE

In the park near the angel of the fountain. At dusk of an evening in May, in the first few years of this Century.

Alma, as a child of ten, comes into the scene. She wears a middy blouse and has ribboned braids. She already has the dignity of an adult; there is a quality of extraordinary delicacy and tenderness or spirituality in her, which must set her distinctly apart from other children. She has a habit of holding her hands, one cupped under the other in a way similar to that of receiving the wafer at Holy Communion. This is a habit that will remain with her as an adult. She stands like that in front of the stone angel for a few moments; then bends to drink at the fountain.

While she is bent at the fountain, John, as a child, enters. He shoots a pea-shooter at Alma's bent-over back. She utters a startled cry and whirls about. He laughs.

JOHN. Hi, Preacher's daughter. (*He advances toward her*) I been looking for you.

ALMA (*hopefully*). You have?

JOHN. Was it you that put them handkerchiefs on my desk? (*Alma
smiles uncertainly*) Answer up!

ALMA. I put a box of handkerchiefs on your desk.

JOHN. I figured it was you. What was the idea, Miss Priss?

ALMA. You needed them.

JOHN. Trying to make a fool of me?

ALMA. Oh, no!

JOHN. Then what was the idea?

ALMA. You have a bad cold and your nose has been running all week.
It spoils your appearance.

JOHN. You don't have to look at me if you don't like my appearance.

ALMA. I like your appearance.

JOHN (*coming closer*). Is that why you look at me all the time?

ALMA. I—don't!

JOHN. Oh, yeh, you do. You been keeping your eyes on me all the time.
Every time I look around I see them cat eyes of yours looking at me.
That was the trouble today when Miss Blanchard asked you where
the river Amazon was. She asked you twice and you still didn't answer
because you w' lookin' at me. What's the idea? What've'y' got on y'
mind anyhow?

ALMA. I was only thinking how handsome you'd be if your face wasn't
dirty. You know why your face is dirty? Because you don't use a handkerchief and you wipe your nose on the sleeve of that dirty old sweater.

JOHN (*indignantly*). Hah!

ALMA. That's why I put the handkerchiefs on your desk and I wrapped
them up so nobody would know what they were. It isn't my fault that
you opened the box in front of everybody!

JOHN. What did you think I'd do with a strange box on my desk? Just
leave it there till it exploded or something? Sure I opened it up. I
didn't expect to find no—*handkerchiefs!*—in it . . .

ALMA (*in a shy trembling voice*). I'm sorry that you were embarrassed.
I honestly am awfully sorry that you were embarrassed. Because I
wouldn't embarrass you for the world!

JOHN. Don't flatter yourself that I was embarrassed. I don't embarrass
that easy.

ALMA. It was stupid and cruel of those girls to laugh.

JOHN. Hah!

ALMA. They should all realize that you don't have a mother to take
care of such things for you. It was a pleasure to me to be able to do

something for you, only I didn't want you to know it was me who did it.

JOHN. Hee-haw! Ho-hum! Take 'em back! (*He snatches out the box and thrusts it toward her.*)

ALMA. *Please* keep them.

JOHN. What do I want with them?

(*She stares at him helplessly. He tosses the box to the ground and goes up to the fountain and drinks. Something in her face mollifies him and he sits down at the base of the fountain with a manner that does not preclude a more friendly relation. The dusk gathers deeper.*)

ALMA. Do you know the name of the angel?

JOHN. Does she have a name?

ALMA. Yes, I found out she does. It's carved in the base, but it's all worn away so you can't make it out with your eyes.

JOHN. Then how do you know it?

ALMA. You have to read it with your fingers. I did and it gave me cold shivers! *You* read it and see if it doesn't give *you* cold shivers! Go on! Read it with your fingers!

JOHN. Why don't you tell me and save me the trouble?

ALMA. I'm not going to tell you.

(JOHN *grins indulgently and turns to the pediment, crouching before it and running his fingers along the worn inscription.*)

JOHN. E?

ALMA. Yes, E is the first letter!

JOHN. T?

ALMA. Yes!

JOHN. E?

ALMA. E!

JOHN. K?

ALMA. No, no, not K!—R! (*He slowly straightens up*)

JOHN. Eternity?

ALMA. *Eternity!*—Didn't it give you the cold shivers?

JOHN. Nahh.

ALMA. Well, it did me!

JOHN. Because you're a preacher's daughter. Eternity. What is eternity?

ALMA (*in a hushed wondering voice*). It's something that goes on and on when life and death and time and everything else is all through with.

JOHN. There's no such thing.

ALMA. There is. It's what people's souls live in when they have left their bodies. My name is Alma and Alma is Spanish for soul. Did you know that?

JOHN. Hee-haw! Ho-hum! Have you ever seen a dead person?

ALMA. No.

JOHN. I have. They made me go in the room when my mother was dying and she caught hold of my hand and wouldn't let me go—and so I screamed and hit her.

ALMA. Oh, you didn't do that.

JOHN (*somberly*). Uh-huh. She didn't look like my mother. Her face was all ugly and yellow and—terrible—bad-smelling! And so I hit her to make her let go of my hand. They told me that I was a devil!

ALMA. You didn't know what you were doing.

JOHN. My dad is a doctor.

ALMA. I know.

JOHN. He wants to send me to college to study to be a doctor but I wouldn't be a doctor for the world. And have to go in a room and watch people dying! . . . Jesus!

ALMA. You'll change your mind about that.

JOHN. Oh, no, I won't. I'd rather *be* a devil, like they called me and go to South America on a boat! . . . Give me one of them handkerchiefs. (*She brings them eagerly and humbly to the fountain. He takes one out and wets it at the fountain and scrubs his face with it*) Is my face clean enough to suit you now?

ALMA. Yes!—Beautiful!

JOHN. *What!*

ALMA. I said "Beautiful"!

JOHN. Well—let's—kiss each other.

(ALMA *turns away.*)

JOHN. Come on, let's just try it!

(*He seizes her shoulders and gives her a quick rough kiss. She stands amazed with one hand cupping the other.*

(*The voice of a child in the distance calls "Johnny! Johnny!"*)

(*He suddenly snatches at her hair-ribbon, jerks it loose and then runs off with a mocking laugh.*

(*Hurt and bewildered,* ALMA *turns back to the stone angel, for comfort. She crouches at the pediment and touches the inscription with her fingers. The scene dims out with music.*)

SCENE ONE

Before the curtain rises a band is heard playing a patriotic anthem, punctuated with the crackle of fireworks.

The scene is the same as for the Prologue. It is the evening of July 4th in a year shortly before the first World War. There is a band concert

and a display of fireworks in the park. During the scene the light changes
from faded sunlight to dusk. Sections of roof, steeples, weathervanes,
should have a metallic surface that catches the mellow light on the back-
drop; when dusk has fallen the stars should be visible.

As the curtain rises, the Rev. and Mrs. Winemiller come in and sit on
the bench near the fountain. Mrs. Winemiller was a spoiled and selfish
girl who evaded the responsibilities of later life by slipping into a state
of perverse childishness. She is known as Mr. Winemiller's "Cross."

MR. WINEMILLER   *(suddenly rising)*. There is Alma, getting on the bandstand! (MRS. WINEMILLER *is dreamily munching popcorn.*)

AN ANNOUNCER'S VOICE   *(at a distance)*. The Glorious Hill Orchestra
brings you Miss Alma Winemiller, The Nightingale of the Delta, singing . . . "La Golondrina."

MR. WINEMILLER   *(sitting back down again)*. This is going to provoke a
lot of criticism.

(The song commences. The voice is not particularly strong, but it has
great purity and emotion. JOHN BUCHANAN *comes along. He is now a*
Promethean figure, brilliantly and restlessly alive in a stagnant society.
The excess of his power has not yet found a channel. If it remains with-
out one, it will burn him up. At present he is unmarked by the dissipa-
tions in which he relieves his demoniac unrest; he has the fresh and shin-
ing look of an epic hero. He walks leisurely before the Winemillers'
bench, negligently touching the crown of his hat but not glancing at
them; climbs the steps to the base of the fountain, then turns and looks
in the direction of the singer. A look of interest touched with irony ap-
pears on his face. A COUPLE, *strolling in the park, pass behind the foun-*
tain.)

THE GIRL.   Look who's by the fountain!

THE MAN.   Bright as a new silver dollar!

JOHN.   Hi, Dusty! Hi, Pearl!

THE MAN.   How'd you make out in that floating crap game?

JOHN.   I floated with it as far as Vicksburg, then sank.

THE GIRL.   Everybody's been calling: "Johnny, Johnny—where's Johnny?"
(JOHN'S *father,* DR. BUCHANAN, *comes on from the right, as* REV. *and* MRS.
WINEMILLER *move off the scene to the left, toward the band music.* DR.
BUCHANAN *is an elderly man whose age shows in his slow and stiff move-*
ments. He walks with a cane. JOHN *sees him coming, but pretends not to*
and starts to walk off.)

DR. BUCHANAN.   John!

JOHN   *(slowly turning around, as the* COUPLE *move off)*. Oh! Hi, Dad.
   . . . *(They exchange a long look)* I—uh—meant to wire you but I
must've forgot. I got tied up in Vicksburg Friday night and just now

got back to town. Haven't been to the house yet. Is everything . . .
going okay? (*He takes a drink of water at the fountain*)

DR. BUCHANAN   (*slowly, in a voice hoarse with emotion*). There isn't any
room in the medical profession for wasters, drunkards and lechers. And
there isn't any room in my house for wasters—drunkards—lechers! (*A
CHILD is heard calling "I sp-yyyyyy!" in the distance*) I married late in
life. I brought over five hundred children into this world before I had
one of my own. And by God it looks like I've given myself the rotten-
est one of the lot. . . . (JOHN *laughs uncertainly*) You will find your
things at the Alhambra Hotel.

JOHN.   Okay. If that's how you want it.

(*There is a pause. The singing comes through on the music.* JOHN *tips
his hat diffidently and starts away from the fountain. He goes a few feet
and his* FATHER *suddenly calls after him.*)

DR. BUCHANAN.   John! (JOHN *pauses and looks back*) Come here.

JOHN.   Yes, Sir? (*He walks back to his* FATHER *and stands before him*)

DR. BUCHANAN   (*hoarsely*). Go to the Alhambra Hotel and pick up your
things and—bring them back to the house.

JOHN   (*gently*). Yes, Sir. If that's how you want it. (*He diffidently extends a hand to touch his* FATHER'S *shoulder.*)

DR. BUCHANAN   (*brushing the hand roughly off*). You! . . . You infernal
whelp, you!

(DR. BUCHANAN *turns and goes hurriedly away.* JOHN *looks after him with
a faint, affectionate smile, then sits down on the steps with an air of relief, handkerchief to forehead, and a whistle of relief. Just then the singing at the bandstand ends and there is the sound of applause.* MRS. WINE-
MILLER *comes in from the left, followed by her* HUSBAND.)

MRS. WINEMILLER.   Where is the ice cream man?

MR. WINEMILLER.   Mother, hush! (*He sees his* DAUGHTER *approaching*)
Here we are, Alma!

(*The song ends. There is applause. Then the band strikes up the Santi-
ago Waltz.*

(ALMA WINEMILLER *enters.* ALMA *had an adult quality as a child and now,
in her middle twenties, there is something prematurely spinsterish about
her. An excessive propriety and self-consciousness is apparent in her
nervous laughter; her voice and gestures belong to years of church entertainment, to the position of hostess in a rectory. People her own age
regard her as rather quaintly and humorously affected. She has grown
up mostly in the company of her elders. Her true nature is still hidden
even from herself. She is dressed in pale yellow and carries a yellow silk
parasol.*

(*As* ALMA *passes in front of the fountain,* JOHN *slaps his hands resound-*

*ingly together a few times. She catches her breath in a slight laughing
sound, makes as if to retreat, with a startled "Oh!", but then goes quickly
to her* PARENTS. *The applause from the crowd continues.*)

MR. WINEMILLER.   They seem to want to hear you sing again, Alma.
(*She turns nervously about, touching her throat and her chest.* JOHN
grins, applauding by the fountain. When the applause dies out, ALMA
sinks faintly on the bench.)

ALMA.   Open my bag, Father. My fingers have frozen stiff! (*She draws a
deep labored breath*) I don't know what came over me—absolute
panic! Never, never again, it isn't worth it—the tortures that I go
through!

MR. WINEMILLER   (*anxiously*). You're having one of your nervous attacks?

ALMA.   My heart's beating so! It seemed to be in my *throat* the whole
time I was singing! (JOHN *laughs audibly from the fountain*) Was it
noticeable, Father?

MR. WINEMILLER.   You sang extremely well, Alma. But you know how I
feel about this, it was contrary to my wishes and I cannot imagine why
you wanted to do it, especially since it seemed to upset you so.

ALMA.   I don't see how anyone could object to my singing at a patriotic
occasion. If I had just sung well! But I barely got through it. At one
point I thought that I wouldn't. The words flew out of my mind. Did
you notice the pause? Blind panic! They really never came back, but
I went on singing—I think I must have been improvising the lyric!
Whew! Is there a handkerchief in it?

MRS. WINEMILLER   (*suddenly*). Where is the ice cream man?

ALMA   (*rubbing her fingers together*). Circulation is slowly coming
back . . .

MR. WINEMILLER.   Sit back quietly and take a deep breath, Alma.

ALMA.   Yes, my handkerchief—now . . .

MRS. WINEMILLER.   Where is the ice cream man?

MR. WINEMILLER.   Mother, there isn't any ice cream man.

ALMA.   No, there isn't any ice cream man, Mother. But on the way
home Mr. Doremus and I will stop by the drug store and pick up a
pint of ice cream.

MR. WINEMILLER.   Are you intending to stay here?

ALMA.   Until the concert is over. I promised Roger I'd wait for him.

MR. WINEMILLER.   I suppose you have noticed who is by the fountain?

ALMA.   *Shhh!*

MR. WINEMILLER.   Hadn't you better wait on a different bench?

ALMA.   This is where Roger will meet me.

MR. WINEMILLER.   Well, Mother, we'll run along now. (MRS. WINEMILLER

has started vaguely toward the fountain, MR. WINEMILLER *firmly re-
straining her)* This way, this way, Mother! *(He takes her arm and
leads her off)*

MRS. WINEMILLER *(calling back, in a high, childish voice).* Strawberry,
Alma. Chocolate, chocolate and strawberry mixed! Not vanilla!

ALMA *(faintly).* Yes, yes, Mother—vanilla . . .

MRS. WINEMILLER *(furiously).* I said *not* vanilla. *(Shouting)* Strawberry!

MR. WINEMILLER *(fiercely).* Mother! We're attracting attention. *(He
propels her forcibly away)*

*(*JOHN *laughs by the fountain.* ALMA *moves her parasol so that it shields
her face from him. She leans back closing her eyes.* JOHN *notices a firecracker by the fountain. He leans over negligently to pick it up. He grins
and lights it and tosses it toward* ALMA's *bench. When it goes off she
springs up with a shocked cry, letting the parasol drop.)*

JOHN *(jumping up as if outraged).* Hey! Hey, you! *(He looks off to
the right.* ALMA *sinks back weakly on the bench.* JOHN *solicitously advances)* Are you all right?

ALMA. I can't seem to—catch my breath! Who threw it?

JOHN. Some little rascal.

ALMA. Where?

JOHN. He ran away quick when I hollered!

ALMA. There ought to be an ordinance passed in this town forbidding
firecrackers.

JOHN. Dad and I treated fifteen kids for burns the last couple of days.
I think you need a little restorative, don't you? *(He takes out a flask)*
Here!

ALMA. What is it?

JOHN. Applejack brandy.

ALMA. No thank you.

JOHN. Liquid dynamite.

ALMA. I'm sure.

*(*JOHN *laughs and returns it to his pocket. He remains looking down at
her with one foot on the end of her bench. His steady, smiling look into
her face is disconcerting her.)*

(In ALMA's *voice and manner there is a delicacy and elegance, a kind of
"airiness," which is really natural to her as it is, in a less marked degree,
to many Southern girls. Her gestures and mannerisms are a bit exaggerated but in a graceful way. It is understandable that she might be accused of "putting on airs" and of being "affected" by the other young
people of the town. She seems to belong to a more elegant age, such as
the Eighteenth Century in France. Out of nervousness and self-consciousness she has a habit of prefacing and concluding her remarks with a little*

breathless laugh. This will be indicated at points, but should be used more freely than indicated; however, the characterization must never be stressed to the point of making her at all ludicrous in a less than sympathetic way.)

ALMA. You're—home for the summer? (JOHN *gives an affirmative grunt*) Summer is not the pleasantest time of year to renew an acquaintance with Glorious Hill—is it? (JOHN *gives an indefinite grunt.* ALMA *laughs airily*) The Gulf wind has failed us this year, disappointed us dreadfully this summer. We used to be able to rely on the Gulf wind to cool the nights off for us, but this summer has been an exceptional season. (*He continues to grin disconcertingly down at her; she shows her discomfiture in flurried gestures*)

JOHN (*slowly*). Are you—disturbed about something?

ALMA. That firecracker was a shock.

JOHN. You should be over that shock by now.

ALMA. I don't get over shocks quickly.

JOHN. I see you don't.

ALMA. You're planning to stay here and take over some of your father's medical practice?

JOHN. I haven't made up my mind about anything yet.

ALMA. I hope so, we all hope so. Your father was telling me that you have succeeded in isolating the germ of that fever epidemic that's broken out at Lyon.

JOHN. Finding something to kill it is more of a trick.

ALMA. You'll do that! He's so positive that you will. He says that you made a special study of bacter—bacter . . .

JOHN. Bacteriology!

ALMA. Yes! At Johns Hopkins! That's in Boston, isn't it?

JOHN. No. Baltimore.

ALMA. Oh, Baltimore. Baltimore, Maryland. Such a beautiful combination of names. And bacteriology—isn't that something you do with a microscope?

JOHN. Well—partly. . . .

ALMA. I've looked through a telescope, but never a microscope. What . . . what do you—see?

JOHN. A—universe, Miss Alma.

ALMA. What kind of a universe?

JOHN. Pretty much the same kind that you saw through the lens of a telescope—a mysterious one. . . .

ALMA. Oh, yes. . . .

JOHN. Part anarchy—and part order!

ALMA. The footprints of God!

JOHN. But not God.

ALMA   (*ecstatically*). To be a doctor! And deal with these mysteries
under the microscope lens . . . I think it is more religious than being
a priest! There is so much suffering in the world it actually makes one
sick to think about it, and most of us are so helpless to relieve it. . . .
But a physician! Oh, my! With his magnificent gifts and training
what a joy it must be to know that he is equipped and appointed to
bring relief to all of this fearful suffering—and fear! And it's an ex-
panding profession, it's a profession that is continually widening its
horizons. So many diseases have already come under scientific control
but the commencement is just—beginning! I mean there is so much
more that is yet to be done, such as mental afflictions to be brought
under control. . . . And with your father's example to inspire you!
Oh, my!

JOHN.   I didn't know you had so many ideas about the medical profession.

ALMA.   Well, I am a great admirer of your father, as well as a patient.
It's such a comfort knowing that he's right next door, within arm's
reach as it were!

JOHN.   Why? Do you have fits? . . .

ALMA.   Fits? (*She throws back her head with a peal of gay laughter*)
Why no, but I do have attacks!—of nervous heart trouble. Which can
be so alarming that I run straight to your father!

JOHN.   At two or three in the morning?

ALMA.   Yes, as late as that, even . . . occasionally. He's very patient with
me.

JOHN.   But does you no good?

ALMA.   He always reassures me.

JOHN.   Temporarily?

ALMA.   Yes . . .

JOHN.   Don't you want more than that?

ALMA.   What?

JOHN.   It's none of my business.

ALMA.   What were you going to say?

JOHN.   You're Dad's patient. But I have an idea . . .

ALMA.   Please go on! (JOHN *laughs a little*) Now you have to go on! You
can't leave me up in the air! What were you going to tell me?

JOHN.   Only that I suspect you need something more than a little tem-
porary reassurance.

ALMA.   *Why?* Why? You think it's more serious than . . . ?

JOHN.   You're swallowing air, Miss Alma.

ALMA.   I'm what?

JOHN.   You're swallowing air, Miss Alma.

ALMA.   I'm swallowing air?

JOHN. Yes, you swallow air when you laugh or talk. It's a little trick that hysterical women get into.

ALMA (*uncertainly*). Ha-ha . . . !

JOHN. You swallow air and it presses on your heart and gives you palpitations. That isn't serious in itself but it's a symptom of something that is. Shall I tell you frankly?

ALMA. Yes!

JOHN. Well, what I think you have is a *doppelganger!* You have a *doppelganger* and the *doppelganger* is badly irritated.

ALMA. Oh, my goodness! I have an irritated *doppelganger!* (*She tries to laugh, but is definitely uneasy*) How awful that sounds! What exactly *is* it?

JOHN. It's none of *my* business. You are not *my* patient.

ALMA. But that's downright wicked of you! To tell me I have something awful-sounding as that, and then refuse to let me know what it is! (*She tries to laugh again, unsuccessfully*)

JOHN. I shouldn't have said anything! I'm not your doctor. . . .

ALMA. Just how did you arrive at this—diagnosis of my case? (*She laughs*) But of course you're teasing me. Aren't you? . . . There, the Gulf wind is stirring! He's actually moving the leaves of the palmetto! And listen to them complaining. . . .

(*As if brought in by this courier from the tropics,* ROSA GONZALES *enters and crosses to the fountain. Her indolent walk produces a sound and an atmosphere like the Gulf wind on the palmettos, a whispering of silk and a slight rattle of metallic ornaments. She is dressed in an almost outrageous finery, with lustrous feathers on her hat, greenish blue, a cascade of them, also diamond and emerald earrings.*)

JOHN (*sharply*). *Who is that?*

ALMA. I'm surprised that you don't know.

JOHN. I've been away quite a while.

ALMA. That's the Gonzales girl. . . . Her father's the owner of the gambling casino on Moon Lake. (ROSA *drinks at the fountain and wanders leisurely off*) She smiled at you, didn't she?

JOHN. I thought she did.

ALMA. I hope that you have a strong character. (*He places a foot on the end of the bench*)

JOHN. Solid rock.

ALMA (*nervously*). The pyrotechnical display is going to be brilliant.

JOHN. The what?

ALMA. The fireworks.

JOHN. Aw!

ALMA. I suppose you've lost touch with most of your *old* friends here.

JOHN (*laconically*). Yeah.

ALMA. You must make some *new* ones! I belong to a little group that meets every ten days. I think you'd enjoy them, too. They're young people with—intellectual and artistic interests. . . .

JOHN (*sadly*). Aw, I see . . . intellectual. . . .

ALMA. You must come!—sometime—I'm going to remind you of it. . . .

JOHN. Thanks. Do you mind if I sit down?

ALMA. Why, certainly not, there's room enough for two! Neither of us are—terribly large in diameter! (*She laughs shrilly.*)

(*A girl's voice is heard calling: "Good-bye, Nellie!" and another answers: "Good-bye!"* NELLIE EWELL *enters——a girl of sixteen with a radiantly fresh healthy quality.*)

ALMA. Here comes someone much nicer! One of my adorable little vocal pupils, the youngest and prettiest one with the least gift for music.

JOHN. I know that one.

ALMA. Hello, there, Nellie dear!

NELLIE. Oh, Miss Alma, your singing was so beautiful it made me cry.

ALMA. It's sweet of you to fib so. I sang terribly.

NELLIE. You're just being modest, Miss Alma. Hello, Dr. John! Dr. John?

JOHN. Yeah?

NELLIE. That book you gave me is too full of long words.

JOHN. Look 'em up in the dictionary, Nellie.

NELLIE. I did, but you know how dictionaries are. You look up one long word and it gives you another and you look up that one and it gives you the long word you looked up in the first place. (JOHN *laughs*) I'm coming over tomorrow for you to explain it all to me. (*She laughs and goes off*)

ALMA. What book is she talking about?

JOHN. A book I gave her about the facts of nature. She came over to the office and told me her mother wouldn't tell her anything and she had to know because she'd fallen in love.

ALMA. Why the precocious little—imp! (*She laughs.*)

JOHN. What sort of a mother has she?

ALMA. Mrs. Ewell's the merry widow of Glorious Hill. They say that she goes to the depot to meet every train in order to make the acquaintance of traveling salesmen. Of course she is ostracized by all but a few of her own type of women in town, which is terribly hard for Nellie. It isn't fair to the child. Father didn't want me to take her as a pupil because of her mother's reputation, but I feel that one has a duty to perform toward children in such—circumstances. . . . And I always say that life is such a mysteriously complicated thing that no one should really presume to judge and condemn the behavior of anyone else!

(*There is a faraway "puff" and a burst of golden light over their heads.*

Both look up. There is a long-drawn "Ahhh . . ." from the invisible crowd. This is an effect that will be repeated at intervals during the scene.)

There goes the first sky-rocket! Oh, look at it burst into a million stars! (JOHN *leans way back to look up and allows his knees to spread wide apart so that one of them is in contact with* ALMA's. *The effect upon her is curiously disturbing.)*

JOHN *(after a moment)* . Do you have a chill?

ALMA. Why, no!—no. Why?

JOHN. You're shaking.

ALMA. Am I?

JOHN. Don't you feel it?

ALMA. I have a touch of malaria lingering on.

JOHN. You have malaria?

ALMA. Never severely, never really severely. I just have touches of it that come and go. *(She laughs airily)*

JOHN *(with a gentle grin)* . Why do you laugh that way?

ALMA. What way?

(JOHN *imitates her laugh.* ALMA *laughs again in embarrassment.)*

JOHN. Yeah. That way.

ALMA. I do declare, you haven't changed in the slightest. It used to delight you to embarrass me and it still does!

JOHN. I guess I shouldn't tell you this, but I heard an imitation of you at a party.

ALMA. Imitation? Of what?

JOHN. You.

ALMA. I?—I? Why, *what* did they imitate?

JOHN. You singing at a wedding.

JOHN. My voice?

JOHN. Your gestures and facial expression!

ALMA. How mystifying!

JOHN. No, I shouldn't have told you. You're upset about it.

ALMA. I'm not in the least upset, I am just mystified.

JOHN. Don't you know that you have a reputation for putting on airs a little—for gilding the lily a bit?

ALMA. I have no idea what you are talking about.

JOHN. Well, some people seem to have gotten the idea that you are just a little bit—affected!

ALMA. Well, well, well, well. *(She tries to conceal her hurt)* That may be so, it may seem so to some people. But since I am innocent of any attempt at affectation, I really don't know what I can do about it.

JOHN. You have a rather fancy way of talking.

ALMA. Have I?

JOHN. Pyrotechnical display instead of fireworks, and that sort of thing.

ALMA. So?

JOHN. And how about that accent?

ALMA. Accent? This leaves me quite speechless! I have sometimes been accused of having a put-on accent by people who disapprove of good diction. My father was a Rhodes scholar at Oxford, and while over there he fell into the natural habit of using the long A where it is correct to use it. I suppose I must have picked it up from him, but it's entirely unconscious. Who gave this imitation at this party you spoke of?

JOHN (*grinning*). I don't think she'd want that told.

ALMA. Oh, it was a *she* then?

JOHN. You don't think a man could do it?

ALMA. No, and I don't think a lady would do it either!

JOHN. I didn't think it would have made you so mad, or I wouldn't have brought it up.

ALMA. Oh, I'm not mad. I'm just mystified and amazed as I always am by unprovoked malice in people. I don't understand it when it's directed at me and I don't understand it when it is directed at anybody else. I just don't understand it, and perhaps it is better not to understand it. These people who call me affected and give these unkind imitations of me—I wonder if they stop to think that I have had certain difficulties and disadvantages to cope with—which may be partly the cause of these peculiarities of mine—which they find so offensive!

JOHN. Now, Miss Alma, you're making a mountain out of a molehill!

ALMA. I wonder if they stop to think that my circumstances are somewhat different from theirs? My father and I have a certain—cross—to bear!

JOHN. What cross?

ALMA. Living next door to us, you should know what cross.

JOHN. Mrs. Winemiller?

ALMA. She had her breakdown while I was still in high school. And from that time on I have had to manage the Rectory and take over the social and household duties that would ordinarily belong to a minister's wife, not his daughter. And that may have made me seem strange to some of my more critical contemporaries. In a way it may have—deprived me of—my youth. . . .

(*Another rocket goes up. Another "Ahhh . . ." from the crowd.*)

JOHN. You ought to go out with young people.

ALMA. I am not a recluse. I don't fly around here and there giving imitations of other people at parties. But I am not a recluse by any manner of means. Being a minister's daughter I have to be more selective

than most girls about the—society I keep. But I do go out now and
then. . . .

JOHN.   I have seen you in the public library and the park, but only two
or three times have I seen you out with a boy and it was always someone like this Roger Doremus.

ALMA.   I'm afraid that you and I move in different circles. If I wished to
be as outspoken as you are, which is sometimes just an excuse for being
rude—I might say that I've yet to see you in the company of a—well, a
—reputable young woman. You've heard unfavorable talk about me in
your circle of acquaintances and I've heard equally unpleasant things
about you in mine. And the pity of it is that you are preparing to be a
doctor. You're intending to practice your father's profession here in
Glorious Hill. *(She catches her breath in a sob)* Most of us have no
choice but to lead useless lives! But you have a gift for scientific research! You have a chance to serve humanity. Not just to go on enduring for the sake of endurance, but to serve a noble, humanitarian cause,
to relieve human suffering. And what do you do about it? Everything
that you can to alienate the confidence of nice people who love and respect your father. While he is devoting himself to the fever at Lyon you
drive your automobile at a reckless pace from one disorderly roadhouse
to another! You say you have seen two things through the microscope,
anarchy and order? Well, obviously *order* is not the thing that impressed you . . . conducting yourself like some overgrown schoolboy
who wants to be known as the wildest fellow in town! And you—a
gifted young doctor—*Magna cum Laude!* *(She turns aside, touching
her eyelids with a handkerchief)* You know what I call it? I call it a
desecration! *(She sobs uncontrollably. Then she springs up from the
bench.* JOHN *catches her hand)*

JOHN.   You're not going to run off, are you?

ALMA.   Singing in public always—always upsets me!—Let go of my
hand. *(He holds on to it, grinning up at her in the deepening dusk.
The stars are coming out in the cyclorama with its leisurely floating
cloud-forms. In the distance the band is playing "La Golondrina")*
Please let go of my hand.

JOHN.   Don't run off mad.

ALMA.   Let's not make a spectacle of ourselves.

JOHN.   Then sit back down.

(A skyrocket goes up. The crowd "Ahhh . . .s.")

ALMA.   You threw that firecracker and started a conversation just in
order to tease me as you did as a child. You came to this bench in order
to embarrass me and to hurt my feelings with the report of that vicious
—imitation! No, let go of my hand so I can leave, now. You've suc-

ceeded in your purpose. I *was* hurt, I *did* make a fool of myself as you intended! So let me go now!

JOHN.   You're attracting attention! Don't you know that I really *like* you, Miss Alma?

ALMA.   No, you don't.

(*Another skyrocket.*)

JOHN.   Sure I do. A lot. Sometimes when I come home late at night I look over at the Rectory. I see something white at the window. Could that be you, Miss Alma? Or, is it your *doppelganger*, looking out of the window that faces my way?

ALMA.   Enough about *doppelganger*—whatever that is!

JOHN.   There goes a nice one, Roman candle they call it!

(*This time the explosion is in back of them. A Roman candle shoots up puffs of rainbow-colored light in back of the stone angel of the fountain. They turn in profile to watch it.*)

JOHN   (*counting the puffs of light*).   Four—five—six—that's all? No— seven!

(*There is a pause.* ALMA *sits down slowly*)

ALMA   (*vaguely*).   Dear me . . . (*She fans herself*)

JOHN.   How about going riding?

ALMA   (*too eagerly*).   When . . . now?

(ROSA GONZALES *has wandered up to the fountain again.* JOHN's *attention drifts steadily toward her and away from* ALMA.)

JOHN   (*too carelessly*).   Oh . . . some afternoon.

ALMA.   Would you observe the speed limit?

JOHN.   Strictly with you, Miss Alma.

ALMA.   Why then, I'd be glad to—John.

(JOHN *has risen from the bench and crosses to the fountain.*)

JOHN.   And wear a hat with a plume!

ALMA.   I don't have a hat with a plume!

JOHN.   Get one!

(*Another skyrocket goes up, and there is another long "Ahhh . . ." from the crowd.* JOHN *saunters up to the fountain.* ROSA *has lingered beside it. As he passes her he whispers something. She laughs and moves leisurely off.* JOHN *takes a quick drink at the fountain, then follows* ROSA, *calling back "Good night" to* ALMA. *There is a sound of laughter in the distance.* ALMA *sits motionless for a moment, then touches a small white handkerchief to her lips and nostrils.* MR. DOREMUS *comes in, carrying a French horn case. He is a small man, somewhat like a sparrow.*)

ROGER.   *Whew!* Golly! Moses!—Well, how did it go, Miss Alma?

ALMA.   How did—what—go?

ROGER   (*annoyed*).   My solo on the French horn.

ALMA   (*slowly, without thinking*).   I paid no attention to it. (*She rises*

slowly and takes his arm) I'll have to hang on your arm—I'm feeling
so dizzy!
(*The scene dims out. There is a final skyrocket and a last "Ahhh . . ."*
from the crowd in the distance. Music is heard, and there is light on
the angel.)

SCENE TWO

Inside the Rectory, which is lighted. Mrs. Winemiller comes in and makes
her way stealthily to the love seat, where she seats herself. Opening her
parasol, she takes out a fancy white-plumed hat which she had concealed
there. Rising, she turns to the mirror on the wall over the love seat and
tries on the hat. She draws a long, ecstatic breath as she places it squarely
on her head. At that moment the telephone rings. Startled, she snatches
off the hat, hides it behind the center table and quickly resumes her seat.
The telephone goes on ringing. Alma comes in to answer it.

ALMA.   Hello. . . . Yes, Mr. Gillam. . . . She did? . . . Are you sure?
. . . How shocking! . . . (MRS. WINEMILLER *now retrieves the hat, seats*
herself in front of ALMA *and puts the hat on*) Thank you, Mr. Gillam
. . . the hat is here.
(MR. WINEMILLER *comes in. He is distracted.*)
MR. WINEMILLER.   Alma! Alma, your mother . . . !
ALMA   (*coming in*). I know, Father, Mr. Gillam just phoned. He told
me she picked up a white plumed hat and he pretended not to notice
in order to save you the embarrassment, so I—told him to just charge
it to us.
MR. WINEMILLER.   That hat looks much too expensive.
ALMA.   It's fourteen dollars. You pay six of it, Father, and I'll pay eight.
(*She gives him the parasol*)
MR. WINEMILLER.   What an insufferable cross we have to bear. (*He re-*
tires despairingly from the room)
(ALMA *goes over to her* MOTHER *and seats her in a chair at the table.*)
ALMA.   I have a thousand and one things to do before my club meeting
tonight, so you work quietly on your picture puzzle or I shall take the
hat back, plume and all.
MRS. WINEMILLER   (*throwing a piece of the puzzle on the floor*).   The
pieces don't fit! (ALMA *picks up the piece and puts it on the table*) The
pieces don't fit!
(ALMA *stands for a moment in indecision. She reaches for the phone,*
then puts it down. Then she takes it up again, and gives a number. The
telephone across the way in the doctor's office rings and that part of the
scene lights up. JOHN *comes in.*)

JOHN   (*answering the phone*) . Hello?

ALMA.   John! (*She fans herself rapidly with a palm leaf clutched in her free hand and puts on a brilliant, strained smile as if she were actually in his presence*)

JOHN.   Miss Alma?

ALMA.   You recognized my voice?

JOHN.   I recognized your laugh.

ALMA.   Ha-ha! How are you, you stranger you?

JOHN.   I'm pretty well, Miss Alma. How're you doing?

ALMA.   Surviving, just surviving! Isn't it fearful?

JOHN.   Uh-huh.

ALMA.   You seem unusually laconic. Or perhaps I should say more than usually laconic.

JOHN.   I had a big night and I'm just recovering from it.

ALMA.   Well, sir, I have a bone to pick with you!

JOHN.   What's that, Miss Alma? (*He drains a glass of bromo*)

ALMA.   The time of our last conversation on the Fourth of July, you said you were going to take me riding in your automobile.

JOHN.   Aw. Did I say that?

ALMA.   Yes indeed you did, sir! And all these hot afternoons I've been breathlessly waiting and hoping that you would remember that promise. But now I know how insincere you are. Ha-ha! Time and again the four-wheeled phenomenon flashes by the Rectory and I have yet to put my—my quaking foot in it!

(MRS. WINEMILLER *begins to mock* ALMA's *speech and laughter.*)

JOHN.   What was that, Miss Alma? I didn't understand you.

ALMA.   I was just reprimanding you, sir! Castigating you verbally! Ha-ha!

MRS. WINEMILLER   (*grimacing*) . Ha-ha.

JOHN.   What about, Miss Alma? (*He leans back and puts his feet on table*)

ALMA.   Never mind. I know how busy you are! (*She whispers*) Mother, hush!

JOHN.   I'm afraid we have a bad connection.

ALMA.   I hate telephones. I don't know why but they always make me laugh as if someone were poking me in the ribs! I swear to goodness they do!

JOHN.   Why don't you just go to your window and I'll go to mine and we can holler across?

ALMA.   The yard's so wide I'm afraid it would crack my voice! And I've got to sing at somebody's wedding tomorrow.

JOHN.   You're going to sing at a wedding?

ALMA. Yes. "The Voice That Breathed O'er Eden!" And I'm as hoarse as a frog! (*Another gale of laughter almost shakes her off her feet*)

JOHN. Better come over and let me give you a gargle.

ALMA. Nasty gargles—I hate them!

MRS. WINEMILLER (*mockingly*). Nasty gargles—I hate them!

ALMA. Mother, shhh!—please! As you no doubt have gathered, there is some interference at this end of the line! What I wanted to say is— you remember my mentioning that little club I belong to?

JOHN. Aw! Aw, yes! Those intellectual meetings!

ALMA. Oh, now, don't call it that. It's just a little informal gathering every Wednesday and we talk about the new books and read things out loud to each other!

JOHN. Serve any refreshments?

ALMA. Yes, we serve refreshments!

JOHN. Any liquid refreshments?

ALMA. Both liquid and solid refreshments.

JOHN. Is this an invitation?

ALMA. Didn't I promise I'd ask you? It's going to be tonight!—at eight at my house, at the Rectory, so all you'll have to do is cross the yard!

JOHN. I'll try to make it, Miss Alma.

ALMA. Don't say try as if it required some Herculean effort! All you have to do is . . .

JOHN. Cross the yard! Uh-huh—reserve me a seat by the punch bowl.

ALMA. That gives me an idea! We *will* have punch, fruit punch, with claret in it. Do you like claret?

JOHN. I just dote on claret.

ALMA. Now you're being sarcastic! Ha-ha-ha!

JOHN. Excuse me, Miss Alma, but Dad's got to use this phone.

ALMA. I won't hang up till you've said you'll come without fail!

JOHN. I'll be there, Miss Alma. You can count on it.

ALMA. Au revoir, then! Until eight.

JOHN. G'bye, Miss Alma.

(JOHN *hangs up with an incredulous grin.* ALMA *remains holding the phone with a dazed smile until the office interior has dimmed slowly out.*)

MRS. WINEMILLER. Alma's in love—in love. (*She waltzes mockingly*)

ALMA (*sharply*). Mother, you are wearing out my patience! Now I am expecting another music pupil and I have to make preparations for the club meeting so I suggest that you . . . (NELLIE *rings the bell*) Will you go up to your room? (*Then she calls sweetly*) Yes, Nellie, coming, Nellie. All right, stay down here then. But keep your attention on your picture puzzle or there will be no ice cream for you after supper!

(She admits NELLIE, *who is wildly excited over something. This scene should be played lightly and quickly.)*

NELLIE. Oh, Miss Alma!

(She rushes past ALMA *in a distracted manner, throws herself on the sofa and hugs herself with excited glee.)*

ALMA. What is it, Nellie? Has something happened at home? (NELLIE *continues her exhilaration)* Oh, now, Nellie, stop that! Whatever it is, it can't be *that* important!

NELLIE *(blurting out suddenly)*. Miss Alma, haven't you ever had— *crushes?*

ALMA. What?

NELLIE. Crushes?

ALMA. Yes—I suppose I have. *(She sits down)*

NELLIE. Did you know that I used to have a crush on *you,* Miss Alma?

ALMA. No, Nellie.

NELLIE. Why do you think that I took singing lessons?

ALMA. I supposed it was because you wished to develop your voice.

NELLIE *(cutting in)*. Oh, you know, and I know, I never had any voice I had a crush on you though. Those were the days when I had crushes on girls. Those days are all over, and now I have crushes on boys. Oh, Miss Alma, you know about Mother, how I was brought up so nobody nice except you would have anything to do with us—Mother meeting the trains to pick up the traveling salesmen and bringing them home to drink and play poker—all of them acting like pigs, pigs, pigs!

MRS. WINEMILLER *(mimicking)*. Pigs, pigs, pigs!

NELLIE. Well, I thought I'd always hate men. Loathe and despise them. But last night— Oh!

ALMA. Hadn't we better run over some scales until you are feeling calmer?

NELLIE *(cutting in)*. I'd heard them downstairs for hours but didn't know who it was—I'd fallen asleep—when all of a sudden my door banged open. He'd thought it was the bathroom!

ALMA *(nervously)*. Nellie, I'm not sure I want to hear any more of this story.

NELLIE *(interrupting)*. Guess who it was?

ALMA. I couldn't possibly guess.

NELLIE. Someone you know. Someone I've seen you with.

ALMA. Who?

NELLIE. The wonderfullest person in all the big wide world! When he saw it was me he came and sat down on the bed and held my hand and we talked and talked until Mother came up to see what had happened to him. You should have heard him bawl her out. Oh, he laid the law down! He said she ought to send me off to a girl's school because she wasn't fit to bring up a daughter! Then she started to bawl him out. You're a fine one to talk, she said, you're not fit to call yourself a doctor. (ALMA *rises abruptly*)

ALMA. John Buchanan?

NELLIE. Yes, of course, Dr. Johnny.

ALMA. Was—with—your—mother?

NELLIE. Oh, he wasn't her beau! He had a girl with him, and Mother had somebody else!

ALMA. Who—did—he—have?

NELLIE. Oh, some loud tacky thing with a Z in her name!

ALMA. Gonzales? Rosa Gonzales?

NELLIE. Yes, that was it! (ALMA *sits slowly back down.*) But him! Oh, Miss Alma! He's the *wonderfullest* person that I . . .

ALMA (*interrupting*). Your mother was right! He isn't fit to call himself a doctor! I hate to disillusion you, but this wonderfullest person is pitiably weak.

(*Someone calls "Johnny" outside.*)

NELLIE (*in hushed excitement*). Someone is calling him now!

ALMA. Yes, these people who shout his name in front of his house are of such a character that the old doctor cannot permit them to come inside the door. And when they have brought him home at night, left him sprawling on the front steps, sometimes at daybreak—it takes two people, his father and the old cook, one pushing and one pulling, to get him upstairs. (*She sits down*) All the gifts of the gods were showered on him. . . . (*The call of "Johnny" is repeated*) But all he cares about is indulging his senses! (*Another call of "Johnny"*)

NELLIE. Here he comes down the steps! (ALMA *crosses toward the window*) Look at him jump!

ALMA. Oh.

NELLIE. Over the banisters. Ha-ha!

ALMA. Nellie, don't lean out the window and have us caught spying.

MRS. WINEMILLER (*suddenly*). Show Nellie how *you* spy on him! Oh, she's a good one at spying. She stands behind the curtain and *peeks* around it, and . . .

ALMA (*frantically*). Mother!

MRS. WINEMILLER. She spies on him. Whenever he comes in at night she rushes downstairs to watch him out of this window!

ALMA (*interrupting her*). Be still!

MRS. WINEMILLER (*going right on*). She called him just now and had a fit on the telephone! (*The OLD LADY cackles derisively.* ALMA *snatches her cigarette from her and crushes it under her foot*) Alma's in love! Alma's in love!

ALMA (*interrupting*). Nellie, Nellie, please go.

NELLIE *(with a startled giggle).* All right, Miss Alma, I'm going. *(She crosses quickly to the door, looking back once with a grin)* Good night, Mrs. Winemiller!

(NELLIE goes out gaily, leaving the door slightly open. ALMA rushes to it and slams it shut. She returns swiftly to MRS. WINEMILLER, her hands clenched with anger.)

ALMA. If ever I hear you say such a thing again, if ever you dare to repeat such a thing in my presence or anybody else's—then it will be the last straw! You understand me? Yes, you understand me! You act like a child, but you have the devil in you. And God will punish you— yes! I'll punish you too. I'll take your cigarettes from you and give you no more. I'll give you no ice cream either. Because I'm tired of your malice. Yes, I'm tired of your malice and your self-indulgence. People wonder why I'm tied down here! They pity me—think of me as an old maid already! In spite of I'm young. Still young! It's you—it's you, you've taken my youth away from me! I wouldn't say that—I'd try not even to think of it—if you were just kind, just simple! But I could spread my life out like a rug for you to step on and you'd step on it, and not even say "Thank you, Alma!" Which is what you've done always—and now you dare to tell a disgusting lie about me—in front of that girl!

MRS. WINEMILLER. Don't you think I hear you go to the window at night to watch him come in and . . .

ALMA. Give me that plumed hat, Mother! It goes back now, it goes back!

MRS. WINEMILLER. *Fight! Fight!*

(ALMA snatches at the plumed hat. MRS. WINEMILLER snatches too. The hat is torn between them. MRS. WINEMILLER retains the hat. The plume comes loose in ALMA's hand. She stares at it a moment with a shocked expression.)

ALMA *(sincerely).* Heaven have mercy upon us!

SCENE THREE

Inside the Rectory.

The meeting is in progress, having just opened with the reading of the minutes by Alma. She stands before the green plush sofa and the others. This group includes Mr. Doremus, Vernon, a willowy younger man with an open collar and Byronic locks, the widow Bassett, and a wistful older girl with a long neck and thick-lensed glasses.

ALMA *(reading).* Our last meeting which fell on July fourteenth . . .

MRS. BASSETT. Bastille Day!

ALMA. Pardon me?

MRS. BASSETT. It fell on Bastille Day! But, honey, that was the meeting before last.

ALMA. You're perfectly right. I seem to be on the wrong page. . . . (*She drops the papers*)

MRS. BASSETT. Butterfingers!

ALMA. Here we are! July twenty-fifth! Correct?

MRS. BASSETT. Correct! (*A little ripple of laughter goes about the circle*)

ALMA (*continuing*). It was debated whether or not we ought to suspend operations for the remainder of the summer as the departure of several members engaged in the teaching profession for their summer vacations . . .

MRS. BASSETT. Lucky people!

ALMA. . . . had substantially contracted our little circle.

MRS. BASSETT. Decimated our ranks!

(*There is another ripple of laughter*)

(JOHN *appears outside the door-frame and rings the bell.*)

ALMA (*with agitation*). Is that—is that—the doorbell?

MRS. BASSETT. It sure did sound like it to me.

ALMA. Excuse me a moment. I think it may be . . .

(*She crosses to the door-frame and makes gesture of opening the door.* JOHN *steps in, immaculately groomed and shining, his white linen coat over his arm and a white Panama hat in his hand. He is a startling contrast to the other male company, who seem to be outcasts of a state in which he is a prominent citizen.*)

ALMA (*shrilly*). Yes, it is—our guest of honor! Everybody, this is Dr. John Buchanan, Jr.

JOHN (*easily glancing about the assemblage*). Hello, everybody.

MRS. BASSETT. I never thought he'd show up. Congratulations, Miss Alma.

JOHN. Did I miss much?

ALMA. Not a thing! Just the minutes—I'll put you on the sofa. Next to me. (*She laughs breathlessly and makes an uncertain gesture. He settles gingerly on the sofa. They all stare at him with a curious sort of greediness*) Well, now! we are completely assembled!

MRS. BASSETT (*eagerly*). Vernon has his verse play with him tonight!

ALMA (*uneasily*). Is that right, Vernon? (*Obviously, it is.* VERNON *has a pile of papers eight inches thick on his knees. He raises them timidly with downcast eyes*)

ROGER (*quickly*). We decided to put that off till cooler weather. Miss Rosemary is supposed to read us a paper tonight on William Blake.

MRS. BASSETT. Those dead poets can keep!

(JOHN *laughs.*)

ALMA (*excitedly jumping up*). Mrs. Bassett, everybody! This is the way I feel about the verse play. It's too important a thing to read under any but ideal circumstances. Not only atmospheric—on some cool evening with music planned to go with it!—but everyone present so that nobody will miss it! Why don't we . . .

ROGER. Why don't we take a standing vote on the matter?

ALMA. Good, good, perfect!

ROGER. All in favor of putting the verse play off till cooler weather, stand up!

(*Everybody rises but* ROSEMARY *and* MRS. BASSETT. ROSEMARY *starts vaguely to rise, but* MRS. BASSETT *jerks her arm.*)

ROSEMARY. Was this a vote?

ROGER. Now, Mrs. Bassett, no rough tactics, please!

ALMA. Has everybody got fans? John, you haven't got one!

(*She looks about for a fan for him. Not seeing one, she takes* ROGER'S *out of his hand and gives it to* JOHN. ROGER *is nonplussed.* ROSEMARY *gets up with her paper.*)

ROSEMARY. The poet—William Blake.

MRS. BASSETT. Insane, insane, that man was a mad fanatic! (*She squints her eyes tight shut and thrusts her thumbs into her ears. The reactions range from indignant to conciliatory*)

ROGER. Now, Mrs. Bassett!

MRS. BASSETT. This is a free country. I can speak my opinion. And I have *read up* on him. Go on, Rosemary. I wasn't criticizing your paper. (*But* ROSEMARY *sits down, hurt*)

ALMA. Mrs. Bassett is only joking, Rosemary.

ROSEMARY. No, I don't want to read it if she feels that strongly about it.

MRS. BASSETT. Not a bit, don't be silly! I just don't see why we should encourage the writings of people like that who have already gone into a drunkard's grave!

VARIOUS VOICES (*exclaiming*). Did he? I never heard that about him. Is that true?

ALMA. Mrs. Bassett is mistaken about that. Mrs. Bassett, you have confused Blake with someone else.

MRS. BASSETT (*positively*). Oh, no, don't tell me. I've read up on him and know what I'm talking about. He traveled around with that Frenchman who took a shot at him and landed them both in jail! Brussels, Brussels!

ROGER (*gaily*). Brussels sprouts!

MRS. BASSETT. That's where it happened, fired a gun at him in a drunken stupor, and later one of them died of T.B. in the gutter! All right. I'm finished. I won't say anything more. Go on with your paper, Rosemary. There's nothing like contact with culture!

(ALMA *gets up.*)

ALMA. Before Rosemary reads her paper on Blake, I think it would be a good idea, since some of us aren't acquainted with his work, to preface the critical and biographical comments with a reading of one of his loveliest lyric poems.

ROSEMARY. I'm not going to read anything at all! Not I!

ALMA. Then let me read it then. (*She takes a paper from* ROSEMARY) . . . This is called "Love's Secret."

(*She clears her throat and waits for a hush to settle.* ROSEMARY *looks stonily at the carpet.* MRS. BASSETT *looks at the ceiling.* JOHN *coughs.*)

> Never seek to tell thy love,
> Love that never told can be,
> For the gentle wind doth move
> Silently, invisibly.
> I told my love, I told my love,
> I told him all my heart.
> Trembling, cold in ghastly fear
> Did my love depart.
>
> No sooner had he gone from me
> Than a stranger passing by,
> Silently, invisibly,
> Took him with a sigh!

(*There are various effusions and enthusiastic applause.*)

MRS. BASSETT. Honey, you're right. That isn't the man I meant. I was thinking about the one who wrote about "the bought red lips." Who was it that wrote about the "bought red lips"?

(JOHN *has risen abruptly. He signals to* ALMA *and points to his watch. He starts to leave.*)

ALMA (*springing up*). John!

JOHN (*calling back*). I have to call on a patient!

ALMA. Oh, John!

(*She calls after him so sharply that the group is startled into silence.*)

ROSEMARY (*interpreting this as a cue to read her paper*). "The poet, William Blake, was born in 1757 . . ."

(ALMA *suddenly rushes to the door and goes out after* JOHN.)

ROGER. Of poor but honest parents.

MRS. BASSETT. No supercilious comments out of you, sir. Go on, Rosemary. (*She speaks loudly*) She has such a beautiful *voice!*

(ALMA *returns inside, looking stunned.*)

ALMA. Please excuse the interruption, Rosemary. Dr. Buchanan had to call on a patient.

MRS. BASSETT (*archly*). I bet I know who the patient was. Ha-ha! That Gonzales girl whose father owns Moon Lake Casino and goes everywhere with two pistols strapped on his belt. Johnny Buchanan will get himself shot in that crowd!

ALMA. Why, Mrs. Bassett, what gave you such an idea? I don't think that John even knows that Gonzales girl!

MRS. BASSETT. He knows her, all right. In the Biblical sense of the word, if you'll excuse me!

ALMA. No, I will not excuse you! A thing like that is inexcusable!

MRS. BASSETT. Have you fallen for him, Miss Alma? Miss Alma has fallen for the young doctor! They tell me he has lots of new lady patients!

ALMA. Stop it! (*She stamps her foot furiously and crushes the palm leaf fan between her clenched hands.*) I won't have malicious talk here! You drove him away from the meeting after I'd bragged so much about how bright and interesting you all were! You put your worst foot forward and simpered and chattered and carried on like idiots, idiots! What am I saying? I—I—please excuse me!

(*She rushes out the inner door.*)

ROGER. I move that the meeting adjourn.

MRS. BASSETT. I second the motion.

ROSEMARY. I don't understand. What happened?

MRS. BASSETT. Poor Miss Alma!

ROGER. She hasn't been herself lately. . . .

(*They all go out. After a moment* ALMA *reenters with a tray of refreshments, looks about the deserted interior and bursts into hysterical laughter. The light dims out.*)

SCENE FOUR

In the doctor's office.

John has a wound on his arm which he is bandaging with Rosa's assistance.

JOHN. Hold that end. Wrap it around. Pull it tight. (*There is a knock at the door. They look up silently. The knock is repeated*) I better answer before they wake up the old man. (*He goes out. A few moments later he returns followed by* ALMA. *He is rolling down his sleeve to conceal the bandage.* ALMA *stops short at the sight of* ROSA.) Wait outside, Rosa. In the hall. But be quiet! (ROSA *gives* ALMA *a challenging look as she withdraws from the lighted area.* JOHN *explains about* ROSA) A little emergency case.

ALMA. The patient you had to call on. (JOHN *grins*) I want to see your father.

JOHN.   He's asleep. Anything I can do?

ALMA.   No, I think not. I have to see your father.

JOHN.   It's two A.M., Miss Alma.

ALMA.   I know, I'm afraid I'll have to see him.

JOHN.   What's the trouble?

(*The voice of* JOHN's *father is heard, calling from above.*)

DR. BUCHANAN.   John! What's going on down there?

JOHN   (*at the door*). Nothing much, Dad. Somebody got cut in a fight.

DR. BUCHANAN.   I'm coming down.

JOHN.   No. Don't! Stay in bed! (*He rolls up his sleeve to show* ALMA *the bandaged wound. She gasps and touches her lips*) I've patched him up, Dad. You sleep!

(JOHN *executes the gesture of closing a door quietly on the hall.*)

ALMA.   You've been in a brawl with that—woman! (JOHN *nods and rolls the sleeve back down.* ALMA *sinks faintly into a chair*)

JOHN.   Is your *doppelganger* cutting up again?

ALMA.   It's your father I want to talk to.

JOHN.   Be reasonable, Miss Alma. You're not that sick.

ALMA.   Do you suppose I would come here at two o'clock in the morning if I were not seriously ill?

JOHN.   It's no telling what you would do in a state of hysteria. (*He puts some powders in a glass of water*) Toss that down, Miss Alma.

ALMA.   What is it?

JOHN.   A couple of little white tablets dissolved in water.

ALMA.   What kind of tablets?

JOHN.   You don't trust me?

ALMA.   You are not in any condition to inspire much confidence. (JOHN *laughs softly. She looks at him helplessly for a moment, then bursts into tears. He draws up a chair beside hers and puts his arm gently about her shoulders*) I seem to be all to pieces.

JOHN.   The intellectual meeting wore you out.

ALMA.   You made a quick escape from it.

JOHN.   I don't like meetings. The only meetings I like are between two people.

ALMA.   Such as between yourself and the lady outside?

JOHN.   Or between you and me.

ALMA   (*nervously*). Where is the . . . ?

JOHN.   Oh. You've decided to take it?

ALMA.   Yes, if you . . .

(*She sips and chokes. He gives her his handkerchief. She touches her lips with it.*)

JOHN.   Bitter?

ALMA.   Awfully bitter.

JOHN. It'll make you sleepy.

ALMA. I do hope so. I wasn't able to sleep.

JOHN. And you felt panicky?

ALMA. Yes. I felt walled in.

JOHN. You started hearing your heart?

ALMA. Yes, like a drum!

JOHN. It scared you?

ALMA. It always does.

JOHN. Sure. I know.

ALMA. I don't think I will be able to get through the summer.

JOHN. You'll get through it, Miss Alma.

ALMA. How?

JOHN. One day will come after another and one night will come after another till sooner or later the summer will be all through with and then it will be fall, and you will be saying, I don't see how I'm going to get through the fall.

ALMA. Oh . . .

JOHN. That's right. Draw a deep breath!

ALMA. Ah . . .

JOHN. Good. Now draw another!

ALMA. Ah . . .

JOHN. Better? Better?

ALMA. A little.

JOHN. Soon you'll be much better. (*He takes out a big silver watch and holds her wrist*) Did y' know that time is one side of the four-dimensional continuum we're caught in?

ALMA. What?

JOHN. Did you know space is curved, that it turns back onto itself like a soap-bubble, adrift in something that's even less than space? (*He laughs a little as he replaces the watch*)

ROSA (*faintly from outside*). Johnny!

JOHN (*looking up as if the cry came from there*). Did you know that the Magellanic clouds are a hundred thousand light years away from the earth? No? (ALMA *shakes her head slightly*) That's something to think about when you worry over your heart, that little red fist that's got to keep knocking, knocking against the big black door.

ROSA (*more distinctly*). Johnny!

(*She opens the door a crack.*)

JOHN. Calla de la boca! (*The door closes and he speaks to* ALMA) There's nothing wrong with your heart but a little functional disturbance, like I told you before. You want me to check it? (ALMA *nods mutely.* JOHN *picks up his stethoscope*)

ALMA. The lady outside, I hate to keep her waiting.

JOHN. Rosa doesn't mind waiting. Unbutton your blouse.

ALMA. Unbutton . . . ?

JOHN. The blouse.

ALMA. Hadn't I better—better come back in the morning, when your father will be able to . . . ?

JOHN. Just as you please, Miss Alma. (*She hesitates. Then begins to unbutton her blouse. Her fingers fumble*) Fingers won't work?

ALMA (*breathlessly*). They are just as if frozen!

JOHN (*smiling*). Let me. (*He leans over her*) Little pearl buttons . . .

ALMA. If your father discovered that woman in the house . . .

JOHN. He won't discover it.

ALMA. It would distress him terribly.

JOHN. Are you going to tell him?

ALMA. Certainly not! (*He laughs and applies the stethoscope to her chest*)

JOHN. Breathe! . . . Out! . . . Breathe! . . . Out!

ALMA. Ah . . .

JOHN. Um-hmmm . . .

ALMA. What do you hear?

JOHN. Just a little voice saying—"Miss Alma is lonesome!" (*She rises and turns her back to him*)

ALMA. If your idea of helping a patient is to ridicule and insult . . .

JOHN. My idea of helping you is to tell you the truth. (ALMA *looks up at him. He lifts her hand from the chair arm*) What is this stone?

ALMA. A topaz.

JOHN. Beautiful stone. . . . Fingers still frozen?

ALMA. A little. (*He lifts her hand to his mouth and blows his breath on her fingers*)

JOHN. I'm a poor excuse for a doctor, I'm much too selfish. But let's try to think about you.

ALMA. Why should you bother about me? (*She sits down*)

JOHN. You know I like you and I think you're worth a lot of consideration.

ALMA. Why?

JOHN. Because you have a lot of feeling in your heart, and that's rare thing. It makes you too easily hurt. Did I hurt you tonight?

ALMA. You hurt me when you sprang up from the sofa and rushed from the Rectory in such—in such mad haste that you left your coat behind you!

JOHN. I'll pick up the coat sometime.

ALMA. The time of our last conversation you said you would take me riding in your automobile sometime, but you forgot to.

JOHN. I didn't forget. Many's the time I've looked across at the Rectory and wondered if it would be worth trying, you and me. . . .

ALMA. You decided it wasn't?

JOHN.   I went there tonight, but it wasn't you and me. . . . Fingers
warm now?

ALMA.   Those tablets work quickly. I'm already feeling drowsy. (*She
leans back with her eyes nearly shut*) I'm beginning to feel almost like
a water lily. A water lily on a Chinese lagoon.

(*A heavy iron bell strikes three.*)

ROSA.   *Johnny?*

(ALMA *starts to rise.*)

ALMA.   I *must* go.

JOHN.   I will call for you Saturday night at eight o'clock.

ALMA.   What?

JOHN.   I'll give you this box of tablets but watch how you take them.
Never more than one or two at a time.

ALMA.   Didn't you say something else a moment ago?

JOHN.   I said I would call for you at the Rectory Saturday night.

ALMA.   Oh . . .

JOHN.   Is that all right?

(ALMA *nods speechlessly. She remains with the box resting in the palm of
her hand as if not knowing it was there.* JOHN *gently closes her fingers
on the box.*)

ALMA.   Oh! (*She laughs faintly*)

ROSA   (*outside*) . *Johnny!*

JOHN.   Do you think you can find your way home, Miss Alma?

(ROSA *steps back into the office with a challenging look.* ALMA *catches her
breath sharply and goes out the side door.*

(JOHN *reaches above him and turns out the light. He crosses to* ROSA *by
the anatomy chart and takes her roughly in his arms. The light lingers
on the chart as the interior dims out.*)

SCENE FIVE

In the Rectory.

*Before the light comes up a soprano voice is heard singing "From the
Land of the Sky Blue Waters."*

*As the curtain rises, Alma gets up from the piano. Mr. and Mrs. Wine-
miller, also, are in the lighted room.*

ALMA.   What time is it, Father? (*He goes on writing. She raises her voice*)
What time is it, Father?

MR. WINEMILLER.   Five of eight. I'm working on my sermon.

ALMA.   Why don't you work in the study?

MR. WINEMILLER.   The study is suffocating. So don't disturb me.

ALMA.   Would there be any chance of getting Mother upstairs if someone should call?

MR. WINEMILLER.   Are you expecting a caller?

ALMA.   Not expecting. There is just a chance of it.

MR. WINEMILLER.   Whom are you expecting?

ALMA.   I said I wasn't expecting anyone, that there was just a possibility . . .

MR. WINEMILLER.   Mr. Doremus? I thought that this was his evening with his mother?

ALMA.   Yes, it is his evening with his mother.

MR. WINEMILLER.   Then who is coming here, Alma?

ALMA.   Probably no one. Probably no one at all.

MR. WINEMILLER.   This is all very mysterious.

MRS. WINEMILLER.   That tall boy next door is coming to see her, that's who's coming to see her.

ALMA.   If you will go upstairs, Mother, I'll call the drug store and ask them to deliver a pint of fresh peach ice cream.

MRS. WINEMILLER.   I'll go upstairs when I'm ready—good and ready, and you can put that in your pipe and smoke it, Miss Winemiller!

(*She lights a cigarette. Mr. Winemiller turns slowly away with a profound sigh.*)

ALMA.   I may as well tell you who might call, so that if he calls there will not be any unpleasantness about it. Young Dr. John Buchanan said he might call.

MRS. WINEMILLER.   See!

MR. WINEMILLER.   You can't be serious.

MRS. WINEMILLER.   Didn't I tell you?

ALMA.   Well, I am.

MR. WINEMILLER.   That young man might come here?

ALMA.   He asked me if he might and I said, yes, if he wished to. But it is now after eight so it doesn't look like he's coming.

MR. WINEMILLER.   If he does come you will go upstairs to your room and I will receive him.

ALMA.   If he does come I'll do no such thing, Father.

MR. WINEMILLER.   You must be out of your mind.

ALMA.   I'll receive him myself. You may retire to your study and Mother upstairs. But if he does come I'll receive him. I don't judge people by the tongues of gossips. I happen to know that he has been grossly misjudged and misrepresented by old busybodies who're envious of his youth and brilliance and charm.

MR. WINEMILLER.   If you're not out of your senses, then I'm out of mine.

ALMA.   I daresay we're all a bit peculiar, Father. . . .

MR. WINEMILLER.   Well, I have had one almost insufferable cross to bear and perhaps I can bear another. But if you think I'm retiring into my study when this young man comes, probably with a whiskey bottle in one hand and a pair of dice in the other, you have another think coming. I'll sit right here and look at him until he leaves. (*He turns back to his sermon*)

(*A whistle is heard outside the open door.*)

ALMA (*speaking quickly*). As a matter of fact I think I'll walk down to the drug store and call for the ice cream myself.

(*She crosses to the door, snatching up her hat, gloves and veil*)

MRS. WINEMILLER. There she goes to him! Ha-ha! (ALMA *rushes out*)

MR. WINEMILLER (*looking up*). Alma! Alma!

MRS. WINEMILLER. Ha-ha-haaaaa!

MR. WINEMILLER. Where is Alma?—Alma! (*He rushes through the door*) Alma!

MRS. WINEMILLER. Ha-ha! Who got fooled? Who got fooled! Ha-haaaa! Insufferable cross yourself, you old—windbag. . . .

(*The curtain comes down.*)

SCENE SIX

A delicately suggested arbor, enclosing a table and two chairs. Over the table is suspended a torn paper lantern. This tiny set may be placed way downstage in front of the two interiors, which should be darkened out, as in the fountain scenes. In the background, as it is throughout the play, the angel of the fountain is dimly visible.

Music from the nearby pavilion of the Casino can be used when suitable for background.

John's voice is audible before he and Alma enter.

JOHN (*from the darkness*). I don't understand why we can't go in the casino.

ALMA. You do understand. You're just pretending not to.

JOHN. Give me one reason.

ALMA (*coming into the arbor*). I am a minister's daughter.

JOHN. That's no reason. (*He follows her in. He wears a white linen suit, carrying the coat over his arm*)

ALMA. You're a doctor. That's a better reason. You can't any more afford to be seen in such places than I can—less!

JOHN (*bellowing*). Dusty!

DUSTY (*from the darkness*). Coming!

JOHN. What are you fishing in that pocketbook for?

ALMA. Nothing.

JOHN. What have you got there?

ALMA. Let go!

JOHN. Those sleeping tablets I gave you?

ALMA. Yes.

JOHN. What for?

ALMA. I need one.

JOHN. *Now?*

ALMA. Yes.

JOHN. Why?

ALMA. Why? Because I nearly died of heart failure in your automobile. What possessed you to drive like that? A demon?

(DUSTY *enters.*)

JOHN. A bottle of vino rosso.

DUSTY. Sure. (*He withdraws*)

JOHN. Hey! Tell Shorty I want to hear the "Yellow Dog Blues."

ALMA. Please give me back my tablets.

JOHN. You want to turn into a dopefiend taking this stuff. I said take one when you need one.

ALMA. I need one now.

JOHN. Sit down and stop swallowing air. (DUSTY *returns with a tall wine bottle and two thin-stemmed glasses*) When does the cock-fight start?

DUSTY. 'Bout ten o'clock, Dr. Johnny.

ALMA. When does *what start?*

JOHN. They have a cock-fight here every Saturday night. Ever seen one?

ALMA. Perhaps in some earlier incarnation of mine.

JOHN. When you wore a brass ring in your nose?

ALMA. Then maybe I went to exhibitions like that.

JOHN. You're going to see one tonight.

ALMA. Oh, no, I'm not.

JOHN. That's what we came here for.

ALMA. I didn't think such exhibitions were legal.

JOHN. This is Moon Lake Casino where anything goes.

ALMA. And you're a frequent patron?

JOHN. I'd say constant.

ALMA. Then I'm afraid you must be serious about giving up your medical career.

JOHN. You bet I am! A doctor's life is walled in by sickness and misery and death.

ALMA. May I be so presumptuous as to inquire what you'll do when you quit?

JOHN. You may be so presumptuous as to inquire.

ALMA. But you won't tell me?

JOHN. I haven't made up my mind, but I've been thinking of South America lately.

ALMA (*sadly*). Oh . . .

JOHN. I've heard that cantinas are lots more fun than saloons, and senoritas are caviar among females.

ALMA. Dorothy Sykes' brother went to South America and was never heard of again. It takes a strong character to survive in the tropics. Otherwise it's a quagmire.

JOHN. You think my character's weak?

ALMA. I think you're confused, just awfully, awfully confused, as confused as I am—but in a different way. . . .

JOHN (*stretching out his legs*). Hee-haw, ho-hum.

ALMA. You used to say that as a child—to signify your disgust!

JOHN (*grinning*). Did I?

ALMA (*sharply*). Don't sit like that!

JOHN. Why not?

ALMA. You look so indolent and worthless.

JOHN. Maybe I am.

ALMA. If you must go somewhere, why don't you choose a place with a bracing climate?

JOHN. Parts of South America are as cool as a cucumber.

ALMA. I never knew that.

JOHN. Well, now you do.

ALMA. Those Latins all dream in the sun—and indulge their senses.

JOHN. Well, it's yet to be proven that anyone on this earth is crowned with so much glory as the one that uses his senses to get all he can in the way of—satisfaction.

ALMA. Self-satisfaction?

JOHN. What other kind is there?

ALMA. I will answer that question by asking you one. Have you ever seen, or looked at, a picture of a Gothic cathedral?

JOHN. Gothic cathedrals? What about them?

ALMA. How everything reaches up, how everything seems to be straining for something out of the reach of stone—or human—fingers? . . . The immense stained windows, the great arched doors that are five or six times the height of the tallest man—the vaulted ceiling and all the delicate spires—all reaching up to something beyond attainment! To me—well, that is the secret, the principle back of existence—the everlasting struggle and aspiration for more than our human limits have placed in our reach. . . . Who was that said that—oh, so beautiful thing!—"All of us are in the gutter, but some of us are looking at the stars!"

JOHN. Mr. Oscar Wilde.

ALMA (*somewhat taken aback*). Well, regardless of who said it, it's still true. Some of us are looking at the stars! (*She looks up raptly and places her hand over his*)

JOHN. It's no fun holding hands with gloves on, Miss Alma.

ALMA. That's easily remedied. I'll just take the gloves off. (*Music is heard*)

JOHN. Christ! (*He rises abruptly and lights a cigarette*) Rosa Gonzales is dancing in the Casino.

ALMA. You *are* unhappy. You hate me for depriving you of the company inside. Well, you'll escape by and by. You'll drive me home and come back out by yourself. . . . I've only gone out with three young men at all seriously, and with each one there was a desert between us.

JOHN. What do you mean by a desert?

ALMA. Oh—wide, wide stretches of uninhabitable ground.

JOHN. Maybe you made it that way by being stand-offish.

ALMA. I made quite an effort with one or two of them.

JOHN. What kind of an effort?

ALMA. Oh, I—tried to entertain them the first few times. I would play and sing for them in the Rectory parlor.

JOHN. With your father in the next room and the door half open.

ALMA. I don't think that was the trouble.

JOHN. What was the trouble?

ALMA. I—I didn't have my heart in it. (*She laughs uncertainly*) A silence would fall between us. You know, a silence?

JOHN. Yes, I know a silence.

ALMA. I'd try to talk and he'd try to talk and neither would make a go of it.

JOHN. Then silence would fall?

ALMA. Yes, the enormous silence.

JOHN. Then you'd go back to the piano?

ALMA. I'd twist my ring. Sometimes I twisted it so hard that the band cut my finger! He'd glance at his watch and we'd both know that the useless undertaking had come to a close. . . .

JOHN. You'd call it quits?

ALMA. Quits is—what we'd call it. . . . One or two times I was rather sorry about it.

JOHN. But you didn't have your heart in it?

ALMA. None of them really engaged my serious feelings.

JOHN. You do have serious feelings—of that kind?

ALMA. Doesn't everyone—sometimes?

JOHN. Some women are cold. Some women are what is called frigid.

ALMA. Do I give that impression?

JOHN. Under the surface you have a lot of excitement, a great deal more than any other woman I have met. So much that you have to carry these sleeping pills with you. The question is why? (*He leans over and lifts her veil*)

ALMA.   What are you doing that for?

JOHN.   So that I won't get your veil in my mouth when I kiss you.

ALMA.   (*faintly*). Do you want to do that?

JOHN.   (*gently*). Miss Alma. (*He takes her arms and draws her to her feet*) Oh, Miss Alma, Miss Alma! (*He kisses her*)

ALMA.   (*in a low, shaken voice*). Not "Miss" any more. Just Alma.

JOHN.   (*grinning gently*). "Miss" suits you better, Miss Alma. (*He kisses her again. She hesitantly touches his shoulders, but not quite to push him away. John speaks softly to her*) Is it so hard to forget you're a preacher's daughter?

ALMA.   There is no reason for me to forget that I am a minister's daughter. A minister's daughter's no different from any other young lady who tries to remember that she *is* a lady.

JOHN.   This lady stuff, is that so important?

ALMA.   Not to the sort of girls that you may be used to bringing to Moon Lake Casino. But suppose that some day . . . (*She crosses out of the arbor and faces away from him*) suppose that some day you—married. . . . The woman that you selected to be your wife, and not only your wife but—the mother of your children! (*She catches her breath at the thought*) Wouldn't you want that woman to be a lady? Wouldn't you want her to be somebody that you, as her husband, and they as her precious children—could look up to with very deep respect? (*There is a pause*)

JOHN.   There's other things between a man and a woman besides respect. Did you know that, Miss Alma?

ALMA.   Yes. . . .

JOHN.   There's such a thing as intimate relations.

ALMA.   Thank you for telling me that. So plainly.

JOHN.   It may strike you as unpleasant. But it does have a good deal to do with—connubial felicity, as you'd call it. There are some women that just give in to a man as a sort of obligation imposed on them by the—cruelty of nature! (*He finishes his glass and pours another*) And there you are.

ALMA.   There *I* am?

JOHN.   I'm speaking generally.

ALMA.   Oh.

(*Hoarse shouts go up from the Casino.*)

JOHN.   The cock-fight has started!

ALMA.   Since you have spoken so plainly, I'll speak plainly, too. There are some women who turn a possibly beautiful thing into something no better than the coupling of beasts!—but love is what you bring to it.

JOHN. You're right about that.

ALMA. Some people bring just their bodies. But there are some people, there are some women, John—who can bring their hearts to it, also— who can bring their souls to it!

JOHN (*derisively*). Souls again, huh?—those Gothic cathedrals you dream of! (*There is another hoarse prolonged shout from the Casino*) Your name is Alma and Alma is Spanish for soul. Some time I'd like to show you a chart of the human anatomy that I have in the office. It shows what our insides are like, and maybe you can show me where the beautiful soul is located on the chart. (*He drains the wine bottle*) Let's go watch the cock-fight.

ALMA. No! (*There is a pause*)

JOHN. I know something else we could do. There are rooms above the Casino. . . .

ALMA (*her back stiffening*). I'd heard that you made suggestions like that to girls that you go out with, but I refused to believe such stories were true. What made you think I might be amenable to such a suggestion?

JOHN. I counted your pulse in the office the night you ran out because you weren't able to sleep.

ALMA. The night I was ill and went to your father for help.

JOHN. It was me you went to.

ALMA. It was your father, and you wouldn't call your father.

JOHN. Fingers frozen stiff when I . . .

ALMA (*rising*). Oh! I want to go home. But I won't go with you. I will go in a taxi! (*She wheels about hysterically*) Boy! Boy! Call a taxi!

JOHN. I'll call one for you, Miss Alma.—Taxi! (*He goes out of the arbor*)

ALMA (*wildly*). You're not a gentleman!

JOHN (*from the darkness*). Taxi!

ALMA. *You're not a gentleman!*

(*As he disappears she makes a sound in her throat like a hurt animal. The light fades out of the arbor and comes up more distinctly on the stone angel of the fountain.*)

PART TWO—A WINTER

SCENE SEVEN

The sky and the southern constellations, almost imperceptibly moving with the earth's motion, appear on the great cyclorama.

The Rectory interior is lighted first, disclosing Alma and Roger Dore-
mus seated on the green plush sofa under the romantic landscape in its
heavy gilt frame. On a tiny table beside them is a cut glass pitcher of
lemonade with cherries and orange slices in it, like a little aquarium of
tropical fish. Roger is entertaining Alma with a collection of photographs
and postcards, mementoes of his mother's trip to the Orient. He is
enthusiastic about them and describes them in phrases his mother must
have assimilated from a sedulous study of literature provided by Cook's
Tours. Alma is less enthusiastic; she is preoccupied with the sounds of a
wild party going on next door at the doctor's home. At present there is
Mexican music with shouts and stamping.

Only the immediate area of the sofa is clearly lighted; the fountain is
faintly etched in light and the night sky walls the interior.

ROGER.   And this is Ceylon, The Pearl of the Orient!

ALMA.   And who is this fat young lady?

ROGER.   That is Mother in a hunting costume.

ALMA.   The hunting costume makes her figure seem bulky. What was
your mother hunting?

ROGER *(gaily)*. Heaven knows what she was hunting! But she found
Papa.

ALMA.   Oh, she met your father on this Oriental tour?

ROGER.   Ha-ha!—yes. . . . He was returning from India with dysentery
and they met on the boat.

ALMA *(distastefully)*. Oh . . .

ROGER.   And here she is on top of a ruined temple!

ALMA.   How did she get up there?

ROGER.   Climbed up, I suppose.

ALMA.   What an active woman.

ROGER.   Oh, yes, active—is no word for it! Here she is on an elephant's
back in Burma.

ALMA.   Ah!

ROGER.   You're looking at it upside down, Miss Alma!

ALMA.   Deliberately—to tease you. *(The doorbell rings)* Perhaps that's
your mother coming to fetch you home.

ROGER.   It's only ten-fifteen. I never leave till ten-thirty.

(MRS. BASSETT *comes in.*)

ALMA.   Mrs. Bassett!

MRS. BASSETT.   I was just wondering who I could turn to when I saw
the Rectory light and I thought to myself, Grace Bassett, you trot
yourself right over there and talk to Mr. Winemiller!

ALMA.   Father has retired.

MRS. BASSETT.   Oh, what a pity. *(She sees* ROGER*)* Hello, Roger! . . . I saw that fall your mother took this morning. I saw her come skipping out of the Delta Planters' Bank and I thought to myself, now isn't that remarkable, a woman of her age and weight so light on her feet? And just at that very moment—*down she went!* I swear to goodness I thought she had broken her hip! Was she bruised much?

ROGER.   Just shaken up, Mrs. Bassett.

MRS. BASSETT.   Oh, how lucky! She certainly must be made out of India rubber! (*She turns to* ALMA) Alma—Alma, if it is not too late for human intervention, your father's the one right person to call up old Dr. Buchanan at the fever clinic at Lyon and let him know!

ALMA.   About—what?

MRS. BASSETT.   You must be stone-deaf if you haven't noticed what's been going on next door since the old doctor left to fight the epidemic. One continual orgy! Well, not five minutes ago a friend of mine who works at the County Courthouse called to inform me that young Dr. John and Rosa Gonzales have taken a license out and are going to be married tomorrow!

ALMA.   Are you—quite certain?

MRS. BASSETT.   Certain? I'm always certain before I speak!

ALMA.   Why would he—do such a thing?

MRS. BASSETT.   August madness! They say it has something to do with the falling stars. Of course it might also have something to do with the fact that he lost two or three thousand dollars at the Casino which he can't pay except by giving himself to Gonzales' daughter. (*She turns to* ALMA) Alma, what are you doing with that picture puzzle?

ALMA   (*with a faint, hysterical laugh*) . The pieces don't fit!

MRS. BASSETT   (*to* ROGER) . I shouldn't have opened my mouth.

ALMA.   Will both of you please go!

(ROGER *goes out.*)

MRS. BASSETT.   I knew this was going to upset you. Good night, Alma. (*She leaves.* ALMA *suddenly springs up and seizes the telephone*)

ALMA.   Long distance. . . . Please get me the fever clinic at Lyon. . . . I want to speak to Dr. Buchanan.

(*The light in the Rectory dims out and light comes on in the doctor's office.* ROSA's *voice is heard calling.*)

ROSA.   *Johnny!*

(*The offstage calling of* JOHN's *name is used throughout the play as a cue for theme music.*

(JOHN *enters the office interior. He is dressed, as always, in a white linen suit. His face has a look of satiety and confusion. He throws himself down in a swivel chair at the desk.*

(ROSA GONZALES *comes in. She is dressed in a Flamenco costume and has been dancing. She crosses and stands before the anatomy chart and clicks her castanets to catch his attention, but he remains looking up at the roofless dark. She approaches him.*)

ROSA. You have blood on your face!

JOHN. You bit my ear.

ROSA. Ohhh . . . (*She approaches him with exaggerated concern*)

JOHN. You never make love without scratching or biting or something. Whenever I leave you I have a little blood on me. Why is that?

ROSA. Because I know I can't hold you.

JOHN. I think you're doing a pretty good job of it. Better than anyone else. Tomorrow we leave here together and Father or somebody else can tell old Mrs. Arbuckle her eighty-five years are enough and she's got to go now on the wings of carcinoma. Dance, Rosa! (*Accordion music is heard. She performs a slow and joyless dance around his chair.* JOHN *continues while she dances*) Tomorrow we leave here together. We sail out of Galveston, don't we?

ROSA. You say it but I don't believe it.

JOHN. I have the tickets.

ROSA. Two pieces of paper that you can tear in two.

JOHN. We'll go all right, and live on fat remittances from your Papa! Ha-ha!

ROSA. Ha-ha-ha!

JOHN. Not long ago the idea would have disgusted me, but not now. (*He catches her by the wrist*) Rosa! Rosa Gonzales! Did anyone ever slide downhill as fast as I have this summer? Ha-ha! Like a greased pig. And yet every evening I put on a clean white suit. I have a dozen. Six in the closet and six in the wash. And there isn't a sign of depravity in my face. And yet all summer I've sat around here like *this,* remembering last night, anticipating the next one! The trouble with me, I should have been *castrated!* (*He flings his wine glass at the anatomy chart. She stops dancing*) Dance, Rosa! Why don't you dance? (ROSA *shakes her head dumbly*) What is the matter, Rosa? Why don't you go on dancing? (*The accordion continues; he thrusts her arm savagely over her head in the Flamenco position*)

ROSA (*suddenly weeping*). I can't dance any more! (*She throws herself to the floor, pressing her weeping face to his knees. The voice of her* FATHER *is heard, bellowing, in the next room*)

GONZALES. The sky is the limit!

(JOHN *is sobered.*)

JOHN. Why does your father want me for a son-in-law?

ROSA (*sobbing*). I want you—I, I want you!

JOHN (*raising her from the floor*). Why do you?

ROSA (*clinging to him*). Maybe because—I was born in Piedras Negras, and grew up in a one room house with a dirt floor, and all of us had to sleep in that one room, five Mexicans and three geese and a little game-cock named Pepe! Ha-ha! (*She laughs hysterically*) Pepe was a good fighter! That's how Papa began to make money, winning bets on Pepe! Ha-ha! We all slept in the one room. And in the night, I would hear the love-making. Papa would grunt like a pig to show his passion. I thought to myself, how dirty it was, love-making, and how dirty it was to be Mexicans and all have to sleep in one room with a dirt floor and not smell good because there was not any bathtub! (*The accordion continues*)

JOHN. What has that got to do with . . . ?

ROSA. Me wanting you? You're tall! You smell good! And, oh, I'm so glad that you never grunt like a pig to show your passion! (*She embraces him convulsively*) Ah, but *quien sabe!* Something might happen tonight, and I'll wind up with some dark little friend of Papa's.

GONZALES (*imperiously*). Rosa! Rosa!

ROSA. Si, si, Papa, aqui estoy!

GONZALES (*entering unsteadily*). The gold beads . . . (*He fingers a necklace of gold beads that* ROSA *is wearing*) Johnny . . . (*He staggers up to* JOHN *and catches him in a drunken embrace*) Listen! When my girl Rosa was little she see a string of gold bead and she want those gold bead so bad that she cry all night for it. I don' have money to buy a string of gold bead so next day I go for a ride up to Eagle Pass and I walk in a dry good store and I say to the man: "Please give me a string a gold bead." He say: "Show me the money!" And I reach down to my belt and I pull out—not the money—but this! (*He pulls out a revolver*) Now—now I have money, but I still have this! (*Laughing*) She got the gold bead. Anything that she want I get for her with this (*He pulls out a roll of bills*) or this! (*He waves the revolver*)

JOHN (*pushing* GONZALES *away*). Keep your stinking breath out of my face, Gonzales!

ROSA. Dejalo, dejalo, Papa!

GONZALES (*moving unsteadily to the couch, with* ROSA *supporting him*). Le doy la tierra y si la tierra no basta—le doy el cielo! (*He collapses onto the couch*) The sky is the limit!

ROSA (*to* JOHN). Let him stay there. Come on back to the party.

(ROSA *leaves the room.* JOHN *goes over to the window facing the Rectory and looks across. The light comes up in the Rectory living room as* ALMA *enters, dressed in a robe. She goes to the window and looks across at the doctor's house. As* ALMA *and* JOHN *stand at the windows looking toward each other through the darkness music is heard. Slowly, as if drawn by the music,* JOHN *walks out of his house and crosses over to the Rectory.*

ALMA *remains motionless at the window until* JOHN *enters the room, behind her. The music dies away and there is a murmur of wind. She slowly turns to face* JOHN.)

JOHN.   I took the open door for an invitation. The Gulf wind is blowing tonight . . . cools things off a little. But my head's on fire. . . . (ALMA *says nothing.* JOHN *moves a few steps toward her*) The silence? (ALMA *sinks onto the love seat, closing her eyes*) Yes, the enormous silence. (*He goes over to her*) I will go in a minute, but first I want you to put your hands on my face. . . . (*He crouches beside her*) Eternity and Miss Alma have such cool hands. (*He buries his face in her lap. The attitude suggests a stone* Pietà. ALMA's *eyes remain closed*)

(*On the other side of the stage* DR. BUCHANAN *enters his house and the light builds a little as he looks around in the door of his office. The love theme music fades out and the Mexican music comes up strongly, with a definitely ominous quality, as* ROSA *enters the office from the other side.*)

ROSA.   Johnny! (*She catches sight of* DR. BUCHANAN *and checks herself in surprise*) Oh! I thought you were Johnny! . . . But you are Johnny's father. . . . I'm Rosa Gonzales!

DR. BUCHANAN.   I know who you are. What's going on in my house?

ROSA   (*nervously*).   John's giving a party because we're leaving tomorrow. (*Defiantly*) Yes! Together! I hope you like the idea, but if you don't, it don't matter, because *we* like the idea and my father likes the idea.

GONZALES   (*drunkenly, sitting up on the couch*).   The sky is the limit! (DR. BUCHANAN *slowly raises his silver-headed cane in a threatening gesture.*)

DR. BUCHANAN.   Get your—swine out of—my house; (*He strikes* GONZALES *with his cane*)

GONZALES   (*staggering up from the couch in pain and surprise*).   Aieeee!

ROSA   (*breathlessly, backing against the chart of anatomy*).   No! No, Papa!

DR. BUCHANAN   (*striking at the chest of the bull-like man with his cane*).   Get your swine out, I said! Get them out of my house!
(*He repeats the blow. The drunken Mexican roars with pain and surprise. He backs up and reaches under his coat.*)

ROSA   (*wildly and despairingly*).   No, no, no, no, no, no!
(*She covers her face against the chart of anatomy. A revolver is fired. There is a burst of light. The cane drops. The music stops short. Everything dims out but a spot of light on* ROSA *standing against the chart of anatomy with closed eyes and her face twisted like that of a tragic mask.*)

ROSA   (*senselessly*).   Aaaaaahhhhhh . . . Aaaaaahhhhhh . . .

(The theme music is started faintly and light disappears from everything but the wings of the stone angel.)

Scene Eight

The doctor's office.
    The stone angel is dimly visible above.
    John is seated in a hunched position at the table. Alma enters with a coffee tray. The sounds of a prayer come through the inner door.

JOHN. What is that mumbo-jumbo your father is spouting in there?
ALMA. A prayer.
JOHN. Tell him to quit. We don't want that wornout magic.
ALMA. You may not want it, but it's not a question of what you want any more. I've made you some coffee.
JOHN. I don't want any.
ALMA. Lean back and let me wash your face off, John. *(She presses a towel to the red marks on his face)* It's such a fine face, a fine and sensitive face, a face that has power in it that shouldn't be wasted.
JOHN. Never mind that. *(He pushes her hand away)*
ALMA. You have to go in to see him.
JOHN. I couldn't. He wouldn't want me.
ALMA. This happened because of his devotion to you.
JOHN. It happened because some meddlesome Mattie called him back here tonight. Who was it did that?
ALMA. I did.
JOHN. It *was* you then!
ALMA. I phoned him at the fever clinic in Lyon as soon as I learned what you were planning to do. I wired him to come here and stop it.
JOHN. You brought him here to be shot.
ALMA. You can't put the blame on anything but your weakness.
JOHN. *You* call me weak?
ALMA. Sometimes it takes a tragedy like this to make a weak person strong.
JOHN. You—white-blooded spinster! You so right people, pious pompous mumblers, preachers and preacher's daughter, all muffled up in a lot of wornout magic! And I was supposed to minister to your neurosis, give you tablets for sleeping and tonics to give you the strength to go on mumbling your wornout mumbo-jumbo!
ALMA. Call me whatever you want, but don't let your father hear your drunken shouting. *(She tries to break away from him)*

JOHN. Stay here! I want you to look at something. (*He turns her about*) This chart of anatomy, look!

ALMA. I've seen it before. (*She turns away*)

JOHN. You've never dared to look at it.

ALMA. Why should I?

JOHN. You're scared to.

ALMA. You must be out of your senses.

JOHN. You talk about weakness but can't even look at a picture of human insides.

ALMA. They're not important.

JOHN. That's your mistake. You think you're stuffed with rose-leaves. Turn around and look at it, it may do you good!

ALMA. How can you behave like this with your father dying and you so . . .

JOHN. Hold still!

ALMA. . . . so much to blame for it!

JOHN. No more than you are!

ALMA. At least for this little while . . .

JOHN. Look here!

ALMA. . . . you could feel some shame!

JOHN. (*with crazy, grinning intensity*). Now listen here to the anatomy lecture! This upper story's the brain which is hungry for something called truth and doesn't get much but keeps on feeling hungry! This middle's the belly which is hungry for food. This part down here is the sex which is hungry for love because it is sometimes lonesome. I've fed all three, as much of all three as I could or as much as I wanted— You've fed none—nothing. Well—maybe your belly a little—watery subsistence— But love or truth, nothing but—nothing but hand-me-down notions!—attitudes!—poses. (*He releases her*) Now you can go. The anatomy lecture is over.

ALMA. So that is your high conception of human desires. What you have here is not the anatomy of a beast, but a man. And I—I reject your opinion of where love is, and the kind of truth you believe the brain to be seeking!—There is something not shown on the chart.

JOHN. You mean the part that Alma is Spanish for, do you?

ALMA. Yes, that's not shown on the anatomy chart! But it's there, just the same, yes, there! Somewhere, not seen, but there. And it's *that* that I loved you with—that! Not what you mention!—Yes, did love you with, John, did nearly *die* of when you hurt me! (*He turns slowly to her and speaks gently*)

JOHN. I wouldn't have made love to you.

ALMA (*uncomprehendingly*). What?

JOHN. The night at the Casino—I wouldn't have made love to you.

Even if you had consented to go upstairs I couldn't have made love to you. *(She stares at him as if anticipating some unbearable hurt)* Yes, yes! Isn't that funny? I'm more afraid of your soul than you're afraid of my body. You'd have been as safe as the angel of the fountain —because I wouldn't feel *decent* enough to touch you. . . .

(MR. WINEMILLER *comes in.*)

MR. WINEMILLER. He's resting more easily now.

ALMA. Oh . . . *(She nods her head.* JOHN *reaches for his coffee cup)* It's cold. I'll heat it.

JOHN. It's all right.

MR. WINEMILLER. Alma, Dr. John wants you.

ALMA. I . . .

MR. WINEMILLER. He asked if you would sing for him.

ALMA. I—couldn't—now!

JOHN. Go in and sing to him, Miss Alma!

(MR. WINEMILLER *withdraws through the outer door.* ALMA *looks back at* JOHN *hunched over the coffee cup. He doesn't return her look. She passes into the blurred orange space beyond the inner door, leaving it slightly open. After a few minutes her voice rises softly within, singing.* JOHN *suddenly rises. He crosses to the door, shoves it slowly open and enters.)*

JOHN *(softly and with deep tenderness)* . Father?

(The light dims out in the house, but lingers on the stone angel.)

SCENE NINE

The cyclorama is the faint blue of a late afternoon in autumn. There is band-music—a Sousa march, in the distance. As it grows somewhat louder, Alma enters the Rectory interior in a dressing gown and with her hair hanging loose. She looks as if she had been through a long illness, the intensity drained, her pale face listless. She crosses to the window frame but the parade is not in sight so she returns weakly to the sofa and sits down closing her eyes with exhaustion.

The Rev. and Mrs. Winemiller enter the outer door frame of the Rectory, a grotesque-looking couple. Mrs. Winemiller has on her plumed hat, at a rakish angle, and a brilliant scarf about her throat. Her face wears a roguish smile that suggests a musical comedy pirate. One hand holds the minister's arm and with the other she is holding an ice cream cone.

MR. WINEMILLER. Now you may let go of my arm, if you please! She was on her worst behavior. Stopped in front of the White Star Pharmacy on Front Street and stood there like a mule; wouldn't budge till I bought her an ice cream cone. I had it wrapped in tissue paper because she had promised me that she wouldn't eat it till we got home.

The moment I gave it to her she tore off the paper and walked home licking it every step of the way!—just—just to humiliate me! (MRS. WINEMILLER *offers him the half-eaten cone, saying "Lick?"*) No, thank you!

ALMA. Now, now, children.

(MR. WINEMILLER's *irritation shifts to* ALMA.)

MR. WINEMILLER. Alma! Why don't you get dressed? It hurts me to see you sitting around like this, day in, day out, like an invalid when there is nothing particularly wrong with you. I can't read your mind. You may have had some kind of disappointment, but you must not make it an excuse for acting as if the world had come to an end.

ALMA. I have made the beds and washed the breakfast dishes and phoned the market and sent the laundry out and peeled the potatoes and shelled the peas and set the table for lunch. What more do you want?

MR. WINEMILLER (*sharply*). I want you to either get dressed or stay in your room. (ALMA *rises indifferently, then her father speaks suddenly*) At night you get dressed. Don't you? Yes, I heard you slipping out of the house at two in the morning. And that was not the first time.

ALMA. I don't sleep well. Sometimes I have to get up and walk for a while before I am able to sleep.

MR. WINEMILLER. What am I going to tell people who ask about you?

ALMA. Tell them I've changed and you're waiting to see in what way.

(*The band music becomes a little louder.*)

MR. WINEMILLER. Are you going to stay like this indefinitely?

ALMA. Not indefinitely, but you may wish that I had.

MR. WINEMILLER. Stop twisting that ring! Whenever I look at you you're twisting that ring. Give me that ring! I'm going to take that ring off your finger! (*He catches her wrist. She breaks roughly away from him*)

MRS. WINEMILLER (*joyfully*). Fight! Fight!

MR. WINEMILLER. Oh, I give up!

ALMA. That's better. (*She suddenly crosses to the window as the band music gets louder*) Is there a parade in town?

MRS. WINEMILLER. Ha-ha—yes! They met him at the station with a great big silver loving-cup!

ALMA. Who? Who did they . . . ?

MRS. WINEMILLER. That boy next door, the one you watched all the time!

ALMA. Is that true, Father?

MR. WINEMILLER (*unfolding his newspaper*). Haven't you looked at the papers?

ALMA. No, not lately.

MR. WINEMILLER (*wiping his eyeglasses*). These people are grasshoppers, just as likely to jump one way as another. He's finished the work his father started, stamped out the fever and gotten all of the glory. Well, that's how it ˙is in this world. Years of devotion and sacrifice are over- looked an' forgotten while someone young an' lucky walks off with the honors!

(ALMA *has crossed slowly to the window. The sun brightens and falls in a shaft through the frame.*)

ALMA (*suddenly crying out*). There he is! (*She staggers away from the window. There is a roll of drums and then silence.* ALMA *now speaks faintly*) What . . . happened? Something . . . struck me! (MR. WINE-MILLER *catches her arm to support her*)

MR. WINEMILLER. *Alma . . .* I'll call a doctor.

ALMA. No, no, don't. Don't call anybody to help me. I want to die! (*She collapses on the sofa*)

(*The band strikes up again and recedes down the street. The Rectory interior dims out. Then the light is brought up in the doctor's office.* JOHN *enters, with his loving-cup. He is sprucely dressed and his whole manner suggests a new-found responsibility. While he is setting the award on the table, removing his coat and starched collar,* NELLIE EWELL *appears in the door behind him. She stands by the anatomy chart and watches him until he discovers her presence.* NELLIE *has abruptly grown up, and wears very adult clothes, but has lost none of her childish impudence and brightness.* JOHN *gives a startled whistle as he sees her.* NELLIE *giggles.*)

JOHN. High heels, feathers . . . and paint!

NELLIE. Not paint!

JOHN. Natural color?

NELLIE. Excitement.

JOHN. Over what?

NELLIE. Everything! You! You here! Didn't you see me at the depot? I shouted and waved my arm off! I'm home for Thanksgiving.

JOHN. From where?

NELLIE. Sophie Newcombe's. (*He remains staring at her, unbelieving. At last she draws a book from under her arm*) Here is that nasty book you gave me last summer when I was pretending such ignorance of things!

JOHN. Only pretending?

NELLIE. Yes. (*He ignores the book. She tosses it on the table*) . . . Well? (JOHN *laughs uneasily and sits on the table*) Shall I go now, or will you look at my tongue? (*She crosses to him, sticking out her tongue*)

JOHN. Red as a berry!

NELLIE. Peppermint drops! Will you have one? (*She holds out a sack*)

JOHN. Thanks. (NELLIE *giggles as he takes one*) What's the joke, Nellie?

NELLIE. They make your mouth so sweet!

JOHN. So?

NELLIE. I always take one when I hope to be kissed.

JOHN *(after a pause)*. Suppose I took you up on that?

NELLIE. I'm not scared. Are you?

(He gives her a quick kiss. She clings to him, raising her hand to press his head against her own. He breaks free after a moment and turns the light back on.)

JOHN *(considerably impressed)*. Where did you learn such tricks?

NELLIE. I've been away to school. But they didn't teach me to love.

JOHN. Who are you to be using that long word?

NELLIE. That isn't a long word!

JOHN. No? *(He turns away from her)* Run along Nellie before we get into trouble.

NELLIE. Who's afraid of trouble, you or me?

JOHN. I am. Run along! Hear me?

NELLIE. Oh, I'll go. But I'll be back for Christmas!

(She laughs and runs out. He whistles and wipes his forehead with a handkerchief.)

SCENE TEN

An afternoon in December. At the fountain in the park. It is very windy.

Alma enters. She seems to move with an effort against the wind. She sinks down on the bench.

A widow with a flowing black veil passes across the stage and pauses by Alma's bench. It is Mrs. Bassett.

MRS. BASSETT. Hello, Alma.

ALMA. Good afternoon, Mrs. Bassett.

MRS. BASSETT. Such wind, such wind!

ALMA. Yes, it nearly swept me off my feet. I had to sit down to catch my breath for a moment.

MRS. BASSETT. I wouldn't sit too long if I were you.

ALMA. No, not long.

MRS. BASSETT. It's good to see you out again after your illness.

ALMA. Thank you.

MRS. BASSETT. Our poor little group broke up after you dropped out.

ALMA *(insincerely)*. What a pity.

MRS. BASSETT. You should have come to the last meeting.

ALMA. Why, what happened?

MRS. BASSETT. Vernon read his verse play!

ALMA. Ah, how was it received?

MRS. BASSETT. Maliciously, spitefully and vindictively torn to pieces, the way children tear the wings of butterflies. I think next spring we might reorganize. (*She throws up her black-gloved hands in a deploring gesture*)

(NELLIE EWELL *appears. She is dressed very fashionably and carrying a fancy basket of Christmas packages.*)

NELLIE. Miss Alma!

MRS. BASSETT (*rushing off*). Goodbye!

NELLIE. Oh, there you are!

ALMA. Why Nellie . . . Nellie Ewell!

NELLIE. I was by the Rectory. Just popped in for a second; the holidays are so short that every minute is precious. They told me you'd gone to the park.

ALMA. This is the first walk I've taken in quite a while.

NELLIE. You've been ill!

ALMA. Not ill, just not very well. How you've grown up, Nellie.

NELLIE. It's just my clothes. Since I went off to Sophie Newcombe I've picked out my own clothes, Miss Alma. When Mother had jurisdiction over my wardrobe, she tried to keep me looking like a child!

ALMA. Your voice is grown-up, too.

NELLIE. They're teaching me diction, Miss Alma. I'm learning to talk like you, long A's and everything, such as "cahn't" and "bahth" and "lahf" instead of "laugh." Yesterday I slipped. I said I "lahfed and lahfed till I nearly died laughing." Johnny was so amused at me!

ALMA. Johnny?

NELLIE. Your nextdoor neighbor!

ALMA. Oh! I'm sure it must be a very fashionable school.

NELLIE. Oh yes, they're preparing us to be young ladies in society. What a pity there's no society here to be a young lady in . . . at least not for me, with Mother's reputation!

ALMA. You'll find other fields to conquer.

NELLIE. What's this I hear about *you*?

ALMA. I have no idea, Nellie.

NELLIE. That you've quit teaching singing and gone into retirement.

ALMA. Naturally I had to stop teaching while I was ill and as for retiring from the world . . . it's more a case of the world retiring from me.

NELLIE. I know somebody whose feelings you've hurt badly.

ALMA. Why, who could that be, Nellie?

NELLIE. Somebody who regards you as an angel!

ALMA. I can't think who might hold me in such esteem.

NELLIE. Somebody who says that you refused to see him.

ALMA. I saw nobody. For several months. The long summer wore me out so.

NELLIE. Well, anyhow, I'm going to give you your present. (*She hands her a small package from the basket*)

ALMA. Nellie, you shouldn't have given me anything.

NELLIE. I'd like to know why not!

ALMA. I didn't expect it.

NELLIE. After the trouble you took with my horrible voice?

ALMA. It's very sweet of you, Nellie.

NELLIE. Open it!

ALMA. Now?

NELLIE. Why, sure.

ALMA. It's so prettily wrapped I hate to undo it.

NELLIE. I love to wrap presents and since it was for you, I did a specially dainty job of it.

ALMA (*winding the ribbon about her fingers*). I'm going to save this ribbon. I'm going to keep this lovely paper too, with the silver stars on it. And the sprig of holly . . .

NELLIE. Let me pin it on your jacket, Alma.

ALMA. Yes, do. I hardly realized that Christmas was coming. . . . (*She unfolds the paper, revealing a lace handkerchief and a card*) What an exquisite handkerchief.

NELLIE. I hate to give people handkerchiefs, it's so unimaginative.

ALMA. I love to get them.

NELLIE. It comes from Maison Blanche!

ALMA. Oh, does it really?

NELLIE. Smell it!

ALMA. Sachet *Roses!* Well, I'm just more touched and pleased than I can possibly tell you!

NELLIE. The card!

ALMA. Card?

NELLIE. You dropped it. (*She snatches up the card and hands it to* ALMA)

ALMA. Oh, how clumsy of me! Thank you, Nellie. "Joyeux Noel . . . to Alma . . . from Nellie and . . . (*She looks up slowly*) John?"

NELLIE. He helped me wrap presents last night and when we came to yours we started talking about you. Your ears must have burned!

(*The wind blows loudly.* ALMA *bends stiffly forward.*)

ALMA. You mean you—spoke well of me?

NELLIE. "Well of"! We raved, simply raved! Oh, he told me the influence you'd had on him!

ALMA. Influence?

NELLIE. He told me about the wonderful talks he'd had with you last summer when he was so mixed up and how you inspired him and you more than anyone else was responsible for his pulling himself together, after his father was killed, and he told me about . . . (ALMA *rises stiffly from the bench*) Where are you going, Miss Alma?

ALMA To drink at the fountain.

NELLIE. He told me about how you came in the house that night like an angel of mercy!

ALMA (*laughing harshly by the fountain*). This is the only angel in Glorious Hill. (*She bends to drink*) Her body is stone and her blood is mineral water.

(*The wind is louder*)

NELLIE. How penetrating the wind is!

ALMA. I'm going home, Nellie. You run along and deliver your presents now. . . .

(*She starts away.*)

NELLIE. But wait till I've told you the wonderfullest thing I . . .

ALMA. I'm going home now. Goodbye.

NELLIE. Oh— Goodbye, Miss Alma.

(*She snatches up her festive basket and rushes in the other direction with a shrill giggle as the wind pulls at her skirts. The lights dim out.*)

SCENE ELEVEN

An hour later. In John's office.

The interior is framed by the traceries of Victorian architecture and there is one irregular section of wall supporting the anatomy chart. Otherwise the stage is open to the cyclorama.

In the background mellow golden light touches the vane of a steeple (a gilded weathercock). Also the wings of the stone angel. A singing wind rises and falls throughout scene.

John is seated at a white enameled table examining a slide through a microscope.

(*A bell tolls the hour of five as* ALMA *comes hesitantly in. She wears a russet suit and a matching hat with a plume. The light changes, the sun disappearing behind a cloud, fading from the steeple and the stone angel till the bell stops tolling. Then it brightens again.*)

ALMA. No greetings? No greetings at all?

JOHN. Hello, Miss Alma.

ALMA (*speaking with animation to control her panic*). How white it is here, such glacial brilliance! (*She covers her eyes, laughing*)

JOHN. New equipment.

ALMA. Everything new but the chart.

JOHN. The human anatomy's always the same old thing.

ALMA. And such a tiresome one! I've been plagued with sore throats.

JOHN. Everyone has here lately. These Southern homes are all improperly heated. Open grates aren't enough.

ALMA. They burn the front of you while your back is freezing!

JOHN. Then you go into another room and get chilled off.

ALMA. Yes, yes, chilled to the bone.

JOHN. But it never gets quite cold enough to convince the damn fools that a furnace is necessary so they go on building without them.

(*There is the sound of wind.*)

ALMA. Such a strange afternoon.

JOHN. Is it? I haven't been out.

ALMA. The Gulf wind is blowing big, white—what do they call them? cumulus?—clouds over! Ha-ha! It seemed determined to take the plume off my hat, like that fox terrier we had once, named Jacob, snatched the plume off a hat and dashed around and around the back yard with it like a trophy!

JOHN. I remember Jacob. What happened to him?

ALMA. Oh, Jacob. Jacob was such a mischievous thief. We had to send him out to some friends in the country. Yes, he ended his days as—a country squire! The tales of his exploits . . .

JOHN. Sit down, Miss Alma.

ALMA. If I'm disturbing you . . . ?

JOHN. No—I called the Rectory when I heard you were sick. Your father told me you wouldn't see a doctor.

ALMA. I needed a rest, that was all. . . . You were out of town mostly. . . .

JOHN. I was mostly in Lyon, finishing up Dad's work in the fever clinic.

ALMA. Covering yourself with sudden glory!

JOHN. Redeeming myself with good works.

ALMA. It's rather late to tell you how happy I am, and also how proud. I almost feel as your father might have felt—if . . . And—are you—happy now, John?

JOHN (*uncomfortably, not looking at her*). I've settled with life on fairly acceptable terms. Isn't that all a reasonable person can ask for?

ALMA. He can ask for much more than that. He can ask for the coming true of his most improbable dreams.

JOHN. It's best not to ask for too much.

ALMA. I disagree with you. I say, ask for all, but be prepared to get nothing! (*She springs up and crosses to the window. She continues*) No, I haven't been well. I've thought many times of something you told me last summer, that I have a *doppelganger*. I looked that up and I found that it means another person inside me, another self, and I don't know whether to thank you or not for making me conscious of

it!—I haven't been well. . . . For a while I thought I was dying, that
that was the change that was coming.

JOHN. When did you have that feeling?

ALMA. August. September. But now the Gulf wind has blown that feeling away like a cloud of smoke, and I know now I'm not dying, that it
isn't going to turn out to be that simple. . . .

JOHN. Have you been anxious about your heart again? (*He retreats to
a professional manner and takes out a silver watch, putting his fingers
on her wrist*)

ALMA. And now the stethoscope? (*He removes the stethoscope from the
table and starts to loosen her jacket. She looks down at his bent head.
Slowly, involuntarily, her gloved hands lift and descend on the crown
of his head. He gets up awkwardly. She suddenly leans toward him
and presses her mouth to his*) Why don't you say something? Has the
cat got your tongue?

JOHN. Miss Alma, what can I say?

ALMA. You've gone back to calling me "Miss Alma" again.

JOHN. We never really got past that point with each other.

ALMA. Oh, yes we did. We were so close that we almost breathed together!

JOHN (*with embarrassment*). I didn't know that.

ALMA. No? Well, I did, I knew it. (*Her hand touches his face tenderly*) You shave more carefully now? You don't have those little razor
cuts on your chin that you dusted with gardenia talcum. . . .

JOHN. I shave more carefully now.

ALMA. So that explains it! (*Her fingers remain on his face, moving
gently up and down it like a blind person reading Braille. He is in-
tensely embarrassed and gently removes her hands from him*) Is it—
impossible now?

JOHN. I don't think I know what you mean.

ALMA. You know what I mean, all right! So be honest with me. One
time I said "no" to something. You may remember the time, and all
that demented howling from the cock-fight? But now I have changed
my mind, or the girl who said "no," she doesn't exist any more, she
died last summer—suffocated in smoke from something on fire inside
her. No, she doesn't live now, but she left me her ring— You see? This
one you admired, the topaz ring set in pearls. . . . And she said to
me when she slipped this ring on my finger—"Remember I died empty-
handed, and so make sure that your hands have *something in them!*"
(*She drops her gloves. She clasps his head again in her hands*) I said,
"But what about pride?"—She said, "Forget about pride whenever it
stands between you and what you must have!" (*He takes hold of her*

wrists) And then I said, "But what if he doesn't want me?" I don't know what she said then. I'm not sure whether she said anything or not—her lips stopped moving—yes, I think she stopped breathing! (*He gently removes her craving hands from his face*) No? (*He shakes his head in dumb suffering*) Then the answer is "no"!

JOHN (*forcing himself to speak*). I have a respect for the truth, and I have a respect for you—so I'd better speak honestly if you want me to speak. (ALMA *nods slightly*) You've won the argument that we had between us.

ALMA. What—argument?

JOHN. The one about the chart.

ALMA. Oh—the chart!

(*She turns from him and wanders across to the chart. She gazes up at it with closed eyes, and her hands clasped in front of her.*)

JOHN. It shows that we're not a package of rose leaves, that every interior inch of us is taken up with something ugly and functional and no room seems to be left for anything else in there.

ALMA. No . . .

JOHN. But I've come around to your way of thinking, that something else is in there, an immaterial something—as thin as smoke—which all of those ugly machines combine to produce and that's their whole reason for being. It can't be seen so it can't be shown on the chart. But it's there, just the same, and knowing it's there—why, then the whole thing—this—this unfathomable experience of ours—takes on a new value, like some—some wildly romantic work in a laboratory! Don't you see?

(*The wind comes up very loud, almost like a choir of voices. Both of them turn slightly,* ALMA *raising a hand to her plumed head as if she were outdoors.*)

ALMA. Yes, I see! Now that you no longer want it to be otherwise you're willing to believe that a spiritual bond can exist between us two!

JOHN. Can't you believe that I am sincere about it?

ALMA. Maybe you are. But I don't want to be talked to like some incurably sick patient you have to comfort. (*A harsh and strong note comes into her voice*) Oh, I suppose I am sick, one of those weak and divided people who slip like shadows among you solid strong ones. But sometimes, out of necessity, we shadowy people take on a strength of our own. I have that now. You needn't try to deceive me.

JOHN. I wasn't.

ALMA. You needn't try to comfort me. I haven't come here on any but equal terms. You said, let's talk truthfully. Well, let's do! Unsparingly, truthfully, even shamelessly, then! It's no longer a secret that I love you. It never was. I loved you as long ago as the time you read the

stone angel's name with your fingers. Yes, I remember the long afternoons of our childhood, when I had to stay indoors to practice my
music—and heard your playmates calling you, "Johnny, Johnny!"
How it went through me, just to hear your name called! And how I
—rushed to the window to watch you jump the porch railing! I stood
at a distance, halfway down the block, only to keep in sight of your
torn red sweater, racing about the vacant lot you played in. Yes, it
had begun that early, this affliction of love, and has never let go of
me since, but keep on growing. I've lived next door to you all the
days of my life, a weak and divided person who stood in adoring awe
of your singleness, of your strength. And that is my story! Now I wish
you would tell *me*—why didn't it happen between us? Why did I fail?
Why did you come almost close enough—and no closer?

JOHN. Whenever we've gotten together, the three or four times that we
have . . .

ALMA. As few as that?

JOHN. It's only been three or four times that we've come face to face.
And each of those times—we seemed to be trying to find something in
each other without knowing what it was that we wanted to find. It
wasn't a body hunger although—I acted as if I thought it might be
the night I wasn't a gentleman—at the Casino—it wasn't the physical
you that I really wanted!

ALMA. I know, you've already . . .

JOHN. You didn't have that to give me.

ALMA. Not at that time.

JOHN. You had something else to give.

ALMA. What did I have?

(JOHN *strikes a match. Unconsciously he holds his curved palm over the
flame of the match to warm it. It is a long kitchen match and it makes a
good flame. They both stare at it with a sorrowful understanding that is
still perplexed. It is about to burn his fingers. She leans forward and
blows it out, then she puts on her gloves.*)

JOHN. You couldn't name it and I couldn't recognize it. I thought it was
just a Puritanical ice that glittered like flame. But now I believe it *was*
flame, mistaken for ice. I still don't understand it, but I know it was
there, just as I know that your eyes and your voice are the two most
beautiful things I've ever known—and also the warmest, although they
don't seem to be set in your body at all. . . .

ALMA. You talk as if my body had ceased to exist for you, John, in spite
of the fact that you've just counted my pulse. Yes, that's it! You tried
to avoid it, but you've told me plainly. The tables have turned, yes,
the tables have turned with a vengeance! You've come around to my
old way of thinking and I to yours like two people exchanging a call

on each other at the same time, and each one finding the other one gone out, the door locked against him and no one to answer the bell! (*She laughs*) I came here to tell you that being a gentleman doesn't seem so important to me any more, but you're telling me I've got to remain a lady. (*She laughs rather violently*) The tables have turned with a vengeance!—The air in here smells of ether—It's making me dizzy . . .

JOHN. I'll open a window.

ALMA. Please.

JOHN. There now.

ALMA. Thank you, that's better. Do you remember those little white tablets you gave me? I've used them all up and I'd like to have some more.

JOHN. I'll write the prescription for you.

(*He bends to write*)

(NELLIE *is in the waiting room. They hear her voice.*)

ALMA. Someone is waiting in the waiting room, John. One of my vocal pupils. The youngest and prettiest one with the least gift for music. The one that you helped wrap up this handkerchief for me. (*She takes it out and touches her eyes with it*)

(*The door opens, first a crack.* NELLIE *peers in and giggles. Then she throws the door wide open with a peal of merry laughter. She has holly pinned on her jacket. She rushes up to* JOHN *and hugs him with childish squeals.*)

NELLIE. I've been all over town just shouting, shouting!

JOHN. Shouting what?

NELLIE. Glad tidings!

(JOHN *looks at* ALMA *over* NELLIE's *shoulder.*)

JOHN. I thought we weren't going to tell anyone for a while.

NELLIE. I couldn't stop myself. (*She wheels about*) Oh, Alma, has he told *you?*

ALMA (*quietly*). He didn't need to, Nellie. I guessed . . . from the Christmas card with your two names written on it!

(NELLIE *rushes over to* ALMA *and hugs her. Over* NELLIE's *shoulder* ALMA *looks at* JOHN. *He makes a thwarted gesture as if he wanted to speak. She smiles desperately and shakes her head. She closes her eyes and bites her lips for a moment. Then she releases* NELLIE *with a laugh of exaggerated gaiety.*)

NELLIE. So, Alma, you were really the first to know!

ALMA. I'm proud of that, Nellie.

NELLIE. See on my finger! This was the present I couldn't tell you about!

ALMA. Oh, what a lovely, lovely solitaire! But solitaire is such a wrong name for it. Solitaire means single and this means *two!* It's blinding, Nellie! Why it . . . hurts my eyes!

(JOHN *catches* NELLIE's *arm and pulls her to him. Almost violently* ALMA *lifts her face; it is bathed in tears. She nods gratefully to* JOHN *for releasing her from* NELLIE's *attention. She picks up her gloves and purse.*)

JOHN. Excuse her, Miss Alma. Nellie's still such a child.

ALMA. (*with a breathless laugh*). I've got to run along now.

JOHN. Don't leave your prescription.

ALMA. Oh, yes, where's my prescription?

JOHN. On the table.

ALMA. I'll take it to the drug store right away!

(NELLIE *struggles to free herself from* JOHN's *embrace which keeps her from turning to* ALMA.)

NELLIE. Alma, don't go! Johnny, let go of me, Johnny! You're hugging me so tight I can't breathe!

ALMA. Goodbye.

NELLIE. Alma! Alma, you know you're going to sing at the wedding! The very first Sunday in spring!—which will be Palm Sunday! "The Voice That Breathed O'er Eden."

(ALMA *has closed the door.* JOHN *shuts his eyes tight with a look of torment. He rains kisses on* NELLIE's *forehead and throat and lips. The scene dims out with music.*)

Scene Twelve

In the park near the angel of the fountain. About dusk:

Alma enters the lighted area and goes slowly up to the fountain and bends to drink. Then she removes a small white package from her pocketbook and starts to unwrap it. While she is doing this, a Young Man comes along. He is dressed in a checked suit and a derby. He pauses by the bench. They glance at each other.

A train whistles in the distance. The Young Man clears his throat. The train whistle is repeated. The Young Man crosses toward the fountain, his eyes on Alma. She hesitates, with the unwrapped package in her hand. Then she crosses toward the bench and stands hesitantly in front of it. He stuffs his hands in his pockets and whistles. He glances with an effect of unconcern back over his shoulder.

Alma pushes her veil back with an uncertain gesture. His whistle dies out. He sways back and forth on his heels as the train whistles again. He suddenly turns to the fountain and bends to drink. Alma slips the package back into her purse. As the young man straightens up, she speaks in a barely audible voice.

ALMA.   The water—is—cool.

THE YOUNG MAN   *(eagerly)*. Did you say something?

ALMA.   I said, the water is cool.

THE YOUNG MAN.   Yes, it sure is, it's nice and cool!

ALMA.   It's always cool.

THE YOUNG MAN.   Is it?

ALMA.   Yes. Yes, even in summer. It comes from deep underground.

THE YOUNG MAN.   That's what keeps it cool.

ALMA.   Glorious Hill is famous for its artesian springs.

THE YOUNG MAN.   I didn't know that.

(The YOUNG MAN *jerkily removes his hands from his pockets. She gathers confidence before the awkwardness of his youth.)*

ALMA.   Are you a stranger in town?

THE YOUNG MAN.   I'm a traveling salesman.

ALMA.   Ah, you're a salesman who travels! *(She laughs gently)* But
    you're younger than most of them are, and not so fat!

THE YOUNG MAN.   I'm just starting out. I travel for Red Goose shoes.

ALMA.   Ah! The Delt's your territory?

THE YOUNG MAN.   From the Peabody Lobby to Cat-Fish Row in Vicks-
    burg.

*(*ALMA *leans back and looks at him under half-closed lids, perhaps a little
suggestively.)*

ALMA.   The life of a traveling salesman is interesting . . . but lonely.

THE YOUNG MAN.   You're right about that. Hotel bedrooms are lonely.

(There is a pause. Far away the train whistles again.)

ALMA.   All rooms are lonely where there is only one person. *(Her eyes
    fall shut)*

THE YOUNG MAN   *(gently)*. You're tired, aren't you?

ALMA.   I? Tired? *(She starts to deny it; then laughs faintly and confesses
    the truth)* Yes . . . a little. . . . But I shall rest now. I've just now
    taken one of my sleeping tablets.

THE YOUNG MAN.   So early?

ALMA.   Oh, it won't put me to sleep. It will just quiet my nerves.

THE YOUNG MAN.   What are you nervous about?

ALMA.   I won an argument this afternoon.

THE YOUNG MAN.   That's nothing to be nervous over. You ought to be
    nervous if you *lost* one.

ALMA.   It wasn't the argument that I wanted to win. . . .

THE YOUNG MAN.   Well, I'm nervous too.

ALMA.   What over?

THE YOUNG MAN.   It's my first job and I'm scared of not making good.

*(The mysteriously sudden intimacy that sometimes occurs between
strangers more completely than old friends or lovers moves them both.*

ALMA *hands the package of tablets to him.*)

ALMA. Then you must take one of my tablets.

THE YOUNG MAN. Shall I?

ALMA. Please take one!

THE YOUNG MAN. Yes, I shall.

ALMA. You'll be surprised how infinitely merciful they are. The prescription number is 96814. I think of it as the telephone number of God! (*They both laugh. He places one of the tablets on his tongue and crosses to the fountain to wash it down*)

THE YOUNG MAN (*to the stone figure*). Thanks, angel. (*He gives her a little salute, and crosses back to* ALMA)

ALMA. Life is full of little mercies like that, not *big* mercies but comfortable *little* mercies. And so we are able to keep on going. . . . (*She has leaned back with half-closed eyes*)

THE YOUNG MAN (*returning*). You're falling asleep.

ALMA. Oh no, I'm not. I'm just closing my eyes. You know what I feel like now? I feel like a water-lily.

THE YOUNG MAN. A water-lily?

ALMA. Yes, I feel like a water-lily on a Chinese lagoon. Won't you sit down? (*The* YOUNG MAN *does*) My name is Alma. Spanish for soul! What's yours?

THE YOUNG MAN. Ha-ha! Mine's Archie Kramer. Mucho gusto, as they say in Spain.

ALMA. Usted habla Espanol, senor?

THE YOUNG MAN. Un poquito! Usted habla Espanol, senorita?

ALMA. Me tambien. Un poquito!

THE YOUNG MAN (*delightedly*). Ha . . . ha . . . ha! Sometimes un poquito is plenty! (ALMA *laughs . . . in a different way than she has ever laughed before, a little wearily, but quite naturally. The* YOUNG MAN *leans toward her confidentially*) What's there to do in this town after dark?

ALMA. There's not much to do in this town after dark, but there are resorts on the lake that offer all kinds of after-dark entertainment. There's one called Moon Lake Casino. It's under new management, now, but I don't suppose its character has changed.

THE YOUNG MAN. What was its character?

ALMA. Gay, very gay, Mr. Kramer. . . .

THE YOUNG MAN. Then what in hell are we sitting here for? Vamonos!

ALMA. Como no, senor!

THE YOUNG MAN. Ha-ha-ha! (*He jumps up*) I'll call a taxi. (*He goes off shouting "Taxi"*)

(ALMA *rises from the bench. As she crosses to the fountain the grave mood of the play is reinstated with a phrase of music. She faces the stone angel and raises her gloved hand in a sort of valedictory salute. Then she turns slowly about toward the audience with her hand still raised in a gesture of wonder and finality as . . . the curtain falls.*)

TWO VIEWS OF SUMMER AND SMOKE

I

R. BRUCE MOODY

Summer and smoke, passion and essence, the flesh and the spirit. . . .

Is John Buchanan the heat of the summer, and Alma Winemiller the spirituel distillation which hangs over it?

Yes, but that would make a play of the conflict of humors, while Tennessee Williams has created in Alma and John characters who contain their own contradictions. In John is the sense, which he sees embodied in Alma, of the essence toward which he knows he must aspire. In Alma lies the strength, which she sees in John, to demand from life the realization of the mundane flesh which she knows she must embody. Alma is the Spanish way of saying soul, and John is Alma's way of saying Jack. At the start, he is the bohemian, she the bourgeois. Yet both contain *Doppelgänger*. At the end, he turns into the bourgeois, and she into the bohemian. He settles down in prim Glorious Hill. She moves on to the Moon Lake Casino.

It is a period piece. It is one of Tennessee Williams's few period pieces. That is to say, it is one of his few plays set in a time through which he himself did not live.

Why does he do this? He does it to utilize the clearer contrasts of a simpler era. Small towns were provincial and agrarian and slept through the days, summer and winter, sure and compact. Good and bad, religion and sensuality, innocence and guilt, these were true antitheses in people's minds; at least they said they were.

Consider what the play would be like if he had set it in the Roaring Twenties. John, as the flaming youth, would have dominated the play, and the play would have been about him. Set it in the 1960s, and Alma would be a square, John someone suffering from an inadmissible lapse of cool, and they both would be much too old.

Yes, they're both pushing thirty; yet that means the author can use mature voices, and to this is added the poignancy of this summer's being

R. Bruce Moody, a native New Yorker and graduate of Columbia College, is a novelist and short story writer. His work has appeared in *The New Yorker* and *Botteghe Oscure*.

Alma's last chance for normal happiness, the moment in her life before confirmed spinsterhood.

For it is Alma's play, and she is one of the most touching of all his heroines and one of the most immediate to us. Tennessee Williams has written only two middle-class plays, this one and *Period of Adjustment*. All the rest are set in either exotic or primitive locales, and to this is added the further exoticism of the persons of them being involved in one way or another with the demimonde, that is to say with a way of life from which a living is made, or may be hoped to be made, through varieties of prostitution. The exoticism of *Summer and Smoke* is that it alone of all his plays is set in Thornton Wilder's Our Town.

Summer and smoke . . . a play filled with elements which balance. The title of the play, the symmetry of the set, balanced by the fulcrum of the statue's hand, a rectory on one side and a physician's office on the other, prologue and epilogue, part one and part two, and a dialogue almost epigrammatic—all reflect these balances.

 . . . the flesh and the spirit. All Tennessee Williams's plays deal with the conflict between the flesh and the spirit. In his early plays, the flesh was sexual magnetism and the spirit tender ideals. In his later plays, sex combines with a hectic materialism and ideals with a sinner's scream for God's aid to embody religious psychodramas of enormous ambition and brilliance.

They fail, as this play failed when it was first done. For Tennessee Williams does not believe what he is tempted, what he wishes, what he longs to believe, that the spirit can surmount the flesh. He sees the real world at its worst and best and is rent by a flesh which is sublime in its ecstasies and a spirit whose ecstasy it is to be sublime.

This conflict is in all his work and is reflected in the governing tone of his plays one by one as he conceived them: of the flesh in his first, *Battle of Angels;* of the spirit in the second, *The Glass Menagerie;* of the flesh in the third, *A Streetcar Named Desire;* of the spirit in the fourth, *Summer and Smoke;* of the flesh in the fifth, *The Rose Tattoo;* of the spirit in the sixth, *Camino Real;* of the flesh in the seventh, *Cat on a Hot Tin Roof.* After *The Glass Menagerie,* those of no matter what tone, which suggested in the end the triumph of the material over the ideal, were his great commercial successes in the Broadway theater, for there a rich and materialistic audience paid to see them. *Summer and Smoke* itself might have been a success there had the playwright contrived, as he did in a later version of it, for John to sleep with Alma and abandon her.

As it is the play is beautiful, and we are fortunate to have it as it is. Its balances are the most delicate he ever conceived and are made perfect by a perfect prose. However, as with so many of his plays, it is upon his female character that he lavishes his greatest interest, best writing, and key scenes, and for all its subtle balances, *Summer and Smoke* is not a masterpiece of balanced construction. It is Alma we care about, not John.

What would have balanced it? Well, John's rebellion begins before the play begins; we do not witness its cause. Perhaps we should, and perhaps we should learn that it is brought out by something in Alma. Or perhaps there's a missing scene. But what scene? Dr. Buchanan's death scene perhaps. Alma faces her demons and goes down, whereas John merely settles with life on fairly acceptable terms, forgoing his exhausting carousals with all those unlikely Mexicans for a middle-class marriage with a pretty but vapid girl. He moves from pleasure into contentment. It is not a very dramatic come-about. Of course, it is right that he do this, but as Alma comes to terms with the god of love, should he not also first come to terms with . . . with what? With God Himself maybe?

Still, the enormous virtues of this play far overshadow its one defect. The play is a poetical play. Tennessee Williams brings to the drama, with its need for verbal concentration, a speech whose suggestive power is usually achieved only by novelists. *Summer and Smoke* was written at the peak of his early lyricism, and its tone dominates its mood like a soft, slow, and balmy Gulf breeze that both relieves and accents the heats and torments of it.

And yet, it is a comedy. Comedy is when you *do not do* what you say you are going to do. Tragedy is when you *do do* what you say you are going to do. Of course, in the epilogue, Scene 12, Alma does do, although not in a way she intended, what she said she was going to do. Well, it is a tragicomedy then. But Tennessee Williams is a great humorist, and his characters reveal themselves in a way so crazy and apt and true that you have to laugh.

And, in a way, Tennessee Williams is funniest when saddest. In the insupportably heartrending penultimate scene of this play, when Alma sees Nellie's ring, she gushes: "Oh, what a lovely solitaire!" All her nascent good manners and prim etiquette come through to both reveal and protect her. "But solitaire is such a wrong name for it. Solitaire means single, and this means *two!*" And we know that being *two,* which Alma so much desired and hoped for, is something which now she can never have. But the writer has not given her a great speech, a soliloquy, a tragic peroration. All he has given her—and it is his special genius that he has done so—is a polite joke! "It's blinding, Nellie! Why it . . . hurts my eyes!" . . .

Remember who Alma is, and how fully the author has created her. She is a real woman, and we sympathize with her. Face the fact also that, although we sympathize with her, it is with John that we unconsciously empathize. Alma is a prude, filled with silly, middle-class half-cocked adages, and if we met her in real life, most of us would not be kind to her; she would annoy us, infuriate us, and we would fall asleep at those Friday night soirees of hers, if we ever went, which we probably would not. We would behave as John does and we would lose her as he does.

But we care about her, because for Alma it is love itself which is at stake. Alma's tragedy is that she knows too well that she and John were meant for one another. John's tragedy is that he does not know it at all. The perfect wife for him is, not Nellie, but Alma! But summer and smoke are not two obviously compatible opposites. The one does not perforce complement the other. There is no *necessary* affinity. Summer and smoke. The one is summer, the other smoke.

II

BEEKMAN H. COTTRELL

Summer and Smoke (1948) is Tennessee Williams's third major play, and although it continues to deal with the same central concerns as did *The Glass Menagerie* (1945) and *A Streetcar Named Desire* (1947), there is an important shift in emphasis. Williams himself gives the impetus to this thematic shift in his production notes for the play. He writes, "There must be a great expanse of sky so that the entire action of the play takes place against it." This everpresent sky implies something which is not present—or, certainly, not stressed—in the two earlier successful plays. The action of *The Glass Menagerie* takes place indoors and in an adjoining alley. Indeed, the Wingfield apartment is cramped and participates in the life outside only by means of an open window or a fire escape. Even when Laura's brother Tom leaves his family and goes out into the world, he is haunted by the constrictions of that St. Louis "home" and is himself trapped by its mood of being shut away from the real life of the world.

There is a bit more of the world—this time New Orleans and its colorful street life—in *A Streetcar Named Desire*. But for its heroine, Blanche Du Bois, there is a sickening sense of being trapped in the Kowalski apartment and its blatant life of the senses. The world knocks on its door in the form of a paperboy, Blanche's suitor Mitch, a flower

Beekman Cottrell, a native of Florida, completed his graduate studies at Columbia. He is chairman of humanities at Carnegie-Mellon University, formerly the Carnegie Institute of Technology.

vendor, or—at the last—the attendants from the sanitarium. But the life and tragedy of the play are confined within the limits of her sister Stella's newly adopted world.

So it is vital to an understanding of *Summer and Smoke* to realize that Williams sees his third drama as being played out against the entire community of Glorious Hill, Mississippi. Our constant awareness is for the wholeness of the stage life, for its constant shifts in and out of homes, offices, living rooms, to the square, to the fountain. Alma Winemiller, unlike Laura and Blanche before her, must learn to cope with a whole world, not just the segment of it she chooses to master. We see Alma trying to expand her soul and encompass the world. She surely does not always succeed. She may, in fact, ultimately fail, but she reaches out into the world as symbolized by the small town, and at the last she does not seem to be defeated.

At least two major concerns permeate all the plays of Tennessee Williams. One is the constant struggle of human beings on earth with two warring forces. As Williams puts it in *Summer and Smoke,* "Part anarchy—and part order!" The other concern has to do with the sensitive people faced with these forces, and the outcome of the confrontation. John says to Alma, "You—white-blooded spinster. . . . You think you're stuffed with rose-leaves," and he is right. Alma does not wish to face the human anatomy chart and all it implies. But Alma has her own kind of rightness, too. "I'm just mystified and amazed as I always am by the unprovoked malice in people." We sympathize with her because she is sensitive and because she is right to be hurt by the thinking and unthinking cruelty of the world.

And so at last she knows she must question the artificial order she has tried to force upon the universe, and she cries out to John, "I've lived next door to you all the days of my life, a weak and divided person who stood in adoring awe of your singleness, of your strength." Yet his strength has been the strength of anarchy, and his chaos, abandoned only at the very end of the play, almost destroys Alma's vulnerable order. Earlier in the play she can say to her father, "Tell them I've changed and you're waiting to see in what way."

She has indeed changed. Her illness, at first feigned and later far more real, symbolizes her new and conscious membership in the ranks of fallible humanity. When she can learn to accept that humanity (and, ironically, when she has worked herself up to a torturing, voluntary offer of it to John), she is ready to face both the unexpected and difficult acceptance of John and Nellie's marriage and the unknown experience with a young man in the park.

In this courage she differs from Laura and Blanche, but she is very like Hannah Jelkes in Williams's later powerful play *The Night of the*

Iguana (1962). Laura retreats to her candles and her glass figurines, while her mother dreams of the jonquil past and gentleman callers. Blanche remains a lady even at the last, even when every shred of her pretension and pride is gone. She too will lose her battle with the world. Anarchy wins for both Laura and Blanche.

Alma's case is different. She may come through; she may be able to accept a world of human compromise and live on, as does Hannah, in modified, ordered sensitivity. It is almost as though Blanche's final speech in *Streetcar* ("Whoever you are—I have always depended on the kindness of strangers.") gives Alma the courage to drive off to the Moon Lake Casino with young Mr. Kramer.

It seems, then, that *Summer and Smoke* moves a philosophical step forward. Giving in can be agonizing, but easy. Readjusting can be agonizing, and difficult. Williams's poetry, his very real people and vivid human situations remain unclouded in this play. We care very much about Alma's plight, and we wish her well. Her solution is less melodramatic than Blanche's, less dreamlike and removed than Laura's. She is a fuller person because of the final scene of the play and what it implies.

Tennessee Williams has created a number of symbolically tragic heroines. Into each have gone several elements: great sensitivity, a sense of standards, a love of beauty, an inability to face the "real" world. But in all of them there is another element—it can be called either willfulness or determination—which makes them much closer to the classical tragic heroines than to victims in a melodrama. In a strange way we admire Laura for her principles and her withdrawal, as we admire Antigone for her fatal decision on the side of superhuman laws. We sympathize deeply with Blanche in her revulsion against her brother-in-law Stanley and his crudity; yet we admire her desperate attempts to hold to standards of gentility and beauty.

Alma Winemiller embodies all these things, and yet we are drawn to her for another reason: She has the courage to try to change. She abjures the total retreat (there is the lesson before her of her mother), whether into seclusion or madness. She faces up to the mysterious force of a Rosa Gonzales and reaches tentatively, with "a gesture of wonder," toward the outer life she has never truly known and perhaps always misjudged. She is the first of the truly daring souls in Williams's plays. After her come Serafina delle Rose from *The Rose Tattoo;* Kilroy and Don Quixote from *Camino Real;* Catherine Holly from *Suddenly Last Summer;* Maggie from *Cat on a Hot Tin Roof;* and Hannah Jelkes, her grandfather Nonno, and Reverend Shannon from *The Night of the Iguana.* Williams continues to dramatize for us facets of a situation we must learn to accept, and Alma quotes Oscar Wilde to prove it: "All of us are in the gutter, but some of us are looking at the stars!" Early in *Summer and Smoke* Alma calls them "the footprints of God," and John answers, "But not God." They are both right, but only partially. One must look at the stars but never neglect or ignore the gutter where he stands.

How does a human being accept this dilemma? Through the sense of human beauty and mystery, of the unrealized potentials for life in the story of Alma Winemiller, Tennessee Williams offers us a compassionate picture of one human soul's movement from isolation toward a sense of communion with the whole of mankind.

ANOUILH

JEAN ANOUILH (1910–   ), A NATIVE OF BORDEAUX, IS ONE OF THE FEW FRENCH PLAYWRIGHTS WHO HAS AVOIDED BECOMING EITHER A PHILOSOPHER-ICONOCLAST OR SIDEWALK CAFE-SEER. STILL IN HIS TEENS WHEN HE ABANDONED HIS LAW STUDIES BECAUSE OF FINANCIAL NEED, HE HAD BEGUN WRITING PLAYS IN HIS SPARE TIME AT SIXTEEN. AT TWENTY-FIVE, ANOUILH ACHIEVED RECOGNITION AS A DRAMATIST, AND SINCE THEN HAS ATTAINED THE STATUS OF FOREMOST FRENCH PLAYWRIGHT. INFLUENCED FIRST BY HIS ELDER CONTEMPORARY, JEAN GIRAUDOUX, AND THEN BY MOLIÈRE, PIRANDELLO, AND BERNARD SHAW, ANOUILH'S WORK HAS CONSISTENTLY GROWN IN SUBTLETY OF THOUGHT, CRAFTSMANSHIP, AND UNIVERSALITY OF APPEAL. A PROLIFIC WRITER, HIS MANY PLAYS INCLUDE *THIEVES' CARNIVAL* (1932); *TIME REMEMBERED* (1939); *ANTIGONE* (1942); *RING ROUND THE MOON* (1947); *THE REHEARSAL* (1950); *THE WALTZ OF THE TOREADORS* (1951); *THE LARK* (1953); AND *POOR BITOS* (1956).

Although it has for its subject the conflict between church and state, Anouilh's *Becket* (1959) neither reflects Christian beliefs nor is a religious play. Rather, the philosophic existentialism which Jean-Paul Sartre formulated during World War II reveals Becket as the existential man, who embraces the role circumstance has imposed upon him, who fulfills himself in that role, not out of a sense of duty, not out of a social or religious or political conscience, but out of a firm commitment to his developing self.

Becket, however, need not necessarily be regarded as the hero of the play, as the prototype of men who have sacrificed their lives to preserve their integrity—and "the honor of God," like Antigone and Joan of Arc (both of whom are subjects of other plays by Anouilh).

Perhaps it is Henry, in fact, who is the focal figure. To be sure, Henry's deeds are often ignoble and unworthy of a king-hero. Yet it is Henry, is it not, who is conscious of historical necessity, of the imperative which a responsible ruler must respond to? Henry's deepest passion was his love for Becket. (Whom did Becket love?) And what is it Henry loves in Becket but the chancellor's refinement and taste, his integrity and wisdom? But Henry was a great king. Anouilh contrasts the virile, capable, and forthright Norman with other European rulers—the ineffectual Louis of France, the devious pope and his scheming cardinal —Henry's major adversaries. *Except for Becket himself!*

Becket, we must remember, has allied himself to issues and causes which might be considered fruitless and reactionary. Would England have gained from replacing Norman government with anarchy? *Should* the Archbishop of Canterbury's authority have been superior to the King's?

The deliberate ambiguities of this play, the questions it raises without assurance of a clear-cut answer are characteristic of the new theater of Sartre, Genêt Ionesco, and Samuel Beckett—whose work both influenced, and was influenced by, fellow Parisian Jean Anouilh.

BECKET

TRANSLATED BY
LUCIENNE HILL

CHARACTERS

HENRY II
THOMAS BECKET
ARCHBISHOP OF CANTERBURY
GILBERT FOLLIOT
BISHOP OF YORK
SAXON PEASANT
HIS SON
GWENDOLEN
1ST ENGLISH BARON
2ND ENGLISH BARON
3RD ENGLISH BARON
4TH ENGLISH BARON
QUEEN MOTHER
THE QUEEN
LOUIS, KING OF FRANCE
THE POPE

ACT ONE

An indeterminate set, with pillars. We are in the cathedral. Center stage: Becket's tomb; a stone slab with a name carved on it. Two sentries come in and take up their position upstage. Then the king enters from the back. He is wearing his crown, and is naked under a big cloak. A page follows at a distance. The king hesitates a moment before the tomb; then removes his cloak with a swift movement and the page takes it away. He falls to his knees on the stone floor and prays, alone, naked, in the middle of the stage. Behind the pillars, in the shadows, one senses the disquieting presence of unseen lookers-on.

KING. Well, Thomas Becket, are you satisfied? I am naked at your tomb and your monks are coming to flog me. What an end to our story! You, rotting in this tomb, larded with my barons' dagger thrusts, and I, naked, shivering in the draughts, and waiting like an idiot for those brutes to come and thrash me. Don't you think we'd have done better to understand each other?
(BECKET *in his Archbishop's robes, just as he was on the day of his death, has appeared on the side of the stage, from behind a pillar. He says softly:*)

BECKET. Understand each other? It wasn't possible.

KING. I said, "In all save the honor of the realm." It was you who taught me that slogan, after all.

BECKET. I answered you, "In all save the honor of God." We were like two deaf men talking.

KING. How cold it was on that bare plain at La Ferté-Bernard, the last time we two met! It's funny, it's always been cold, in our story. Save at the beginning, when we were friends. We had a few fine summer evenings together, with the girls . . .

(*He says suddenly:*)

Did you love Gwendolen, Archbishop? Did you hate me, that night when I said, "I am the King," and took her from you? Perhaps that's what you never could forgive me for?

BECKET (*quietly*). I've forgotten.

KING. Yet we were like two brothers, weren't we—you and I? That night it was a childish prank—a lusty lad shouting "I am the King!" . . . I was so young . . . And every thought in my head came from you, you know that.

BECKET (*gently, as if to a little boy*). Pray, Henry, and don't talk so much.

KING (*irritably*). If you think I'm in the mood for praying at the moment . . .

(BECKET *quietly withdraws into the darkness and disappears during the* KING's *next speech.*)

I can see them through my fingers, spying on me from the aisles. Say what you like, they're an oafish lot, those Saxons of yours! To give oneself over naked to those ruffians! With my delicate skin . . . Even you'd be afraid. Besides, I'm ashamed. Ashamed of this whole masquerade. I need them though, that's the trouble. I have to rally them to my cause, against my son, who'll gobble up my kingdom if I let him. So I've come to make my peace with their Saint. You must admit it's funny. You've become a Saint and here am I, the King, desperately in need of that great amorphous mass which could do nothing, up till now, save lie inert beneath its own enormous weight, cowering under blows, and which is all-powerful now. What use are conquests, when you stop to think? They are England now, because of their vast numbers, and the rate at which they breed—like rabbits, to make good the massacres. But one must always pay the price—that's another thing you taught me, Thomas Becket, when you were still advising me . . . You taught me everything . . . (*Dreamily*) Ah, those were happy times . . . At the peep of dawn—well, our dawn that is, around noon, because we always went to bed very late—you'd come into my room, as I was emerging from the bathhouse, rested, smiling, debonair, as fresh as if we'd never spent the entire night drinking and whoring through the town.

(*He says a little sourly:*)

That's another thing you were better at than me . . .

(*The* PAGE *has come in. He wraps a white towel around the* KING *and proceeds to rub him down. Off stage is heard for the first time—we will hear it often—the gay, ironical Scottish marching song which* BECKET *is always whistling.*

The lighting changes. We are still in the empty cathedral. Then, a moment or so later, BECKET *will draw aside a curtain and reveal the* KING's *room. Their manner, his and the* KING's, *faraway at first, like a memory relived, will gradually become more real.*

THOMAS BECKET, *dressed as a nobleman, elegant, young, charming, in his short doublet and pointed, upturned shoes, comes in blithely and greets the* KING.)

BECKET. My respects, my Lord!

KING (*his face brightening*). Oh, Thomas . . . I thought you were still asleep.

BECKET. I've already been for a short gallop to Richmond and back, my Lord. There's a divine nip in the air.

KING (*his teeth chattering*). To think you actually like the cold! (*To the* PAGE) Rub harder, pig!

(*Smiling,* BECKET *pushes the* PAGE *aside and proceeds to rub the* KING *himself.*)

(*To the* PAGE) Throw a log on the fire and get out. Come back and dress me later.

BECKET. My prince, I shall dress you myself.

(*The* PAGE *goes.*)

KING. Nobody rubs me down the way you do. Thomas, what would I do without you? You're a nobleman, why do you play at being my valet? If I asked my barons to do this, they'd start a civil war!

BECKET (*smiling*). They'll come round to it in time, when Kings have learnt to play their role. I am your servant, my prince, that's all. Helping you to govern or helping you get warm again is part of the same thing to me. I like helping you.

KING (*with an affectionate little gesture*). My little Saxon! At the beginning, when I told them I was taking you into my service, do you know what they all said? They said you'd seize the chance to knife me in the back one day.

BECKET (*smiling as he dresses him*). Did you believe them, my prince?

KING. N . . . no. I was a bit scared at first. You know I scare easily . . . But you looked so well brought up, beside those brutes. However did you come to speak French without a trace of an English accent?

BECKET. My parents were able to keep their lands by agreeing to "collaborate," as they say, with the King your father. They sent me to France as a boy to acquire a good French accent.

KING. To France? Not to Normandy?

BECKET *(still smiling)*. That was their one patriotic conceit. They loathed the Norman accent.

KING *(distinctly)*. Only the accent?

BECKET *(lightly and inscrutably)*. My father was a very severe man. I would never have taken the liberty of questioning him on his personal convictions while he was alive. And his death shed no light on them, naturally. He managed, by collaborating, to amass a considerable fortune. As he was also a man of rigid principles, I imagine he contrived to do it in accordance with his conscience. That's a little piece of sleight of hand that men of principle are very skillful at in troubled times.

KING. And you?

BECKET *(feigning not to understand the question)*. I, my Lord?

KING *(putting a touch of contempt into his voice, for despite his admiration for* THOMAS *or perhaps because of it, he would like to score a point against him occasionally)*. The sleight of hand, were you adept at it too?

BECKET *(still smiling)*. Mine was a different problem. I was a frivolous man, you'll agree? In fact, it never came up at all. I adore hunting and only the Normans and their protégés had the right to hunt. I adore luxury and luxury was Norman. I adore life and the Saxons' only birthright was slaughter. I'll add that I adore honor.

KING *(with faint surprise)*. And was honor reconciled with collaboration too?

BECKET *(lightly)*. I had the right to draw my sword against the first Norman nobleman who tried to lay hands on my sister. I killed him in single combat. It's a detail, but it has its points.

KING *(a little slyly)*. You could always have slit his throat and fled into the forest, as so many did.

BECKET. That would have been uncomfortable, and not a lot of use. My sister would immediately have been raped by some other Norman baron, like all the Saxon girls. Today, she is respected. *(Lightly)* My Lord, did I tell you?—My new gold dishes have arrived from Florence. Will my Liege do me the honor of christening them with me at my house?

KING. Gold dishes! You lunatic!

BECKET. I'm setting a new fashion.

KING. I'm your King and I eat off silver!

BECKET. My prince, your expenses are heavy and I have only my pleasures to pay for. The trouble is I'm told they scratch easily. Still, we'll see. I received two forks as well—

KING. Forks?

BECKET. Yes. It's a new instrument, a devilish little thing to look at— and to use too. It's for pronging meat with and carrying it to your mouth. It saves you dirtying your fingers.

KING. But then you dirty the fork?

BECKET. Yes. But it's washable.

KING. So are your fingers. I don't see the point.

BECKET. It hasn't any, practically speaking. But it's refined, it's subtle. It's very un-Norman.

KING *(with sudden delight)*. You must order me a dozen! I want to see my great fat barons' faces, at the first court banquet, when I present them with that! We won't tell them what they're for. We'll have no end of fun with them.

BECKET *(laughing)*. A dozen! Easy now, my Lord! Forks are very expensive you know! My prince, it's time for the Privy Council.

KING *(laughing too)*. They won't make head nor tail of them! I bet you they'll think they're a new kind of dagger. We'll have a hilarious time!

(They go out, laughing, behind the curtain, which draws apart to reveal the same set, with the pillars. The Council Chamber. The COUNCILORS *stand waiting. The* KING *and* BECKET *come in, still laughing.)*

KING *(sitting in a chair)*. Gentlemen, the Council is open. I have summoned you here today to deal with this refusal of the clergy to pay the absentee tax. We really must come to an understanding about who rules this kingdom, the Church—

(The ARCHBISHOP *tries to speak.)*

just a moment, Archbishop!—or me! But before we quarrel, let us take the good news first. I have decided to revive the office of Chancellor of England, keeper of the Triple Lion Seal, and to entrust it to my loyal servant and subject Thomas Becket.

*(*BECKET *rises in surprise, the color draining from his face.)*

BECKET. My Lord . . . !

KING *(roguishly)*. What's the matter, Becket? Do you want to go and piss already? True, we both had gallons to drink last night!

(He looks at him with delight.)

Well, that's good! I've managed to surprise you for once, little Saxon.

BECKET *(dropping on one knee, says gravely)*. My Liege, this is a token of your confidence of which I fear I may not be worthy. I am very young, frivolous perhaps—

KING. I'm young too. And you know more than all of us put together.

(*To the others.*) He's read books, you know. It's amazing the amount
he knows. He'll checkmate the lot of you! Even the Archbishop! As
for his frivolity, don't let him fool you! He drinks strong wine, he likes
to enjoy himself, but he's a lad who thinks every minute of the time!
Sometimes it embarrasses me to feel him thinking away beside me. Get
up, Thomas. I never did anything without your advice anyway. No-
body knew it, now everybody will, that's all.
(*He bursts out laughing, pulls something out of his pocket and gives it to*
BECKET.)
There. That's the Seal. Don't lose it. Without the Seal, there's no more
England and we'll all have to go back to Normandy. Now, to work!
(*The* ARCHBISHOP *rises, all smiles, now the first shock is over.*)
ARCHBISHOP. May I crave permission to salute, with my Lord's approval, my young and learned archdeacon here? For I was the first—
I am weak enough to be proud of pointing it out—to notice him and
take him under my wing. The presence at this Council, with the pre-
ponderant title of Chancellor of England, of one of our brethren—
our spiritual son in a sense—is a guarantee for the Church of this
country, that a new era of agreement and mutual understanding is
dawning for us all and we must now, in a spirit of confident co-
operation—
KING (*interrupting*). Etc., etc. . . . Thank you, Archbishop! I knew
this nomination would please you. But don't rely too much on Becket
to play your game. He is my man.
(*He turns to* BECKET, *beaming.*)
Come to think of it, I'd forgotten you were a deacon, little Saxon.
BECKET (*smiling*). So had I, my prince.
KING. Tell me—I'm not talking about wenching, that's a venial sin—
but on the odd occasions when I've seen you fighting, it seems to me
you have a mighty powerful sword arm, for a priest! How do you reconcile that with the Church's commandment forbidding a priest to
shed blood?
BISHOP OF OXFORD (*prudently*). Our young friend is only a deacon, he
has not yet taken all his vows, my Lord. The Church in its wisdom
knows that youth must have its day and that—under the sacred pretext of war—a holy war, I mean, of course, young men are permitted
to—
KING (*interrupting*). All wars are holy wars, Bishop! I defy you to find
me a serious belligerent who doesn't have Heaven on his side, in theory. Let's get back to the point.
ARCHBISHOP. By all means, your Highness.
KING. Our customs demand that every landowner with sufficient acreage
to maintain one must send a man-at-arms to the quarterly review of

troops, fully armed and shield in hand, or pay a tax in silver. Where is my tax?

BISHOP OF OXFORD. *Distingo,* your Highness.

KING. Distinguish as much as you like. I've made up my mind. I want my money. My purse is open, just drop it in.

(*He sprawls back in his chair and picks his teeth. To* BECKET.)

Thomas, I don't know about you, but I'm starving. Have them bring us something to eat.

(BECKET *makes a sign to the* SENTRY *who goes out. A pause. The* ARCHBISHOP *rises.*)

ARCHBISHOP. A layman who shirks his duty to the State, which is to assist his Prince with arms, should pay the tax. Nobody will question that.

KING (*jovially*). Least of all the clergy!

ARCHBISHOP (*continuing*). A churchman's duty to the State is to assist his Prince in his prayers, and in his educational and charitable enterprises. He cannot therefore be liable to such a tax unless he neglects those duties.

BISHOP OF OXFORD. Have we refused to pray?

KING (*rising in fury*). Gentlemen! Do you seriously think that I am going to let myself be swindled out of more than two thirds of my revenues with arguments of that sort? In the days of the Conquest, when there was booty to be had, our Norman abbots tucked up their robes all right. And lustily too! Sword in fist, hams in the saddle, at cockcrow or earlier! "Let's go to it, Sire! Out with the Saxon scum! It's God's will! It's God's will!" You had to hold them back then! And on the odd occasions when you wanted a little Mass, they never had the time. They'd mislaid their vestments, the churches weren't equipped —any excuse to put it off, for fear they'd miss some of the pickings while their backs were turned!

ARCHBISHOP. Those heroic days are over. It is peacetime now.

KING. Then pay up! I won't budge from that.

(*Turning to* BECKET.)

Come on, Chancellor, say something! Has your new title caught your tongue?

BECKET. May I respectfully draw my Lord Archbishop's attention to one small point?

KING (*grunting*). Respectfully, but firmly. You're the Chancellor now.

BECKET (*calmly and casually*). England is a ship.

KING (*beaming*). Why, that's neat! We must use that, sometime.

BECKET. In the hazards of seafaring, the instinct of self-preservation has always told men that there must be one and only one master on board ship. Mutinous crews who drown their captain always end up, after a short interval of anarchy, by entrusting themselves body and soul to one of their number, who then proceeds to rule over them, more harshly sometimes than their drowned captain.

ARCHBISHOP. My Lord Chancellor—my young friend—there is in fact a saying—the captain is sole master after God.

(*He thunders suddenly, with a voice one did not suspect from that frail body:*)

After God!

(*He crosses himself. All the* BISHOPS *follow suit. The wind of excommunication shivers through the Council. The* KING, *awed, crosses himself too and mumbles, a little cravenly.*)

KING. Nobody's trying to question God's authority, Archbishop.

BECKET (*who alone has remained unperturbed*). God steers the ship by inspiring the captain's decisions. But I never heard tell that He gave His instructions directly to the helmsman.

(GILBERT FOLLIOT, *Bishop of London, rises. He is a thin-lipped, venomous man.*)

FOLLIOT. Our young Chancellor is only a deacon—but he is a member of the Church. The few years he has spent out in the tumult of the world cannot have made him forget so soon that it is through His Church Militant and more particularly through the intermediary of our Holy Father the Pope and his Bishops—his qualified representatives—that God dictates His decisions to men!

BECKET. There is a chaplain on board every ship, but he is not required to determine the size of the crew's rations, nor to take the vessel's bearings. My Reverend Lord the Bishop of London—who is the grandson of a sailor they tell me—cannot have forgotten that point either.

FOLLIOT (*yelping*). I will not allow personal insinuations to compromise the dignity of a debate of this importance! The integrity and honor of the Church of England are at stake!

KING (*cheerfully*). No big words, Bishop. You know as well as I do that all that's at stake is its money. I need money for my wars. Will the Church give me any, yes or no?

ARCHBISHOP (*cautiously*). The Church of England has always acknowledged that it was its duty to assist the King, to the best of its ability, in all his needs.

KING. There's a fine speech. But I don't like the past tense, Archbishop. There's something so nostalgic about it. I like the present. And the future. Are you going to pay up?

ARCHBISHOP. Your Highness, I am here to defend the privileges which your illustrious forefather William granted to the Church of England. Would you have the heart to tamper with your forefather's work?

KING. May he rest in peace. His work is inviolable. But where he is now he doesn't need money. I'm still on earth unfortunately, and I do.

FOLLIOT. Your Highness, this is a question of principle!

KING. I'm levying troops, Bishop! I have sent for 1,500 German foot soldiers, and three thousand Swiss infantry to help fight the King of
France. And nobody has ever paid the Swiss with principles.

BECKET *(rises suddenly and says incisively)*. I think, your Highness,
that it is pointless to pursue a discussion in which neither speaker is
listening to the other. The law and custom of the land give us the
means of coercion. We will use them.

FOLLIOT *(beside himself)*. Would you dare—you whom she raised from
the obscurity of your base origins—to plunge a dagger in the bosom of
your Mother Church?

BECKET. My Lord and King has given me his Seal with the Three Lions
to guard. My mother is England now.

FOLLIOT *(frothing, and slightly ridiculous)*. A deacon! A miserable
deacon nourished in our bosom! Traitor! Little viper! Libertine! Syco-
phant! Saxon!

KING. My Reverend friend, I suggest you respect my Chancellor, or else
I'll call my guards.

(He has raised his voice a little toward the end of this speech. The
GUARDS *come in.)*

(Surprised) Why, here they are! Oh, no, it's my snack. Excuse me,
gentlemen, but around noon I need something to peck at or I tend
to feel weak. And a King has no right to weaken, I needn't tell you that.
I'll have it in my chapel, then I can pray directly afterwards. Come and
sit with me, son.

(He goes out taking BECKET *with him. The three* PRELATES *have risen,*
deeply offended. They move away, murmuring to one another, with
sidelong glances in the direction in which the KING *went out.)*

FOLLIOT. We must appeal to Rome! We must take a firm line!

YORK. My Lord Archbishop, you are the Primate of England. Your
person is inviolate and your decisions on all matters affecting the
Church are law in this country. You have a weapon against such intransigence: excommunication.

BISHOP OF OXFORD. We must not use it save with a great deal of prudence, Reverend Bishop. The Church has always triumphed over the
centuries, but it has triumphed prudently. Let us bide our time. The
King's rages are terrible, but they don't last. They are fires of straw.

FOLLIOT. The little self-seeker he has at his elbow now will make it his
business to kindle them. And I think, like the Reverend Bishop, that
only the excommunication of that young libertine can reduce him to
impotence.

*(*BECKET *comes in.)*

BECKET. My Lords, the King has decided to adjourn his Privy Council. He thinks that a night of meditation will inspire your Lordships with a wise and equitable solution—which he authorizes you to come and submit to him tomorrow.

FOLLIOT (*with a bitter laugh*). You mean it's time for the hunt.

BECKET (*smiling*). Yes, my Lord Bishop, to be perfectly frank with you, it is. Believe me, I am personally most grieved at this difference of opinion and the brutal form it has taken. But I cannot go back on what I said as Chancellor of England. We are all bound, laymen as well as priests, by the same feudal oath we took to the King as our Lord and Sovereign; the oath to preserve his life, limbs, dignity and honor. None of you, I think, has forgotten the words of that oath?

ARCHBISHOP (*quietly*). We have not forgotten it, my son. No more than the other oath we took, before that—the oath to God. You are young, and still uncertain of yourself, perhaps. Yet you have, in those few words, taken a resolution the meaning of which has not escaped me. Will you allow an old man, who is very close to death, and who, in this rather sordid argument, was defending more perhaps than you suspect—to hope, as a father, that you will never know the bitterness of realizing, one day, that you made a mistake.

(*He holds out his ring and* BECKET *kisses it.*)

I give you my blessing, my son.

(BECKET *has knelt. Now he rises and says lightly:*)

BECKET. An unworthy son, Father, alas. But when is one worthy? And worthy of what?

(*He pirouettes and goes out, insolent and graceful as a young boy.*)

FOLLIOT (*violently*). Such insults to your Grace cannot be tolerated! This young rake's impudence must be crushed!

ARCHBISHOP (*thoughtfully*). He was with me for a long time. His is a strange, elusive nature. Don't imagine he is the ordinary libertine that outward appearances would suggest. I've had plenty of opportunity to observe him, in the bustle of pleasure and daily living. He is as it were detached. As if seeking his real self.

FOLLIOT. Break him, my Lord, before he finds it! Or the clergy of this country will pay dearly.

ARCHBISHOP. We must be very circumspect. It is our task to see into the hearts of men. And I am not sure that this one will always be our enemy.

(*The* ARCHBISHOP *and the three* BISHOPS *go out. The* KING *is heard calling off stage.*)

KING. Well, son, have they gone? Are you coming hunting?

(*Trees come down from the flies. The black velvet curtain at the back opens on a clear sky, transforming the pillars into leafless trees of a for-*

est in winter. Bugles. The lights have gone down. When they go up again, the KING *and* BECKET *are on horseback, each with a hawk on his gauntleted wrist. Torrential rain is heard.*)

KING. Here comes the deluge. (*Unexpectedly*) Do you like hunting this way, with hawks?

BECKET. I don't much care to delegate my errands. I prefer to feel a wild boar on the end of my spear. When he turns and charges there's a moment of delicious personal contact when one feels, at last, responsible for oneself.

KING. It's odd, this craving for danger. Why are you all so hell-bent on risking your necks for the most futile reasons?

BECKET. One has to gamble with one's life to feel alive.

KING. Or dead! You make me laugh.

(*To his hawk:*)

Quiet, my pretty, quiet! We'll take your hood off in a minute. You couldn't give much of a performance under all these trees. I'll tell you one creature that loves hawking anyway, and that's a hawk! It seems to me we've rubbed our backsides sore with three hours' riding, just to give them this royal pleasure.

BECKET (*smiling*). My Lord, these are Norman hawks. They belong to the master race. They have a right to it.

KING (*suddenly, as he reins his horse*). Do you love me, Becket?

BECKET. I am your servant, my prince.

KING. Did you love me when I made you Chancellor? I wonder sometimes if you're capable of love. Do you love Gwendolen?

BECKET. She is my mistress, my prince.

KING. Why do you put labels onto everything to justify your feelings?

BECKET. Because, without labels, the world would have no shape, my prince.

KING. Is it so important for the world to have a shape?

BECKET. It's essential, my prince, otherwise we can't know what we're doing.

(*Bugles in the distance.*)

The rain is getting heavier, my Lord! Come, let us shelter in that hut over there.

(*He gallops off. After a second of confused indecision, the* KING *gallops after him, holding his hawk high and shouting:*)

KING. Becket! You didn't answer my question!

(*He disappears into the forest. Bugles again. The four* BARONS *cross the stage, galloping after them, and vanish into the forest. Thunder. Lightning. A hut has appeared to one side of the stage.* BECKET *is heard shouting:*)

BECKET. Hey there! You! Fellow! Can we put the horses under cover in

your barn? Do you know how to rub down a horse? And have a look
at the right forefoot of messire's horse. I think the shoe is loose. We'll
sit out the storm under your roof.

(*After a second, the* KING *enters the hut, followed by a hairy* SAXON *who,
cap in hand, bows repeatedly, in terrified silence.*)

KING   (*shaking himself*) . What a soaking! I'll catch my death!

(*He sneezes.*)

All this just to keep the hawks amused!

(*Shouting at the* MAN:)

What are you waiting for? Light a fire, dog! It's freezing cold in this
shack.

(*The* MAN, *terror-stricken, does not move. The* KING *sneezes again. To*
BECKET:)

What is he waiting for?

BECKET.   Wood is scarce, my Lord. I don't suppose he has any left.

KING.   What—in the middle of the forest?

BECKET.   They are entitled to two measures of dead wood. One branch
more and they're hanged.

KING.   (*astounded*) . Really? And yet people are always complaining
about the amount of dead wood in the forests. Still, that's a problem
for my intendants, not me.

(*Shouting at the* MAN:)

Run and pick up all the wood you can carry and build us a roaring
fire! We won't hang you this time, dog! (*The* PEASANT, *terrified, dares
not obey.* BECKET *says gently:*)

BECKET.   Go, my son. Your King commands it. You've the right.

(*The* MAN *goes out, trembling, bowing to the ground, repeatedly.*)

KING.   Why do you call that old man your son?

BECKET.   Why not? You call him dog, my prince.

KING.   It's a manner of speaking. Saxons are always called "dog." I can't
think why, really. One could just as well have called them "Saxon"!
But that smelly old ragbag your son!

(*Sniffing.*)

What on earth can they eat to make the place stink so—dung?

BECKET.   Turnips.

KING.   Turnips—what are they?

BECKET.   Roots.

KING   (*amused*) . Do they eat roots?

BECKET.   Those who live in the forests can't grow anything else.

KING.   Why don't they move out into the open country then?

BECKET.   They would be hanged if they left their area.

KING.   Oh, I see. Mark you, that must make life a lot simpler, if you
know you'll be hanged at the least show of initiative. You must ask

yourself far fewer questions. They don't know their luck! But you still
haven't told me why you called the fellow your son?

BECKET (*lightly*). My prince, he is so poor and bereft and I am so
strong beside him, that he really is my son.

KING. We'd go a long way with that theory!

BECKET. Besides, my prince, you're appreciably younger than I am and
you call me "son" sometimes.

KING. That's got nothing to do with it. It's because I love you.

BECKET. You are our King. We are all your sons and in your hands.

KING. What, Saxons too?

BECKET (*lightly, as he strips off his gloves*). England will be fully built,
my prince, on the day the Saxons are your sons as well.

KING. You are a bore today! I get the feeling that I'm listening to the
Archbishop. And I'm dying of thirst. Hunt around and see if you can't
find us something to drink. Go on, it's your son's house!

(BECKET *starts looking, and leaves the room after a while. The* KING *looks
around too, examining the hut with curiosity, touching things with
grimaces of distaste. Suddenly he notices a kind of trap door at the foot
of a wall. He opens it, thrusts his hand in and pulls out a terrified* GIRL.
He shouts:)

Hey, Thomas! Thomas!

(BECKET *comes in.*)

BECKET. Have you found something to drink, Lord?

KING (*holding the* GIRL *at arm's length*). No. Something to eat. What
do you say to that, if it's cleaned up a bit?

BECKET (*coldly*). She's pretty.

KING. She stinks a bit, but we could wash her. Look, did you ever see
anything so tiny? How old would you say it was—fifteen, sixteen?

BECKET (*quietly*). It can talk, my Lord.

(*Gently, to the* GIRL:)

How old are you?

(*The* GIRL *looks at them in terror and says nothing.*)

KING. You see? Of course it can't talk!

(*The* MAN *has come back with the wood and stops in the doorway,
terrified.*)

How old is your daughter, dog?

(*The* MAN *trembles like a cornered animal and says nothing.*)

He's dumb as well, that son of yours. How did you get him—with a
deaf girl? It's funny the amount of dumb people I meet the second I
set foot out of my palace. I rule over a kingdom of the dumb. Can you
tell me why?

BECKET. They're afraid, my prince.

KING. I know that. And a good thing too. The populace must live in fear, it's essential. The moment they stop being afraid they have only one thought in mind—to frighten other people instead. And they adore doing that! Just as much as we do! Give them a chance to do it and they catch up fast, those sons of yours! Did you never see a peasants' revolt? I did once, in my father's reign, when I was a child. It's not a pretty sight.

(*He looks at the* MAN, *exasperated.*)

Look at it, will you? It's tongue-tied, it's obtuse, it stinks and the country is crawling with them!

(*He seizes the* GIRL *who was trying to run away.*)

Stay here, you!

(*To* BECKET:)

I ask you, what use is it?

BECKET (*smiling*). It scratches the soil, it makes bread.

KING. Pooh, the English eat so little of it . . . At the French Court, yes, I daresay—they fairly stuff it down! But here!

BECKET (*smiling*). The troops have to be fed. For a King without troops . . .

KING (*struck by this*). True enough! Yes, that makes sense. There must be some sort of reason in all these absurdities. Well well, you little Saxon philosopher, you! I don't know how you do it, but you'll turn me into an intelligent man yet! The odd thing is, it's so ugly and yet it makes such pretty daughters. How do you explain that, you who can explain it all?

BECKET. At twenty, before he lost his teeth and took on that indeterminate age the common people have, that man may have been handsome. He may have had one night of love, one minute when he too was a King, and shed his fear. Afterwards, his pauper's life went on, eternally the same. And he and his wife no doubt forgot it all. But the seed was sown.

KING (*dreamily*). You have such a way of telling things . . .

(*He looks at the* GIRL.)

Do you think she'll grow ugly too?

BECKET. For sure.

KING. If we made her a whore and kept her at the palace, would she stay pretty?

BECKET. Perhaps.

KING. Then we'd be doing her a service, don't you think?

BECKET (*coldly*). No doubt.

(*The* MAN *stiffens.* THE GIRL *cowers, in terror. The* BROTHER *comes in, somber-faced, silent, threatening.*)

KING. Would you believe it? They understand every word, you know! Who's that one there?

BECKET (*taking in the situation at a glance*). The brother.

KING. How do you know?

BECKET. Instinct, my Lord.

(*His hand moves to his dagger.*)

KING (*bawling suddenly*). Why are they staring at me like that? I've had enough of this! I told you to get something to drink, dog!

(*Terrified, the* MAN *scuttles off.*)

BECKET. Their water will be brackish. I have a gourd of juniper juice in my saddlebag. (*To the* BROTHER) Come and give me a hand you! My horse is restive.

(*He seizes the* BOY *roughly by the arm and hustles him out into the forest, carelessly whistling his little marching song. Then, all of a sudden, he hurls himself onto him. A short silent struggle.* BECKET *gets the* BOY's *knife away; he escapes into the forest.* BECKET *watches him go for a second, holding his wounded hand. Then he walks around the back of the hut. The* KING *has settled himself on a bench, with his feet up on another, whistling to himself. He lifts the* GIRL's *skirts with his cane and examines her at leisure.*)

KING (*in a murmur*). All my sons! . . .

(*He shakes himself.*)

That Becket! He wears me out. He keeps making me think! I'm sure it's bad for the health.

(*He gets up,* BECKET *comes in followed by the* MAN.)

What about that water? How much longer do I have to wait?

BECKET. Here it is, my Lord. But it's muddy. Have some of this juniper juice instead.

KING. Drink with me.

(*He notices* BECKET's *hand, wrapped in a blood-stained cloth.*)

What's the matter? You're wounded!

BECKET (*hiding his hand*). No doubt about it, that horse of mine is a nervous brute. He can't bear his saddle touched. He bit me.

KING (*with a hearty, delighted laugh*). That's funny! Oh, that's very funny! Milord is the best rider in the Kingdom! Milord can never find a stallion with enough spirit for him! Milord makes us all look silly at the jousts, with his fancy horsemanship, and when he goes to open his saddlebags he gets himself bitten! Like a page!

(*He is almost savagely gleeful. Then suddenly, his gaze softens.*)

You're white as a sheet, little Saxon . . . Why do I love you? . . . It's funny, I don't like to think of you in pain. Show me that hand. A horse bite can turn nasty. I'll put some of that juniper gin on it.

BECKET (*snatching his hand away*). I already have, my Lord, it's nothing.

KING. Then why do you look so pale? Show me your hand.

BECKET (*with sudden coldness*). It's an ugly wound and you know you hate the sight of blood.

KING   (*steps back a little, then exclaims with delight*) . All this just to
fetch me a drink! Wounded in the service of the King! We'll tell the
others you defended me against a wild boar and I'll present you with a
handsome gift this evening. What would you like?

BECKET   (*softly*) . This girl.

(*He adds after a pause:*)

I fancy her.

(*A pause.*)

KING   (*his face clouding over*) . That's tiresome of you. I fancy her too.
And where that's concerned, friendship goes by the board.

(*A pause. His face takes on a cunning look.*)

All right, then. But favor for favor. You won't forget, will you?

BECKET.   No, my prince.

KING.   Favor for favor; do you give me your word as a gentleman?

BECKET.   Yes, my prince.

KING   (*draining his glass, suddenly cheerful*) . Done! She's yours. Do
we take her with us or shall we have her sent?

BECKET.   I'll send two soldiers to fetch her. Listen. The others have
caught up.

(*A troop of men-at-arms have come riding up behind the shack during the
end of the scene.*)

KING   (*to the* MAN) . Wash your daughter, dog, and kill her fleas. She's
going to the palace. For Milord here, who's a Saxon too. You're pleased
about that, I hope?

(*To* BECKET *as he goes:*)

Give him a gold piece. I'm feeling generous this morning.

(*He goes out. The* MAN *looks at* BECKET *in terror.*)

BECKET.   No one will come and take your daughter away. Keep her
better hidden in future. And tell your son to join the others, in the
forest, he'll be safer there, now. I think one of the soldiers saw us.
Here!

(*He throws him a purse and goes out. When he has gone, the* MAN
snatches up the purse, then spits venomously, his face twisted with hate.)

MAN.   God rot your guts! Pig!

GIRL   (*unexpectedly*) . He was handsome, that one. It is true he's taking
me to the palace?

MAN.   You whore! You Norman's trollop!

(*He hurls himself onto her and beats her savagely. The* KING, BECKET *and
the* BARONS *have galloped off, amid the sound of bugles. The hut and the
forest backcloth disappear. We are in* BECKET'S *palace.*

FOOTMEN *push on a kind of low bed-couch, with cushions and some stools.
Upstage, between two pillars, a curtain behind which can be seen the
shadows of banqueting* GUESTS. *Singing and roars of laughter. Downstage,
curled up on the bed,* GWENDOLEN *is playing a string instrument. The*

curtain is drawn aside. BECKET *appears. He goes to* GWENDOLEN *while the banqueting and the laughter, punctuated by hoarse incoherent snatches of song, go on upstage.* GWENDOLEN *stops playing.*)

GWENDOLEN. Are they still eating?

BECKET. Yes. They have an unimaginable capacity for absorbing food.

GWENDOLEN *(softly, beginning to play again)*. How can my Lord spend his days and a large part of his nights with such creatures?

BECKET *(crouching at her feet and caressing her)*. If he spent his time with learned clerics debating the sex of angels, your Lord would be even more bored, my kitten. They are as far from the true knowledge of things as mindless brutes.

GWENDOLEN *(gently, as she plays)*. I don't always understand everything my Lord condescends to say to me . . . What I do know is that it is always very late when he comes to see me.

BECKET *(caressing her)*. The only thing I love is coming to you. Beauty is one of the few things which don't shake one's faith in God.

GWENDOLEN. I am my Lord's war captive and I belong to him body and soul. God has willed it so, since He gave the Normans victory over my people. If the Welsh had won the war I would have married a man of my own race, at my father's castle. God did not will it so.

BECKET *(quietly)*. That belief will do as well as any, my kitten. But, as I belong to a conquered race myself, I have a feeling that God's system is a little muddled. Go on playing.

(GWENDOLEN *starts to play again. Then she says suddenly:*)

GWENDOLEN. I'm lying. You are my Lord, God or no God. And if the Welsh had been victorious, you could just as easily have stolen me from my father's castle. I should have come with you.

(She says this gravely. BECKET *rises abruptly and moves away. She looks up at him with anguished eyes and stops playing.*)

Did I say something wrong? What is the matter with my Lord?

BECKET. Nothing. I don't like being loved. I told you that.

(The curtain opens. The KING *appears.*)

KING *(a little drunk)*. Well, son, have you deserted us? It worked! I told you! They've tumbled to it! They're fighting with your forks! They've at last discovered that they're for poking one another's eyes out. They think it's a most ingenious little invention. You'd better go in, son, they'll break them in a minute.

(BECKET *goes behind the curtain to quieten his* GUESTS. *He can be heard shouting:*)

Gentlemen, gentlemen! No, no, they aren't little daggers. No, truly— they're for pronging meat . . . Look, let me show you again.

(Huge roars of laughter behind the curtain. The KING *has moved over to* GWENDOLEN. *He stares at her.*)

KING.   Was that you playing, while we were at table?

GWENDOLEN   *(with a deep curtsy)* . Yes, my Lord.

KING.   You have every kind of accomplishment, haven't you? Get up. *(He lifts her to her feet, caressing her as he does so. She moves away, ill at ease. He says with a wicked smile:)*

KING.   Have I frightened you, my heart? We'll soon put that right.

(He pulls the curtain aside.)

Hey there, Becket! That's enough horseplay, my fat lads! Come and hear a little music. When the belly's full, it's good to elevate the mind a bit.

(To GWENDOLEN:*)*

Play!

(The four BARONS, *bloated with food and drink, come in with* BECKET. GWENDOLEN *has taken up her instrument again. The* KING *sprawls on the bed, behind her. The* BARONS, *with much sighing and puffing, unclasp their belts and sit down on stools, where they soon fall into a stupor.* BECKET *remains standing.)*

Tell her to sing us something sad. I like sad music after dinner, it helps the digestion.

(He hiccups.)

You always feed us far too well, Thomas. Where did you steal that cook of yours?

BECKET.   I bought him, Sire. He's a Frenchman.

KING.   Really? Aren't you afraid he might poison you? Tell me, how much does one pay for a French cook?

BECKET.   A good one, like him, costs almost as much as a horse, my Lord.

KING   *(genuinely outraged)* . It's outrageous! What is the country coming to! No man is worth a horse! If I said "favor for favor"— remember?—and I asked you to give him to me, would you?

BECKET.   Of course, my Lord.

KING   *(with a smile, gently caressing* GWENDOLEN*)* . Well, I won't. I don't want to eat too well every day; it lowers a man's morale. Sadder, sadder, my little doe.

(He belches.)

Oh, that venison! Get her to sing that lament they composed for your mother, Becket. It's my favorite song.

BECKET.   I don't like anyone to sing that lament, my Lord.

KING.   Why not? Are you ashamed of being a Saracen girl's son? That's half your charm, you fool! There must be some reason why you're more civilized than all the rest of us put together! I adore that song.

*(GWENDOLEN *looks uncertainly at* BECKET. *There is a pause. Then the* KING *says coldly:)*

That's an order, little Saxon.

BECKET   (*inscrutably, to* GWENDOLEN). Sing.
(*She strikes a few opening chords, while the* KING *makes himself comfortable beside her, belching contentedly. She begins:*)
GWENDOLEN   (*singing*).

> Handsome Sir Gilbert
> Went to the war
> One fine morning in May
> To deliver the heart
> Of Lord Jesus our Savior,
> From the hands of the Saracens.
> Woe! Woe! Heavy is my heart
> At being without love!
> Woe! Woe! Heavy is my heart
> All the livelong day!

KING   (*singing*).

> All the livelong day! Go on!

GWENDOLEN.   As the battle raged
> He swung his mighty sword
> And many a Moor fell dead
> But his trusty charger
> Stumbled in the fray
> And Sir Gilbert fell.
> Woe! Woe! Heavy is my heart!
> At being without love!
> Woe! Woe! Heavy is my heart
> All the livelong day.
>
> Wounded in the head
> Away Gilbert was led
> To the Algiers market
> Chained hand and foot
> And sold there as a slave.

KING   (*singing, out of tune*).

> All the livelong day!

GWENDOLEN.   A Saracen's daughter
> Lovely as the night
> Lost her heart to him
> Swore to love him always
> Vowed to be his wife.

Woe! Woe! Heavy is my heart
At being without love!
Woe! Woe! Heavy is my heart
All the livelong day—

KING   (*interrupting*). It brings tears to my eyes, you know, that story. I
look a brute but I'm soft as swansdown really. One can't change one's
nature. I can't imagine why you don't like people to sing that song. It's
wonderful to be a love child. When I look at my august parents' faces,
I shudder to think what must have gone on. It's marvelous to think of
your mother helping your father to escape and then coming to join
him in London with you inside her. Sing us the end, girl. I adore the
end.

GWENDOLEN   (*softly*).
Then he asked the holy Father
For a priest to baptize her
And he took her as his wife
To cherish with his life
Giving her his soul
To love and keep alway.

Gay! Gay! Easy is my heart
At being full of love
Gay! Gay! Easy is my heart
To be loved alway.

KING   (*dreamily*). Did he really love her all his life? Isn't it altered a
bit in the song?

BECKET.   No, my prince.

KING   (*getting up, quite saddened*). Funny, it's the happy ending that
makes me feel sad . . . Tell me, do you believe in love, Thomas?

BECKET   (*coldly*). For my father's love for my mother, Sire, yes.

(*The* KING *has moved over to the* BARONS *who are now snoring on their
stools. He gives them a kick as he passes.*)

KING.   They've fallen asleep, the hogs. That's their way of showing their
finer feelings. You know, my little Saxon, sometimes I have the impression that you and I are the only sensitive men in England. We
eat with forks and we have infinitely distinguished sentiments, you
and I. You've made a different man of me, in a way . . . What you
ought to find me now, if you loved me, is a girl to give me a little
polish. I've had enough of whores.

(*He has come back to* GWENDOLEN. *He caresses her a little and then says
suddenly:*)

Favor for favor—do you remember?

(*A pause.*)

BECKET (*pale*). I am your servant, my prince, and all I have is yours. But you were also gracious enough to say I was your friend.

KING. That's what I mean! As one friend to another it's the thing to do!

(*A short pause. He smiles maliciously, and goes on caressing* GWENDOLEN *who cowers, terrified.*)

You care about her then? Can you care for something? Go on, tell me, tell me if you care about her?

(BECKET *says nothing. The* KING *smiles.*)

You can't tell a lie. I know you. Not because you're afraid of lies— I think you must be the only man I know who isn't afraid of anything —not even Heaven—but because it's distasteful to you. You consider it inelegant. What looks like morality in you is nothing more than esthetics. Is that true or isn't it?

BECKET (*meeting his eyes, says softly*). It's true, my Lord.

KING. I'm not cheating if I ask for her, am I? I said "favor for favor" and I asked you for your word of honor.

BECKET (*icily*). And I gave it to you.

(*A pause. They stand quite still. The* KING *looks at* BECKET *with a wicked smile.* BECKET *does not look at him. Then the* KING *moves briskly away.*)

KING. Right. I'm off to bed. I feel like an early night tonight. Delightful evening, Becket. You're the only man in England who knows how to give your friends a royal welcome.

(*He kicks the slumbering* BARONS.)

Call my guards and help me wake these porkers.

(*The* BARONS *wake with sighs and belches as the* KING *pushes them about, shouting:*)

Come on, Barons, home! I know you're connoisseurs of good music, but we can't listen to music all night long. Happy evenings end in bed, eh Becket?

BECKET (*stiffly*). May I ask your Highness for a brief moment's grace?

KING. Granted! Granted! I'm not a savage. I'll wait for you both in my litter. You can say good night to me downstairs.

(*He goes out, followed by the* BARONS. BECKET *stands motionless for a while under* GWENDOLEN's *steady gaze. Then he says quietly:*)

BECKET. You will have to go with him, Gwendolen.

GWENDOLEN (*composedly*). Did my Lord promise me to him?

BECKET. I gave him my word as a gentleman that I would give him anything he asked for. I never thought it would be you.

GWENDOLEN. If he sends me away tomorrow, will my Lord take me back?

BECKET. No.

GWENDOLEN.   Shall I tell the girls to put my dresses in the coffer?

BECKET.   He'll send over for it tomorrow. Go down. One doesn't keep
the King waiting. Tell him I wish him a respectful good night.

GWENDOLEN   (*laying her viol on the bed*). I shall leave my Lord my
viol. He can almost play it now.

(*She asks, quite naturally:*)

My Lord cares for nothing, in the whole world, does he?

BECKET.   No.

GWENDOLEN   (*moves to him and says gently*). You belong to a conquered
race too. But through tasting too much of the honey of life, you've
forgotten that even those who have been robbed of everything have
one thing left to call their own.

BECKET   (*inscrutably*). Yes, I daresay I had forgotten. There is a gap
in me where honor ought to be. Go now.

(GWENDOLEN *goes out.* BECKET *stands quite still. Then he goes to the bed,
picks up the viol, looks at it, then throws it abruptly away. He pulls off
the fur coverlet and starts to unbutton his doublet. A* GUARD *comes in,
dragging the Saxon* GIRL *from the forest, whom he throws down in the
middle of the room. The* KING *appears.*)

KING   (*hilariously*). Thomas, my son! You'd forgotten her! You see how
careless you are! Luckily I think of everything. It seems they had to
bully the father and the brother a tiny bit to get her, but anyway,
here she is. You see?—I really am a friend to you, and you're wrong
not to love me. You told me you fancied her. I hadn't forgotten that,
you see. Sleep well, son!

(*He goes out, followed by the* GUARD. *The* GIRL, *still dazed, looks at* BECKET
*who has not moved. She recognizes him, gets to her feet and smiles at
him. A long pause, then she asks with a kind of sly coquetry:*)

GIRL.   Shall I undress, my Lord?

BECKET   (*who has not moved*). Of course.

(*The* GIRL *starts to undress.* BECKET *looks at her coldly, absent-mindedly
whistling a few bars of his little march. Suddenly he stops, goes to the*
GIRL, *who stands there dazed and half naked, and seizes her by the
shoulders.*)

I hope you're full of noble feelings and that all this strikes you as
pretty shabby?

(*A* SERVANT *runs in wildly and halts in the doorway speechless. Before he
can speak, the* KING *comes stumbling in.*)

KING   (*soberly*). I had no pleasure with her, Thomas. She let me lay
her down in the litter, limp as a corpse, and then suddenly she pulled
out a little knife from somewhere. There was blood everywhere . . .
I feel quite sick.

(BECKET *has let go of the* GIRL. *The* KING *adds, haggard:*)
  She could easily have killed me instead!
(*A pause. He says abruptly:*)
  Send that girl away. I'm sleeping in your room tonight. I'm frightened.
(BECKET *motions to the* SERVANT, *who takes away the half-naked* GIRL. *The* KING *has thrown himself, fully dressed, onto the bed with an animal-like sigh.*)
  Take half the bed.
BECKET.   I'll sleep on the floor, my prince.
KING.   No. Lie down beside me. I don't want to be alone tonight.
(*He looks at him and murmurs:*)
  You loathe me, I shan't even be able to trust you now . . .
BECKET.   You gave me your Seal to keep, my prince. And the Three Lions
  of England which are engraved on it keep watch over me too.
(*He snuffs out the candles, all save one. It is almost dark.*)
KING   (*his voice already thick with sleep*). I shall never know what
  you're thinking . . .
(BECKET *has thrown a fur coverlet over the* KING. *He lies down beside him and says quietly:*)
BECKET.   It will be dawn soon, my prince. You must sleep. Tomorrow
  we are crossing to the Continent. In a week we will face the King of
  France's army and there will be simple answers to everything at last.
(*He has lain down beside the* KING. *A pause, during which the* KING's
snoring gradually increases. Suddenly, the KING *moans and tosses in his sleep.*)
KING   (*crying out*). They're after me! They're after me! They're armed
  to the teeth! Stop them! Stop them!
(BECKET *sits up on one elbow. He touches the* KING, *who wakes up with a great animal cry.*)
BECKET.   My prince . . . my prince . . . sleep in peace. I'm here.
KING.   Oh . . . Thomas, it's you . . . They were after me.
(*He turns over and goes back to sleep with a sigh. Gradually he begins to snore again, softly.* BECKET *is still on one elbow. Almost tenderly, he draws the coverlet over the* KING.)
BECKET.   My prince . . . If you were my true prince, if you were one of
  my race, how simple everything would be. How tenderly I would love
  you, my prince, in an ordered world. Each of us bound in fealty to the
  other, head, heart and limbs, with no further questions to ask of oneself, ever.
(*A pause. The* KING's *snores grow louder.* BECKET *sighs and says with a little smile:*)
  But I cheated my way, a twofold bastard, into the ranks, and found a

place among the conquerors. You can sleep peacefully though, my
prince. So long as Becket is obliged to improvise his honor, he will
serve you. And if one day, he meets it face to face . . .
(*A short pause.*)
But where is Becket's honor?
(*He lies down with a sigh, beside the* KING. *The* KING's *snores grow louder
still. The candle sputters. The lights grow even dimmer . . .*)

ACT TWO

*The curtain rises on the same set of arching pillars, which now repre-
sents a forest in France. The King's tent, not yet open for the day, is set
up among the trees. A Sentry stands some way off.*

*It is dawn. Crouched around a campfire, the four Barons are having
their morning meal, in silence. After a while, one of them says:*

1ST BARON.   This Becket then, who is he?
(*A pause. All four are fairly slow in their reactions.*)
2ND BARON   (*surprised at the question*).   The Chancellor of England.
1ST BARON.   I know that! But who is he, exactly?
2ND BARON.   The Chancellor of England, I tell you! The Chancellor of
England is the Chancellor of England! I don't see what else there is to
inquire into on that score.
1ST BARON.   You don't understand. Look, supposing the Chancellor of
England were some other man. Me, for instance . . .
2ND BARON.   That's plain idiotic.
1ST BARON.   I said supposing. Now, I would be Chancellor of England
but I wouldn't be the same Chancellor of England as Becket is. You
can follow that, can you?
2ND BARON   (*guardedly*). Yes . . .
1ST BARON.   So, I *can* ask myself the question.
2ND BARON.   What question?
1ST BARON.   Who is this man Becket?
2ND BARON.   What do you mean, who is this man Becket? He's the
Chancellor of England.
1ST BARON.   Yes. But what I'm asking myself is who is he, as a man?
2ND BARON   (*looks at him and says sorrowfully*).   Have you got a pain?
1ST BARON.   No, why?
2ND BARON.   A Baron who asks himself questions is a sick Baron. Your
sword—what's that?
1ST BARON.   My sword?
2ND BARON.   Yes.

1ST BARON (*putting his hand to the hilt*). It's my sword! And anyone who thinks different—

2ND BARON. Right. Answered like a nobleman. We peers aren't here to ask questions. We're here to give answers.

1ST BARON. Right then. Answer me.

2ND BARON. Not to questions! To orders. You aren't asked to think in the army. When you're face to face with a French man-at-arms, do you ask yourself questions?

1ST BARON. No.

2ND BARON. Does he?

1ST BARON. No.

2ND BARON. Does he?

1ST BARON. No.

2ND BARON. You just fall to and fight. If you started asking each other questions like a pair of women, you might as well bring chairs onto the battlefield. If there are any questions to be asked you can be sure they've been asked already, higher up, by cleverer heads than yours.

1ST BARON (*vexed*). I meant I didn't like him, that's all.

2ND BARON. Why couldn't you say so then? That we'd have understood. You're entitled not to like him. I don't like him either, come to that. To begin with, he's a Saxon.

1ST BARON. To begin with!

3RD BARON. One thing you can't say though. You can't say he isn't a fighter. Yesterday when the King was in the thick of it, after his squire was killed, he cut his way right through the French, and he seized the King's banner and drew the enemy off and onto himself.

1ST BARON. All right! He's a good fighter!

3RD BARON (*to* 2ND BARON). Isn't he a good fighter?

2ND BARON (*stubbornly*). Yes. But he's a Saxon.

1ST BARON (*to the* 4TH BARON, *who has so far said nothing*). How about you, Regnault? What do you think of him?

4TH BARON (*placidly, swallowing his mouthful of food*). I'm waiting.

1ST BARON. Waiting for what?

4TH BARON. Till he shows himself. Some sorts of game are like that: you follow them all day through the forest, by sounds, or tracks, or smell. But it wouldn't do any good to charge ahead with drawn lance; you'd just spoil everything because you don't know for sure what sort of animal it is you're dealing with. You have to wait.

1ST BARON. What for?

4TH BARON. For whatever beast it is to show itself. And if you're patient it always does in the end. Animals know more than men do, nearly always, but a man has something in him that an animal hasn't got: he knows how to wait. With this man Becket—I'll wait.

1ST BARON.   For what?

4TH BARON.   For him to show himself. For him to break cover.

(*He goes on eating*)

   The day he does, we'll know who he is.

(BECKET's *little whistled march is heard off stage.* BECKET *comes in, armed.*)

BECKET.   Good morning to you, Gentlemen.

(*The four* BARONS *rise politely, and salute.*)

   Is the King still asleep?

1ST BARON   (*stiffly*). He hasn't called yet.

BECKET.   Has the camp marshal presented his list of losses?

1ST BARON.   No.

BECKET.   Why not?

2ND BARON   (*surlily*). He was part of the losses.

BECKET.   Oh?

1ST BARON.   I was nearby when it happened. A lance knocked him off his horse. Once on the ground, the foot soldiers dealt with him.

BECKET.   Poor Beaumont. He was so proud of his new armor.

2ND BARON.   There must have been a chink in it then. They bled him white. On the ground. French swine!

BECKET   (*with a slight shrug*). That's war.

1ST BARON.   War is a sport like any other. There are rules. In the old days, they took you for ransom. A Knight for a Knight. That was proper fighting!

BECKET   (*smiling*). Since one has taken to sending the foot soldiery against the horses with no personal protection save a cutlass, they're a little inclined to seek out the chink in the armor of any Knight unwise enough to fall off his horse. It's repulsive, but I can understand them.

1ST BARON.   If we start understanding the common soldiery war will be butchery plain and simple.

BECKET.   The world is certainly tending towards butchery, Baron. The lesson of this battle, which has cost us far too much, is that we will have to form platoons of cutthroats too, that's all.

1ST BARON.   And a soldier's honor, my Lord Chancellor, what of that?

BECKET   (*dryly*). A soldier's honor, Baron, is to win victories. Let us not be hypocritical. The Norman nobility lost no time in teaching those they conquered that little point. I'll wake the King. Our entry into the city is timed for eight o'clock and the *Te Deum* in the cathedral for a quarter past nine. It would be bad policy to keep the French Bishop waiting. We want these people to collaborate with a good grace.

1ST BARON   (*grunting*). In my day, we slaughtered the lot and marched in afterwards.

BECKET.   Yes, into a dead city! I want to give the King living cities to increase his wealth. From eight o'clock this morning, I am the French people's dearest friend.

1ST BARON.   What about England's honor, then?

BECKET *(quietly)*. England's honor, Baron, in the final reckoning, has always been to succeed.

(He goes into the KING's *tent smiling. The four* BARONS *look at each other, hostile.)*

1ST BARON *(muttering.)* What a mentality!

4TH BARON *(sententiously)*. We must wait for him. One day, he'll break cover.

(The four BARONS *move away.* BECKET *lifts the tent flap and hooks it back. The* KING *is revealed, in bed with a* GIRL.)

KING *(yawning)*. Good morning, son. Did you sleep well?

BECKET.   A little memento from the French on my left shoulder kept me awake, Sire. I took the opportunity to do some thinking.

KING *(worriedly)*. You think too much. You'll suffer for it, you know! It's because people think that there are problems. One day, if you go on like this, you'll think yourself into a dilemma, your big head will present you with a solution and you'll jump feet first into a hopeless mess—which you'd have done far better to ignore, like the majority of fools, who know nothing and live to a ripe old age. What do you think of my little French girl? I must say, I adore France.

BECKET *(smiling)*. So do I, Sire, like all Englishmen.

KING.   The climate's warm, the girls are pretty, the wine is good. I intend to spend at least a month here every winter.

BECKET.   The only snag is, it's expensive! Nearly 2,000 casualties yesterday.

KING.   Has Beaumont made out his total?

BECKET.   Yes. And he added himself to the list.

KING.   Wounded?

*(*BECKET *does not answer. The* KING *shivers. He says somberly:)*

I don't like learning that people I know have died. I've a feeling it may give Death ideas.

BECKET.   My prince, shall we get down to work? We haven't dealt with yesterday's dispatches.

KING.   Yesterday we were fighting! We can't do everything.

BECKET.   That was a holiday! We'll have to work twice as hard today.

KING.   Does it amuse you—working for the good of my people? Do you mean to say you love all those folk? To begin with they're too numerous. One can't love them, one doesn't know them. Anyway, you're lying, you don't love anything or anybody.

BECKET (*tersely*) . There's one thing I do love, my prince, and that I'm sure of. Doing what I have to do and doing it well.

KING (*grinning*) . Always the es—es . . . What's your word again? I've forgotten it.

BECKET. Esthetics?

KING. Esthetics! Always the esthetic side, eh?

BECKET. Yes, my prince.

KING (*slapping the* GIRL's *rump*) . And isn't that esthetic too? Some people go into ecstasies over cathedrals. But this is a work of art too! Look at that—round as an apple . . .

(*Quite naturally, as if he were offering him a sweetmeat:*)
Want her?

BECKET (*smiling*) . Business, my Lord!

KING (*pouting like a schoolboy*) . All right. Business. I'm listening. Sit down.

(BECKET *sits down on the bed, beside the* KING, *with the* GIRL *like a fascinated rabbit in between them.*)

BECKET. The news is not good, my prince.

KING (*with a careless wave of the hand*) . News never is. That's a known fact. Life is one long web of difficulties. The secret of it—and there is one, brought to perfection by several generations of worldly-wise philosophers—is to give them no importance whatever. In the end one difficulty swallows up the other and you find yourself ten years later still alive with no harm done. Things always work out.

BECKET. Yes. But badly. My prince, when you play tennis, do you simply sit back and let things work out? Do you wait for the ball to hit your racket and say "It's bound to come this way eventually"?

KING. Ah, now just a minute. You're talking about things that matter. A game of tennis is important, it amuses me.

BECKET. And suppose I were to tell you that governing can be as amusing as a game of tennis? Are we going to let the others smash the ball into our court, my prince, or shall we try to score a point, both of us, like two good English sportsmen?

KING (*suddenly roused by his sporting instinct*) . The point, Begod, the point! You're right! On the court, I sweat and strain, I fall over my feet, I half kill myself, I'll cheat if need be, but I never give up the point!

BECKET. Well then, I'll tell you what the score is, so far. Piecing together all the information I have received from London since we've been on the Continent, one thing strikes me, and that is: that there exists in England a power which has grown until it almost rivals yours, my Lord. It is the power of your clergy.

KING. We did get them to pay the tax. That's something!

BECKET. Yes, it's a small sum of money. And they know that Princes can always be pacified with a little money. But those men are past masters at taking back with one hand what they were forced to give with the other. That's a little conjuring trick they've had centuries of practice in.

KING (*to the* GIRL). Pay attention, my little sparrow. Now's your chance to educate yourself. The gentleman is saying some very profound things!

BECKET (*in the same flippant way*). Little French sparrow, suppose you educate us instead. When you're married—if you do marry despite the holes in your virtue—which would you prefer, to be mistress in your own house or to have your village priest laying down the law there?

(*The* KING, *a little peeved, gets up on his knees on the bed and hides the bewildered* GIRL *under an eiderdown.*)

KING. Talk sense, Becket! Priests are always intriguing, I know that. But I also know that I can crush them any time I like.

BECKET. Talk sense, Sire. If you don't do the crushing now, in five years' time there will be two Kings in England, the Archbishop of Canterbury and you. And in ten years' time there will be only one.

KING (*a bit shamefaced*). And it won't be me?

BECKET (*coldly*). I rather fear not.

KING (*with a sudden shout*). Oh, yes, it will! We Plantagenets hold on to our own! To horse, Becket, to horse! For England's glory! War on the faithful! That will make a change for us!

(*The eiderdown starts to toss. The* GIRL *emerges, disheveled, and red in the face.*)

GIRL (*pleadingly*). My Lord! I can't breathe!

(*The* KING *looks at her in surprise. He had clearly forgotten her. He bursts out laughing.*)

KING. What are you doing there? Spying for the clergy? Be off. Put your clothes on and go home. Give her a gold piece, Thomas.

(*The* GIRL *picks up her rags and holds them up in front of her.*)

GIRL. Am I to come back to the camp tonight, my Lord?

KING (*exasperated*). Yes. No. I don't know! We're concerned with the Archbishop now, not you! Be off.

(*The* GIRL *disappears into the back portion of the tent. The* KING *cries:*) To horse, Thomas! For England's greatness! With my big fist and your big brain we'll do some good work, you and I! (*With sudden concern*) Wait a second. You can never be sure of finding another one as good in bed.

(*He goes to the rear of the tent and cries:*)

Come back tonight, my angel! I adore you! You have the prettiest eyes in the world!

(*He comes downstage and says confidentially to* BECKET:)

You always have to tell them that, even when you pay for it, if you
want real pleasure with them. That's high politics, too!
(*Suddenly anxious, as his childish fear of the clergy returns.*)
What will God say to it all, though? After all, they're *His* Bishops!

BECKET (*with an airy gesture*). We aren't children. You know one can
always come to some arrangement with God, on this earth. Make haste
and dress, my prince. We're going to be late.

KING (*hurrying out*). I'll be ready in a second. Do I have to shave?

BECKET (*smiling*). It might be as well, after two days' fighting.

KING. What a fuss for a lot of conquered Frenchmen! I wonder sometimes if you aren't a bit too finicky, Thomas.

(*He goes out.* BECKET *closes the tent just as two* SOLDIERS *bring on a*
YOUNG MONK, *with his hands tied.*)

BECKET. What is it?

SOLDIER. We've just arrested this young monk, my Lord. He was loitering round the camp. He had a knife under his robe. We're taking
him to the Provost.

BECKET. Have you got the knife?

(*The* SOLDIER *hands it to him.* BECKET *looks at it, then at the little* MONK.)
What use do you have for this in your monastery?

MONK. I cut my bread with it!

BECKET (*amused*). Well, well. (*To the* SOLDIERS) Leave him to me. I'll
question him.

SOLDIER. He's turbulent, my Lord. He struggled like a very demon. It
took four of us to get his knife away and tie him up. He wounded the
Sergeant. We'd have finished him there and then, only the Sergeant
said there might be some information to be got out of him. That's
why we're taking him to the Provost.

(*He adds:*)
That's just to tell you he's a spiteful devil.

BECKET (*who has not taken his eyes off the little* MONK.) Very well.
Stand off.

(*The* SOLDIERS *move out of earshot.* BECKET *goes on looking at the* BOY,
and playing with the knife.)
What are you doing in France? You're a Saxon.

MONK (*crying out despite himself*). How do you know?

BECKET I can tell by your accent. I speak Saxon very well, as well as
you speak French. Yes, you might almost pass for a Frenchman—to un-
practiced ears. But I'd be careful. In your predicament, you'd do as
well to be taken for a Frenchman as a Saxon. It's less unpopular.
(*A pause.*)

MONK (*abruptly*). I'm prepared to die.

BECKET (*smiling*). After the deed. But before, you'll agree it's stupid.

(He looks at the knife which he is still holding between two fingers.)
   Where are you from?
MONK   *(venomously)*. Hastings!
BECKET.   Hastings. And who was this kitchen implement intended for?
(No answer.)
   You couldn't hope to kill more than one man with a weapon of this sort. You didn't make the journey for the sake of an ordinary Norman soldier, I imagine.
(The little MONK does not answer.)
   (Tersely) Listen to me, my little man. They're going to put you to the torture. Have you ever seen that? I'm obliged to attend professionally from time to time. You think you'll have the necessary strength of spirit, but they're terribly ingenious and they have a knowledge of anatomy that our imbecilic doctors would do well to emulate. One always talks. Believe me, I know. If I can vouch that you've made a full confession, it will go quicker for you. That's worth considering.
(The MONK does not answer.)
   Besides, there's an amusing detail to this affair. You are directly under my jurisdiction. The King gave me the deeds and livings of all the abbeys in Hastings when he made me Chancellor.
MONK   *(stepping back)*. Are you Becket?
BECKET.   Yes.
(He looks at the knife with faint distaste.)
   You don't only use it to cut your bread. Your knife stinks of onion, like any proper little Saxon's knife. They're good, aren't they, the Hastings onions?
(He looks at the knife again with a strange smile.)
   You still haven't told me who it was for.
(The MONK says nothing.)
   If you meant it for the King, there was no sense in that, my lad. He has three sons. Kings spring up again like weeds! Did you imagine you could liberate your race single-handed?
MONK.   No.
(He adds dully:)
   Not my race. Myself.
BECKET.   Liberate yourself from what?
MONK.   My shame.
BECKET   *(with sudden gravity)*. How old are you?
MONK.   Sixteen.
BECKET   *(quietly)*. The Normans have occupied the island for a hundred years. Shame is an old vintage. Your father and your grandfather drank it to the dregs. The cup is empty now.
MONK   *(shaking his head)*. No.

(*A shadow seems to cross* BECKET's *eyes. He goes on, quietly:*)

BECKET.   So, one fine morning, you woke in your cell to the bell of the first offices, while it was still dark. And it was the bells that told you, a boy of sixteen, to take the whole burden of shame onto yourself?

MONK   (*with the cry of a cornered animal*). Who told you that?

BECKET   (*softly*). I told you I was a polyglot. (*Indifferently*) I'm a Saxon too, did you know that?

MONK   (*stonily*). Yes.

BECKET   (*smiling*). Go on. Spit. You're dying to.

(*The* MONK *looks at him, a little dazed, and then spits.*)

BECKET   (*smiling*). That felt good, didn't it? (*Tersely*) The King is waiting. And this conversation could go on indefinitely. But I want to keep you alive, so we can continue it one of these days.

(*He adds lightly:*)

It's pure selfishness, you know. Your life hasn't any sort of importance for me, obviously, but it's very rare for Fate to bring one face to face with one's own ghost, when young. (*Calling*) Soldier!

(*The* SOLDIER *comes back and springs clanking to attention.*)

Fetch me the Provost. Run!

(*The* SOLDIER *runs out.* BECKET *comes back to the silent* YOUNG MONK.)

Delightful day, isn't it? This early-morning sun, hot already under this light veil of mist . . . A beautiful place, France. But I'm like you, I prefer the solid mists of the Sussex downs. Sunshine is luxury. And we belong to a race which used to despise luxury, you and I.

(*The* PROVOST MARSHAL *of the camp comes in, followed by the* SOLDIER. *He is an important personage, but* BECKET *is inaccessible, even for a* PROVOST MARSHAL, *and the man's behavior shows it.*)

Sir Provost, your men have arrested this monk who was loitering round the camp. He is a lay brother from the convent of Hastings and he is directly under my jurisdiction. You will make arrangements to have him sent back to England and taken to the convent, where his Abbot will keep him under supervision until my return. There is no specific charge against him, for the moment. I want him treated without brutality, but very closely watched. I hold you personally responsible for him.

PROVOST.   Very good, my Lord.

(*He motions to the* SOLDIERS. *They surround the little* MONK *and take him away without a further glance from* BECKET. *Left alone,* BECKET *looks at the knife, smiles, wrinkles his nose and murmurs, with faint distaste:*)

BECKET.   It's touching, but it stinks, all the same.

(*He flings the knife away, and whistling his little march goes toward the tent. He goes in, calling out lightheartedly:*)

Well, my prince, have you put on your Sunday best? It's time to go

We mustn't keep the Bishop waiting!

(*A sudden joyful peal of bells. The tent disappears as soon as* BECKET *has gone in. The set changes. A backcloth representing a street comes down from the flies. The permanent pillars are there, but the* SOLDIERS *lining the route have decorated them with standards. The* KING *and* BECKET *advance into the city, on horseback, preceded by two* TRUMPETERS; *the* KING *slightly ahead of* BECKET *and followed by the four* BARONS. *Acclamations from the crowd. Bells, trumpets throughout the scene.*)

KING (*beaming as he waves*). Listen to that! They adore us, these French!

BECKET. It cost me quite a bit. I had money distributed among the populace this morning. The prosperous classes are at home, sulking, of course.

KING. Patriots?

BECKET. No. But they would have cost too much. There are also a certain number of your Highness' soldiers among the crowd, in disguise, to encourage any lukewarm elements.

KING. Why do you always make a game of destroying my illusions? I thought they loved me for myself! You're an amoral man, Becket. (*Anxiously*) Does one say amoral or immoral?

BECKET (*smiling*). It depends what one means.

KING. She's pretty, look—the girl on the balcony to the right there. Suppose we stopped a minute . . .

BECKET. Impossible. The Bishop is waiting in the cathedral.

KING. It would be a lot more fun than going to see a Bishop!

BECKET. My Lord, do you remember what you have to say to him?

KING (*waving to the crowd*). Yes, yes, yes! As if it mattered what I say to a French Bishop, whose city I've just taken by force!

BECKET. It matters a great deal. For our future policy.

KING. Am I the strongest or am I not?

BECKET. You are, today. But one must never drive one's enemy to despair. It makes him strong. Gentleness is better politics. It saps virility. A good occupational force must not crush, it must corrupt.

KING (*waving graciously*). What about my pleasure then? Where does that enter into your scheme of things? Suppose I charged into this heap of frog-eaters now instead of acting the goat at their *Te Deum?* I can indulge in a bit of pleasure, can't I? I'm the conqueror.

BECKET. That would be a fault. Worse, a failing. One can permit oneself anything, Sire, but one must never indulge.

KING. Yes, Papa, right, Papa. What a bore you are today. Look at that little redhead there, standing on the fountain! Give orders for the procession to follow the same route back.

(*He rides on, turning his horse to watch the* GIRL *out of sight. They have*

gone by, the four BARONS *bringing up the rear. Organ music. The standards disappear, together with the* SOLDIERS. *We are in the cathedral. The
stage is empty.*
*The organ is heard. Swelling chords. The organist is practicing in the
empty cathedral. Then a sort of partition is pushed on, which represents
the sacristy.*
The KING, *attired for the ceremony, the* BARONS, *an unknown* PRIEST *and
a* CHOIRBOY *come in. They seem to be waiting for something. The* KING
sits impatiently on a stool.)

KING.   Where's Becket? And what are we waiting for?

1ST BARON.   He just said to wait, my Lord. It seems there's something not
quite in order.

KING *(pacing about ill-humoredly)*. What a lot of fuss for a French
Bishop! What do I look like, I ask you, hanging about in this sacristy
like a village bridegroom!

4TH BARON.   I quite agree, my Lord! I can't think why we don't march
straight in. After all, it's your cathedral now. *(Eagerly)* What do you
say, my Lord? Shall we just draw our swords and charge?

KING *(going meekly back to his stool with a worried frown)*. No.
Becket wouldn't like it. And he's better than we are at knowing the
right thing to do. If he told us to wait, there must be a good reason.
*(*BECKET *hurries in.)*

Well, Becket, what's happening? We're freezing to death in here!
What do the French think they're at, keeping us moldering in this
sacristy?

BECKET.   The order came from me, Sire. A security measure. My police
are certain that a French rising was to break out during the ceremony.
(The KING *has risen. The* 2ND BARON *has drawn his sword. The other
three follow suit.)*

2ND BARON.   God's Blood!

BECKET.   Put up your swords. The King is safe in here. I have put guards
on all the doors.

2ND BARON.   Have we your permission to go in and deal with it, my
Lord? We'll make short work of it!

3RD BARON.   Just say the word, Sire! Shall we go?

BECKET *(curtly)*. I forbid you. There aren't enough of us. I am bringing fresh troops into the city and having the cathedral evacuated.
Until that is done, the King's person is in your keeping, gentlemen.
But sheathe your swords. No provocation, please. We are at the mercy
of a chance incident and I still have no more than the fifty escort men-
at-arms in the city.

KING *(tugging at* BECKET's *sleeve)*. Becket! Is that priest French?

BECKET. Yes. But he is part of the Bishop's immediate entourage. And the Bishop is our man.

KING. You know how reliable English Bishops are! So I leave you to guess how far we can trust a French one! That man has a funny look in his eyes.

BECKET. Who, the Bishop?

KING. No. That priest.

BECKET (*glances at the* PRIEST *and laughs*). Of course, my prince, he squints! I assure you that's the only disturbing thing about him! It would be tactless to ask him to leave. Besides, even if he had a dagger, you have your coat of mail and four of your Barons. I must go and supervise the evacuation of the nave.

(*He starts to go. The* KING *runs after him.*)

KING. Becket!

(BECKET *stops.*)

The choirboy?

BECKET (*laughing*). He's only so high!

KING. He may be a dwarf. You never know with the French.

(*Drawing* BECKET *aside.*)

Becket, we talked a little flippantly this morning. Are you sure God isn't taking his revenge?

BECKET (*smiling*). Of course not. I'm afraid it's simply my police force taking fright and being a little overzealous. Policemen have a slight tendency to see assassins everywhere. They only do it to make themselves important. Bah, what does it matter? We'll hear the *Te Deum* in a deserted church, that's all.

KING (*bitterly*). And there was I thinking those folk adored me. Perhaps you didn't give them enough money.

BECKET. One can only buy those who are for sale, my prince. And those are just the ones who aren't dangerous. With the others, it's wolf against wolf. I'll come back straightaway and set your mind at rest.

(*He goes out. The* KING *darts anxious looks on the* PRIEST *as he paces up and down muttering his prayers.*)

KING. Baron!

(*The* 4TH BARON *is nearest the* KING. *He steps forward.*)

4TH BARON (*bellowing as usual*). My Lord?

KING. Shush! Keep an eye on that man, all four of you, and at the slightest move, leap on him.

(*There follows a little comic dumbshow by the* KING *and the* PRIEST, *who is beginning to feel uneasy too. A sudden violent knocking on the sacristy door. The* KING *starts.*)

Who is it?

(*A* SOLDIER *comes in.*)

SOLDIER.   A messenger from London, my Lord. They sent him on here from the camp. The message is urgent.

KING   (*worried*) . I don't like it. Regnault, you go and see.

(*The* 4TH BARON *goes out and comes back again, reassured.*)

4TH BARON.   It's William of Corbeil, my Lord. He has urgent letters.

KING.   You're sure it *is* him? It wouldn't be a Frenchman in disguise? That's an old trick.

4TH BARON   (*roaring with laughter*) . I know him, Sire! I've drained more tankards with him than there are whiskers on his face. And the old goat has plenty!

(*The* KING *makes a sign. The* 4TH BARON *admits the* MESSENGER, *who drops on one knee and presents his letters to the* KING.)

KING.   Thank you. Get up. That's a fine beard you have, William of Corbeil. Is it well stuck on?

MESSENGER   (*rising, bewildered*) . My beard, Sire?

(*The* 4TH BARON *guffaws and slaps him on the back.*)

4TH BARON.   You old porcupine you!

(*The* KING *has glanced through the letters.*)

KING.   Good news, gentlemen! We have one enemy less.

(RECKET *comes in. The* KING *cries joyfully:*)

Becket!

BECKET.   Everything is going according to plan, my prince. The troops are on their way. We've only to wait here quietly, until they arrive.

KING   (*cheerfully*) . You're right, Becket, everything is going according to plan. God isn't angry with us. He has just recalled the Archbishop.

BECKET   (*in a murmur*) . That little old man . . . How could that feeble body contain so much strength?

KING.   Now, now, now! Don't squander your sorrow, my son. I personally consider this an excellent piece of news!

BECKET.   He was the first Norman who took an interest in me. He was a true father to me. God rest his soul.

KING.   He will! After all the fellow did for Him, he's gone to Heaven, don't worry. Where he'll be definitely more use to God than he was to us. So it's definitely for the best.

(*He pulls* BECKET *to him.*)

Becket! My little Becket, I think the ball's in our court now! This is the time to score a point.

(*He seizes his arm, tense and quite transformed.*)

An extraordinary idea is just creeping into my mind, Becket. A master stroke! I can't think what's got into me this morning, but I suddenly feel extremely intelligent. It probably comes of making love with a

French girl last night. I am subtle, Becket, I am profound! So profound it's making my head spin. Are you sure it isn't dangerous to think too hard? Thomas, my little Thomas! Are you listening to me?

BECKET (*smiling at his excitement*). Yes, my prince.

KING (*as excited as a little boy*). Are you listening carefully? Listen, Thomas! You told me once that the best ideas are the stupidest ones, but the clever thing is to think of them! Listen, Thomas! Tradition prevents me from touching the privileges of the Primacy. You follow me so far?

BECKET. Yes, my prince . . .

KING. But what if the Primate is my man? If the Archbishop of Canterbury is for the King, how can his power possibly incommodate me?

BECKET. That's an ingenious idea, my prince, but you forget that his election is a free one.

KING. No! You're forgetting the Royal Hand! Do you know what that is? When the candidate is displeasing to the Throne the King sends his Justicer to the Conclave of Bishops and it's the King who has the final say. That's an old custom too, and for once, it's in my favor! It's fully a hundred years since the Conclave of Bishops has voted contrary to the wishes of the King.

BECKET. I don't doubt it, my Lord. But we all know your Bishops. Which one of them could you rely on? Once the Primate's miter is on their heads, they grow dizzy with power.

KING. Are you asking me, Becket? I'll tell you. Someone who doesn't know what dizziness means. Someone who isn't even afraid of God. Thomas, my son, I need your help again and this time it's important. I'm sorry to deprive you of French girls and the fun of battle, my son, but pleasure will come later. You are going over to England.

BECKET. I am at your service, my prince.

KING. Can you guess what your mission will be?

(*A tremor of anguish crosses* BECKET's *face at what is to come.*)

BECKET. No, my prince.

KING. You are going to deliver a personal letter from me to every Bishop in the land. And do you know what those letters will contain, my Thomas, my little brother? My royal wish to have you elected Primate of England.

(BECKET *has gone deathly white. He says with a forced laugh:*)

BECKET. You're joking, of course, my Lord. Just look at the edifying man, the saintly man whom you would be trusting with these holy functions!

(*He has opened his fine coat to display his even finer doublet.*)

Why, my prince, you really fooled me for a second!

(*The* KING *bursts out laughing.* BECKET *laughs too, rather too loudly in his relief.*)

A fine Archbishop I'd have made! Look at my new shoes! They're the latest fashion in Paris. Attractive, that little upturned toe, don't you think? Quite full of unction and compunction, isn't it, Sire?

KING (*suddenly stops laughing*). Shut up about your shoes, Thomas. I'm in deadly earnest. I shall write those letters before noon. You will help me.

(BECKET, *deathly pale, stammers:*)

BECKET. But my Lord, I'm not even a priest!

KING (*tersely*). You're a deacon. You can take your final vows tomorrow and be ordained in a month.

BECKET. But have you considered what the Pope will say?

KING (*brutally*). I'll pay the price!

(BECKET, *after an anguished pause, murmurs:*)

BECKET. My Lord, I see now that you weren't joking. Don't do this.

KING. Why not?

BECKET. It frightens me.

KING (*his face set and hard*). Becket, this is an order!

(BECKET *stands as if turned to stone. A pause. He murmurs:*)

BECKET (*gravely*). If I become Archbishop, I can no longer be your friend.

(*A burst of organ music in the cathedral. Enter an* OFFICER.)

OFFICER. The church is now empty, my Lord. The Bishop and his clergy await your Highness' good pleasure.

KING (*roughly to* BECKET). Did you hear that, Becket? Pull yourself together. You have an odd way of taking good news. Wake up! They say we can go in now.

(*The procession forms with the* PRIEST *and the* CHOIRBOY *leading.* BECKET *takes his place, almost reluctantly, a pace or so behind the* KING.)

BECKET (*in a murmur*). This is madness, my Lord. Don't do it. I could not serve both God and you.

KING (*looking straight ahead, says stonily*). You've never disappointed me, Thomas. And you are the only man I trust. You will leave tonight. Come, let's go in.

(*He motions to the* PRIEST. *The procession moves off and goes into the empty cathedral, as the organ swells.*

A moment's darkness. The organ continues to play. Then a dim light reveals BECKET'S *room. Open chests into which two* SERVANTS *are piling costly clothes.*)

2ND SERVANT (*who is the younger of the two*). The coat with the sable trimming as well?

1ST SERVANT. Everything! You heard what he said!

2ND SERVANT   (*grumbling*). Sables! To beggars! Who'll give them alms if they beg with that on their backs! They'll starve to death!

1ST SERVANT   (*cackling*). They'll eat the sables! Can't you understand, you idiot! He's going to sell all this and give them the money!

2ND SERVANT.   But what will he wear himself? He's got nothing left at all!

(BECKET *comes in, wearing a plain gray dressing gown.*)

BECKET.   Are the chests full? I want them sent over to the Jew before tonight. I want nothing left in his room but the bare walls. Gil, the fur coverlet!

1ST SERVANT   (*regretfully*). My Lord will be cold at night.

BECKET.   Do as I say.

(*Regretfully, the* 1ST SERVANT *takes the coverlet and puts it in the chest.*) Has the steward been told about tonight's meal? Supper for forty in the great hall.

1ST SERVANT.   He says he won't have enough gold plate, my Lord. Are we to mix it with the silver dishes?

BECKET.   Tell him to lay the table with the wooden platters and earthenware bowls from the kitchens. The plate has been sold. The Jew will send over for it late this afternoon.

1ST SERVANT   (*dazed*). The earthenware bowls and the wooden platters. Yes, my Lord. And the steward says could he have your list of invitations fairly soon, my Lord. He only has three runners and he's afraid there won't be time to—

BECKET.   There are no invitations. The great doors will be thrown open and you will go out into the street and tell the poor they are dining with me tonight.

1ST SERVANT   (*appalled*). Very good, my Lord.

(*He is about to go.* BECKET *calls him back.*)

BECKET.   I want the service to be impeccable. The dishes presented to each guest first, with full ceremony, just as for princes. Go now.

(*The two* SERVANTS *go out.* BECKET, *left alone, casually looks over one or two articles of clothing in the chests. He murmurs:*)

I must say it was all very pretty stuff.

(*He drops the lid and bursts out laughing.*)

A prick of vanity! The mark of an upstart. A truly saintly man would never have done the whole thing in one day. Nobody will ever believe it's genuine.

(*He turns to the jeweled crucifix above the bed and says simply:*)

I hope You haven't inspired me with all these holy resolutions in order to make me look ridiculous, Lord. It's all so new to me. I'm setting about it a little clumsily perhaps.

(*He looks at the crucifix and with a swift gesture takes it off the wall.*)

And you're far too sumptuous too. Precious stones around your bleed-
ing Body . . . I shall give you to some poor village church.
(*He lays the crucifix on the chest. He looks around the room, happy,
lighthearted, and murmurs:*)
It's like leaving for a holiday. Forgive me, Lord, but I never enjoyed
myself so much in my whole life. I don't believe You are a sad God.
The joy I feel in shedding all my riches must be part of Your divine
intentions.
(*He goes behind the curtain into the antechamber where he can be heard
gaily whistling an old English marching song. He comes back a second
later, his bare feet in sandals, and wearing a monk's coarse woolen robe.
He draws the curtain across again and murmurs:*)
BECKET.   There. Farewell, Becket. I wish there had been something I
had regretted parting with, so I could offer it to You.
(*He goes to the crucifix and says simply:*)
Lord, are You sure You are not tempting me? It all seems far too easy.
(*He drops to his knees and prays.*)

ACT THREE

*A room in the king's palace. The two queens, the Queen Mother and the
Young Queen, are on stage, working at their tapestry. The king's two
sons, one considerably older than the other, are playing in a corner, on
the floor. The king is in another corner, playing at cup-and-ball. After
several unsuccessful attempts to catch the ball in the cup, he throws down
the toy and exclaims irritably:*

KING.   Forty beggars! He invited forty beggars to dinner!
QUEEN MOTHER.   The dramatic gesture, as usual! I always said you had
misplaced your confidence, my son.
KING (*pacing up and down*).   Madam, I am very particular where I place
my confidence. I only ever did it once in my whole life and I am still
convinced I was right. But there's a great deal we don't understand!
Thomas is ten times more intelligent than all of us put together.
QUEEN MOTHER (*reprovingly*).   You are talking about royalty, my son.
KING (*grunting*).   What of it? Intelligence has been shared out on a
different basis.
YOUNG QUEEN.   It seems he has sold his gold plate and all his rich
clothes to a Jew. He wears an ordinary homespun habit now.
QUEEN MOTHER.   I see that as a sign of ostentation, if nothing worse! One
can become a saintly man, certainly, but not in a single day. I've never
liked the man. You were insane to make him so powerful.

KING   (*crying out*). He is my friend!

QUEEN MOTHER   (*acidly*). More's the pity.

YOUNG QUEEN.   He is your friend in debauchery. It was he who lured you away from your duty towards me. It was he who first took you to the whorehouses!

KING   (*furious*). Rubbish, Madam! I didn't need anybody to lure me away from my duty towards you. I made you three children, very conscientiously. Phew! My duty is done for a while.

YOUNG QUEEN   (*stung*). When that libertine loses the evil influence he has on you, you will come to appreciate the joys of family life again. Pray Heaven he disobeys you!

KING.   The joys of family life are limited, Madam. To be perfectly frank, you bore me. You and your eternal backbiting, over your everlasting tapestry, the pair of you! That's no sustenance for a man!

(*He trots about the room, furious, and comes to a halt behind their chairs.*)

If at least it had some artistic merit. My ancestress Mathilda, while she was waiting for her husband to finish carving out his kingdom, now *she* embroidered a masterpiece—which they left behind in Bayeux, more's the pity. But that! It's beyond belief it's so mediocre.

YOUNG QUEEN   (*nettled*). We can only use the gifts we're born with.

KING.   Yes. And yours are meager.

(*He glances out of the window once more to look at the time, and says with a sigh:*)

I've been bored to tears for a whole month. Not a soul to talk to. After his nomination, not wanting to seem in too indecent a hurry, I leave him alone to carry out his pastoral tour. Now, back he comes at last, I summon him to the palace and he's late.

(*He looks out of the window again and exclaims:*)

Ah! Someone at the sentry post!

(*He turns away, disappointed.*)

No, it's only a monk.

(*He wanders about the room, aimlessly. He goes over to join the CHIL-DREN, and watches them playing for a while.*)

(*Sourly*) Charming babes. Men in the making. Sly and obtuse already. And to think one is expected to be dewy-eyed over creatures like that, merely because they aren't yet big enough to be hated or despised. Which is the elder of you two?

ELDER BOY   (*rising*). I am, Sir.

KING.   What's your name again?

ELDER BOY.   Henry III.

KING   (*sharply*). Not yet, Sir! Number II is in the best of health. (*To the* QUEEN) You've brought them up well! Do you think of yourself as

Regent already? And you wonder that I shun your bedchamber? I
don't care to make love with my widow.

(*An* OFFICER *comes in.*)

OFFICER.   A messenger from the Archbishop, my Lord.

KING   (*beside himself with rage*). A messenger! A messenger! I summoned
the Archbishop Primate in person!

(*He turns to the* WOMEN, *suddenly uneasy, almost touching.*)

Perhaps he's ill? That would explain everything.

QUEEN MOTHER   (*bitterly*). That's too much to hope for.

KING   (*raging*). You'd like to see him dead, wouldn't you, you females—
because he loves me? If he hasn't come, it's because he's dying! Send
the man in, quickly! O my Thomas . . .

(*The* OFFICER *goes and admits the* MONK. *The* KING *hurries over to him.*)

Who are you? Is Becket ill?

MONK   (*falling on one knee*). My Lord, I am William son of Etienne,
secretary to his Grace the Archbishop.

KING.   Is your master seriously ill?

MONK.   No, my Lord. His Grace is in good health. He has charged me
to deliver this letter with his deepest respects—and to give your Highness this.

(*He bows lower and hands something to the* KING.)

KING   (*stunned*). The Seal? Why has he sent me back the Seal?

(*He unrolls the parchment and reads it in silence. His face hardens. He
says curtly, without looking at the* MONK:)

You have carried out your mission. Go.

(*The* MONK *rises and turns to go.*)

MONK.   Is there an answer from your Highness for his Grace the Archbishop?

KING   (*harshly*). No!

(*The* MONK *goes out. The* KING *stands still a moment, at a loss, then flings
himself onto his throne, glowering. The* WOMEN *exchange a conspiratorial
look. The* QUEEN MOTHER *rises and goes to him.*)

QUEEN MOTHER   (*insidiously*). Well, my son, what does your friend say
in his letter?

KING   (*bawling*). Get out! Get out, both of you! And take your royal
vermin with you! I am alone!

(*Frightened, the* QUEENS *hurry out with the children. The* KING *stands
there a moment, reeling a little, as if stunned by the blow. Then he
collapses onto the throne and sobs like a child.*)

(*Moaning*) O my Thomas!

(*He remains a moment prostrate, then collects himself and sits up. He
looks at the Seal in his hand and says between clenched teeth:*)

You've sent me back the Three Lions of England, like a little boy who

doesn't want to play with me any more. You think you have God's
honor to defend now! I would have gone to war with all England's
might behind me, and against England's interests, to defend you, little
Saxon. I would have given the honor of the Kingdom laughingly . . .
for you . . . Only I loved you and you didn't love me . . . that's the
difference.

(*His face hardens. He adds between clenched teeth:*)

Thanks all the same for this last gift as you desert me. I shall learn to
be alone.

(*He goes out. The lights dim.* SERVANTS *remove the furniture. When the
lights go up again, the permanent set, with the pillars, is empty.
A bare church; a man half hidden under a dark cloak is waiting behind
a pillar. It is the* KING. *Closing chords of organ music. Enter* GILBERT
FOLLIOT, *Bishop of London, followed by his* CLERGY. *He has just said
Mass. The* KING *goes to him.*)

Bishop . . .

FOLLIOT   (*stepping back*) . What do you want, fellow?

(*His acolytes are about to step between them, when he exclaims:*)

The King!

KING.   Yes.

FOLLIOT.   Alone, without an escort, and dressed like a common squire?

KING.   The King nevertheless. Bishop, I would like to make a confession.

FOLLIOT   (*with a touch of suspicion*) . I am the Bishop of London. The
    King has his own Confessor. That is an important Court appointment
    and it has its prerogatives.

KING.   The choice of priest for Holy Confession is open, Bishop, even
    for a King.

(FOLLIOT *motions to his* CLERGY, *who draw away.*)

Anyway, my confession will be short, and I'm not asking for absolution.
I have something much worse than a sin on my conscience, Bishop: a
mistake. A foolish mistake.

(FOLLIOT *says nothing.*)

I ordered you to vote for Thomas Becket at the Council of Clarendon.
I repent of it.

FOLLIOT   (*inscrutably*) . We bowed before the Royal Hand.

KING.   Reluctantly, I know. It took me thirteen weeks of authority and
    patience to crush the small uncrushable opposition of which you were
    the head, Bishop. On the day the Council met you looked green. They
    told me you fell seriously ill afterwards.

FOLLIOT   (*impenetrably*) . God cured me.

KING.   Very good of Him. But He is rather inclined to look after His
    own, to the exclusion of anyone else. He let me fall ill without lifting
    a finger! And I must cure myself without divine intervention. I have

the Archbishop on my stomach. A big hard lump I shall have to vomit back. What does the Norman clergy think of him?

FOLLIOT *(reserved)*. His Grace seems to have the reins of the Church of England well in hand. Those who are in close contact with him even say that he behaves like a holy man.

KING *(with grudging admiration)*. It's a bit sudden, but nothing he does ever surprises me. God knows what the brute is capable of, for good or for evil. Bishop, let us be frank with each other. Is the Church very interested in holy men?

FOLLIOT *(with the ghost of a smile)*. The Church has been wise for so long, your Highness, that she could not have failed to realize that the temptation of saintliness is one of the most insidious and fearsome snares the devil can lay for her priests. The administration of the realm of souls, with the temporal difficulties it carries with it, chiefly demands, as in all administrations, competent administrators. The Roman Catholic Church has its Saints, it invokes their benevolent intercession, it prays to them. But it has no need to create others. That is superfluous. And dangerous.

KING. You seem to be a man one can talk to, Bishop. I misjudged you. Friendship blinded me.

FOLLIOT *(still impenetrable)*. Friendship is a fine thing.

KING *(suddenly hoarse)*. It's a domestic animal, a living, tender thing. It seems to be all eyes, forever gazing at you, warming you. You don't see its teeth. But it's a beast with one curious characteristic. It is only after death that it bites.

FOLLIOT *(prudently)*. Is the King's friendship for Thomas Becket dead, your Highness?

KING. Yes, Bishop. It died quite suddenly. A sort of heart failure.

FOLLIOT. A curious phenomenon, your Highness, but quite frequent.

KING *(taking his arm suddenly)*. I hate Becket now, Bishop. There is nothing more in common between that man and me than this creature tearing at my guts. I can't bear it any more. I shall turn it loose on him. But I am the King; what they conventionally call my greatness stands in my way. I need somebody.

FOLLIOT *(stiffening)*. I do not wish to serve anything but the Church.

KING. Let us talk like grown men, Bishop. We went in hand in hand to conquer, pillage and ransom England. We quarrel, we try to cheat each other of a penny or two, but Heaven and Earth still have one or two common interests. Do you know what I have just obtained from the Pope? His Blessing to go and murder Catholic Ireland, in the name of the Faith. Yes, a sort of crusade to impose Norman barons and clergy on the Irish, with our swords and standards solemnly blessed as if we were to give the Turks a drubbing. The only condition: a little piece of silver per household per year, for St. Peter's pence, which the native clergy of Ireland is loath to part with and which I have undertaken to make them pay. It's a mere pittance. But at the end of the year it will add up to a pretty sum. Rome knows how to do her accounts.

FOLLIOT *(terror-stricken)*. There are some things one should never say, your Highness: one should even try not to know about them, so long as one is not directly concerned with them.

KING *(smiling)*. We are alone, Bishop, and the church is empty.

FOLLIOT. The church is never empty. A little red lamp burns in front of the High Altar.

KING *(impatiently)*. Bishop, I like playing games, but only with boys of my own age! Do you take me for one of your sheep, holy pastor? The One whom that little red lamp honors read into your innermost heart and mine a long time ago. Of your cupidity and my hatred, He knows all there is to know.

(FOLLIOT *withdraws into his shell. The* KING *cries irritably:*)

If that's the way you feel you must become a monk, Bishop! Wear a hair shirt on your naked back and go and hide yourself in a monastery to pray! The Bishopric of London, for the pure-hearted son of a Thames waterman, is too much, or too little!

(A pause.)

FOLLIOT *(impassively)*. If, as is my duty, I disregard my private feelings, I must admit that his Grace the Archbishop has so far done nothing which has not been in the interests of Mother Church.

KING *(eying him, says jovially)*. I can see your game, my little friend. You mean to cost me a lot of money. But I'm rich—thanks to Becket, who has succeeded in making you pay the Absentee Tax. And it seems to me eminently ethical that a part of the Church's gold should find its way, via you, back to the Church. Besides, if we want to keep this on a moral basis, Holy Bishop, you can tell yourself that as the greatness of the Church and that of the State are closely linked, in serving me, you will in the long run be working for the consolidation of the Catholic Faith.

FOLLIOT *(contemplating him with curiosity)*. I had always taken your Highness for a great adolescent lout who cared only for his pleasure.

KING. One can be wrong about people, Bishop. I made the same mistake. *(With a sudden cry)* O my Thomas . . .

FOLLIOT *(fiercely)*. You love him, your Highness! You still love him! You love that mitered hog, that impostor, that Saxon bastard, that little guttersnipe!

KING *(seizing him by the throat)*. Yes, I love him! But that's my affair, priest! All I confided to you was my hatred. I'll pay you to rid me of him, but don't ever speak ill of him to me. Or we'll fight it out as man to man.

FOLLIOT. Highness, you're choking me!

KING *(abruptly releasing him)*. We will meet again tomorrow, my Lord Bishop, and we'll go over the details of our enterprise together. You will be officially summoned to the palace on some pretext or other— my good works in your London Diocese, say—where I am your chief parishioner. But it won't be the poor and needy we'll discuss. My poor can wait. The Kingdom they pin their hopes on is eternal.

(The KING *goes out.* GILBERT FOLLIOT *remains motionless. His* CLERGY *join him timidly. He takes his crook and goes out with dignity, but not before one of his Canons has discreetly adjusted his miter, which was knocked askew in the recent struggle.*

They have gone out.

The lighting changes. Curtains between the pillars. The episcopal palace.

Morning. A PRIEST *enters, leading two* MONKS *and the* YOUNG MONK *from the convent of Hastings.)*

PRIEST. His Grace will receive you here.

(The two MONKS *are impressed. They push the* YOUNG MONK *about a little.)*

1ST MONK. Stand up straight. Kiss his Grace's ring and try to answer his questions with humility, or I'll tan your backside for you!

2ND MONK. I suppose you thought he'd forgotten all about you? The great never forget anything. And don't you act proud with him or you'll be sorry.

(Enter BECKET, *wearing a coarse monk's robe.)*

BECKET. Well, brothers, is it fine over in Hastings?

(He gives them his ring to kiss.)

1ST MONK. Foggy, my Lord.

BECKET *(smiling)*. Then it's fine in Hastings. We always think fondly of our Abbey there and we intend to visit it soon, when our new duties grant us a moment's respite. How has this young man been behaving? Has he given our Abbot much trouble?

2ND MONK. A proper mule, my Lord. Father Abbot tried kindness, as you recommended, but he soon had to have recourse to the dungeon and bread and water, and even to the whip. Nothing has any effect. The stubborn little wretch is just the same; all defiance and insults. He has fallen into the sin of pride. Nothing I know of will pull him out of that!

1ST MONK. Save a good kick in the rump perhaps—if your Grace will pardon the expression. *(To the* BOY) Stand up straight.

BECKET *(to the* BOY) *.* Pay attention to your brother. Stand up straight. As a rule the sin of pride stiffens a man's back. Look me in the face.

(The YOUNG MONK *looks at him.)*

Good.

*(*BECKET *looks at the boy for a while, then turns to the* MONKS.)

You will be taken to the kitchens where you can refresh yourselves before you leave, brothers. They have orders to treat you well. Don't spurn our hospitality; we relieve you, for today, of your vows of abstinence, and we fondly hope you will do honor to our bill of fare. Greet your father Abbot in Jesus on our behalf.

2ND MONK *(hesitantly)* . And the lad?

BECKET. We will keep him here.

1ST MONK. Watch out for him, your Grace. He's vicious.

BECKET *(smiling)* . We are not afraid.

(The MONKS *go out.* BECKET *and the* YOUNG MONK *remain, facing each other.)*

Why do you hold yourself so badly?

YOUNG MONK. I don't want to look people in the face any more.

BECKET. I'll teach you. That will be your first lesson. Look at me.

(The BOY *gives him a sidelong glance.)*

Better than that.

(The BOY *looks at him.)*

Are you still bearing the full weight of England's shame alone? Is it that shame which bends your back like that?

YOUNG MONK. Yes.

BECKET. If I took over half of it, would it weigh less heavy?

(He motions to the PRIEST*)* .

Show in their Lordships the Bishops. You'll soon see that being alone is not a privilege reserved entirely for you.

(The BISHOPS *come in.* BECKET *leads the* YOUNG MONK *into a corner.)*

You stay here in the corner and hold my tablets. I ask only one thing. Don't leap at their throats; you'd complicate everything.

(He motions to the BISHOPS *who remain standing.)*

FOLLIOT. Your Grace, I am afraid this meeting may be a pointless one. You insisted—against our advice—on attacking the King openly. Even before the three excommunications which you asked us to sanction could be made public, the King has hit back. His Grand Justicer Richard de Lacy has just arrived in your antechamber and is demanding to see you in the name of the King. He is the bearer of an official order summoning you to appear before his assembled Council within twenty-four hours and there to answer the charges made against you.

BECKET. Of what is the King accusing me?

FOLLIOT.   Prevarication. Following the examination of accounts by his Privy Council, his Highness demands a considerable sum still outstanding on your administration of the Treasury.

BECKET.   When I resigned the Chancellorship I handed over my ledgers to the Grand Justicer who acquitted me of all subsequent dues and claims. What does the King demand?

OXFORD.   Forty thousand marks in fine gold.

BECKET   (*smiling*). I don't believe there was ever as much money in all the coffers of all England in all the time I was Chancellor. But a clever clerk can soon change that . . . The King has closed his fist and I am like a fly inside it.

(*He smiles and looks at him.*)

I have the impression, gentlemen, that you must be feeling something very akin to relief.

YORK.   We advised you against open opposition.

BECKET.   William of Aynsford, incited by the King, struck down the priest I had appointed to the Parish of his Lordship's See, on the pretext that his Highness disapproved of my choice. Am I to look on while my priests are murdered?

FOLLIOT.   It is not for you to appoint a priest to a free fief! There is not a Norman, layman or cleric, who will ever concede that. It would mean reviewing the entire legal system of the Conquest. Everything can be called into question in England except the fact that it was conquered in 1066. England is the land of law and of the most scrupulous respect for the law; but the law begins at that date only, or England as such ceases to exist.

BECKET.   Bishop, must I remind you that we are men of God and that we have an Honor to defend, which dates from all eternity?

OXFORD   (*quietly*). This excommunication was bad policy, your Grace. William of Aynsford is a companion of the King.

BECKET   (*smiling*). I know him very well. He's a charming man. I have drained many a tankard with him.

YORK   (*yelping*). And his wife is my second cousin!

BECKET.   That is a detail I deplore, my Lord Bishop, but he has killed one of my priests. If I do not defend my priests, who will? Gilbert of Clare has indicted before his court of justice a churchman who was under our exclusive jurisdiction.

YORK.   An interesting victim I must say! He deserved the rope a hundred times over. The man was accused of rape and murder. Wouldn't it have been cleverer to let the wretch hang—and have peace?

BECKET.   "I bring not peace but the sword." Your Lordship must I'm sure have read that somewhere. I am not interested in what this man is guilty of. If I allow my priests to be tried by a secular tribunal; if I let Robert de Vere abduct our tonsured clerics from our monasteries, as he has just done, on the grounds that the man was one of his serfs who had escaped land bondage, I don't give much for our freedom and our chances of survival in five years' time, my Lord. I have excommunicated Gilbert of Clare, Robert de Vere and William of Aynsford. The Kingdom of God must be defended like any other Kingdom. Do you think that Right has only to show its handsome face for everything to drop in its lap? Without Might, its old enemy, Right counts for nothing.

YORK. What Might? Let us not indulge in empty words. The King is Might and he is the law.

BECKET. He is the written law, but there is another, unwritten law, which always makes Kings bend the neck eventually.

(*He looks at them for a moment and smiles.*)

I was a profligate, gentlemen, perhaps a libertine, in any case, a worldly man. I loved living and I laughed at all these things. But you passed the burden on to me and now I have to carry it. I have rolled up my sleeves and taken it on my back and nothing will ever make me set it down again. I thank your Lordships. The council is adjourned and I have made my decision. I shall stand by these three excommunications. I shall appear tomorrow before the King's supreme court of Justice.

(*The* BISHOPS *look at one another in surprise, then bow and go out.* BECKET *turns to the* YOUNG MONK:)

Well, does the shame weigh less heavy now?

YOUNG MONK. Yes.

BECKET (*leading him off and laughing*). Then stand up straight!

(*The drapes close. Distant trumpets. The* KING *comes out from behind the curtains and turns to peep through them at something. A pause. Then* GILBERT FOLLIOT *comes hurrying in.*)

KING. What's happening? I can't see a thing from up here.

FOLLIOT. Legal procedure is taking its course, your Highness. The third summons has been delivered. He has not appeared. In a moment he will be condemned in absentia. Once prevarication is established, our Dean the Bishop of Chichester will go to see him and communicate according to the terms of the ancient Charter of the Church of England, our corporated repudiation of allegiance, absolving us of obedience to him—and our intention to report him to our Holy Father the Pope. I shall then, as Bishop of London, step forward and publicly accuse Becket of having celebrated, in contempt of the King, a sacrilegious Mass at the instigation of the Evil Spirit.

KING (*anxiously*). Isn't that going rather far?

FOLLIOT. Of course. It won't fool anyone, but it always works. The assembly will then go out to vote, in order of precedence, and return a verdict of imprisonment. The sentence is already drawn up.

KING. Unanimously?

FOLLIOT. We are all Normans. The rest is your Highness' concern. It will merely be a matter of carrying out the sentence.

KING (*staggering suddenly*). O my Thomas!

FOLLIOT (*impassively*). I can still stop the machine, your Highness.

KING (*hesitates a second then says*). No. Go.

(FOLLIOT *goes out. The* KING *goes back to his place, behind the curtain. The two* QUEENS *come into the room, and join the* KING. *All three stand and peer through the curtain. A pause.*)

YOUNG QUEEN. He's doomed, isn't he?

KING (*dully*). Yes.

YOUNG QUEEN. At last!

(*The* KING *turns on her, his face twisted with hate.*)

KING. I forbid you to gloat!

YOUNG QUEEN. At seeing your enemy perish—why not?

KING (*frothing*). Becket is my enemy, but in the human balance, bastard as he is, and naked as his mother made him, he weighs a hundred times more than you do, Madam, with your crown and all your jewels and your august father the Emperor into the bargain. Becket is attacking me and he has betrayed me. I am forced to fight him and crush him, but at least he gave me, with open hands, everything that is at all good in me. And you have never given me anything but your carping mediocrity, your everlasting obsession with your puny little person and what you thought was due to it. That is why I forbid you to smile as he lies dying!

YOUNG QUEEN. I gave you my youth! I gave you your children!

KING (*shouting*). I don't like my children! And as for your youth—that dusty flower pressed in a hymnbook since you were twelve years old, with its watery blood and its insipid scent—you can say farewell to that without a tear. With age, bigotry and malice may perhaps give some spice to your character. Your body was an empty desert, Madam! —which duty forced me to wander in alone. But you have never been a wife to me! And Becket was my friend, red-blooded, generous and full of strength!

(*He is shaken by a sob.*)

O my Thomas!

(*The* QUEEN MOTHER *moves over to him.*)

QUEEN MOTHER (*haughtily*). And I, my son, I gave you nothing either, I suppose?

KING (*recovers his composure, glares at her and says dully*). Life. Yes. Thank you. But after that I never saw you save in a passage, dressed for a Ball, or in your crown and ermine mantle, ten minutes before official ceremonies, where you were forced to tolerate my presence. I have always been alone, and no one on this earth has ever loved me except Becket!

QUEEN MOTHER *(bitterly)*. Well, call him back! Absolve him, since he loves you! Give him supreme power then! But do something!

KING. I am. I'm learning to be alone again, Madam. As usual.

(A PAGE *comes in, breathless.)*

Well? What's happening? How far have they got?

PAGE. My Liege, Thomas Becket appeared just when everyone had given him up; sick, deathly pale, in full pontifical regalia and carrying his own heavy silver cross. He walked the whole length of the hall without anyone daring to stop him, and when Robert Duke of Leicester, who was to read out his sentence, began the consecrated words, he stopped with a gesture and forbade him, in God's name, to pronounce judgment against him, his spiritual Father. Then he walked back through the crowd, which parted for him in silence. He has just left.

KING *(unable to hide his delight)*. Well played, Thomas! One point to you.

(He checks himself, embarrassed, and then says:)

And what about my Barons?

PAGE. Their hands flew to their swords with cries of "Traitor! Perjurer! Arrest him! Miserable wretch! Hear your sentence!" But not one of them dared move, or touch the sacred ornaments.

KING *(with a roar)*. The fools! I am surrounded by fools and the only intelligent man in my Kingdom is against me!

PAGE *(continuing his story)*. Then, on the threshold, he turned, looked at them coldly as they shouted in their impotence, and he said that not so long ago he could have answered their challenge sword in hand. Now he could no longer do it, but he begged them to remember that there was a time when he met strength with strength.

KING *(jubilantly)*. He could beat them all! All, I tell you! On horseback, on foot, with a mace, with a lance, with a sword! In the lists they fell to him like ninepins!

PAGE. And his eyes were so cold, and so ironic—even though all he had in his hand was his episcopal crook—that one by one, they fell silent. Only then did he turn and go out. They say he has given orders to invite all the beggars of the city to sup at his house tonight.

KING *(somberly)*. And what about the Bishop of London, who was going to reduce him to powder? What about my busy friend Gilbert Folliot?

PAGE. He had a horrible fit of rage trying to incite the crowd, he let out a screech of foul abuse and then he fainted. They are bringing him round now.

(*The* KING *suddenly bursts into a shout of irrepressible laughter, and, watched by the two outraged* QUEENS, *collapses into the* PAGE'*s arms, breathless and helpless with mirth.*)

KING. It's too funny! It's too funny!

QUEEN MOTHER (*coldly*) . You will laugh less heartily tomorrow, my son. If you don't stop him, Becket will reach the coast tonight, ask asylum of the King of France and jeer at you, unpunished, from across the Channel.

(*She sweeps out with the* YOUNG QUEEN. *Suddenly, the* KING *stops laughing and runs out.*

The light changes. Curtains part. We are at the Court of LOUIS, KING OF FRANCE. *He is sitting in the middle of the courtroom, very erect on his throne. He is a burly man with intelligent eyes.*)

LOUIS (*to his* BARONS) . Gentlemen, we are in France and a fart on England's King—as the song goes.

1ST BARON. Your Majesty cannot *not* receive his Ambassadors Extraordinary!

LOUIS. Ordinary, or extraordinary, I am at home to all ambassadors. It's my job. I shall receive them.

1ST BARON. They have been waiting in your Majesty's anteroom for over an hour, Sire.

LOUIS. Let them wait. That's *their* job. An ambassador is made for pacing about an antechamber. I know what they are going to ask me.

2ND BARON. The extradition of a felon is a courtesy due from one crowned head to another.

LOUIS. My dear man, crowned heads can play the little game of courtesy but nations owe each other none. My right to play the courteous gentleman stops where France's interests begin. And France's interests consist in making things as difficult as possible for England—a thing England never hesitates to do to us. The Archbishop is a millstone round Henry Plantagenet's neck. Long live the Archbishop! Anyway, I like the fellow.

2ND BARON. My gracious sovereign is master. And so long as our foreign policy permits us to expect nothing of King Henry—

LOUIS. For the time being, it is an excellent thing to stiffen our attitude. Remember the Montmirail affair. We only signed the peace treaty with Henry on condition that he granted to spare the lives of the refugees from Brittany and Poitou whom he asked us to hand over to him. Two months later all of them had lost their heads. That directly touched my personal honor. I was not strong enough at the time, so I had to pretend I hadn't heard of these men's execution. And I continued to lavish smiles on my English cousin. But praise God our affairs have taken a turn for the better. And today *he* needs *us*. So I will now proceed to remember my honor. Show in the ambassadors.

(*Exit* 1ST BARON. *He comes back with* FOLLIOT *and the* DUKE OF ARUNDEL.)

1ST BARON.   Permit me to introduce to your Majesty the two envoys extraordinary from his Highness Henry of England; his Grace the Bishop of London and the Duke of Arundel.

LOUIS   (*with a friendly wave to the* DUKE). Greetings to you, Milord. I have not forgotten your amazing exploits at the last tournament at Calais. Do you still wield a lance as mightily as you did, Milord?

ARUNDEL   (*with a gratified bow*). I hope so, Sire.

LOUIS.   We hope that our friendly relations with your gracious master will allow us to appreciate your jousting skill again before long, on the occasion of the forthcoming festivities.

(FOLLIOT *has unrolled a parchment.*)

Bishop, I see you have a letter for us from your master. We are listening.

FOLLIOT   (*bows again and starts to read*). "To my Lord and friend Louis, King of the French; Henry, King of England, Duke of Normandy, Duke of Aquitaine and Count of Anjou: Learn that Thomas, former Archbishop of Canterbury, after a public trial held at my court by the plenary assembly of the Barons of my realm has been found guilty of fraud, perjury and treason towards me. He has forthwith fled my Kingdom as a traitor, and with evil intent. I therefore entreat you not to allow this criminal, nor any of his adherents, to reside upon your territories, nor to permit any of your vassals to give help, support or counsel to this my greatest enemy. For I solemnly declare that your enemies or those of your Realm would receive none from me or my subjects. I expect you to assist me in the vindication of my honor and the punishment of my enemy, as you would wish me to do for you, should the need arise."

(*A pause.* FOLLIOT *bows very low and hands the parchment to the* KING *who rolls it up casually and hands it to one of the* BARONS.)

LOUIS.   Gentlemen, we have listened attentively to our gracious cousin's request and we take good note of it. Our chancellery will draft a reply which will be sent to you tomorrow. All we can do at the moment, is express our surprise. No news had reached us of the presence of the Archbishop of Canterbury on our domains.

FOLLIOT   (*tersely*). Sire, the former Archbishop has taken refuge at the Abbey of St. Martin, near Saint-Omer.

LOUIS   (*still gracious*). My Lord Bishop, we flatter ourselves that there is some order in our Kingdom. If he were there, we would certainly have been informed.

(*He makes a gesture of dismissal. The* AMBASSADORS *bow low and go out backwards, ushered out by the* 1ST BARON. *Immediately,* LOUIS *says to the* 2ND BARON:)

    Show in Thomas Becket and leave us.

(*The* 2ND BARON *goes out and a second later admits* THOMAS, *dressed in a monk's robe.* THOMAS *drops onto one knee. The* BARON *goes out.*)

    (*Kindly*) Rise, Thomas Becket. And greet us as the Primate of England. The bow is enough—and if I know my etiquette, you are entitled to a slight nod of the head from me. There, that's done. I would even be required to kiss your ring, if your visit were an official one. But I have the impression that it isn't, am I right?

BECKET   (*with a smile*). No, Sire. I am only an exile.

LOUIS   (*graciously*). That too is an important title, in France.

BECKET.   I am afraid it is the only one I have left. My property has been seized and distributed to those who served the King against me; letters have been sent to the Duke of Flanders and all his Barons enjoining them to seize my person. John, Bishop of Poitiers, who was suspected of wanting to grant me asylum, has just been poisoned.

LOUIS   (*smiling*). In fact you are a very dangerous man.

BECKET.   I'm afraid so.

LOUIS   (*unperturbed*). We like danger, Becket. And if the King of France started being afraid of the King of England, there would be something sadly amiss in Europe. We grant you our royal protection on whichever of our domains it will please you to choose.

BECKET.   I humbly thank your Majesty. I must, however, tell you that I cannot buy this protection with any act hostile to my country.

LOUIS.   You do us injury. That was understood. You may be sure we are practiced enough in the task of Kingship not to make such gross errors in our choice of spies and traitors. The King of France will ask nothing of you. But . . . There is always a but, as I'm sure you are aware, in politics.

(BECKET *looks up. The* KING *rises heavily onto his fat legs, goes to him and says familiarly:*)

    I am only responsible for France's interests, Becket. I really can't afford to shoulder those of Heaven. In a month or a year I can summon you back here and tell you, just as blandly, that my dealings with the King of England have taken a different turn and that I am obliged to banish you.

(*He slaps him affably on the back, his eyes sparkling with intelligence and asks, with a smile:*)

    I believe you have dabbled in politics too, Archbishop?

BECKET   (*smiling*). Yes, Sire. Not so very long ago.

LOUIS   (*jovially*). I like you very much. Mark you, had you been a French

Bishop, I don't say I wouldn't have clapped you in prison myself. But in the present circumstances, you have a right to my royal protection. Do you value candor, Becket?

BECKET. Yes, Sire.

LOUIS. Then we are sure to understand each other. Do you intend to go to see the Holy Father?

BECKET. Yes, Sire, if you give me your safe conduct.

LOUIS. You shall have it. But a word in your ear—as a friend. (Keep this to yourself, won't you?—don't go and stir up trouble for me with Rome.) Beware of the Pope. He'll sell you for thirty pieces of silver. The man needs money.

(*The lights dim. A curtain closes. Two small rostrums, bearing the* POPE *and the* CARDINAL, *are pushed on stage, to a light musical accompaniment. The* POPE *is a thin, fidgety little man with an atrocious Italian accent. The* CARDINAL *is swarthy, and his accent is even worse. The whole effect is a little grubby, among the gilded splendor.*)

POPE. I don't agree, Zambelli! I don't agree at all! It's a very bad plan altogether. We will forfeit our honor all for 3,000 silver marks.

CARDINAL. Holy Father, there is no question of forfeiting honor, but merely of taking the sum offered by the King of England and thereby gaining time. To lose that sum and give a negative answer right away would solve neither the problems of the Curia, nor those of Thomas Becket—nor even, I am afraid, those of the higher interests of the Church. To accept the money—the sum is meager, I agree, and cannot be viewed as a factor in our decision—is merely to make a gesture of appeasement in the interests of peace in Europe. Which has always been the supreme duty of the Holy See.

POPE (*concerned*). If we take money from the King, I cannot possibly receive the Archbishop, who has been waiting here in Rome for a whole month for me to grant him an audience.

CARDINAL. Receive the money from the King, Very Holy Father, and receive the Archbishop too. The one will neutralize the other. The money will remove all subversive taint from the audience you will grant the Archbishop and on the other hand, the reception of the Archbishop will efface whatever taint of humiliation there may be in accepting the money.

POPE (*gloomily*). I don't want to receive him at all. I gather he is a sincere man. I am always disconcerted by people of that sort. They leave me with a bad taste in my mouth.

CARDINAL. Sincerity is a form of strategy, just like any other, Holy Father. In certain very difficult negotiations, when matters are not going ahead and the usual tactics cease to work, I have been known to use it myself. The great pitfall, of course, is if your opponent starts being sincere at the same time as you. Then the game becomes horribly confusing.

POPE. You know what they say Becket's been meaning to ask me?—in the month he's spent pacing about my antechamber?

CARDINAL (*innocently*). No, Holy Father.

POPE (*impatiently*). Zambelli! Don't play the fox with me! It was you who told me!

CARDINAL (*caught out*). I beg your pardon, Holy Father, I had forgotten. Or rather, as Your Holiness asked me the question, I thought you had forgotten and so I took a chance and—

POPE (*irritably*). Zambelli, if we start outmaneuvering each other to no purpose, we'll be here all night!

CARDINAL (*in confusion*). Force of habit, your Holiness. Excuse me.

POPE. To ask me to relieve him of his rank and functions as Archbishop of Canterbury—that's the reason Becket is in Rome! And do you know why he wants to ask me that?

CARDINAL (*candidly for once*). Yes, Holy Father.

POPE (*irritably*). No, you do not know! It was your enemy Rapallo who told me!

CARDINAL (*modestly*). Yes, but I knew it just the same, because I have a spy in Rapallo's palace.

POPE (*with a wink*). Culograti?

CARDINAL. No. Culograti is only my spy in his master's eyes. By the man I have spying on Culograti.

POPE (*cutting short the digression*). Becket maintains that the election of Clarendon was not a free one, that he owes his nomination solely to the royal whim and that consequently the honor of God, of which he has now decided he is the champion, does not allow him to bear this usurped title any longer. He wishes to be nothing more than an ordinary priest.

CARDINAL (*after a moment's thought*). The man is clearly an abyss of ambition.

POPE. And yet he knows that we know that his title and functions are his only safeguard against the King's anger. I don't give much for his skin wherever he is, when he is no longer Archbishop!

CARDINAL (*thoughtfully*). He's playing a deep game. But I have a plan. Your Holiness will pretend to believe in his scruples. You will receive him and relieve him of his titles and functions as Primate, then, immediately after, as a reward for his zeal in defending the Church of England, you will reappoint him Archbishop, in right and due form this time. We thus avert the danger, we score a point against him—and at the same time a point against the King.

POPE. That's a dangerous game. The King has a long arm.

CARDINAL.   We can cover ourselves. We will send secret letters to the English court explaining that this new nomination is a pure formality and that we herewith rescind the excommunications pronounced by Becket; on the other hand, we will inform Becket of the existence of these secret letters, swearing him to secrecy and begging him to consider them as null and void.

POPE *(getting muddled)*. In that case, perhaps there isn't much point in the letters being secret?

CARDINAL. Yes, there is. Because that will allow us to maneuver with each of them as if the other was ignorant of the contents, while taking the precaution of making it known to them both. The main thing is for them not to know that we know they know. It's so simple a child of twelve could grasp it!

POPE.   But Archbishop or no, what are we going to do with Becket?

CARDINAL *(with a lighthearted wave of his hand)*. We will send him to a convent. A French convent, since King Louis is protecting him—to the Cistercians say, at Pontigny. The monastic rule is a strict one. It will do that onetime dandy a world of good! Let him learn real poverty! That will teach him to be the comforter of the poor!

POPE.   That sounds like good advice, Zambelli. Bread and water and nocturnal prayers are an excellent remedy for sincerity.

(He muses a moment.)

The only thing that puzzles me, Zambelli, is why you should want to give me a piece of good advice . . .

(The CARDINAL *looks a little embarrassed.*

The little rostra go as they came and the curtain opens revealing a small, bare cell, center stage. BECKET *is praying before a humble wooden crucifix. Crouching in a corner, the* YOUNG MONK *is playing with a knife.)*

BECKET. Yet it would be simple enough. Too simple perhaps. Saintliness is a temptation too. Oh, how difficult it is to get an answer from You, Lord! I was slow in praying to You, but I cannot believe that others, worthier than I, who have spent years asking You questions, have been better than myself at deciphering Your real intentions. I am only a beginner and I must make mistake after mistake, as I did in my Latin translations as a boy, when my riotous imagination made the old priest roar with laughter. But I cannot believe that one learns Your language as one learns any human tongue, by hard studying, with a dictionary, a grammar and a set of idioms. I am sure that to the hardened sinner, who drops to his knees for the first time and murmurs Your name, marveling, You tell him all Your secrets, straightaway, and that he understands. I have served You like a dilettante, surprised that I could still find my pleasure in Your service. And for a long time I was on my

guard because of it. I could not believe this pleasure would bring me one step nearer You. I could not believe that the road could be a happy one. Their hair shirts, their fasting, their bells in the small hours summoning one to meet You, on the icy paving stones, in the sick misery of the poor ill-treated human animal—I cannot believe that all these are anything but safeguards for the weak. In power and in luxury, and even in the pleasures of the flesh, I shall not cease to speak to You, I feel this now. You are the God of the rich man and the happy man too, Lord, and therein lies Your profound justice. You do not turn away Your eyes from the man who was given everything from birth. You have not abandoned him, alone in his ensnaring facility. And he may be Your true lost sheep. For Your scheme of things, which we mistakenly call Justice, is secret and profound and You plumb the hidden depths of poor men's puny frames as carefully as those of Kings. And beneath those outward differences, which blind us, but which to You are barely noticeable; beneath the diadem or the grime, You discern the same pride, the same vanity, the same petty, complacent preoccupation with oneself. Lord, I am certain now that You meant to tempt me with this hair shirt, object of so much vapid self-congratulation! this bare cell, this solitude, this absurdly endured winter-cold—and the conveniences of prayer. It would be too easy to buy You like this, at so low a price. I shall leave this convent, where so many precautions hem You round. I shall take up the miter and the golden cope again, and the great silver cross, and I shall go back and fight in the place and with the weapons it has pleased You to give me. It has pleased You to make me Archbishop and to set me, like a solitary pawn, face to face with the King, upon the chessboard. I shall go back to my place, humbly, and let the world accuse me of pride, so that I may do what I believe is my life's work. For the rest, Your will be done.
(*He crosses himself.*

The YOUNG MONK *is still playing with his knife. Suddenly he throws it and watches as it quivers, embedded in the floor.*)

ACT FOUR

The King of France's Court. King Louis comes in, holding Becket familiarly by the arm.

LOUIS.   I tell you, Becket, intrigue is an ugly thing. You keep the smell about you for ages afterwards. There is a return of good understanding between the Kingdom of England and Ourselves. Peace in that direction assures me of a great advantage in the struggle which I will shortly have to undertake against the Emperor. I must protect my rear by a truce with Henry Plantagenet, before I march towards the East. And, needless to say, you are one of the items on the King's bill of charges. I can even tell you, that apart from yourself, his demands are negligible. (*Musingly*) Curious man. England's best policy would have been to take advantage of the Emperor's aggressive intentions and close the other jaw of the trap. He is deliberately sacrificing this opportunity for the pleasure of seeing you driven out. He really hates you, doesn't he?

BECKET (*simply*). Sire, we loved each other and I think he cannot forgive me for preferring God to him.

LOUIS. Your King isn't doing his job properly, Archbishop. He is giving way to passion. However! He has chosen to score a point against you, instead of against me. You are on his bill, I have to pay his price and banish you. I do not do so without a certain shame. Where are you thinking of going?

BECKET. I am a shepherd who has remained too long away from his flock. I intend to go back to England. I had already made my decision before this audience with your Majesty.

LOUIS (*surprised*). You have a taste for martyrdom? You disappoint me. I thought you more healthy-minded.

BECKET. Would it be healthy-minded to walk the roads of Europe, and beg a refuge where my carcass would be safe? Besides, where would I be safe? I am a Primate of England. That is a rather showy label on my back. The honor of God and common sense, which for once coincide, dictate that instead of risking the knife thrust of some hired assassin, on the highway, I should go and have myself killed—if killed I must be—clad in my golden cope, with my miter on my head and my silver cross in my hand, among my flock in my own cathedral. That place alone befits me.

(*A pause.*)

LOUIS. I daresay you're right. (*He sighs*) Ah, what a pity it is to be a King, sometimes, when one has the surprise of meeting a man! You'll tell me, fortunately for me, that men are rare. Why weren't you born on this side of the Channel, Becket? (*He smiles*) True, you would no doubt have been a thorn in *my* side then! The honor of God is a very cumbersome thing.

(*He muses for a moment and then says abruptly:*)

Who cares, I'll risk it! I like you too much. I'll indulge in a moment's humanity. I am going to try something, even if your master does seize on the chance to double his bill. After all, banishing you would merely have cost me a small slice of honor . . . I am meeting Henry in a day or two, at La Ferté-Bernard, to seal our agreement. I shall try to persuade him to make his peace with you. Should he agree, will you be willing to talk with him?

BECKET. Sire, ever since we stopped seeing each other, I have never ceased to talk to him.

(Blackout. Prolonged blare of trumpets. The set is completely removed. Nothing remains but the cyclorama around the bare stage. A vast, arid plain, lashed by the wind. Trumpets again.

Two SENTRIES *are on stage, watching something in the distance.)*

SENTRY. Open those eyes of yours, lad! And drink it all in. You're new to the job, but you won't see something like this every day! This a historic meeting!

YOUNG SENTRY. I daresay, but it's perishing cold! How long are they going to keep us hanging about?

SENTRY. We're sheltered by the wood here, but you can bet they're even colder than we are, out there in the plain.

YOUNG SENTRY. Look! They've come up to each other! I wonder what they're talking about?

SENTRY. What do you think they're talking about, muttonhead? Inquiring how things are at home? Complaining about their chilblains? The fate of the world, that's what they're arguing about! Things you and I won't ever understand. Even the words those bigwigs use—why, you wouldn't even know what they meant!

(They go off. The lights go up. BECKET *and the* KING, *on horseback, are alone in the middle of the plain, facing each other.*

Throughout the scene, the winter blizzard wails like a shrill dirge beneath their words. And during their silences, only the wind is heard.)

KING. You look older, Thomas.

BECKET. You too, Highness. Are you sure you aren't too cold?

KING. I'm frozen stiff. You love it of course! You're in your element, aren't you? And you're barefooted as well!

BECKET *(smiling)* . That's my latest affectation.

KING. Even with these fur boots on, my chilblains are killing me. Aren't yours, or don't you have any?

BECKET *(gently)* . Of course.

KING *(cackling)*. You're offering them up to God, I hope, holy monk?

BECKET *(gravely)* . I have better things to offer Him.

KING *(with a sudden cry)* . If we start straightaway, we're sure to quarrel! Let's talk about trivial things. You know my son is fourteen? He's come of age.

BECKET. Has he improved at all?

KING. He's a little idiot and sly like his mother. Becket, don't you ever marry!

BECKET (*smiling*). The matter has been taken out of my hands. By you, Highness! It was you who had me ordained!

KING (*with a cry*). Let's not start yet, I tell you! Talk about something else!

BECKET (*lightly*). Has your Highness done much hunting lately?

KING (*snarling*). Yes, every day! And it doesn't amuse me any more.

BECKET. Have you any new hawks?

KING (*furiously*). The most expensive on the market! But they don't fly straight.

BECKET. And your horses?

KING. The Sultan sent me four superb stallions for the tenth anniversary of my reign. But they throw everyone! Nobody has managed to mount one of them, yet!

BECKET (*smiling*). I must see what I can do about that some day.

KING. They'll throw you too! And we'll see your buttocks under your robe! At least, I hope so, or everything would be too dismal.

BECKET (*after a pause*). Do you know what I miss most, Sire? The horses.

KING. And the women?

BECKET (*simply*). I've forgotten.

KING. You hypocrite. You turned into a hypocrite when you became a priest. (*Abruptly*) Did you love Gwendolen?

BECKET. I've forgotten her too.

KING. You did love her! That's the only way I can account for it.

BECKET (*gravely*). No, my prince, in my soul and conscience, I did not love her.

KING. Then you never loved anything, that's worse! (*Churlishly*) Why are you calling me your prince, like in the old days?

BECKET (*gently*). Because you have remained my prince.

KING (*crying out*). Then why are you doing me harm?

BECKET (*gently*). Let's talk about something else.

KING. Well, what? I'm cold.

BECKET. I always told you, my prince, that one must fight the cold with the cold's own weapons. Strip naked and splash yourself with cold water every morning.

KING. I used to when you were there to force me into it. I never wash now. I stink. I grew a beard at one time. Did you know?

BECKET (*smiling*). Yes. I had a hearty laugh over it.

KING. I cut it off because it itched.

(*He cries out suddenly, like a lost child:*)

Becket, I'm bored!

BECKET (*gravely*). My prince. I do so wish I could help you.

KING. Then what are you waiting for? You can see I'm dying for it!

BECKET   (*quietly*). I'm waiting for the honor of God and the honor of
the King to become one.

KING.   You'll wait a long time then!

BECKET.   Yes. I'm afraid I will.

(*A pause. Only the wind is heard.*)

KING   (*suddenly*). If we've nothing more to say to each other, we might
as well go and get warm!

BECKET.   We have everything to say to each other, my prince. The opportunity may not occur again.

KING.   Make haste, then. Or there'll be two frozen statues on this plain
making their peace in a frozen eternity! I am your King, Becket! And
so long as we are on this earth you owe me the first move! I'm prepared to forget a lot of things but not the fact that I am King! You
yourself taught me that.

BECKET   (*gravely*). Never forget it, my prince. Even against God. You
have a different task to do. You have to steer the ship.

KING.   And you—what do you have to do?

BECKET.   Resist you with all my might, when you steer against the wind.

KING.   Do you expect the wind to be behind me, Becket? No such luck!
That's the fairy-tale navigation! God on the King's side? That's never
happened yet! Yes, once in a century, at the time of the Crusades,
when all Christendom shouts "It's God's will!" And even then! You
know as well as I do what private greeds a Crusade covers up, in nine
cases out of ten. The rest of the time, it's a head-on wind. And there
must be somebody to keep the watch!

BECKET.   And somebody else to cope with the absurd wind—and with
God. The tasks have been shared out, once and for all. The pity of it
is that it should have been between us two, my prince—who were
friends.

KING   (*crossly*). The King of France—I still don't know what he hopes
to gain by it—preached at me for three whole days for me to make my
peace with you. What good would it do you to provoke me beyond
endurance?

BECKET.   None.

KING.   You know that I am the King, and that I must act like a King!
What do you expect of me? Are you hoping I'll weaken?

BECKET.   No. That would prostrate me.

KING.   Do you hope to conquer me by force then?

BECKET.   You are the strong one.

KING.   To win me round?

BECKET.   No. Not that either. It is not for me to win you round. I have
only to say no to you.

KING.   But you must be logical, Becket!

BECKET. No, that isn't necessary, my Liege. We must only do—absurdly—what we have been given to do—right to the end.

KING. Yet I know you well enough, God knows. Ten years we spent together, little Saxon! At the hunt, at the whorehouse, at war; carousing all night long the two of us; in the same girl's bed, sometimes . . . and at work in the Council Chamber too. Absurdly. That word isn't like you.

BECKET. Perhaps. I am no longer like myself.

KING (*derisively*). Have you been touched with grace?

BECKET (*gravely*). Not by the one you think. I am not worthy of it.

KING. Did you feel the Saxon in you coming out, despite Papa's good collaborator's sentiments?

BECKET. No. Not that either.

KING. What then?

BECKET. I felt for the first time that I was being entrusted with something, that's all—there in that empty cathedral, somewhere in France, that day when you ordered me to take up this burden. I was a man without honor. And suddenly I found it—one I never imagined would ever become mine—the honor of God. A frail, incomprehensible honor, vulnerable as a boy-King fleeing from danger.

KING (*roughly*). Suppose we talked a little more precisely, Becket, with words I understand? Otherwise we'll be here all night. I'm cold. And the others are waiting for us on the fringes of this plain.

BECKET. I am being precise.

KING. I'm an idiot then! Talk to me like an idiot! That's an order. Will you lift the excommunication which you pronounced on William of Aynsford and others of my liegemen?

BECKET. No, Sire, because that is the only weapon I have to defend this child, who was given, naked, into my care.

KING. Will you agree to the twelve proposals which my Bishops have accepted in your absence at Northampton, and notably to forego the much-abused protection of Saxon clerics who get themselves tonsured to escape land bondage?

BECKET. No, Sire. My role is to defend my sheep. And they are my sheep. (*A pause.*)

Nor will I concede that the Bishops should forego the right to appoint priests in their own dioceses, nor that churchmen should be subject to any but the Church's jurisdiction. These are my duties as a pastor—which it is not for me to relinquish. But I shall agree to the nine other articles in a spirit of peace, and because I know that you must remain King—in all save the honor of God. (*A pause.*)

KING (*coldly*). Very well. I will help you defend your God, since that is your new vocation, in memory of the companion you once were to me—in all save the honor of the Realm. You may come back to England, Thomas.

BECKET.   Thank you, my prince. I meant to go back in any case and give myself up to your power, for on this earth, you are my King. And in all that concerns this earth, I owe you obedience.

(*A pause.*)

KING   (*ill at ease*). Well, let's go back now. We've finished. I'm cold.

BECKET   (*Dully*). I feel cold too, now.

(*Another pause. They look at each other. The wind howls.*)

KING   (*suddenly*). You never loved me, did you, Becket?

BECKET.   In so far as I was capable of love, yes, my prince, I did.

KING.   Did you start to love God?

(*He cries out:*)

You mule! Can't you ever answer a simple question?

BECKET   (*quietly*). I started to love the honor of God.

KING   (*somberly*). Come back to England. I give you my royal peace. May you find yours. And may you not discover you were wrong about yourself. This is the last time I shall come begging to you.

(*He cries out:*)

I should never have seen you again! It hurts too much.

(*His whole body is suddenly shaken by a sob.*)

BECKET   (*goes nearer to him; moved*). My prince—

KING   (*yelling*). No! No pity! It's dirty. Stand away from me! Go back to England! It's too cold out here!

(BECKET *turns his horse and moves nearer to the* KING.)

BECKET   (*gravely*). Farewell, my prince. Will you give me the kiss of peace?

KING.   No! I can't bear to come near you! I can't bear to look at you! Later! Later! When it doesn't hurt any more!

BECKET.   I shall set sail tomorrow. Farewell, my prince. I know I shall never see you again.

KING   (*his face twisted with hatred*). How dare you say that to me after I gave you my royal word? Do you take me for a traitor?

(BECKET *looks at him gravely for a second longer, with a sort of pity in his eyes. Then he slowly turns his horse and rides away. The wind howls.*)

KING.   Thomas!

(*But* BECKET *has not heard. The* KING *does not call a second time. He spurs his horse and gallops off in the other direction. The lights fade. The wind howls.*

The lights change. Red curtains fall. BECKET's *whistled march is heard off stage during the scene change.*

The curtains open. Royal music. KING HENRY's *palace somewhere in*

France. The two QUEENS, *the* BARONS *and* HENRY's SON *are standing around the dinner table, waiting. The* KING, *his eyes gleaming maliciously, looks at them and then exclaims:*)

KING. Today, gentlemen, I shall not be the first to sit down! (*To his* SON, *with a comic bow*) You are the King, Sir. The honor belongs to you. Take the high chair. Today I shall wait on *you!*

QUEEN MOTHER (*with slight irritation*). My son!

KING. I know what I'm doing, Madam! (*With a sudden shout*) Go on, you great loon, look sharp! You're the King, but you're as stupid as ever!

(*The* BOY *flinches to avoid the blow he was expecting and goes to sit in the* KING's *chair, sly and rather ill at ease.*)

Take your places, gentlemen! I shall remain standing. Barons of England, here is your second King. For the good of our vast domains, a kingly colleague had become a necessity. Reviving an ancient custom, we have decided to have our successor crowned during our lifetime and to share our responsibilities with him. We ask you now to give him your homage and to honor him with the same title as Ourself.

(*He makes a sign. Two* SERVANTS *have brought in a haunch of venison on a silver charger. The* KING *serves his* SON.)

YOUNG QUEEN (*to her* SON). Sit up straight! And try to eat properly for once, now that you've been raised to glory!

KING (*grunting as he serves him*). He hasn't the face for it! He's a little slyboots and dim-witted at that. However, he'll be your King in good earnest one day, so you may as well get used to him. Besides it's the best I had to offer.

QUEEN MOTHER (*indignantly*). Really, my son! This game is unworthy of you and of us. You insisted on it—against my advice—at least play it with dignity!

KING (*rounding on her in fury*). I'll play the games that amuse me, Madam, and I'll play them the way I choose! This mummery, gentlemen, which is, incidentally, without any importance at all— (if your new King fidgets let me know, I'll give him a good kick up his train) — will at the very least have the appreciable result of showing our new friend, the Archbishop, that we can do without him. If there was one ancient privilege the Primacy clung to, tooth and nail, it was its exclusive right to anoint and consecrate the Kings of this realm. Well, it will be that old toad the Archbishop of York—with letters from the Pope authorizing him to do so—I paid the price!—who, tomorrow, will crown our son in the cathedral! What a joke that's going to be!

(*He roars with laughter amid the general silence.*)

What a tremendous, marvelous joke! I'd give anything to see that Archbishop's face when he has to swallow that! (*To his* SON) Get down from there, you imbecile! Go back to the bottom of the table and take your victuals with you! You aren't officially crowned until tomorrow.

(*The* boy *picks up his plate and goes back to his place, casting a cowed, smoldering look at his* father. *Watching him, says jovially*)

What a look! Filial sentiments are a fine thing to see, gentlemen! You'd like to be the real King, wouldn't you, you young pig? You'd like that number III after your name, eh, with Papa good and stiff under his catafalque! You'll have to wait a bit! Papa is well. Papa is very well indeed!

QUEEN MOTHER. My son, God knows I criticized your attempts at reconciliation with that wretch, who has done us nothing but harm . . . God knows I understand your hatred of him! But do not let it drag you into making a gesture you will regret, merely for the sake of wounding his pride. Henry is still a child. But you were not much older when you insisted on reigning by yourself, and in opposition to me. Ambitious self-seekers—and there is never any scarcity of those around Princes—can advise him, raise a faction against you and avail themselves of this hasty coronation to divide the Kingdom! Think it over, there is still time.

KING. We are still alive, Madam, and in control! And nothing can equal my pleasure in imagining my proud friend Becket's face when he sees the fundamental privilege of the Primacy whisked from under his nose! I let him cheat me out of one or two articles the other day, but I had something up my sleeve for him!

QUEEN MOTHER. Henry! I bore the weight of state affairs longer than you ever have. I have been your Queen and I am your mother. You are answerable for the interests of a great Kingdom, not for your moods. You already gave far too much away to the King of France, at La Ferté-Bernard. It is England you must think of, not your hatred—or disappointed love—for that man.

KING (*in a fury*). Disappointed love—disappointed love? What gives you the right, Madam, to meddle in my loves and hates?

QUEEN MOTHER. You have a rancor against the man which is neither healthy nor manly. The King your father dealt with his enemies faster and more summarily than that. He had them killed and said no more about it. If Thomas Becket were a faithless woman whom you still hankered after, you would act no differently. Sweet Jesu, tear him out of your heart once and for all!

(*She bawls suddenly:*)

Oh, if I were a man!

KING (*grinning*). Thanks be to God, Madam, he gave you dugs. Which I never personally benefited from. I suckled a peasant girl.

QUEEN MOTHER   (*acidly*). That is no doubt why you have remained so lumpish, my son.

YOUNG QUEEN.   And haven't I a say in the matter? I tolerated your mistresses, Sir, but do you expect me to tolerate everything? Have you ever stopped to think what kind of woman I am? I am tired of having my life encumbered with this man. Becket! Always Becket! Nobody ever talks about anything else here! He was almost less of a hindrance when you loved him. I am a woman. I am your wife and your Queen. I refuse to be treated like this! I shall complain to my father, the Duke of Aquitaine! I shall complain to my uncle, the Emperor! I shall complain to all the Kings of Europe, my cousins! I shall complain to God!

KING   (*shouting rather vulgarly*). I should start with God! Be off to your private chapel, Madam, and see if He's at home.

(*He turns to his mother, fuming.*)

And you, the other Madam, away to your chamber with your secret councilors and go and spin your webs! Get out, both of you! I can't stand the sight of you! I retch with boredom whenever I set eyes on you! And young Henry III too! Go on, get out!

(*He chases him out with kicks, yelling:*)

Here's my royal foot in your royal buttocks! And to the devil with my whole family, if he'll have you! Get out, all of you! Get out! Get out!

(*The* QUEENS *scurry out, with a great rustling of silks. He turns to the* BARONS *who all stand watching him, terror-stricken.*)

(*More calmly*) Let us drink, gentlemen. That's about all one can do in your company. Let us get drunk, like men, all night; until we roll under the table, in vomit and oblivion.

(*He fills their glasses and beckons them closer.*)

Ah, my four idiots! My faithful hounds! It's warm beside you, like being in a stable. Good sweat! Comfortable nothingness!

(*He taps their skulls.*)

Not the least little glimmer inside to spoil the fun. And to think that before he came I was like you! A good fat machine for belching after drink, for pissing, for mounting girls and punching heads. What the devil did you put into it, Becket, to stop the wheels from going round? (*Suddenly to the* 2ND BARON) Tell me, do you think sometimes, Baron?

2ND BARON.   Never, Sire. Thinking has never agreed with an Englishman. It's unhealthy. Besides, a gentleman has better things to do.

KING   (*sitting beside them, suddenly quite calm*). Drink up, gentlemen. That's always been considered a healthy thing to do.

(*He fills the goblets.*)

Has Becket landed? I'm told the sea has been too rough to cross these last few days.

1st baron   (*somberly*) . He has landed, Sire, despite the sea.

king.   Where?

1st baron.   On a deserted stretch of coast, near Sandwich.

king.   So God did not choose to drown him?

1st baron.   No.

king   (*he asks in his sly, brutish way*) . Was nobody there waiting for
him? There must be one or two men in England whom he can't call
his friends!

1st baron.   Yes. Gervase, Duke of Kent, Regnouf de Broc and Regnault
de Garenne were waiting for him. Gervase had said that if he dared to
land he'd cut off his head with his own hands. But the native Englishmen from all the coastal towns had armed themselves to form an escort
for the Archbishop. And the Dean of Oxford went to meet the Barons
and charged them not to cause bloodshed and make you look a traitor,
seeing that you had given the Archbishop a safe conduct.

king   (*soberly*) . Yes, I gave him a safe conduct.

1st baron.   All along the road to Canterbury, the peasants, the artisans
and the small shopkeepers came out to meet him, cheering him and
escorting him from village to village. Not a single rich man, not a single Norman, showed his face.

king.   Only the Saxons?

1st baron.   Poor people armed with makeshift shields and rusty lances.
Riffraff. Swarms of them though, all camping around Canterbury, to
protect him. (*Gloomily*) Who would have thought there were so many
people in England!

(*The* king *has remained prostrate without uttering a word. Now he suddenly jumps up and roars:*)

king.   A miserable wretch who ate my bread! A man I raised up from
nothing! A Saxon! A man loved! (*Shouting like a madman*) I loved
him! Yes, I loved him! And I believe I still do! Enough, O God!
Enough! Stop, stop, O God, I've had enough!

(*He flings himself down on the couch, sobbing hysterically; tearing at the
horsehair mattress with his teeth, and eating it. The* barons, *stupefied,
go nearer to him.*)

1st baron   (*timidly*) . Your Highness . . .

king   (*moaning, with his head buried in the mattress*) . I can do nothing! I'm as limp and useless as a girl! So long as he's alive, I'll never be
able to do a thing. I tremble before him astonished. And I am the
King! (*With a sudden cry*) Will no one rid me of him? A priest! A
priest who jeers at me and does me injury! Are there none but cowards
like myself around me? Are there no men left in England? Oh, my
heart! My heart is beating too fast to bear!

(*He lies, still as death on the torn mattress. The four* barons *stand around speechless. Suddenly, on a percussion instrument, there rises a rhythmic beating, a sort of muffled tom-tom which is at first only the agitated heart-beats of the* KING, *but which swells and grows more insistent. The four* BARONS *look at each other. Then they straighten, buckle their sword belts, pick up their helmets and go slowly out, leaving the* KING *alone with the muffled rhythm of the heartbeats, which will continue until the murder. The* KING *lies there prostrate, among the upturned benches, in the deserted hall. A torch splutters and goes out. He sits up, looks around, sees they have gone and suddenly realizes why. A wild, lost look comes into his eyes. A moment's pause then he collapses on the bed with a long broken moan.*)

KING. O my Thomas!

(*A second torch goes out. Total darkness. Only the steady throb of the heartbeats is heard. A dim light. The forest of pillars again. Canterbury Cathedral. Upstage a small alter, with three steps leading up to it, half screened by a grill. In a corner downstage* BECKET, *and the* YOUNG MONK, *who is helping him on with his vestments. Nearby, on a stool, the Archbishop's miter. The tall silver cross is leaning against a pillar.*)

BECKET. I must look my best today. Make haste.

(*The* MONK *fumbles with the vestments. The muffled tom-tom is heard distantly at first, then closer.*)

MONK. It's difficult with all those little laces. It wants a girl's hands.

BECKET (*softly*) . A man's hands are better, today. Never mind the laces. The alb, quickly. And the stole. And then the cope.

MONK (*conscientiously*) . If it's worth doing it's worth doing well.

BECKET. You're quite right. If it's worth doing it's worth doing well. Do up all the little laces, every one of them. God will give us time.

(*A pause. The* BOY *struggles manfully on, putting out his tongue in concentration. The throbbing grows louder.*)

(*Smiling*) Don't pull your tongue out like that!

(*He watches the* BOY *as he works away.*)

MONK (*sweating but content*) . There. That's all done. But I'd rather cleaned out our pigsty at home! It's not half such hard work!

BECKET. Now the alb.

(*A pause.*)

Were you fond of your pigs?

MONK (*his eyes lighting up*) . Yes, I was.

BECKET. At my father's house, we had some pigs too, when I was a child. (*Smiling*) We're two rough lads from Hastings, you and I! Give me the chasuble.

(BECKET *kisses the chasuble and slips it over his head. He looks at the* BOY *and says gently:*)

Do you miss your knife?

MONK.   Yes.

(*Pause.*)

Will it be today?

BECKET   (*gravely*). I think so, my son. Are you afraid?

MONK.   Oh, no. Not if we have time to fight. All I want is the chance to strike a few blows first; so I shan't have done nothing but receive them all my life. If I can kill one Norman first—just one, I don't want much —one for one, that will seem fair and right enough to me.

BECKET   (*with a kindly smile*). Are you so very set on killing one?

MONK.   One for one. After that, I don't much care if I *am* just a little grain of sand in the machine. Because I know that by putting more and more grains of sand in the machine, one day it will come grinding to a stop.

BECKET   (*gently*). And on that day, what then?

MONK.   We'll set a fine, new, well-oiled machine in the place of the old one and this time we'll put the Normans into it instead.

(*He asks, quite without irony:*)

That's what justice means, isn't it?

(BECKET *smiles and does not answer him.*)

BECKET.   Fetch me the miter.

(*He says quietly, as the* BOY *fetches it:*)

O Lord, You forbade Peter to strike a blow in the Garden of Olives. But I shall not deprive him of that joy. He has had too few joys in his short span on earth. (*To the* BOY) Now give me my silver cross. I must hold it.

MONK   (*passing it to him*). Lord, it's heavy! A good swipe with that and they'd feel it! My word, I wish I could have it!

BECKET   (*stroking his hair*). Lucky little Saxon! This black world will have been in order to the end, for you.

(*He straightens, grave once more.*)

There. I'm ready, all adorned for Your festivities, Lord. Do not, in this interval of waiting, let one last doubt enter my soul.

(*During this scene, the throbbing has grown louder. Now it mingles with a loud knocking on the door. A* PRIEST *runs in wildly.*)

PRIEST.   Your Grace! There are four armed men outside! They say they must see you on behalf of the King. I've barricaded the door but they're breaking it in! They've got hatchets! Quickly! You must go into the back of the church and have the choir gates closed! They're strong enough, they'll hold!

BECKET   (*calmly*). It is time for Vespers, William. Does one close the choir gates during Vespers? I never heard of such a thing.

PRIEST   (*nonplused*). I know, but . . .

BECKET.   Everything must be the way it should be. The choir gates will remain open. Come, boy, let us go up to the altar. This is no place to be.

(*He goes toward the altar, followed by the* YOUNG MONK. *A great crash. The door has given way. The four* BARONS *come in, in their helmets. They fling down their hatchets and draw their swords.* BECKET *turns to face them, grave and calm, at the foot of the altar. They stop a moment, uncertain and disconcerted; four statues, huge and threatening. The tomtom has stopped. There is nothing now but a heavy silence.* BECKET *says simply:*)

Here it comes. The supreme folly. This is its hour.

(*He holds their eyes. They dare not move. He says coldly:*)

One does not enter armed into God's house. What do you want?

1ST BARON   (*thickly*) . Your death.

(*A pause.*)

2ND BARON   (*thickly*) . You bring shame to the King. Flee the country or you're a dead man.

BECKET   (*softly*) . It is time for the service.

(*He turns to the altar and faces the tall crucifix without paying any further attention to them. The throbbing starts again, muffled. The four* MEN *close in like automata. The* YOUNG MONK *suddenly leaps forward brandishing the heavy silver cross in order to protect* BECKET, *but one of the* BARONS *swings his sword and fells him to the ground.* BECKET *murmurs, as if in reproach:*)

Not even one! It would have given him so much pleasure, Lord. (*With a sudden cry*) Oh how difficult You make it all! And how heavy Your honor is to bear!

(*He adds, very quietly:*)

Poor Henry.

(*The four* MEN *hurl themselves onto him. He falls at the first blow. They hack at his body, grunting like woodcutters. The* PRIEST *has fled with a long scream, which echoes in the empty cathedral.*
Blackout.
On the same spot. The KING, *naked, on bended knees at* BECKET's *tomb, as in the first scene. Four* MONKS *are whipping him with ropes, almost duplicating the gestures of the* BARONS *as they killed* BECKET.)

KING   (*crying out*) . Are you satisfied now, Becket? Does this settle our account? Has the honor of God been washed clean?

(*The four* MONKS *finish beating him, then kneel down and bow their heads. The* KING *mutters—one feels it is part of the ceremony:*)

Thank you. Yes, yes, of course, it was agreed, I forgive you. Many thanks.

(*The* PAGE *comes forward with a vast cloak, which the* KING *wraps around himself. The* BARONS *surround the* KING *and help him to dress, while the*

BISHOPS *and the* CLERGY, *forming a procession, move away solemnly up-stage to the strains of the organ. The* KING *dresses hurriedly, with evident bad temper, aided by his* BARONS. *He grimaces ill-humoredly and growls:*) The pigs! The Norman Bishops just went through the motions, but those little Saxon monks—my word, they had their money's worth!
(*A* BARON *comes in. A joyful peal of bells is heard.*)

BARON.   Sire, the operation has been successful! The Saxon mob is yelling with enthusiasm outside the cathedral, acclaiming your Majesty's name in the same breath as Becket's! If the Saxons are on our side now, Prince Henry's followers look as though they have definitely lost the day.

KING   (*with a touch of hypocritical majesty beneath his slightly loutish manner*).   The honor of God, gentlemen, is a very good thing, and taken all in all, one gains by having it on one's side. Thomas Becket, who was our friend, used to say so. England will owe her ultimate victory over chaos to him, and it is our wish that, henceforward, he should be honored and prayed to in this Kingdom as a saint. Come, gentlemen. We will determine, tonight, in Council, what posthumous honors to render him and what punishment to deal out to his murderers.

1ST BARON   (*imperturbably*).   Sire, they are unknown.

KING   (*inpenetrably*).   Our justice will seek them out, Baron, and you will be specially entrusted with this inquiry, so that no one will be in any doubt as to our Royal desire to defend the honor of God and the memory of our friend from this day forward.

(*The organ swells triumphantly, mingled with the sound of the bells and the cheering of the crowds as they file out.*)

WRITING A PLAY ABOUT BECKET

JEAN ANOUILH

I am not a serious man, I wrote *Becket* by chance. I had bought on the quays of the Seine—where, in curious little stalls set up on the parapet, old gentlemen of another age sell old books to other old gentlemen and to the very young—*The Conquest of England by the Normans*, by Augustin Thierry, an historian of the Romantic school, forgotten today and scrapped; for history, too, has its fashions.

I did not expect to read this respectable work, which I assumed would be boring. I had bought it because it had a pretty green binding and I needed a spot of green on my shelves. All the same, when I returned home I skimmed through the book (I am well-mannered with old books) and I happened upon the chapters that tell the story of Becket, some thirty pages, which one might have taken to be fiction except that the bottoms of the pages were jammed with references in Latin from the chroniclers of the twelfth century.

I was dazzled. I had expected to find a saint—I am always a trifle distrustful of saints, as I am of great theatre stars—and I found a man.

The idea of writing a play about it skirted my mind, as the idea to become a fencing champion had done in my childhood. Just as I was reminding myself that I was not a serious man and that probably this was not for me, the telephone rang. I began to exchange the latest news about a family that held for me not the faintest glimmer of interest; then I was told that dinner was served and at the same time I would have to take strong measures against my son who had just laid low both his sisters with his bare fists; I was reminded at the same time of the evening mail, which contained letters from two spongers and three actresses (the three who were miraculously destined to play all the feminine leads in my plays); then came a sinister gray envelope, a note from my tax collector . . . I completely forgot about Becket.

The following winter, green decidedly did not look well on my shelves in Paris and I bought an admirable red Balzac, first edition; I took *The Conquest of England by the Normans* to a mountain chalet where the shelves were a little empty.

One evening I was playing a game of solitaire, a game that for twenty years I have failed to bring off: my young wife, wearied by the endless spectacle of my failures, the extent of which she is only partially aware, decided to go up to bed and asked me for a book with which to read herself to sleep. I removed one of the green volumes on the shelves behind me and told her, "Read the story of Becket, it is beautiful," and I continued to fail at my solitaire, a gauge of my serenity and self-confidence. (The day that I succeed, the shock will be so great that I will probably have to be locked up in a psychiatric ward.)

An hour passed by the tick-tock of the Swiss cuckoo clock I have taught to play mischief with time; and I was in a state of remorse over that extra shot of whiskey and those last cigarettes of the day; the ones that will probably kill you in the end, which in fact no longer give you any pleasure. My wife appeared at the top of the stairs in her pajamas. She had tears in her eyes.

I was about to defend myself when I realized the tears had actually nothing to do with me. She simply told me (and I can still recall the emotion expressed in her face at that moment), "Oh, how beautiful it is! Why don't you make a play of it? It's absolutely you!"

I muttered something; I went up to bed and the next day at 8 o'clock I started, without a plan, to write the first word. Everything was marshaled in my mind. It was already written, I had only to copy it out. In fifteen happy days I finished the first part.

Then I returned to Paris, where I have never written anything; except my first play, necessitated by poverty, and that play, incidentally, provided me with the means for writing my second one in the country.

In the meantime, life went on as usual in Paris; rehearsals for another play; the doubt came back. The second part of Becket was undoable. The troubles between the Pope and the king of France; this undercurrent conflict that lasted through seven years of exile, ending in the sham reconciliation on the plain at Ferté-Bernard and finally death in the cathedral, a subject already magnificently treated by Eliot. This was certainly not for me.

The following summer, having left Paris, I started a short play, *The Fair at Empoigne,* which will be produced this winter by Jean-Louis Barrault. I completed it very easily. I felt myself in good form, my appetite whetted rather than satiated by the work. Talent is like a faucet; while it is open, one must write. Inspiration is a farce that poets have invented to give themselves importance. It was still only the middle of the summer and it was absolutely necessary that I write something else.

My wife reappeared, this time smiling, on the threshold of the bottom of the garden of a house we had rented on a beach in the Landes. She said to me simply but firmly: "You are ridiculous; finish *Becket.*"

I have always feared ridicule; and for this specific reason and, incidentally, to please her, I started the very next day on the second part of the play, a scene with some facile comedy lines that I habitually write to give myself courage and to prove to myself that the work is, after all, not as important as one would like to pretend. Things fell into their place of themselves, and in fifteen days I finished *Becket.*

Altogether shamefaced at the idea of having written an historical play, I gave it to an historian friend of mine to read, and he roared with laughter, saying: "Are you unaware that history, like everything else on this earth, makes progress? In Augustin Thierry's time one could believe that Becket was of Saxon origin; but for over fifty years we have had proof that he was a good Norman. He was from the vicinity of Rouen and was in fact called Bequet."

A large part of the subject of my play was based on the fact that Becket was of the vanquished race. A serious man at this point would have torn out his hair; then he would have rewritten his play on a more exact historical basis.

I decided that if history in the next fifty years should go on making progress it will perhaps rediscover that Becket was indubitably of Saxon origin; in any case, for this drama of friendship between two men, between the king and his friend, his companion in pleasure and in work (and this is what gripped me about the story), this friend whom he could not cease to love though he became his worst enemy the night he was named archbishop—for this drama it was a thousand times better that Becket remained a Saxon.

I changed nothing; I had the play performed three months later in Paris. It had a great success and I noticed that no one except my historian friend was aware of the progress of history.

All this was part and parcel of my increasingly involved technique for unsuccessful solitaire, which has been protecting me for close to thirty years against the extreme hazards of this profession.

ALBEE

EDWARD ALBEE (1928–   ) WAS STILL AN INFANT WHEN HE WAS ADOPTED BY THE SON AND HEIR OF THEATER OWNER E. F. ALBEE. SENT TO LAWRENCEVILLE AND CHOATE, AND TO TRINITY COLLEGE, WHERE HE REMAINED FOR A YEAR AND A HALF, HE BECAME ALIENATED FROM THE LIFE OF UPPER-CLASS SUBURBIA. AT TWENTY HE LEFT HOME AND SECURITY TO LIVE IN NEW YORK AND WRITE POETRY, EXISTING FOR A DECADE ON A SMALL INHERITANCE WHOSE INCOME HE AUGMENTED BY WORKING AT MENIAL JOBS. AT TWENTY-NINE, HE WROTE HIS FIRST PLAY, *THE ZOO STORY.* PREMIERED IN BERLIN IN 1959, IT WAS PRO-DUCED IN NEW YORK THE FOLLOWING YEAR, ESTABLISHING ALBEE AS A MAN OF THE THEATER. HIS SUBSEQUENT WORK HAS INCLUDED *THE AMERICAN DREAM* (1960); *WHO'S AFRAID OF VIRGINIA WOOLF?* (1962); *TINY ALICE* (1965); AND *A DELICATE BALANCE* (1966), WHICH WAS AWARDED THE PULITZER PRIZE IN 1967.

The Zoo Story, however it is interpreted, is a work of extraordinary compassion and pathos. The description in the stage directions of Jerry anticipates and illuminates the catastrophe which concludes the play. He is obviously a hustler, a man whose precarious livelihood depends on gratuities given in return for sexual services. But how does Albee protect him from our contempt? How does Albee evoke our compassion?

The title *The Zoo Story* is clearly close to the thematic center of the play. Is it possible that Jerry has come to understand that the circum-stances of his life have isolated and encaged him? Do not the experiences with his landlady and her dog bring him to a realization of what his life has been, and what it might have been and what it now can never be-come? Jerry is a man who has been offered love but who has never ac-cepted love. How is the fact that he is emotionally crippled made mani-fest?

Peter's function in the play does not become entirely clear until the very last few moments. Then we are aware that *The Zoo Story* has to do with expiation, redemption, and vicarious atonement. Does such a theme seem suitable or grotesque, involving, as it would seem, an en-counter between an unsavory "transient" and a self-satisfied member of the establishment?

The Zoo Story has been related to the theater of the absurd, to the new drama which rejects the realism of Ibsen and Chekhov. To what ex-tent does *The Zoo Story* seem to differ in technique from other plays in this anthology? We note that even though *The Zoo Story* is a work which evokes our compassion, causing us to say: "Oh, the pity of it," it is intentionally comic. The new theater, whose principal exponents are Samuel Beckett, Eugene Ionesco, Jean Genêt, and Michel de Ghelde-rode, expresses the sense of the absurdity of human existence through "black comedy." Could we begin to formulate a description of new direc-tions in the theater from an analysis of *The Zoo Story?*

THE ZOO STORY

THE PLAYERS

PETER: *A man in his early forties, neither fat nor gaunt, neither handsome nor homely. He wears tweeds, smokes a pipe, carries horn-rimmed glasses. Although he is moving into middle age, his dress and his manner would suggest a man younger.*

JERRY: *A man in his late thirties, not poorly dressed, but carelessly. What was once a trim and lightly muscled body has begun to go to fat; and while he is no longer handsome, it is evident that he once was. His fall from physical grace should not suggest debauchery; he has, to come closest to it, a great weariness.*

The Scene: It is Central Park; a Sunday afternoon in summer; the present. There are two park benches, one toward either side of the stage; they both face the audience. Behind them: foliage, trees, sky. At the beginning, Peter is seated on one of the benches.

(Stage Directions: As the curtain rises, Peter is seated on the bench stage-right. He is reading a book. He stops reading, cleans his glasses, goes back to reading. Jerry enters.)

JERRY. I've been to the zoo. (PETER *doesn't notice.*) I said, I've been to the zoo. MISTER, I'VE BEEN TO THE ZOO!

PETER. Hm? . . . What? . . . I'm sorry, were you talking to me?

JERRY. I went to the zoo, and then I walked until I came here. Have I been walking north?

PETER *(puzzled)*. North? Why . . . I . . . I think so. Let me see.

JERRY *(pointing past the audience)*. Is that Fifth Avenue?

PETER. Why yes; it is.

JERRY. And what is that cross street there; that one, to the right?

PETER. That? Oh, that's Seventy-fourth Street.

JERRY. And the zoo is around Sixty-fifth Street; so, I've been walking north.

PETER *(anxious to get back to his reading)*. Yes; it would seem so.

JERRY. Good old north.

PETER *(lightly, by reflex)*. Ha, ha.

JERRY *(after a slight pause)*. But not due north.

PETER. I . . . well, no, not due north; but, we . . . call it north. It's northerly.

JERRY *(watches as* PETER, *anxious to dismiss him, prepares his pipe)*. Well, boy; you're not going to get lung cancer, are you?

PETER *(looks up, a little annoyed, then smiles)*. No, sir. Not from this.

JERRY. No, sir. What you'll probably get is cancer of the mouth, and then you'll have to wear one of those things Freud wore after they took one whole side of his jaw away. What do they call those things?

PETER (*uncomfortable*). A prosthesis?

JERRY. The very thing! A prosthesis. You're an educated man, aren't you? Are you a doctor?

PETER. Oh, no; no. I read about it somewhere; *Time* magazine I think. (*He turns to his book.*)

JERRY. Well, *Time* magazine isn't for blockheads.

PETER. No. I suppose not.

JERRY (*after a pause*). Boy, I'm glad that's Fifth Avenue there.

PETER (*vaguely*). Yes.

JERRY. I don't like the west side of the park much.

PETER. Oh? (*Then, slightly wary, but interested*) Why?

JERRY (*offhand*). I don't know.

PETER. Oh. (*He returns to his book*).

JERRY (*He stands for a few seconds, looking at* PETER, *who finally looks up again, puzzled*). Do you mind if we talk?

PETER (*obviously minding*). Why . . . no, no.

JERRY. Yes you do; you do.

PETER (*puts his book down, his pipe out and away, smiling*). No, really; I don't mind.

JERRY. Yes you do.

PETER (*finally decided*). No; I don't mind at all, really.

JERRY. It's . . . it's a nice day.

PETER (*stares unnecessarily at the sky*). Yes. Yes, it is; lovely.

JERRY. I've been to the zoo.

PETER. Yes, I think you said so . . . didn't you?

JERRY. You'll read about it in the papers tomorrow, if you don't see it on your TV tonight. You have TV, haven't you?

PETER. Why yes, we have two; one for the children.

JERRY. You're married!

PETER (*with pleased emphasis*). Why, certainly.

JERRY. It isn't a law, for God's sake.

PETER. No . . . no, of course not.

JERRY. And you have a wife.

PETER (*bewildered by the seeming lack of communication*). Yes!

JERRY. And you have children.

PETER. Yes; two.

JERRY. Boys?

PETER. No, girls . . . both girls.

JERRY. But you wanted boys.

PETER. Well . . . naturally, every man wants a son, but . . .

JERRY (*lightly mocking*). But that's the way the cookie crumbles?

PETER (*annoyed*). I wasn't going to say that.

JERRY. And you're not going to have any more kids, are you?

PETER *(a bit distantly)*. No. No more. *(Then back, and irksome)* Why did you say that? How would you know about that?

JERRY. The way you cross your legs, perhaps; something in the voice. Or maybe I'm just guessing. Is it your wife?

PETER *(furious)*. That's none of your business! *(A silence)* Do you understand? *(JERRY nods.* PETER *is quiet now)* Well, you're right. We'll have no more children.

JERRY *(softly)*. That *is* the way the cookie crumbles.

PETER *(forgiving)*. Yes . . . I guess so.

JERRY. Well, now; what else?

PETER. What were you saying about the zoo . . . that I'd read about it, or see . . . ?

JERRY. I'll tell you about it, soon. Do you mind if I ask you questions?

PETER. Oh, not really.

JERRY. I'll tell you why I do it; I don't talk to many people—except to say like: give me a beer, or where's the john, or what time does the feature go on, or keep your hands to yourself, buddy. You know—things like that.

PETER. I must say I don't . . .

JERRY. But every once in a while I like to talk to somebody, really *talk;* like to get to know somebody, know all about him.

PETER *(Lightly laughing, still a little uncomfortable)*. And am I the guinea pig for today?

JERRY. On a sun-drenched Sunday afternoon like this? Who better than a nice married man with two daughters and *,* . . uh . . . a dog? *(PETER shakes his head)* No? Two dogs. *(PETER shakes his head again)* Hm. No dogs? *(PETER shakes his head, sadly)* Oh, that's a shame. But you look like an animal man. CATS? *(PETER nods his head, ruefully)* Cats! But, that can't be your idea. No, sir. Your wife and daughters? *(PETER nods his head)* Is there anything else I should know?

PETER *(He has to clear his throat.)* There are . . . there are two para-keets. One . . . uh . . . one for each of my daughters.

JERRY. Birds.

PETER. My daughters keep them in a cage in their bedroom.

JERRY. Do they carry disease? The birds.

PETER. I don't believe so.

JERRY. That's too bad. If they did you could set them loose in the house and the cats could eat them and die, maybe. *(PETER looks blank for a moment, then laughs)* And what else? What do you do to support your enormous household?

PETER. I . . . uh . . . I have an executive position with a . . . a small publishing house. We . . . uh . . . we publish textbooks.

JERRY. That sounds nice; very nice. What do you make?

PETER   (*still cheerful*) . Now look here!

JERRY.   Oh, come on.

PETER.   Well, I make around eighteen thousand a year, but I don't carry
more than forty dollars at any one time . . . in case you're a . . . a
holdup man . . . ha, ha, ha.

JERRY   (*ignoring the above*) . Where do you live? (PETER *is reluctant*)
Oh, look; I'm not going to rob you, and I'm not going to kidnap
your parakeets, your cats, or your daughters.

PETER   (*too loud*) . I live between Lexington and Third Avenue, on
Seventy-fourth Street.

JERRY.   That wasn't so hard, was it?

PETER.   I didn't mean to seem . . . ah . . . it's that you don't really
carry on a conversation; you just ask questions. and I'm . . . I'm normally . . . uh . . . reticent. Why do you just stand there?

JERRY.   I'll start walking around in a little while, and eventually I'll sit
down. (*Recalling*) Wait until you see the expression on his face.

PETER.   What? Whose face? Look here; is this something about the zoo?

JERRY   (*distantly*) . The what?

PETER.   The zoo; the zoo. Something about the zoo.

JERRY.   The zoo?

PETER.   You've mentioned it several times.

JERRY   (*still distant, but returning abruptly*) . The zoo? Oh, yes; the
zoo. I was there before I came here. I told you that. Say, what's the
dividing line between upper-middle-middle-class and lower-upper-
middle-class?

PETER.   My dear fellow, I . . .

JERRY.   Don't my dear fellow me.

PETER   (*unhappily*) . Was I patronizing? I believe I was; I'm sorry. But,
you see, your question about the classes bewildered me.

JERRY.   And when you're bewildered you become patronizing?

PETER.   I . . . I don't express myself too well, sometimes. (*He attempts
a joke on himself*) I'm in publishing, not writing.

JERRY   (*amused, but not at the humor*) . So be it. The truth *is: I* was
being patronizing.

PETER.   Oh, now; you needn't say that.

(*It is at this point that* JERRY *may begin to move about the stage with
slowly increasing determination and authority, but pacing himself, so
that the long speech about the dog comes at the high point of the arc.*)

JERRY.   All right. Who are your favorite writers? Baudelaire and J. P.
Marquand?

PETER   (*wary*) . Well, I like a great many writers; I have a considerable
. . . catholicity of taste, if I may say so. Those two men are fine, each
in his way. (*Warming up.*) Baudelaire, of course . . . uh . . . is by

far the finer of the two, but Marquand has a place . . . in our . . . uh . . . national . . .

JERRY.   Skip it.

PETER.   I . . . sorry.

JERRY.   Do you know what I did before I went to the zoo today? I walked all the way up Fifth Avenue from Washington Square; all the way.

PETER.   Oh; you live in the Village! (*This seems to enlighten* PETER.)

JERRY.   No, I don't. I took the subway down to the Village so I could walk all the way up Fifth Avenue to the zoo. It's one of those things a person has to do; sometimes a person has to go a very long distance out of his way to come back a short distance correctly.

PETER   (*Almost pouting*). Oh, I thought you lived in the Village.

JERRY.   What were you trying to do? Make sense out of things? Bring order? The old pigeonhole bit? Well, that's easy; I'll tell you. I live in a four-story brownstone roominghouse on the upper West Side between Columbus Avenue and Central Park West. I live on the top floor; rear; west. It's a laughably small room, and one of my walls is made of beaverboard; this beaverboard separates my room from another laughably small room, so I assume that the two rooms were once one room, a small room, but not necessarily laughable. The room beyond my beaverboard wall is occupied by a colored queen who always keeps his door open; well, not always, but *always* when he's plucking his eyebrows, which he does with Buddhist concentration. This colored queen has rotten teeth, which is rare, and he has a Japanese kimono, which is also pretty rare; and he wears this kimono to and from the john in the hall, which is pretty frequent. I mean, he goes to the john a lot. He never bothers me, and he never brings anyone up to his room. All he does is pluck his eyebrows, wear his kimono and go to the john. Now, the two front rooms on my floor are a little larger, I guess; but they're pretty small, too. There's a Puerto Rican family in one of them, a husband, a wife, and some kids; I don't know how many. These people entertain a lot. And in the other front room, there's somebody living there, but I don't know who it is. I've never seen who it is. Never. Never ever.

PETER   (*embarrassed*). Why . . . why do you live there?

JERRY   (*from a distance again*). I don't know.

PETER.   It doesn't sound like a very nice place . . . where you live.

JERRY.   Well, no; it isn't an apartment in the East Seventies. But, then again, I don't have one wife, two daughters, two cats and two parakeets. What I do have, I have toilet articles, a few clothes, a hot plate that I'm not supposed to have, a can opener, one that works with a key, you know; a knife, two forks, and two spoons, one small, one large; three plates, a cup, a saucer, a drinking glass, two picture frames, both empty, eight or nine books, a pack of pornographic playing cards, regular deck, an old Western Union typewriter that prints nothing but capital letters, and a small strongbox without a lock which has in it . . . what? Rocks! Some rocks . . . sea-rounded rocks I picked up on the beach when I was a kid. Under which . . . weighed down . . . are some letters . . . please letters . . . please why don't you do this, and please when will you do that letters. And when letters, too. When will you write? When will you come? When? These letters are from more recent years.

PETER *(stares glumly at his shoes, then)*. About those two empty picture frames . . . ?

JERRY. I don't see why they need any explanation at all. Isn't it clear? I don't have pictures of anyone to put in them.

PETER. Your parents . . . perhaps . . . a girl friend . . .

JERRY. You're a very sweet man, and you're possessed of a truly enviable innocence. But good old Mom and good old Pop are dead . . . you know? . . . I'm broken up about it, too . . . I mean really. BUT. That particular vaudeville act is playing the cloud circuit now, so I don't see how I can look at them, all neat and framed. Besides, or, rather, to be pointed about it, good old Mom walked out on good old Pop when I was ten and a half years old; she embarked on an adulterous turn of our southern states . . . a journey of a year's duration . . . and her most constant companion . . . among others, among many others . . . was a Mr. Barleycorn. At least, that's what good old Pop told me after he went down . . . came back . . . brought her body north. We'd received the news between Christmas and New Year's, you see, that good old Mom had parted with the ghost in some dump in Alabama. And, without the ghost . . . she was less welcome. I mean, what was she? A stiff . . . a northern stiff. At any rate, good old Pop celebrated the New Year for an even two weeks and then slapped into the front of a somewhat moving city omnibus, which sort of cleaned things out family-wise. Well no; then there was Mom's sister, who was given neither to sin nor the consolations of the bottle. I moved in on her, and my memory of her is slight excepting I remember still that she did all things dourly: sleeping, eating, working, praying. She dropped dead on the stairs to her apartment, my apartment then, too, on the afternoon of my high school graduation. A terribly middle-European joke, if you ask me.

PETER. Oh, my; oh, my.

JERRY. Oh, your what? But that was a long time ago, and I have no feeling about any of it that I care to admit to myself. Perhaps you can see, though, why good old Mom and good old Pop are frameless. What's your name? Your first name?

PETER. I'm Peter.

JERRY. I'd forgotten to ask you. I'm Jerry.

PETER *(with a slight, nervous laugh)*. Hello, Jerry.

JERRY *(nods his hello)*. And let's see now; what's the point of having a girl's picture, especially in two frames? I have two picture frames, you remember. I never see the pretty little ladies more than once, and most of them wouldn't be caught in the same room with a camera. It's odd, and I wonder if it's sad.

PETER. The girls?

JERRY. No. I wonder if it's sad that I never see the little ladies more than once. I've never been able to have sex with, or, how is it put? . . . make love to anybody more than once. Once; that's it. . . . Oh, wait; for a week and a half, when I was fifteen . . . and I hang my head in shame that puberty was late . . . I was a h-o-m-o-s-e-x-u-a-l. I mean, I was queer . . . *(Very fast)* . . . queer, queer, queer . . . with bells ringing, banners snapping in the wind. And for those eleven days, I met at least twice a day with the park superintendent's son . . . a Greek boy, whose birthday was the same as mine, except he was a year older. I think I was very much in love . . . maybe just with sex. But that was the jazz of a very special hotel, wasn't it? And now; oh, do I love the little ladies; really, I love them. For about an hour.

PETER. Well, it seems perfectly simple to me. . . .

JERRY *(angry)*. Look! Are you going to tell me to get married and have parakeets?

PETER *(angry himself)*. Forget the parakeets! And stay single if you want to. It's no business of mine. I didn't start this conversation in the . . .

JERRY. All right, all right. I'm sorry. All right? You're not angry?

PETER *(laughing)*. No, I'm not angry.

JERRY *(relieved)*. Good. *(Now back to his previous tone)* Interesting that you asked me about the picture frames. I would have thought that you would have asked me about the pornographic playing cards.

PETER *(with a knowing smile)*. Oh, I've seen those cards.

JERRY. That's not the point. *(Laughs)* I suppose when you were a kid you and your pals passed them around, or you had a pack of your own.

PETER. Well, I guess a lot of us did.

JERRY. And you threw them away just before you got married.

PETER. Oh, now; look here. I didn't *need* anything like that when I got older.

JERRY. No?

PETER *(embarrassed)*. I'd rather not talk about these things.

JERRY. So? Don't. Besides, I wasn't trying to plumb your post-adolescent sexual life and hard times; what I wanted to get at is the value difference between pornographic playing cards when you're a kid, and pornographic playing cards when you're older. It's that when you're a kid you use the cards as a substitute for a real experience, and when you're older you use real experience as a substitute for the fantasy. But I imagine you'd rather hear about what happened at the zoo.

PETER (*enthusiastic*). Oh, yes; the zoo. (*Then, awkward*) That is . . . if you. . . .

JERRY. Let me tell you about why I went . . . well, let me tell you some things. I've told you about the fourth floor of the roominghouse where I live. I think the rooms are better as you go down, floor by floor. I guess they are; I don't know. I don't know any of the people on the third and second floors. Oh, wait! I do know that there's a lady living on the third floor, in the front. I know because she cries all the time. Whenever I go out or come back in, whenever I pass her door, I always hear her crying, muffled, but . . . very determined. Very determined indeed. But the one I'm getting to, and all about the dog, is the landlady. I don't like to use words that are too harsh in describing people. I don't like to. But the landlady is a fat, ugly, mean, stupid, unwashed, misanthropic, cheap drunken bag of garbage. And you may have noticed that I very seldom use profanity, so I can't describe her as well as I might.

PETER. You describe her . . . vividly.

JERRY. Well, thanks. Anyway, she has a dog, and I will tell you about the dog, and she and her dog are the gatekeepers of my dwelling. The woman is bad enough; she leans around in the entrance hall, spying to see that I don't bring in things or people, and when she's had her mid-afternoon pint of lemon-flavored gin she always stops me in the hall, and grabs ahold of my coat or my arm, and she presses her disgusting body up against me to keep me in a corner so she can talk to me. The smell of her body and her breath . . . you can't imagine it . . . and somewhere, somewhere in the back of that pea-sized brain of hers, an organ developed just enough to let her eat, drink, and emit, she has some foul parody of sexual desire. And I, Peter, I am the object of her sweaty lust.

PETER. That's disgusting. That's . . . horrible.

JERRY. But I have found a way to keep her off. When she talks to me, when she presses herself to my body and mumbles about her room and how I should come there, I merely say: but, Love; wasn't yesterday enough for you, and the day before? Then she puzzles, she makes slits of her tiny eyes, she sways a little, and then, Peter . . . and it is at this moment that I think I might be doing some good in that tormented house . . . a simple-minded smile begins to form on her unthinkable face, and she giggles and groans as she thinks about yesterday and the day before; as she believes and relives what never happened. Then, she motions to that black monster of a dog she has, and she goes back to her room. And I am safe until our next meeting.

PETER. It's so . . . unthinkable. I find it hard to believe that people such as that really *are*.

JERRY *(lightly mocking)*. It's for reading about, isn't it?

PETER *(seriously)*. Yes.

JERRY. And fact is better left to fiction. You're right, Peter. Well, what I have been meaning to tell you about is the dog; I shall, now.

PETER *(nervously)*. Oh, yes; the dog.

JERRY. Don't go. You're not thinking of going, are you?

PETER. Well . . . no, I don't think so.

JERRY *(as if to a child)*. Because after I tell you about the dog, do you know what then? Then . . . then I'll tell you about what happened at the zoo.

PETER *(laughing faintly)*. You're . . . you're full of stories, aren't you?

JERRY. You don't *have* to listen. Nobody is holding you here; remember that. Keep that in your mind.

PETER *(irritably)*. I know that.

JERRY. You do? Good.

(The following long speech, it seems to me, should be done with a great deal of action, to achieve a hypnotic effect on PETER, *and on the audience, too. Some specific actions have been suggested, but the director and the actor playing* JERRY *might best work it out for themselves.)*

ALL RIGHT. *(As if reading from a huge billboard)* THE STORY OF JERRY AND THE DOG! *(Natural again)* What I am going to tell you has something to do with how sometimes it's necessary to go a long distance out of the way in order to come back a short distance correctly; or, maybe I only think that it has something to do with that. But, it's why I went to the zoo today, and why I walked north . . . northerly, rather . . . until I came here. All right. The dog, I think I told you, is a black monster of a beast: an oversized head, tiny, tiny ears, and eyes . . . bloodshot, infected, maybe; and a body you can see the ribs through the skin. The dog is black, all black; all black except for the bloodshot eyes, and . . . yes . . . and an open sore on its . . . *right* forepaw; that is red, too. And, oh yes; the poor monster, and I do believe it's an old dog . . . it's certainly a misused one . . . almost always has an erection . . . of sorts. That's red, too. And . . . what else? . . . oh, yes; there's a gray-yellow-white color, too, when he bares his fangs. Like this: Grrrrrr! Which is what he did when he saw me for the first time . . . the day I moved in. I worried about that animal the very first minute I met him. Now, animals don't take to me like Saint Francis had birds hanging off him all the time. What I mean is:

animals are indifferent to me . . . like people (*He smiles slightly*)
. . . most of the time. But this dog wasn't indifferent. From the very
beginning he'd snarl and then go for me, to get one of my legs. Not
like he was rabid, you know; he was sort of a stumbly dog, but he
wasn't half-assed, either. It was a good, stumbly run; but I always
got away. He got a piece of my trouser leg, look, you can see right
here, where it's mended; he got that the second day I lived there; but,
I kicked free and got upstairs fast, so that was that. (*Puzzles*) I still
don't know to this day how the other roomers manage it, but you
know what I *think:* I think it had to do only with me. Cozy. So. Anyway, this went on for over a week, whenever I came in; but never
when I went out. That's funny. Or, it *was* funny. I could pack up and
live in the street for all the dog cared. Well, I thought about it up in
my room one day, one of the times after I'd bolted upstairs, and I
made up my mind. I decided: First, I'll kill the dog with kindnss, and
if that doesn't work . . . I'll just kill him. (PETER *winces*) Don't react
Peter; just listen. So, the next day I went out and bought a bag of
hamburgers, medium rare, no catsup, no onion; and on the way home
I threw away all the rolls and kept just the meat.
(*Action for the following, perhaps*)
When I got back to the roominghouse the dog was waiting for me. I
half opened the door that led into the entrance hall, and there he was;
waiting for me. It figured. I went in, very cautiously, and I had the
hamburgers, you remember; I opened the bag, and I set the meat down
about twelve feet from where the dog was snarling at me. Like so! He
snarled; stopped snarling; sniffed; moved slowly; then faster, then
faster toward the meat. Well, when he got to it he stopped, and he
looked at me. I smiled; but tentatively, you understand. He turned his
face back to the hamburgers, smelled, sniffed some more, and then . . .
RRRAAAAGGGGGHHHH, like that . . . he tore into them. It was
as if he had never eaten anything in his life before, except like garbage.
Which might very well have been the truth. I don't think the landlady
ever eats anything but garbage. But. He ate all the hamburgers, almost
all at once, making sounds in his throat like a woman. *Then,* when
he'd finished the meat, the hamburger, and tried to eat the paper,
too, he sat down and smiled. I think he smiled; I know cats do. It was
a very gratifying few moments. Then, BAM, he snarled and made for
me again. He didn't get me this time, either. So, I got upstairs, and I
lay down on my bed and started to think about the dog again. To be
truthful, I was offended, and I was damn mad, too. It was six perfectly
good hamburgers with not enough pork in them to make it disgusting.
I was offended. But, after a while, I decided to try it for a few more
days. If you think about it, this dog had what amounted to an antip-

athy toward me; really. And I wondered if I mightn't overcome this antipathy. So, I tried it for five more days, but it was always the same: snarl, sniff; move; faster; stare; gobble; RAAGGGHHH; smile; snarl; BAM. Well, now; by this time Columbus Avenue was strewn with hamburger rolls and I was less offended than disgusted. So, I decided to kill the dog.

(PETER *raises a hand in protest*)

Oh, don't be so alarmed, Peter; I didn't succeed. The day I tried to kill the dog I bought only one hamburger and what I thought was a murderous portion of rat poison. When I bought the hamburger I asked the man not to bother with the roll, all I wanted was the meat. I expected some reaction from him, like: we don't sell no hamburgers without rolls; or, wha' d'ya wanna do, eat it out'a ya han's? But no; he smiled benignly, wrapped up the hamburger in waxed paper, and said: A bite for ya pussy-cat? I wanted to say: No, not really; it's part of a plan to poison a dog I know. But, you can't say "a dog I know" without sounding funny; so I said, a little too loud, I'm afraid, and too formally: YES, A BITE FOR MY PUSSY-CAT. People looked up. It always happens when I try to simplify things; people look up. But that's neither hither nor thither. So. On my way back to the rooming-house, I kneaded the hamburger and the rat poison together between my hands, at that point feeling as much sadness as disgust. I opened the door to the entrance hall. and there the monster was, waiting to take the offering and then jump me. Poor bastard; he never learned that the moment he took to smile before he went for me gave me time enough to get out of range. BUT, there he was; malevolence with an erection, waiting. I put the poison patty down, moved toward the stairs and watched. The poor animal gobbled the food down as usual, smiled, which made me almost sick, and then, BAM. But, I sprinted up the stairs, as usual, and the dog didn't get me, as usual. AND IT CAME TO PASS THAT THE BEAST WAS DEATHLY ILL. I knew this because he no longer attended me, and because the landlady sobered up. She stopped me in the hall the same evening of the attempted murder and confided the information that God had struck her puppy-dog a surely fatal blow. She had forgotten her bewildered lust, and her eyes were wide open for the first time. They looked like the dog's eyes. She sniveled and implored me to pray for the animal. I wanted to say to her: Madam, I have myself to pray for, the colored queen, the Puerto Rican family, the person in the front room whom I've never seen, the woman who cries deliberately behind her closed door, and the rest of the people in all roominghouses, everywhere; besides, Madam, I don't understand how to pray. But . . . to simplify things . . . I told her I would pray. She looked up. She said that I was a liar, and

that I probably wanted the dog to die. I told her, and there was so
much truth here, that I didn't want the dog to die. I didn't, and not
just because I'd poisoned him. I'm afraid that I must tell you I wanted
the dog to live so that I could see what our new relationship might
come to.

(PETER *indicates his increasing displeasure and slowly growing antago-
nism.*)

Please understand, Peter; that sort of thing is important. You must
believe me; it *is* important. We have to know the effect of our actions.
(*Another deep sigh*) Well, anyway; the dog recovered. I have no idea
why, unless he was a descendant of the puppy that guarded the gates
of hell or some such resort. I'm not up on my mythology. (*He pronounces the word myth-o-logy*) Are you?

(PETER *sets to thinking, but* JERRY *goes on.*)

At any rate, and you've missed the eight-thousand-dollar question,
Peter; at any rate, the dog recovered his health and the landlady recovered her thirst, in no way altered by the bow-wow's deliverance.
When I came home from a movie that was playing on Forty-second
Street, a movie I'd seen, or one that was very much like one or several
I'd seen, after the landlady told me puppykins was better, I was so hoping for the dog to be waiting for me. I was . . . well, how would you
put it . . . enticed? . . . fascinated? . . . no, I don't think so . . .
heart-shatteringly anxious, that's it; I was heart-shatteringly anxious to
confront my friend again.

(PETER *reacts scoffingly.*)

Yes, Peter; friend. That's the only word for it. I was heart-shatteringly
et cetera to confront my doggy friend again. I came in the door and
advanced, unafraid, to the center of the entrance hall. The beast was
there . . . looking at me. And, you know, he looked better for his
scrape with the nevermind. I stopped; I looked at him; he looked at
me. I think . . . I think we stayed a long time that way . . . still,
stone-statue . . . just looking at one another. I looked more into his
face than he looked into mine. I mean, I can concentrate longer at
looking into a dog's face than a dog can concentrate at looking into
mine, or into anybody else's face, for that matter. But during that
twenty seconds or two hours that we looked into each other's face, we
made contact. Now, here is what I had wanted to happen: I loved the
dog now, and I wanted him to love me. I had tried to love, and I had
tried to kill, and both had been unsuccessful by themselves. I hoped
. . . and I don't really know why I expected the dog to understand
anything, much less my motivations . . . I hoped that the dog would
understand.

(PETER *seems to be hypnotized.*)

It's just . . . it's just that . . . (JERRY *is abnormally tense, now*)
. . . it's just that if you can't deal with people, you have to make a
start somewhere. WITH ANIMALS! (*Much faster now, and like a
conspirator*) Don't you see? A person has to have some way of dealing
with SOMETHING. If not with people . . . if not with people . . .
SOMETHING. With a bed, with a cockroach, with a mirror . . .
no, that's too hard, that's one of the last steps. With a cockroach,
with a . . . with a . . . with a carpet, a roll of toilet paper . . .
no, not that, either . . . that's a mirror, too; always check bleed-
ing. You see how hard it is to find things? With a street corner,
and too many lights, all colors reflecting on the oily-wet streets . . .
with a wisp of smoke, a wisp . . . of smoke . . . with . . . with pornographic playing cards, with a strongbox . . . WITHOUT A LOCK
. . . with love, with vomiting, with crying, with fury because the
pretty little ladies aren't pretty little ladies, with making money with
your body which is an act of love and I could prove it, with howling
because you're alive; with God. How about that? WITH GOD WHO
IS A COLORED QUEEN WHO WEARS A KIMONO AND PLUCKS
HIS EYEBROWS, WHO IS A WOMAN WHO CRIES WITH DE-
TERMINATION BEHIND HER CLOSED DOOR . . . with God
who, I'm told, turned his back on the whole thing some time ago . . .
with . . . some day, with people. (JERRY *sighs the next word heavily*)
People. With an idea; a concept. And where better, where ever better
in this humiliating excuse for a jail, where better to communicate one
single, simple-minded idea than in an entrance hall? Where? It would
be A START! Where better to make a beginning . . . to understand
and just possibly be understood . . . a beginning of an understanding,
than with . . .
(*Here* JERRY *seems to fall into almost grotesque fatigue.*)
   . . . than with A DOG. Just that; a dog.
(*Here there is a silence that might be prolonged for a moment or so;
then* JERRY *wearily finishes his story.*)
A dog. It seemed like a perfectly sensible idea. Man is a dog's best
friend, remember. So: the dog and I looked at each other. I longer
than the dog. And what I saw then has been the same ever since.
Whenever the dog and I see each other we both stop where we are. We
regard each other with a mixture of sadness and suspicion, and then
we feign indifference. We walk past each other safely; we have an understanding. It's very sad, but you'll have to admit that it is an understanding. We had made many attempts at contact, and we had failed.
The dog has returned to garbage, and I to solitary but free passage. I
have not returned. I mean to say, I have *gained* solitary free passage,
if that much further loss can be said to be gain. I have learned that

neither kindness nor cruelty by themselves, independent of each other, creates any effect beyond themselves; and I have learned that the two combined, together, at the same time, are the teaching emotion. And what is gained is loss. And what has been the result: the dog and I have attained a compromise; more of a bargain, really. We neither love nor hurt because we do not try to reach each other. And, *was* trying to feed the dog an act of love? And, perhaps, was the dog's attempt to bite me *not* an act of love? If we can so misunderstand, well then, why have we invented the word love in the first place?

(*There is silence.* JERRY *moves to* PETER's *bench and sits down beside him. This is the first time* JERRY *has sat down during the play.*)

The Story of Jerry and the Dog: the end.

(PETER *is silent.*)

Well, Peter? (JERRY *is suddenly cheerful*) Well, Peter? Do you think I could sell that story to the *Reader's Digest* and make a couple of hundred bucks for *The Most Unforgettable Character I've Ever Met?* Huh?

(JERRY *is animated, but* PETER *is disturbed.*)

Oh, come on now, Peter; tell me what you think.

PETER   (*numb*). I . . . I don't understand what . . . I don't think I . . . (*Now, almost tearfully*) Why did you tell me all of this?

JERRY.   Why not?

PETER.   I DON'T UNDERSTAND!

JERRY   (*furious, but whispering*). That's a lie.

PETER.   No. No, it's not.

JERRY   (*quietly*). I tried to explain it to you as I went along. I went slowly; it all has to do with . . .

PETER.   I DON'T WANT TO HEAR ANY MORE. I don't understand you, or your landlady, or her dog. . . .

JERRY.   *Her* dog! I thought it was my . . . No. No, you're right. It *is* her dog. (*Looks at* PETER *intently, shaking his head*) I don't know what I was thinking about; of course you don't understand. (*In a monotone, wearily*) I don't live in your block; I'm not married to two parakeets, or whatever your setup is. I am a *permanent transient,* and my home is the sickening roominghouses on the West Side of New York City, which is the greatest city in the world. Amen.

PETER.   I'm . . . I'm sorry; I didn't mean to . . .

JERRY.   Forget it. I suppose you don't quite know what to make of me, eh?

PETER   (*a joke*). We got all kinds in publishing. (*Chuckles*)

JERRY.   You're a funny man. (*He forces a laugh*) You know that? You're a very . . . a richly comic person.

PETER   (*modestly, but amused*). Oh, now, not really. (*Still chuckling*)

JERRY. Peter, do I annoy you, or confuse you?

PETER (*lightly*). Well, I must confess that this wasn't the kind of afternoon I'd anticipated.

JERRY. You mean, I'm not the gentleman you were expecting.

PETER. I wasn't expecting anybody.

JERRY. No, I don't imagine you were. But I'm here, and I'm not leaving.

PETER (*consulting his watch*). Well, you may not be, but I must be getting home soon.

JERRY. Oh, come on; stay a while longer.

PETER. I really should get home; you see . . .

JERRY (*tickles* PETER's *ribs with his fingers*). Oh, come on.

PETER (*He is very ticklish; as* JERRY *continues to tickle him his voice becomes falsetto.*) No, I . . . OHHHHH! Don't do that. Stop, Stop. Ohhh, no, no.

JERRY. Oh, come on.

PETER (*as* JERRY *tickles*). Oh, hee, hee, hee. I must go. I . . . hee, hee, hee. After all, stop, stop, hee, hee, hee, after all, the parakeets will be getting dinner ready soon. Hee, hee. And the cats are setting the table. Stop, stop, and, and . . . (PETER *is beside himself now*) . . . and we're having . . . hee, hee . . . uh . . . ho, ho, ho.

(JERRY *stops tickling* PETER, *but the combination of the tickling and his own mad whimsy has* PETER *laughing almost hysterically. As his laughter continues, then subsides,* JERRY *watches him, with a curious fixed smile.*)

JERRY. Peter?

PETER. Oh, ha, ha, ha, ha, ha. What? What?

JERRY. Listen, now.

PETER. Oh, ho, ho. What . . . what is it, Jerry? Oh, my.

JERRY (*mysteriously*). Peter, do you want to know what happened at the zoo?

PETER. Ah, ha, ha. The what? Oh, yes; the zoo. Oh, ho, ho. Well, I had my own zoo there for a moment with . . . hee, hee, the parakeets getting dinner ready, and the . . . ha, ha, whatever it was, the . . .

JERRY (*calmly*). Yes, that was very funny, Peter. I wouldn't have expected it. But do you want to hear about what happened at the zoo, or not?

PETER. Yes. Yes, by all means; tell me what happened at the zoo. Oh, my. I don't know what happened to me.

JERRY. Now I'll let you in on what happened at the zoo; but first, I should tell you why I went to the zoo. I went to the zoo to find out more about the way people exist with animals, and the way animals exist with each other, and with people too. It probably wasn't a fair test, what with everyone separated by bars from everyone else, the animals for the most part from each other, and always the people from the animals. But, if it's a zoo, that's the way it is. (*He pokes* PETER *on the arm*) Move over.

PETER   (*friendly*). I'm sorry, haven't you enough room? (*He shifts a little.*)

JERRY   (*smiling slightly*). Well, all the animals are there, and all the people are there, and it's Sunday and all the children are there. (*He pokes* PETER *again.*) Move over.

PETER   (*patiently, still friendly*). All right.

(*He moves some more, and* JERRY *has all the room he might need.*)

JERRY.   And it's a hot day, so all the stench is there, too, and all the balloon sellers, and all the ice cream sellers, and all the seals are barking, and all the birds are screaming. (*Pokes* PETER *harder*) Move over!

PETER   (*beginning to be annoyed*). Look here, you have more than enough room! (*But he moves more, and is now fairly cramped at one end of the bench.*)

JERRY.   And I am there, and it's feeding time at the lion's house, and the lion keeper comes into the lion cage, one of the lion cages, to feed one of the lions. (*Punches* PETER *on the arm, hard*) MOVE OVER!

PETER   (*very annoyed*). I can't move over any more, and stop hitting me. What's the matter with you?

JERRY.   Do you want to hear the story? (*Punches* PETER's *arm again.*)

PETER   (*flabbergasted*). I'm not so sure! I certainly don't want to be punched in the arm.

JERRY   (*punches* PETER's *arm again*). Like that?

PETER.   Stop it! What's the matter with you?

JERRY.   I'm crazy, you bastard.

PETER.   That isn't funny.

JERRY.   Listen to me, Peter. I want this bench. You go sit on the bench over there, and if you're good I'll tell you the rest of the story.

PETER   (*flustered*). But . . . whatever for? What *is* the matter with you? Besides, I see no reason why I should give up this bench. I sit on this bench almost every Sunday afternoon, in good weather. It's secluded here; there's never anyone sitting here, so I have it all to myself.

JERRY   (*softly*). Get off this bench, Peter; I want it.

PETER   (*almost whining*). No.

JERRY.   I said I want this bench, and I'm going to have it. Now get over there.

PETER.   People can't have everything they want. You should know that; it's a rule; people can have some of the things they want, but they can't have everything.

JERRY   (*laughs*). Imbecile! You're slow-witted!

PETER.   Stop that!

JERRY.   You're a vegetable! Go lie down on the ground.

PETER   (*intense*). Now *you* listen to me. I've put up with you all afternoon.

JERRY.   Not really.

PETER.   LONG ENOUGH. I've put up with you long enough. I've listened to you because you seemed . . . well, because I thought you wanted to talk to somebody.

JERRY.   You put things well; economically, and yet . . . oh, what is the word I want to put justice to your . . . JESUS, you make me sick . . . get off here and give me my bench.

PETER.   MY BENCH!

JERRY   (*pushes* PETER *almost, but not quite, off the bench*). Get out of my sight.

PETER   (*regaining his position*). God da . . . mn you. That's enough! I've had enough of you. I will not give up this bench; you can't have it, and that's that. Now, go away.

(JERRY *snorts but does not move.*)

   Go away, I said.

(JERRY *does not move.*)

   Get away from here. If you don't move on . . . you're a bum . . . that's what you are. . . . If you don't move on, I'll get a policeman here and make you go.

(JERRY *laughs, stays.*)

   I warn you, I'll call a policeman.

JERRY   (*softly*). You won't find a policeman around here; they're all over on the west side of the park chasing fairies down from trees or out of the bushes. That's all they do. That's théir function. So scream your head off; it won't do you any good.

PETER.   POLICE! I warn you, I'll have you arrested. POLICE! (*Pause*) I said POLICE! (*Pause*) I feel ridiculous.

JERRY.   You look ridiculous: a grown man screaming for the police on on a bright Sunday afternoon in the park with nobody harming you. If a policeman *did* fill his quota and come sludging over this way he'd probably take you in as a nut.

PETER   (*with disgust and impotence*). Great God, I just came here to read, and now you want me to give up the bench. You're mad.

JERRY.   Hey, I got news for you, as they say. I'm on your precious bench, and you're never going to have it for yourself again.

PETER   (*furious*). Look, you; get off my bench. I don't care if it makes any sense or not. I want this bench to myself; I want you OFF IT!

JERRY   (*mocking*). Aw . . . look who's mad.

PETER.   GET OUT!

JERRY.   No.

PETER.   I WARN YOU!

JERRY.   Do you know how ridiculous you look *now?*

PETER   (*His fury and self-consciousness have possessed him*). It doesn't matter. (*He is almost crying*) GET AWAY FROM MY BENCH!

JERRY.   Why? You have everything in the world you want; you've told me about your home, and your family, and *your own* little zoo. You have everything, and now you want this bench. Are these the things men fight for? Tell me, Peter, is this bench, this iron and this wood, is this your honor? Is this the thing in the world you'd fight for? Can you think of anything more absurd?

PETER.   Absurd? Look, I'm not going to talk to you about honor, or even try to explain it to you. Besides, it isn't a question of honor; but even if it were, you wouldn't understand.

JERRY   (*contemptuously*). You don't even know what you're saying, do you? This is probably the first time in your life you've had anything more trying to face than changing your cats' toilet box. Stupid! Don't you have any idea, not even the slightest, what other people *need?*

PETER.   Oh, boy, listen to you; well, you don't need this bench. That's for sure.

JERRY.   Yes; yes, I do.

PETER   (*quivering*). I've come here for years; I have hours of great pleasure, great satisfaction, right here. And that's important to a man. I'm a responsible person, and I'm a GROWNUP. This is my bench, and you have no right to take it away from me.

JERRY.   Fight for it, then. Defend yourself; defend your bench.

PETER.   You've *pushed* me to it. Get up and fight.

JERRY.   Like a man?

PETER   (*still angry*). Yes, like a man, if you insist on mocking me even further.

JERRY.   I'll have to give you credit for one thing: you *are* a vegetable, and a slightly nearsighted one, I think . . .

PETER.   THAT'S ENOUGH. . . .

JERRY.   . . . but, you know, as they say on TV all the time—you know —and I mean this, Peter, you have a certain dignity; it surprises me. . . .

PETER.   STOP!

JERRY   (*rises lazily*). Very well, Peter, we'll battle for the bench, but we're not evenly matched.

(*He takes out and clicks open and ugly-looking knife.*)

PETER   (*suddenly awakening to the reality of the situation*). You *are* mad! You're stark raving mad! YOU'RE GOING TO KILL ME!

(*But before* PETER *has time to think what to do,* JERRY *tosses the knife at* PETER'*s feet.*)

JERRY.   There you go. Pick it up. You have the knife and we'll be more evenly matched.

PETER (*horrified*). No!

JERRY (*rushes over to* PETER, *grabs him by the collar;* PETER *rises; their faces almost touch*). Now you pick up that knife and you fight with me. You fight for your self-respect; you fight for that goddamned bench.

PETER (*struggling*). No! Let . . . let go of me! He . . . Help!

JERRY (*slaps* PETER *on each "fight"*). You fight, you miserable bastard; fight for that bench; fight for your parakeets; fight for your cats, fight for your two daughters; fight for your wife; fight for your manhood, you pathetic little vegetable. (*Spits in* PETER'*s face*) You couldn't even get your wife with a male child.

PETER (*breaks away, enraged*). It's a matter of genetics, not manhood, you . . . you monster.

(*He darts down, picks up the knife and backs off a little; he is breathing heavily.*)

I'll give you one last chance; get out of here and leave me alone!

(*He holds the knife with a firm arm, but far in front of him, not to attack but to defend.*)

JERRY (*sighs heavily*). So be it!

(*With a rush he charges* PETER *and impales himself on the knife. Tableau: For just a moment, complete silence,* JERRY *impaled on the knife at the end of* PETER'*s still firm arm. Then* PETER *screams, pulls away, leaving the knife in* JERRY. JERRY *is motionless, on point. Then he, too, screams, and it must be the sound of an infuriated and fatally wounded animal. With the knife in him, he stumbles back to the bench that* PETER *had vacated. He crumbles there, sitting, facing* PETER, *his eyes wide in agony, his mouth open.*)

PETER (*whispering*). Oh my God, oh my God, oh my God. . . .

(*He repeats these words many times, very rapidly.*)

JERRY (JERRY *is dying; but now his expression seems to change. His features relax, and while his voice varies, sometimes wrenched with pain, for the most part he seems removed from his dying. He smiles.*)

Thank you, Peter. I mean that, now; thank you very much.

(PETER'*s mouth drops open. He cannot move; he is tranfixed.*)

Oh, Peter, I was so afraid I'd drive you away. (*He laughs as best he can.*) You don't know how afraid I was you'd go away and leave me. And now I'll tell you what happened at the zoo. I think . . . I think this is what happened at the zoo . . . I think. I think that while I was at the zoo I decided that I would walk north . . . northerly, rather . . . until I found you . . . or somebody . . . and I decided that I would talk to you . . . I would tell you things . . . and things that I would tell you would . . . Well, here we are. You see? Here we *are*. But . . . I don't know . . . could I have planned all this? No . . . no, I couldn't have. But I think I did. And now I've told you what you wanted to know, haven't I? And now you know all about what happened at the zoo. And now you know what you'll see in your TV, and the face I told you about . . . you remember . . . the face I told you about . . . my face, the face you see right now. Peter . . . Peter? . . . Peter . . . thank you. I came unto you (*He laughs, so faintly*) and you have comforted me. Dear Peter.

PETER   (*almost fainting*). Oh my God!

JERRY.   You'd better go now. Somebody might come by, and you don't want to be here when anyone comes.

PETER   (*does not move, but begins to weep*). Oh my God, oh my God.

JERRY   (*most faintly, now; he is very near death*). You won't be coming back here any more, Peter; you've been dispossessed. You've lost your bench, but you've defended your honor. And Peter, I'll tell you something now; you're not really a vegetable; it's all right, you're an animal. You're an animal, too. But you'd better hurry now, Peter. Hurry, you'd better go . . . see?

(JERRY *takes a handkerchief and with great effort and pain wipes the knife handle clean of fingerprints*).

Hurry away, Peter.

(PETER *begins to stagger away*).

Wait . . . wait, Peter. Take your book . . . book. Right here . . . beside me . . . on your bench . . . my bench, rather. Come . . . take your book.

(PETER *starts for the book, but retreats.*)

Hurry . . . Peter.

(PETER *rushes to the bench, grabs the book, retreats*).

Very good, Peter . . . very good. Now . . . hurry away.

(PETER *hesitates for a moment, then flees, stage-left.*)

Hurry away. . . . (*His eyes are closed now*) Hurry away, your parakeets are making the dinner . . . the cats . . . are setting the table . . .

PETER   (*off stage*). (*A pitiful howl*) OH MY GOD!

JERRY   (*his eyes still closed, he shakes his head and speaks; a combination of scornful mimicry and supplication*).

Oh . . . my . . . God.

(*He is dead.*)

WHICH THEATRE IS THE ABSURD ONE?

EDWARD ALBEE

A theatre person of my acquaintance—a man whose judgment must be respected, though more for the infallibility of his intuition than for his reasoning—remarked just the other week, "The Theatre of the Absurd has had it; it's on its way out; it's through."

Now this, on the surface of it, seems to be a pretty funny attitude to be taking toward a theatre movement which has, only in the past couple of years, been impressing itself on the American public consciousness. Or is it? Must we judge that a theatre of such plays as Samuel Beckett's *Krapp's Last Tape,* Jean Genêt's *The Balcony* (both long, long runners off-Broadway) and Eugène Ionesco's *Rhinoceros*—which, albeit in a hoked-up production, had a substantial season *on* Broadway—has been judged by the theatre public and found wanting?

And shall we have to assume that The Theatre of the Absurd Repertory Company, currently playing at New York's off-Broadway Cherry Lane Theatre—presenting works by Beckett, Ionesco, Genêt, Arrabal, Jack Richardson, Kenneth Koch, and myself—being the first such collective representation of the movement in the United States, is also a kind of farewell to the movement? For that matter, just what *is* The Theatre of the Absurd?

Well, let me come at it obliquely. When I was told, about a year ago, that I was considered a member in good standing of The Theatre of the Absurd I was deeply offended. I was deeply offended because I had never heard the term before and I immediately assumed that it applied to the theatre uptown—Broadway.

What (I was reasoning to myself) could be more absurd than a theatre in which the esthetic criterion is something like this: A "good" play is one which makes money; a "bad" play (in the sense of "Naughty! Naughty!" I guess) is one which does not; a theatre in which performers have plays rewritten to correspond to the public relations image of themselves; a theatre in which playwrights are encouraged (what a funny word!) to think of themselves as little cogs in a great big wheel; a theatre in which imitation has given way to imitation of imitation; a theatre in which London "hits" are, willy-nilly, in a kind of reverse of chauvinism, greeted in a manner not unlike a colony's obeisance to the Crown; a theatre in which real estate owners and theatre party managements predetermine the success of unknown quantities; a theatre in which everybody scratches and bites for billing as though it meant access to the last bomb shelter on earth; a theatre in which, in a given season, there was not a single performance of a play by Beckett, Brecht, Chekhov, Genêt, Ibsen, O'Casey, Pirandello, Shaw, Strindberg—or Shakespeare? What, indeed, I thought, could be more absurd than that? (My conclusions . . . obviously.)

For it emerged that The Theatre of the Absurd, aside from being the title of an excellent book by Martin Esslin on what is loosely called the avant-garde theatre, was a somewhat less than fortunate catch-all phrase to describe the philosophical attitudes and theatre methods of a number of Europe's finest and most adventurous playwrights and their followers.

I was less offended, but still a little dubious. Simply: I don't like labels; they can be facile and can lead to nonthink on the part of the public. And unless it is understood that the playwrights of The Theatre of the Absurd represent a group only in the sense that they seem to be doing something of the same thing in vaguely similar ways at approximately the same time—unless this is understood, then the labeling itself will be more absurd than the label.

Playwrights, by nature, are grouchy, withdrawn, envious, greedy, suspicious and, in general, quite nice people—and the majority of them wouldn't be caught dead in a colloquy remotely resembling the following:

> IONESCO (*At a Left Bank café table, spying* BECKETT *and* GENÊT *strolling past in animated conversation*). Hey! Sam! Jean!
>
> GENÊT. Hey, it's Eugene! Sam, it's Eugene!
>
> BECKETT. Well, I'll be damned. Hi there, Eugene boy.
>
> IONESCO. Sit down, kids.
>
> GENÊT. Sure thing.
>
> IONESCO (*rubbing his hands together*). Well, what's new in The Theatre of the Absurd?
>
> BECKETT. Oh, less than a lot of people think. (*They all laugh*).

Etc. No. Not very likely. Get a playwright alone sometime, get a few drinks in him, and maybe he'll be persuaded to sound off about his "intention" and the like—and hate himself for it the next day. But put a group of playwrights together in a room, and the conversation—if there is any—will, more likely than not, concern itself with sex, restaurants, and the movies.

Very briefly, then—and reluctantly, because I am a playwright and would much rather talk about sex, restaurants, and the movies—and stumblingly, because I do not pretend to understand it entirely, I will try to define The Theatre of the Absurd. As I get it, The Theatre of the Absurd is an absorption-in-art of certain existentialist and post-existentialist philosophical concepts having to do, in the main, with man's attempts to make sense for himself out of his senseless position in a world which makes no sense—which makes no sense because the moral, religious, political, and social structures man has erected to "illusion" himself have collapsed.

Albert Camus put it this way: "A world that can be explained by reasoning, however faulty, is a familiar world. But in a universe that is suddenly deprived of illusions and of light, man feels a stranger. His is an irremediable exile, because he is deprived of memories of a lost homeland as much as he lacks the hope of a promised land to come. This divorce between man and his life, the actor and his setting, truly constitutes the feeling of Absurdity."

And Eugène Ionesco says this: "Absurd is that which is devoid of purpose. . . . Cut off from his religious, metaphysical, and transcendental roots, man is lost; all his actions become senseless, absurd, useless."

And to sum up the movement, Martin Esslin writes, in his book *The Theatre of the Absurd:* "Ultimately, a phenomenon like The Theatre of the Absurd does not reflect despair or a return to dark irrational forces but expresses modern man's endeavor to come to terms with the world in which he lives. It attempts to make him face up to the human condition as it really is, to free him from illusions that are bound to cause constant maladjustment and disappointment. . . . For the dignity of man lies in his ability to face reality in all its senselessness; to accept it freely, without fear, without illusions—and to laugh at it."

Amen.

(And while we're on the subject of Amen, one wearies of the complaint that The Theatre of the Absurd playwrights alone are having at God these days. The notion that God is dead, indifferent, or insane—a notion blasphemous, premature, or academic depending on your persuasion—while surely a tenet of some of the playwrights under discussion, is, it seems to me, of a piece with Mr. Tennessee Williams' description of the Deity, in *The Night of the Iguana,* as "a senile delinquent.")

So much for the attempt to define terms. Now, what of this theatre? What of this theatre in which, for example, a legless old couple live out their lives in twin ashcans, surfacing occasionally for food or conversation (Samuel Beckett's *Endgame*); in which a man is seduced, and rather easily, by a girl with three well-formed and functioning noses (Eugène Ionesco's *Jack, or The Submission*); in which, on the same stage, one group of Negro actors is playing at pretending to be Negro (Jean Genêt's *The Blacks*) ?

What of this theatre? Is it, as it has been accused of being, obscure, sordid, destructive, anti-theatre, perverse, and absurd (in the sense of foolish)? Or is it merely, as I have so often heard it put, that, "This sort of stuff is too depressing, too . . . too mixed-up; I go to the theatre to relax and have a good time."

I would submit that it is this latter attitude—that the theatre is a place to relax and have a good time—in conflict with the purpose of The Theatre of the Absurd—which is to make a man face up to the human condition as it really is—that has produced all the brouhaha and the dissent. I would submit that The Theatre of the Absurd, in the sense that it is truly the contemporary theatre, facing as it does man's condition as it is, is the Realistic theatre of our time; and that the supposed Realistic theatre—the term used here to mean most of what is done on Broadway—in the sense that it panders to the public need for self-congratulation and reassurance and presents a false picture of ourselves to ourselves, is, with an occasional very lovely exception, really and truly The Theatre of the Absurd.

And I would submit further that the health of a nation, a society, can be determined by the art it demands. We have insisted of television and our movies that they not have anything to do with anything, that they be our never-never land; and if we demand this same function of our live theatre, what will be left of the visual-auditory arts—save the dance (in which nobody talks) and music (to which nobody listens)?

It has been my fortune, the past two or three years, to travel around a good deal, in pursuit of my career—Berlin, London, Buenos Aires, for example; and I have discovered a couple of interesting things. I have discovered that audiences in these and other major cities demand of their commercial theatre—and get—a season of plays in which the froth and junk are the exception and not the rule. To take a case: in Berlin, in 1959, Adamov, Genêt, Beckett, and Brecht (naturally) were playing the big houses; this past fall, Beckett again, Genêt again, Pinter twice, etc. To take another case: in Buenos Aires there are over a hundred experimental theatres.

These plays cannot be put on in Berlin over the head of a protesting or an indifferent audience; these experimental theatres cannot exist in Buenos Aires without subscription. In the end—and it must always come down to this, no matter what other failings a theatre may have—in the end a public will get what it deserves, and no better.

I have also discovered, in my wanderings, that young people throng to what is new and fresh in the theatre. Happily, this holds true in the United States as well. At the various colleges I have gone to to speak I have found an eager, friendly, and knowledgeable audience, an audience which is as dismayed by the Broadway scene as any proselytizer for the avant-garde. I have found among young people an audience which is not so preconditioned by pap as to have cut off half of its responses. (It is interesting to note, by the way, that if an off-Broadway play has a substantial run, its audiences will begin young and grow older; as the run goes on, cloth coats give way to furs, walkers and subway riders to taxi-takers. Exactly the opposite is true on Broadway.)

The young, of course, are always questioning values, knocking the status quo about, considering shibboleths to see if they are pronounceable. In time, it is to be regretted, most of them—the kids—will settle down to their own version of the easy, the standard; but in the meanwhile . . . in the meanwhile they are a wonderful, alert, alive, accepting audience.

And I would go so far as to say that it is the responsibility of everyone who pretends any interest at all in the theatre to get up off their six-ninety seats and find out what the theatre is *really* about. For it is a lazy public which produces a slothful and irresponsible theatre.

Now, I would suspect that my theatre-friend with the infallible intuition is probably right when he suggests that The Theatre of the Absurd (or the avant-garde theatre, or whatever you want to call it) as it now stands is on its way out. Or at least is undergoing change. All living organisms undergo constant change. And while it is certain that the nature of this theatre will remain constant, its forms, its methods—its devices, if you will—most necessarily will undergo mutation.

This theatre has no intention of running downhill; and the younger playwrights will make use of the immediate past and mold it to their own needs. (Harold Pinter for example, could not have written *The Caretaker* had Samuel Beckett not existed, but Pinter is, nonetheless, moving in his own direction.) And it is my guess that the theatre in the United States will always hew more closely to the post-Ibsen/Chekhov tradition than does the theatre in France, let us say. It is our nature as a country, a society. But we will experiment, and we will expect your attention.

For just as it is true that our response to color and form was forever altered once the impressionist painters put their minds to canvas, it is just as true that the playwrights of The Theatre of the Absurd have forever altered our response to the theatre.

And one more point: The avant-garde theatre is fun; it is free-swinging, bold, iconoclastic, and often wildly, wildly funny. If you will approach it with childlike innocence—putting your standard responses aside, for they do not apply—if you will approach it on its own terms, I think you will be in for a liberating surprise. I think you may no longer be content with plays that you can't remember halfway down the block. You will not only be doing yourself some good, but you will be having a great time, to boot. And even though it occurs to me that such a fine combination must be sinful, I still recommend it.